ninth edition

The Systematic Design of Instruction

Walter Dick
Florida State University, Emeritus

Lou Carey
University of South Florida, Emeritus

James O. Carey
University of South Florida, Emeritus

Pearson

Acknowledgments of third-party content appear on the appropriate page within the text.
Photo Credit: p. 307: Nyul/123RF; p. 309: Gabriel Blaj/Alamy Stock Photo; p. 457: Lisa Young/123RF, Andy Dean/123RF, Thomas M Perkins/Shutterstock, HONGQI ZHANG/123RF; p. 458: Claudiodivizia/123RF, Pejo/123RF, Karel Miragaya/123RF; p. 459: Lisa Young/123RF, Dragon Images/Shutterstock, Andy Dean/123RF; COV: Philsajonesen/Vetta/ Getty Images.

Library of Congress Cataloging-in-Publication Data

Names: Dick, Walter, author. | Carey, Lou, author. | Carey, James O, author.
Title: The systematic design of instruction / Walter Dick, Florida State University, Emeritus, Lou Carey, University of South Florida, Emeritus, James O. Carey, University of South Florida, Emeritus.
Description: Ninth edition. | Hoboken, NJ: Pearson, [2022] | Includes bibliographical references and index. | Summary: "The Systematic Design of Instruction, 9th ed., introduces you simply and clearly to the fundamentals of ID, namely the concepts and procedures for analyzing, designing, developing, and formatively evaluating instruction. The text is designed to aid your learning in several ways. The intuitive chapter organization explains each step in the design process through easily understandable sections, including (1) Objectives, (2) Overview, (3) Concepts, (4) Evaluation and Revision, (5) Examples, (6) Case Study, (7) Professional and Historical Perspectives, (8) Process Flowcharts, (9) Practice, and (10) Feedback. Every chapter leads you through a step of the model, presenting carefully illustrated academic and business applications and background research. The contemporary design examples also help you link current theoretical concepts to practical applications. Sample rubrics and exercises provide tools you can use when designing instruction to connect theory to your own real-life applications. Finally, annotated references direct you to resources that help amplify and reinforce each concept in the ID process"-- Provided by publisher.
Identifiers: LCCN 2020054895 (print) | LCCN 2020054896 (ebook) | ISBN 9780135824146 (paperback) | ISBN 9780135824139 (epub)
Subjects: LCSH: Instructional systems--Design. | Lesson planning.
Classification: LCC LB1028.38 .D53 2022 (print) | LCC LB1028.38 (ebook) | DDC 371.3--dc23
LC record available at https://lccn.loc.gov/2020054895
LC ebook record available at https://lccn.loc.gov/2020054896

3 2021

ISBN 10: 0-13-582414-1
ISBN 13: 978-0-13-582414-6

Preface

Not so many years ago, instruction was typically created by professors or trainers who simply developed and delivered lectures based on their research, experience, and expertise. Instructional emphasis has shifted dramatically from expert lectures to interactive instruction. This instruction focuses on the main purposes for and anticipated outcomes of the learning, the nature of the environment where acquired knowledge and skills would be used, and the particular characteristics of the learners in relation to the discipline and environment. Effective instruction today requires careful and systematic analysis as well as description of the intertwined elements that affect successful learning and requires integral evaluation and refinement throughout the creative process.

The elegance of a generic systematic instructional design (ID) process is its inherent ability to remain current by accommodating emerging technologies, theories, discoveries, or procedures. For example, performance analysis and needs assessment reveal new institutional needs and new performance requirements that must now be accommodated in the instruction; analysis and description of the performance context uncover novel constraints and new technologies. Likewise, thoughtful analysis of present learners discloses characteristics not previously observed, and analysis of new instructional delivery options enables more efficient and cost-effective combinations of media and teaching–learning methods. The inquiry and analysis phases inherent in each step of a systematic ID model help ensure that the resulting decisions and designs are current, practical, and effective.

The Systematic Design of Instruction, 9th ed., introduces you simply and clearly to the fundamentals of ID, namely the concepts and procedures for analyzing, designing, developing, and formatively evaluating instruction. The text is designed to aid your learning in several ways. The intuitive chapter organization explains each step in the design process through easily understandable sections, including (1) Objectives, (2) Overview, (3) Concepts, (4) Evaluation and Revision, (5) Examples, (6) Case Study, (7) Professional and Historical Perspectives, (8) Process Flowcharts, (9) Practice, and (10) Feedback. Every chapter leads you through a step of the model, presenting carefully illustrated academic and business applications and background research. The contemporary design examples also help you link current theoretical concepts to practical applications. Sample rubrics and exercises provide tools you can use when designing instruction to connect theory to your own real-life applications. Finally, annotated references direct you to resources that help amplify and reinforce each concept in the ID process.

Acquiring the ID ideas and skills presented here will undoubtedly change the way you approach creating instruction. This is not a textbook to be read and memorized but is meant to be used for you to create effective instruction. You learn a systematic, thoughtful, inquiry-based approach to creation that helps ensure the success of those who use your instruction. For learning ID most effectively, we suggest that you choose a relatively small instructional goal in your own discipline and context and then, as you study each chapter, apply the steps in the model to designing instruction for your personal goal—in other words, this can be a learning-by-doing textbook. This helps ensure that you can take the ID model from this learning experience and make it an integral part of your own ID practices.

New to This Edition

In this edition, we retain the features that seem most important to readers of previous editions as well as add new perspectives and features that keep the text current within the discipline, including the following new materials within each chapter:

- An introductory overview that introduces the ideas covered in each chapter.
- An evaluation and revision section that contains both evaluation strategies and a rubric for evaluating instructional design products through each step in the model.
- An elaborated example from a business perspective.
- Professional and historical perspectives.
- Flowcharts of design procedures for each step in the model.

In addition to these new features, this edition includes:

- Additional attention to:
  - learning and portable digital devices.
  - the relationship between transfer of learning and the performance context.
  - the theoretical bases of learning in designing and developing instruction.
- Additional tables that help summarize and organize concepts.
- Application of ID concepts through multiple examples in business and education and a serial case study for adult learners in a university setting. The case study is carried through the steps of the design model in each chapter of the book.
- A plan with case study examples for using constructivist learning environments in cognitive ID.
- Updated references and recommended readings with annotations.
- A complete case study in the appendices (in addition to the one contained in the text) that details the products of design and development activities for each step in the model for a school curriculum goal on writing composition.

Pedagogical Features

There are many pedagogical features within each chapter, including:

- The Dick and Carey instructional design model is keyed to steps in each chapter.
- A chapter overview to help readers focus on critical content in each chapter.
- Careful use of subordination in titles and subtitles to cue organization of content.
- Tables and figures to illustrate or highlight content in each chapter.
- A rubric for readers to use to self assess products developed at each step in the design model.
- Case studies and examples that flow through each chapter.
- Task analysis flowcharts of main steps within each chapter.
- Practice and feedback for main steps within each chapter.

The text also includes a detailed table of contents, glossary, and index of key terms and important individuals.

Instructor Resources

There is a complete *Instructors' Manual for the Systematic Design of Instruction.* It includes:

- The instructional strategy and activities for the course.
- Course schedules for ten- and fifteen-week semesters.

- Strategies for evaluating student products.
- Strategies for using the instructors' manual.
- The test item bank for the course that includes both verbal information and intellectual skills items.

Each chapter the manual includes:

- Preinstructional activities.
- Performance objectives and their relevance to instructional designers.
- Prerequisite information and skills for each chapter.
- Content presentation (instructional goal analysis for chapter tasks).
- Phases of the Dick and Carey Model.
- Inputs and outputs for each step in the Dick and Carey Model.
- A rubric for evaluating products developed.
- A business-related case Study.

Brief Contents

Contents

chapter 2
Identifying Instructional Goals Using Front-End Analysis 18

chapter 3
Conducting a Goal Analysis 48

chapter 7
Developing Assessment Instruments 154

chapter 8
Planning the Instructional Strategy: Theoretical Bases 194

chapter 9

Planning Logistics and Management for the Instructional Strategy 248

To the Instructor

The *Instructors' Manual for The Systematic Design of Instruction* is a Word document available for download from the publisher's Instructor's Resource Center. As professors teaching an ID course using this textbook, you may copy the *Instructors' Manual for The Systematic Design of Instruction* and paste it into your course management system (e.g., Compass, Blackboard). If you do not know how to access the Instructor's Resource Center online to obtain these materials, contact your Pearson representative for instructions.

The Instructors' Manual for The Systematic Design of Instruction contains important information for those teaching the course, including:

- Course Management Plans for ten-week and fifteen-week terms.
- Suggestions for providing either an information-based or a product-based learning experience.
- Course management suggestions for web-based delivery.
- Goals and objectives for each step in the model.
- Illustrations of preinstructional materials.
- Goal analyses for each step in the model.
- Rubrics for evaluating ID and development products for each step in the model.
- Practice and feedback, including concept quizzes and application quizzes for each chapter of the text.

In the spirit of constructive feedback, always an important component of the systematic design process, the authors welcome reactions from readers about ways in which the text may be strengthened to better meet their needs. Please send comments to the authors at the following e-mail addresses:

Walter Dick	wdick@penn.com
Lou Carey	jim.lou.carey@gmail.com
James O. Carey	jamesocarey@gmail.com

chapter 1

Introduction to Instructional Design

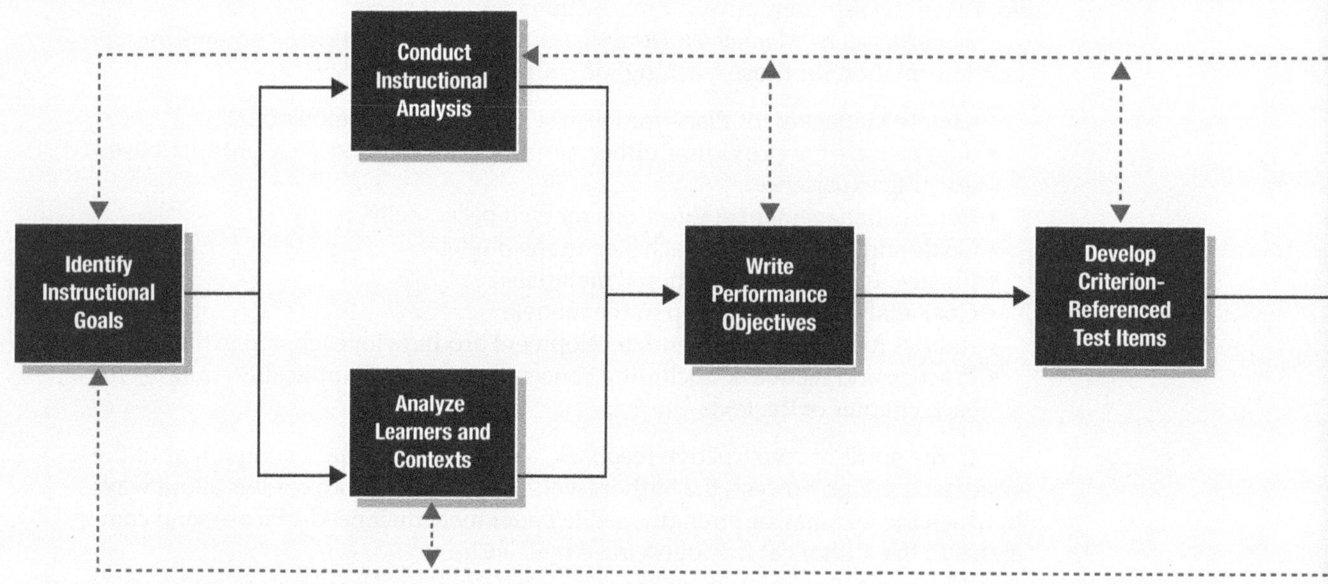

The Dick and Carey Systems Approach Model for Designing Instruction

In a contemporary e-learning or distance-education course, students are brought together with an instructor (perhaps) and are guided through textbook or online content by class activities such as online exercises, question/answer/discussion boards, projects, and interaction with classmates. If student attitudes, achievement, and completion rates are not up to desired levels, such variations as substituting a more interesting textbook, requiring student work groups, or enhancing real-time interaction with the instructor may be tried. If those or other solutions fail to improve outcomes, the instructor or course manager may reorganize the content on the web e-learning portal or, believing that "e-learning isn't for everyone," may simply make no changes at all.

Attempts to improve student achievement by tinkering with this or that component of a course can be frustrating, often leading an instructor or course manager to explain low performance as a student

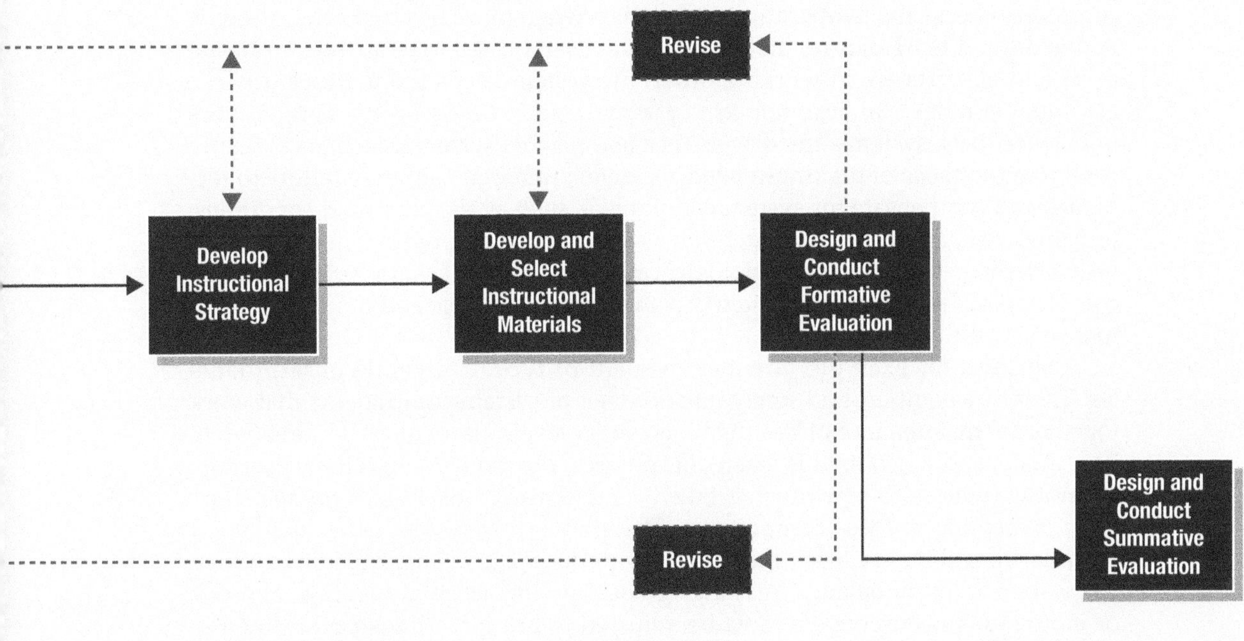

problem—the students lack the necessary background, aren't smart enough, aren't motivated, or don't have the study habits and perseverance to succeed. However, rather than piecemeal fixes or frustrated rationalizations, a more productive approach is to view e-learning—and, indeed, all purposeful teaching and learning—as systematic processes in which every component is crucial to successful learning. The instructor, learners, materials, instructional activities, delivery system, and learning and performance environments interact and work with each other to bring about desired student learning outcomes. Changes in one component can affect other components as well as the eventual learning outcomes; failure to account adequately for conditions within a single component can doom the entire instructional process. Israelite (2004, 2006) characterizes e-learning shortfalls in corporate training as a failure to use *systems thinking*—for example, the investment in high-tech learning management systems and delivery technologies frequently has not been accompanied by thorough consideration of other instructional components such as the design of effective learning experiences. Israelite's perspective is usually referred to as the *systems point of view*, and advocates typically use systems thinking to analyze performance problems and design instruction.

The Systems Point of View

Let's first consider what is meant by a *system*. The term *system* has become very popular as what we do becomes increasingly interrelated with what other people do. A system is technically a set of interrelated parts, all of which work together toward a defined goal. The parts of the system depend on each other for input and output, and the entire system uses feedback to determine if its desired goal has been reached. If it has not, then the system is modified until it reaches the goal. The most easily understood systems are those we create and can control rather than those that occur naturally. For example, you probably have a heating and cooling system in your home in which various components work together to produce a desired temperature. The thermostat is the feedback mechanism through which the system constantly checks the temperature and signals when more heat or cold is needed. At the desired temperature, the system shuts itself off. As long as the thermostat is set and all parts are in working order, the system keeps the temperature in a comfortable range. An automobile's braking system, however, by using a more fallible feedback system—the driver—is a less reliable system. Mechanical failure is seldom the cause of braking-related accidents; rather, it is human failure to recognize and compensate for system components such as slippery road conditions, impaired vision, or distracted attention to a cell phone or a radio while driving in heavy traffic. When human physiological and psychological characteristics are key components of a system, the system becomes less predictable and more difficult to manage for the desired results.

Consider, for example, the management of type 1 (juvenile onset) diabetes. There is a complex and finely balanced set of system components that work together for maintenance of healthy blood sugar levels, particularly (1) diet (what, how much, and when food is eaten), (2) physical exertion, (3) emotional exertion, (4) insulin (when and how much is taken), and (5) each individual's unique metabolic processing of these components. The goal of this system is a stable blood sugar level, and the feedback mechanism is periodic blood sugar readings. When the system is out of balance, readings go outside the acceptable range, and one or more system components must be adjusted to bring readings up or down as needed. Controlling this system might seem to be a daunting task in the presence of human individual differences. The systems approach, however, enables professionals to identify interacting components of diabetes care, establish normal human ranges for each component as starting points for care, and then adjust and fine-tune a care regimen as needed to accommodate individual differences. An accepted perspective for professionals in diabetes care is that the system is dynamic rather than static, requiring continuous monitoring as individuals grow, age, and change their lifestyles.

The Systems Approach to Instructional Design

The instructional process itself can be viewed as a system whose purpose is to bring about learning. The components of the system are the learners, the instructor, the instructional materials and activities, the learning environment, and the environment in which new skills will be applied, all interacting to achieve the goal. For example, in a traditional classroom, the instructor might guide students through sample problems in the textbook or student manual. To determine whether learning is taking place, a quiz is administered at the end of the class. In the instructional system, the quiz is equivalent to the blood sugar readings in diabetes care. If student achievement is not satisfactory, then components must be modified to make the system more effective and bring about the desired learning outcomes.

The systems view of instruction sees the important roles of all the components in the process. They must all interact effectively, just as the parts in a system of diabetes care must interact effectively to bring about desired outcomes. Success depends not on any one component in the system but rather on a determination of the contributions of each component to the desired outcome. There must be a clear assessment of the effectiveness of the system in bringing about learning and a mechanism to make changes if learning fails to occur. As in the example of diabetes care, instructional systems include the human component and are therefore complex and dynamic, requiring constant monitoring and adjustment.

Thus far, our discussion of the instructional process has focused only on the *learning moment*, when instructors, instructional materials and activities, and learners come together with the goal that learning will occur. What about the preparation for the instructional process? How does the instructor decide what to do and when? It is not surprising that someone with a systems view sees the preparation, implementation, evaluation, and revision of instruction as one integrated process. In the broadest systems sense, a variety of sources provide input to the preparation of the instruction. The output is some product or combination of products and procedures that are implemented. The results are used to determine whether the system should be changed and, if so, how.

Instructional Design (ID) Models

The purpose of this book is to describe a systems approach for the design, development, implementation, and evaluation of instruction. This is not a physical system, such as home heating and air conditioning, but a procedural system. We must emphasize that there is no single systems approach model for designing instruction. A number of models bear the label *systems approach,* and all share most of the same basic components. Collectively, these design models and the processes they represent are referred to as *instructional systems development (ISD). Instructional design (ID)* is used as an umbrella term that includes all phases of the ISD process. These terms all become clear as you begin to use the instructional design process.

Instructional design models are based, in part, on many years of research on the learning process. Each component of a model is based on theory and, in most instances, on research demonstrating the effectiveness of that component. The purpose for the model is to help you learn, understand, analyze, and improve your practice of the discipline, but all models are oversimplified representations. As you grow in understanding, don't confuse the representation with the reality. The graphical arrangement of boxes and arrows, for example, implies a linear process flow, but any experienced instructional designer will attest that in practice, the process most often looks more like the circular, continuous improvement model in Figure 1.1 or the concurrent processes model in Figure 1.2 that is useful when

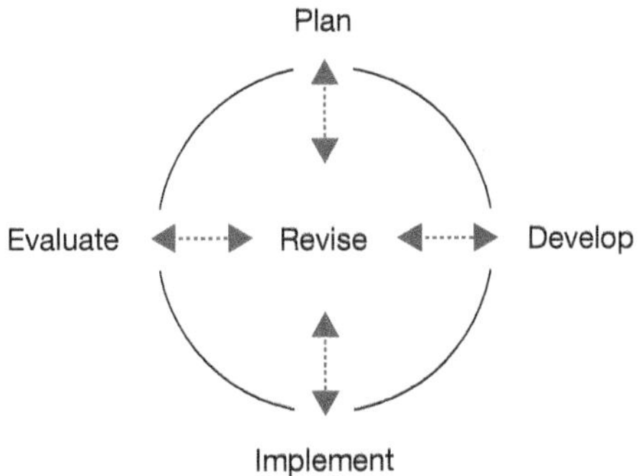

Figure 1.1 Continuous Improvement Cycle

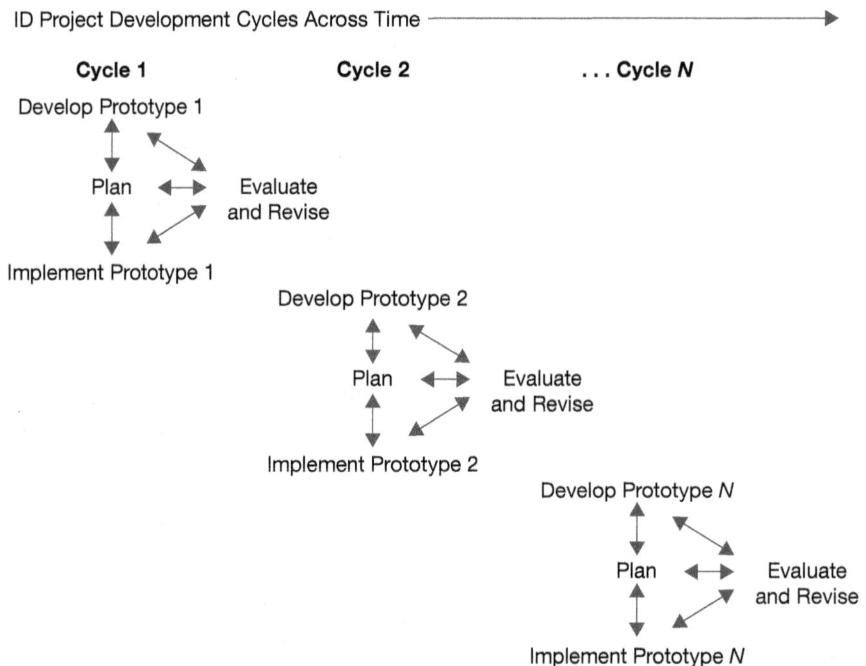

Figure 1.2 Concurrent ID Process in Rapid Prototype Development

planning, development, implementation, and revision all occur at the same time or in multiple cycles of simultaneous activities. If you are new to the field of instructional design, these figures may not make a lot of sense now but will come into focus later in the book.

The Dick and Carey Model of Instructional Design

The systems approach model presented in this book is less complex than some but incorporates the major components common to all models, including analysis, design, development, implementation, and evaluation. We describe a series of steps, all of which receive input from preceding steps and provide output for the next steps. All components work together to either produce effective instruction or, if the system evaluation component signals a failure, determine how instruction can be improved.

The model as presented here is based not only on theory and research but also on a considerable amount of practical experience in its application. In the section that follows, we present the general systems-approach model in much the same way as a practical cookbook recipe—you do this and then you do that. When you begin to use a recipe in your own kitchen, however, it takes on greater meaning. In essence, your use of your own kitchen, your own ingredients, and your own personal touch results in a unique product. You may change the recipe, take shortcuts, substitute ingredients, and perform steps out of sequence. So it is with instructional designers—in the beginning, they use a model such as the one presented in this book as a scaffold to support their analysis, design, development, implementation, and evaluation work. As students and practitioners of instructional design become more experienced and proficient, they replace the scaffold with their own unique solution strategies for the multidimensional problems they encounter in designing instruction. As in any complex endeavor, those who fail to make the jump from dependence to independence never master the discipline and are, at best, good technicians.

The Dick and Carey model was introduced in the first edition of *The Systematic Design of Instruction* in 1978, and a simple Google search for "Dick and Carey model" will provide a glimpse of its presence in the discipline from that first publication to this day. As you begin designing instruction, trust the model—it has worked for countless students and professionals. As you grow in knowledge and experience, trust yourself! The flexibility, insight, and creativity required for original solutions reside in experienced users and professionals—not in models. The Dick and Carey Model is only a representation of practices in the discipline of instructional design. It gives us a way to distinguish the practices within the broader discipline, similar to distinguishing the individual trees within a forest, but mastering a discipline requires that we "see the forest for the trees." In his book *The Fifth Discipline: The Art and Practice of the Learning Organization*, Peter Senge (1990) accurately defines and depicts what it means to practice a discipline:

> By "discipline" I mean . . . a body of theory and technique that must be studied and mastered to be put into practice. A discipline is a developmental path for acquiring certain skills or competencies. As with any discipline, from playing the piano to electrical engineering, some people have an innate "gift," but anyone can develop proficiency through practice. To practice a discipline is to be a lifelong learner. You "never arrive"; you spend your life mastering disciplines. . . . Practicing a discipline is different from emulating a model. (pp. 10–11)

Components of the Dick and Carey Model

Identify Instructional Goal(s)

The first step in the model is to determine what new information and skills you want learners to have mastered when they have completed your instruction, expressed as goals. The instructional goals may be derived from a list of goals, from a performance analysis, from a needs assessment, from practical experience with learning difficulties of students, from the analysis of people who are doing a job, or from some other requirement for new instruction.

Conduct Instructional Analysis

After you have identified the instructional goal, you determine step-by-step what people are doing when they perform that goal as well as look at subskills needed for complete mastery of the goal. The final step in the instructional analysis process is to determine what skills, knowledge, and attitudes, known as *entry skills*, are needed by learners to be successful in the new instruction. For example, students need to know the concepts of radius and diameter in order to compute the area and the circumference of a circle, so those concepts are entry skills for instruction on computing area and circumference.

Analyze Learners and Contexts

In addition to analyzing the instructional goal, there is a parallel analysis of the learners, the context in which they learn the skills, and the context in which they use them. Learners' current skills, preferences, and attitudes are determined along with the characteristics of the instructional setting and the setting in which the skills will eventually be used. This crucial information shapes a number of the succeeding steps in the model, especially the instructional strategy.

Write Performance Objectives

Based on the instructional analysis and the description of entry skills, you write specific statements of what learners will be able to do when they complete the instruction. These statements, derived from the skills identified in the instructional analysis, identify the skills to be learned, the conditions under which the skills will be demonstrated, and the criteria for successful performance.

Develop Assessment Instruments

Based on the objectives you have written, you develop assessments that are parallel to and that measure the learners' ability to perform what you describe in the objectives. Major emphasis is placed on relating the kind of skills described in the objectives to the assessment requirements. The range of possible assessments for judging learners' achievement of critical skills across time includes objective tests, alternative assessments, live performances, measures of attitude formation, and portfolios that are collections of objective and alternative assessments that document learners' progress over time.

Develop Instructional Strategy

Based on information from the five preceding steps, a designer identifies a theoretically based strategy to use in the instruction to achieve the learning goal. The strategy emphasizes activation of internal mental processes that will foster student learning, including:

- preinstructional activities, such as stimulating motivation and focusing attention;
- presentation of new content with examples and demonstrations;
- active learner participation and practice with feedback on how they are doing; and
- follow-through activities that assess students' learning and relate the newly learned skills to real-world applications.

The strategy is based on current theories of learning and results of learning research, the characteristics of the media used to engage learners, the content to be learned, and the characteristics of the learners who participate in the instruction. These features are used to plan necessary logistics and management, develop or select materials, and plan instructional activities.

Develop and Select Instructional Materials

In this step, the instructional strategy is used to produce the instruction and typically includes guidance for learners, instructional materials, and assessments. (In using the term *instructional materials,* we include all forms of instruction such as instructor's guides, student reading lists, PowerPoint presentations, case studies, videos, podcasts, computer-based multimedia formats, and web pages for distance learning.) The decision to develop original materials depends on the types of learning outcomes, the availability of existing relevant materials, and developmental resources available to you. Criteria for selecting from among existing materials are also provided.

Design and Conduct Formative Evaluation of Instruction

Following completion of a draft of the instruction, a series of evaluations is conducted to collect data used to identify problems with the instruction or opportunities to make the instruction better, called *formative* because its purpose is to help create and improve instructional processes and products. The three types of formative evaluation are referred to as *one-to-one evaluation, small-group evaluation,* and *field trial evaluation,* each of which provides the designer with a different set of information that can be used to improve instruction. Similar techniques can be applied to the formative evaluation of existing materials or classroom instruction.

Revise Instruction

The final step in the design and development process (and the first step in a repeat cycle) is revising the instruction. Data from the formative evaluation are summarized and interpreted to identify difficulties experienced by learners in achieving the objectives and to relate these difficulties to specific deficiencies in the instruction. The dotted line in the figure at the beginning of this chapter (labeled "Revise") indicates that the data from a formative evaluation are not simply used to revise the instruction itself but are used to reexamine the validity of the instructional analysis and the assumptions about the entry skills and characteristics of learners. It also may be necessary to reexamine statements of performance objectives and test items in light of formative data. The instructional strategy is reviewed, and finally all of these considerations are incorporated into revisions of the instruction to make it a more effective learning experience. In actual practice, a designer does not wait to begin revising until all analysis, design, development, and evaluation work is completed; rather, the designer is constantly making revisions in previous steps based on what has been learned in subsequent steps. Revision is not a discrete event that occurs at the end of the ID process but an ongoing process of using information to reassess assumptions and decisions. If you have had any previous experience with the Dick and Carey model, you will note a minor change in the model in this ninth edition of the book. The dotted revision line now extends all the way back to identifying instructional goals, and the revision lines to each step in the model are now double-ended arrows depicting the inevitable flow of evaluation and revision activities that are ongoing throughout design and development. This concept has always been implicit in our writing about the model, but with this revision we make it a more explicit part of the model.

Design and Conduct Summative Evaluation

Although summative evaluation is the culminating evaluation of the effectiveness of instruction, it generally is not a part of the design process. It is an evaluation of the absolute or relative value of the instruction and occurs only after the instruction has been formatively evaluated and sufficiently revised to meet the standards of the designer. Because the summative evaluation is sometimes not conducted by the designer of the instruction but instead by an independent evaluator, this component is not considered an integral part of the instructional design process per se.

Procedures used for summative evaluation are receiving more attention today than in previous years because of increased interest in the transfer of knowledge and skills from training settings to the workplace. This type of evaluation answers questions related to whether the instruction provided solved the problems it was designed to solve. There is also increased interest in the effectiveness of e-learning across organizations, states, and countries. For example, will e-learning developed for learners in Utah, which is very transportable electronically, be effective for students in the Caribbean or China? What would experts in learning conclude about the instructional strategies within very attractive materials that were developed "a world away"? Terms such as *learner verification, materials effectiveness,* and *assurances of materials effectiveness* are resurfacing now that materials transportability is much more economical and effortless.

Using the Systems Approach Model

The model described in detail in succeeding chapters is presented as a graphic on the first two pages of each chapter. Ten interconnected boxes represent sets of theories, procedures, and techniques used by the instructional designer to design, develop, evaluate, and revise instruction. The dotted line indicates iterative cycles of evaluation and revision that can occur in each step of the model. The left to right flow of steps, however, does indicate a preferred sequence of design and development based on the logic of ID and the input-output relationships among the steps in the process. We believe it is important for those new to this discipline who are enrolled in a class or studying this text independently to follow the main flow of steps in the model as they begin an ID project. If you follow a career path in this discipline, be assured that you will adapt any ID model to fit the resources and constraints present in future projects. Our model of instructional design is referred to as a *systems approach model*, and it brings together in one coherent whole many concepts that you may have already encountered in a variety of educational situations. For example, you undoubtedly have heard of *performance objectives* and may have already written some yourself. Such terms as *criterion-referenced testing* and *instructional strategy* may also be familiar. The model shows how these terms, and the processes associated with them, are interrelated and how these procedures can be used to produce effective instruction.

The instructional strategy component of our model describes how the designer uses information from analyzing what is to be taught to formulate a plan for connecting learners with the *instruction* being developed with the ID model. Throughout this text, we define the term *instruction* quite broadly as purposeful activity intended to cause, guide, or support learning. As such, instruction encompasses such activities as traditional group lecture/discussion, computer-based drill and practice, moderated small-group online case-study analysis, individualized discovery learning, or group problem solving mediated through avatar characters in a computer-generated virtual world. The range of activities that can serve as instruction is limited only by the imagination of teachers, designers, and students. Now that you have read descriptions of the Dick and Carey model, consider some important questions about its use.

Why Use the Systems Approach?

Empirical and Replicable Perhaps the most important reason for using the systems approach is that it is an empirical and replicable process. In the process of systematically designing instruction, data are collected to determine whether any parts of the instruction are not working, and if yes, it is revised until it does work. Instruction can be designed for a single delivery or for use on multiple occasions with multiple learners with predictable results. It is worth the time and effort to develop, evaluate, and revise instruction because the lessons learned can often provide guidance for adapting it for different learners in different contexts, scaling it for different audience sizes, and delivering it with different media.

Accountability Laws Among the reasons that systematic approaches to instructional design are effective is the required focus on what learners are to know or do when the instruction is concluded. Without this precise statement, subsequent planning and implementation steps can become unclear and ineffective. This focus on outcomes is pertinent for all public schools because of the contemporary political climate in education. The most recent standards/accountability movement began with a number of states passing laws establishing tests and performance standards for judging student, school, and school district performance and was cemented when Congress passed the No Child Left Behind Act of 2001 followed by the National Governors Association Common Core Standards initiative in 2009 and the Every Student Succeeds Act (ESSA) of 2015. These programs mandate state-level development and implementation of assessments of basic skills at selected grade levels, and some state and district-level administrators have adopted assessment results as standards for distributing performance awards to districts, schools, and classroom teachers. A systems approach to instruction is a powerful tool for planning successful standards-based education because of the tight alignment among learning outcomes, student characteristics, instructional activities, and assessments.

Connectedness among Components Another reason for using the systems approach is the interlocking connection between each component, especially the relationship between instructional strategy and desired learning outcomes. Instruction specifically targeted on the skills and knowledge to be learned helps supply the appropriate conditions for these learning outcomes. Stated another way, the range of instructional activities cannot be loosely related or unrelated to what is to be learned.

Outcomes-Based The systems approach is an outcomes-based approach to instruction because it begins with a clear understanding of the new knowledge and skills that students will learn. Although widely adopted among educators at all levels, the systems approach finds even more numerous applications in business and industry, government, nonprofits, nongovernmental organizations, and the military, where there is a premium on both efficiency of instruction and quality of learner performance, with high payoffs for both.

Careful attention is paid to determining what learners must already know (prerequisite knowledge and skills) in order to begin the instruction as well as what must be learned during instruction (enabling knowledge and skills). The instruction is focused on the skills to be learned and is presented under the best conditions for learning. The learner is evaluated fairly, with instruments that measure the skills and knowledge described in the objectives, and the results are used to revise the instruction so that it will be even more effective the next time it is used with learners. Following this process causes the designer to focus on the needs and skills of the learners and the environment in which new skills will be used and results in the creation of effective instruction that transfers to real applications on the job.

For Which Instructional Types and Learner Groupings Is the Systems Approach Appropriate?

Types of Instruction The systems approach to designing instruction includes the planning, development, implementation, and evaluation of instruction. Part of this process is choosing the type of instruction. In some instances, it is most appropriate to have an instructor deliver the instruction; in other situations, a variety of media may be used. In every instance, the systems approach is an invaluable tool for identifying what is to be taught, determining how to teach it, and evaluating the instruction to find out whether it is effective.

Learner Groupings The procedure described in this text for developing an instructional strategy is a generic one. Although systematically designed instruction is not necessarily individualized, a primary application of the systems approach to instructional design is for self-paced, independent learning. Useful for developing simple tutorial instruction for individual students, the systems approach is equally applicable to problem-solving assignments for small groups of students or complex digital multimedia for distance delivery to a mass audience over the web. The procedure easily fits the requirements of any preferred medium of instruction, noting that most research suggests that it is the analysis process and the instructional strategies, rather than the delivery mode, that determine instructional success. The systems approach is a generic planning process that ensures that materials developed for any type of instruction or student grouping are responsive to the needs of learners and effective in achieving the desired learning outcomes.

The reader should be careful to distinguish between the process of designing instruction and the delivery of that instruction. The systems approach is basically a design process, whereas types of instruction, instructional media, and individualized versus group activity are all decisions made within the design process. Ideally, there are no predetermined assumptions about these decisions because a major part of the design process is to determine how the instruction can be delivered most effectively.

Who Should Use the Systems Approach?

ID Professionals The ISD approach can benefit a diverse range of professionals whose full- or part-time activity is to create instruction effective for a given learning outcome with a particular learner population. The instruction is often designed and packaged for use with many learners over a period of time, whether in business, industry, government, social services, the military, or personnel divisions, as well as in instructional support service centers in junior colleges, universities, and some public school districts. Professional titles used by ID professionals include *instructional designer, instructional technologist, human performance technologist, educational technologist, trainer* or *training specialist*, and *human resource development specialist*. (In 2002, a task force was convened within the International Society for Performance Improvement [ISPI] to develop a process and performance standards for certifying ID professionals. The certification program is in place and awards the designation *Certified Performance Technologist* [CPT] to successful applicants.)

The ID professional sometimes works with a team of specialists to develop the instruction, often including a content specialist, an instructional technologist, an evaluation specialist, and a manager (who is often the instructional designer). The team approach draws on the expertise of specialists to produce a product that none could produce alone. In these settings, there is a premium placed on interpersonal skills because seemingly everyone has ideas on how best to do what needs to be done.

Professors and Instructors This book is suitable for university professors, military instructors, corporate trainers, and instructors in any other setting who are interested in improving the effectiveness of their instruction. We are convinced that the model and procedures are equally applicable in both school and nonschool settings. Instructional design skills are critical for those designing instruction for web delivery.

Teachers As you study the instructional design model and perhaps use it to design specific instruction, you will find that it takes both time and effort. If you are a teacher, you may find yourself saying, "I could never use this process to prepare all my instruction," and you would probably be correct. The individual instructor with day-to-day instructional responsibilities can use the complete process to develop only small amounts of instruction at any given time because of the level of detail included in each step. However, even such limited use can expand any teacher's instructional repertoire. Also, teachers can select and apply some of the steps or even pieces of a single step as appropriate for different instructional planning needs. As you work through the book, however, your goal should be to master the level of detail contained in each step because mastery of the full model establishes the experience and insight to select the right pieces of the instructional design process properly according to specific instructional needs. What you learn in this book is a theory-based, systematic way of viewing the teaching–learning process. The ID model provides tools that you can tuck away in a mental toolbox along with all of the other tools that you have picked up through your academic training and your experience. Using these tools helps you sharpen your focus on instructional practices that tend to predict successful learning in students.

We have found that almost every teacher who has studied the process has come away with two reactions: The first is that they will certainly begin immediately to use some of the components in the model, if not all of them. The second reaction is that their approach to instruction will never be the same because of the insights they have gained from using the process. (The reader may be somewhat skeptical at this point; be sure to consider your own reactions after you have used this approach.)

Our examples of various aspects of the application of the systematic design process include instructional contexts for all age groups, from young children to mature adults. We use the terms *teacher, instructor,* and *designer* interchangeably throughout the book because we truly believe they are interchangeable.

As you read through the chapters that follow, you will find in the Examples sections a business-related plan for retirees on recreational golf. In the Case Study sections, there are materials on group leadership skills for adult learners in graduate school. The appendices contain another complete case study in language arts for middle school students. These examples are carried through each step of the design model at the point it is introduced. Analyzing case studies from differing contexts will aid your transfer of the design skills to your own instructional goal and subsequent design work. These particular studies were chosen because you will be able to "look through" the obvious content of the examples to see the more abstract instructional design processes illustrated.

Professional and Historical Perspectives

You have seen that the instructional design process we describe in this book requires detailed Analysis, Design, Development, Implementation, and Evaluation activities. As such, the Dick and Carey model is one of many that belong in the ADDIE family. One will find frequent reference in professional literature to the ADDIE instructional design model when there is no such singular entity; rather, the use of the term is just an acknowledgment that a particular ID practice has incorporated analysis, design, development, implementation, and evaluation. A group of ID models that shared these components evolved in the 1960s and 1970s with the interest in systems thinking in professional, technical, and military training. Recent research into what instructional designers do in their jobs confirms the relevance and value of ADDIE components in contemporary ID practice, if not in the exact placement in a specific ID process (e.g., York & Ertmer, 2016). A few of the many ADDIE ID models that influence ID practice today are described by Merrill (2013), Morrison et al. (2019), Rothwell et al. (2016), Smith and Ragan (2020), and van Merriënboer and Kirschner (2018). Some of the graphic depictions of these and other contemporary ID models have very different appearances, but they all specify or imply the five ADDIE components.

Our original approach to the instructional strategy component of the model was heavily influenced by the work of Robert Gagné's *The Conditions of Learning* (1965), which incorporated cognitive information-processing views of learning that assume most human behavior to be very complex and controlled primarily by a person's internal mental processes rather than external stimuli and reinforcements. Instruction is seen as organizing and providing sets of information, examples, experiences, and activities that guide, support, and augment students' internal mental processes. Learning occurs when students incorporate new information and schemes into their memories that enable new capabilities. This would be the *cognitivist* view of learning and instruction. Gagné further developed cognitive views in later editions of *The Conditions of Learning* (1970, 1977, 1985). His influence as one of the founders of the instructional systems development discipline is described in Richey's (2000) book *The Legacy of Robert M. Gagné.*

Constructivism is a pedagogical philosophy that has influenced the thinking of many instructional designers. Although constructivist thinking varies broadly on many issues, the central point is the view of learning as a unique product "constructed" by each individual learner combining new information and experiences with existing knowledge. In fact, this view is shared by all cognitive psychologists who take their understanding of human learning and memory from information processing theories such as that described by Atkinson and Shiffrin (1960). Where *constructivists* diverge is in their views on some ontological issues regarding the nature of reality and the consequences for some epistemological issues about how new knowledge is acquired. This all boils down to constructivist prescriptions for instruction containing minimal learning guidance, whereas cognitivist prescriptions would typically be for instruction containing more learning guidance. Implications for designing instruction will be explored further in Chapter 8 along with some commentary on *learning sciences* and *design-based research.*

Throughout this text, readers will find predominately a cognitivist view of teaching and learning. They will also see elements of constructivist thinking adapted as appropriate for the varieties of learners, learning outcomes, learning contexts, and performance contexts that are discussed.

The Dick and Carey model incorporates an eclectic set of tools drawn from major theoretical positions and is an effective design framework for guiding pedagogical practices within all foundational orientations. Although some instructional theorists may question the model as recommending practices counter to their pedagogical practices, the authors counsel an open-minded view and believe that most instructional design processes advocated in the model, when used by expert professionals, are essentially neutral. That is, master teachers and instructional designers can translate their own views of learning theory into pedagogical practices based on their own decisions about goals, students, and learning environments. Because the model depicts a set of generic ID practices, it has been adapted successfully by teachers, instructional designers, educational technologists, military trainers, and performance technologists in all kinds of settings.

For those interested in more historical context, Reiser's (2001a, 2001b) articles on the history of instructional design and technology provide a good review of the origins and development of the field.

References and Recommended Readings

At the end of each chapter, carefully selected references are listed. The books and articles supplement the description in the chapter or focus in more detail on an important concept that has been presented.

The references listed for this first chapter are somewhat different. These are a mixture of current books in the field of instructional design or works that have direct implications for the practice of instructional design along with a selection of classic texts and articles. Many of the topics in this text also appear in these referenced texts, which vary in depth and breadth of coverage of topics but should help expand your knowledge and understanding of the instructional design field.

Note: The first three references are out of order alphabetically, because they are open-access, online resources that provide broad coverage of many topics in this text and extended readings on related subjects.

Clark, D. R. *The performance juxtaposition site*. http://nwlink.com/~donclark/index.html

Culatta, R., & Kearsley, G. Instructional design.org. https://www.instructionaldesign.org

West, R. E. *Foundations of learning and instructional design technology: The past, present, and future of learning and instructional design technology*. EdTech Books. https://edtechbooks.org/lidtfoundations

Atkinson, R. C., & Shiffrin, R. M. (1968). Human memory: A proposed system and its control processes. In K. W. Spence & J. T. Spence (Eds.), *The psychology of learning and motivation (Volume 2)* (pp. 89–195). Academic Press.

Banathy, B. H. (1968). *Instructional systems*. Fearon Publishers. A classic text placing instruction in a systems context.

Blanchard, P. N., & Thacker, J. W. (Eds.). (2019). *Effective training: Systems, strategies, and practices* (6th ed.). Chicago Business Press. Presents useful combination of theory and practical examples from professional and technical training.

Branch, R. M., Lee, H., & Tseng, S. S. (Eds.). (2019). *Educational media and technology yearbook: Volume 42*. Springer. Describes current information on associations, organizations, and degree programs in the field of educational technology. Includes sections on trends and issues, and virtual and augmented reality.

Craik, F. I. M., & Lockhart, R. S. (1972). Levels of processing: A framework for memory research. *Journal of Verbal Learning and Verbal Behavior, 11*, 671–684.

Driscoll, M. P. (2005). *Psychology of learning for instruction* (3rd ed.). Allyn & Bacon. Describes contemporary approaches to learning that focus on instruction.

Duffy, T. M., & Jonassen, D. H. (Eds.). (1992). *Constructivism and the technology of instruction*. Lawrence Erlbaum Associates. Provides a comprehensive review of varying perspectives on constructivism.

Ely, D. P. (1996). *Classic writings on instructional technology*. Libraries Unlimited. Describes the people and writings that shaped instructional technology.

Ertmer, P. A., & Newby, T. J. (1993). Behaviorism, cognitivism, constructivism: Comparing critical features from an instructional design perspective. *Performance Improvement Quarterly, 6*(4), 50–72. Compares three theoretical bases with guidelines for instructional designers.

Ertmer, P. A., Quinn, J. A., & Glazewski, K. D. (Eds.). (2019). *The ID casebook: Case studies in instructional design* (5th ed.). Pearson. Provides an array of examples of the application of instructional design processes to real-world problems in K–12, postsecondary, and corporate settings.

Fleming, M. L., & Levie, W. H. (1993). *Instructional message design: Principles from the cognitive and behavioral sciences* (2nd ed.). Educational Technology Publications. A classic text still used in designing displays and interfaces for contemporary media technologies.

Gagné, R. M. (1985). *The conditions of learning* (4th ed.). Holt, Rinehart and Winston. Details the linkage between cognitive learning theory and instructional practices in the final edition of this classic book.

Gagné, R. M. (1977). *The conditions of learning* (3rd ed.). Holt, Rinehart & Winston.

Gagné, R. M. (1970). *The conditions of learning* (2nd ed.). Holt, Rinehart & Winston.

Gagné, R. M. (1965). *The conditions of learning* (1st ed.). Holt, Rinehart & Winston. The original text of Gagné's theory linking types of learning to instructional practice.

Gagné, R. M., & Medsker, K. L. (1996). *The conditions of learning: Training applications*. Harcourt Brace College Publishers. Presents same model as Gagné's original text by this name, but with the addition of examples from business and industry.

Gagné, R. M., Wager, W. W., Golas, K. C., & Keller, J. M. (2004). *Principles of instructional design* (5th ed.). Wadsworth/Thomson Learning. Includes two new chapters on technology and online learning. This is the first new edition of this classic book since 1992.

Hannafin, M. J., Hannafin, K. M., Land, S. M., & Oliver, K. (1997). Grounded practice and the design of constructivist learning environments. *Educational Technology Research and Development*, *45*(3), 101–117. Presents a carefully reasoned argument for grounding instructional practice in theoretical foundations—regardless of the particular practice that one espouses.

Hannum, W. (2005). Instructional systems development: A 30-year retrospective. *Educational Technology Magazine*, *45*(4), 5–21.

Israelite, L. (2004). We thought we could, we think we can, and lessons along the way. In E. Masie (Ed.), *Learning: Rants, raves, and reflections.* Jossey-Bass Pfeiffer. Presents a human resource development executive's systems-based view of the importance of maintaining instructional design integrity within the technology decisions and subsequent materials development performed by professional and technical trainers.

Israelite, L. (Ed.). (2006). *Lies about learning.* ASTD Press. Chapter 13 focuses on identifying goals before choosing solutions.

Koszalka, T. A., Russ-Eft, D. F., & Reiser, R. A. (2013). *Instructional design competencies: The standards* (4th ed.). Information Age Publishing. Contains revised standards and competencies from the International Board of Standards for Training, Performance, and Instruction.

Medsker, K. L., & Holdsworth, K. M. (Eds.) (2007). *Models and strategies for training design.* John Wiley & Sons. Focuses on ID models in training settings. This is a print-on-demand book.

Merrill, M. D. (2013). *First principles of instruction.* Pfeiffer. Argues that wide-ranging instructional design theories all include five fundamentally similar principles.

Morrison, G. R., Ross, S. M., & Kalman, H. K. (2019). *Designing effective instruction* (8th ed.). Wiley. Covers many current instructional design concepts as well as planning for project management and instructional implementation.

Newby, T. J., Stepich, D. A., Lehman, J. D., Russell, J. D., & Todd. A. (2010). *Educational technology for teaching and learning* (4th ed.). Pearson. Focuses on integrating instruction and technology for the classroom, including planning and developing instruction, grouping learners, selecting delivery formats (including distance learning), managing, and evaluating instruction.

Piskurich, G. M. (2015). *Rapid instructional design: Learning ID fast and right* (3rd ed.). Wiley. Describes an instructional design process "how to" with lots of tips and examples rather than a book about rapid-prototyping methods in instructional design.

Reiser, R. A. (2001a). A history of instructional design and technology: Part I: A history of instructional media. *Educational Technology Research and Development* 49(1), 53–64.

Reiser, R. A. (2001b). A history of instructional design and technology: Part II: A history of instructional design. *Educational Technology Research and Development* 49(2), 57–67.

Reiser, R. A., & Dempsey, J. V. (Eds.). (2017). *Trends and issues in instructional design and technology* (4th ed.). Pearson.

Richey, R. C. (Ed.). (2000). *The legacy of Robert M. Gagné.* ERIC Clearinghouse on Information and Technology. Presents a biographical and historical retrospective that includes five of Gagné's key research papers.

Richey, R. C., & Klein, J. D. (2007). *Design and development research: Methods, strategies, and issues.* Routledge. Describes methods and strategies for conducting design and development research, including product and tool research and model research.

Rothwell, W. J., Benscoter, G. M., King, M., & King, S. B. (2016). *Mastering the instructional design process: A systematic approach* (5th ed.). Wiley. Describes the instructional design process and focuses on professional and technical training.

Senge, P. (1990). *The fifth discipline: The art and practice of the learning organization.* Currency Doubleday. Identifies systems thinking as the fifth in a set of five disciplines required for growth and development of learning organizations. A modern management classic.

Silber, K. H., & Foshay, W. R. (2010). *Handbook of improving performance in the workplace. Instructional design and training delivery.* Pfeiffer. Describes standard principles and evidence-based practices for designing instruction and delivering training.

Smith, P. L., & Ragan, T. J. (2020). *Instructional design* (4th ed.). Wiley. Describes instructional strategies for various learning outcomes.

Spector, J. M., Merrill, M. D., Elen, J., & Bishop, M. J. (2013). *Handbook of research on educational communications and technology* (4th ed.). Springer. Describes new and emerging educational technologies.

Van Merriënboer, J. J. G., & Kirschner, P. A. (2018). *Ten steps to complex learning: A systematic approach to four-component instructional design* (3rd ed.). Routledge.

Visscher-Voerman, I., & Gustafson, K. L. (2004). Paradigms in the theory and practice of education and training design. *Educational Technology, Research, and Development*, 52(2), 69–89.

York, C. S., & Ertmer, P. A. (2016). Examining instructional design principles applied by experienced designers in practice. *Performance Improvement Quarterly*, 29(2), 169–192.

chapter 2

Identifying Instructional Goals Using Front-End Analysis

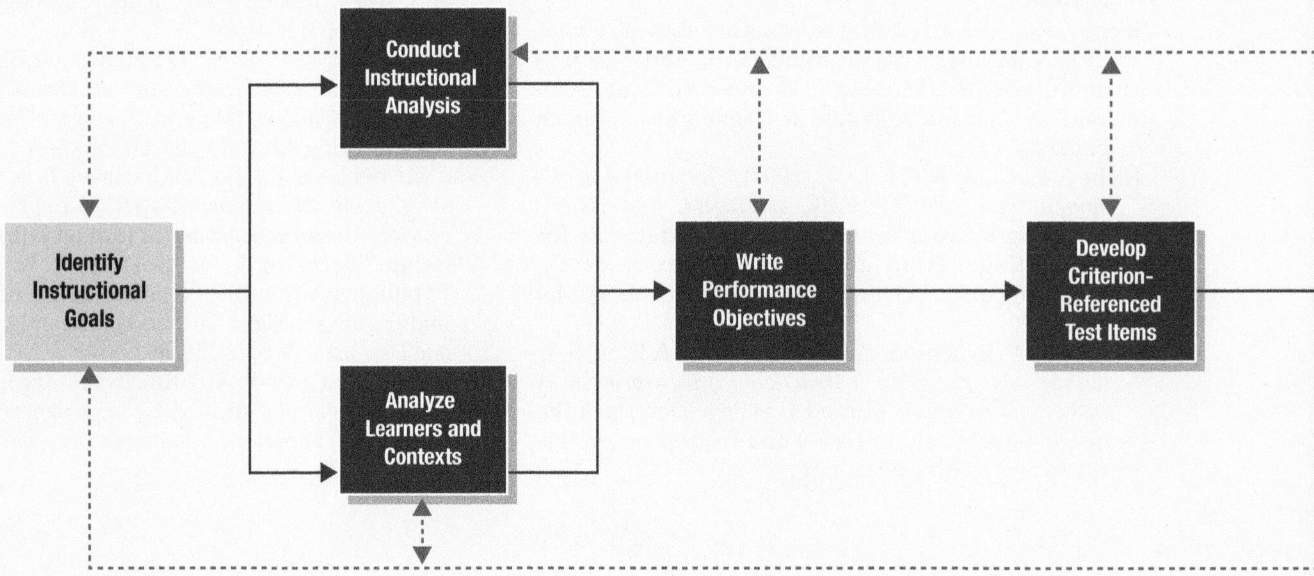

Objectives

- Identify instructional goals.
- Describe how front-end analysis, performance analysis, needs assessment, and job analysis are used in identifying instructional goals.
- Clarify instructional goals.
- Evaluate instructional goals for congruence with organizational needs, feasibility, and clarity.
- Write an instructional goal that meets the criteria for initiating the development of instructional materials.

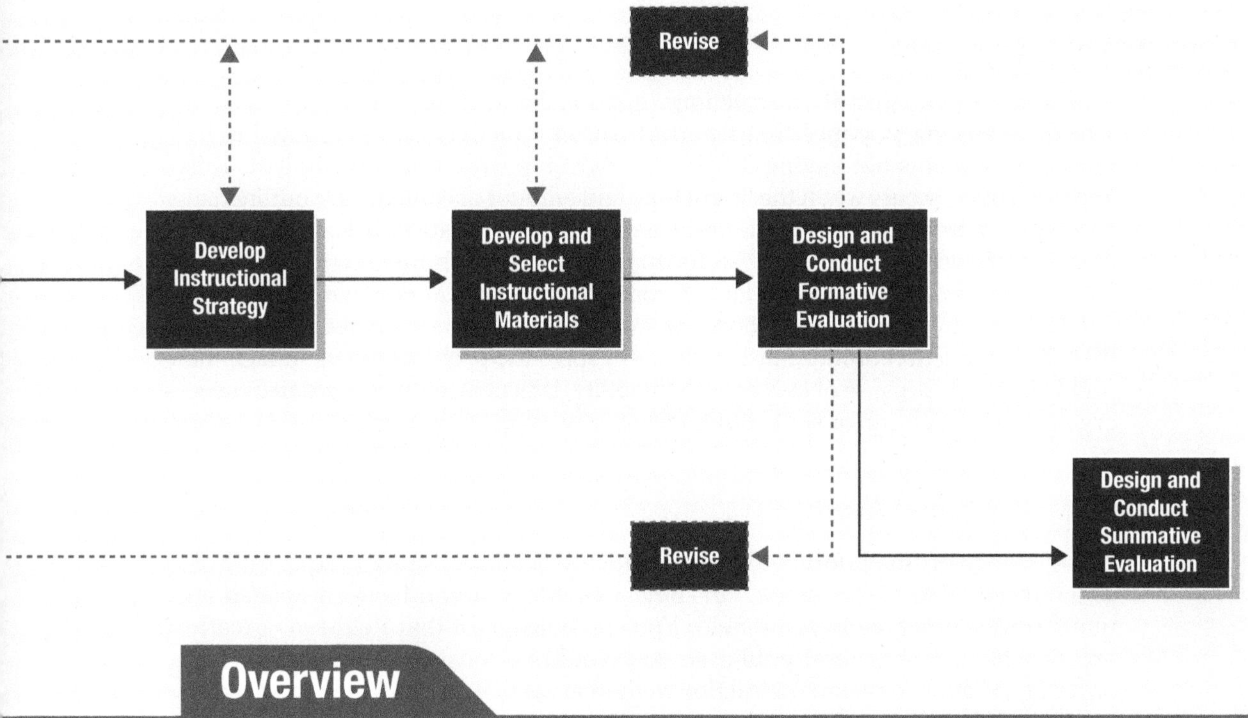

Overview

Instructional goals are clear statements of behaviors that learners are to demonstrate as a result of instruction. Typically derived through a front-end analysis process and intended to address problems that can be resolved most efficiently through instruction, instructional goals provide the foundation for all subsequent instructional design activities. Instructional goals are selected and refined through a rational process that requires answering questions about a particular problem and need, the context wherein the problem and need reside, the availability of resources to design and develop the instruction, and the clarity of the goal statement.

Concepts

Identifying Instructional Goals

Instructional goals are descriptions of capabilities learners are to achieve, or what they will be able to do, as a result of specific instruction. Such capabilities are the desired outcome of specific teaching and learning activities. Perhaps the most critical event in the instructional design process is identifying the instructional goal. If done improperly, even elegant instruction may not serve the organization's or the intended learners' real needs. Without accurate goals, designers run the risk of planning instructional solutions for which needs do not really exist. There are many ways to identify instructional goals, but four common methods are the content outline, subject-matter expert, administrative mandate, and performance technology approaches.

It is important to distinguish between instructional goals and broader social, institutional, and organizational goals. Such broader goals could include ensuring equitable access by all citizens to a city's public resources, graduating 70 percent of matriculating freshman students within four years, or raising customers' positive call center experience ratings from 70 to 90 percent. If it is determined that people working in these contexts will need new skills for their organization to reach those goals, then instructional goals will be identified.

Content Outline Approach

A common way to identify instructional goals is the content outline approach, in which convincing evidence that a performance problem exists is assumed to be caused by students not having learned the right type or amount of content. This approach often occurs when the "right type and amount of content" are outlined in predefined curriculum standards and frameworks, corporate policies, equipment manuals, training manuals, and so forth. One danger with this method is being locked into content standards that may no longer be relevant or that never were adequate solutions for organizational or social needs. Another danger is assuming that new instruction or more instruction will solve the problem when, in fact, the problem may be because of lack of accountability, lack of incentives, outdated tools, organizational culture, or some other factor.

The Subject-Matter Expert Approach

Every reader of this book could be considered a subject-matter expert (SME, pronounced "S M E" or "smee") in some area. Most of you have completed an undergraduate degree in some field. Your knowledge of that field now greatly exceeds that of the general public, so you would be considered an SME. When SMEs are asked to develop instruction in their areas of expertise, they most likely consider their own learning on the subject. Depending on their evaluation of their own knowledge, they try either to replicate it for students or to improve it. The instructional goals established by SMEs often contain words such as *know* and *understand* with regard to content information. This approach to the teaching–learning process assumes that students need to learn what the SME knows and emphasizes the communication of information from instructor to student in the instructional process.

The Administrative Mandate Approach

It often happens that goals are identified for initiating the ID process simply because some administrative authority (e.g., a person, a panel, a board, an agency, a work team, a supervisor, or a program manager) issues a mandate that training for the selected goals will occur. Goals selected by mandate can be valid if appropriate planning and insight were exercised by the administrator on whose authority the training is based or if an instructional designer can exercise political savvy and negotiating skills to confirm or redirect goals after the fact. Unfortunately, there often is little latitude for negotiation, and this "ready-fire-aim" approach frequently misses the mark. Note that some goals selected through mandate can be valid by definition when required by federal or state law, by union contract, by safety requirements for new employee hires, and so forth. Such goals are true mandates and usually go straight to the training department. The public school student performance standards enacted by state legislatures are also examples of true mandates in public education and are passed down to school districts and schools for implementation.

Performance Technology Approach

Instructional designers favor the performance technology approach, in which instructional goals are set in response to problems or opportunities within an organization. This is also referred to as *human performance* technology and *performance improvement*. There are no preconceived notions of what must be learned, of what will be included in an instructional package, or that, in fact, there is any need for instruction at all. Designers attempt to work with those responsible for ensuring that an organization is meeting its quality and productivity goals. These concerns apply to any organization, private or public.

Private organizations are motivated to meet productivity goals, stockholders' expectations, and their clients' and customers' needs. Public agencies, including public schools, share this motivation and also strive to meet the needs for which taxpayers have mandated the expenditure of public funds. To the extent they are not doing so, changes must be made, and the crucial issue becomes determining the correct modifications. Dessinger et al. (2012) provide an informative overview of the current model of performance technology endorsed by the International Society for Performance Improvement (ISPI).

Notice that these four approaches are not mutually exclusive; that is, a designer could take a performance technology approach while also studying existing content outlines, consulting subject-matter experts, and reviewing relevant administrative mandates.

Front-End Analysis

The Dick and Carey model we use throughout this text is a guide to the design, development, and revision of instruction. It has long been accepted that careful front-end analysis is absolutely critical prior to initiating the design of instruction. *Front-end analysis* is an umbrella term for several processes used for arriving at valid instructional goals by evaluating instructional needs and identifying alternative approaches to meeting those needs. It includes a variety of activities including but not limited to performance analysis, needs assessment, job analysis, and instructional goal evaluation. Mastery of front-end analysis skills is not a goal of this text; rather, it is assumed that an instructional systems design program would include coursework and experiences in evaluation, needs assessment, and performance analysis.

Figure 2.1 helps clarify how the skills that you are learning in this text fit into the front-end analysis phase of more complex, larger-scale training and curriculum development projects. For most instructional design efforts in school and university settings and for many professional and technical training projects, the overview and examples of front-end analysis in this chapter will serve the novice designer well.

If you are a student using this book, you may be designing and developing a unit or lesson of instruction as one of the requirements for your class. If that is the case, you might start your project at the "Conduct Needs Assessment as Required" step in Figure 2.1 and then go straight to "Identify Goal 1 for Initiating the Design of Instruction." To provide a broader context for instructional design

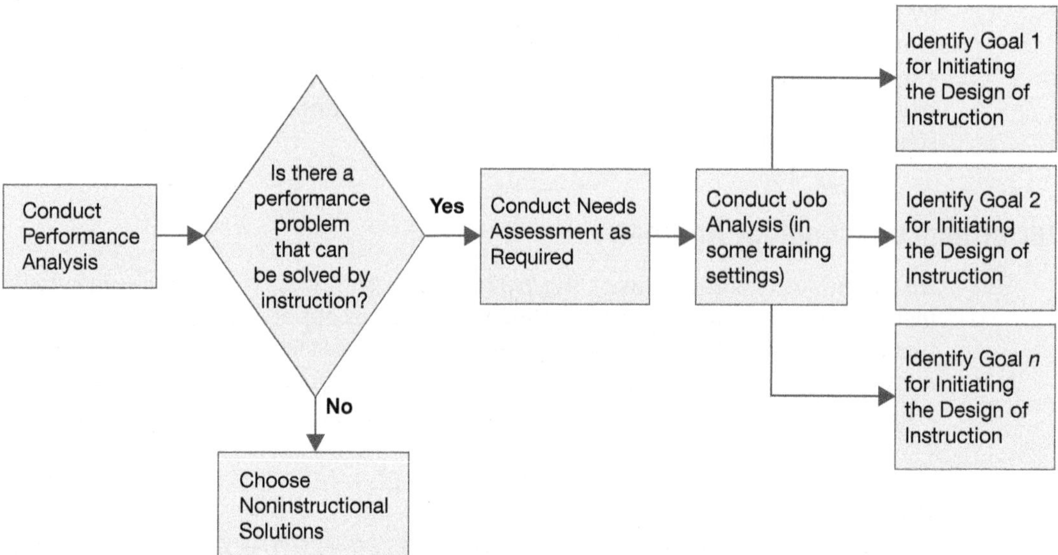

Figure 2.1 Front-End Analysis for Complex Training and Curriculum Development Contexts

in the discussions that follow, we will briefly step through the front-end analysis tasks in Figure 2.1 with examples from business and public schools.

Performance Analysis

Performance analysis is defined as an analytical process used to locate, analyze, and correct job or product performance problems. It is basically a scientific method or research approach to identifying and clarifying problems, the causes of the problems, and possible solutions. This involves careful definition, observation, data gathering, and interpretation. A main concern for the instructional designer is whether the solutions for the performance problems identified involve training or some other operation. Figure 2.2 contains a diagram of main steps in performance analysis.

When viewing the main steps listed in Figure 2.2, readers will immediately realize that they are a version of a generic problem-solving strategy focused on the issue of performance analysis. Public and private organizations are continually

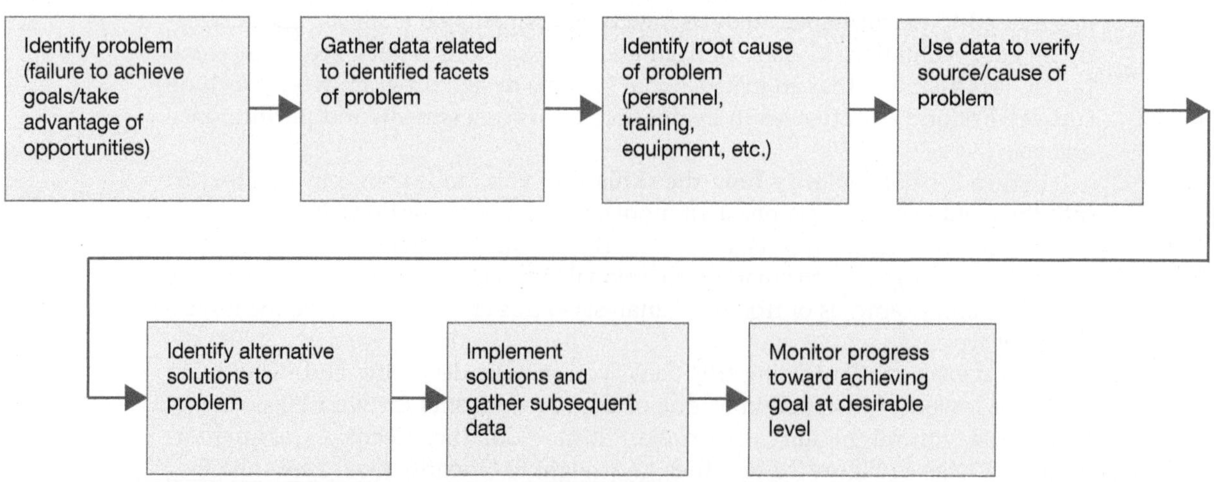

Figure 2.2 Main Steps in Performance Analysis

faced with problems that senior officers and managers must identify and solve. Problems reflect a failure to achieve certain organizational goals or to take advantage of opportunities. Those failures are often seen as resulting from a lack of or improper use of skills; thus, it is not unusual for an officer to identify a problem and assume that training is the solution. Such problems are often presented to the training department with the request that they develop training to solve the problem.

Even when a direct request for training has not been made, the response to someone saying, "I've got a problem!" has often been, "OK, let's do a performance analysis and find out what training we can provide." Performance analysis is an indispensable tool for solving problems, but a performance technologist would take a different mindset into the problem situation and do some analysis before deciding that training should be provided. In common terminology, this mindset is called *critical thinking*. Being a critical thinker is both an attitude and an intellectual skill—that is, one must choose to act like and master the analytical techniques used by a critical thinker. Some of these attitudes and techniques include being open-minded, being objective, seeking causes, viewing a problem from multiple perspectives, giving a fair hearing to evidence on multiple perspectives, suspending judgment until all pertinent information has been heard, listening to contrary views, and changing a conclusion in the face of compelling information. Applying critical-thinking attitudes and skills is more difficult from within an organization than from outside. That is why outside consultants are sometimes hired to conduct strategic planning and performance analysis activities. Instructional designers, however, are most often part of the organization in which they practice their profession, so must cultivate this critical thinking mindset to be effective performance analysts.

Robinson and Robinson (2008) proposed a *performance relationship map* for organizing information gathered during a performance analysis. Review their questions in Table 2.1 and relate them to the performance analysis business example that follows.

Performance Analysis in a Business Setting To explain performance analysis further, let's consider an example from professional and technical training. In our example, the head of a large information systems (IS) division came to the training manager and said, "The customer service call center has grown so fast that we can't keep up with all of the service orders on their computer workstations. Instead of hiring more service technicians, corporate personnel wants me to accept six

Table 2.1 Robinson and Robinson Questions for Consideration in a Performance Analysis

1. What is the problem originally voiced?
2. Is the problem related to a core organizational outcome?
3. Are there established operational goals for this outcome?
4. Is the operational goal being met?
5. Is there an operational need?
6. Have job performance standards been set for achieving the operational goal?
7. Are job performance standards being met?
8. Is there a job performance need?
9. Are there external factors outside the control of local management that are contributing to the operational and job performance needs (e.g., government regulations, corporate hiring freeze, labor contract, corporation's national contract with communication service provider)?
10. Are there internal factors within the control of local management that are contributing to job performance needs?
11. Are there solutions for the performance needs?

transfers from other divisions who are scheduled for termination due to downsizing. I'm going to start screening candidates for transfer, but I know they won't have the skills we need. I want you to decide whether we should train them ourselves in desktop troubleshooting and repair or send them outside for training." The training manager replied, "Thanks for the heads-up. I'll check with the customer service manager and get back to you tomorrow morning." The training manager did some homework that night, and the next morning she diplomatically proposed a performance analysis rather than a quick jump into a training program. The director of information systems agreed to hold up the screening process, but only for a week and a half, saying, "Go ahead and see what you can do." Some of the steps she took and information she learned over the next ten days are as follows:

- The computer breakdown problem was in the customer service call center, which had expanded rapidly with many new customer representatives and computer purchases. Current staffing in IS was not sufficient to keep up with the workstation troubleshooting and repair needs.
- One of the business goals for the customer service unit was to improve customer relations.
- One operational target for improved customer relations was customer satisfaction with 96 percent of telephone contact opportunities.
- To reach the satisfaction target, the customer service division had set performance standards of "maximum of three automated call menu selections before reaching a live representative" and "maximum average wait time of 90 seconds before reaching a live representative." (There were other performance standards, but these are the only ones we consider here.)
- When the training manager checked the most recent customer follow-up data, she found that satisfaction with telephone contact was running at 76 percent, and when she checked telephone log tracking reports, she found that average wait time was just over two and a half minutes and wait time for 17 percent of calls was over five minutes. Clearly, a business goal of the customer service unit and a target performance standard were not being met.
- The training manager checked computer workstation problem reports, downtime, and repair logs in IS and found that hiring and training new computer techs to get workstations repaired and back online sooner would, indeed, decrease service interruptions in the call center and thereby lower average caller wait time.

But were there other solutions? Here is what the training manager found when she suspended judgment pending additional information, began to analyze the system of components and relationships among components that could be contributing to the performance problem, and entertained the possibility of alternatives to a training solution.

- She took another look at the telephone logs and checked a sample of transaction records, and then she took time to sit down and chat with customer service representatives in the break room about their day-to-day job successes and frustrations. She discovered that about a quarter of all calls going to the experienced customer service representatives with specialized training were simple information requests that could be handled by a receptionist-level person without a computer workstation and that the representatives were annoyed by those requests.
- The representatives also told her that their workstation software seemed "kind of flaky," so she looked again at the workstation problem reports and repair logs and found that about 20 percent of downtime was due to simple configuration fixes and crash reboots that customer service representatives were not trained to identify and fix.

- She then spent some time with the manager of the computer repair shop and found that computer purchases had barely kept up with the growth of the customer service call center and that IS did not have much shelf inventory to swap a working computer for a broken computer.

At the end of her ten days of performance analysis, the training manager, the head of information systems, and the customer service manager had a meeting and decided to try the following strategies for solving the performance problem and helping the customer service unit achieve its business goal:

- The training manager agreed to work with the telephone systems person in IS to improve call screening by clarifying the contents of the menu choices in the automated answering scripts and by adding another choice in two of the three menu levels. These changes would route a greater percentage of simple information requests to a pool of the newer, less-experienced customer service representatives.
- The training manager agreed to work with IS on a job aid for each workstation, a small laminated card with a decision tree of simple "If this happened, then do that" suggestions for computer "first aid." She also agreed to do a brief interactive training piece that would be available on the company's intranet to step the customer service representatives through the terminology and the process in the decision tree.
- IS decided to accelerate its computer purchase schedule to create some shelf inventory of machines that could be configured and available for service while broken units were being repaired.
- All agreed that it would be a good idea to allow some time for implementing and evaluating the proposed solutions and, in the meantime, to hire temporary computer technicians if needed from an outside employment services agency.

In solving the performance problem described in our example, the training director followed a *performance relationship map* formulated by Robinson and Robinson (2008) for organizing performance analysis efforts. The strategy of the relationship map is to relate a problem that has been voiced to a core organizational or business outcome and then check operational goals and performance standards related to that outcome. Table 2.2 is a summary in question and answer form of the relationship map process for performance analysis.

The purpose of a performance analysis study as depicted in Table 2.2 is to acquire information in order to verify problems and identify solutions. The outcome of a performance analysis study is a clear description of a problem in terms of failure to achieve desired organizational results and the corresponding desired and actual employee performance, evidence of the causes of the problem, and suggested cost-effective solutions. Note that although an instructional designer may guide or participate in a performance analysis study, there is no assumption that instruction will be a component of the solution. These studies are often team efforts, and the results reflect what is possible when drawing upon a wide range of organizational resources. An important lesson in this example of performance analysis is that the process involved more than reviews of performance statistics. It required delving into the content of the problem and soliciting contributions from those involved therein. Another important consideration in selecting a solution is cost, and instruction is often one of the more expensive alternative solutions. Experience has shown that under careful analysis, many organizational problems that previously were addressed by training are now solved via multicomponent solutions that may or may not include training. If part of the solution is training on new skills or rejuvenating existing skills, then plans for a needs assessment and an instructional design project are made.

Table 2.2 Application of the Robinson and Robinson (2008) Performance Relationship Map

Performance Analysis Question	Performance Analysis Answer
1. What is the problem that was originally voiced?	1. A training program for six new computer techs for desktop troubleshooting and repair in the customer service call center.
2. Is the voiced problem related to a core organizational outcome?	2. Yes: Improve customer relations.
3. Are there established operational goals for this outcome?	3. Yes: 96 percent customer satisfaction with service contacts by telephone (desired status).
4. Is the operational goal being met?	4. No: 76 percent customer satisfaction with service contacts by telephone (actual status).
5. Is there an operational need?	5. Yes: Eliminate the 20 percentage point gap between the desired status and the actual status.
6. Have job performance standards been set for achieving the operational goal?	6. Yes: Maximum of three automated call menu selections and maximum average wait time of ninety seconds before reaching a live service representative (desired status).
7. Are job performance standards being met?	7. No: Average wait time more than two and a half minutes and wait time for 17 percent of calls more than five minutes (actual status).
8. Is there a job performance need?	8. Yes: Eliminate the sixty-second gap between the desired status and the actual status.
9. Are there external factors outside the control of local management that are contributing to operational and job performance needs (e.g., government regulations, corporate hiring freeze, labor contract, corporation's national contract with telephone service provider)?	9. No: Operational and job performance needs appear to be within the control of local management.
10. Are there internal factors within the control of local management that are contributing to job performance needs?	10. Yes: Work flow, logistics, employee skills, person hours.
11. Are there solutions for the performance needs?	11. Yes: Work flow—redesign call routing. Logistics—accelerate computer acquisitions. Employee skills—create job aid with training. Person hours—hire technicians from temp agency.

Performance Analysis in a Public School Setting The term *performance analysis* is seldom used in public schools, but the same kind of critical thinking is applied routinely to solve problems involving administrator, teacher, and student performance. For an example focusing on student performance, assume the principal of an elementary school was reviewing results from the state standards test and saw that fifth-grade students were well below the state average for finding and using information resources and that low performance on this section of the test was pulling down the overall fifth-grade performance profile. The principal explained the student performance problem to the assistant principal (AP) for curriculum and said, "We need in-service training for the fifth-grade teachers and the media specialist in information literacy skills. Will you please arrange it?" The AP said she would take care of it, but before she looked into scheduling in-service training, she did some investigating. Here are some of the steps she took and information she found:

- She checked the state standards and found that an *information-literate person* recognizes when information will help solve a problem, chooses the best sources for valid and timely information, organizes and synthesizes the new information, and writes and displays the information appropriately for the problem. (*Information literacy* is the current term for library skills or research skills.)
- She compared the state benchmarks and skills in information literacy with sample test items and old exams that had been released to the public. The benchmarks and test items required both recall of information and application of information and concepts to solve problem scenarios. The test items seemed to be valid measures of the skills.
- She looked at scheduling and found that each class rotated through the media center once a week for forty minutes of contact time. She talked with the media specialist, who invited her to sit in on several fifth-grade classes during their media center visits and noted that the students had only fifteen to twenty minutes for learning information skills after getting organized and settled down, checking books in, browsing for new books, checking new books out, and taking Accelerated Reader quizzes. The fifteen to twenty minutes of instructional time did seem to be relevant; students were focused and on task, but she didn't see students actively participating in solving information literacy problems. She also did not observe much follow-up when the students went back to their classrooms.

After her investigation, the AP briefed the principal on some tentative conclusions and decided to meet with the fifth-grade teachers and the media specialist. In the meeting, she became convinced they all had a good grasp of information literacy skills, but none were very pleased with how they were teaching the content. They all believed they did not have time to go beyond a simple descriptive level and work with the students on applying the skills to solve the types of problem scenarios on the state test. The teachers admitted they did not spend much time in the classroom following up on the instruction in the media center because of pressure to keep test scores up in reading, writing, and arithmetic, confirming the AP's observations of what was happening in the media center and the classrooms. The group concurred on the need for raising students' state test performance on using information resources and, agreeing they had to change their instructional practices, decided on the following action plan:

- Free the media specialist to attend the fifth-grade teachers' group meetings for collaboratively planning a strategy for embedding information skills within classroom language arts instruction.
- Free the media specialist for team teaching time in the fifth-grade classrooms.
- Upgrade from the desktop to the networked version of Accelerated Reader software so students could take AR tests and monitor progress in their own classrooms, thus freeing up instructional time during class visits to the media center.
- Implement an intensive learning improvement program with a combination of direct instruction, problem-solving scenarios, learning guidance as needed, embedded assessments, remediation, and enrichment.

The AP reported to the principal that she and the teachers believed they had a plan for solving the state test performance problem, but it would require some resources. The principal concurred and said the money was available for the software upgrade. Freeing the media specialist would be more difficult, but money for a part-time media center clerk might be available from the PTA, the School Improvement Team's discretionary funds, a district budget for performance improvement projects, or a combination of those sources.

Although the AP would not have described her investigation as performance analysis, she was using good, solid problem-solving methods to look for the causes of the students' poor test performance. By working closely with those most involved in the problem context, she discovered that in-service training would not have improved student test scores. The media specialist and teachers knew the content and how to teach it; however, the constraints in their school schedule prevented them from doing so. The need was for changes freeing sufficient time for students to learn application of the information literacy skills.

The examples from business and education both illustrate instances where instruction was not the primary solution for a problem. When instruction is indeed the solution or part of the solution, then needs assessment is an important tool for getting the instructional design process on track for effective results.

Needs Assessment

The logic of needs assessment can be summarized as a simple equation:

Desired status – Actual status = Need

Needs assessment is sometimes called *discrepancy analysis*. The discrepancy is the observed difference between the desired status and the actual status. The processes involved in conducting a large-scale needs assessment can be very sophisticated, but the logic of needs assessment is simple. Needs assessment logic is used as a tool in the performance analysis in Table 2.2. For example, look at steps 3 through 5 and then at steps 6 through 8. There are three components of needs assessment logic. The first is establishing a standard or goal referred to as the *desired status*. The second component is determining the actual status or existing level of performance on the standard or goal, and the third component is identifying the gap between desired status and actual status, thereby describing a need. This gap is referred to as the *discrepancy*. For example:

Desired Status	Actual Status	Discrepancy
90% on-time arrivals for city busses	77% on-time arrivals	13% more on-time arrivals
10 fiction books in the school library for each student enrolled	8 fiction books per student	2 more fiction books per student
40% gross profit margin on hardware sales	43% gross profit margin	Exceeded desired status, no discrepancy
95% pass rate for students taking functional literacy exam	81% of students passing	14% more students passing

It has been noted that managers or executives often describe problems in terms of *actual status*, or the way things are now. Examples are "Our deliveries are late," "Not enough of our students go to the district spelling bee," "Our sales are down," and "Too many of our students are failing the basic skills test." For actual status and performance to have meaning in needs assessment, the investigator must establish standards for a desired status and then further identify exactly how late the deliveries are, how many students made the district spelling bee, how far sales are down, and what percentage of the students are failing the basic skills test.

Careful descriptions of both desired and actual status are required because a *gap* or *need* is defined as a comparison between the two. The gap of greatest consequence is in organizational results. If it turns out that there is no gap, then there is no need and no change is required, and obviously there is no requirement for new instruction or training. This is the situation whenever any organizational officer (including a school board member) surveys a situation and indicates that it is satisfactory—the desired and actual are the same or the actual exceeds the desired, and there is no need for change.

We have seen that needs assessment logic is one of the tools used in performance analysis. If performance analysis indicates that training is one of the best solutions for a performance problem, then needs assessment is used again; it is called *training needs assessment* or *learning needs assessment*, and it results in instructional goals for beginning an instructional design project. Recall that in the example of the customer service performance analysis, the training director noted that 20 percent of computer downtime was due to simple configuration fixes and crash reboots with which customer service representatives were not familiar. She decided that this was a training problem and volunteered to develop a job aid and training for workstation "first aid." At this point, she would probably turn the task over to an instructional designer, whose first thought would be "What are the real scope and nature of the performance problem that I want to solve through training?" Training needs assessment could help him answer his question. He could apply the three components of needs assessment logic: (1) working with subject-matter experts in IS to develop realistic standards for workstation first aid performance by customer service representatives (desired status); (2) studying work orders and maintenance logs and observing, interviewing, and perhaps testing customer service representatives (actual status); and (3) describing the gaps between standards for performance and actual performance levels (needs). Through this needs assessment work, the project manager could state a job performance standard for use by management in tracking the success of training and an instructional goal for beginning an ID project. The job performance standard could be "Customer service representatives will solve 95 percent of simple desktop configuration and crash reboot problems," and the instructional goal could be "Using a decision tree job aid, customer service representatives will diagnose simple desktop configuration and crash reboot problems and fix the problems without help from coworkers, supervisors, or IS technicians." Chevalier (2010) provides a cautionary note about stating instructional goals, suggesting that there are instances when interim goals that do not address the entire gap between actual and desired levels of performance are appropriate.

Needs Assessment in a Public School Setting It is not unusual to hear principals say their teachers *need* to know more about mobile computing. As a result, a workshop is provided so teachers can all become more competent. In this situation, teacher skills should be viewed as a means to an end: to turn out more competent students. If the real needs assessment issue is "What are the desired mobile computing skill levels and the actual mobile computing skill levels of the students?" and "If there is a gap and a need here, then what are the various solutions to upgrade those skills?" a workshop for all teachers may or may not be the best solution. We should examine gaps in organizational results rather than internal processes when we begin to identify needs and make plans for spending organizational resources to meet these needs.

Needs assessment is a critical component of the total design process. Trainers and educators must be aware that the creation of unnecessary instruction has a tremendous cost in dollars and encourages detrimental attitudes in students involved in pointless learning activities and managers paying for training that does not solve problems. Therefore, more emphasis is being placed on front-end analysis, performance analysis, and other approaches for identifying needs more accurately. In the past, it was common for survey instruments to be the major means of identifying and documenting training needs. Today, surveys are being supplemented or supplanted with more collaborative engagement with all who interact within the context of the need, including insightful interviews, focus groups, direct observations of performers, and analysis of performance data collected in the setting where training is being considered.

Job Analysis and Task Analysis

An important component of front-end analysis is *job analysis,* or the process of gathering, analyzing, and synthesizing descriptions of what people do in their jobs. Job analysis is a managerial activity that gained popularity in the late 1800s and early 1900s with time-and-motion studies and has evolved to serve many roles within the human resource development function, including (1) human resource forecasting and planning; (2) selecting and recruiting personnel; (3) ensuring equality of employment opportunity; (4) designing performance reviews; (5) developing compensation plans; (6) designing and redesigning jobs; and (7) planning training, job aids, performance support systems, and employee development. Current descriptions of what people do in their jobs are particularly useful in an era of constant, rapid, technological change and job dislocation because descriptions of what people do provide a baseline for making decisions about redesigning jobs for organizational effectiveness, personal productivity, and job satisfaction. A typical process used to perform job analysis includes:

- creating an initial list of job tasks,
- surveying experts and job incumbents about the accuracy of the task named,
- summarizing those tasks reported as critical,
- naming high-priority tasks for further review, and
- performing a task analysis for tasks judged as high priority.

Create Initial List of Job Tasks In creating an initial list of job tasks for a particular job, the job is first characterized in general terms according to the people who work in the job and the environment surrounding the job. Following this description, there are typically two ways one can begin to establish the characteristics of a job: one way is to have experts actually observe experienced workers performing the job and list the tasks they see performed; another way is to have those performing the job list all the steps they take as they perform the tasks. Regardless of the method used to derive the initial list of tasks, they are grouped according to common characteristics into categories called *duties* and then used to create an inventory.

Identify High-Priority Tasks After the task inventory is assembled, it is screened by asking subject-matter experts and job holders whether the tasks really are a part of the job, and the list is revised based on their judgments. The refined list of tasks is formatted as a survey, response scales and directions are added, and the survey is pilot tested. High-priority response scales include such questions as "Is this a task that you perform as part of your job?" "How frequently do you perform this task?" "What percentage of your workday do you spend on this task?" "How critical is this task to the success of your job?" and "How difficult is this task to perform?" Following a final review and revision, the survey is duplicated and distributed to a sample of job holders.

After return of the surveys, responses are summarized on a task-by-task basis, and high-priority tasks are chosen for further review. All of the processes described thus far in this general sequence are called *job analysis.*

Perform a Task Analysis Task analysis work is complex, very labor-intensive, and time-consuming; therefore, it is usually done only when specifically required for job design and redesign and for the design and development of critical training.

When job analysis is conducted in professional, technical, and military training contexts, it is usually to answer questions about what job performance really is and to focus training resources on tasks that offer a high probability of gains in job efficiency, effectiveness, and satisfaction. Task analysis is often essential when new equipment, machinery, software, and processes are introduced into medical, industrial, business, and military enterprises.

The process of task analysis has several more steps, including:

1. The tasks chosen for further review are broken down into component elements.
2. The relationships among elements are detailed.
3. The tools and conditions involved in performing each element are described.
4. The standards for successful performance are written.

At that point, priorities would be assigned, and the instructional design process would begin.

In summary, instructional goals are ideally derived through a process of performance analysis that establishes rather broad indications of a problem that can be solved by providing instruction. Then a needs assessment is conducted to determine more specifically what performance deficiencies will be addressed, and an instructional goal is stated. Sometimes further examination of that goal is undertaken, either in the context of a curriculum or a job analysis. As a result, more refined specific statements of instructional goals emerge that focus on what learners are able to do and the context in which they are able to do it. Regardless of the procedure used to generate a goal, it is almost always necessary for the designer to clarify and sometimes amplify the goal in order for it to serve as a firm starting point for the instructional design process. Many goals are abstract or fuzzy, and designers must learn how to cope effectively with them.

Clarity in Instructional Goals

Designers must avoid writing fuzzy instructional goals and recognize a vague, nonspecific goal when encountered. A fuzzy *goal* is generally some abstract statement about an internal state of the learner, such as *appreciating, having an awareness of, knowing how,* and *sensing*. These kinds of terms often appear in goal statements, but the designer does not know what they mean because there is no indication of what learners would be doing if they achieved this goal.

Describe Successful Learner Performance

Designers assume that at the successful completion of their instruction, students should be able to demonstrate that they have achieved the goal, but if the goal is so unclear that it is not apparent what successful performance would be, then further analysis must be undertaken.

The following five steps are recommended to clarify a vague goal:

1. Write down the instructional goal.
2. Generate a list of all the behaviors the learners should perform to demonstrate that they have achieved the goal.
3. Analyze the expanded list of behaviors and select those that best reflect achievement of the goal.
4. Incorporate the selected behaviors into a statement or statements that describe what the learners will demonstrate.
5. Examine the revised goal statement and judge whether learners who demonstrate the behaviors will have accomplished the initial broad goal.

If the answer to question 5 is yes, then you have clarified the goal; you have developed one or more goal statements that collectively represent the achievement of an important goal. The designer should be aware of this type of goal analysis procedure because many critical educational and training goals are not initially stated as clear and concise descriptions of performances of learners. They often are stated in terms that are quite meaningful (in general) to the originator but have no specifics that the designer can use for developing instruction. Such goals should not be discarded as being useless; instead, an analysis should be undertaken to identify specific performance outcomes that are implied by the goal. Often, it is helpful to use a number of knowledgeable people in the process so that you see the range of ideas that can emerge from the goal and the need for consensus on specific behaviors if truly successful instruction is to be developed.

Describe Learners, Context, and Tools

Whereas the most important aspect of an instructional goal is the description of what learners will be able to do, that description is not complete without an indication of (1) who the learners are, (2) the context in which they will use the skills, and (3) the tools that will be available. These considerations will be addressed more fully in Chapter 5, but a preliminary description of these aspects is important at this point.

Learners The designer must be clear about exactly who the learners will be rather than making vague statements or allusions to groups of learners. It is not unheard of for a design project to come to a halt when it is discovered that there is no audience for the instruction. In essence, the instruction has no market. Is there an adequate number of learners to try out new instructional materials? The characteristics of the people who will be participating in the instruction are extremely important as the designer begins to analyze exactly what skills must be included in the instruction. What are their current skill levels, their abilities, and their motivation for undertaking the instruction?

Performance Context and Tools Likewise, from the very beginning, a project designer must be clear about the context in which the skills will be used and whether any aids or tools will be available. For example, they might be working at a desk or be on their feet talking to a customer. They could be working in an office under supervision or out in the field alone. Will they be working independently or on a team?

An important aspect of the performance context is the tools available to aid the work. For example, what software is available for a construction estimator meeting a potential client at a job site? Must some information be available from memory, or will a mobile app provide everything the estimator needs to get the job done?

Information about the performance context, including tools, is extremely important for the designer to analyze exactly what skills must be included in the instruction. Eventually, the information will be used to select instructional strategies to promote the use of the skills, not only in the learning context but also in the context in which they are eventually intended for application on the job.

A complete goal statement should describe the following:

- the learners,
- what learners will be able to do in the performance context,
- the performance context in which the skills will be applied, and
- the tools that will be available to the learners in the performance context.

An example of a complete goal statement would be the following: "The Acme Call Center operators will be able to use the Client Helper Support System to provide information to customers who contact the call center." All four components of a goal statement are included in this statement.

Evaluation and Revision

Evaluating Instructional Goals

Sometimes the goal-setting process is not totally rational; that is, it does not follow a systematic front-end analysis process. The instructional designer must be aware that instructional design takes place in a specific context that includes a number of political and economic considerations as well as technical or academic ones. Stated in another way, powerful people and vested interests often determine priorities, and finances almost always determine the limitations of what can be done on an instructional design project. Any selection of instructional goals must be done through an iterative evaluation process. Careful front-end analysis is anything but a linear sequence of activities; rather, it is a sequence of formative evaluations and revisions. As each process is undertaken, new information becomes available, and deeper understanding of the performance problem develops, requiring reevaluation and perhaps refinement of the instructional goal. This circular iterative cycle repeats until designers are secure in their instructional goal assumptions and ready to move on to in-depth analysis of learners and contextual factors. Those analyses may in turn spur additional evaluations of one's instructional goal and subsequent revisions.

Selection and refinement of instructional goals is often shaped using three primary criteria:

1. Is the instructional goal **congruent** with the organization's needs?
2. Will **contextual factors** support development of instruction for the goal?
3. Is the instructional goal **clear** and understood by all stakeholders?

These criteria are of great importance to the institution or organization that will undertake the development as well as to the designer who is considering the project.

Congruence with Organizational Needs We cannot overemphasize the importance of being able to relate logically and persuasively the goals of instruction to documented performance gaps within an organization or opportunities that could benefit an organization. When instruction is developed for a client, the client must be convinced that if learners achieve the instructional goals, then a significant organizational problem will be solved or an opportunity will be realized through the use of the new skills. This kind of reasoning is applicable to the development of instruction in business, the military, nonprofits, government, public schools, and other public agencies.

Contextual Factors The rationale for an instructional goal may help garner support from decision makers, but the designer and managers must be assured that contextual factors will support both the development of the instruction and its delivery. A first concern is whether the **content is stable**. The designer should determine whether the content is stable enough to warrant the cost of developing instruction for it. If it will be out of date in six months, then extensive instructional development is probably not warranted unless there is an extremely critical short-term need.

Another concern is the **designer's own expertise** in the subject matter of the instruction that will be developed. Experienced professional designers often work in teams involved in a content area that is, at least initially, totally foreign to them. The ability and willingness to work in teams is one of the most important characteristics of a successful designer. A great deal of content learning must take place before the designer can work effectively. For those just learning the design process, it is preferable to begin with a content area in which they already have subject-matter expertise. It is a lot easier to learn one new set of skills, namely instructional design skills, than it is to learn two new sets of skills—both content and process—at the same time. Yet another concern related to designers is whether there are enough designers, technology specialists, content experts, and other team members to develop the instruction.

Most designers would agree that there seldom is **sufficient time** to develop instruction. One reason is that predicting the amount of time required to carry out a project is difficult. Another is that organizations often want something "yesterday!"

Not only is it difficult to predict how long it will take to develop instruction, but it is also difficult to predict how long learners will take to master the instructional goals (i.e., how long the instruction will last). No readily accepted rules of thumb relate instructional (or learning) time to skills mastered. So many factors are involved that time estimates are difficult to make.

The most likely scenario is that the designer is told, "You have three weeks to develop a four-hour workshop." Until an organization has experience in making these decisions, they are based on immediate conditions in the work setting. Certainly, the designer can shorten or lengthen instruction to fit the time available, but the primary instructional concern is to select the best possible instructional strategies for teaching the skills that must be mastered and then determine how much time is required. Obviously, we can make more accurate learning-time estimates after several tryouts of the instruction.

It is assumed that learners will be available to use the completed instruction, but the instructional design process depends heavily on the **availability of learners** to try out the instruction during development. Without access to appropriate learners, the designer will be unable to implement the total design process. A few learners are needed to try out rough draft versions of the instruction. If they are not available, then the designer will have to alter the ID process and may want to reconsider the validity of the need.

If you have chosen (or are required) to design an instructional package as you work through the chapters of this book, the process will consume many hours of your time. Before you finalize your selection of an instructional goal, it will be helpful to review the criteria listed in the following rubric.

Rubric for Evaluating Instructional Goals

The rubric that follows contains a summary of the criteria you can use to evaluate and refine your instructional goals. It includes the main areas of congruence with the organization's needs, the feasibility of the goal, and its clarity.

Designer note: If an element is not relevant for your project, mark NA for not applicable in the No column.

No	Some	Yes	**A. Congruence with Organization Needs** Is/are the instructional goal statement(s):
___	___	___	1. Linked clearly to an identified problem in the organization?
___	___	___	2. Linked clearly to documented performance gaps?
___	___	___	3. Clearly a solution to the problem?
___	___	___	4. Acceptable to those who approve the instructional effort?

B. Contextual Factors Will development of instruction for the goal be feasible given:

___ ___ ___ 1. Stable content/skills over time to warrant investment/resources?
___ ___ ___ 2. Sufficient designer expertise in instructional goal area?
___ ___ ___ 3. Sufficient personnel to design/develop/deliver instruction?
___ ___ ___ 4. Sufficient time to design/develop/deliver instruction?
___ ___ ___ 5. Sufficient budget to design, develop, and deliver instruction?
___ ___ ___ 6. An adequate number of learners for development/delivery?

C. Clarity Do the instructional goal statement(s) describe the:

___ ___ ___ 1. Actions of the learners (what they will be able to do)?
___ ___ ___ 2. Content clearly?
___ ___ ___ 3. Intended learners?
___ ___ ___ 4. Performance context?
___ ___ ___ 5. Tools available to learners in performance context?

D. Other

___ ___ ___ 1.
___ ___ ___ 2.

An appropriate, feasible, and clearly stated instructional goal should be the product of these activities. Using this clarified statement of learner outcomes, you are ready to conduct a goal analysis, which is described in Chapter 3.

Examples

An example procedure used to develop instructional goals may help you formulate or evaluate your own goals. The example, providing friendly customer service in a banking context, is based on an identified problem, needs assessment activities, and a prescribed solution to the problem. It has its own scenario to help clarify the context of the problem and the process used to identify the goals. There are additional examples for your consideration in the case study of this chapter and in the case study located in the appendices.

Providing Customer Service

For this example, a local bank noticed a problem with low customer satisfaction ratings in its branch offices, primarily from customers completing lobby transactions with tellers and with customer service representatives. Informal performance analysis indicated that a satisfaction problem did indeed exist, stemming from customers' perceptions that bank personnel were often impersonal and sometimes short in their dealings. Unable to determine immediately whether bank personnel did not know how or did not take the time to interact in a polite, friendly, and businesslike manner, further investigation revealed a common feeling of needing to hurry through a transaction so that other customers would not be kept waiting. However, an even more significant factor was that many employees did not know simple routines for courteous business interactions and did not have strategies for maintaining personalized contact with customers during high-volume times in the lobby. Training would certainly be part of an effective solution, and the following instructional goal was identified:

Personnel will know the value of courteous, friendly service.

Although we can all agree that the intentions of this goal are sound, it can be classified as fuzzy and should be clarified. Simply because a goal is fuzzy does not mean it is not worthwhile. Just the opposite—it may be very worthwhile, as in this particular case of a goal that is common to many banks, even though it may still need some work.

First, the phrase *will know the value of* can be changed to *will demonstrate* in order to communicate better what is expected of personnel. Second, we must determine exactly what personnel are expected to demonstrate. We can begin this task by dividing the comprehensive term *service* into more interpretable main parts. We chose to define service as (1) a greeting to the customer, (2) a business transaction, and (3) a conclusion. Even with these two relatively minor changes, the goal is much clearer.

Original Goal	Restated Goal
Personnel will know the value of friendly service.	Personnel will demonstrate courteous, friendly behavior while greeting customers, transacting business, and concluding transactions.

Although the goal is much better in the new form, there are still two terms, *courteous* and *friendly*, that remain to be clarified. By relating these two concepts to each of the three stages of service that have been identified, we can further clarify the goal. Remember the five steps included in making a fuzzy goal clearer:

1. Write the goal on paper.
2. Brainstorm to identify the behaviors learners would demonstrate to reflect their achievement of the goal.
3. Sort through the stated behaviors and select those that best represent the goal.
4. Incorporate the behaviors into a statement that describes what the learner will be able to do.
5. Evaluate the resulting statement for its clarity and relationship to the original fuzzy notion.

To help with the brainstorming process of identifying behaviors implied by "courteous and friendly," we described behaviors specific to each of the three stages of service. We also decided to consider behaviors that could be classified as discourteous and unfriendly in a bank setting. The behaviors bank personnel *could* demonstrate and *should not* demonstrate to be considered courteous and friendly are listed in Table 2.3. The descriptions of courteous and discourteous behaviors can be given to bank administrators for additions, deletions, and further clarification.

When the list of representative behaviors is as complete as you can make it, review it at each stage of service to identify key behaviors that best represent the instructional goal. Based on the sample list, we restate the instructional goal as follows. All three forms of the goal are included to enable comparisons for completeness and clarity.

Original Goal Personnel will know the value of courteous, friendly service.

Revised Version Personnel will demonstrate courteous, friendly behavior while greeting customers, transacting business, and concluding transactions.

Final Goal

- Personnel will demonstrate courteous, friendly behavior while greeting customers, transacting business, and concluding transactions by initiating conversation, personalizing comments, focusing attention, assisting with forms, and concluding with a "thanks" and a wish for the customer's well-being.

Table 2.3 Friendly and Courteous Behaviors during Business Transactions with Customers

Greeting the Customer

DO	DON'T
1. Initiate greeting to customer (e.g., "Hello," "Good morning").	1. Wait for customer to speak first.
2. Say something to customer to make service appear personal: (a) use customer's name whenever possible; (b) say, "It's good to see you again" or "We haven't seen you for a while."	2. Treat customer like a stranger or someone you have never seen before.
3. If you must complete a prior transaction before beginning work, smile, verbally excuse yourself, and say you will only need a moment to finish your current task.	3. Simply continue working on a task and fail to look up or acknowledge a customer until you are ready.
4. Inquire, "How may I help you today?"	4. Wait for customer to initiate conversation about service needed.

Transacting Business

DO	DON'T
1. Attend to the customers currently waiting in your line. If you must leave your station, simply inform newly arriving customers that your line is closing and invite them to begin waiting in an alternate line.	1. Shuffle customers to another line after they have waited in yours for a while.
2. Listen attentively to the customer as he or she explains problem or service desired.	2. Interrupt customers when you believe you know what they are going to say and can see by the paperwork the type of transaction they wish.
3. Keep the customer's business as the primary focus of attention during transaction.	3. Chat with employees or other customers, thereby delaying the current customer.
4. Complete any missing information on the form yourself, explaining to the customer what you have added and why.	4. Simply inform customers they have incorrectly or incompletely filled out a form, thereby making it their problem.
5. Give complete, clear instructions for additional forms that the customer should complete.	5. Simply say, "Complete these other forms and then come back."

Concluding Transaction

DO	DON'T
1. Inquire whether they need any additional services today.	1. Dismiss a customer by focusing your eyes on the next customer in line.
2. Thank the customer for his or her business.	2. Act like you have done him or her a favor by completing the transaction.
3. Verbally respond to any comments that the customer may have initiated (e.g., the weather, a holiday or upcoming vacation, your outfit or hairstyle, new decorations).	3. Let customer-initiated comments drop as though unnoticed.
4. Conclude with a wish for the customer's well-being (e.g., "Take care," "Have a nice trip," "Have a nice day," "Hurry back.").	4. Allow customers to walk away without a final comment or wish for their well-being.

- *Learners, contexts, and tools:* The learners (personnel) are all bank employees who work directly with customers either in person, by telephone, or through written correspondence. The context is most typically the bank facility and spontaneous, interactive work with customers. Personnel will have no communication aids available to assist them in interacting with customers.

Although the final goal reflects only a subset of the behaviors generated during the brainstorming process, those selected convey the basic intention of the instructional goal. The complete list of courteous and discourteous behaviors that was generated should be saved as input for subsequent instructional analysis activities.

This example, related to clarifying a fuzzy goal, demonstrates that although taking a first step toward goal clarification can result in a clearer instructional goal, it may still be open to interpretation by instructional designers or instructors. Sometimes the goal must be clarified further by defining the actual behaviors to be demonstrated within each of the general categories included in the instructional goal.

A final concern when identifying instructional goals is the context in which the behavior will be performed. The instructional goal for bank personnel implies that the ultimate performance will be with customers in a bank. The performance context in which the goal is accomplished will have important implications for the instructional strategy.

Case Study

Group Leadership Training

This case study on group leadership training will serve as a running example to help the reader put the ID process together and will be included toward the end of every chapter between the Examples and the Professional and Historical Perspectives sections. Training effective group leaders is a common need in organizations ranging from education to business, industry, military, government, and community groups. Regardless of the context, any course of action dependent on productive group process requires effective group leadership. The setting for our case study is a master's degree program within a leadership department on a college campus. The following paragraphs describe planning decisions based on performance analysis, needs assessment, the instructional goal, information for clarifying the instructional goal, and criteria for establishing instructional goals.

Performance Analysis

The department chair noted that data summaries from exit interviews and surveys of graduating students indicate that students do not feel confident or comfortable leading group discussions aimed at solving an organization's problems. Although they believe it is a critical professional skill for them, they do not believe it was included in their coursework or addressed as a part of their internships or projects during the program. The chair of the program, realizing that this was one of the department's primary goals, thought surely it was included somewhere in the program. Not wanting to replicate coursework or proliferate courses, she examined syllabi on record for the courses and studied the nature of students' self-selected internships for the past two semesters. She interviewed faculty in the department regarding areas where this skill is currently taught and learned that the department previously required a semester-long communications course in the College of Arts and Sciences. This course had been eliminated four years ago in an effort to streamline the curriculum. At that time, faculty agreed to include a unit on communication within several of the leadership department's remaining courses.

She then attended an annual meeting of the department's curriculum advisory board made up of professionals from education, business, government, and other constituent agencies throughout the state where the department's graduates were employed. This group reviews the department's current goals and recommends others related to trends and needs within their organizations. Prior to this meeting, she asked them to investigate the importance of the skill "Leading group discussions aimed at identifying and solving the organization's problems" for their employees. In addition, she wanted their perceptions of their employees' abilities in performing this skill within their organizations. The advisory board reported that the skill was critical for their employees and that new hires were often deficient in this area.

Needs Assessment

The department's curriculum committee was provided with data from graduates' exit interviews and surveys and the department's advisory board recommendations. Committee members were charged with analyzing data from these groups, surveying current students, and discussing the issue with faculty from the communications department. They concluded that (1) the leader was the key person in determining the effectiveness of problem-solving groups, (2) leaders of the most effective groups had well-developed group discussion leadership skills, and (3) there was a chronic deficit of effective group leaders among the current students. They set about determining where within the existing curriculum and courses a unit on leading group problem-solving meetings could be added. They concluded that the goal did not merit a semester-long course, and they recommended instead a one-credit-hour mini-course that could be offered in conjunction with internships, between regular terms, or as a short summer course.

The department, on the recommendation of the curriculum committee, requested funds to develop a blended, web-based and classroom instructional mini-course of about four weeks' duration. The instruction was to focus on group discussion leadership skills. Support for development was requested from the college's technology support unit and the college's computer-based learning center. Development stipends were requested for one faculty member and four graduate assistants in the areas of instructional design, communications, educational technology, and leadership. The funds were granted.

Clarifying the Instructional Goal

The instructional goal is (1) a clear, general statement of learner outcomes that is (2) related to an identified problem and needs assessment and (3) achievable through instruction rather than some more efficient means such as enhancing motivation of employees.

What Is the Instructional Goal? In this instance, the instructional goal is for master's students in the leadership department to demonstrate effective discussion group leadership skills in problem-solving meetings. These discussions should be focused on encouraging colleagues to attend meetings, helping them identify problems on campus and in the community, and planning programs to help reduce identified problems.

What Is the Relationship between the Goal and the Needs Assessment Study? The instructional goal is directly linked to the needs assessment study and to the curriculum committee's recommendations about effective leadership at the campus and community levels. It is also directly related to evidence that effective discussion group leadership was highly correlated with effective groups within organizations.

Does Instruction Appear to Be the Most Effective Way to Achieve the Goal? Developing effective discussion group leadership skills is directly related to instruction and practice, and these competencies are not likely to be developed through cursory coursework or activities within internships.

Who Are the Learners? The learners are master's-level students enrolled in a course in the leadership department. They have various undergraduate degree areas of study; they are at varying places within the department's coursework sequence; and they have developed varying group leadership skills through community organizations, membership in quality teams at work, or formal employment as managers or supervisors. Some will have had instruction in small-group leadership at the undergraduate level. They have selected leadership as a major area of study, so they are motivated to acquire or refine their skills as a leader among their colleagues.

In What Context Will the Skills Be Used? Leaders will use their group discussion skills in planning for meetings on campus and in the community and in providing leadership for the discussions that occur during the meetings. These meetings may occur on campus or in a variety of education, business, community, or government organizations.

What Tools Are Available to Aid Learners' Performance in the Actual Context? There is no formal support for further developing and refining discussion group leadership skills other than practice, practice, practice. Some organizations may have staff development personnel to aid group leaders; others will not have them.

Readers are reminded that an additional case study is located in the appendices. These materials are beneficial in part because they are collected together rather than spread through the chapters of the text. Readers can easily progress from one design document to the next and see the progress of the design. The case study begins with an example of front-end analysis and development of instructional goals. It is important to remind you that our purpose in using these particular case studies is not to teach how to lead meetings or to write sentences. These examples were chosen to be completely transparent so you can "look through" the familiar content to the design concepts and skills. It is extremely difficult to learn unfamiliar content using other unfamiliar content.

Professional and Historical Perspectives

A systematic analysis of what people do and how they do it was in evidence in business and manufacturing in time-and-motion studies in the late 1800s and formalized in Taylor's *The Principles of Scientific Management* (1915). The whole idea of systematic analysis of efficiency and productivity in organizations was the genesis for the intensive research on training methods during World War I and on learning and training during World War II in both military and private sectors. Systematic thinking about the human factor in organizational productivity fostered the first cohesive examination of human performance technology (HPT) in Gilbert's (1978) behavioral engineering model. HPT has evolved over the past forty years and is now a mature discipline that is part of most human resources functions in private and public enterprise.

Identifying, clarifying, and analyzing goals has been as much a part of public education as of HPT. Political, social, and economic goals have always been part of public education, but the goals of particular interest here are those that state desired outcomes of the teaching and learning process. As long as there has been schooling, there have been achievement tests, and achievement tests are de facto definitions of learning outcomes. Achievement testing in schools began in the mid-19th century, proliferated as standardized tests in the early 20th century, and progressed to the nationwide availability of the Iowa Test of Basic Skills in the 1940s. Standardized achievement testing became a way of measuring normative learning outcomes by reporting students' percentile rank, grade-level standing, and changes in standing from beginning to end of a school year. These standardized test measures are germane to our interest in identifying goals.

If standardized tests are valid measures of students' achievement, then it is an easy transition to use those measures to hold schools accountable for students' achievement. Accountability, however, required setting standards for goals for what students should know and be able to do as a result of schooling. Goals and subordinate competencies were written for most traditional subjects across the grade levels, first in the outcomes-based education movement that started in the late 1980s and faded in the early 1990s. The standards-based education movement began with federal reauthorization of ESEA (1994) and continued with Goals 2000 (1990), No Child Left Behind (2001), Common Core (2010), and Every Student Succeeds (2015). Testing companies had to reconfigure their tests to align with national and state goals and enable student-by-student measures of competence on each goal. These high-stakes achievement tests have encountered social and political headwinds, resulting in shifting goals and changing standards for judging student competence at local, state, and national levels. Accountability, however, is still a guiding principle in public education today. In Chapter 6, we will explore the use of different types of tests for measuring learners' mastery of goals and objectives.

Readers using this book as part of a graduate degree program in instructional systems design or instructional technology may find that coursework in evaluation, performance analysis, and needs assessment is part of their program of study. Others wanting in-depth preparation in front-end analysis should refer to this list of selected resources. The full citations are at the end of this chapter.

Performance Analysis Brethower (2007), Mager and Pipe (1997), Robinson and Robinson (2008), Rossett (2009), Van Tiem et al. (2012).

Needs Assessment Chevalier (2010), Sleezer et al. (2014), Kaufman (1998), Kaufman and Guerra-Lopez (2013).

Job Analysis Brannick et al. (2007) and Jonassen et al. (1999).

Evaluation Brown and Seidner (2012), Kirkpatrick and Kirkpatrick (2006), and Russ-Eft and Preskill (2009).

Case Studies in Front-End Analysis Ertmer et al.'s *ID Casebook* (2019) and *Analyzing Performance Problems* by Mager and Pipe (1997). The Mager and Pipe resource describes a useful decision process for identifying performance problems caused by circumstances other than instruction. Their process is distilled into a straightforward flowchart that is easy to understand and apply. Lundberg et al. (2010) describe a case study of performance analysis in a retail customer service setting wherein training proved to be a small part of an overall performance solution. Others wanting in-depth preparation in front-end analysis should refer to the references at the end of this chapter.

Process Flowcharts

Identifying Instructional Goals

This section contains flowcharts in Figures 2.3 through 2.6 that will assist you in reviewing the tasks required to identify instructional goals. The flowcharts will also help you summarize the information from the chapter and provide guidance for your design work.

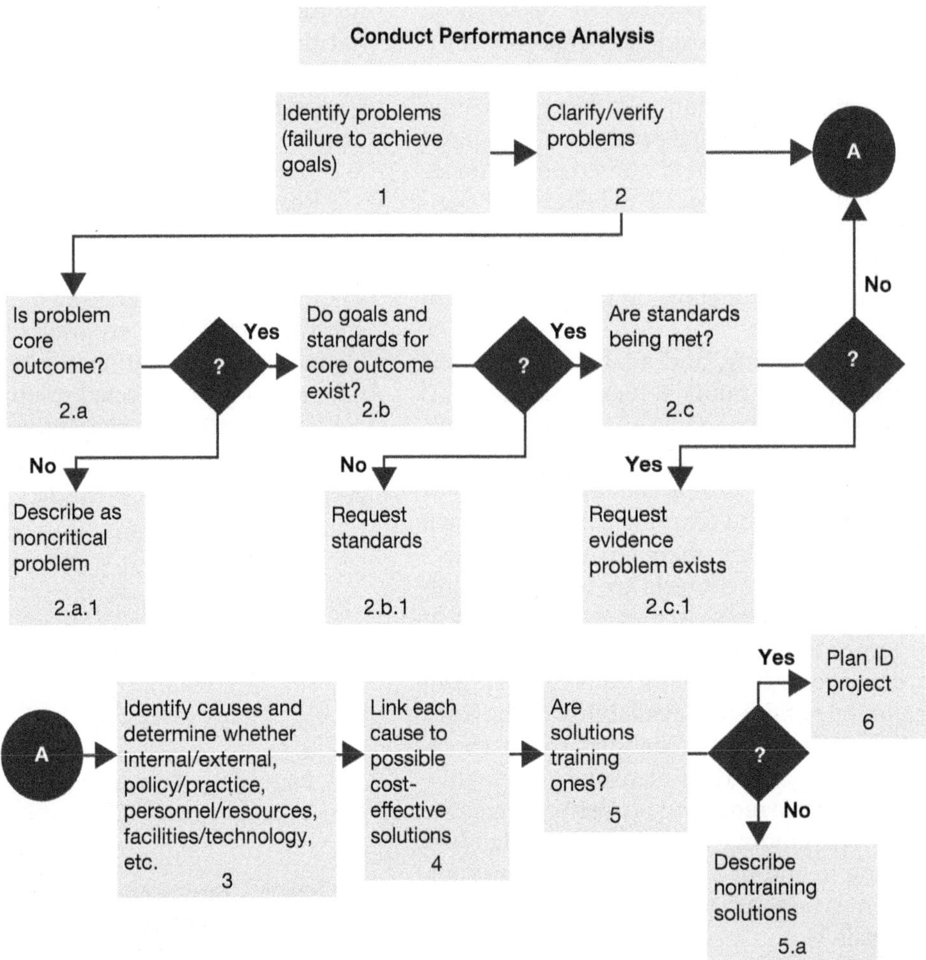

Figure 2.3 Conduct a Performance Analysis

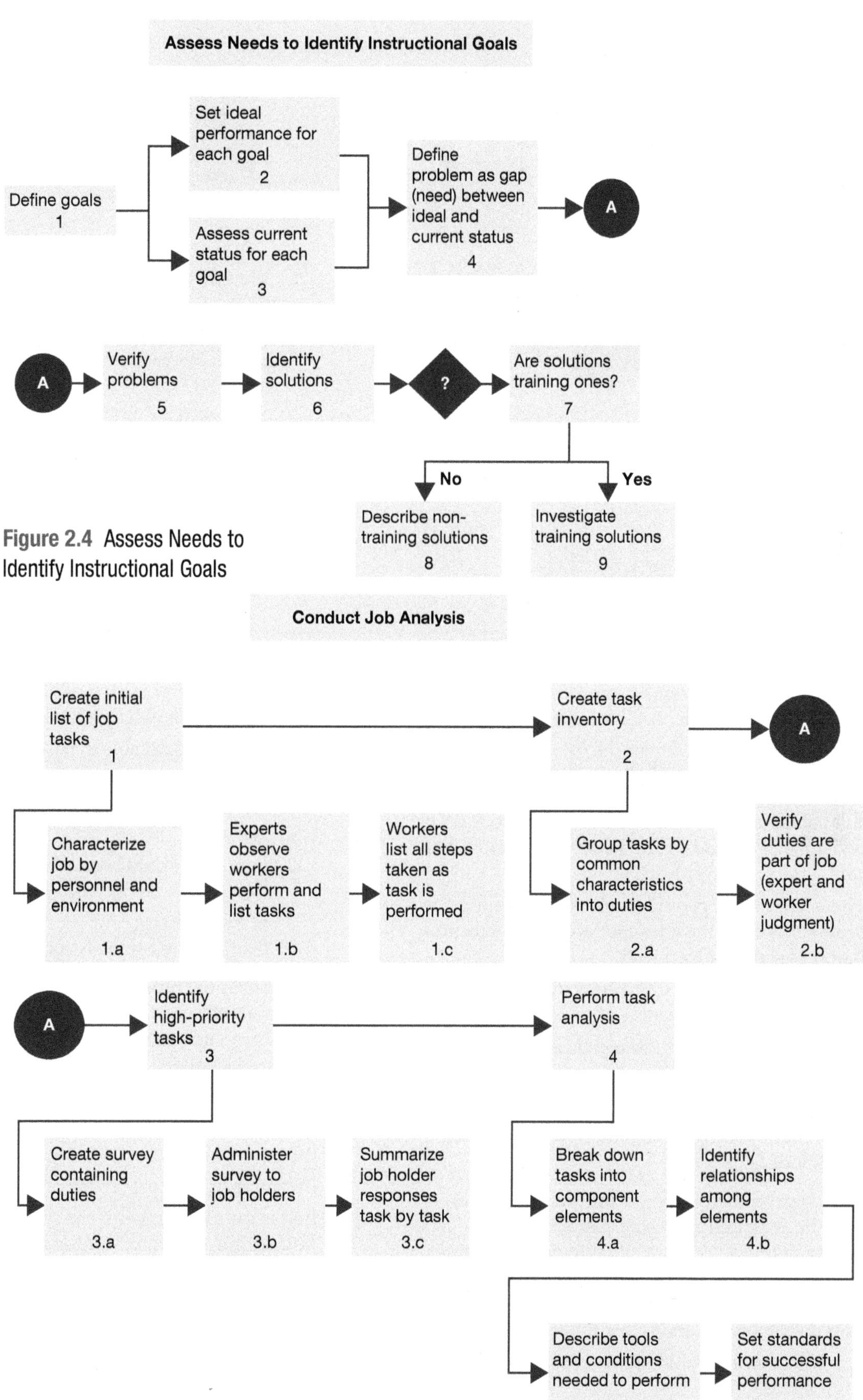

Figure 2.4 Assess Needs to Identify Instructional Goals

Figure 2.5 Tasks for Conducting a Job Analysis

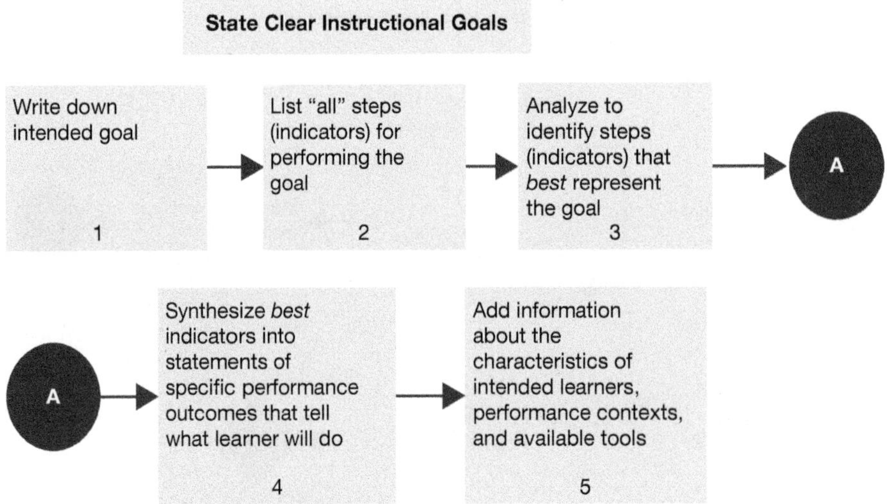

Figure 2.6 State Clear Instructional Goals

Practice

The following list contains several instructional goals that may or may not be appropriate based on the criteria for writing acceptable instructional goals stated in this chapter. Read each goal and determine whether it is correct as written or should be revised. If you believe it can be revised given the information available, revise it and compare your work with the revisions provided in the Feedback section that follows.

1. The district will provide in-service training for teachers prior to the administration and interpretation of standardized tests.
2. Students will understand how to punctuate a variety of simple sentences.
3. Salespersons will learn to use time management forms.
4. Teachers will assign one theme each week.
5. Customers will understand how to balance a checkbook.

The first step in developing a unit of instruction is to state the instructional goal. Several criteria can be used to help you select a suitable goal statement. From the following list of possible considerations for selection, identify all those that are relevant to a designer's selection of an instructional goal.

_____ 6. Personal knowledge and skills in content area

_____ 7. Stable content area

_____ 8. Time required for writing instruction versus the importance of students possessing that knowledge or skill

_____ 9. Students available to try out materials for clarity and revision purposes

_____ 10. Areas in which students have difficulty learning

_____ 11. Few materials available on the topic though instruction is considered important

_____ 12. Content area is fairly logical

An instructional goal must be stated as clearly as possible. From the following lists of considerations, select all those within each section that are important for writing instructional goals.

13. Clear statement of behavior
    a. Behavior required of the student is obvious in the goal.
    b. Behavior in the goal can be observed.
    c. Behavior in the goal can be measured to determine whether students have reached the goal.
14. Clear versus fuzzy goals
    a. Instructional goal includes a clearly stated behavior.
    b. Any limitations that will be imposed on the behavior are stated clearly.

15. Time
    a. Approximate instructional time required for students to reach goal.
    b. Approximate time you can devote to developing and revising instruction.
16. Following a district-wide needs assessment on middle school students' writing skills, teachers decided to design special instruction that focused students on:
    - Writing a variety of sentence types based on sentence purpose.
    - Using a variety of sentence structures that vary in complexity.
    - Using a variety of punctuation to match sentence type and complexity.

    Through instruction focused directly on the problems identified in the needs assessment, they hoped to change the current pattern of simplistic similarity found in students' compositions. Write an instructional goal for the instruction that can be used in the special unit on writing composition.
17. Write an instructional goal for which you would like to develop a unit of instruction, and evaluate it using the rubric suggested for evaluating instructional goals.

Feedback

1. The instructional goal should be revised because it describes what the district is expected to accomplish rather than the teachers. The goal could be rewritten in the following way to reflect two units of instruction commonly provided by school districts. Notice the behavior to be exhibited by teachers has been clarified.
    - Teachers will administer selected standardized tests according to the procedures described in the test manual.
    - Teachers will interpret student performance on both individual and class profile sheets that are provided by the test maker.
2. The goal should be revised because the words *will understand* are too general. The goal could be rewritten to clarify exactly the behavior students will use to demonstrate that they understand how to punctuate sentences. In addition, the specific punctuation marks to be included in the lesson and used by students are included in the goal.
    - Students will punctuate a variety of simple sentences using periods, question marks, and exclamation points.
3. *Learn to use* states the intended outcome of instruction, but behavior used to describe what sales personnel will actually do might be clarified as follows:
    - Sales personnel will complete time management forms using daily, weekly, and monthly schedules.
4. This is not an instructional goal but a description of the process teachers will use to enable students to practice composition skills; it totally ignores the nature of the skills students are expected to acquire during practice. Not enough information is included in the statement to enable the instructional goal to be rewritten.
5. The phrase *will understand* in the goal is imprecise. The instructional goal could be clarified as follows:
    - Customers will balance a checkbook using check stubs or a check register and a monthly bank statement.

6–12. If you selected all of the criteria, you are correct. Each criterion is an important consideration in developing an instructional goal. With regard to personal knowledge of the topic, experienced instructional designers often work with SMEs from a variety of context areas in which the designer has no expertise.

13–15. All considerations listed are important.

16. Compare your instructional goal for writing composition with this one: In written composition, students will: (1) use a variety of sentence types and accompanying punctuation based on the purpose and mood of the sentence and (2) use a variety of sentence types and accompanying punctuation based on the complexity or structure of the sentence. You should examine all the information related to the front-end analysis for the school curriculum case study

located in Appendix A, which reflects the beginning point for a complete instructional design case study in a school context. Readers currently working in schools or planning to work in schools should benefit from this school-based example.

17. Refer to the criteria for evaluating instructional goals listed in the rubric for evaluating instructional goals shown earlier. Evaluate your topic using each of the following criteria statements:
    - Does your goal meet each criterion?
    - If it does not meet a particular criterion, can it be revised to do so?
    - If it does not meet a particular criterion and cannot be revised to do so, you may wish to write another instructional goal and try again.

    You may need help in determining whether your goal meets some of the criteria for topic selection, such as need or interest, possibly by discussing these issues with colleagues and students. Libraries and the Internet are good sources for determining whether materials on your topic are available and the nature of the available materials. Revise and rewrite your instructional goal as needed to meet the above criteria.

    You may check the clarity of your goal by asking colleagues and intended learners to interpret verbally the instructional goal you have written. Do they interpret the goal and the required behavior exactly as you intended? You may need to revise.

    If your goal is too big for the instructional time available (thirty minutes, one hour, two hours, etc.), consider dividing the goal into its logical major parts, reword each part as an instructional goal, and then select the part most suited to your needs and time constraints.

    If your goal is too small for the amount of time you desire, consider the skills the student will need to enter your instruction and the skills the student will be ready to learn as a result of completing it. By considering skills related to your goal in this fashion, you can identify the appropriate instruction to include for a specific period of time. Of course, you should revise your instructional goal to include more skills or information as required.

    Rewrite your instructional goal if necessary, and begin Chapter 3 after you have developed a clear, behaviorally stated instructional goal that you estimate will fit the desired amount of instructional time.

References and Recommended Reading

Barbazette, J. (2006). *Training needs assessment: Methods, tools, and techniques*. Pfeiffer.

Brannick, M., Levine, E. L., & Morgeson, F. P. (2007). *Job analysis: Methods, research, and applications for human resource management* (2nd ed.). Sage Publications. Thorough treatment of functions and methods of job analysis in the workplace.

Brethower, D. (2007). *Performance analysis: Knowing what to do and how*. HRD Press. Employs systems approach in performance analysis and includes tools and job aids.

Brown, S. M., & Seidner, C. J. (Eds.). (2012). *Evaluating corporate training: Models and issues*. Springer. Contains a section on evaluation contexts and models that have relevance for front-end analysis.

Chevalier, R. (Ed.). (2010). Gap analysis revisited. *Performance Improvement, 49*(7): 5–7. Proposes setting reasonable goals and using milestone measures to assess progress in reaching the goals.

Dessinger, J. C., Moseley, J. L., & Van Tiem, D. M. (2012). Performance improvement/HPT model: Guiding the process. *Performance Improvement, 51*(3), 10–17. Describes the history and use of the HTP model and includes a performance tool for selecting interventions.

Earle, R. S. (1990). Performance technology: A new perspective for the public schools. *Performance Improvement Quarterly, 3*(4): 3–11. Recommends application of human performance technology for review and solutions to problems in public education.

Educational Technology Magazine, 43(1). (2003). Special issue on perspectives on training and performance improvement in business.

Ertmer, P. A., Quinn, J., & Glazewski, K. D. (Eds.). (2019). *The ID casebook: Case studies in instructional design* (5th ed.). Routledge.

Gagné, R. M., Wager, W. W., Golas, K. C., & Keller, J. M. (2004). *Principles of instructional design* (5th ed.). Wadsworth/Thomson Learning. Educational goals are related to instructional outcomes, especially as they relate to different categories of learning.

Gilbert, T. F. (1978). *Human competence: Engineering worthy performance*. McGraw-Hill.

Jonassen, D. H., Tessmer, M., & Hannum, W. H. (1999). *Task analysis methods for instructional design*. Lawrence Erlbaum Associates. The book has a chapter on job task analysis and discussion of value of task analysis for setting goals.

Kaufman, R. (1998). *Strategic thinking: A guide to identifying and solving problems* (revised). American Society for Training & Development and the International Society for Performance Improvement.

Kaufman, R., & Guerra-Lopez, I. (2013). *Needs assessment for organizational success*. ASTD Press. Discusses front-end analysis and tools needed to achieve successful, measurable results.

Kirkpatrick, D. L., & Kirkpatrick, J. D. (2006). *Evaluating training programs: The four levels* (3rd ed.). Berrett-Koehler. Presents four levels of evaluation for training programs including reaction, learning, behavior, and results and includes case studies.

Lundberg, C., Elderman, J. L., Ferrell, P., & Harper, L. (2010). Data gathering and analysis for needs assessment: A case study. *Performance Improvement 49*(8), 27–34. Describes data gathering methods and procedures for data analysis in a business case study.

Mager, R. F. (1997). *Goal analysis* (3rd ed.). CEP Press. This brief book describes a process used by the author to help groups clearly identify goals for their instruction. It is over twenty years old but provides clear logic for goal analysis.

Mager, R. F., & Pipe, P. (1997). *Analyzing performance problems* (3rd ed.). CEP Press. Latest edition of a classic that describes an approach to determining if training is the solution to a performance problem or if other solutions should be implemented.

Pershing, J. A. (Ed.). (2006). *Handbook of human performance technology: Principles, practices, and potential* (3rd ed.). Pfeiffer.

Richey, R. C., Kline, J. D., & Tracey, M. W. (2010). *The instructional design knowledge base: Theory, research, and practice*. Taylor and Francis. Describes classic and current theories as frameworks for instructional design practice.

Robinson, D. G., & Robinson, J. C. (2008). *Performance consulting: Moving beyond training* (2nd ed.). Berrett-Koehler.

Rosenberg, M. (1990, January). Performance technology: Working the system. *Training*, 43–48. One of the early defining articles on performance technology.

Rossett, A. (2009). *First things fast*. Pfeiffer. Approaches to determining if a performance problem exists in an organization.

Rothwell, W. J., Benscoter, B., King, M., & King, S. B. (2015). *Mastering the instructional design process: A systematic approach* (5th ed.). Wiley. Includes a focus on HPT and includes analyzing needs, learners, work settings, and work and successfully managing instructional design projects.

Russ-Eft, D., & Preskill, H. (2009). *Evaluation in organizations: A systematic approach to enhancing learning, performance, and change* (2nd ed.). Basic Books. Describes assessment tools and procedures needed to evaluate the effectiveness of programs.

Russ-Eft, D. F., & Sleezer, C. M. (Eds.). (2019). *Case studies in needs assessment*. Sage.

Silber, K. H., & Foshay, W. R. (Eds.). (2010). *Handbook of improving performance in the workplace. Volume one, Instructional Design and Training Delivery*. Pfeiffer.

Sleezer, C. M., Russ-Eft, D. F., & Gupta, K. (2014). *A practical guide to needs assessment* (3rd ed.). Wiley. Provides a complete model of needs assessment including chapters on management and numerous job aids.

Stolovitch, H. D., & Keeps, E. J. (2004). *Front end analysis and return on investment toolkit*. Jossey-Bass/Pfeiffer. This toolkit with job aids and examples facilitates analyzing training efforts on the front end as well as evaluating worth and return on investment (ROI) on the back end of ISD.

Taylor, F. W. (1915). *The principles of scientific management*. Harper & Brothers.

Van Tiem, D. M., Moseley, J. L., & Dessinger, J. C. (2012). *Fundamentals of performance technology: A guide to improving people, process, and performance* (3rd ed.). Pfeiffer. Describes methods for impacting organizational change using the human performance technology (HPT) model, includes case studies.

Watkins, R., & Leigh, D. (Eds.). (2010). *Handbook of improving performance in the workplace. Volume two, Selecting and Implementing Performance Interventions*. Pfeiffer.

chapter 3

Conducting a Goal Analysis

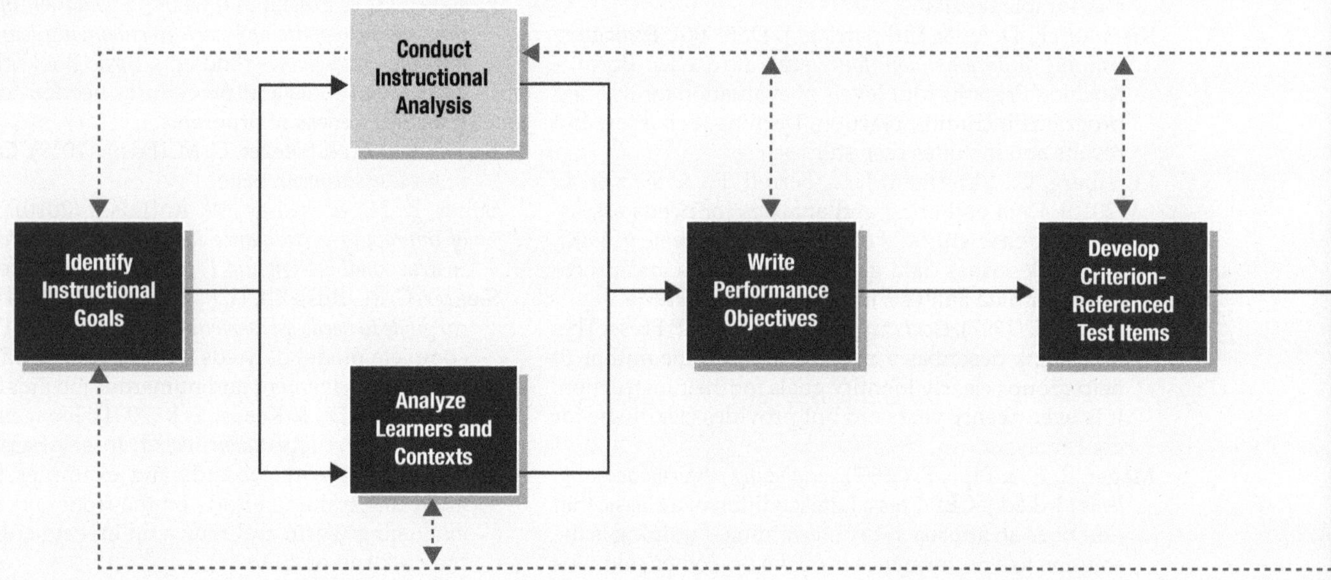

Objectives

- Classify instructional goals in the following domains: intellectual skill, psychomotor skill, attitude, and verbal information.
- Perform a goal analysis to identify the major steps required to accomplish an instructional goal.

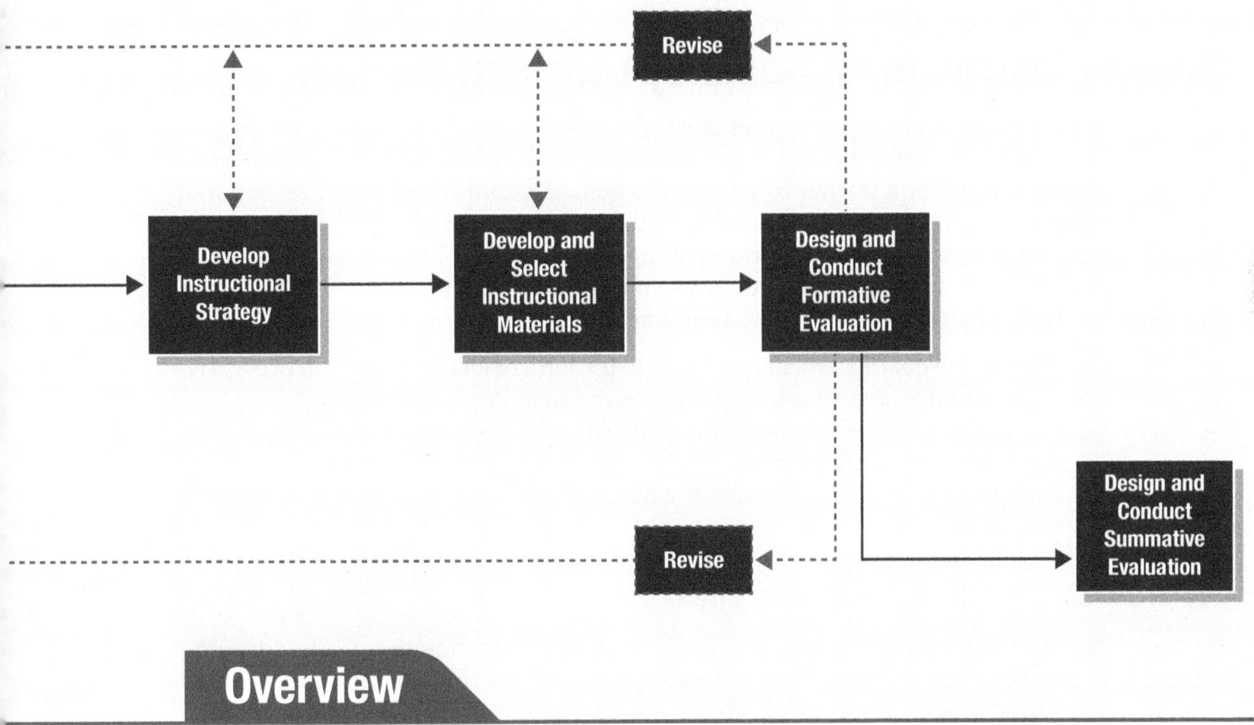

Overview

The goal analysis process is begun only after you have a clear statement of the instructional goal. The first step in the goal analysis process is to classify the goal into one of the four domains of learning: an attitude, an intellectual skill, verbal information, or a psychomotor skill.

The second step in goal analysis is to identify the major steps that learners must perform to demonstrate they have achieved the goal. These major steps should include both the skill performed and relevant content, and they should be sequenced in the most efficient order. For intellectual skill and psychomotor goals, as well as most attitudes, a sequential diagram of the steps to be taken is appropriate. An analysis of verbal information will usually result in a set of topics that can be organized by chronology or by other inherent relationships such as parts of a whole, simple to complex, or familiar to unfamiliar. Remember that perfect frameworks of skills required for a goal are rarely created on the first attempt. Your initial product should be viewed as a draft and should be subjected to evaluation and refinement. Specific problems to look for during the evaluation include steps that are not a natural part of the process, too small or too large, or misplaced in the sequence.

Concepts

Notice the diagram of the Dick and Carey instructional design model at the beginning of this chapter. As we move from one chapter to the next in describing the instructional design process, note that the step being discussed is highlighted in the diagram. Also, recall that we begin this step of the design process with a goal that has already been identified and stated. The goal could have been identified through performance analysis and needs assessment or by consulting a state's school performance standards or federal workplace safety standards. However it was derived, the goal should be a clear statement of what learners will be able to do.

Classify Instructional Goals by Learning Domain

An **instructional analysis** is a set of procedures that, when applied to an instructional goal, identifies the relevant steps for performing a goal and the subordinate skills required for a learner to achieve the goal. A **subordinate skill** is a skill that must be achieved in order to learn some higher-level skill by facilitating or providing positive transfer for the learning of higher-level skills. This chapter focuses on goal analysis, and Chapter 4 illustrates subordinate skills analysis.

Goal analysis includes three fundamental steps:

1. Classify the goal statement according to the kind of learning that will occur. The different categories of learning are referred to as *domains of learning*.
2. For intellectual and psychomotor skills, identify and sequence the major steps required to perform the goal.
3. For verbal information, identify the major clusters of information that learners must recall.

Gagné's (1985) Domains of Learning Outcomes

The four domains of learning are intellectual skills, psychomotor skills, attitudes, and verbal information. Instructional goals are categorized into one of these domains because of the implications for goal analysis and the selection of the appropriate subordinate skills analysis techniques discussed in Chapter 4.

Intellectual Skills Defined as skills that require the learner to do some unique cognitive activity, intellectual skills are unique in the sense that the learner must be able to solve a problem or perform an activity with previously unencountered information or examples. The four most common types of intellectual skills are making discriminations, forming concepts, applying rules, and solving problems.

It is important to be able to identify the various levels of intellectual skills. With these skills, the learner can classify things according to labels and characteristics, can apply a rule, and can select and apply a variety of rules in order to solve problems. Any goal that requires a learner to manipulate symbolic information in some way is an intellectual skill.

Discrimination. Discriminations are primarily simple, low-level learning by which we know whether things are the same or different. We actively teach young children to discriminate between the same and different colors, shapes, textures, sounds, temperatures, tastes, and so forth. Discriminations are seldom taught as individual learning outcomes to older children and adults except in specialized instances such as sounds in foreign language and music, colors and odors in chemistry, and kinesthetic "feel" in athletics. Discriminations are, however, important building blocks that we put together as we learn concepts. Just think of the important discriminations that are involved as a child learns the concept of hot burner and the rule "Don't touch the burner if it is hot!"

Concepts. Learning *concepts* essentially means being able to identify examples as being members of a certain classification. If the concept is baseball equipment, then the learner must be able to determine whether various examples of equipment are baseball equipment. Note that the learner might be asked to identify an actual object or even a picture or description of the object. The learner would have to have mastered the concept by learning the characteristics of baseball equipment that distinguish it from all other sporting equipment and from other objects as well.

Rules. Concepts are combined to produce rules. An example of a rule is "$a^2 + b^2 = c^2$." In this rule, the learner has to have the concepts of *a*, *b*, and *c*, squaring, adding, and square root. The rule shows the relationships among these concepts. The knowledge of the rule is tested by giving the learner a variety of values for *a* and *b* and asking for the value of *c*. The learner must follow a series of steps to produce the correct answer.

Problem Solving. The highest level of intellectual skill is *problem solving*, and there are two types of problems: **well-structured problem solving** and **ill-structured problem solving**. The well-structured problem is more typical and is usually considered an application problem. The learner is asked to apply a number of concepts and rules to solve a well-defined problem. Typically, the preferred way of going about determining what the solution should be is for the learner (or problem solver) to be given many details about a situation, a suggestion of what rules and concepts might apply, and an indication of what the characteristics of the solution will be. For example, algebra problems are well-structured problems with a preferred process, involve a variety of concepts and rules, and have a "correct" answer.

Researchers also classify some problems as ill structured in which not all the data required for a solution are readily available to the learner or even the nature of the goal is not clear. Multiple processes can be used to reach a solution, and no one solution is considered the "correct" one, even though the general properties of an adequate solution may be known. There is no better example of an ill-structured problem than the instructional design process itself. We rarely know all the critical elements that pertain to the formulation of the need for the instruction or the learners who will receive the instruction. There are various methods of analysis and strategies for presenting the instruction, and there are a variety of ways to assess the effectiveness of the instruction.

Most of the instruction created by instructional designers is in the domain of intellectual skills. It is important to be able to classify learning outcomes according to the various levels of skills and to determine whether the instructional goal could be improved or made more appropriate for learners by elevating it to a higher level of intellectual skill outcome.

Psychomotor Skills Psychomotor skills are characterized by learners executing physical actions, with or without equipment, to achieve specified results. In certain situations, there may be a lot of "psycho" in the psychomotor goal—that is, there may be a great deal of mental or cognitive activity that must accompany the motor activity. However, for purposes of instructional analysis, if the learner must learn to execute new, nontrivial motor skills or performance depends on the skillful execution of a physical skill, we refer to it as a *psychomotor goal*. Consider the following examples: Being able to throw a baseball is a psychomotor skill that requires repeated practice for mastery. Panning smoothly with a video camera to follow a moving object while maintaining correct lead space in the video frame requires practice for mastery; however, programming a DVR to record a late-night program, in which touching the buttons on a remote control is a trivial motor skill, is essentially an *intellectual skill*, meaning that extended practice in touching the buttons is not required for mastery and will not improve the ability to record the late-night program.

Attitudes If we express a goal statement in terms of having learners choose to do something, then that goal should be classified as an attitudinal goal. Attitudes are usually described as the tendency to make particular choices or decisions. For example, we would like individuals to choose to be good employees, choose to protect the environment, and choose to eat nourishing food. To identify an attitudinal goal, determine whether the learners have a choice to make and whether the goal indicates the direction in which the decision is to be influenced.

Another characteristic of attitudinal goals is that they probably will not be achieved at the end of the instruction. They are quite often long-term goals that are extremely important but very difficult to evaluate in the short term. As you examine an attitudinal goal, note that the only way we can determine whether learners have "achieved" an attitude is by having them do something—a psychomotor skill, an intellectual skill, or verbal information; therefore, instructional goals that focus on attitudes can be viewed as influencing the learner to choose, under certain circumstances, to perform an intellectual or a psychomotor skill or to state certain verbal information. This view of attitudes aligns well with current thinking about teaching dispositions as educational goals. It is well understood that there is a clear distinction between knowing how to do something and choosing to do it. For example, knowing how to report bullying on the playground or illegal practices in mortgage loan processing is necessary but not sufficient for action; a disposition toward (i.e., a choice for) social conscience, fair play, and ethical behavior is also required.

Verbal Information For tasks that are classified as verbal information, there is no symbolic manipulation—no problem solving or rule applying. In essence, verbal information goals require the learners to provide specific responses to relatively specific questions. You can usually spot a verbal information goal by the verb that is used. Often the learner must *state, list*, or *describe*. It is assumed that the information to be stated or listed will be taught in the instruction; therefore, the task for the learner is to store the information in memory during the instruction and remember it for the test or when needed for some related task.

Review each of the following abbreviated goal statements:

1. Given a bank statement and a checkbook, balance the checkbook.
2. Set up and operate a digital video camera.
3. Choose to make lifestyle decisions that reflect positive lifelong health concerns.
4. Given a list of cities, name the state of which each is the capital.

Each of these goals might serve as the starting point for instructional design, and the question then becomes "How do we determine what skills must be learned in order to achieve these goals?" The first step is to categorize the goal into one of Gagné's (1985) domains of learning.

Let's consider goal 1, which deals with balancing a checkbook. By nearly anyone's definition, this is a problem-solving task and is therefore classified as an intellectual skill. The following would also be classified as intellectual skills: applying the rule for computing sales tax and classifying a variety of creatures as either mammals or reptiles.

The second goal listed—setting up and operating a digital video camera—is classified as a **psychomotor skill** because it involves the coordination of mental and physical activity. In this case, equipment must be manipulated in a very specific way to produce a quality video image successfully. Other examples would include putting a golf ball and operating an electric paint sprayer.

In the third example concerning choosing a healthy lifestyle, the learner definitely has a choice to make, and regardless of whether they understand factors that make up a healthy lifestyle, they may or may not choose to follow them. Other examples include choosing not to text while driving and choosing to contribute to a local charity.

The last of our sample goals reflects verbal information and requires the learner to name the state for which each of the cities is the capital. There are many ways to teach such a skill and several ways the learner might try to learn it. Other examples of verbal information include reciting a poem, recalling an address, or associating objects with their names.

Cognitive Strategies Readers familiar with Gagné's work know that he described a fifth domain of learning—**cognitive strategies**. Cognitive strategies are the metaprocesses that we use to manage our thinking about things and manage our own learning. Some strategies are as straightforward as mentally repeating the name of new acquaintances several times while visualizing their faces so that you can call them by name the next time you meet them. A more complex cognitive strategy is figuring out how to organize, cluster, remember, and apply new information from a chapter that will be included on a test. Now consider the very complex combination of ill-structured problems and cognitive strategies used by a civil engineer in laying out a section of farmland for housing development. The engineer must:

1. Have command of a vast array of physical and intellectual tools, such as computer-assisted design; geographic information system databases; land surveying; soil analysis; hydrology; and water, sewer, gas, and electrical utilities systems.
2. Have command of a variety of "textbook" engineering strategies for the range of problems encountered in a land-development project.
3. Manage cooperative team efforts for in-house and consulting specialists in environmental, legal, and architectural matters.
4. Organize, manage, and apply all of those tools, solution strategies, and collaboration skills in a formerly unencountered environment. Some tools are useful; some are not. Some solutions work; others are rejected or modified. Some project team members will contribute quickly and reliably; others might require more direction and maintenance. In the end, the final site development is a one-of-a-kind product of the engineer's ability to orchestrate a variety of resources toward the solution of a unique problem.

The civil engineer in this example manages the internal thinking processes required to organize, attack, and solve the multidimensional problems in laying out the housing development, all the while learning new strategies for accomplishing the work assigned. This civil engineer's work can be compared directly with an instructional designer's work, as described previously. Both are engaged in solving ill-structured problems. For the instructional design processes described in this text, we place cognitive strategies with problem solving at the top of the intellectual skills grouping.

We mention cognitive strategies here for completeness and to avoid confusion but have deliberately omitted the terminology from the chapters that follow because for our purposes cognitive strategies can be treated similarly to ill-structured problem solving and taught as intellectual skills.

Performing an Instructional Goal Analysis

It is important to recognize that the amount of instruction required to teach an instructional goal will vary tremendously from one goal to another. Some goals represent skills that can be taught in less than an hour, whereas other goals may take many hours for students to achieve. The smaller the goal, the easier it is to do a precise analysis of what is to be learned. After we identify the domain of the goal, it is necessary to be more specific in indicating what the learner will be doing when performing the goal.

Procedures for Analyzing Intellectual and Psychomotor Skills

The best technique for analyzing a goal that is either an intellectual skill or a psychomotor skill is to describe, in step-by-step fashion, exactly what a person would be doing when performing the goal. This is not as easy as it first may sound. The person may perform physical activities that are easy to observe, as in a psychomotor skill. However, the person may process *mental steps* that must be executed before there is any overt behavior, as in an intellectual skill. For example, it may be quite easy to observe the psychomotor steps used to clean a paintbrush and spray equipment but almost impossible to observe directly all the intellectual steps that a person might follow to determine how much paint would be required to cover a building.

As you go through the process of describing the exact steps that a person might take in performing a goal, you may find that one of the steps requires a decision followed by several alternate paths that can be pursued (and, therefore, must be learned). For example, in cleaning a paintbrush, you might find at one point in the cleaning process that the paint will not come out, so an alternative technique must be applied. Similarly, in attempting to solve the mathematics problems related to area and required paint, it may be necessary first to classify the problems as *type A* (smooth surface requiring less paint) or *type B* (rough surface requiring more paint). Based on that outcome, one of two very different techniques might be used to solve the problem. The point is that the learner must be taught both how to make the decision and how to perform all the alternative steps required to reach the goal.

Goal analysis is the visual display of the specific steps the learner would do when performing the instructional goal. Each step is stated in a box as shown in the flow diagram:

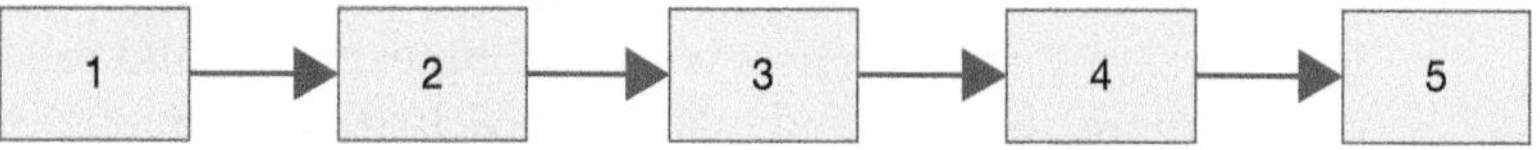

What this diagram indicates is that a learner who had the tools available as described in the goal statement could perform the goal by first doing step 1, which might be adding two numbers or might be striking a particular key on a keyboard. After doing step 1, the learner then performs step 2 and then steps 3, 4, and 5. After doing step 5, the process is complete and, if done properly, is considered a demonstration of the performance of the goal.

This sounds straightforward, and it is until you start doing an analysis of your own goal. Then questions arise about how large a step should be. How much can be included in one step? The answer depends primarily on the learner. If the instruction is for very young students or older students who have not "learned how to learn," then the steps should be quite small. If the same topic is being taught to older, more proficient learners, the same skills are included, but they would likely be combined into larger steps. Take a close look at the systems design model at the beginning of this chapter and note that the "Conduct Instructional Analysis" step we are now describing is depicted as a parallel activity with the "Analyze Learners and Contexts" step rather than as a preceding or following activity. The process of analyzing learners is described in Chapter 5; however, it is important to recognize that elements of that step can be completed simultaneously with goal analysis and that using detailed knowledge of learners while doing a goal analysis results in more useful and realistic work. Remember that the chapter-by-chapter sequence found in this text is designed to lead you through the process of learning to use a systems design model. As you become proficient at instructional design, you will gain a better feel for the sequential, parallel, and cyclical relationships among the steps in the model, and you will gain confidence in applying your own strategies for organizing and sequencing your instructional design work.

Regardless of how large the steps should be, the statement of each step must include a verb that describes an observable behavior. In our example, we used the verbs *adding* and *striking*. These are behaviors we can observe, or, in the case of adding, we can observe the answer written down. What we cannot see, for example, are people reading or listening; there is no direct result or product. If these are part of the goal, then the step should indicate what learners will identify from what they read or hear. Each step should have an observable outcome.

Another behavior that we cannot observe directly is decision making. Obviously, it is a mental process based on a set of criteria. The decision-making steps are often critical to the performance of a goal, and depending on what decision is made, a different set of skills is used. If reaching the goal includes decision making, the decision step should be placed in a diamond with the alternate decision paths shown.

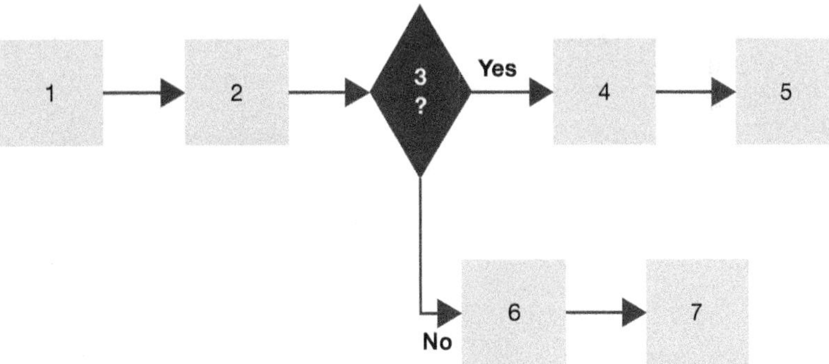

Let's walk through this diagram of the performance of a goal. The performer does step 1 and step 2 sequentially. Then a decision must be made, such as answering the question "Does the estimate exceed $300?" or "Is the word spelled correctly on the screen?" If the answer is yes, then the learner continues with steps 4 and 5. Alternatively, if the answer is no, then the learner does steps 6 and 7.

Several important characteristics about decisions should be noted. First, a decision can be a step in the goal analysis process. The decision is written out with an appropriate verb and displayed in a diamond in the diagram. Second, there must be at least two different skills to be learned and performed based on the outcome of the decision. An example not requiring a decision diamond is one in which a step requires the learner to "Select an apple" and the next step to "Peel the apple." The learner might be taught criteria to use for selecting an apple, but regardless of the apple selected, the next step is always to peel it. There are no alternative next steps, and no diamond is used in the diagram.

If we alter the apple example, the step in the diamond might be to distinguish between ripe and unripe apples. After the distinction is made, the ripe apples might be treated in one manner and the unripe in another. Clearly, the learner must be able to distinguish between the two types of apples and then be able to perform the appropriate procedure depending on the ripeness of the apple. Note that the question in the diamond is "Is the apple ripe?" This implies learner ability to make this distinction. If it is likely that students can already do this, then no teaching is required; students are simply told to do this at the appropriate point in the instruction. However, in some cases, it is necessary to treat this as a skill—"The learner will be able to distinguish between ripe and unripe apples"—and eventually to provide instruction for this skill, just as you would for any other steps in the goal analysis process.

Notice also that the numbers in the boxes do not necessarily indicate the sequence in which all of the steps will be performed. In the example, if a person does steps 4 and 5 as a result of the decision made at step 3, then the person would not do steps 6 and 7. The opposite is also true. Also note that step 3, because it is in a diamond, must be a question. The answer to the question leads one to different steps or skills.

Several other conventions about diagramming a goal are useful to know, such as what to do if you run out of space. Suppose you are working across the page and need room for more boxes. Obviously, you can turn the page on its side. Another solution, shown in the following diagram, is to use a circle after the last box on the line to indicate the point where the process breaks and then reconnects to the boxes after an identical lettered circle. The letter in the circle is arbitrary but should not be the same as any other letter used elsewhere in your analysis diagram. In our example, we use the letter M. It is not necessary to draw any connecting lines from one circle with an M to the identical circle because the reader can locate easily the next circle with the same letter in it.

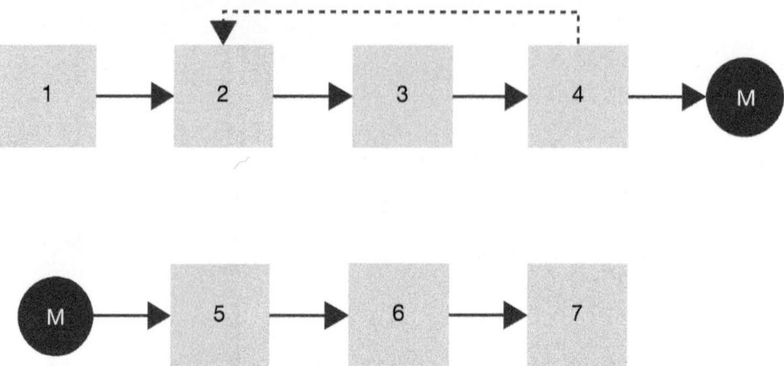

Another solution to the space problem is to drop down to the next line with your boxes and proceed backward from right to left with the description and numbering. As long as the line and arrows indicate the direction of flow, this is acceptable. The arrows are critical to the interpretation of the diagram. Also note the use of the dotted line in the preceding diagram, which means that when the goal is being performed, it is possible to go back to any number of earlier steps and come forward through the sequence again. Examine the diagram carefully to see the logic of the process being described.

As you analyze your goal, you may find that you have difficulty knowing exactly how much should be included in each step. As a general rule at this stage, there are typically at least five steps but not more than fifteen steps for one to two hours of instruction. If you have fewer than five, perhaps you have not been specific enough in describing the steps. If you have more than fifteen steps, then either you have taken too large a chunk to be analyzed or you have listed the steps in too much detail. A very general rule of thumb is to review and revise the steps until you have five to fifteen steps for every one to two hours of instruction.

Procedures for Analyzing Verbal Information Goals

For analyzing instructional goals classified as verbal information, you begin the analysis process by thinking, "Now let's see, what will the students be doing? I guess I will ask them to list the major bones in the body, to describe the major causes of bone injuries, and so forth. I'll just ask them on a test to do this, and they'll write down their answers." In a sense, there is no intellectual or psychomotor procedure other than the presentation of a test question and the retrieval of the answer. There is no problem solving with the information nor any decision making required of the learner. Doing the goal analysis is similar to preparing an outline of the topics contained in the goal, but there is no sequence of steps per se. Boxes can be used to indicate the major topics within the goal, but no arrows are used to indicate a sequence of steps to be performed.

With no procedure to follow, how does the designer sequence verbal information skills? The best sequence for verbal information skills is chronological when a natural chronology can be identified. When there is no natural ordering among the topics, then they should be sequenced based on the inherent relationships among them; for example, spatial, from easy to complex, from familiar to unfamiliar, common content areas, and so forth.

Procedures for Analyzing Attitudinal Goals

When the instructional goal is classified as an attitude, then it is necessary to identify the behavior that will be exhibited when the attitude is demonstrated. Is the behavior an intellectual skill or a psychomotor skill? If so, use the procedural flowchart process described previously. However, if the attitude demonstration constitutes verbal information, then your goal analysis should be a list or outline of the major topics contained in the information.

In summary, goal analysis for intellectual and psychomotor skills is an analysis of the steps to be performed, whereas for a verbal information goal, it is a list of the major topics to be learned; either approach can be used for an attitudinal goal depending on how the desired attitude will be exhibited.

More Suggestions for Identifying Steps within a Goal

If you cannot state your goal in terms of sequential steps, perhaps it has not been stated clearly in terms of the outcome behavior required. If it has been stated clearly and you still have difficulty, there are several procedures you can use to help identify the steps, including:

1. Describe for yourself the kind of test item or assessment you could use to determine whether the learners could perform your goal.
2. Think about the steps that the learner must go through to respond to your assessment or test.
3. "Test" yourself; that is, observe yourself, both in the physical and mental sense, performing the goal.
4. Jot down notes about each of the steps you go through and the decisions you must make. These are the steps you would record as the goal analysis.
5. Find others who you know can do it and ask them the steps they would follow. Compare their steps with yours. Often, there are differences that you should consider in the final representation of the goal.

6. Observe others performing your goal. What steps do they follow?
7. Consult written materials such as textbooks, technical reports, equipment manuals, software instructions, users' guides, policies and procedures booklets, and so forth to determine how the skills in your goal are described.
8. Talk with employees or supervisors who currently perform or manage performance of the goal in the workplace.
9. For selected skills, you could even look up "how to" videos on websites such as YouTube or VideoJug, remembering, of course, always to question the authority of this type of resource.

In professional and technical training, the jobsite (what we call the *performance context* in Chapter 5) is a good place for observing experts performing the goal and for finding existing manuals that document job performance standards. Recall that analyzing contexts is a parallel activity to conducting a goal analysis in the Dick and Carey model and is very pertinent to the goal analysis.

As an aside, refer for a moment to Figure 2.1 on page 22 and note the step labeled "Conduct Job Analysis" right before the goals are identified. In professional and technical training settings, the results of a job analysis might be available to the instructional designer for use in doing a goal analysis. Stated simply, the results of a job analysis are a report of the findings from a very careful and detailed examination of the types of job performance information described in the previous paragraph. There are circumstances, however, in which detailed information for goal analysis simply is not available when you are asked to begin developing instruction. Take, for example, the case when new training materials are being developed at the same time that a new piece of robotic equipment or software is being developed so that the manuals, training, and new product can be brought to market simultaneously. When time to market is critical for gaining a competitive advantage, a company will not want to delay product introduction while the training department completes the product package. This circumstance necessitates the *rapid prototyping* approach to instructional design described in Chapter 10. Although these procedures may produce a series of steps that seem very simple to you, remember that you are the SME; they probably will not be so simple or obvious to the uninformed learner.

Evaluation and Revision

Evaluating and Revising a Goal Analysis

Doing a goal analysis obviously requires the designer to either have extensive knowledge about the goal or be working with someone who does. This need for knowledge may have a downside if the designer has already taught the topic or goal in a regular classroom setting. We have routinely observed that novice designers tend to list the steps they would follow in teaching a goal rather than the steps that a learner should use in performing the goal. Teaching and performing are different. Verbs to watch for in your description of the steps in your goal analysis are *describe, list, say*, and so forth. These are almost never part of performing psychomotor, intellectual, or attitude goals but rather are words useful in describing how we would teach something. We will reach that point later in the instructional design process; for now, we only want to portray, in graphic form, the steps that someone would follow if they were performing your goal.

Another problem in conducting a goal analysis is the inclusion of skills and information that are "near and dear" to the designer but are not really required for the performance of the goal. Designers with a lot of experience in a topic area may be subject to this problem, or, more likely, it arises when the designer is working with a SME who insists on including a certain topic, skill, or information. This becomes a political issue that can be resolved only through negotiation.

Rubric for Evaluating a Goal Analysis

The following summary rubric can be used to evaluate the quality of your instructional goal analysis. It contains sections for rating the main steps, the diagramming strategy, and other criteria you may identify for your project.

Designer note: If an element is not relevant for your project, mark NA in the No column.

No	Some	Yes	
			A. Steps Statements Is/are the
____	____	____	1. Verb (behavior/action) included?
____	____	____	2. Outcomes visible/observable?
____	____	____	3. Content focused/clear?
____	____	____	4. Steps focused on learner actions rather than trainer/teacher actions?
____	____	____	5. Size chunks comparable in scope, appropriate for learners?
____	____	____	6. Steps important/main step in goal?
____	____	____	7. Relationships between/among steps clear?
____	____	____	8. Relationships among steps reflected in the sequence?
____	____	____	9. Redundancy among/between steps avoided?
____	____	____	10. (Other)
			B. Diagramming Is/are the
____	____	____	1. Main steps placed in boxes, left to right on page?
____	____	____	2. Decision points illustrated by a diamond, question, and branch answers (e.g., yes, no) with arrows leading to next step?
			3. Sequencing clearly illustrated with
____	____	____	a. Arrows between steps?
____	____	____	b. Numbering system for main steps indicating flow?
____	____	____	c. Pairs of matching circles with matching letters for breaks in lines?
			C. Other
____	____	____	1.
____	____	____	2.

The final product of your goal analysis should be a diagram of skills that provides an overview of what learners will be doing when they perform the instructional goal. This framework is the foundation for the subordinate skills analysis described in Chapter 4.

Examples

The first phase of performing an instructional analysis involves two major steps: (1) classifying the goal into a domain of learning and (2) performing a goal analysis by identifying and sequencing the major steps required to perform the goal. Table 3.1 shows four sample instructional goals and a list of the four learning domains described previously. First, we classify each goal into one of the domains, and then we identify and sequence the major steps required to perform the goal.

Table 3.1 Sample Instructional Goals and Learning Domains

Sample Goals	Learning Domain
1. Interpret performance score distributions using frequency polygons.	Intellectual skills—making discriminations, using learning concepts, using rules, and solving problems
2. Putt a golf ball.	Psychomotor skills—physical activity, which usually includes mental activity as well
3. Choose to maximize personal safety while staying in a hotel.	Attitudes—making particular choices or behaving in a manner that implies an underlying belief or preference
4. Describe the five parts of a material safety data sheet (MSDS) that are most important for jobsite safety.	Verbal information—stating facts, providing specific information (e.g., naming objects)

Intellectual Skills Goals

Examine the first goal listed in Table 3.1— interpret performance score distributions using frequency polygons. This goal is classified as an *intellectual skill* because learners are required to learn concepts, follow rules, and solve problems in performing the goal. The main steps for this intellectual skill goal are illustrated in Figure 3.1.

With the goal classified, we should identify the major steps required to perform the goal and the best sequence for the steps. A good way for the designer to proceed is to examine a frequency polygon to identify its components. Working left to right, write down the steps it would take to create the polygon. Undoubtedly the learner would begin by creating the two axes (step 1) and then adding the frequencies on the vertical side (1.1) and the scores on the horizontal side (1.2). The dots in the intersections of scores and frequencies would be added (1.3), and then the dots would be connected (1.4) to make the shape of the distribution clear. Finally, the implications of the shape for describing or evaluating the performance would follow (step 2).

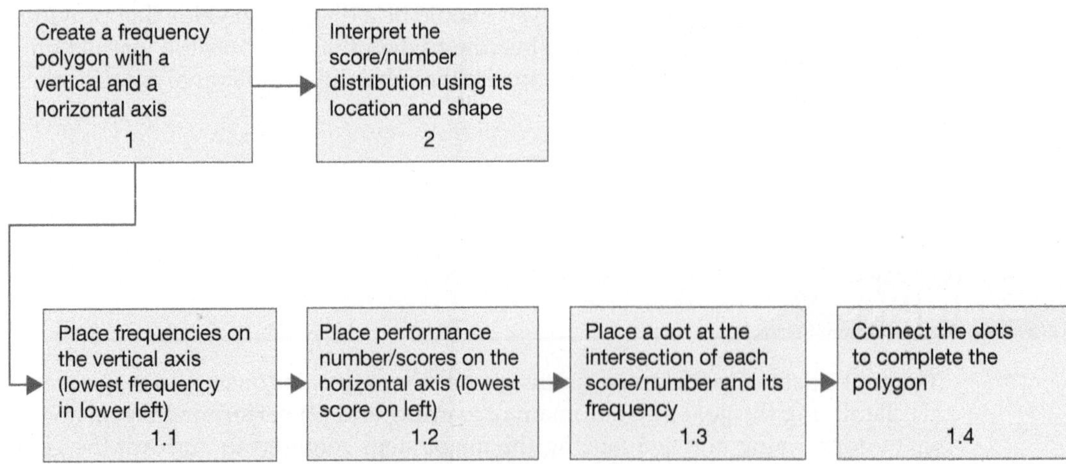

Figure 3.1 Goal Analysis for an Intellectual Skill

Goal: Interpret performance score distributions using frequency polygons.

Psychomotor Skills Goals

The second instructional goal presented in Table 3.1, putting a golf ball, should be classified as a *psychomotor skill* because both mental planning and physical execution of the plan are required to putt the ball into the cup. Neither banging the ball around the green nor simply "willing" the ball into the cup will accomplish the task. Rather, mental planning and calculating, combined with accurately executing the stroke based on mental calculations, are required.

Now that we have the putting goal classified by domain, we next identify and sequence the major steps learners take to execute the goal, shown in Figure 3.2. As we watch a golfer preparing to putt the ball, we notice some mental planning activities appear to occur. The steps that follow planning simply provide a broad overview of the complete task from beginning to end. The sequence we have at this point provides us with the framework we need to identify the subordinate skills required to perform each of the steps already identified.

Attitudinal Goals

The third goal listed in Table 3.1, choosing to maximize personal safety while staying in a hotel, is classified as an *attitudinal goal* because it implies choosing a course of action based on an underlying attitude or belief. What would learners be doing if they were exhibiting behavior demonstrating safety consciousness while staying in a hotel? The first step to building a framework for this goal is to visit several hotels and inquire about safety features provided, resulting in identifying the three possible main areas of concern:

1. Hotel fires
2. Personal safety while in hotel room
3. Protection of valuable possessions

Figure 3.3 shows the major steps for maximizing personal safety in relation to hotel fires. This series of steps reflects the actual behaviors performed by a person who chooses to maximize fire safety precautions while at a hotel. Each of these major steps could be broken down further, but, for now, they indicate what a person should be doing to perform the first part of this goal. A similar analysis should be done for the second and third components of the goal related to personal safety and protecting valuable possessions.

Verbal Information Goals

The fourth instructional goal in Table 3.1, describing the five parts of a material safety data sheet (MSDS) that are most important for jobsite safety, is classified as a *verbal information goal* because learners are required to recall specific information about the contents of a document. An MSDS is a federally mandated information

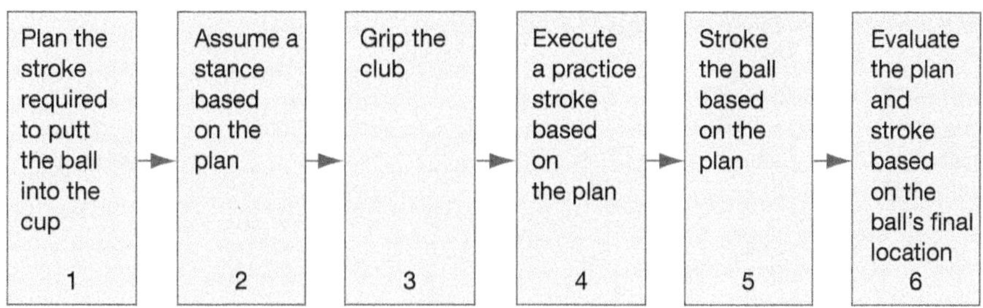

Figure 3.2 Goal Analysis for a Psychomotor Skill

Goal: Putt a golf ball.

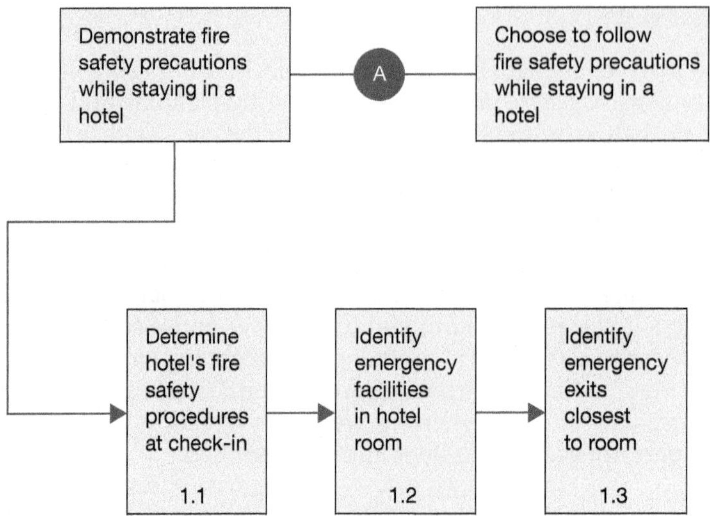

Figure 3.3 Goal Analysis for an Attitude Skill

Goal: Choose to maximize personal safety while staying in a hotel.

sheet provided to customers by chemical manufacturers. Performing this goal requires knowledge of five topics, as illustrated in Figure 3.4. Note that for a verbal information goal, these are not "steps" in the sense that one goes from one activity to the next. There is no mandated order inherent in the information, so the goal analysis simply numbers the major clusters of information in the same order they appear on an MSDS. That would likely be the same order in which the information would be covered during the instruction.

Typical First Approach to Goal Analysis

When reading a text such as this, the instructional goal diagrams may appear to have simply flowed from the word processors of the authors. When the reader initially applies the process, however, it does not always seem to work as smoothly and easily. It might be useful to show a typical "first pass" at goal analysis and to point out some of the problems that can be avoided.

Examine Figure 3.5, which shows the analysis of a wordy goal related to the initial use of a word-processing program. It appears that the analyst did not say, "How should I perform this goal?" but seemed to ask, "How should I teach this goal?" We might want to explain some background information to begin the instruction. However, at this point, we want to list only the steps in actual performance of the goal. Performing the goal in Figure 3.5 does not require an explanation of operating systems; thus, step 1 should be eliminated.

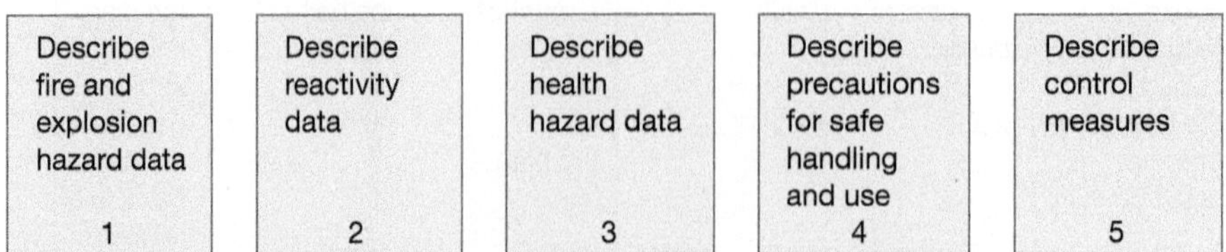

Figure 3.4 Goal Analysis for a Verbal Information Skill

Goal: Describe the five parts of a material safety data sheet (MSDS) that are most important for workplace safety (OSHA Form 174).

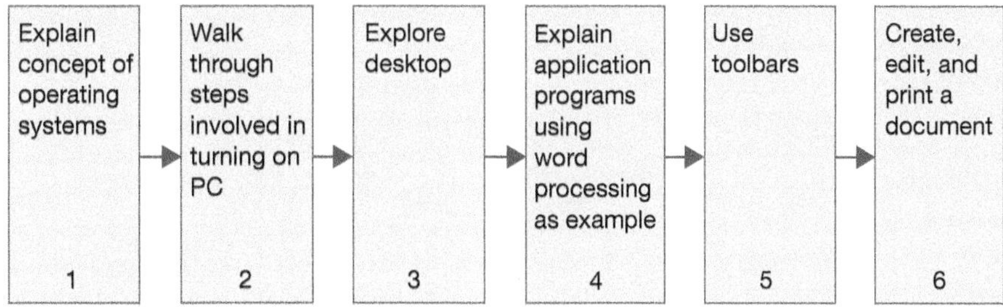

Figure 3.5 Faulty Goal Analysis of an Intellectual Skill Related to Word Processing

Goal: Boot up PCs; describe operating systems; and create, edit, and print a document using a word-processing application.

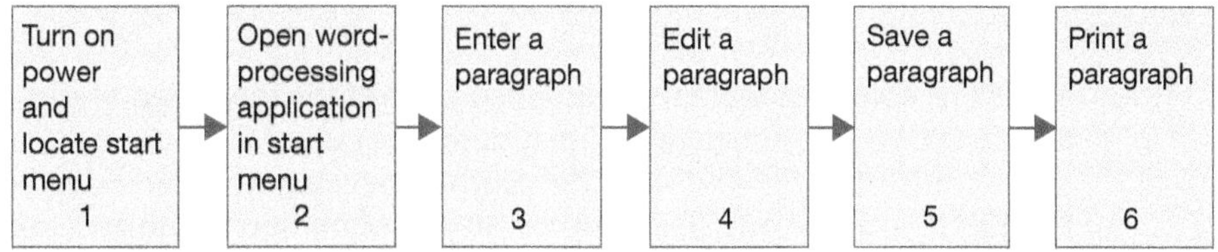

Figure 3.6 Revised Goal Analysis for a Word-Processing Goal

Goal: Operate a word-processing application by entering, editing, and printing a brief document.

Step 2 appears to be a general step related to getting the system up and running. It should be revised to express what the learner would be doing—namely, turning on the power and locating the start menu. Step 3 should be eliminated because it is a general process for first-time users that should only appear as a substep.

Concerning step 4, the expert who was performing the goal would never stop to explain what an application program is. This may be a subordinate skill somewhere in the instruction, but it does not belong here; thus, it too should be eliminated. All we want to do is note the steps in getting the word-processing application working. Moving on to step 5 puts us back on track, but what is meant by "Use toolbars"? It should be dropped as well because the substance of the goal is included in step 6.

Finally, step 6 includes creating, editing, and printing a document. This is much too large a step for a goal analysis and should be broken down into the following separate steps: create a file, enter a paragraph of prose, edit a paragraph, and print a paragraph.

Given this analysis, we would rewrite the goal as follows: Operate a word-processing application by entering, editing, and printing a brief document. The revised steps are shown in Figure 3.6. It looks considerably different from the initial analysis of Figure 3.5. Also, note that as you review the steps necessary to carry out the goal, no one step is equivalent to performing the goal; all the steps must be performed in sequence to demonstrate the ability to perform the goal.

Case Study

Group Leadership Training

Recall from the Case Study section of Chapter 2 the instructional goal selected by the instructional designer: "Demonstrate effective discussion group leadership skills." This goal is now brought forward for goal analysis in this chapter. The goal is classified as an intellectual skill because it requires learning concepts and rules

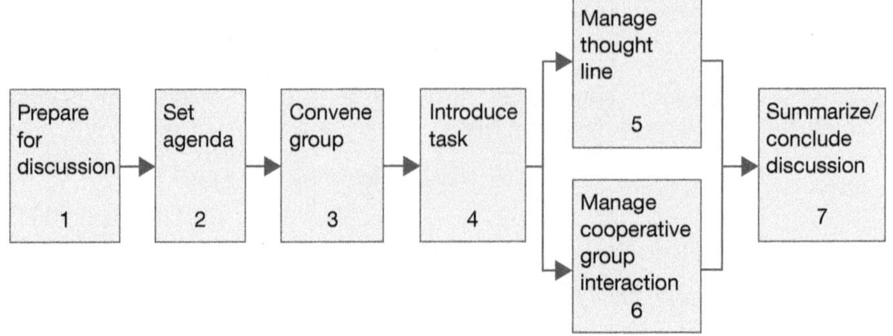

Figure 3.7 Goal Analysis for an Intellectual Skill

Goal: Demonstrate effective discussion group leadership skills.

as well as solving problems. The seven main steps identified to perform this goal and the planned sequence are included in Figure 3.7. There is a natural flow of tasks from left to right because the product developed at each step becomes input for the subsequent one. This step-by-step explanation of the general instructional goal makes subsequent instructional analysis activities much easier.

Professional and Historical Perspectives

In the mid-1950s, Benjamin Bloom (1956) and his colleagues published *The Taxonomy of Educational Objectives* as a framework for classifying student learning outcomes according to his views on the complexity of different kinds of skills. Bloom's taxonomy is a popular scheme for categorizing learning in both school and business settings, so we include it here and compare it in Table 3.2 with Gagné's types of

Table 3.2 Types of Learning Required in Bloom's Domains of Learning Outcomes

Bloom THESE DOMAINS OF LEARNING OUTCOMES	**Gagné** REQUIRE THESE TYPES OF LEARNING
Psychomotor Domain	Psychomotor Skills
Affective Domain	Attitude Skills
Cognitive Domain: Knowledge	Verbal Information Skills
Cognitive Domain: Comprehension	Intellectual Skills: Primarily concepts with some rules
Cognitive Domain: Application	Intellectual Skills: Primarily rules with some problem solving
Cognitive Domain: Analysis	Intellectual Skills: Primarily well-defined problem solving
Cognitive Domain: Synthesis	Intellectual Skills: Primarily ill-defined problem solving with some elements of cognitive strategies
Cognitive Domain: Evaluation	Intellectual Skills: Primarily ill-defined problem solving with some elements of cognitive strategies

Note: Most of Bloom's categories within the cognitive domain require combinations of skills. This table is intended to be illustrative rather than a definitive statement of the skills therein.

learning. Those familiar with Bloom's categories may wish to use the table for translating from Bloom to Gagné. We use Gagné's scheme throughout the book because his categories provide guidance for how to analyze goals and subskills and how to develop instructional strategies that are most effective in bringing about learning. More recently, Anderson et al. (2001) modified some of Bloom's terminology and configured his taxonomy as a matrix to visually relate the knowledge level to other levels of the cognitive domain.

Process Flowcharts

Identifying Instructional Goals

This section contains two flowcharts, Figure 3.8 and Figure 3.9, that will assist you in reviewing the tasks required to conduct an instructional goal analysis. These flowcharts will help you summarize the information from the chapter and provide guidance for your design work.

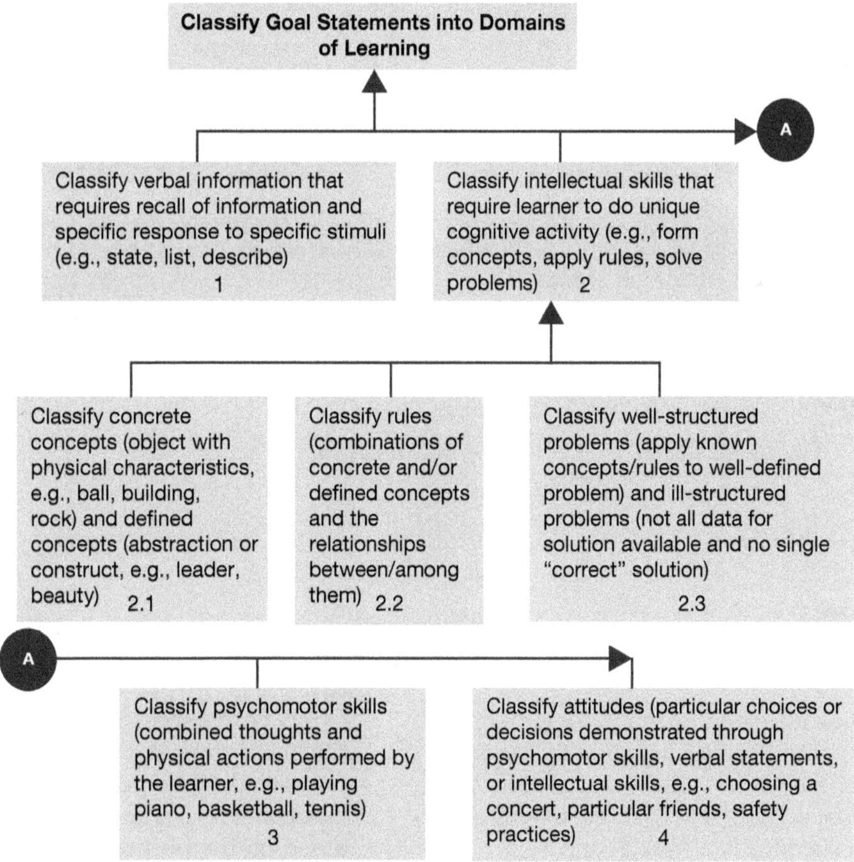

Figure 3.8 Classify Goal Statements into Domains of Learning

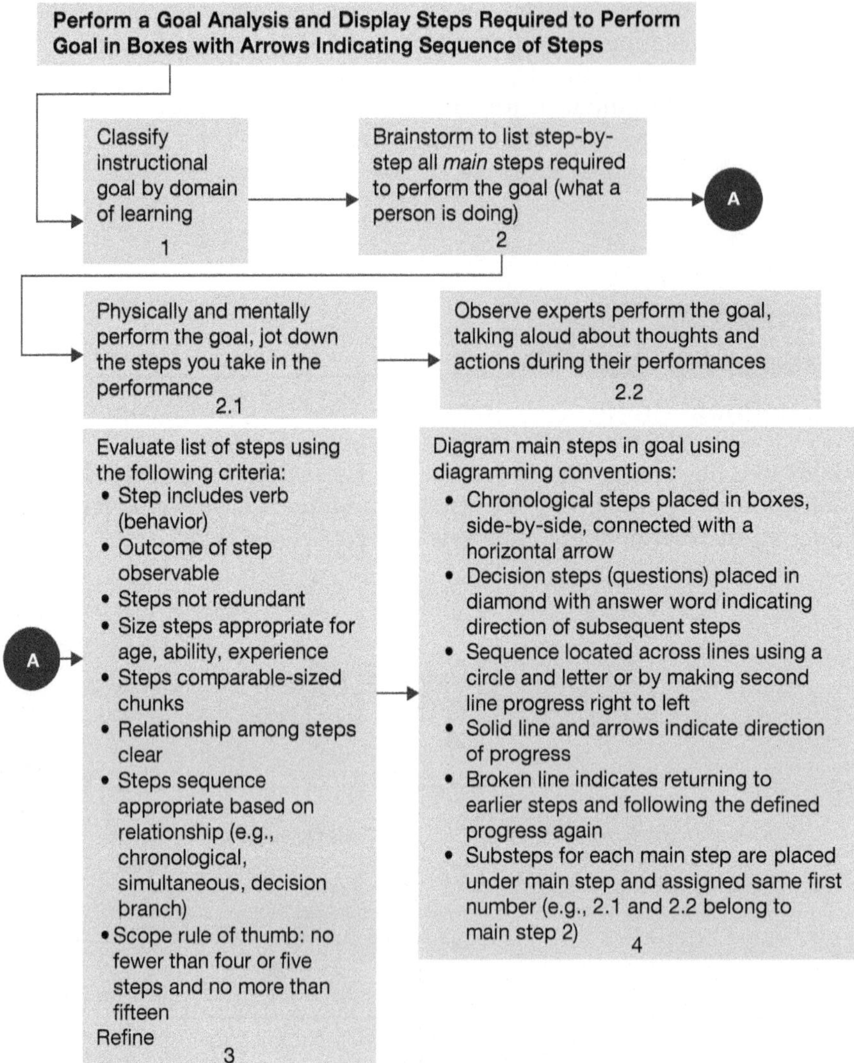

Figure 3.9 Tasks for Performing a Goal Analysis

Practice

1. Table 3.3 contains a list of learning domains and instructional goals. Read each goal in the second column and classify it using the learning domains listed in the first column. For each goal, write the rationale you used to classify each one.
2. On separate sheets of paper, identify and sequence the major areas of activity implied by instructional goals 1, 2, and 3 in Table 3.3.
3. On a separate sheet of paper, identify and sequence the major steps implied by the following instructional goal: Write a composition (1) using a variety of sentence types and accompanying punctuation based on the purpose and mood of the sentence and (2) using a variety of sentence types and accompanying punctuation based on the complexity or structure of the sentence. Use the rubric in this chapter to guide and evaluate your work.

Table 3.3 Classify Instructional Goals by Learning Domain

Learning Domain	Sample Instructional Goal	Rationale
A. Psychomotor Skill	______ 1. Name parts of the human body using common terminology.	
B. Intellectual Skill	______ 2. Separate an egg yolk from the egg white using the shell as a tool.	
C. Verbal Information	______ 3. Choose to behave safely while flying on airplanes.	
D. Attitude		

Feedback

1. Compare your work with the examples provided in Table 3.4.
2. Compare your decisions about what constitutes the major steps and sequences for each of the three instructional goals listed in Figures 3.10 through 3.12. Your analyses will be slightly different from ours because there usually is no one way to analyze the steps in a goal, and the wording always varies.

   The first goal, naming parts of the human body (Figure 3.10), does not have a chronology of events that can be used to develop a logical framework. An organizing method must be identified that enables us to cluster or group information in a logical manner. We chose to organize the content using a "parts of a whole" plan (i.e., main areas of the body). We then selected a sequence for the areas by moving from the top to the bottom—for example, head, arms, hands, trunk, legs, and feet. Note that the words are not connected with arrows because these are not sequential steps that must be performed.

   The psychomotor skill required to crack an egg and separate the yolk from the white (Figure 3.11) has a natural sequence of events. The shell cannot be pulled apart until it is broken, and the egg white cannot be separated until the shell is pulled apart. Like most psychomotor tasks, this one requires practice. The only way your mind can tell your hands how hard to tap the shell or how fast to pour the yolk is to practice the skill. Incorrect estimations and translations result in squashed shells and broken yolks.

   The instructional goal on airplane safety (Figure 3.12) has a sequence of sorts that does help with this goal. Carry-on items are stored, and then attention is given to safety announcements. The announcements help in locating safety features on the plane. Then it is necessary to keep the seat belt on and to limit one's alcohol intake.
3. Compare your goal analysis for writing sentences with the one located in Appendix B.

Table 3.4 Feedback for Classifying Instructional Goals

Learning Domain	Sample Instructional Goal	Rationale
A. Psychomotor Skill B. Intellectual Skill C. Verbal Information D. Attitude	C 1. Name parts of the human body using common terminology.	Requires associating a name with a part of the body. Each part of the body has one name. It does not require anything but recalling labels or names.
	A 2. Separate an egg yolk from egg white using the shell as a tool.	Requires mental planning and accurate translation of mental plans into physical actions.
	D 3. Choose to behave safely while flying on airplanes.	Behavior implies an underlying attitude about safety.

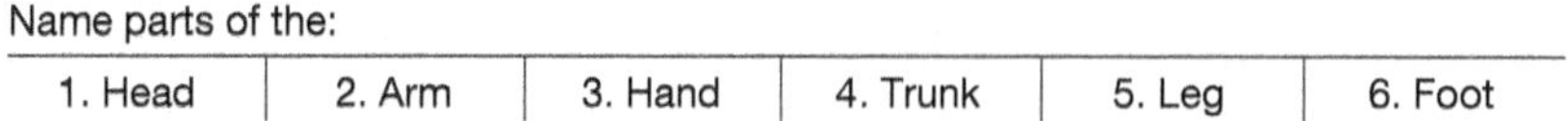

Figure 3.10 Goal Analysis for a Verbal Information Skill
Goal: Name parts of the human body using common terminology.

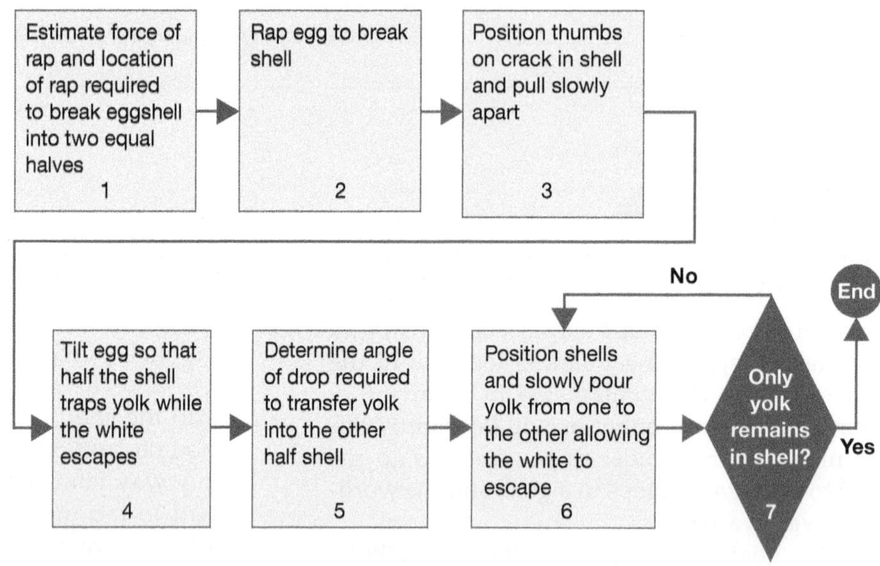

Figure 3.11 Goal Analysis for a Psychomotor Skill
Goal: Separate an egg yolk from the egg white using the shell as a tool.

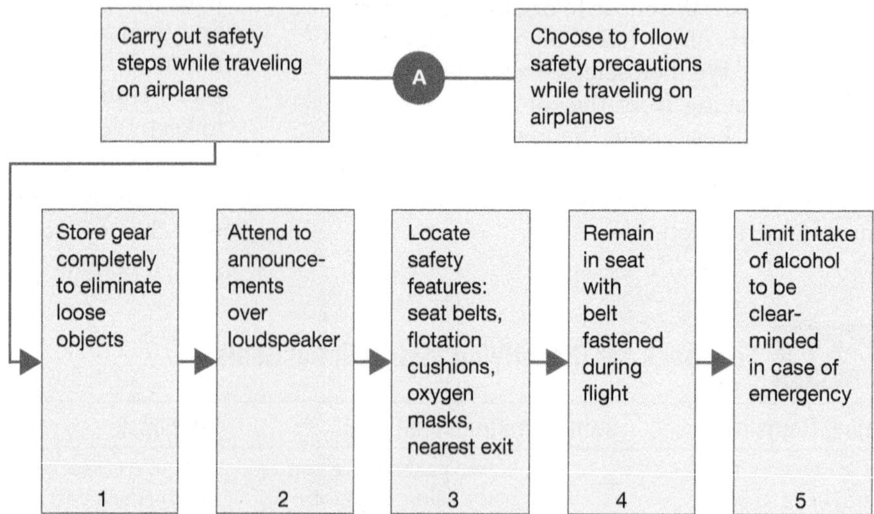

Figure 3.12 Goal Analysis for an Attitudinal Skill
Goal: Choose to behave safely while flying on airplanes.

References and Recommended Readings

Anderson, L. W., Krathwohl, D. R., Airasian, P. W., Kruikshank, K. A., Mayer, R. E., Pintrich, P. R., Raths, J., & Wittrock, M. C. (2001). *A taxonomy for learning, teaching, and assessing: A revision of Bloom's taxonomy of educational objectives*. Pearson.

Bloom, B., Englehart, M., Furst, E., Hill, W., & Krathwohl, D. (1956). *Taxonomy of educational objectives: The classification of educational goals: Handbook 1: The cognitive domain*. W. H. Freeman.

Clark, R. C., & Mayer, R. E. (2013). *Scenario-based e-learning: Evidence-based guidelines for online workforce learning*. Pfeiffer. Provides a good example of cognitive task analysis in professional and technical training, including classification of goals into learning domains.

Crandall, B., Klein, G., & Hoffman, R. R. (2006). *Working minds: A practitioner's guide to cognitive task analysis*. MIT Press. Includes methods and tools for collecting and analyzing data about how people do things.

Gagné, R. (1985). *Conditions of learning* (4th ed.). Holt, Rinehart and Winston. A classic regarding many aspects of instructional design, including the domains of learning and hierarchical analysis.

Gagné, R. M., Wager, W. W., Golas, K. C., & Keller, J. M. (2004). *Principles of instructional design* (5th ed.). Wadsworth/Thomson Learning. Provides a number of examples of the application of instructional analysis to intellectual skills.

Hackos, J. T., & Redish, J. C. (1998). *User and task analysis for interface design*. Wiley. Describes observational techniques for task analysis that have direct application for goal analysis.

Jonassen, D. H., Tessmer, M., & Hannum, W. (1999). *Task analysis procedures for instructional design*. Lawrence Erlbaum Associates. Excellent overview and "how to" guide to instructional design applications of a wide range of techniques for instructional analysis. This book is currently available as an e-book through netLibrary.

Loughner, P., & Moller, L. (1998). The use of task analysis procedures by instructional designers. *Performance Improvement Quarterly*, *11*(3), 79–101.

Mager, R. (1997). *Goal analysis: How to clarify your goals so you can actually achieve them*. The Center for Effective Performance. The title accurately describes the contents of this instructional design classic.

Mellon, C. (1997). Goal analysis: Back to the basics. *Tech Trends*, *42*(5), 38–42.

chapter 4

Identifying Subordinate and Entry Skills

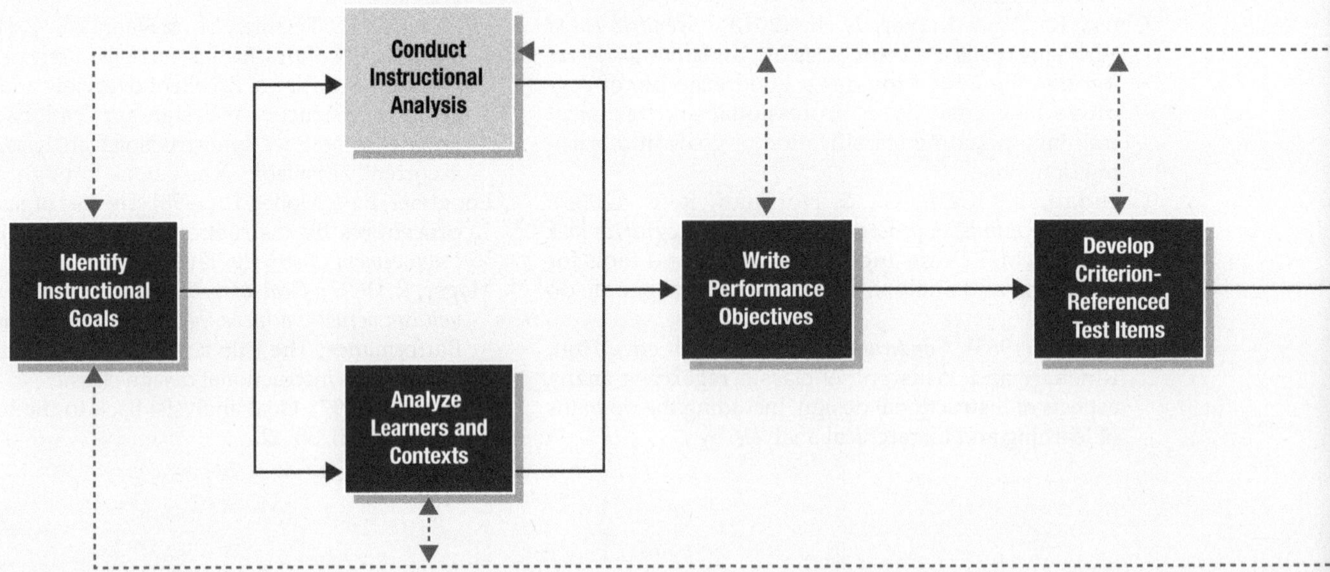

Objectives

- Describe approaches to subordinate skills analysis including hierarchical, procedural, cluster, and combination techniques.
- Describe the relationships among the subordinate skills identified through subordinate skills analysis, including entry skills.
- Apply subordinate skills analysis techniques to steps in the goal analysis and identify entry skills as appropriate.

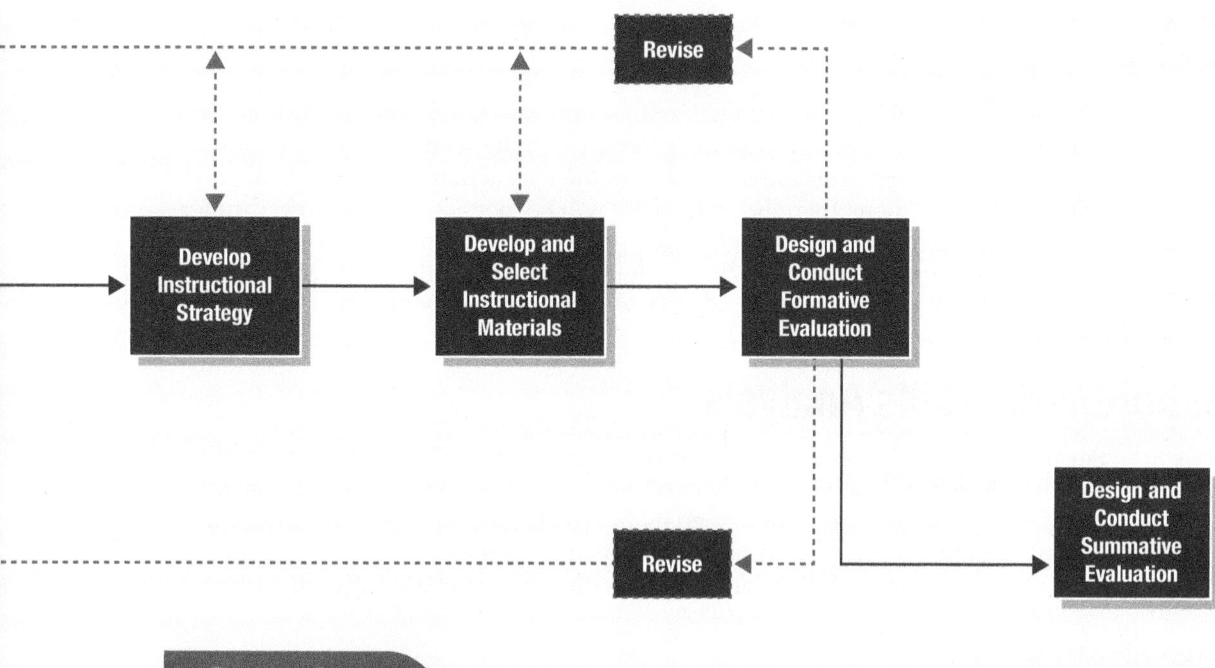

Overview

The next task is to identify what the learner must *know* and be able to *do* in order to achieve each of the main steps in an instructional goal. This process is called a subordinate skills analysis. Before beginning a subordinate skills analysis, it is necessary to have a clear description of the main tasks learners must perform in order to accomplish the instructional goal. The derivation of these major steps was described in Chapter 3. To conduct a subordinate skills analysis, you must analyze each of the major steps in a goal.

Different analysis techniques are used with different types of instructional goals. Intellectual and psychomotor skills are analyzed using hierarchical and procedural analysis. If a step is verbal information, a cluster analysis should be done. Goal analysis of an attitude identifies the behaviors exhibited if someone holds that attitude.

For each of the skills identified during this subordinate skills analysis, the process is repeated; that is, each of the identified subordinate skills is analyzed to identify its respective subordinate skills. This step-down process is used until you believe that no further subordinate skills remain to be identified. At this point, the designer identifies the entry skills required of learners by drawing a dotted line below those skills to be taught and above those that will not. The skills identified in the analysis that will not be taught are referred to as *entry skills*.

The final product of the subordinate skills analysis is a framework of the subordinate skills required to perform each main step of the instructional goal. The total instructional analysis includes the instructional goal, the main steps required to accomplish the goal, the subordinate skills required to accomplish each main step, and the entry skills. This framework of skills is the foundation for all subsequent instructional design activities.

It is important to evaluate the analysis of learning tasks before proceeding to the next phase of design activities because many hours of work remain to be completed. The quality of the analysis directly affects the ease with which succeeding design activities can be performed and the quality of the eventual instruction. Producing an accurate and clear analysis of tasks typically requires several iterations and refinements.

Concepts

The second step in the instructional analysis process is referred to as *subordinate skills analysis*. The purpose is to identify the appropriate set of subordinate skills for each step. If required skills are omitted from the instruction and many students do not already have them, then the instruction will be ineffective. However, if superfluous skills are included, the instruction will take more time than it should, and the unnecessary skills may actually interfere with learning the required skills. The identification of either too many or too few skills can be a problem.

Subordinate Skills Analysis

Several processes are used to identify subordinate skills. We describe each of the techniques and indicate how they can be applied to various types of goals. We begin with "pure" goals—that is, goals in which the steps are only intellectual or psychomotor skills. Complex goals, however, often involve several domains. A combination approach that can be used with complex goals is also described.

Hierarchical Analysis

The **hierarchical analysis** approach is used to analyze individual steps in the goal analysis that are classified as intellectual or psychomotor skills. To understand the hierarchical approach, consider an instructional goal that requires the learner to justify the recommendation that a particular piece of real estate should be purchased at a particular time. This is an intellectual skill goal, and it requires learning a number of rules and concepts related to the assessment of property values, the effect of inflation on property values, the financial status of the buyer, and the buyer's short- and long-term investment goals. The skills in each of these areas depend on knowledge of the basic concepts used in the financial and real estate fields. In this example, it is extremely important to identify and teach each of the critical rules and concepts prior to teaching the steps for analyzing a particular real estate purchase situation and making a recommendation.

How does the designer go about identifying the subordinate skills a student must learn in order to achieve a higher-level intellectual skill? The hierarchical analysis technique suggested by Gagné (1985) consists of asking the question "What must the student already know so that, with a minimal amount of instruction, this task can be learned?" By answering this question, the designer can identify one or more critical subordinate skills required of the learner prior to attempting instruction on the step itself. After these subordinate skills have been identified, the designer then asks the same question with regard to each of them, namely, "What is it that the student must already know how to do, the absence of which would make it impossible to learn this subordinate skill?" resulting in identifying one or more additional subordinate skills. If this process is continued with increasingly lower levels of subordinate skills, one quickly reaches a very basic level of performance, such as being able to recognize whole numbers or being able to recognize letters.

To get a visual understanding of how the designer "builds" the hierarchical analysis, consider the generic hierarchy shown in Figure 4.1. Here, a *rule* serves as the immediate subordinate skill required to learn a particular problem-solving skill. It is important to understand that box 2 represents one step in performing the goal. After the rule has been identified (box 2.4), the designer then asks, "What must the student know how to do in order to learn the rule?" The answer is that the student must learn two concepts, which are represented in boxes 2.2 and 2.3. When asked, "What must the student know how to do to learn the concept in box 2.2?" the answer is nothing, so no additional skills are listed. For box 2.3, the question results in the identification of a relevant discrimination, which is shown in box 2.1. Figure 4.1 represents how the analysis appears when laid out in a diagram and is consistent with Gagné's hierarchy of intellectual skills. Gagné notes that in order to learn how to perform problem-solving skills, learners must first know how to apply the rules that are required to solve the problem. The immediate subskills to the instructional goal are the rules that must be applied in the problem situation.

Further, Gagné notes that rules are based on recognizing the components or concepts that are combined in the rules. In other words, in order to learn the relationship among "things," you must be able to classify them. The subordinate skills

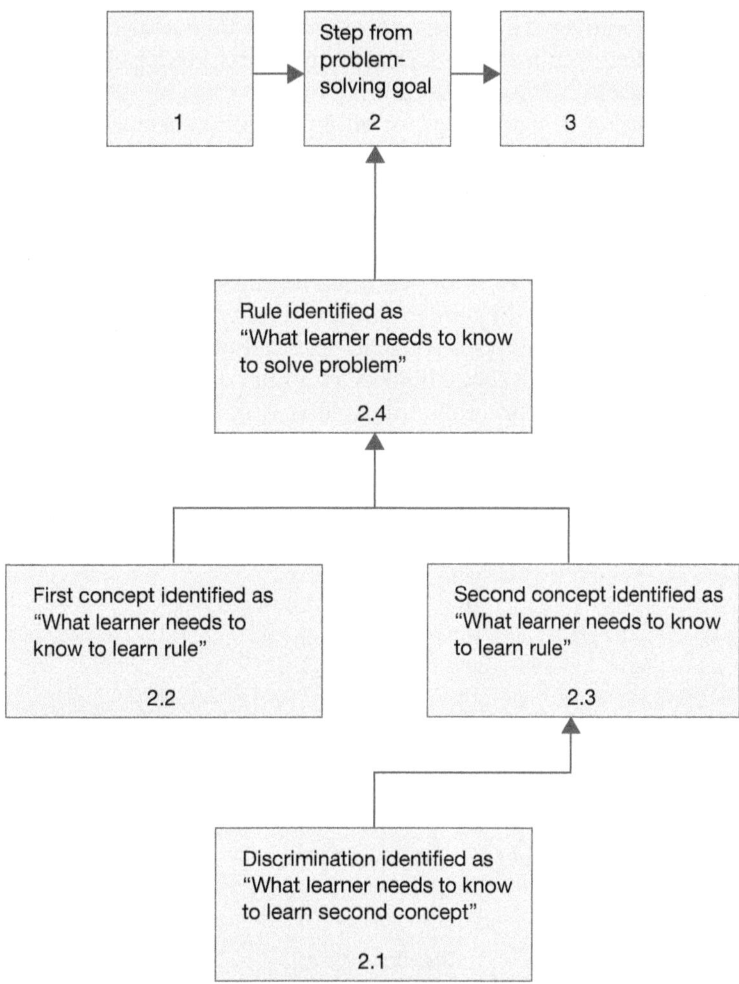

Figure 4.1 Hypothetical Hierarchical Analysis of a Step from a Problem-Solving Goal

required for any given rule are typically classifying the concepts used in the rules. Finally, the learner must be able to discriminate whether a particular example is relevant to the concept.

This hierarchy of skills is helpful to the designer because it can be used to suggest the type of specific subordinate skills required to support any particular step in the goal. If the step is a problem-solving skill (or selecting and using a number of rules), then the subskills should include the relevant rules, concepts, and discriminations. However, if the application of a single rule is being taught, then only the subordinate concepts and discriminations are taught.

To apply the hierarchical approach to the steps in the goal analysis, the designer applies it to each step in the goal, including any decision steps. The question "What must the learner know or do in order to learn to do the first step in performing the goal?" is repeated for each of the subskills for the first step and then for each of the remaining steps in the goal. If this approach is used with the hypothetical problem-solving goal shown in Figure 4.1, the result might resemble that shown in Figure 4.2.

Observe in Figure 4.2 that the same subskills have been identified as in the original methodology suggested by Gagné. The fact that no subskills are listed for steps 1, 3, and 4 indicates the designer's determination that there are no relevant skills the learner must master before being taught these steps. This is often a perfectly reasonable assumption.

An example resulting from using the hierarchical instructional analysis technique appears in Figure 4.3. In the diagram, it can be seen that step 8 from the goal analysis requires students to estimate to the nearest one-hundredth of a unit (±0.01) a designated point on a linear scale marked only in tenths. Three subordinate skills have been identified for step 8, related to estimating a point to the nearest hundredth on a scale marked only in tenths units, dividing that scale into subunits, and identifying a designated point on a particular scale. Each of these skills has subordinate skills that are identified.

The use of hierarchical analysis is also illustrated in Figure 4.4. Notice that the cognitive task performed by the learner is shown in the four successive substeps labeled 1 through 4 from the goal analysis. In this particular example, the subordinate skills are the same as those identified for the same skill in Figure 4.3; however, it should be noted that they are organized somewhat differently.

These particular analyses were not devised on the basis of one attempt at the process—or even two or three. It takes a number of attempts at identifying the vertical subordinate skills and their interrelationships before you can be satisfied that all the relevant skills are identified and stated appropriately. It is almost impossible to know when an appropriate and valid hierarchical analysis of an instructional goal has been achieved.

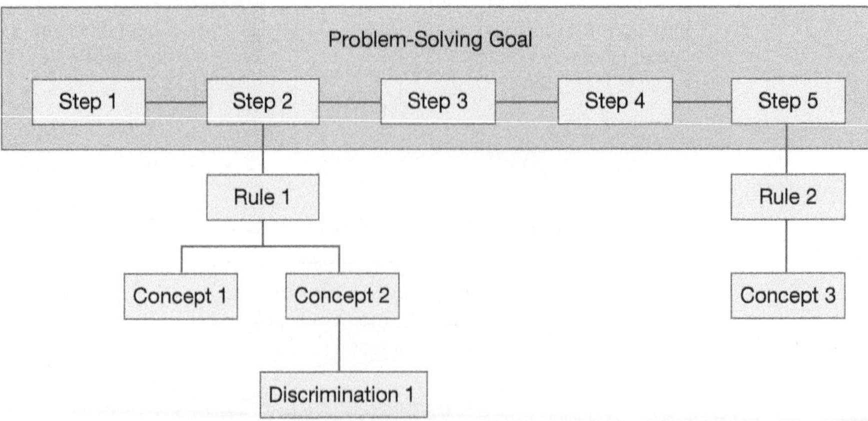

Figure 4.2 Hypothetical Hierarchical Analysis of Steps in a Problem-Solving Goal

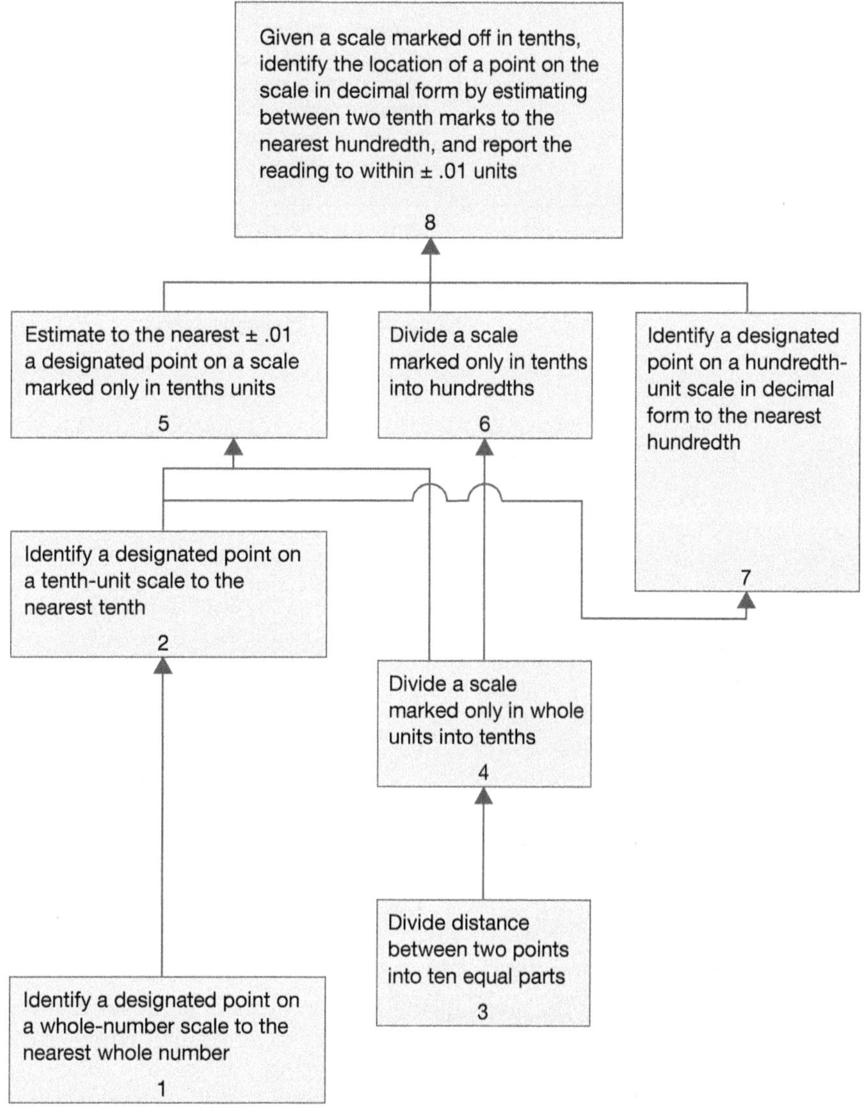

Figure 4.3 Subordinate Skills Analysis for Scale-Reading Example

After you are satisfied that you have identified all the subskills required for students to master your instructional goal, it is time to diagram your analysis using the following conventions:

1. The instructional goal is stated at the top. All the steps in the goal appear in numbered boxes below the instructional goal.
2. All subordinate intellectual skills appear in boxes that are attached via lines coming from the tops and bottoms of boxes.
3. Verbal information and attitudinal skills are attached to intellectual and motor skills via horizontal lines (shown in subsequent sections).
4. Arrows indicate that the flow of skills is upward toward the goal.
5. If two lines should not intersect, then use an arch, as shown for the line between boxes 2 and 7 in Figure 4.3. The interpretation is that the skill in step 2 is required for steps 5 and 7 but not step 6.
6. Statements of all subordinate skills, including decisions, should include verbs that indicate what the student must be able to do. Avoid boxes that include only nouns.
7. In actual applications, hierarchies are not necessarily symmetrical, and they can take on all kinds of shapes. There is no one correct appearance for a hierarchy.

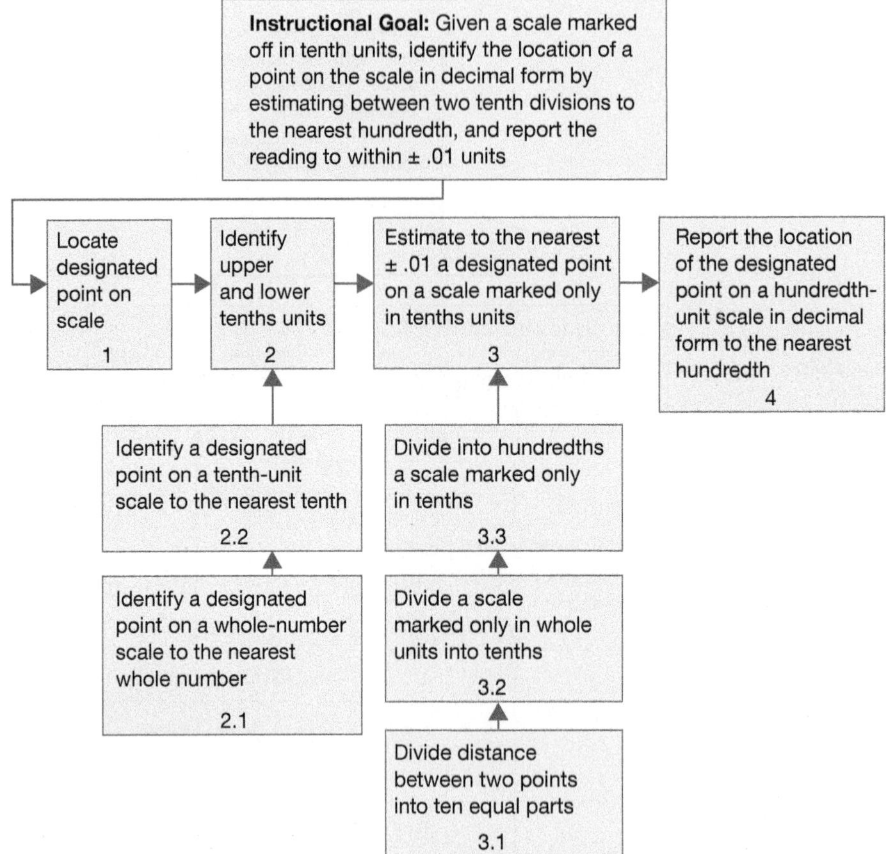

Figure 4.4 Hierarchical Analysis of Steps in a Goal Analysis

8. If one of the steps in the goal analysis is a question and is represented by a decision diamond, it is necessary to determine whether there are subordinate skills required to make that decision.

Doing a hierarchical analysis for each step is not easy because we are not accustomed to thinking about the content of instruction from this point of view. One way to proceed is to ask, "What mistake might students make if they were learning this particular skill?" Often, the answer to this question is the key to identifying the appropriate subordinate skills for the skill in question. The kinds of misunderstandings that students might have indicate the understandings, also known as *skills*, that they must have. For example, if students might err because they become confused between stalactites and stalagmites, then an important subordinate skill is the ability to classify examples of these two entities.

It is important to review your analysis several times, making sure that you have identified all the subskills required for learners to master the instructional goal. At this point, you should again use the backward-stepping procedure, from the highest and most complex skill in your hierarchy to the lowest and simplest skills required by your learners. This allows you to determine whether you have included all the necessary subskills. It may be possible to check the adequacy of your back-stepping analysis by starting with the simplest skills in your hierarchy and working upward through the subskills to the most complex skills. You should also ask the following questions: Have I included subskills in the analysis that:

1. Relate to the identification of basic concepts, such as objects or object qualities? (Example: Can a tetrahedron be identified?)

2. Enable learners to identify abstractions by means of a definition? (Example: Can the student explain what a city is or show what an emulsion is?)
3. Enable learners to apply rules? (Example: Can the student make verbs in a sentence agree with subjects or simplify mixed fractions?)
4. Enable learners to learn how to solve problems demonstrating mastery of the instructional goal?

You may be able to identify subskills you have omitted by using these questions to evaluate your instructional analysis.

As you proceed with the instructional analysis, it is important to have a clear idea of the distinction between the steps and substeps of performing a goal and subordinate skills. The steps and substeps are the activities that an expert or a competent person would describe as the steps in the performance. The subordinate skills are not necessarily identified by a competent person when describing the process. These are the skills and knowledge that learners must learn before they can perform the steps in the goal.

Procedural Analysis

Sometimes when looking at the steps in a goal analysis for intellectual or psychomotor skills, one or more of the steps in the goal analysis is found to contain an additional set of mental or physical steps. When this is the case, simply list the skills from left to right in the same step-by-step manner as was done for the original goal analysis, as shown in the following diagram.

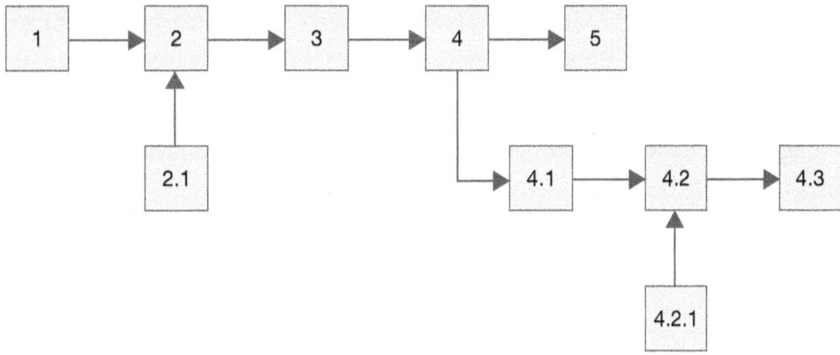

Steps 1 through 5 are the original steps in the goal analysis. Step 2.1 is subordinate to step 2, as in any typical hierarchical relationship. Steps 4.1, 4.2, and 4.3 are subskills of step 4 in that they detail the three additional procedural steps of which step 4 is composed. Step 4.2.1 is subordinate to step 4.2 in a normal hierarchical relationship.

Consider the following examples of steps in an instructional goal. The first is "Place jack under bumper of car." Although this could be described as a series of steps for an adult population, it is probably best represented as one step in the process of changing a tire on a car. But what about a problem-solving step, like "Conduct needs assessment"? This is a step in a goal of designing instruction that surely is too large to be a single step for any audience. It should be broken down into steps such as "Describe ideal status," "Design instruments for data collection," "Collect data to document current status," and "Determine gap between ideal status and current status." Now consider this final example: Suppose one of the steps in a goal analysis is "Boil water." Most adults should know what to do, or they could be taught quickly. For learners who are young children, it may be necessary to list the substeps as "Get pan from cupboard," "Fill with water," "Place pan on burner," "Turn on burner," "Is water bubbling?" and "Remove pan." This is an extremely simple example, but it illustrates how substeps are identified.

Cluster Analysis for Verbal Information

Cluster analysis is used when the instructional goal or a main subskill in the goal requires learning verbal information. We demonstrated previously that it makes little sense to try to do a goal analysis of a verbal information goal because no logical procedure is inherent in the goal. Instead, you move directly to the identification of information needed to achieve the goal.

How do you identify the subordinate skills that should be taught? The answer is almost always apparent from the statement of the goal itself. If the student must be able to identify the states associated with each capital city, then there are fifty subskills, one associated with each state and its capital. It would be useless to write those out as part of the analysis because they could be reproduced easily from a text. In contrast, the subskills are sometimes not as apparent, as in the goal "List five major causes of inflation." The answer may depend on a particular economic theory. In this case, it might be worth listing the five major reasons as part of what we refer to as a *cluster analysis*.

The most meaningful analysis of a verbal information goal is to identify the major categories of information that are implied by the goal. Are there ways that the information can be clustered best? The state capitals might be clustered according to geographic regions; the bones of the body might be clustered by major parts of the body, such as head, arms, legs, and trunk. If the goal were to be able to list all the Major League Baseball cities, they might be clustered by American and National leagues and then by divisions.

How do you diagram a cluster analysis? One way is to use the hierarchical technique with the goal at the top and each major cluster as a subskill, clearly labeled as a verbal information cluster analysis and not a hierarchy. It is just as easy to use an outline format and simply list each of the clusters.

It is sometimes embarrassing for teacher–designers to find that when instructional analysis techniques are used, an instructional goal that they have often taught and for which they would like to develop systematically designed instruction is, in fact, simply verbal information. They can feel guilty that they are not teaching rules and problem solving, but this guilt is sometimes misplaced. There are times when the acquisition of verbal information is critically important. For example, learning vocabulary in a foreign language is verbal information that is the foundation of learning a very complex set of communication skills. The verbal information we must learn as children or as adults is the vehicle we use to develop much more complex concepts and rules. Verbal information goals should not be automatically discarded on discovery but considered for their relevance to other important educational goals. Verbal information is the knowledge base called on when we execute our how-to intellectual skills.

Analysis Techniques for Attitude Goals

In order to determine the subordinate skills for an attitudinal goal, the designer should ask, "What must learners do when exhibiting this attitude?" and "Why should they exhibit this attitude?" The answer to the first question is almost always a psychomotor or an intellectual skill. The purpose of the goal is to get the learner to choose to do either a psychomotor or an intellectual skill; therefore, the first half of the analysis for an attitudinal goal requires hierarchical analysis techniques, which aids in identifying the subskills required if the learner chooses to do them. If the learner is to choose to train for an Ironman competition, then it is necessary to teach the learner effective training routines. If the learner is to choose to critique a certain body of literature, then the student must learn to comprehend and analyze it.

The second part of the analysis is "Why should the learner make a particular choice?" The answer is usually verbal information that may be either analyzed using a separate cluster analysis or integrated into the basic hierarchical analysis that was done for the first half of the analysis. The verbal information constitutes the persuasive part of attitude shaping, along with modeling and reinforcement, and it should be included as an integral part of the instructional analysis.

To represent an attitude on an instructional analysis chart, simply write the attitude goal in a box beside the psychomotor or intellectual skill goal to be analyzed. Connect the two main boxes with a line like this:

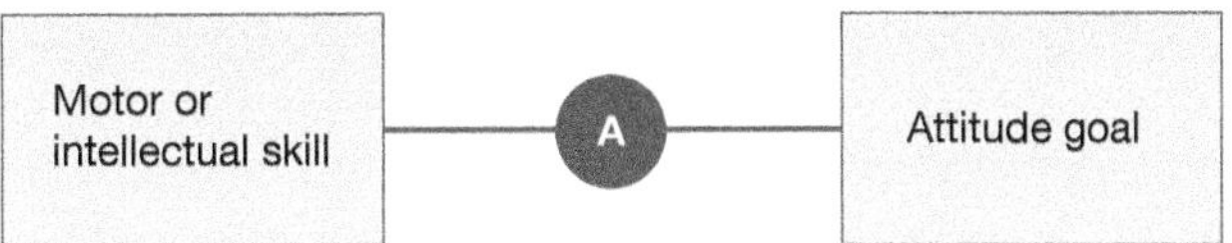

This connecting line shows that the motor or intellectual skill is supporting the attitudinal goal. At this point, it is obvious that we are beginning to combine the various analysis techniques. These combinations, sometimes called *information maps*, are described next.

Analysis Techniques for Combination Domains

We have already described how an attitudinal goal can be analyzed using a hierarchical analysis. It is quite common to find that the instructional analysis process results in identifying a combination of subordinate skills from several domains for a goal that was classified as belonging to only one domain.

Consider, for example, the combination of intellectual skills and verbal information. It is not unusual when doing a hierarchical analysis to identify knowledge that the learner should know. Just knowing something is not an intellectual skill as we have defined it here and therefore would not, by the rules, appear on an intellectual skills hierarchy. However, it is often important that this knowledge, which is verbal information, appear as a part of the analysis of what must be learned to achieve the instructional goal. Standard practice is that the verbal information be shown in the diagram with a connecting line, like this:

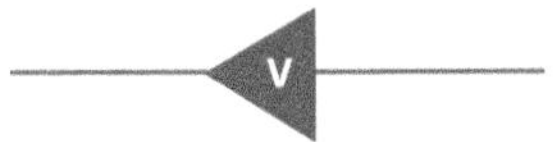

This indicates that the verbal information in the right-hand box is used in support of the intellectual skill in the left-hand box. In a hierarchy, it might look like this:

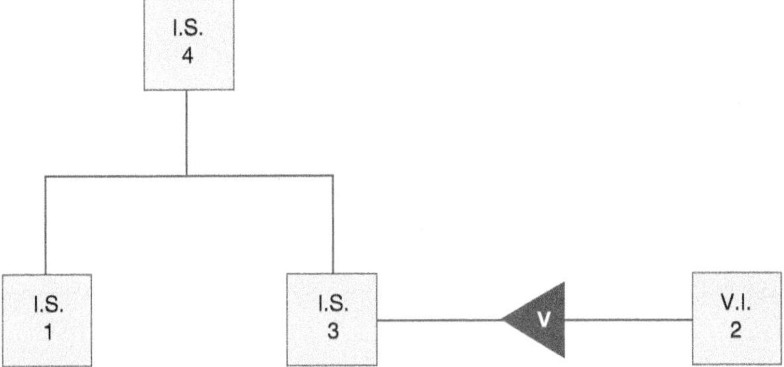

Boxes 1, 3, and 4 represent intellectual skills, whereas box 2 is verbal information.

What happens if you put all the diagramming techniques together? It is conceivable that an attitude goal with a psychomotor component might require subordinate intellectual skills and verbal information and look something like this:

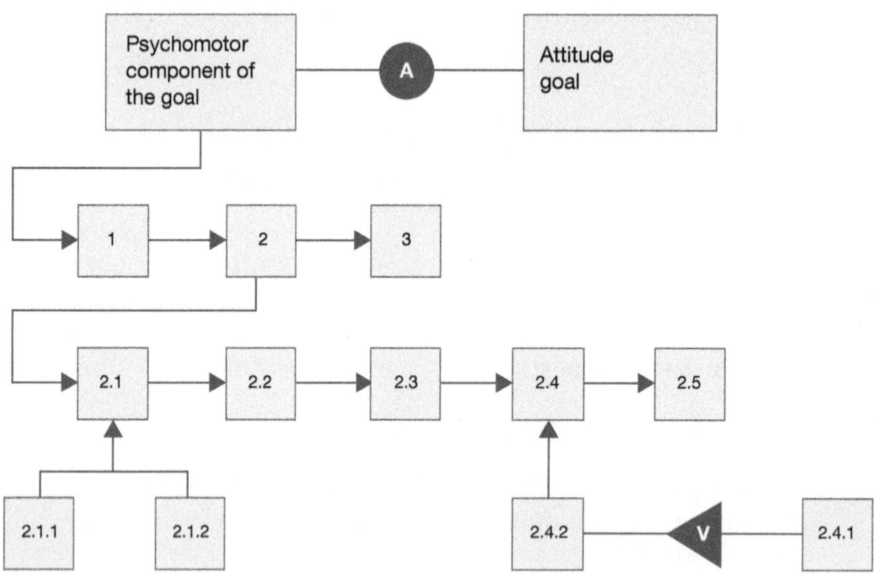

The diagram indicates that the primary goal is for learners to develop an attitude that will be demonstrated by the execution of some psychomotor skill. The psychomotor skill is composed of three steps—1, 2, and 3. A subskill analysis of skill 2 indicates that it includes five steps, 2.1 through 2.5. Two intellectual skills, 2.1.1 and 2.1.2, are subordinate to step 2.1. The intellectual skill 2.4.2 requires verbal information, 2.4.1, to support step 2.4.

Instructional Analysis Diagrams

At this point, let's review the diagramming procedures for doing an instructional analysis. The first step, of course, is to classify your instructional goal and perform a goal analysis as described in Chapter 3. Then select the appropriate technique(s) for identifying the subordinate skills.

Type of Goal or Step	Type of Subordinate Skills Analysis
Intellectual skill	Hierarchical*
Psychomotor skill	Hierarchical*
Verbal information	Cluster
Attitude	Hierarchical* and/or cluster

*Note that hierarchical analyses can contain sequences of procedural steps.

As the designer proceeds with the analysis, the subordinate skills are displayed visually in diagrams. When diagrammed, any particular set of subskills required to reach an instructional goal can have a variety of structural appearances. The following diagram is generally used to represent a goal analysis. There are no subordinate skills, so all the skills are diagrammed in one continuous line.

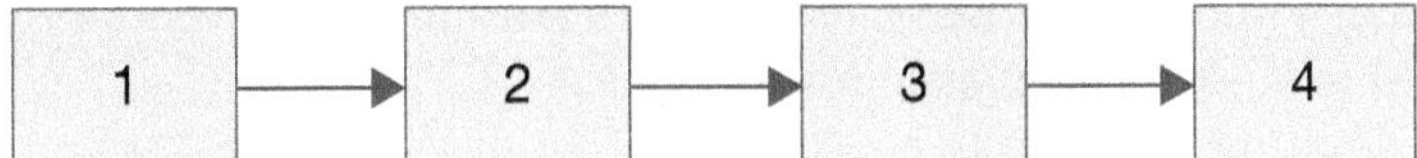

It is also traditional to place superordinate skills above the skills on which they are dependent so the reader automatically recognizes the implied learning relationship of the subskills. This is illustrated in the following diagram. Notice that subskills 1.1, 1.2, and 1.3 do not depend on each other but that learning skill 1 requires the previous learning of 1.1, 1.2, and 1.3. Objectives 2, 3, and 4 are not interdependent, but 4.1 and 4.2 must be learned prior to 4.

Instructional goal

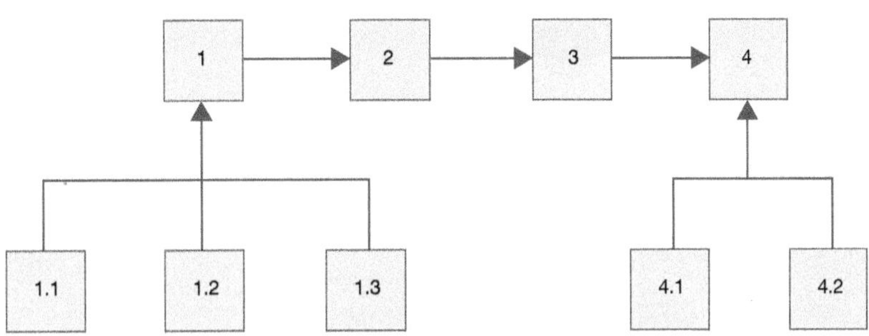

The following diagram illustrates the dependence of subsequent skills on those preceding them.

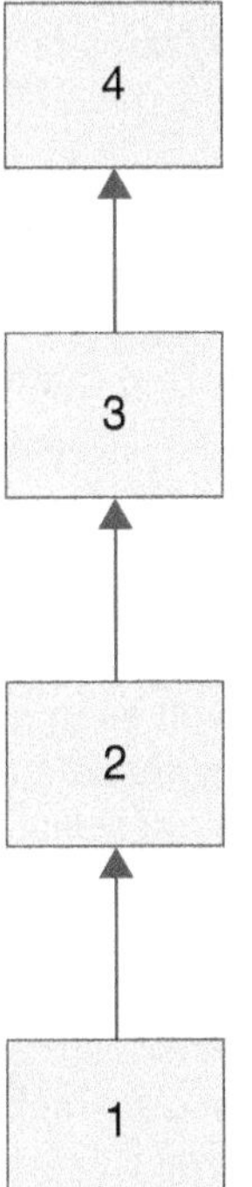

The student must learn subskill 1 in order to learn to perform subskill 2. Likewise, before subskill 4 can be learned, subskills 1, 2, and 3 must be mastered; thus, these skills form a hierarchy. Note, this does not mean that 1, 2, 3, and 4 are performed in sequence. If they were, then they would be the substeps of a superordinate skill and would be diagrammed as follows:

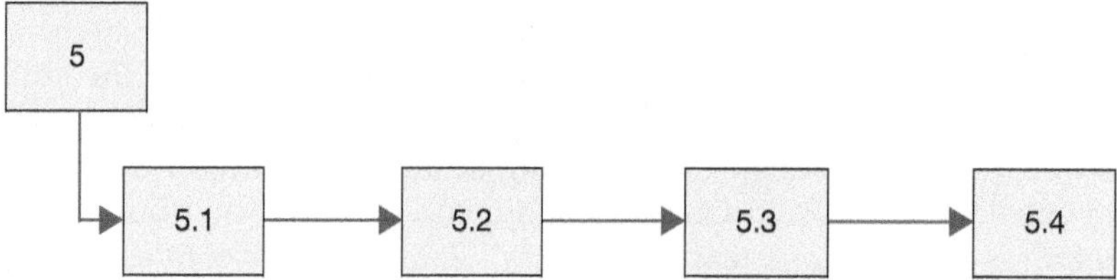

In addition, we noted that attitudinal goals can be indicated by the following:

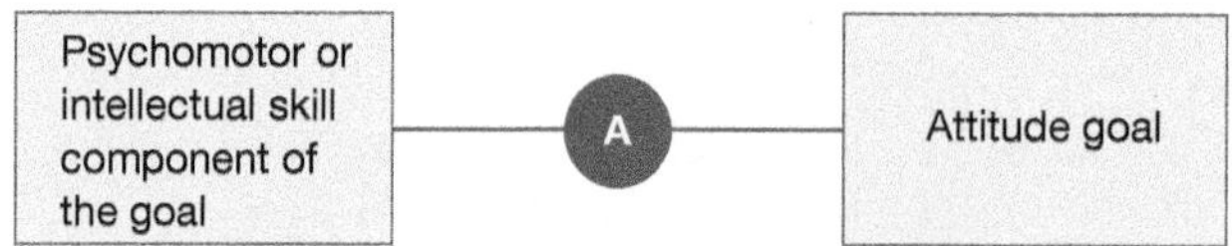

Verbal information is indicated by connecting it to an intellectual skill via a line and a triangle containing the letter V.

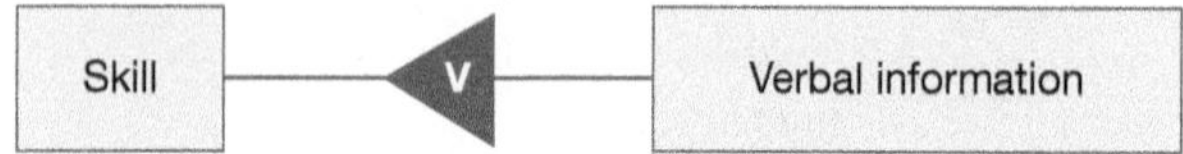

Skill in using these diagramming conventions should help you grasp the implied relationship of subskills in an instructional analysis diagram. The order for learning each skill is also implied through the sequencing of skills.

Take note of the numbers that appear in the various diagrams of subordinate skills. Do not interpret them to mean more than they do. At this point in the instructional design process, the numbers in the boxes are used simply as a shorthand method for referring to the box; they do not necessarily represent the sequence in which the skills are taught. Using these numbers, we can discuss the relationship between box 7 and box 5 without describing the skills involved. We should not be thinking about how we will teach these skills but rather ensuring that we have the correct skills included in our analysis. At a later point in the design process, it will be necessary to decide on the instructional sequence for the skills, and you may wish to renumber the skills at that time.

Why is the instructional analysis process so critical to the design of instruction? It is a process the instructional designer can use to identify those skills really needed by the learner to achieve the instructional goal as well as to help exclude unnecessary skills. This may not appear to be a terribly strong argument when considered in light of a particular instructional goal that you might select. You might believe that you are so thoroughly familiar with the content and skills required of the learner that this type of analysis is superfluous. Remember, however, that as experts we often go through many steps and subskills automatically without thinking of them as we perform the skill. These are steps and subskills that can easily be overlooked when designing instruction for naïve learners. Consider also that as you become involved in a variety of instructional design projects, you cannot be a subject-matter expert in all areas. It is necessary to engage in analytic processes of this type with a variety of subject-matter specialists to identify the critical skills that result in efficient and effective instruction.

Cognitive Task Analysis

Recall that we introduced the topics of job analysis and job task analysis in Chapter 2. There is a methodology called **cognitive task analysis (CTA)** that belongs with the concepts of job analysis and job task analysis, and it fits into our discussion in this chapter on identifying subordinate skills. Practitioners developed CTA methods because they understood that there are many mental processes going on inside an employee's head when performing a complex job and that much of this processing could not be detected by simple observation of the employee performing the tasks. Some mentally challenging tasks may even be performed totally in the mind of the employee and could result in nothing more than a single new line of computer code or a verbal statement such as "Insert that needle right here!"

Early practitioners of CTA were in the field of human factors analysis and ergonomics, but the practice is now also used in front-end analysis in instructional design. It is particularly used in training and performance technology as well as other design settings. The process of CTA includes observation and interview: observation to capture and record job procedures and interviews to capture and record the conceptual knowledge necessary to perform the job. Observations and interviews are with known expert performers of the job, and the observations and interviews are structured and rigorous.

One reason for this discussion of CTA is the similarities between it and the instructional design process you are studying in this text. The observational and analytical techniques used in CTA are often found in front-end analysis, goal analysis, and subordinate skills analysis in instructional design (ID). The product of CTA is an array of goals, subgoals, and tasks that characterize the skills required to perform a job, and the array is most often hierarchical or a combination of procedural and hierarchical, just as described in this chapter. Clark et al. (2013) suggest that other products of CTA should include (1) a description of the context in which the skill will be performed, along with notation of tools needed for performing the skill; (2) precise statements of the performance; and (3) a description of the criteria to be used to assess the performance. (You will note when reading Chapter 6 that these are the same three components in a three-part objective: conditions, behavior, and criteria.) Because the aims of CTA are the same as those in the first few steps of ID—that is, job analysis, goals, goal analysis, subordinate skills, and performance objectives—it is easy to understand why the processes and products of CTA and ID are so similar.

CTA has been used most frequently for analyzing complex tasks in which precision performance is required. The results of CTA are used to begin development of many different types of training solutions, from simple job aids and text-based materials to instructor-mediated learning and e-learning. Because CTA can be expensive and time consuming, it is often applied in the development of more complex types of training and human factors solutions, such as electronic performance support systems, training simulators, human–machine and human–computer interface designs, and computer-based simulations and expert systems. Readers interested in more details about CTA may want to start with the chapter in the *Handbook of Research on Educational Communications and Technology* by Clark et al. (2013). For more depth, Crandall et al. (2006) is a good resource on the topic.

Concept Mapping

Another analytical procedure associated with learning task analysis is *concept mapping*, which is the graphical representation of how conceptual knowledge is structured. It can take the form of flowcharts, hierarchies, circles, or spider webs, with lines connecting the concepts to show their relationships to each other. We mention concept mapping here because of its association with instructional analysis but view it as more appropriate for use as an instructional method for teaching intellectual skills than as an analytical method in instructional design. The popular WebQuest hyperlinking model is a good example of using concept mapping, or *webbing*, in a teaching and learning application. Novak (2009), however, gave structure to concept mapping in the 1960s and describes applications in human performance technology in recent writings.

Entry Skills

The instructional analysis process serves another important function not yet discussed: It helps the designer identify exactly what learners must already know or be able to do before they begin the instruction, called *entry skills* because learners must already have mastered them in order to learn the new skills included in the instruction.

The procedure used to identify entry skills is directly related to the subordinate skills analysis process. You know that with the hierarchical analysis you ask, "What must the learner know or be able to do to learn this skill?" The answer to this question is one or more subordinate skills. With each successive set of subordinate skills, the skills will become more basic, and the bottom of the hierarchy will contain very basic skills.

Assume you have a highly developed hierarchy representing the array of skills required to take a learner from the most basic level of understanding up to your instructional goal. It is likely, however, that your learners already have some of these skills, making it unnecessary to teach all the skills in the extended hierarchy. To identify the entry skills for your instruction, examine the hierarchy or cluster analysis and identify those skills that a majority of the learners have already mastered before beginning your instruction. Draw a dotted line above these skills in the analysis chart. The skills that appear above the dotted line are those you must teach in your instruction, whereas those below the line are entry skills.

Why are entry skills so important? They are the initial building blocks for your instruction, the basis from which learners can begin to acquire the skills presented in your instruction. Without these skills, a learner will have a very difficult time trying to learn from your instruction. Entry skills are a key component in the design process. An example of how entry skills can be identified through the use of a hierarchy appears in Figure 4.5. This is basically the same hierarchy that appeared in Figure 4.3; however, three more skills have been added to the analysis chart. A dotted line has been drawn across the page indicating that all skills above the line will be taught in the instructional materials. All the skills listed below the line are assumed to be skills already attained by students before beginning the instruction.

Each skill below the line was derived directly from a superordinate skill that already appeared on the instructional analysis chart, derived by asking the question "What must the learner be able to do to learn this skill?" Note that even the entry skills identified in Figure 4.5 have a hierarchical relationship to each other. The *derived skills* (skills that must be mastered in order to learn skills 1 and 7 but are not taught in this instruction) include the ability to interpret whole and decimal numbers. Students must have mastered these skills before they begin the instruction on reading a scale.

The description thus far relates entry skills to a hierarchical instructional analysis. Similarly, if a cluster or combination approach is used in which subordinate skills and knowledge are identified, then the identification process can be continued until basic skills are identified and so indicated by the dotted line.

How you identify the specific entry skills for your materials depends on where you stopped when you conducted your instructional analysis. If you identified only those tasks and skills that you plan to include in the instructional materials, then you must take each of the lowest skills in the hierarchy and determine

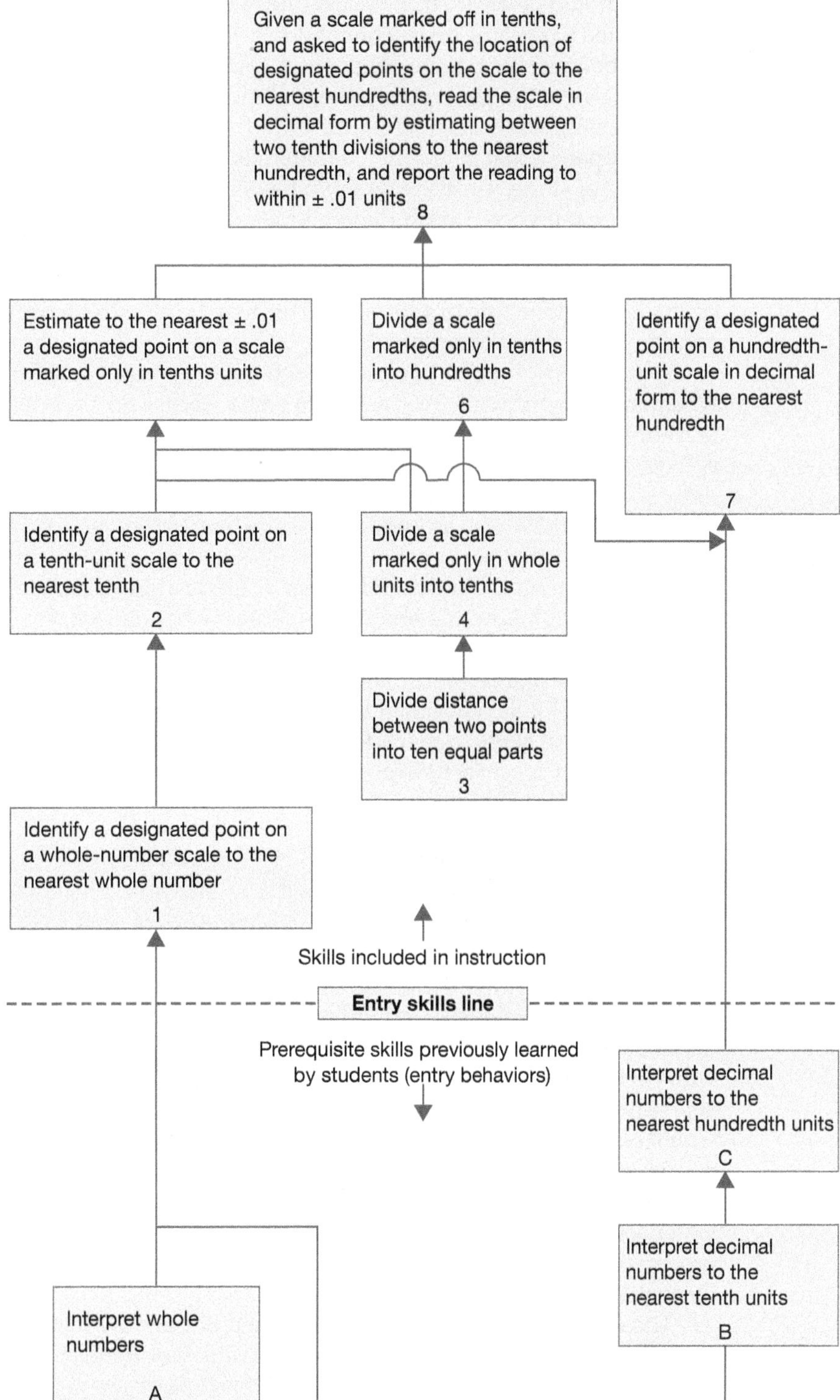

Figure 4.5 Instructional Analysis for Scale Reading Example

the subordinate skills associated with them. These are listed on your instructional analysis chart beneath a line that clearly differentiates them from subordinate skills to be included in the instructional materials. If your subordinate skills analysis were already carried out to the point of identifying basic low-level skills, then it should be possible for you simply to draw a dotted line through the chart above those skills that you assume most learners have already acquired.

You should be aware that the examples we use rather clearly describe specific skills related to specific instructional goals. There are some descriptors of learners that may be considered to be either entry skills for a particular instructional unit or as descriptive of the general target population. Consider the question of students' reading levels.

It is apparent that instructional materials typically depend heavily on the reading ability of students; students must have some minimum level of reading ability to become involved with the materials. Is the specification of reading level a description of a general characteristic of the learners, or is it a specific entry skill that students must possess before beginning instruction? Clear arguments could be made on either side of this issue. You may be able to identify other skills that would produce similar problems.

A possible technique to classify such an ability appropriately is to determine whether it is worthwhile or feasible to test a learner for that particular skill prior to permitting the learner to begin the instruction. If the answer to that question is "Yes, it would be worth the time to test the learner," then you have probably defined a specific entry behavior. If, however, it seems inappropriate to test the skill of the learner (such as giving a reading test) before instruction, then the factor you have identified is probably better classified as a general characteristic of the learners for whom the unit is intended. There is more discussion on this point in the chapter that follows on analyzing learners and contexts.

Also note that when developing instructional materials about topics of general interest that emphasize information objectives, there sometimes are apparently no required entry skills other than the ability to read the materials and to use appropriate reasoning skills to reach the instructional goal. If you have identified such an area, then it is perfectly legitimate to indicate that although the materials are intended for a certain group of learners, there are no specific entry skills required to begin the instruction.

The Tentativeness of Entry Skills

The identification of entry skills is one of the real danger spots in the instructional design process because the designer is making assumptions about both what the learners do not currently know and what they should already know. Obviously, the designer can err in one of two directions, and each has consequences. For example, with curriculum materials designed for only gifted students, the subordinate skills analysis dotted line separating skills to be taught from skills assumed to be known would be placed relatively high on the chart, suggesting that learners already have mastered most of the skills described on the chart. When the assumed entry skills are not already mastered by the majority of the target population, the instructional materials lose their effectiveness for a large number of learners. Without adequate preparation in the entry skills, learners' efforts are inefficient and frustrating, and the materials are ineffective.

The second error occurs when the dotted line is drawn too low on the instructional analysis, presuming that learners have few or none of the skills required to achieve the instructional goal. An error of this type seriously depresses motivation and is costly both in terms of developing instructional materials not really needed by learners and in terms of the time required for learners to study skills they have already mastered.

It should be noted that the designer is making a set of assumptions at this early point about the learners who will use the instruction. If time is available, a tryout sample of group members should be tested and interviewed to determine if most of them have the entry skills derived from the subskills analysis. Procedures for doing this are discussed in Chapters 11 and 12. If time does not permit this, then the assumptions must be tested at a later time in the development process.

Delaying this verification of entry skills, however, can lead to a situation in which a lot of development has taken place improperly because of a mismatch between the learner and the instruction.

If the alignment between the entry skills of the learners and the skills planned for inclusion in the instruction is not a good fit, then a fundamental question must be answered: Is specific content being taught, or is the target population being taught? If it is the former, then little or no change is required in entry skills. One simply keeps looking until a group of learners with the right entry skills is found. Your instruction is for them! If your purpose is to teach a specific group of learners, however, then the instruction must be modified by the addition or subtraction of instruction to match the entry skills that do exist within the group. There is no one correct answer to this dilemma. Each situation must be considered in light of the needs assessment that resulted in the creation of the instructional goal.

In the same manner, it is often found that only some of the intended learners have the entry skills. What accommodation can be made for this situation? It may be possible to have several "starting points" within the instruction, and learners' scores on entry skills tests can be used to place them at the appropriate starting point. Or the solution may again be that the instruction was designed for learners with certain entry skills. Those who do not have these skills must master them somewhere else before beginning the instruction. There are usually no easy answers to this all-too-common situation.

Evaluation and Revision

Evaluating and Revising Subordinate and Entry Skills

It is important to evaluate the analysis of learning tasks before proceeding to the next phase of design activities because many hours of work remain to be completed. The quality of the analysis directly affects the ease with which succeeding design activities can be performed and the quality of the eventual instruction. Specific criteria to use in evaluating the analysis include whether:

- all relevant tasks are identified,
- superfluous tasks are eliminated,
- the relationships among the tasks are clearly designated through the configuration of tasks on the chart, and
- the placement of lines is used to connect the tasks.

Producing an accurate and clear analysis of tasks typically requires several iterations and refinements.

In evaluating the tasks identified for an instructional goal, you should question whether they accurately reflect the goal. Are they comprehensive or limited to having students learn how to make discriminations or identify concepts? Although these skills are obviously important, it may be necessary to modify the goal statement by requiring students to use a rule or to solve problems that require the use of the concepts and discriminations that you originally stated in your goal.

You may also find that you have included skills that are nice to know but are not really required in order to achieve your goal. Many designers begin with the attitude that these skills are important and should be included. In the end, superfluous tasks often confuse learners or unnecessarily increase the length of the instruction, which can cause the instruction for more important tasks to be rushed or omitted because of time constraints. It is not necessary to include everything you know about a topic; the whole point of using goal analysis is to identify just what the learner must know to be successful—nothing more and nothing less. Although it is sometimes tempting not to do so, our best advice is to let the analysis identify the skills for you. It is absolutely the best starting point.

Rubric for Evaluating Subordinate and Entry Skills

Following is a rubric for evaluating subordinate and entry skills. The three sections of criteria include skills statements, diagramming, and other criteria you may identify for your goal analysis project.

Designer note: If an element is not relevant for your project, mark NA in the No column.

No	Some	Yes	
			A. Intellectual and Psychomotor Skills Does the analysis:
___	___	___	1. Identify critical rules and concepts for main steps in goal?
___	___	___	2. Illustrate the hierarchical relationship among skills by:
___	___	___	a. Progressing downward from problem solving to rules, to concepts, to discriminations?
___	___	___	b. Using upward pointing arrows to link hierarchical skills?
___	___	___	c. Using codes—e.g., 4.2 (step 4 skill 2)—to link related skills?
___	___	___	3. Have procedural subskills linked to main steps using procedural boxes left to right, arrows, and skills code numbers?
___	___	___	4. Have required verbal information linked to appropriate skill?
			B. Verbal Information Does the analysis:
___	___	___	1. Use main areas of content as headings?
___	___	___	2. Use appropriate size chunks/depth for learners?
___	___	___	3. Present information in logical order (e.g., spatial, chronological, familiar to unfamiliar)?
___	___	___	4. Avoid noncritical information?
___	___	___	5. Use appropriate format for scope (e.g., matrix, cluster, box, outline)?
___	___	___	6. Link information directly to related attitude or skill using "V" triangle?
			C. Attitudes Are attitudes clearly linked to appropriate:
___	___	___	1. Behaviors that reflect the attitude (positive and negative)?
___	___	___	2. Verbal information needed to support the attitude?
___	___	___	3. Psychomotor skills needed to act in certain ways?
___	___	___	4. Intellectual skills needed to reason appropriately (e.g., what to do, rewards, consequences)?
___	___	___	5. Skills and attitudes using "A" circle and horizontal lines?
			D. Other
___	___	___	1.
___	___	___	2.

Examples

In this section, we illustrate combination analysis procedures for a psychomotor skill and an attitude. In the case study that follows, there are two examples of combination analysis procedures for intellectual skills and verbal information.

Subordinate Skills Analysis of a Psychomotor Skill

Instructional Goal Putt a golf ball into the cup.

Psychomotor skills usually require a combination of intellectual and motor skills, and the intellectual skills often require supporting verbal information. The chronological procedure to follow in putting a golf ball is illustrated in Figure 4.6 (continued from Figure 3.2, p. 61). At this point, we must continue the

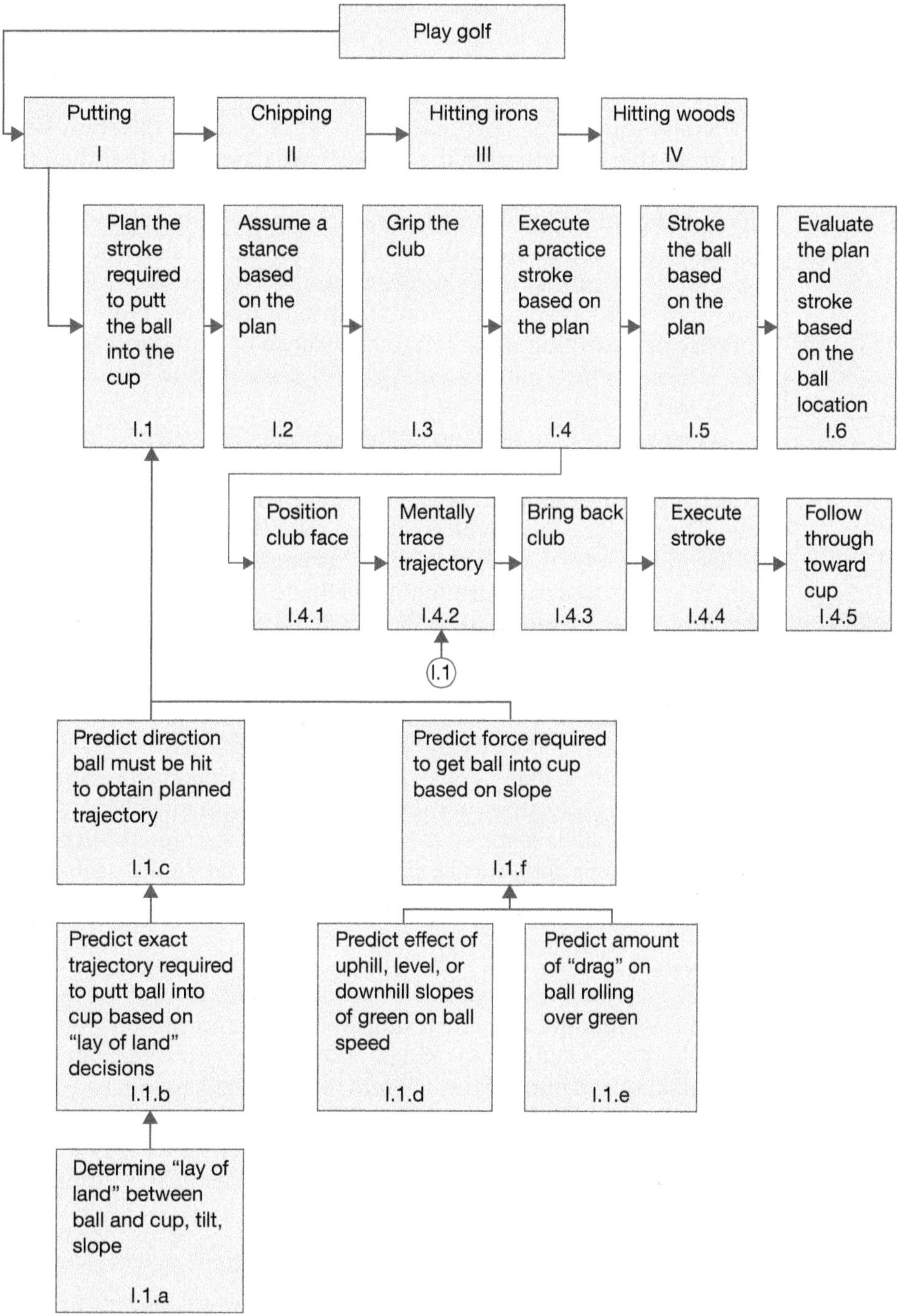

Figure 4.6 Hierarchical Analysis of First Step in Psychomotor Skill of Putting a Golf Ball

Goal: Putt a golf ball.

Type of Learning: Psychomotor

instructional analysis to identify the subordinate skills and information required to perform each step previously identified. As an illustration, we first analyze the subordinate skills required to perform step I.1: Plan the stroke required to putt the ball into the cup.

Note in the diagram that the subordinate skills required to plan the stroke are all intellectual skills—the psychological component of the psychomotor skill. The motor component occurs when the golfer translates the plan into action. Observing someone putting, the designer can readily see the motor part of the skill, whereas the mental part remains hidden. All the mental activity required to plan the stroke should be completed prior to moving to step I.2: Assume a stance based on the plan.

The first step in this psychomotor skill is an intellectual skill, so we apply the hierarchical analysis procedure. In response to the question "What must the learner be able to do to plan the stroke?" we determine that the plan consists of predictions on the direction the ball should be hit and the amount of force with which it should be hit. In turn, direction of the putt depends on knowing the required trajectory of the ball, which in turn depends on knowledge of the "lay of the land." A similar analysis has been used to identify the subordinate skills associated with determining how hard to hit the ball. Note that for simplicity other factors affecting direction and distance of putts on a specific green have been left out of the analysis (e.g., type of grass, "grain," time of day, moisture, and so forth).

Two items are of importance in this example: First, step I.1 in the goal—namely, making a plan about how to hit the ball—is a step that cannot be taught until learners can apply rules about direction and force and their accompanying subordinate skills. These skills can then be combined into the step of making a plan.

Second, examining the five subskills beneath step 1.4, you should again go through the process of determining whether each is an intellectual skill, and, if so, whether further hierarchical analysis is required. Steps I.4.1, I.4.3, I.4.4, and I.4.5 are motor skills that should require no further analysis. Step I.4.2 is an intellectual skill, however, and requires the use of the plan as well as all the accompanying subordinate skills listed for step I.1. It is not necessary to repeat all these skills in the chart. This dependency can be noted by simply putting a I.1 in a circle under step I.4.2 to indicate that all of step I.1 must be learned before this step.

Each of the other steps in the putting procedure must be analyzed to identify the subordinate skills required to perform it. Skill is acquired through both accurate mental predictions and practice at translating the predictions into physical actions. Much practice is required for accurate translations.

Identification of Entry Skills for Putting Identifying appropriate entry skills for the putting instruction depends on the current skill level of the learner. We would probably not identify any entry skills for "weekend duffers" who enjoy playing golf without knowledge and skill beyond how to score the game and successive approximations of putting the ball into the cup. For experienced golfers with skill, however, we could place the entry skills line between the subordinate skills for step I (subskills I.1 through I.6) and main step I. The only way to know for sure is to observe sample learners from the target group actually putting the ball.

Subordinate Skills Analysis of an Attitudinal Goal

The attitudinal goal analysis example that follows illustrates one technique you could use to develop an instructional analysis for such a goal. Starting with the goal statement, the necessary skills and information are identified in a step-by-step sequence.

Instructional Goal The learner will choose to maximize personal safety while staying in a hotel.

The choice to follow safety precautions while registered in a hotel requires that learners know about potential dangers to themselves, know the procedures to follow, and then actually follow the procedures. The attitudinal instructional goal is introduced in Chapter 3, and preliminary analysis and sequence decisions are illustrated in Figure 3.3 (p. 62).

To continue the analysis, we focus only on fire hazards. What procedures should a hotel occupant follow to minimize the risk of being harmed during a hotel fire? We identified a procedure that contains three basic steps, placed in a sequence that fits a natural order of events.

1. Inquire about hotel's fire safety rules, procedures, and precautions when checking into the hotel.
2. Check emergency facilities in assigned room.
3. Check emergency exits closest to room.

The next step is to analyze the information and skills an individual needs to accomplish each step. Remember that one important component of shaping an attitude, and thereby increasing the chances that people will demonstrate the desired behavior, is to provide them with information about why they should act in a certain way. In your analysis of these tasks, be sure to include reasons that each should be accomplished.

Begin with the first task. Why should someone request fire safety information? Reasons include facts about death and injury as a result of fires in hotels. Facts about the frequency of hotel fires, additional hazards in high-rise hotels, or perhaps the number of persons killed or injured annually in hotel fires could be included. The purpose of this information is to get their attention and help them realize that they, too, are at risk while registered in hotels.

Moreover, they must be able to judge whether the hotel's reported safety precautions and procedures are adequate, which means they need information about routine fire safety precautions they can expect to find in hotels. Thus, the first task in our procedure includes supporting information describing why patrons should gather fire safety information about hotels and what they should expect to find. The first subordinate skill and the supporting information could be diagrammed as follows:

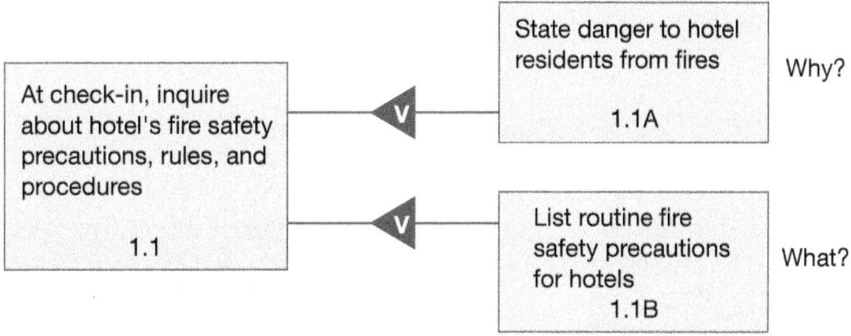

If we observe hotel patrons inquiring about fire safety procedures while checking into the hotel, we could infer correctly that they were choosing to maximize their personal safety while staying in the hotel (our original attitudinal goal).

From here, move to the second subordinate skill: Check emergency facilities in assigned room. Again, they must know why they should do this and what they could expect to find, which could be diagrammed as follows:

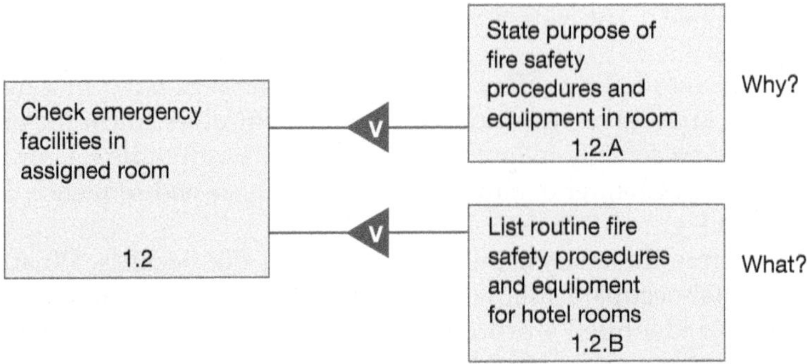

The third subordinate skill is related to why hotel guests should check emergency exits close to their assigned rooms and what they should expect to see, as shown next:

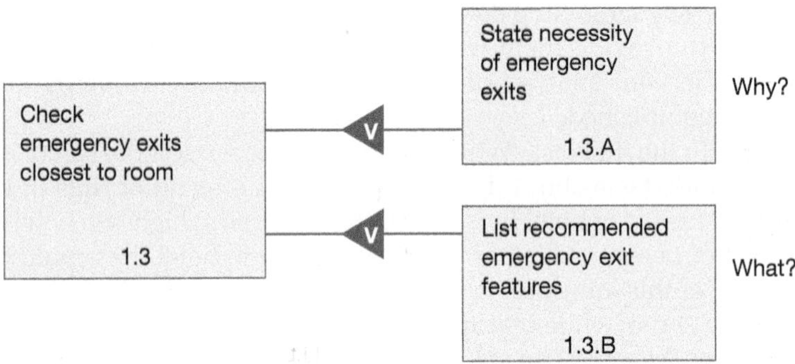

A completed analysis for the fire precaution skill appears in Figure 4.7. Notice in the diagram that the main subordinate skills are placed horizontally. Blocks of information required to perform each step in the procedure are connected to the appropriate box using this symbol:

After completing the analysis of skills 2 and 3, it would be wise to check each set of subordinate skills to determine whether they are related to the original attitudinal goal. If patrons were performing the tasks as specified, could we infer that they were demonstrating an attitude toward maximizing their personal safety while staying in a hotel? If the answer is yes, then we have not strayed from our original goal.

Identification of Entry Skills for Personal Safety Now, review the attitude instructional analysis on personal safety in a hotel included in Figure 4.7. Where would you place the entry skills line? Assume that all steps in the procedures, and the information required for each step, are needed; therefore, it is unnecessary to include an entry skills line in the diagram.

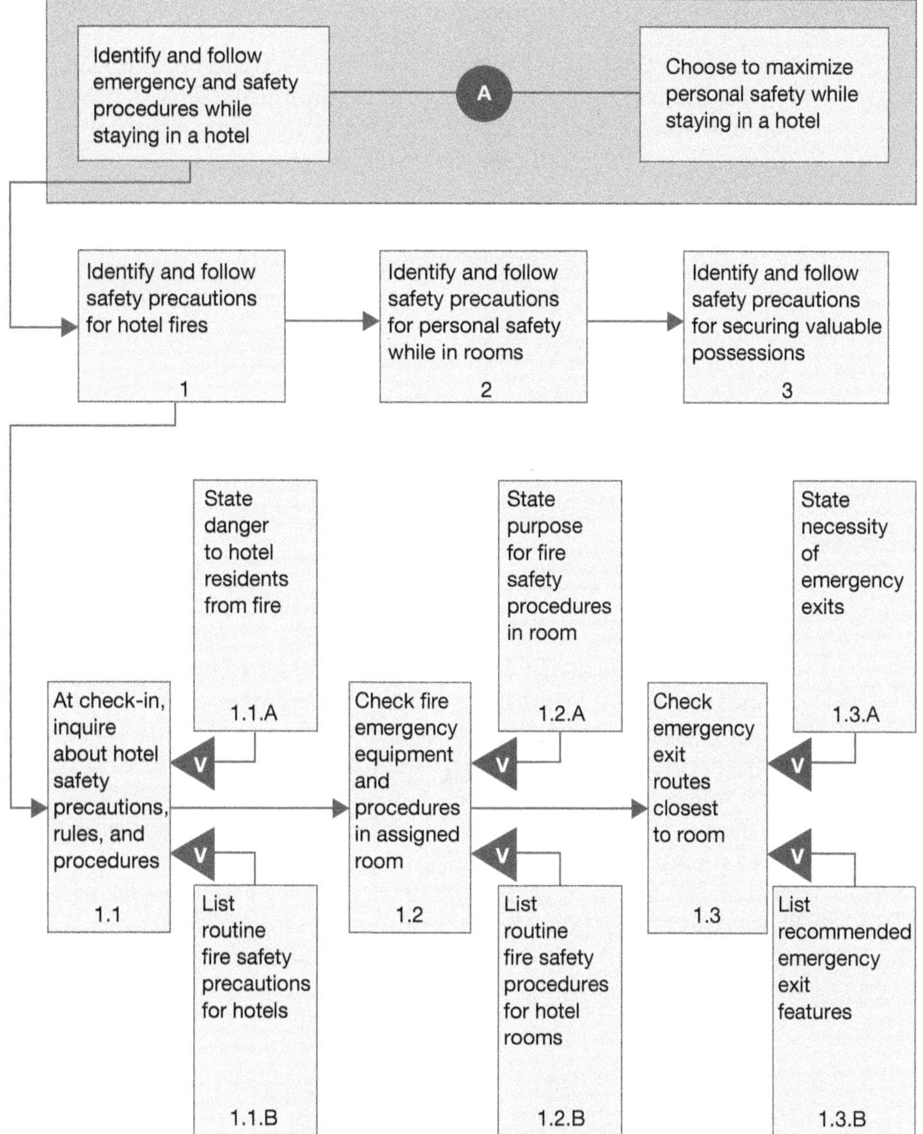

Figure 4.7 Subordinate Skills Analysis of Selected Component of an Attitudinal Instructional Goal

Case Study

Group Leadership Training

We continue now with the case study on group leadership training for group leaders. Only part of the goal analysis work begun in Chapter 3 is selected for more detailed subskills analysis work here because complete analyses of all steps in the goal would become too lengthy and unwieldy for inclusion in this text. We illustrate subskills analysis for both intellectual skills and verbal information.

Hierarchical Analysis of an Intellectual Skill

Instructional Goal Demonstrate effective discussion group leadership skills.

The hierarchical approach is used to continue the instructional analysis of main step 6, manage cooperative group interaction, from the goal analysis shown in Figure 3.7 (p. 64). Recall that the goal analysis had seven main steps.

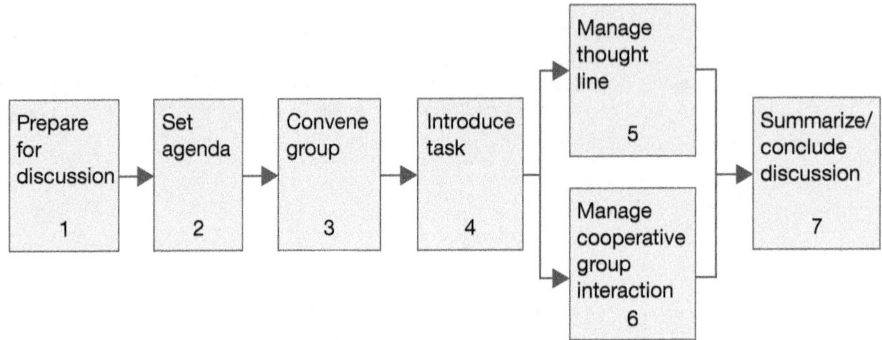

For main skill 6, the instructional designer identified three main discussion leader actions as behaviors that aid in managing cooperative group interaction—*engender cooperative member behaviors, defuse blocking behaviors of members*, and *alleviate group stress during a meeting*. These three actions are illustrated and sequenced in the following diagram.

Because they are not related hierarchically, there is some latitude in how they are sequenced. *Engender cooperative member action* is listed first because it is the most straightforward and positive of the three actions; *defusing blocking behaviors* is listed second because it is a complement to positive actions, and *alleviate group stress* is listed last. In main step 6, the learner integrates the three subordinate skills to manage cooperative group interaction.

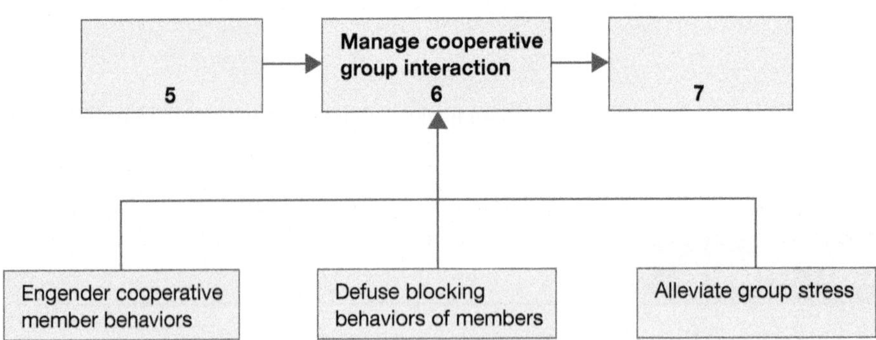

We continue the hierarchical analysis by identifying the skills subordinate to each of the management skills, focusing on one task at a time. Beginning with the first, for leaders to engender cooperative behaviors, they must be able to recognize strategies for engendering cooperative behavior and to recognize group members' cooperative actions. More specifically, they must be able to name strategies for encouraging cooperative interaction and name member actions that facilitate cooperative interaction. Because these latter tasks are verbal information, they are connected to their respective classification tasks using verbal information symbols, diagrammed as follows:

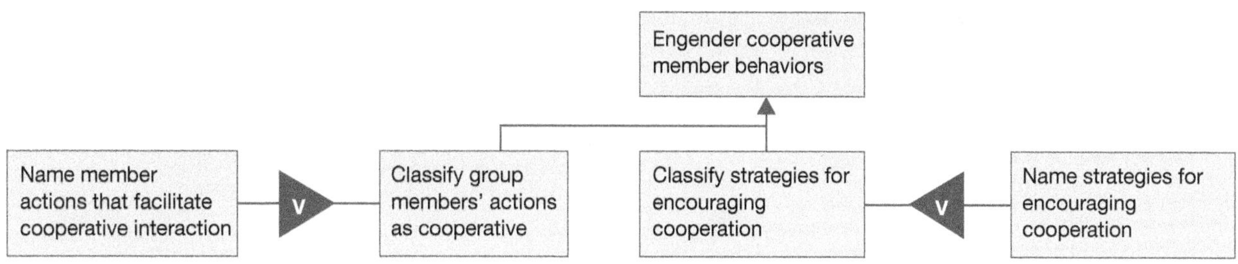

Next, let's turn our attention to the second task in the diagram: Defuse blocking behaviors of group discussion members. To demonstrate this skill, leaders must classify strategies for defusing blocking behaviors as well as group member actions that block cooperative interaction. Each of these behaviors has a verbal information component consisting of naming defusing strategies and naming member actions that block cooperative interaction, as the following diagram illustrates:

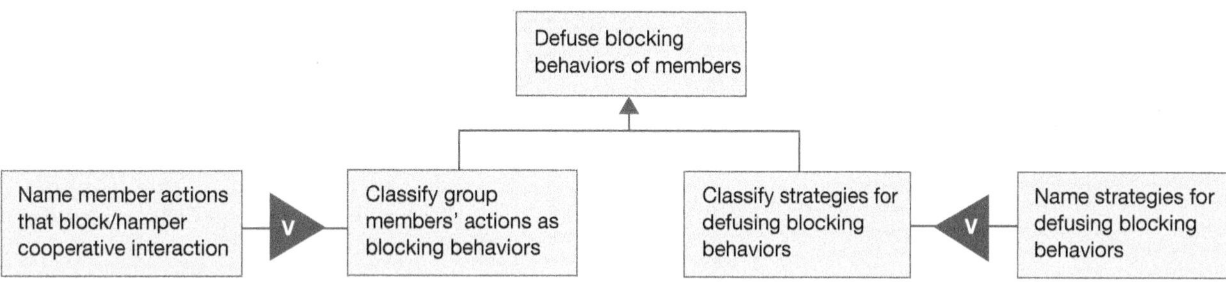

We are now ready for the third skill: Alleviate group stress. Similar to the first two tasks, leaders must classify leader actions for alleviating group stress and symptoms of group stress. These two tasks are supported by verbal information tasks related to naming the strategies and naming the symptoms, which can be diagrammed as follows:

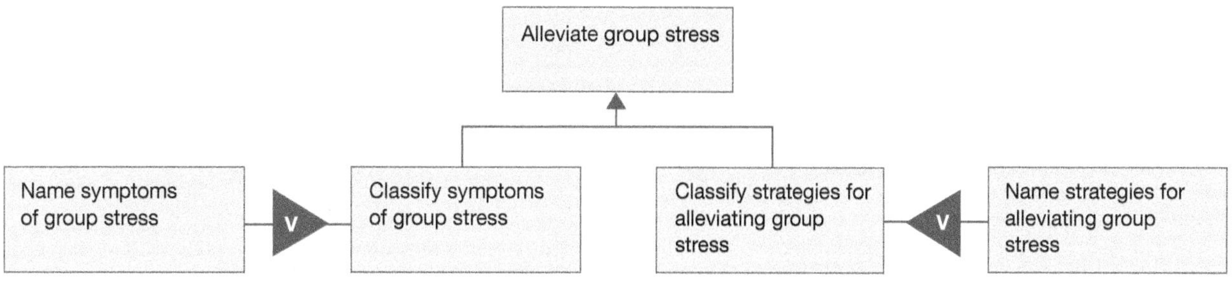

A completed draft of the analysis thus far is included in Figure 4.8 to demonstrate the relationship among subtasks in the hierarchy. First, notice that the original seven steps provide an overview and step-by-step sequence for the instructional goal written at the top of the diagram. Second, notice the hierarchical substructure beneath step 6 that identifies the subordinate skills in the hierarchy for only step 6. Third, notice that the three group management steps have been arranged horizontally (subordinate skills 6.5, 6.10, and 6.15), implying that they are not hierarchically related. To complete the instructional analysis for the instructional goal, identify the information to be included in the remaining verbal information tasks and the subordinate skills for the other major steps identified in the instructional goal. As you can see from this example, a thorough analysis of an intellectual skill can become quite elaborate.

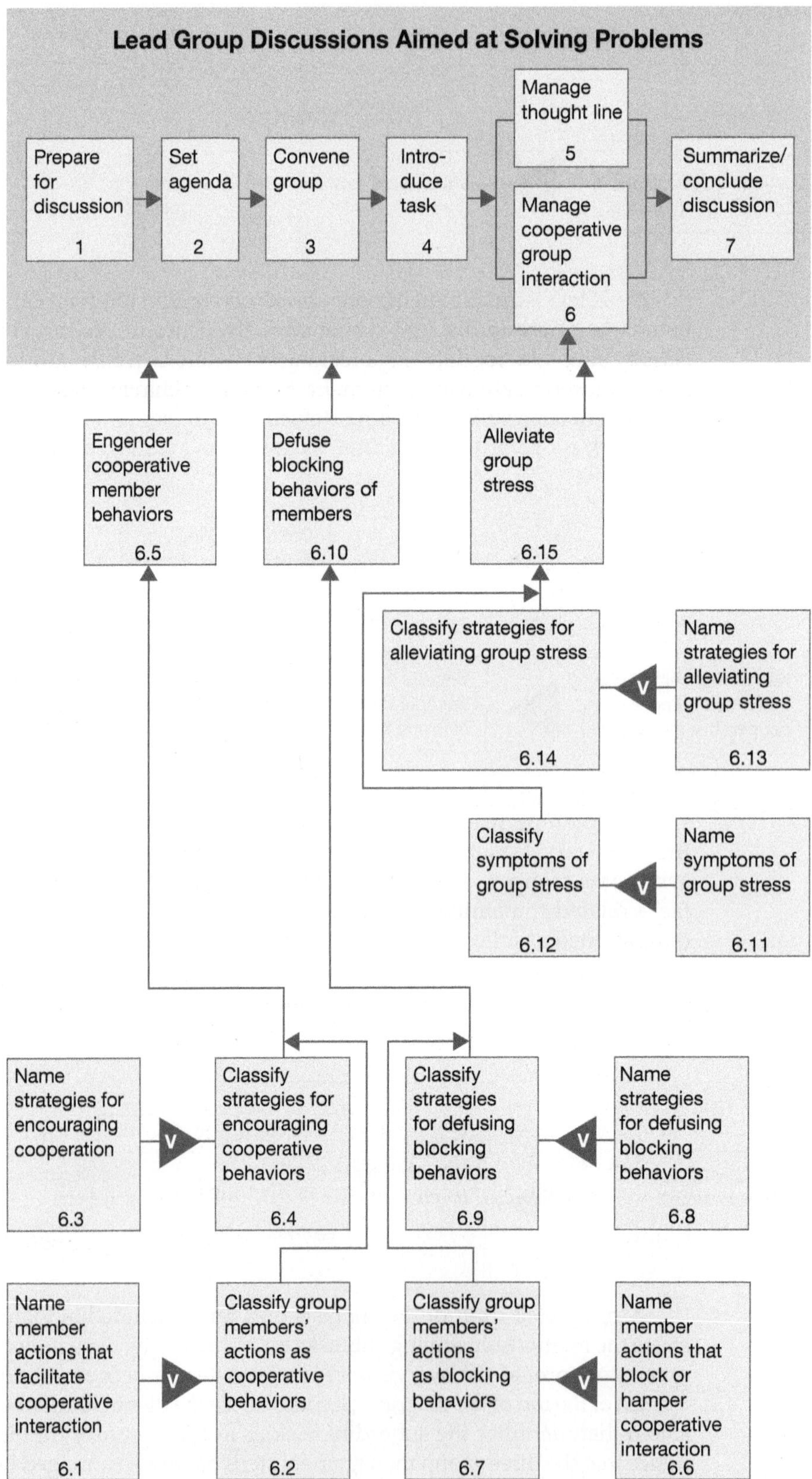

Figure 4.8 Hierarchical Analysis of Cooperative Interaction Portion of Group Discussion Goal

Cluster Analysis for Verbal Information Subordinate Skills

Subordinate Skills Name member actions that facilitate cooperative interaction, and name member actions that block or hamper cooperative interaction.

Although some instructional goals are verbal information tasks, more often we must perform an analysis of verbal information subordinate skills that are embedded within an intellectual skills hierarchy. Table 4.1 contains a cluster analysis for two of the verbal information subordinate skills tasks in the managing cooperative group discussion analysis depicted in Figure 4.8. Verbal information for subskill 6.1, name member actions that facilitate cooperative interaction, and subskill 6.6, name member actions that block or hamper cooperative interaction, are included. Task 6.1 contains one cluster of information: spontaneous actions when introducing and reacting to new ideas. Task 6.6 contains two clusters of information: spontaneous, unplanned actions and planned, purposeful actions. Each of the three clusters has its own column in Table 4.1.

Identification of Entry Skills

Next, consider the hierarchical instructional analysis in leading group discussions in Figure 4.8. Which tasks do you believe should be labeled *entry skills* for the masters' level students? For this heterogeneous group, two skills in Figure 4.9 should be labeled. Recall the target population has various undergraduate majors; most have only cursory training in group discussion skills, and few have experience serving as chairs for various committees at work and in the community. It is possible that all skills beneath 6.5, 6.10, and 6.15 could be classified as entry skills; however, the instructional designer should check this assumption carefully prior to proceeding to these higher-level skills. Should all skills beneath these three skills be classified as entry skills, then the instruction for this group could focus on practicing these leadership skills in interactive groups with detailed feedback on their verbal and nonverbal management actions during the meetings.

In summary, it is important to evaluate the analysis of learning tasks before proceeding to the next phase of design activities, because many hours of work remain to be completed. The quality of the analysis directly affects the ease with which succeeding design activities can be performed and the quality of the eventual instruction. Specific criteria to use in evaluating the analysis include whether:

- all relevant tasks are identified,
- superfluous tasks are eliminated,
- the relationships among the tasks are clearly designated through the configuration of tasks on the chart, and
- the placement of lines used to connect the tasks is appropriate.

Producing an accurate and clear analysis of tasks typically requires several iterations and refinements.

Figure 4.10 summarizes the major concepts from Chapters 3 and 4. The goal is translated into a diagram of steps and substeps via the goal analysis process. Those steps, in turn, are used to derive the subordinate skills and the entry skills for the goal. The overall process is referred to as an *instructional analysis*. Careful instructional analysis can be complex and time consuming. In large ID projects in which there is pressure to complete new curriculum materials or get a product to market, designers sometimes use rapid prototyping techniques to speed up the overall ID process. There is an overview of these techniques in Chapter 9.

Table 4.1 Cluster Analysis of Verbal Information Tasks for Goal on Leading Group Discussion

Name Member Actions That Facilitate Cooperative Interaction 6.1

Spontaneous, Unplanned Actions:

6.1.1 When introducing and reacting to new ideas:

1. Treats all members' ideas fairly (impartiality) and with due consideration
2. Comes with open mind
3. Listens and considers others' comments
4. Volunteers information and ideas
5. Expects others to have sincere motives
6. Invites others to participate
7. Demonstrates goodwill constantly
8. Resists pressures to conform
9. Appreciates loyalties members feel toward others and other groups

6.1.2 When *ideas* are questioned by group members:

1. Admits personal errors in ideas, judgment
2. Resists tendency to abandon ideas too quickly
3. Explains ideas further to enable fair examination
4. Helps modify ideas for group acceptance

Name Member Actions That Block or Hamper Cooperative Interaction 6.6

Spontaneous, Unplanned Actions:

6.6.1 When introducing and reacting to new ideas:

1. Neglects comments made by colleagues who:
   a. Rarely speak
   b. Lack influence
2. Neglects comments because they:
   a. Are poorly phrased
   b. Are unpopular
   c. Lack immediate appeal
3. Accepts ideas too quickly due to:
   a. Desire to make quick progress
   b. Advocacy by popular, articulate, experienced member (favoritism)
   c. Desire to be considered cooperative
   d. Novelty
4. Comes with fully formed conclusions
5. Proposes and exhorts
6. Only remarks when invited
7. Misconstrues others' motives
8. Neglects others' comments, ideas
9. Rewards/punishes others for ideas
10. Pressures others to conform
11. Demeans members' loyalties to others

6.6.2 When *ideas* are questioned by group members:

1. Refuses to admit personal error
2. Shows dogmatic commitment to own ideas
3. Views questions as personal attack (oversensitive)
4. Reacts to questions defensively

Planned, Purposeful Actions:

6.6.3 Attempts to control others by building a personal image through:

1. Adopting a sage role ("I've been here longer, and I know"); remains quiet early and then saves the group with reasonable recommendations
2. Dropping names, places, experiences
3. Collusion (feeding cues to colleagues, opening opportunities for each other)
4. Moving faster than others, suggests solutions before others get started
5. Taking extreme position, then moving to center to appear cooperative
6. Over responding (listening and responding to feign cooperativeness)
7. Showing specious earnestness ("That's such a gooood idea yooou have!")
8. Using trendy language for popular appeal

6.6.4 Attempts to control others by inducing feelings of inadequacy in them through:

1. Using technical language unnecessarily
2. Demanding definitions repetitively
3. Displaying studied disregard of another's comments (going back to previous speaker as though nothing was said)
4. Usurping leader's functions repeatedly

6.6.5 Attempts to control others by delaying work of group through:

1. Summarizing unnecessarily at short intervals
2. Cautioning against moving too fast
3. Deceptively showing deliberation and adjustment (posture/gestures)

6.6.6 Attempts to control others by putting them off balance through:

1. Inappropriately changing pace, tone, volume
2. Distorting another's ideas to make them appear contradictory, extreme, unreasonable
3. Abruptly switching from logic to sentimentality
4. Disparaging important matters with over casual reaction or verbal minimization
5. Studied misrepresentation

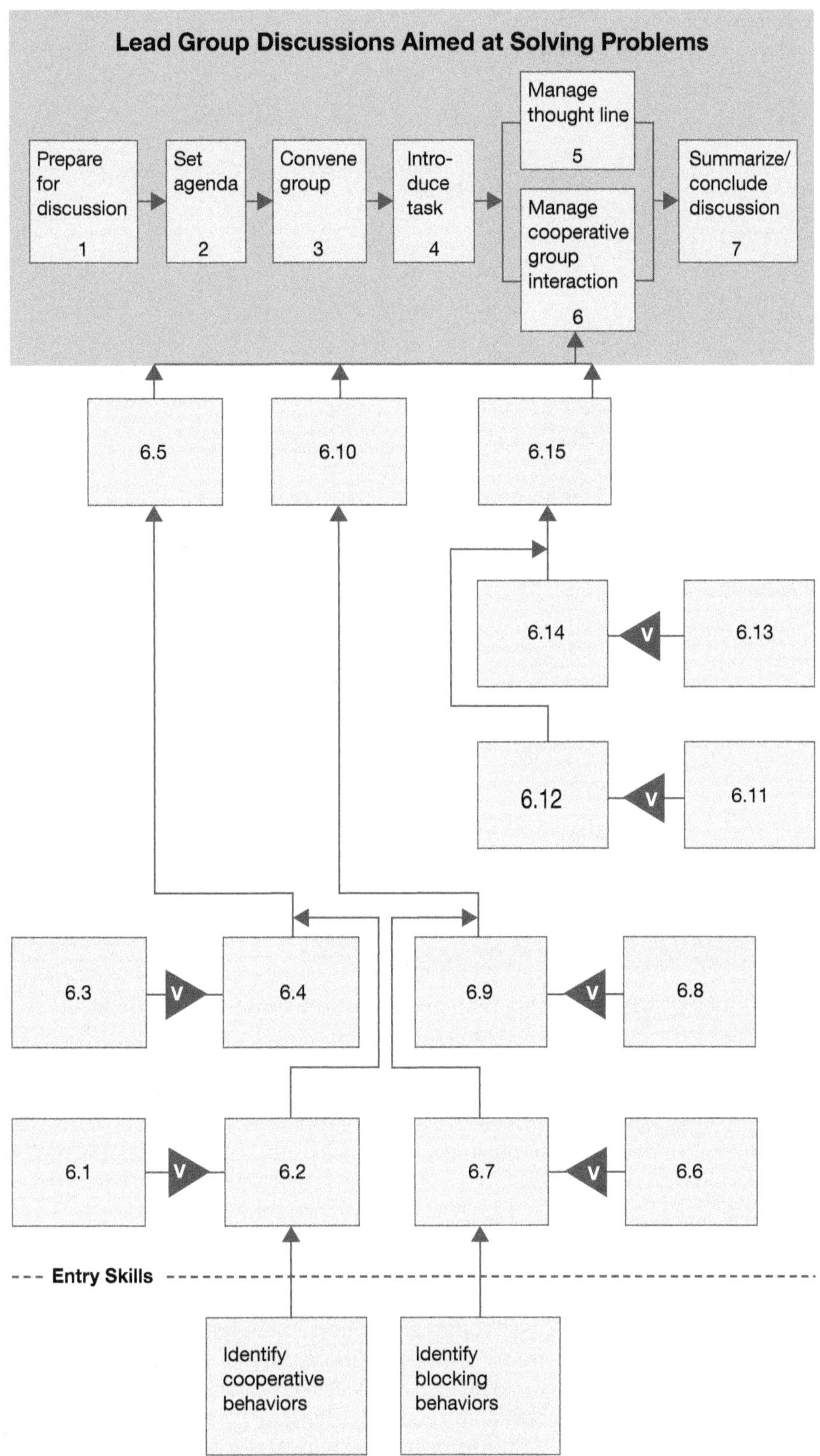

Figure 4.9 Entry Skills Line Added to Instructional Analysis for Group Discussion Goal

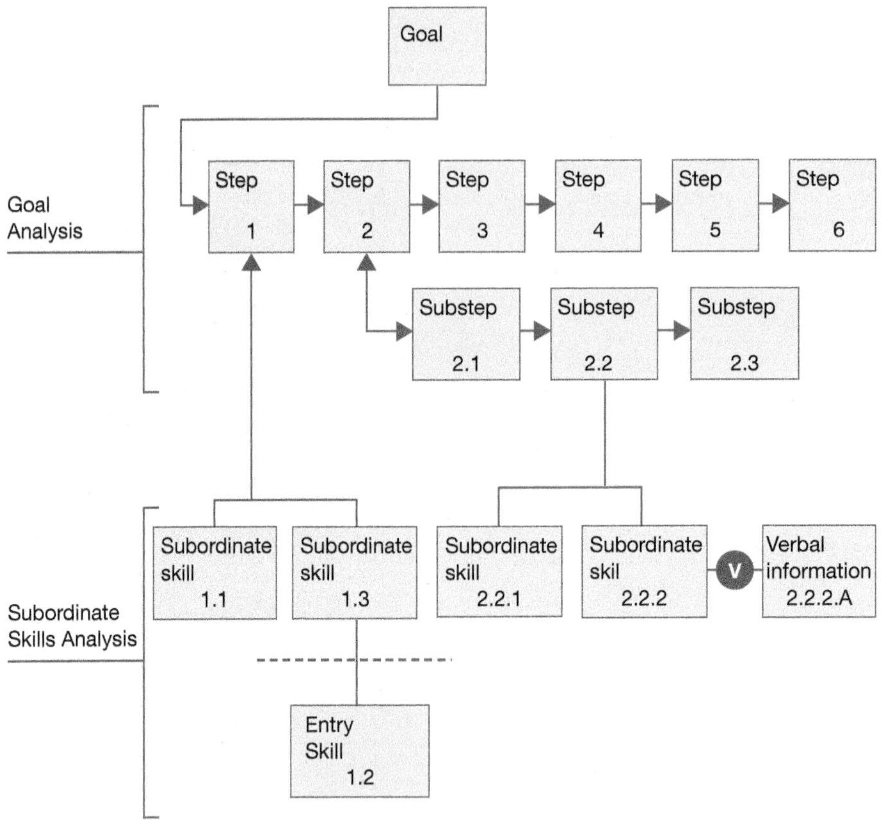

Figure 4.10 Components of the Instructional Analysis Process

Professional and Historical Perspectives

You may recall from Chapter 2 the discussions of job analysis and task analysis; that is, describing the mental and physical actions that a person actually does when performing a job. These terms have specific meaning in human performance technology, where one needs to know what employees do before determining how to make job performance more efficient and effective. As technology changes the workplace, job and task analysis are critical for designing new jobs and redesigning old jobs. We may think of this technological revolution as a 21st-century phenomenon, but technological change is what drove the industrial revolutions of the 18th and 19th centuries when economies moved from their agricultural and handicraft base toward a manufacturing base. The new technologies, instead of being digital, were innovations in power generation and delivery, machinery design, mechanization and mechanical automation, the factory system, the production line, and new ways of organizing production and the work that people did. Time and motion studies and efficiency studies were developed to help managers understand and improve production processes, and "efficiency experts" became the early precursors to today's industrial and organizational psychologists. Task analysis methods were employed effectively by military psychologists and training developers during World War II to prepare soldiers for changing equipment, responsibilities, and tactics; and by industry to manage the changeover from peacetime to wartime production. Task analysis is still a core methodology used today in business management, manufacturing, training and development, and high tech.

The task analysis techniques you have studied in this chapter are *learning task analysis*. After a job or skill has been clearly described using *job task analysis*, then one uses learning task analysis to determine the component skills that one would need to learn in order to perform the job or skill. The results of learning task analysis become the content and process structure for which instruction will be developed. The job task analysis work done during World War II pointed out the critical nature of entry behaviors, subordinate skills, and hierarchical relationships among subskills that are important components of the instructional design process.

Process Flowcharts

Identifying Subordinate and Entry Skills

This section contains three flowcharts, Figures 4.11, 4.12, and 4.13. They will assist you in reviewing the tasks required to identify subordinate and entry skills for your instructional goal. They will also help you summarize the information from the chapter and provide guidance for your design work.

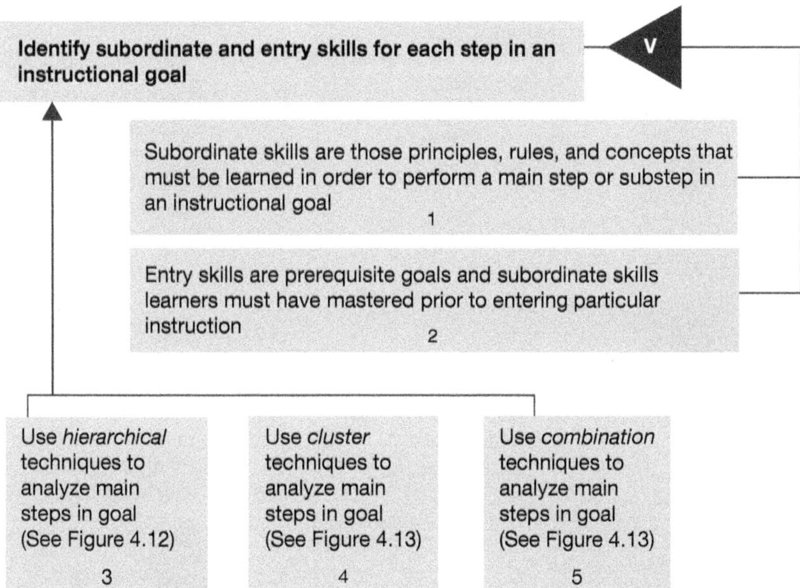

Figure 4.11 Identify Subordinate and Entry Skills for Each Step in an Instructional Goal

Practice

In the exercises that follow, you are asked to complete a subordinate skills analysis for psychomotor, intellectual, and verbal information goals. The topics and goals used in the examples are purposely different from those used in previous examples. Working with new goals at this point provides you with a broader base of experience that should be beneficial when you select a topic and goal of your own.

Work through each example, and then compare your analysis with the sample one in the Feedback section. If your analysis is different, locate the differences and determine whether you would like to make any revisions in yours. You may like your analysis better than the sample provided, but you should be able to explain and justify the differences.

1. Do an instructional analysis for the following psychomotor skill.

   Topic Changing a tire

   Demonstrate your ability to do a procedural analysis by identifying the subskills required to perform step 2 for the following instructional goal on tire changing.

   Instructional Goal Change the tire on an automobile.

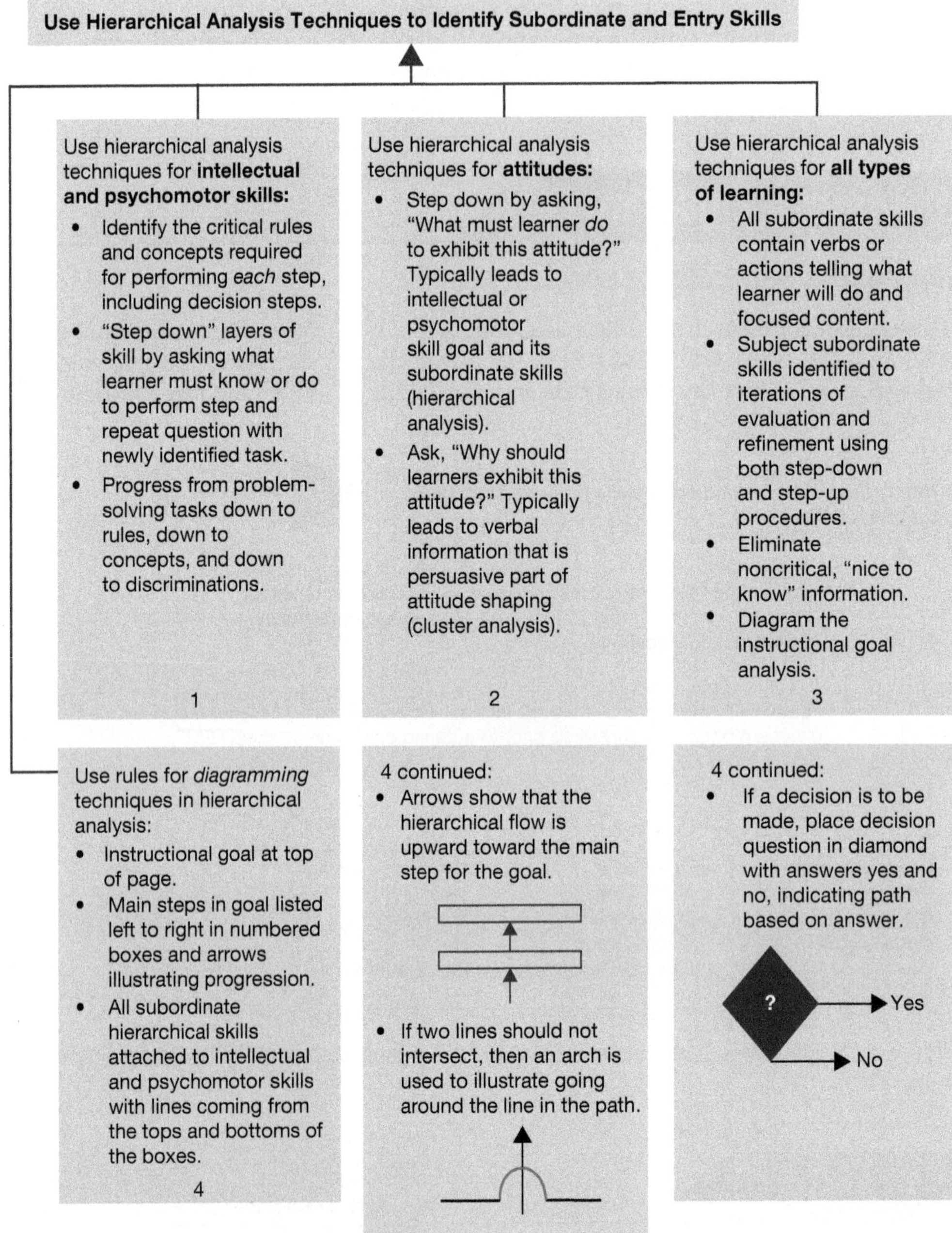

Figure 4.12 Use Hierarchical Analysis Techniques to Identify Subordinate and Entry Skills

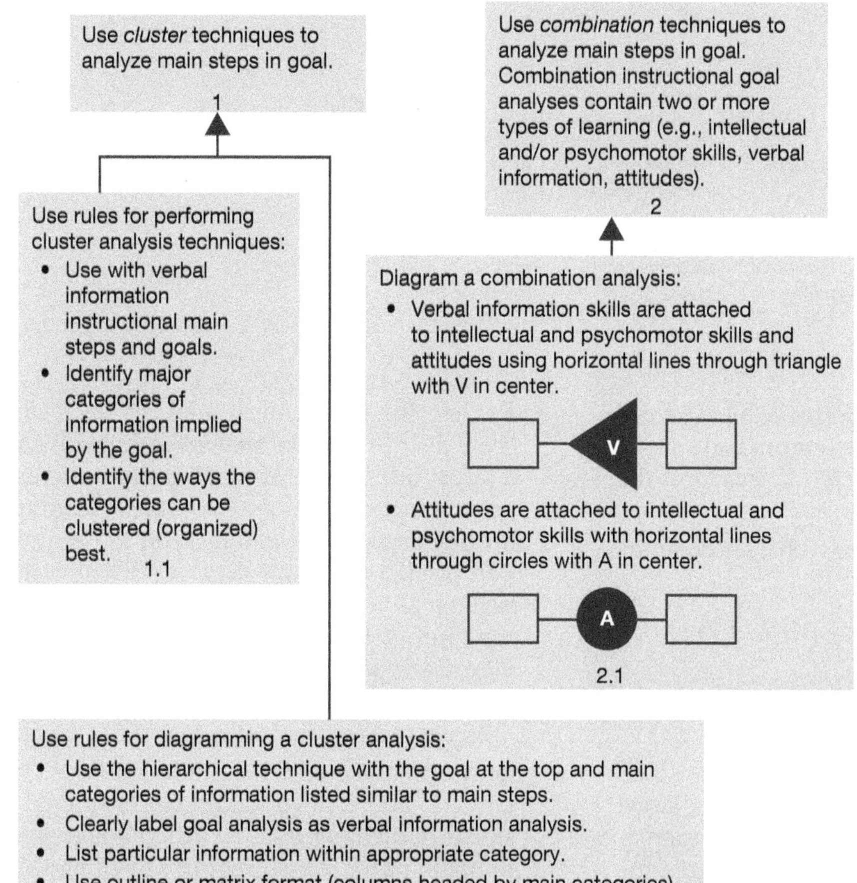

Figure 4.13 Use Cluster and Combination Techniques to Analyze Main Steps in an Instructional Goal

Practice Continued

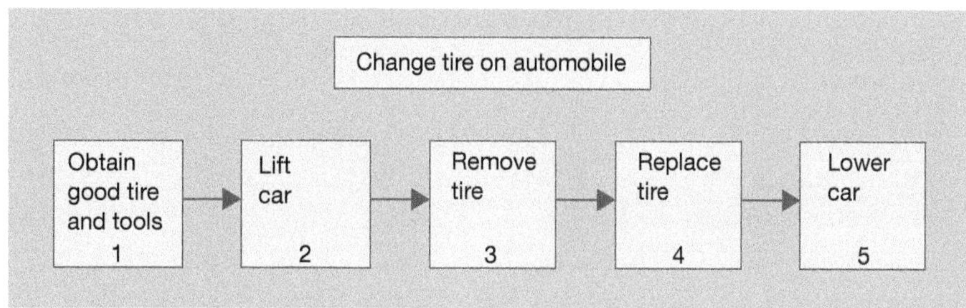

2. Complete a hierarchical analysis for the following intellectual skill.

   Topic Measure/score distributions

Instructional Goal Interpret measure/score distributions using frequency polygons.

Recall the main steps for this instructional goal from Figure 3.1 are:

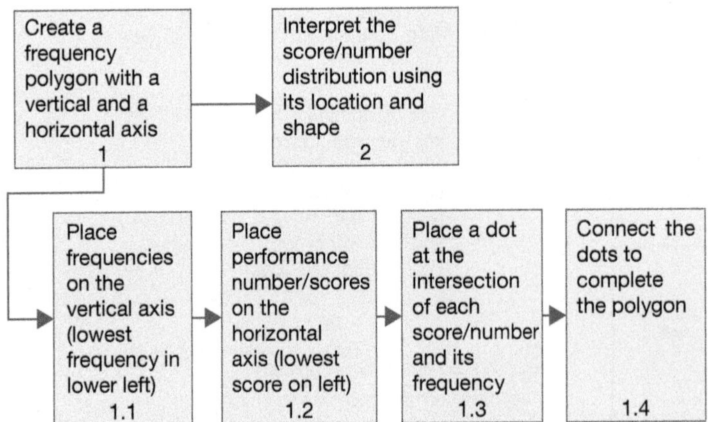

Demonstrate your ability to do a hierarchical analysis by identifying the subordinate skills required to perform main step 2, Interpret the distribution using its location and shape.

3. Complete a cluster analysis for verbal information.

   Topic Parts of the body.

   Instructional Goal Name the parts of the body using common terminology.

   One strategy for this analysis is to proceed from the head to the feet.

4. Review the psychomotor instructional analysis on changing a tire in Figure 4.14, assuming a target population of high school juniors with temporary driver's licenses. For any steps in the procedure, identify the entry skills you believe are relevant for this analysis. Modify the procedural analysis in the diagram to reflect your work.

5. Review the hierarchical analysis on measure/score distributions located in Figure 4.15. Assume a target population of ninth-grade students who are average and above average in reading and arithmetic skills. Which tasks in the analysis do you predict are entry skills, and which do you believe should be included in instruction for the ninth-grade group? Modify the diagram in Figure 4.15 to reflect your work.

6. Consider the verbal information on naming parts of the human body in Figure 4.16. Assume a target population of third-grade students. Which tasks do you believe should be considered entry skills? Remember that the task requires students to name parts, which requires spelling. Modify Figure 4.16 to show your work.

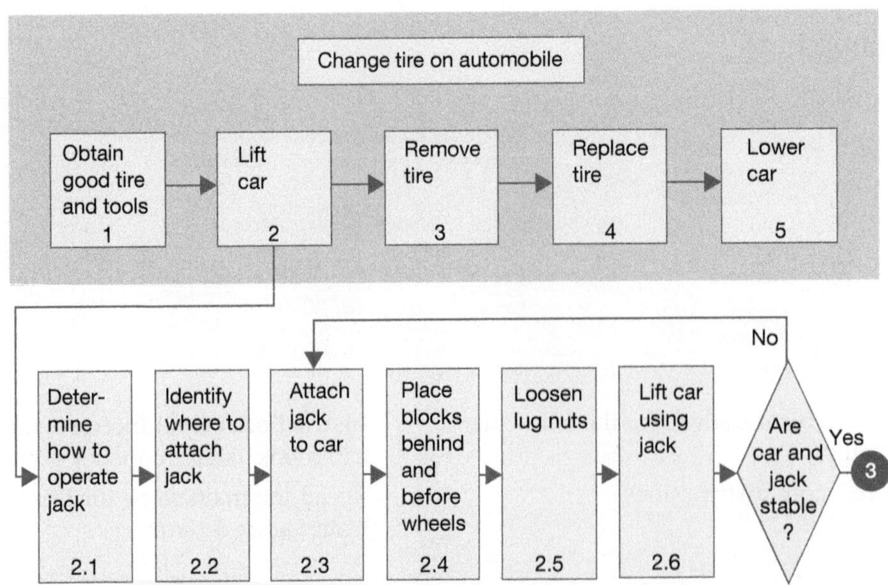

Figure 4.14 Instructional Analysis for Changing an Automobile Tire

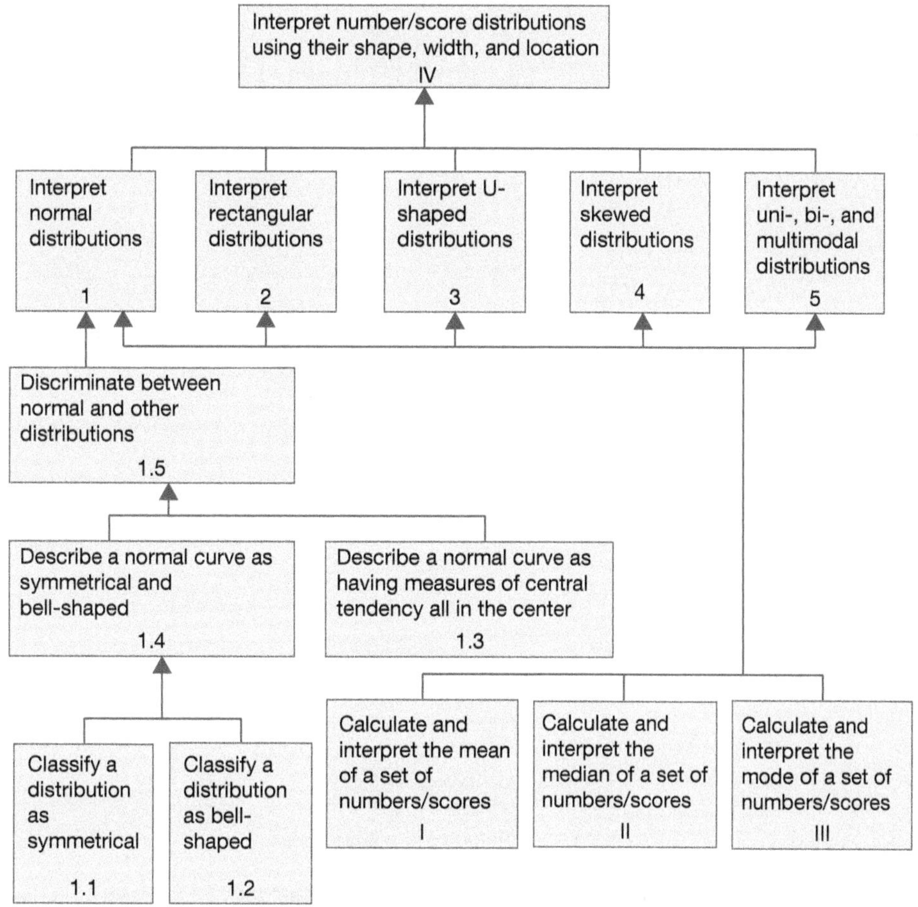

Figure 4.15 Subordinate Skill Analysis for an Intellectual Skill: Instructional Goal: Interpret measure/score distributions using frequency polygons, Main step IV: Interpret measure/score distributions using their shape, width, and location

Feedback

1. Compare your subskills analysis for changing a tire with the one shown in Figure 4.14. You may also have identified some subskills below the skills labeled 2.1 through 2.6. For example, it is necessary to know the rule that *Lug nuts loosen by turning counterclockwise* to complete step 2.5 successfully.
2. Compare your hierarchical analysis for interpreting measure/score distributions with the one shown in Figure 4.15. Analyze and determine whether you can explain differences between your work and that shown in the figure.
3. Compare your verbal information cluster analysis on parts of the body with the one shown in Figure 4.16.
4. No subordinate skills are included in the instructional analysis on changing a tire that should be designated as entry skills for this high school learner group.
5. Probably five subordinate skills in the instructional analysis for interpreting performance score distributions should be considered entry skills: subordinate skills I.A, II.A, and II.A, presumably all taught in previous units, as well as subordinate skills 2.1.4 and 2.1.5.
6. Entry skills identified for the verbal information cluster analysis include the ability to discriminate among the head, arms, hands, trunk, leg, and foot. Correct spelling of terms is covered in the instruction; thus, it is not included as an entry skill.

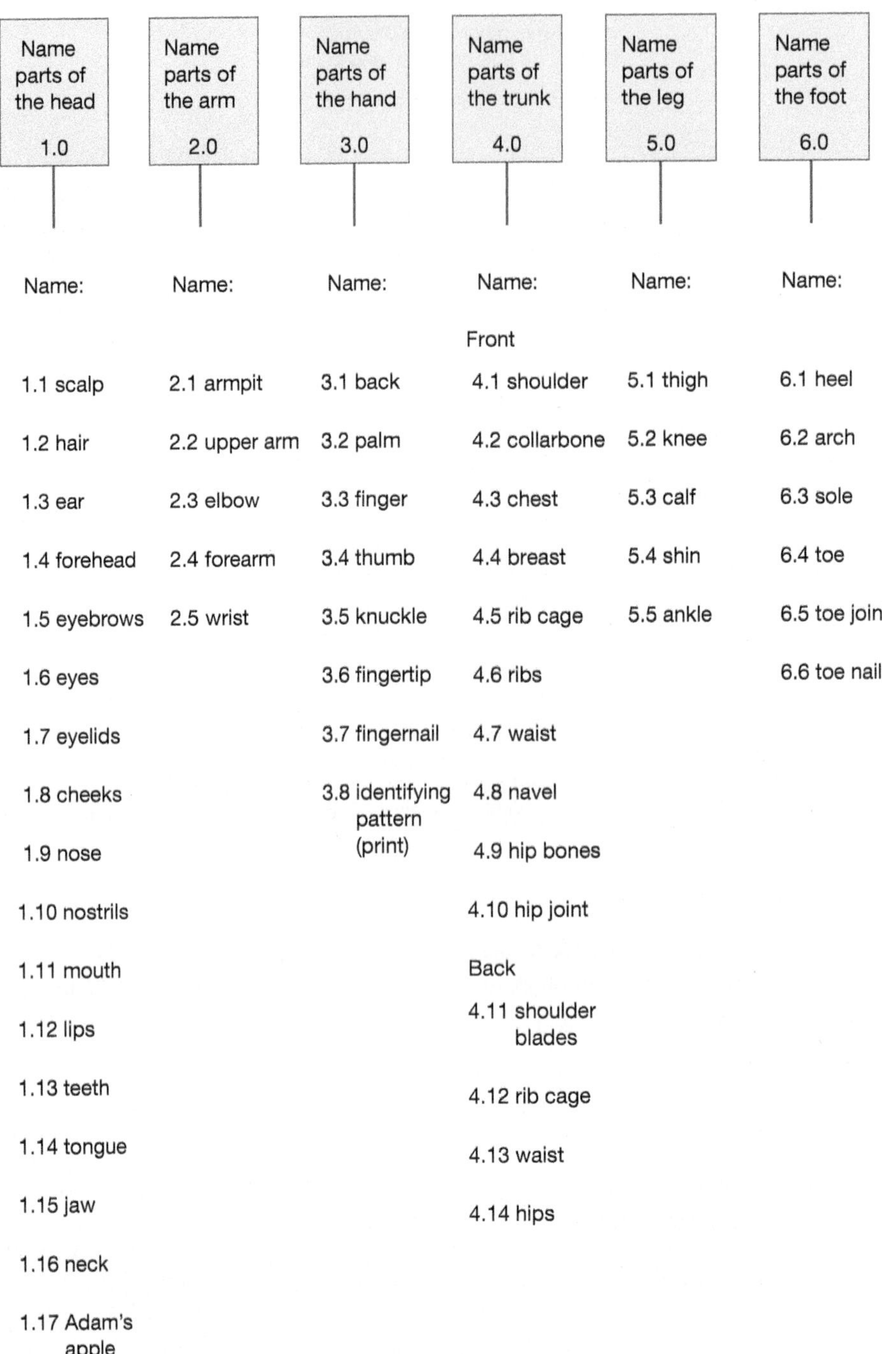

Figure 4.16 Cluster Analysis of a Verbal Information Task

Goal: Name the various parts of the human body.

Type of Learning: Verbal Information

References and Recommended Readings

Adams, A. E., Rogers, W. A., & Fisk, A. D. (2013). Skill components of task analysis. *Instructional Science, 41*(6), 1009–1046. Report of a study of task analysis skills performed by novices under three different conditions and comparisons with performances by experienced practitioners.

Annett, J., & Neville, A. S. (Eds.) (2000). *Task analysis.* Taylor & Francis. Annett originated many of the concepts from cognitive task analysis and hierarchical task analysis in the study of human factors and ergonomics.

Clark, R. E., Feldon, D., vanMerrienboer, J., Yates, K., & Early, S. (2013). Cognitive task analysis. In J. M. Spector, M. D. Merrill, J. J. G. vanMerrienboer, & M. P. Driscol (Eds.), *Handbook of research on educational communications and technology* (4th ed.). Lawrence Erlbaum Associates. Describes cognitive task analysis in practice and research, and presents research and reviews on issues in CTA.

Crandall, B., Klein, G., & Hoffman, R. R. (2006). *Working minds: A practitioner's guide to cognitive task analysis.* MIT Press. Describes tools for collecting, summarizing, and communicating data about cognitive processes.

Gagné, R. M. (1962). Military training and principles of learning. *American Psychologist, 17*(2), 83–91. Based on his extensive work with the military, Gagné focuses on the centrality of task analysis, sequencing tasks, and relationships among tasks.

Gagné, R. M. (1985). *Conditions of learning* (4th ed.). Holt, Rinehart and Winston. Describes classic instructional design, including the domains of learning and hierarchical analysis.

Gagné, R. M., Wager, W. W., Golas, K. C., & Keller, J. M. (2004). *Principles of instructional design* (5th ed.). Wadsworth/Thomson Learning. Provides a number of examples of the application of hierarchical analysis to intellectual skills.

Gottfredson, C. (2002, June/July). Rapid task analysis: The key to developing competency-based e-learning. *The E-Learning Developer's Journal.* http://www.elearningguild.com/pdf/2/062502DST.pdf. Details a procedure with examples for instructional analysis.

Jonassen, D. H. (1997). Instructional design models for well-structured and ill-structured problem-solving learning outcomes. *Educational Technology Research and Development, 45*(1), 65–94. Includes a step-wise look at approaches to solving well-structured and ill-structured problems that can be used during instructional analysis.

Jonassen, D. H., Tessmer, M., & Hannum, W. (1999). *Task analysis procedures for instructional design.* Lawrence Erlbaum Associates. Provides an excellent overview and how-to guide to instructional design applications of a wide range of techniques for job and task analysis. This book is currently available as an e-book through netLibrary.

Lee, J., & Reigeluth, C. M. (2003). Formative research on the heuristic task analysis process. *Educational Technology Research and Development, 51*(4), 5–24. Describes task analysis methods for complex cognitive tasks and proposes the need for various interview strategies, various experts, and skilled task analysts.

Loughner, P., & Moller, L. (1998). The use of task analysis procedures by instructional designers. *Performance Improvement Quarterly, 11*(3), 79–101. Provides another look at task analysis for the instructional designer.

Mager, R. (1997). *Goal analysis: How to clarify your goals so you can actually achieve them.* The Center for Effective Performance. Describes the utility of clarifying instructional goals prior to goal analysis.

Novak, J. D. (2009). *Learning, creating, and using knowledge: Concept maps as facilitative tools in schools and corporations* (2nd ed.). Routledge. Describes the use of concept maps in instructional design.

Reigeluth, C. M. (1983). Current trends in task analysis: The integration of task analysis and instructional design. *Journal of Instructional Development, 6*(4), 24–35. Although more than thirty years old, this article is still a good description of how task analysis is integrated into the instructional design process.

Shepard, A. (2000). *Hierarchical task analysis.* Taylor & Francis. Describes cognitive task analysis and focuses on hierarchical configurations of job analysis in business and industrial settings.

Shipley, S. L., Stephen, J. S., & Tawfit, A. A. (2018). Revisiting the historical roots of task analysis in instructional design. *Tech Trends, 62*, 319–320. A brief summary of where task analysis originated and where it is going in the future.

chapter 5

Analyzing Learners and Contexts

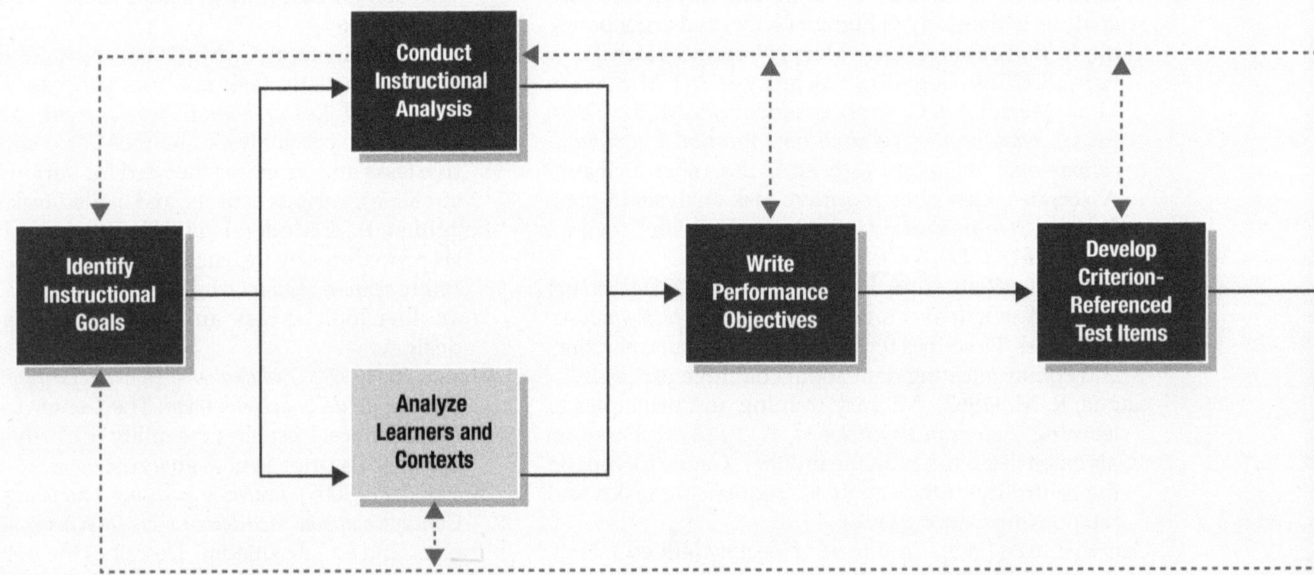

Objectives

- Analyze and describe the general characteristics of a target population.
- Analyze and describe the contextual characteristics of the performance setting (location where acquired skills will be performed).
- Analyze and describe the contextual characteristics of the learning setting (location where instruction will occur).
- Evaluate instructional analysis work in light of learner and context information and revise as indicated.

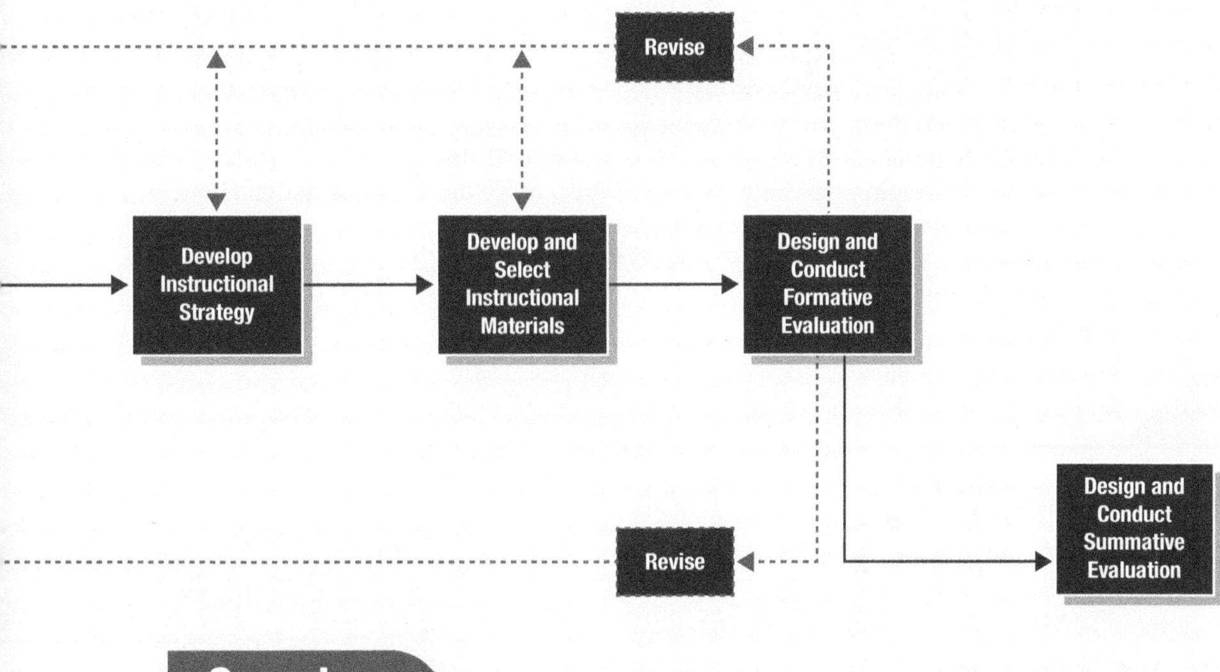

Overview

To begin this stage of instructional design, you should have completed or be working on the goal analysis and the subordinate skills analysis including the identification of entry skills. You should also have general ideas about the target population for which instruction is to be developed, using general descriptions such as kindergarten children, seventh graders, college freshmen, ambulance drivers, or automobile operators convicted of reckless driving following a serious accident.

There are two main analyses undertaken in this chapter: *learner analysis* and *context analysis*. During learner analysis the instructional designer identifies the general characteristics that members of the target population bring to the instruction, such as reading levels; attention span; previous experience; motivation levels; attitudes toward school, training, or work; and performance levels in previous instructional situations. Another important characteristic is the extent and context of related knowledge and skills that members of the target population already possess. One outcome from these target group analysis activities is a description of learner characteristics that facilitates later design considerations, such as appropriate contexts, motivational information and activities, materials formatting, and the amount of material to be presented at one time.

During performance context analysis, the designer describes the environment in which learners will actually use the information and skills prescribed in the instructional goal when they resume their natural roles as students, employees, citizens, or clients. Performance context features important to describe include whether the learner receives managerial or supervisory support in the performance context, the physical and social aspects of the performance site, the tools and technologies provided in the performance site, and the relevance of the information and skills to be learned to the performance site.

The final task in context analysis is to describe the learning context—that is, the "space" in which teaching and learning activities will occur, whether it is a classroom, a laboratory, an on-the-job setting, a learning management system, or a cell phone screen. Critical issues in the learning context are discovered through a review of resources that could support instruction and constraints that could inhibit instruction or limit instructional options. Both resources and constraints are usually analyzed in such categories as finances, personnel, time, facilities, equipment, and local culture. In addition, the compatibility of the learning context with your instructional needs and the learners' needs should be described. Finally, the feasibility of simulating the performance site within the learning site should be considered. The closer you can simulate the performance site, the more likely learners will be able to transfer and implement newly acquired skills.

Finally, in keeping with our systems approach, we use the information about learners and contexts to evaluate, and possibly revise, our instructional goal framework. This is accomplished by having persons knowledgeable about the learners and contexts judge the feasibility of your instructional analysis given your learners and contexts.

Concepts

Learner Analysis

Let's begin by considering the learners for any given set of instruction, referred to as the *target population*—also referred to as the *target audience* or *target group*—the ones you want to reach with the appropriate instruction.

Target Population

The target population is described by such identifiers as age, grade level, topic being studied, job experience, or job position. For example, a set of materials might be intended for systems programmers, fifth-grade reading classes, middle managers, or high school principals. These examples are typical of the descriptions usually available for instructional materials. However, the instructional designer must go beyond these general descriptions and be much more specific about the skills required of the learners for whom the materials are intended.

What information must designers know about their target population? Useful information about the target population includes (1) entry skills, (2) prior knowledge of the topic area, (3) attitudes toward content and potential delivery system, (4) academic motivation, (5) educational and ability levels, (6) general learning preferences, (7) attitudes toward the organization giving the instruction, and (8) group characteristics, including diversity (e.g., gender, race, culture, health, and special needs). The following paragraphs elaborate each of these categories.

Entry Skills Prior to beginning instruction in most fields of study, target population members must have already mastered specific skills (i.e., entry skills) in order to master the learning goal. These skills should be defined clearly, and learners' actual status on these skills should be verified during the instructional development process. The research literature also describes other characteristics of learners that can influence the outcome of instruction. They can be categorized as either specific or general in nature and relate to learners' knowledge, experience, and attitudes.

Prior Knowledge of Topic Area Much of the current learning research emphasizes the importance of determining what learners already know about the topic to be taught; rarely are they completely unaware or lacking in at least some knowledge of the subject. Further, they often have partial knowledge or misconceptions about the topic. During instruction, learners interpret new content in light of the associations they can make with their prior learning. They construct new knowledge by building on their prior understanding; therefore, it is extremely important for the designer to determine the range and nature of prior knowledge.

Attitudes Toward Content and Potential Delivery Systems Learners may have impressions or attitudes about the topic to be taught and perhaps even how it might be delivered. For example, the salesman may have no interest in mastering the rules and techniques required for keeping a rational database up-to-date by entering notes taken in the field into a laptop or desktop at the end of the day or workweek. They might, however, be interested in learning new skills if the company provides them with an app for entering data in the field on a tablet or smartphone that will sync with a network computer for automated data entry. The designer should determine, from a sample set of learners, the range of prior experience and attitudes toward the content area to be covered in the instruction. Designers should also determine learners' expectations regarding how the instruction might be delivered. Learners who had a bad e-learning experience with an ill-conceived and badly supported learning management system might be skeptical about taking more training in a similar system.

Academic Motivation Many instructors consider the motivation level of learners the most important factor in successful instruction. Teachers report that when learners have little motivation or interest in the topic, learning is almost impossible. Keller (2008) developed a model of the different types of motivation necessary for successful learning and suggested how to use this information to design effective instruction. Called the **ARCS model** (attention, relevance, confidence, and satisfaction), it is discussed in detail in Chapter 8; it is used here to show how to obtain information from learners during the learner analysis.

Keller suggests asking learners questions such as these: How relevant is this instructional goal to you? What aspects of the goal interest you most? How confident are you that you could learn to perform the goal successfully? How satisfying would it be to you to be able to perform the goal? The answers to these questions provide insight into the target population and into potential problem areas in the design of instruction. Do not assume that learners are very interested in the topic, find it relevant to their interests or job, feel confident that they can learn it, and will be satisfied when they do. These assumptions are almost never valid. It is important to find out how learners feel before you design the instruction so that accommodations can be planned before it is being delivered.

Educational and Ability Levels Determine the achievement and general ability levels of the learners. Are members of your target group, compared with their peers, homogeneous (similar) above average, average, or below average in their achievement? Are they somewhat heterogeneous (different), meaning they cross two of these levels, or are they heterogeneous, meaning they cross all these levels? This information provides insight into the kinds of instructional experiences they may have had and perhaps their ability to cope with new and different approaches to instruction.

General Learning Preferences Find out about the target population's learning skills and preferences and their willingness to explore new modes of learning. In other words, are these learners seemingly fixated on the lecture/discussion approach to learning, or have they experienced success with seminar-style classes, case studies, small-group problem-based learning, or independent e-learning courses? Much has been written about *learning styles* and assessing a student's personal learning style so that instruction can be adapted for maximum effectiveness. Research indicates that personal styles can be identified, but such styles are often derived from learners' expressions of personal preferences for listening, viewing, reading, small-group discussion, and so forth, rather than measurement of psychological traits that predict how a student learns best. We treat learning styles as an aspect of learning preferences until a body of research emerges that confirms practical gains in learning efficiency, effectiveness, and attitudes through individualizing instruction based on identification of learning styles.

Attitudes Toward Training Organization Determine the target population's attitudes toward the organization providing the instruction. Do they have a positive, constructive view of both management and their peers, or are they somewhat cynical about senior leadership and their ability to provide appropriate training? Researchers have indicated that such attitudes are substantial predictors of the success of instruction in terms of the likelihood of newly learned skills being used on the job. Those with positive attitudes about the organization and their peers are more likely to use the skills.

Group Characteristics Including Diversity and Special Needs A careful analysis of the learners provides two additional kinds of information that can be influential in the design of instruction. The first is the degree of heterogeneity or diversity within the target population on important variables. Such variables might include but not be limited to gender, race, culture, health, special needs, communication preferences, native language, and perhaps political beliefs, religion, and sexual orientation. Of course, designers must be careful when characterizing learners by political beliefs, religion, and sexual orientation. The designer must take care to characterize a group using only factors that are justifiably important to the instructional goal and to the learning and performance contexts. If such information cannot be gathered and used with sensitivity, then it should not be gathered. Obviously, finding ways to accommodate diversity is important.

Instructional designers must be familiar with American laws related to individuals with special needs and ensure that their performance and learning contexts can accommodate those needs. These laws include:

Americans with Disabilities Act (ADA)	Individuals with Disabilities Education Act (IDEA)	Section 504 of the Rehabilitation Act
This civil rights law prohibits discrimination in schools, workplaces, and public spaces on the basis of disability.	This law requires schools to provide special education and related services to children who need them.	This civil rights law prohibits discrimination in schools that receive federal funding on the basis of disability.

The second kind of information is an overall impression of the target population based on direct interactions with them. This is not simply accepting a stereotypical description or a management description of the learners; it requires interaction with learners in order to develop an impression of what they know and how they feel.

In some instances, the description of group characteristics is made more challenging by some contemporary e-learning methods. For example, how does one characterize a group of 5,000 students who have just enrolled in a massively open online course (MOOC)? Perhaps an online utility such as SurveyMonkey could be used to tally data on biographical information, education level, career interests, and motivational factors. Perhaps a sample of the whole group could be taken to develop an in-depth profile of a prototypical learner, known as developing **personas**—that is, fictional persons who represent predominant characteristics of intended learners.

Regardless of how the information is collected, these learner variables are used to select and develop the objectives for instruction, and they especially influence various components of the instructional strategy. They help the designer develop a motivational strategy for the instruction and suggest various types of examples that can be used to illustrate points, ways in which the instruction may (or may not) be delivered, and ways to make the practice of skills relevant for learners.

Tryout Learners It is important to make a distinction between the target population and what we refer to as *tryout learners*. The target population is an abstract representation of the widest possible range of users, such as college students, fifth graders, or adults. Tryout learners, in contrast, are learners available to the designer while the instruction is being developed. It is assumed that these tryout learners are members of the target population—that is, they are college students, fifth graders, and adults, respectively. However, the tryout learners are specific college students, fifth graders, or adults. While the designer is preparing the instruction for the target population, the tryout learners serve as representatives of that group in order to plan the instruction and to determine how well the instruction works after it is developed.

Data for Learner Analysis

There are various ways to collect data about learners. One method involves a site visit for structured interviews with managers, instructors, and learners. These interviews might yield valuable information about learners' entry skills, personal goals, attitudes about the content and training organization, and self-reported skill levels. During the site visit, the designer could also observe learners in the performance and instructional contexts. Either on-site or using distance technology, designers could administer surveys and questionnaires to obtain similar information about learners' interests, goals, attitudes, and self-reported skills. In addition to self-report and supervisor judgment, designers could administer pretests to identify learners' actual entry skills and prior knowledge and skills.

Output What should result from your learner analysis activities? The output should include a careful summary of the learners in all the categories just described. This information will be referenced by you and others throughout the remainder of the design process.

Performance Context Analysis

During context analysis, the designer should focus on the characteristics of the performance setting where the acquired skills are to be used eventually. Instruction should be part of satisfying a need that has been derived from a needs assessment, which should be based on identifying performance problems that can be solved through instruction or opportunities that instruction can provide for an organization. The instruction must contribute to meeting an identified need by providing learners with skills and attitudes that will be used, if not in the workplace, certainly somewhere other than the learning environment. Seldom is something learned simply to demonstrate mastery on a test at the end of the instruction; therefore, as designers, it is important for us to know the environment in which our learners will be using their new skills. For higher-order learning, a careful context analysis is critical for aiding the designer in recreating authentic elements of the performance context during instruction and enabling the learner to build optimal conceptual frameworks for learning and remembering. Accurate performance context analysis should enable the designer to develop a more authentic learning experience, thereby enhancing the learners' motivation, sense of instructional relevance, and transfer of new knowledge and skills to the work setting. In fact, the reason for analyzing the performance context before the learning context is to ensure, to the greatest extent possible, that requirements for applying the new skills are present while new skills are being learned.

Communications technologies are changing our concepts of the performance context. A call center employee's context may be so much within the computer screen and headset that the physical surroundings are marginalized. A lineman for an electric utility company may be high up in a bucket truck but using a tablet to access performance support to solve the problem he or she has found. An employee may be at home teleworking as a preferred work style or as necessitated by a short-term health or transportation problem. Analyzing a distributed performance context is complicated because one must consider the actual context, which can be a moving target, as well as the "home base" context where an employee ultimately reports and the dynamics of interactions between the two. Regardless of whether the performance context is traditional or physically and intellectually distributed, instructional designers should consider several factors: managerial or supervisory support, physical aspects of the site, social aspects of the site, and relevance of the skills to be learned to the workplace.

Managerial or Supervisory Support

We must learn about the organizational support that learners can expect to receive when using the new skills. Research indicates that one of the strongest predictors of use of new skills in a new setting (called **transfer of learning**) is the support received by the learner. If managers, supervisors, or peers ignore or punish those using new skills, then use of the new skills will cease. If personnel recognize and praise those using new skills and demonstrate how the skills are contributing to progress within the organization, then skills will be used, and it is hoped that their use will address the problem identified in the original needs assessment.

If managers' support is not present, then the designer (or the training organization) has an added problem associated with this project, namely recruiting their support. It is often helpful to include managers in project planning, ask them to serve as subject-matter experts, and perhaps ask them to serve as mentors or coaches for the learners during training and when they return to the workplace.

Physical and Social Aspects of the Site

The second aspect of the context analysis is to assess the physical context in which the skills will be used. Will their use depend on equipment, facilities, tools, timing, or other resources? This information can be used to design the training so that skills can be practiced in conditions as similar as possible to those in the workplace.

Understanding the social context in which skills are to be applied is critical for designing effective instruction. In analyzing social aspects, some relevant questions to ask include the following: Will learners work alone or as team members?

Will they work independently in the field, or will they be presenting ideas in staff meetings or supervising employees? Are the skills to be learned already used proficiently by others in the organization, or will these learners be the first?

Relevance of Skills to Workplace To ensure that new skills meet identified needs, we should assess the relevance of the skills to be learned by employees currently working in the performance site. This is a reality check to ensure that instruction really will be the solution, or part of a solution, to the needs that were originally identified. Designers should assess whether physical, social, or motivational constraints to the use of the new skills exist. Physical constraints might include lack of workspace, outdated equipment, inadequate time or scheduling, or too few personnel. For example, it would do little good to provide customer service training for a receptionist who has a constant stream of customers, all four telephone lines lit, and a thirty-minute delay for customers with appointments. Likewise, training in new instructional software is irrelevant for teachers who have severely outdated computers in their classrooms that won't run current software applications.

Data for Performance Context Analysis

Although some instructional analyses can be done in the office, context analyses require designers to observe in the appropriate setting. These observations influence the entire future course of the project because they provide critical information not only for direct input to the project but also for enhancing the skills and knowledge of designers.

On-site visits for purposes of context analysis should be planned well in advance, and one or more visits should be made. Ideally, these visits should occur at the same time that instructional analysis is being conducted. The sites will be situation specific, and some may have been identified in the needs assessment.

The purpose for the visits is to gather data from potential learners and managers and to observe the work environment where the new skills will be used. The basic data-gathering procedures include interviews and observations. The interviews should be conducted using written questions that focus on the issues presented in this chapter. Answers to the questions are situation or project specific and depend on the unique nature of each setting.

Output The major outputs of this phase of the study are (1) a description of the physical and organizational environment where the skills will be used and (2) a list of any special factors that may facilitate or interfere with the learners' use of the new skills. Similar to the learner analysis information, this output will be used as a reference by the instructional designer and others throughout the remainder of the design project.

Learning Context Analysis

Two aspects to the analysis of the learning context determine what is and what should be. The "what is" is a review of the setting in which instruction will take place. This might be only one site, such as a college classroom or corporate training center, or it could be one of many sites that a client has available. It could also be on the job with job aids, coaching, or electronic performance support. In fact, it could be anytime, anywhere with mobile technologies. The "what should be" is facilities, communications, hardware, software, expertise, personnel, logistics, and any other resources required for adequate support of the intended instruction.

In the learning context analysis, the focus is on the following: (1) the compatibility of the site with instructional requirements, (2) the adaptability of the site for simulating aspects of the workplace or performance site, (3) the adaptability of the site for using a variety of instructional strategies and training delivery approaches, and (4) the constraints present that may affect the design and delivery of instruction. The following paragraphs briefly elaborate each of these areas.

Compatibility of Site with Instructional Requirements

In the instructional goal statement prepared in the first step of the model, the tools and other support items required to perform the goal are listed. Does the learning environment that you are visiting include these tools? Can it accommodate them if they are provided? The most common "tools" today are probably computers and smart mobile devices. Even when not germane to the specific task to be learned, computers, tablets, and smartphones are frequently used as the medium for learning the task, for communications about the task, and for tracking achievement, so the issue of technology in the learning context requires careful analysis.

Specific tools may also be required for learning and performing tasks in academic, professional, and technical settings. Tools may be as simple as a mallet and chisel or as complex as a computer-controlled robot on a production line or imaging equipment in a medical clinic. The availability and compatibility of tools in the learning context are critical to effective instruction. We are reminded of a colleague who tells of taking piano lessons during World War II when resources and pianos were scarce in her neighborhood. She recalls walking to her lesson with a cardboard piano keyboard folded under her arm and practicing fingering for scales and popular songs. She agrees that little transfer occurred between the learning and performance contexts and also reports serious problems with her motivation.

Adaptability of Site to Simulate Workplace Another issue is the compatibility of the training environment with the work environment. In training, an attempt must be made to simulate those factors from the work environment that are critical to performance. Is it possible to do so in the designated training context? What must be changed or added?

Adaptability for Delivery Approaches The list of tool requirements from the goal statement indicates the "what should be" with regard to the learning context and, obviously, for the performance context as well. There may be other limitations or requirements that should be noted at this point in the analysis; these relate to organizational mandates that have been placed on your instruction. The organization may have decided that the instruction must be deliverable in typical corporate training centers in the United States, that the instruction must be deliverable by web to employees' desktops worldwide, or that the instruction is intended for the "typical" fourth-grade classroom. Determine what delivery approach can be used in the proposed instructional sites.

Learning Site Constraints Affecting Design and Delivery For whatever reason, a management decision may have been made upfront that this instruction be delivered using a specific learning technology. The decision may not have been made based on an analysis of the capability of the technology to deliver the desired instruction. In such cases, the context analysis of the learning environment becomes critically important. Many of the compatibility issues that once plagued digital technology in learning environments are disappearing as increasingly more education and training materials are developed in HTML or ported to HTML from special purpose materials development software. Regardless of the strides that have been made in compatibility, it is still critical that the development of the instruction never be initiated before addressing such matters. Most experienced designers have, at one time or another, regretted the omission of constraints analysis in the design process.

In an ideal situation, the location of the training and the means of delivering it would be decided based on an analysis of the requirements for teaching the instructional goal. In the extreme, some argue that training should not be delivered until the individual has need of it. It should be delivered just in time where needed in the workplace, not in a group setting in a classroom. Traditional practice is a long way from that vision. An instructor teaching twenty to twenty-four learners in a classroom is still the predominant method of corporate training. Public education is teacher-led with typically twenty to forty students. However, more e-learning is being accessed from the web at home, at a workstation, or on a tablet. The instruction can be individualized or can be set in a virtual learning community using real-time interaction with other students, a group leader, or an instructor. The new skills being learned may even be supported by performance support software on the student's desktop or on a mobile device in the job site. Such systems are a very real part of current training technology and make systematic design principles even more applicable for the development of efficient and effective instruction.

Data for Learning Context Analysis

The analysis of the learning context is similar, in many ways, to that of the workplace. The major purpose of the analysis is to identify available facilities and limitations of the setting. The procedure for analyzing the learning context is to schedule visits to one or more training sites and schedule interviews with instructors, managers of the sites, and learners, if appropriate. As with performance context analysis, have interview questions prepared in advance. If the learners are similar to those who will be taking your instruction, they may be able to provide valuable information about their use of the site. It is also important to observe the site in use and to imagine its use for your instruction. In addition, determine any limitations on your use of the site and the potential impact on your project. For instruction that will not be site-based, it is still important to interview managers and learners in addition to the obvious need to review the learning technology, infrastructure, and personnel needed to deliver the instruction.

Output The major outputs of the learning context analysis are (1) a description of the extent to which the site can be used to deliver training on skills that will be required for transfer to the workplace and (2) a list of any limitations that may have serious implications for the project. This information will be used to initiate, verify, or change decisions throughout the remainder of the design project.

Public School Contexts

Before summarizing this section, it is worth reviewing learner and context analysis from the perspective of the designer who will be developing instruction for public schools. Designers who support learner and learning environment analyses may believe that they are already familiar with them in the public school sector and that no further analysis is necessary. We encourage you to renew your experience base by doing the proposed analyses with learners, teachers, and typical classrooms.

The importance cannot be overemphasized of analyzing the context in which skills learned in school classrooms will ultimately be used. Those who work in vocational education see the immediate relevance of this step to their design efforts. They want to provide vocational graduates with skills that can be used and supported in the workplace. However, consider something like fifth-grade science instruction. What is the "performance site" for skills learned in such a course? One way to answer the question is to identify where the skills will be used next in the curriculum and talk with those teachers about the contexts in which the skills are used and about how well prepared students have been in these skills in the past.

Another analysis of the performance context relates to the use of the skills and knowledge outside the school. Why are the students learning these skills? Do they have any application in the home or the community, in hobby or recreational interests, in vocational or higher educational pursuits, or in development of "life skills"? If so, note performance context applications carefully and bring them to the instructional strategy stage of design. These applications are exactly what is needed to boost motivation, provide context for new content and examples, and design practice activities that are seen as relevant by students. In essence, we believe the learner and context analysis step in the instructional design model is just as important to the public school designer as it is to someone working with adult populations in diverse training and work environments.

Evaluation and Revision

Evaluating and Revising the Instructional Analysis

Most designers review and revise design analyses before the first draft of instruction is created. One component of the design process for which a preliminary tryout can be made is the instructional analysis. The reason we discuss the tryout in this chapter, rather than in Chapter 10, is the tryout can occur at the same time the designer is conducting the learner and context analyses. Those analyses bring the designer into contact with potential learners or recent learners who can review the instructional analysis with the designer.

The instructional analysis diagram indicates the goal, the steps required to perform the goal, the subordinate skills, and the required entry skills. In order to review the reasonableness of your analysis, select several people who have the characteristics of the target population. Sit with each person and explain what the analysis means. State the goal, and explain what someone would do if he or she were able to do it. You might provide an example in which you go through the steps. Then explain how each of the sets of subskills supports one or more of the steps in the goal. Explain what is meant by *entry skills*, and ask whether the person knows or can do each of the entry skills you have listed for your instruction.

What is the purpose of this explanation? You hear yourself explaining your ideas as you have represented them in the analysis. Sometimes just the act of explaining the analysis leads to insights about duplications, omissions, unclear relationships, illogical sequences, or unneeded information. Almost without regard to what the learner says during the explanation, you may find changes you want to make.

In addition to your personal reactions, you must see how a learner from the target population reacts to the skills you will be teaching. You will be *explaining* and not *teaching*, but you should stop occasionally to ask questions of the learner. Does the learner understand what you are talking about? How would the learner describe it in his or her own words? Can the learner perform the entry skills? These questions focus on the task, but you can include learner analysis questions as well, asking if he or she understands the relevance of the skills, has knowledge of the topic area, or sees how learning and using the skills will alleviate a problem or need.

If you do this review with several learners, perhaps somewhat divergent in their backgrounds and experiences but still members of the target population, you will gain information to refine the instructional analysis.

You might also explain your materials to supervisors in the work setting to obtain their input. Supervisors can provide insights from both content-expert and context-feasibility perspectives. Input from target learners and supervisors aids revising the instructional analysis before you begin the next phase of the design process, writing performance objectives and assessments, which depend entirely on information from the instructional, learner, and context analyses.

This description of an early review and revision of instructional analysis work highlights the iterative nature of the ID process. Recall that in a system, the components interact; a change in inputs from one component affects the outputs of another component. As instructional designers do their work, they frequently "circle back" to fine-tune earlier decisions based on new information discovered as they progress through the ID process.

Rubric for Evaluating Analysis of Learners and Contexts

The following rubric is a summary of the criteria you can use to evaluate statements of learners' characteristics (achievement, experience, and attitudes), performance, and instructional contexts.

Designer note: If an element is not relevant for your project, mark NA in the No column.

No	Some	Yes	**I. Learner Characteristics**
			A. Achievement and Ability Does the description include relevant information for instruction related to goal, subordinate skills, and entry behaviors, for:
____	____	____	1. Age?
____	____	____	2. Grade/education level?
____	____	____	3. Achievement level?
____	____	____	4. Ability level?
			B. Experience Does the description include a summary of learners':
____	____	____	1. Current job?
____	____	____	2. Prior experience?
____	____	____	3. Entry skills?
____	____	____	4. Prior knowledge of topic area?
			C. Attitudes Does the description include a summary of learners':
____	____	____	1. Attitudes toward content?
____	____	____	2. Attitudes toward delivery system?
____	____	____	3. Academic motivation (attention, relevance, confidence, satisfaction)?
____	____	____	4. Expectations for instruction?
____	____	____	5. Learning preferences?
____	____	____	6. Attitude about training organization?
____	____	____	7. Group characteristics (overall impression)?
			D. Diversity Does the analysis describe learners':
____	____	____	1. Age?
____	____	____	2. Culture?
____	____	____	3. Race?
____	____	____	4. Gender?
____	____	____	5. Background and experience?
____	____	____	6. Health, exceptionalities?
____	____	____	7. Other?
			E. Special Needs Does the description include a summary of learners':
____	____	____	1. Americans with Disabilities Act (ADA) considerations?
____	____	____	2. Individuals with Disabilities Education Act (IDEA) considerations?
____	____	____	3. Section 504 of the Rehabilitation Act considerations?
____	____	____	4. Physical needs?
____	____	____	5. Emotional needs?
____	____	____	6. Mental needs?
____	____	____	7. Special equipment, facilities, time, etc., needs?
____	____	____	8. Other?

_____ _____ _____ **II. Performance Context** Does the analysis include whether:
_____ _____ _____ A. Goal is based on needs assessment and identified problem or opportunity?
_____ _____ _____ B. Project has managerial support?
_____ _____ _____ C. Physical aspects are positive or a constraint (circle one)?
_____ _____ _____ D. Social aspects of site are positive or a constraint (circle one)?
_____ _____ _____ E. Goal and skills are relevant to target group and managers?
_____ _____ _____ F. Other?

III. Learning Context Does the analysis include whether the site:
_____ _____ _____ A. Is compatible with instructional requirements?
_____ _____ _____ B. Can be adapted to simulate workplace?
_____ _____ _____ C. Can be adapted to accommodate planned delivery approaches?
_____ _____ _____ D. Has constraint that will affect instructional design and delivery?
_____ _____ _____ E. Can be adapted to accommodate learners' needs?
_____ _____ _____ F. Other?

Examples

Identifying learner characteristics and the contextual characteristics of the performance and learning settings is an important early step in designing instruction. In this section, we illustrate how learner characteristics, the performance context, and the learning context can be described using a two-dimensional matrix format that allows designers to record a lot of information in a limited amount of space and to find it readily as they work on various aspects of the instruction. Table 5.1 is an

Table 5.1 Example Form for Analyzing Learner Characteristics

Information Categories	Data Sources	Learner Characteristics
1. Entry skills	Interview target learners, supervisors; Pretest	
2. Prior knowledge of topic area	Interview target learners, supervisors; Observe in performance setting; Pretest	
3. Attitudes toward content	Interviews Questionnaires Observations	
4. Attitudes toward potential delivery system	Interviews Questionnaires Observations	
5. Motivation for instruction (ARCS)	Interviews Questionnaires Observations	
6. Educational and ability levels	Interviews Questionnaires Observations	
7. General learning preferences	Interviews Questionnaires Observations	
8. Attitudes toward training organization	Interviews Questionnaires Observations	
9. General group characteristics a. Heterogeneity b. Size c. Overall impressions	Interviews Questionnaires Records	

Table 5.2 Example Form for Analyzing Performance Context

Information Categories	Data Sources	Performance Site Characteristics
1. Managerial/ supervisory support	**Interviews:** Current persons holding position, supervisors, administrators **Organization Records:**	Reward system (intrinsic—personal growth opportunities; extrinsic—financial, promotion, recognition) Amount (time) and nature of direct supervision Evidence of supervisor commitment (time, resources)
2. Physical aspects of site	**Interviews:** Current persons holding position, supervisors, administrators **Observations:** Observe one to three sites considered typical	Facilities: Resources: Equipment: Timing:
3. Social aspects of site	**Interviews:** Current persons holding position, supervisors, administrators **Observations:** Observe typical person performing skills at sites selected	Supervision: Interaction: Others using skills effectively:
4. Relevance of skills to workplace	**Interviews:** Current persons holding position, supervisors, administrators **Observations:** Observe typical person performing skills at sites selected	Meet identified needs: Current applications: Future applications:

example form for analyzing learner characteristics, Table 5.2 is an example form for analyzing the performance context, and Table 5.3 is an example form for analyzing the learning context. The first and second columns of each table list suggestions for categories of information and data sources that could be more or less important in your analyses depending on the learners and contexts under consideration. For specific examples of how these forms would be filled out, see the following case study and the case studies in Appendix D.

Case Study

Group Leadership Training

Learner and context analyses are critical in instances where heterogeneous groups of learners who are not known to the instructional designer will be learning in unfamiliar contexts and performing their new skills in self-regulated contexts. This is the situation in the group leadership training example in this case study. Recall that the goal for this case study is for master's degree students in the leadership department to demonstrate effective discussion group leadership skills in problem-solving meetings. Recall also the learner characteristics from the group leadership scenario in Chapter 2. To summarize their characteristics, they are:

- homogeneous (similar) in that they are all master's-level graduate students, have the same leadership major, and are motivated to learn strategies that advance them in their leadership careers.
- heterogeneous (different or diverse) in that they have different undergraduate majors, ages, work experiences, career aspirations, genders, and cultures.

Table 5.3 Example Form for Analyzing Learning Context

Information Categories	Data Sources	Learning Site Characteristics
1. Number/nature of sites	**Interviews:** Managers **Site visits:** **Observations:**	Number: Facilities: Equipment: Resources: Constraints: Other:
2. Site compatibility with instructional needs	**Interviews:** Managers, instructors **Site visits:** **Observations:**	Instructional strategies: Delivery approaches: Time: Personnel: Other:
3. Site compatibility with learner needs	**Interviews:** Managers, instructors, learners **Site visits:** **Observations:**	Location (distance): Conveniences: Space: Equipment: Other:
4. Feasibility for simulating workplace	**Interviews:** Managers, instructors, learners **Site visits:** **Observations:**	Supervisory characteristics: Physical characteristics: Social characteristics: Other:

Learner Analysis

Table 5.4 elaborates this general description. Column 1 names the categories of information considered, column 2 names data sources for obtaining the information, and column 3 contains information specific to the students as they enter the group leadership instruction. Notice, as you read through the categories, how you begin to form a picture of the group of students.

Performance Context Analysis

A performance context analysis is shown in Table 5.5. Again, information categories are listed in column 1, data sources are included in column 2, and performance site characteristics are described in column 3. Gathering such information about the arena in which group leaders work aids designers in choosing the best instructional strategies to use for maximizing the transfer of skills to the performance site. In this case, the leaders are working on campus and in education, business, government, and nonprofit arenas gathering information, organizing meetings and programs, and performing group management tasks during formal and informal meetings. They typically work independently, and they are loosely supervised within their organizations; often, they are the supervisors.

Learning Context Analysis

Table 5.6 contains a learning context analysis for the group leadership instructional goal. A list of the information categories appears in column 1, the data sources in column 2, and learning context characteristics in column 3. From this information, we can infer that the design team has a very good instructional situation.

Table 5.4 Description of Learner Characteristics for Master's Students in the Leadership Department

Information Categories	Data Sources	Learner Characteristics
1. Entry skills	**Interviews and Observations:** Three current employers of department alumni, three alumni, various department faculty, and three graduating students **Test Data:** Graduation surveys and exit interviews No test data currently exists prior to course development	**Performance Setting:** Most students have little prior experience as meeting chairpersons, and most have no prior experience in serving as the leader in problem-solving discussions. Learners have served as problem-solving group members in work- or community-related committee meetings; however, most have had no formal training in leading problem solving through interactive discussions. **Learning Setting:** Target students are skilled learners having successfully completed several years of higher education. They have experience in web-based and blended instruction as well as small group instruction and problem-based learning courses.
2. Prior knowledge of topic area	**Interviews and Observations:** Same as above	Learners have general knowledge of the group leadership area from participating as members in group discussions and from observing different leaders they have had through the years. As adults who have interacted more or less successfully with colleagues, they possess, at least at an awareness level, many of the skills required to be effective discussion leaders.
3. Attitudes toward content	**Interviews and Observations:** Same as above	Learners are enrolled in a master's-level leadership program and believe the group problem-solving skills are beneficial and will help them become good leaders and contributing members of team efforts. They also believe that acquiring the group leadership skills will help them ensure that their committee meetings will be effective and productive.
4. Attitudes toward potential delivery system	**Interviews and Observations:** Same as above	Learners have experience learning through live lectures, web-based instruction, and live group problem-solving simulations. They like the convenience of the web-based instruction, and they believe the simulations will be helpful.
5. Motivation for instruction (ARCS)	**Interviews and Observations:** Same as above **Questionnaires:** Sent to all current students in the leadership department	Learners are positive about their choice of major and are anxious to develop/refine their leadership skills. They believe the problem-solving group leadership skills are relevant to their current and future jobs, and they are confident they can become effective group discussion leaders. These factors, along with the interactive nature of the instruction, should help ensure that learners are attentive during instruction.
6. Educational and ability levels	**Interviews and Observations:** Same as above **Records:** Biographical data from program application forms **Test Data:** No test data on leading groups currently exists for master's students in the department	**Education Levels:** All learners are master's-level students in a leadership department; however, they vary in their undergraduate majors, ages, work experience, and focus for their eventual work. Some want to work on campus in areas such as student personnel, recruitment, orientation, and student services. Others want to work in public schools as principals, leaders in curriculum or personnel, safety, and athletics. Still others plan to work in business and government. **Ability Levels:** Students are proficient learners with high ability levels. Besides academic progress, learners' interpersonal skills are a concern. Based on experiences with current and prior students in the program, it seems that learners are heterogeneous with some high in interpersonal skills, some moderate, and some low. Some have a cooperative leadership philosophy while others seem to be quite autocratic.

Information Categories	Data Sources	Learner Characteristics
7. General learning preferences	**Attitude Data:** Student responses on program admissions survey **Interviews and Observations:** Thirty percent of current students in the program	Learners are experienced with a variety of learning formats; however, they prefer not to be publicly "put on the spot" until they are completely clear about faculty expectations and the skills they are to demonstrate in a course. In instructional settings, they prefer a short cycle of (1) presentation (What do you expect of me?), (2) private rehearsal (How can I best accomplish this?), and then (3) interactive "on the spot" simulations. They like problem-based learning, interaction/progress with real people and problems, and simulations. They like to be involved.
8. Attitudes toward training organization	**Interviews:** Same as above	Respondents have positive feelings about the faculty and program, about web-based instruction, and about the college's computer learning center. All think the course is a good idea for helping them plan and manage meetings within their organizations. They also believe the course will help them become acquainted with other students in the department and others across campus. They expressed hope these relationships will help them build an interpersonal network of support.
9. General group characteristics a. Heterogeneity b. Size c. Overall impressions	**Interviews:** Department students and faculty **Department Records:** Needs assessment, history with students, biographical forms **Observations:** Three alumni conducting problem-solving meetings on campus	**Heterogeneity:** Learners are heterogeneous in that they come from various undergraduate schools and majors; come from a wide variety of work settings and areas of expertise; have varying years of work experience; and represent a mix of age, gender, and cultural backgrounds. **Size:** There will be a total of twenty learners enrolled in the course to maximize learning efficiency for live group interactive work. **Overall impressions:** Instruction will need to be efficient, effective, and convenient.

Table 5.5 Description of Performance Context for Group Leadership Instruction

Information Categories	Data Sources	Performance Site Characteristics
1. Managerial/supervisory support	**Interviews:** Three members of the program advisory council, three current faculty, and the department chair **Records:**	Supervision of program leaders is minimal as they are typically employed as supervisors. Supervision mainly takes the form of receiving current information for the organization and directives from higher-level management. For example, they attend leadership councils for the organization; learn of current issues and problems; and receive organizational bulletins, materials, and information from the employer's website. They receive immediate notification of current problems in their areas, details of those problems, and statistical summaries of targeted problems.
2. Physical aspects of site	**Interviews:** Same as above **Observations:** Attended three meetings in different organizations within the local community	**Facilities:** Most organizations employing alumni provide quality conference rooms for staff meetings, and meetings typically occur within those rooms. **Resources:** Employers provide for resources required (meeting announcements, materials distributed to attendees, etc.) for operating the meetings.

Information Categories	Data Sources	Performance Site Characteristics
		Equipment: No particular equipment is required for the meetings. When needed, technology support is provided through the organizations' training departments. **Timing:** Meetings are typically scheduled by the leader either biweekly or as needed if a particular situation warrants it.
3. Social aspects of site	**Interviews:** Same as above **Observations:** Same as above	**Supervision:** The alumni have no supervision during the conduct of the meeting. **Interaction:** The alumni are interacting actively with colleagues who attend the meetings. This interaction is as a leader to manage the work of the group. The alumni can invite other experts to meetings as the topic to be discussed warrants. **Others effectively using skills:** There are others effectively using discussion leadership skills in the meetings. They have developed these skills through their educational programs, in the workplace, or in other community settings. It is interesting to see the skillful blocking and diversion behaviors demonstrated by some of their colleagues during meetings.
4. Relevance of skills to workplace	**Interviews:** Same as above **Observations:** Same as above **Records:** Reviewed needs assessment study describing characteristics of effective/ineffective leaders	**Meet identified needs:** The leadership instruction should meet identified needs of improving the effectiveness of leaders in the problem solving/solutions meetings. New leaders will be able to use the skills for their first meeting session, and the skills will serve them well in future meetings.

Table 5.6 Description of Learning Context for Master's Student Leaders

Information Categories	Data Sources	Learning Site Characteristics
1. Number/nature of sites	**Interviews:** Managers **Site Visits:** **Observations:**	**Number:** Five conference rooms are available within the department and college for interactive group simulations. **Facilities:** The web-based, individualized instruction can be accessed by learners in their homes, in most places on campus with Wi-Fi, and through cellular connections with smart devices. They also have opportunities to access the materials in various computer centers in the college and across campus. The interactive group sessions are to occur in a classroom within the leadership department and in the five available conference rooms. **Equipment:** Typical classrooms and conference rooms contain whiteboards, projection screens, and LCD projectors for computer display projection onto screens, and newsprint pads and stands.

Information Categories	Data Sources	Learning Site Characteristics
		Resources: The college is providing funding to create blended web-based and interactive conference instruction. Once developed and field-tested, the department will be responsible for maintaining the instruction. The price of continuing the instruction should be covered through student tuition and department funds. **Constraints:** 1. The conference rooms are often busy. Scheduling interactive group sessions may be difficult; however, there is less use evenings and weekends when planned instruction will occur. 2. The regular faculty available in the future may not be content experts in group discussion leadership. Faculty without these skills who wish to teach the course within the leadership department may need to upgrade their skills in the communications department, an additional faculty member with communication expertise may need to be employed, or the instruction may need to be delivered by faculty from the communications department.
2. Site compatibility with instructional needs	**Interviews:** Managers, Instructors **Site Visits:** **Observations:**	**Instructional strategies:** A variety of instructional strategies can be employed including self-study online materials, computer-based instruction, classroom presentations and discussion, and simulated small-group discussion sessions in conference rooms. **Delivery approaches:** Support is available for production and use of all typical print and nonprint materials. Support is also available for Internet-based instruction and other computer-based multimedia formats. **Time:** The majority of instructional time will occur as independent web-based learning. Time required in the department for interactive group meetings is limited to twelve hours (a one-credit-hour course). This time is initially planned to be four weekly sessions of three hours. **Personnel:** One faculty member and four graduate assistants (leadership, communications, technology, and instructional design) will develop the course. This team will be supported by personnel in the college's computer learning center and the educational technology support center.
3. Site compatibility with learner needs	**Interviews:** Managers, Instructors, Learners **Site Visits:** **Observations:**	**Location (distance):** The campus is located centrally within the county area, making transportation for group sessions as convenient as possible for students. **Conveniences:** Restaurants are located on campus, and there is a coffee shop within the college. **Space:** The classrooms can be used for larger group meetings and the conference rooms for smaller group meetings. **Equipment:** Student leaders will be responsible for gathering any equipment they need for their planned meetings.
4. Feasibility for simulating workplace	**Interviews:** Managers, Instructors, Learners **Site Visits:** **Observations:**	**Supervisory characteristics:** This cannot be simulated since leaders will have no supervision and little support in the workplace. **Physical characteristics:** The physical characteristics can be simulated since leaders will typically hold their staff meetings in the employers' conference rooms. **Social characteristics:** Within their organizations, learners will work as the leaders of interactive group discussions. These discussions with learners as leaders can readily be simulated in the department.

The importance of the instructional goal and the political/social priority currently attached to it has created the financial and professional resources, facilities, equipment, and personnel to provide quality instructional products and instruction. The only apparent limitations placed on the designers are those related to balancing time, learning efficiency, and cost-effectiveness.

Professional and Historical Perspectives

Historically, educational psychologists have examined an array of individual difference variables and their relationship to learning. Studies of intelligence and personality traits fill the literature. From an instructional design perspective, we want to know which variables significantly affect the achievement of the group of learners we will instruct, because designers create instruction for groups of learners having common characteristics. In this chapter, we identify a set of variables indicated by research to affect learning. By describing your learners in terms of these variables, you can modify your instructional strategy to enhance learning.

We encourage you to think beyond the accepted textbook and study guide approach to instruction, which has led to the criticism that much education emphasizes factual recall over conceptual understanding and textbook problems over authentic application. Constructivist theorists have been justifiably sharp in their criticism of teaching/learning activities that are abstracted from, and thus not relevant to, authentic physical, social, and problem contexts. This leads not only to diminution of learner motivation but also to inability to transfer learning for application in meaningful, real-life problem situations outside the learning context.

Advances in instructional technology and diverse learning and work environments have increased the importance of considering these factors in designing new instruction. While the traditional lecture mode in a training facility or school classroom remains a cost-effective format, this is changing rapidly and dramatically. Such changes will lead to research beyond learner characteristics when developing learning-effective and cost-effective instruction.

Process Flowcharts

Analyzing Learners and Contexts

To aid your work, the main tasks for analyzing (1) learner characteristics, (2) the performance context, and (3) the learning context are illustrated in Figures 5.1, 5.2, and 5.3. Figure 5.4 illustrates tasks for evaluating and revising your instructional analysis to this point.

Practice

The main instructional design concepts in this chapter are learner analysis, performance context analysis, learning context analysis, and the evaluation/revision of the instructional analysis. In the exercises that follow, the purposes for each of these design activities are named, data to be gathered for each are described, and data collection procedures are identified. For each of the analysis statements, identify the related type(s) of analysis. If the element named is associated with more than one type of analysis, place the letters of all types involved in the space preceding the element. If it is not associated with any, place the letter *d* in the space.

a. Learner analysis
b. Performance context analysis
c. Learning context analysis
d. None of these

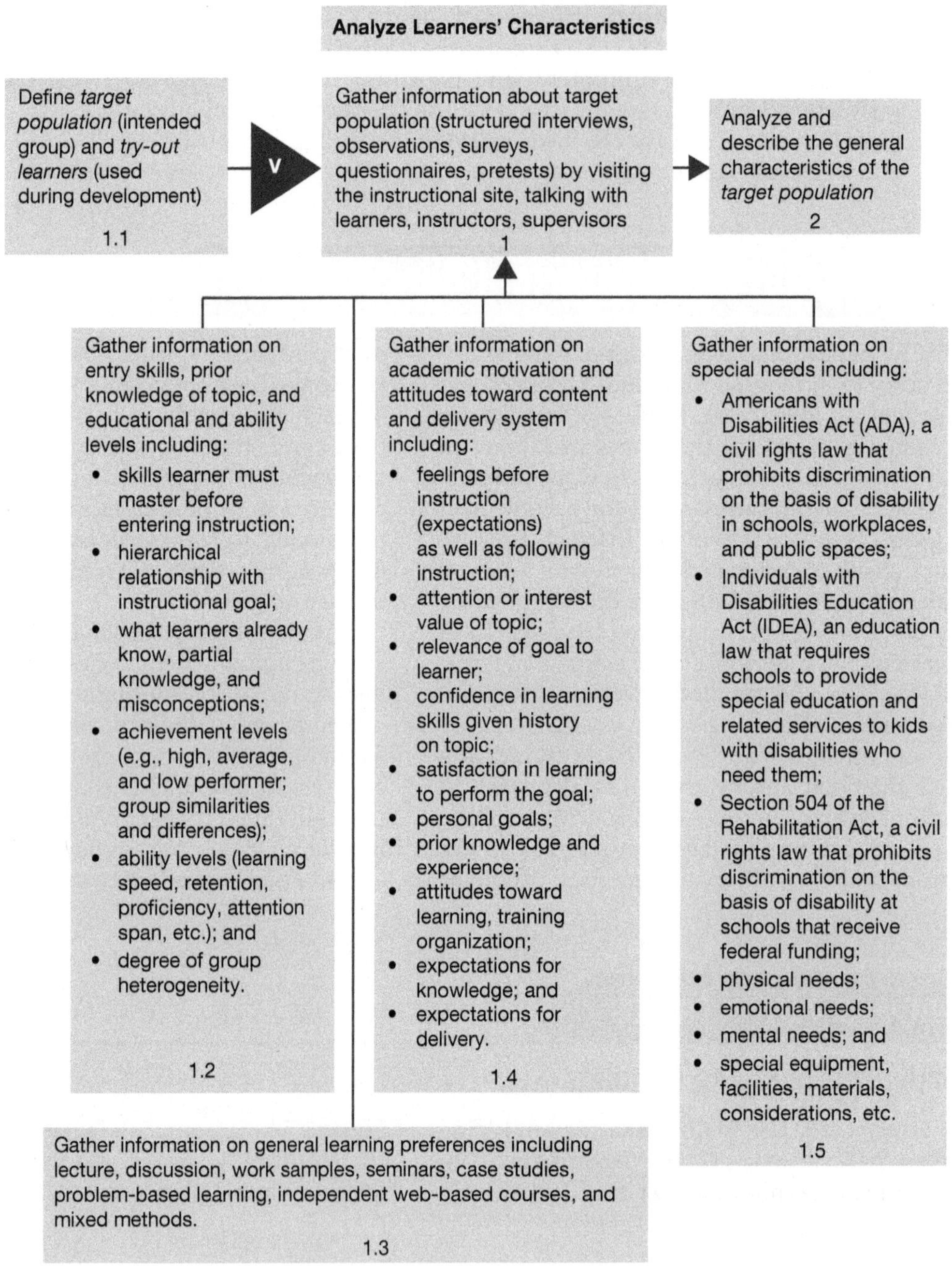

Analyze Learners' Characteristics

Define *target population* (intended group) and *try-out learners* (used during development)
1.1

V

Gather information about target population (structured interviews, observations, surveys, questionnaires, pretests) by visiting the instructional site, talking with learners, instructors, supervisors
1

Analyze and describe the general characteristics of the *target population*
2

Gather information on entry skills, prior knowledge of topic, and educational and ability levels including:

- skills learner must master before entering instruction;
- hierarchical relationship with instructional goal;
- what learners already know, partial knowledge, and misconceptions;
- achievement levels (e.g., high, average, and low performer; group similarities and differences);
- ability levels (learning speed, retention, proficiency, attention span, etc.); and
- degree of group heterogeneity.

1.2

Gather information on academic motivation and attitudes toward content and delivery system including:

- feelings before instruction (expectations) as well as following instruction;
- attention or interest value of topic;
- relevance of goal to learner;
- confidence in learning skills given history on topic;
- satisfaction in learning to perform the goal;
- personal goals;
- prior knowledge and experience;
- attitudes toward learning, training organization;
- expectations for knowledge; and
- expectations for delivery.

1.4

Gather information on special needs including:

- Americans with Disabilities Act (ADA), a civil rights law that prohibits discrimination on the basis of disability in schools, workplaces, and public spaces;
- Individuals with Disabilities Education Act (IDEA), an education law that requires schools to provide special education and related services to kids with disabilities who need them;
- Section 504 of the Rehabilitation Act, a civil rights law that prohibits discrimination on the basis of disability at schools that receive federal funding;
- physical needs;
- emotional needs;
- mental needs; and
- special equipment, facilities, materials, considerations, etc.

1.5

Gather information on general learning preferences including lecture, discussion, work samples, seminars, case studies, problem-based learning, independent web-based courses, and mixed methods.
1.3

Figure 5.1 Analyze Learners' Characteristics

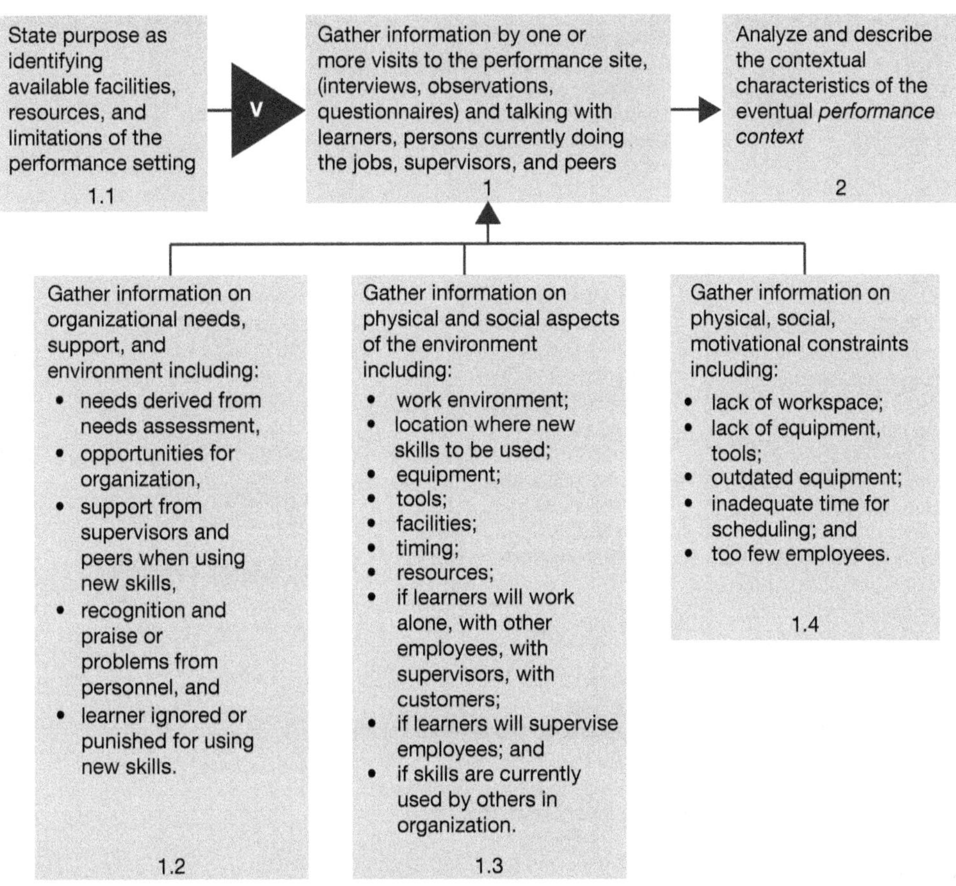

Figure 5.2 Analyze Performance Context

Practice Continued

Purposes for Analysis

______ 1. Identify facilities, resources, and limitations of site

______ 2. Examine relevance of skills to workplace

______ 3. Describe learners' entry skills

______ 4. Review instructional equipment and systems

______ 5. Describe social aspects of site

______ 6. Describe learners' motivation for learning

Information Gathered for Analysis

______ 7. Skills and experience of trainers and teachers

______ 8. Attitudes of managers toward instructional content

______ 9. Relevance of skills to workplace

______ 10. Prior knowledge and experiences

______ 11. Number and nature of training sites

______ 12. Attitudes of supervisors and managers toward learners

Persons Involved in Analysis

______ 13. Instructional designers

______ 14. Supervisors or managers

______ 15. Directors, trainers, or teachers

______ 16. Learners

17. Assume that you have been hired by a large school district as an instructional designer. Your first project is to create Internet-based writing instruction for sixth-grade students. Imagine a typical set of sixth-grade students in a very large school district and develop a table of learner characteristics for the project.

18. For the same instructional goal and students, create an analysis table to describe the performance and learning contexts. These are typically the same in a middle school setting.

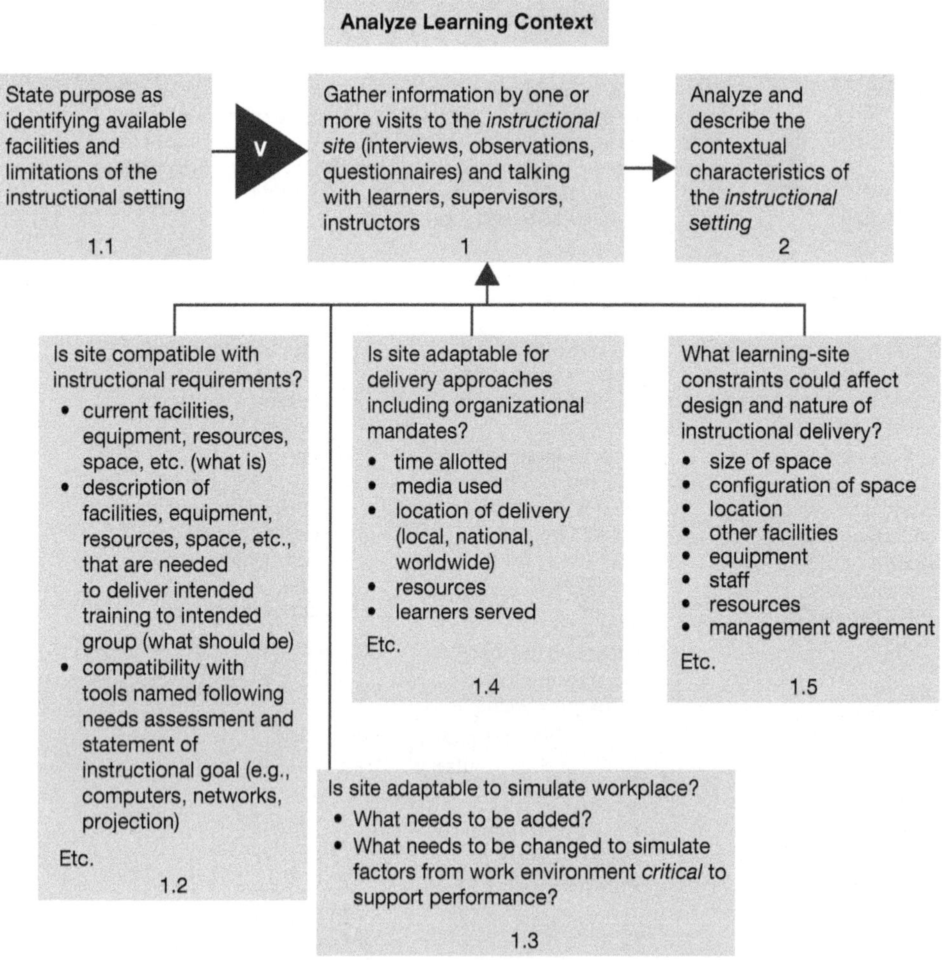

Figure 5.3 Analyze Learning Context

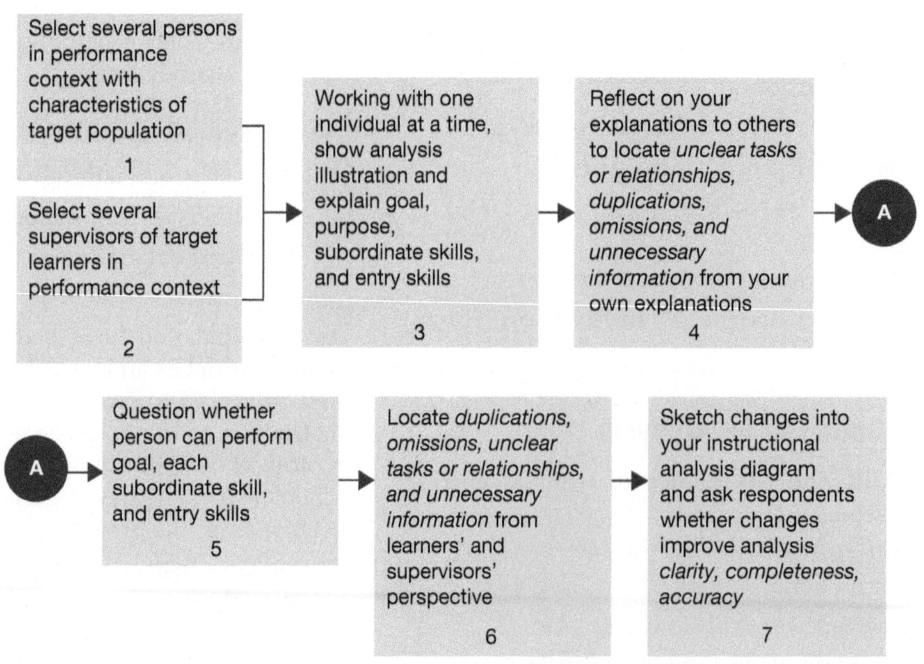

Figure 5.4 Evaluate and Revise Instructional Analysis

Feedback

1. b, c	4. c	7. c	10. a
2. b	5. b, c	8. b	11. c
3. a	6. a	9. b	12. b

13–16. All the individuals named could be involved in each of the three types of analysis.

17. Compare your learner characteristics with those in Appendix D, 1, page 444.

18. Compare your performance/learning context with that in Appendix D, 2, page 445. Remember, your analyses are expected to differ in some ways because this is an ill-structured problem.

References and Recommended Readings

Bursuck, W., & Friend, M. (2018). *Including students with special needs* (8th ed.). Pearson. The orientation is for teachers, but the book provides a variety of strategies and interventions for working with special needs students, including assistive and instructional technologies.

Cennamo, K., & Kalk, D. (2018). *Real world instructional design: An iterative approach to designing learning experiences*. Routledge. Contains a thorough chapter on analyzing learner characteristics in training settings.

Haskell, R. E. (2000). *Transfer of learning: Cognition, instruction, and reasoning*. Academic Press. Addresses problems of how learning is applied and adapted to similar or new performance contexts.

Holton, E. F., & Baldwin, T. T. (Eds.). (2003). *Improving learning transfer in organizations*. Jossey-Bass. Focuses on adult learners and their needs for transfer of learning to the workplace.

Hutchins, H. M. (2009). In the trainer's voice: A study of training transfer practices. *Performance Improvement Quarterly, 22*(1), 69–93. Describes variables that influence transfer of knowledge and skills to the performance context, including learner characteristics, training design characteristics, and work environment.

Kaiser, L., Kaminski, K., & Foley, J. (Eds.). (2013). *Learning transfer in adult education: New directions for adult and continuing education*, Number 137. Jossey-Bass. Describes ways to integrate learning transfer into curricula, syllabi, and practice in adult education.

Keller, J. M. (2008). An integrative theory of motivation, volition, and performance. *Technology, Instruction, Cognition, and Learning, 6*(2), 79–104. Describes a theory (MVP) that incorporates intentions, action control, and information processing within the framework of a systems model.

Keller, J. M. (2010). *Motivational design for learning and performance: The ARCS model approach*. Springer. The full ARCS model with a process for integrating motivational design with instructional design, including worksheets and tools for obtaining audience information and analyzing the audience.

Knowles, M., Holton, E. F., Swanson, R. A., & Robinson, P. A. (2020). *The adult learner: The definitive classic in adult education and human resource development* (9th ed.). Routledge. Latest iteration of Malcolm Knowles's description of the characteristics of adult learners.

Mager, R. F., & Pipe, P. (1997). *Analyzing performance problems* (3rd ed.). CEP Press. The decision flowchart in the text is useful for deciding what aspects of the performance context to include in an analysis.

Mayer, R. E. (2011). Towards a science of motivated learning in technology-supported environments. *Educational Technology Research and Development, 59*(2), 301–308.

McCombs, B. L. (2011). Learner-centered practices: Providing the context for positive learner development, motivation, and achievement. In J. Meece & J. Eccles (Eds.), *Handbook of research on schools, schooling, and human development*. Routledge. Stresses the importance of learner characteristics and the learning context in successful learning.

Park, S. (2018). Motivation theories and instructional design. In R. E. West, *Foundations of learning and instructional design technology: The past, present, and future of learning and instructional design technology*. EdTech Books. https://edtechbooks.org/lidtfoundations/motivation_theories_and_instructional_design. Explores a variety of theories of motivation as they relate to learning and instruction.

Rieber, L. P. (2020). Q methodology in learning, design, and technology: An introduction. *Education Tech Research Dev*. https://doi.org/10.1007/s11423-020-09777-2. Describes a combination of quantitative and qualitative methods for describing selected learner characteristics.

Rothwell, W. J., Benscoter, G. M., King, M., & King, S. B. (2016). *Mastering the instructional design process* (5th ed.). Wiley. Focuses on applications in professional and technical training with good advice on transfer to the performance context.

Rozkowski, M. J., & Soven, M. (2010). Did you learn something useful today? An analysis of how perceived utility relates to perceived learning and their predictiveness of satisfaction with training. *Performance Improvement Quarterly, 23*(2), 71–91. Concludes perceived usefulness was almost as good as amount learned in predicting satisfaction with training.

Tessmer, M., & Harris, D. (1993). *Analysing the instructional setting: Environmental analysis*. Kogan Page. Presents a complete process for examining the environment in which learning will take place.

Tessmer, M., & Richey, R. C. (1997). The role of context in learning and instructional design. *Educational Technology, Research, and Development, 45*, 85–111.

Tobias, S. (2010). Learner characteristics. In R. M. Gagné (Ed.). *Instructional technology: Foundations*. Routledge digital edition. Summarizes areas of research on learner characteristics.

chapter 6

Writing Performance Objectives

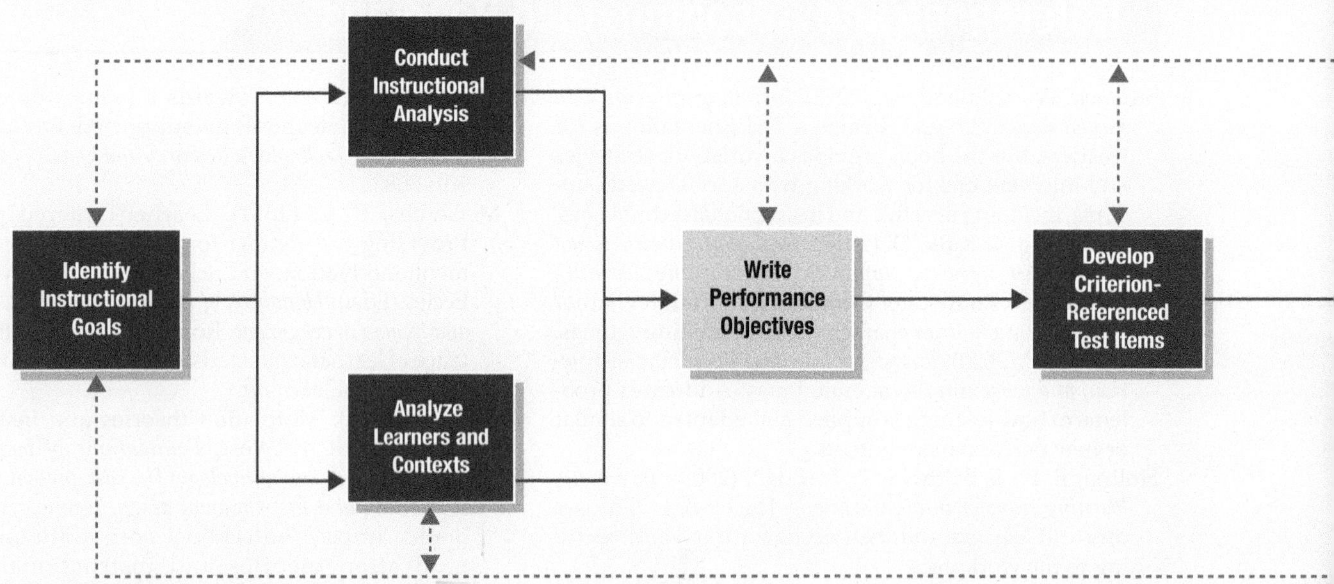

Objectives

- Write an elaborated instructional goal to include pertinent information about the eventual performance context.
- Write a terminal objective appropriate for the instructional context.
- Write performance objectives for subordinate skills that have been identified in an instructional analysis. These objectives should include the subordinate skill to be performed (behavior and content), the conditions under which the skill will be performed, and the criteria to be used to assess learner performance.

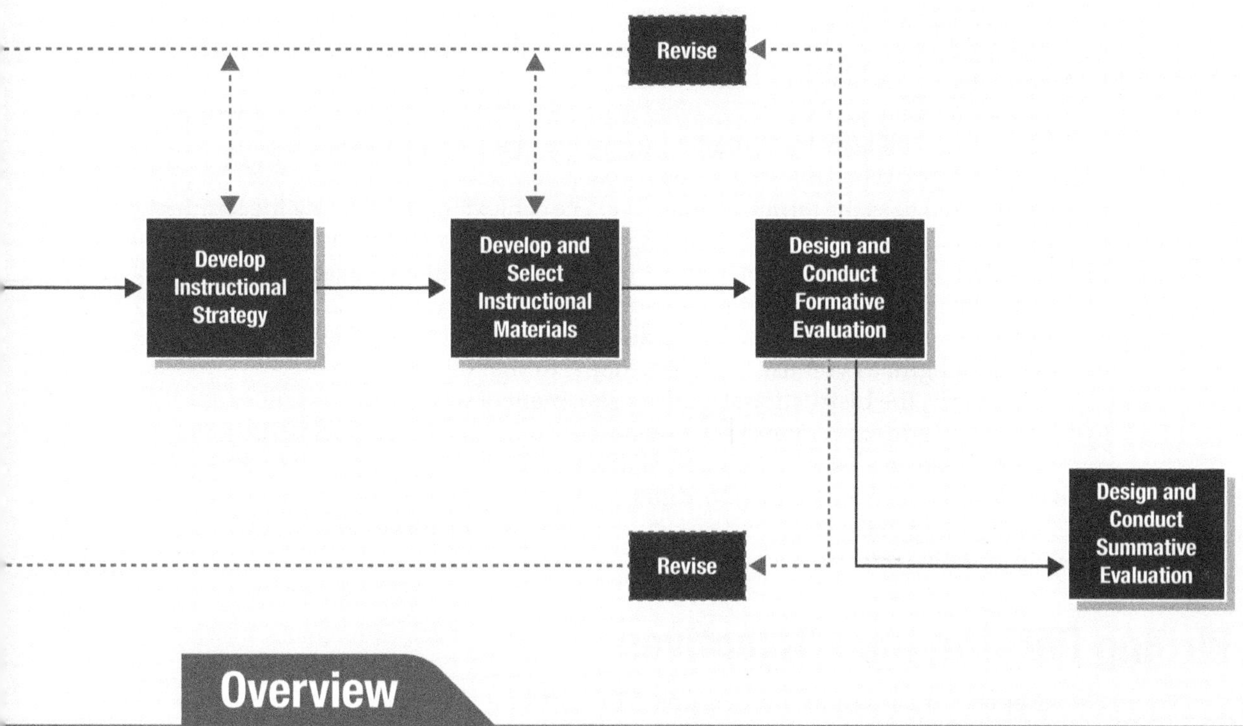

Overview

A performance objective is a clear statement of a skill that students are expected to master. Before beginning to write performance objectives, you should have completed the following design documents: an instructional analysis, a learner analysis, a performance context analysis, and a learning context analysis. With these products as a foundation, you are ready to write performance objectives for your goal, all steps and substeps in that goal, and their respective subordinate skills.

Begin by elaborating your instructional goal statement to include pertinent information about the eventual performance context. With the instructional goal and performance context in mind, convert the goal statement into a terminal objective that describes what students are expected to do at the conclusion of instruction.

To transform each enabling skill into a performance objective, you must add both conditions and criteria to it. In selecting appropriate conditions, you should consider (1) appropriate stimuli and cues to aid the learners' search of their memories for associated information, (2) appropriate characteristics for any required resource materials, (3) appropriate levels of task complexity for the target population, and (4) the relevance or authenticity of the context in which the skill will be performed. For attitudinal objectives, you must also consider circumstances in which the learners are free to make choices without reprisal.

The final task is to specify a criterion or criteria appropriate for the conditions and behavior described as well as appropriate for the developmental level of the target group. When the learners' responses can vary, as they can for tasks in all four learning domains, criteria that describe the characteristics of an acceptable response must be added. These behaviors, however, are very useful for developing required checklists or rating scales. In specifying criteria, designers must be careful not to rely on imprecise criteria, such as *expert judgment.*

Concepts

Perhaps the best-known part of the instructional design model is the writing of performance objectives. Table 6.1 links the steps in the ID process studied thus far to their related types of objectives.

The instructional goal describes what learners will be able to do in a real-world context, outside the learning situation, using the skills and knowledge acquired during instruction. When the instructional goal is converted to a performance objective, it is referred to as the **terminal objective**. The context for performing the terminal objective is created within the learning situation, not the real world. Similarly, the skills derived through an analysis of the steps in a goal are called *subordinate skills.* The objectives describing the skills that pave the way to the achievement of the terminal objective are referred to as **subordinate objectives**. These terms will become meaningful as you use the instructional design model.

In summary, the **instructional goal** is a statement of what students will be able to do in the performance context that you described in Chapter 5. The instructional goal is rephrased as a **terminal objective** describing what students will be able to do in the learning context, and **subordinate objectives** describe the building-block skills, or enabling skills, that students must master on their way to achieving the terminal objective.

Writing Performance Objectives

This chapter's most important concept is the performance objective. Four terms are often used synonymously when describing learner performance. Mager (1997) first used the term *behavioral objective* in 1975 to emphasize that it is a statement describing what the student will be able to do. Some educators strongly objected to this orientation. Other, perhaps more acceptable, terms have been substituted for

Table 6.1 Derivation of Performance Objectives

Step in the ID Process	Results of the Step	Name When Stated as an Objective
Goal Identification (Chapter 2)	Instructional Goal or Goals	Terminal Objective or Objectives
Goal Analysis (Chapter 3)	Major Steps and/or Clusters of Information Required to Master the Goal	Subordinate Objectives
Subordinate Skills Analysis (Chapter 4)	Subskills	Subordinate Objectives
Subordinate Skills Analysis (Chapter 4)	Entry Skills	Subordinate Objectives

behavioral; therefore, much of the literature contains the terms *performance objective, learning objective,* and *instructional objective.* When you see these, you can assume that they are synonymous with behavioral objective. Do not be misled to think that an instructional objective describes what an instructor will be doing. It describes instead the kinds of knowledge, skills, or attitudes that students will be learning. Marken and Morrison (2013) provide an interesting analysis of the terminology associated with objectives from the 1970s.

Performance objectives are derived from the skills in the instructional analysis. One or more objectives should be written for each of the skills identified in the instructional analysis. Sometimes, this includes writing objectives for the skills identified as entry skills. Why should objectives be written for entry skills if they are not included in instruction? Objectives for entry skills form the basis for developing test items to determine whether students actually have the entry skills you assumed they would have, which helps ensure the appropriateness of given instruction for particular students. In addition, these objectives are useful for the designer should it be determined necessary to develop instruction for previously assumed entry skills not actually possessed by the target population.

The Function of Performance Objectives

Performance objectives serve a variety of purposes, not just as statements from which test items and tasks are derived. They have quite different functions for designers, instructors, and learners, and it is important to keep these distinctions in mind.

For the designer, objectives are an integral part of the design process, the means by which the skills in the instructional analysis are translated into complete descriptions of what students will be able to do after completing instruction. Objectives serve as the input documentation for the designer or test construction specialist as they prepare the test and the instructional strategy. It is important that designers have as much detail as possible for these activities.

After the instruction has been prepared for general use, the objectives are used to communicate to both the instructor and the learners what may be learned from the materials. To accomplish this, it is sometimes desirable to either shorten or reword the objectives to express ideas that are clear to learners based on their knowledge of the content. Designers should be aware of this shift in the use of objectives and reflect this distinction in the materials they create.

Parts of an Objective

How are objectives written for the goal statement, steps in the goal, subordinate skills, and entry skills? Mager's (1997) work continues to be the standard for the development of objectives. His prescription for an objective is a statement that includes three major parts. The three major parts are the following:

1. The **skill** identified in the instructional analysis (e.g., write a haiku poem)
2. The prevailing **conditions** while a learner carries out the task (e.g., given five inspirational themes from nature)
3. The **criteria** to be used to evaluate the quality of learner performance (e.g., must contain seventeen syllables arranged in three lines containing five, seven, and five syllables, respectively)

The first part describes the skill identified in the instructional analysis, describing what the learner will be able to do. This component contains both the action and the content or concept. In the distance estimation problem described in Figure 4.3 (p. 75), the skill or behavior is to "identify the location of a point on the scale in decimal form by estimating between two tenth divisions to the nearest hundredth."

The second part of an objective describes the prevailing conditions while a learner carries out the task. Will learners be allowed to use a computer? Will they be given a paragraph to analyze? Will they discuss the problem with friends? These are questions about what will be available to learners when they perform the desired skill. In the distance estimation problem, the conditions are "given a scale marked off in tenths."

The third part of an objective describes the criteria to be used to evaluate learner performance. The criterion is often stated in terms of the limits, or range, of acceptable answers or responses, indicating the tolerance limits for the response. The criterion may also be expressed in terms of a qualitative judgment, such as the inclusion of certain facts in a definition, or a physical performance that has defined characteristics. In the distance estimation problem, the criterion for an acceptable answer is "report the reading to within ±.01 units."

The following statement contains all three parts of the objective: "Given a scale marked off in tenths (condition), identify the location of a point on the scale in decimal form by estimating between two tenth divisions to the nearest hundredth (enabling skill), and report the reading to within ±.01 units (criteria)." Table 6.2 summarizes the parts of a performance objective with more examples.

Caution Sometimes an objective may not convey any real information, even though it may meet the formatting criteria for being an objective. For example, consider the following objective: "Given a multiple-choice test, complete the test and achieve a score of at least nine out of ten correct." Although this may be an exaggerated example, it can be referred to as a *universal objective* in the sense that it appears to meet all the criteria for being an objective and is applicable to almost any cognitive learning situation. It says nothing, however, in terms of the actual conditions or the behavior that is to be learned and evaluated. You should always make sure your objectives are not universal objectives.

Derivation of Actions or Behaviors

It has been stated that objectives are derived directly from the instructional analysis; thus, they must express precisely the types of actions or behaviors already identified in the analysis. If the subskill in the instructional analysis includes, as it should, a clearly identifiable behavior, then the task of writing an objective becomes simply the addition of conditions under which the behavior must be performed and criteria for assessment. For example, if the subskill is "divides a scale into tenths," then a suitable objective might be stated: "Given a scale divided into whole units,

Table 6.2 Parts of a Performance Objective

Conditions (CN)	Behavior (B)	Criteria (CR)
A description of the tools and resources that will be available to the learner when performing the skill	A description of the skill including actions, content, and concepts	A description of acceptable performance of the skill

Examples:

1. In a workteam meeting (CN), manage the line of discussion (B) so the meeting stays on track (CR).
2. Using a web search engine (CN), use Boolean operators (B) to narrow the number of relevant hits by at least half (CR).
3. From memory (CN), describe the emergency response procedure when a gas detection indictor goes off (B), exactly as detailed in the company policy manual (CR).

divide one unit into tenths. The number of subunits must be ten, and the size of all units must be approximately the same."

Sometimes, however, the designer may find that subskill statements are too vague to write a matching objective. In this circumstance, the designer should consider the verbs that may be used to describe behavior carefully. Most intellectual skills can be described by such verbs as *identify, classify, demonstrate,* or *generate.* These verbs, as described by Gagné et al. (2004), refer to such specific activities as grouping similar objects, distinguishing one thing from another, or solving problems. Note that Gagné et al. have not used the verbs *know, understand,* or *appreciate* because they are too vague. When these words are used (inappropriately) in objectives, *know* usually refers to verbal information, *understand* to intellectual skills, and *appreciate* to attitudes. These vague terms should be replaced by more specific performance verbs. Combs et al. (2008) make convincing arguments for precise statements of objectives to facilitate valid assessment of students' learning.

The instructor must review each objective and ask, "Could I observe a learner doing this?" It is impossible to observe a learner "knowing" or "understanding." These verbs are often associated with information that the instructor wants the students to learn. To make it clear to students that they are supposed to learn certain skills, it is preferable to state in the objective exactly how students are to demonstrate that they know or understand the skills. For example, the learner might be required to state that New York and California are approximately 3,000 miles apart. If students are able to state (or write) this fact, it may be inferred that they know it.

Objectives that relate to psychomotor skills usually are easily expressed in terms of a behavior (e.g., running, jumping, driving). When objectives involve attitudes, the learner is usually expected to choose a particular alternative or sets of alternatives. However, it may involve the learner making a choice from among a variety of activities.

Derivation of Conditions

With the knowledge, skill, or attitudinal part of the objective clearly identified, you are ready to specify the conditions part of the objective. *Conditions* refers to the exact set of circumstances and resources that will be available to the learner when the skill is performed. In selecting appropriate conditions, you must consider both the skill to be demonstrated and the characteristics of the target population. You should also consider the purposes that the conditions serve in an objective. These purposes include specifying (1) cues to enable learners to search the information stored in their memory, (2) the characteristics of any *resource material* required to perform the task, (3) control of *task complexity,* and (4) *aiding transfer* from the instructional to the performance context. Several conditions could be used to describe the stimuli learners will be given to aid their recall of verbal information. Consider the following list of stimuli (conditions) and behaviors, each of which could enable learners to demonstrate that they know or can associate the concept with the definition.

Condition		Behavior
Given the term,	→	write the definition.
Given the definition,	→	name the term.
Given the term and a set of alternative definitions,	→	select the most precise definition.
Given an illustration of a concept,	→	name and define the concept illustrated.
Given the term,	→	list its unique physical characteristics.
Given the term,	→	list its functions or roles.

Although each of these conditions is "from memory," it more clearly specifies the nature of the stimulus material or information that learners will be given in order to search their memory for the desired response. Each condition could also imply a paper-and-pencil test, a computer touch screen, or an online interactive form, but merely specifying the method by which the test will be administered as the condition leaves the issue of an appropriate stimulus undefined.

Resource Materials The second purpose for including conditions in an objective is to specify any resource materials that are needed to perform a given task. Such resource materials might include the following: (1) illustrations, such as tables, charts, or graphs; (2) written materials, such as reports, stories, or newspaper articles; (3) physical objects, such as rocks, leaves, slides, machines, or tools; and (4) reference materials such as dictionaries, manuals, databases, textbooks, or the web. Besides naming the resources required, the conditions should specify any unique characteristics the resources should possess.

Control Task Complexity The third purpose for conditions is to control the complexity of a task in order to tailor it to the abilities and experiences of the target population. Consider how the following conditions control the complexity of a map-reading objective.

1. Given a neighborhood map containing no more than six designated places, . . .
2. Given a commercial map of a city, . . .
3. Given a smartphone with GPS, a specified current location, and a specified destination, . . .

Such conditions limit or expand the complexity of the same task to make it appropriate for a given target group.

Aiding Transfer The fourth purpose for conditions is aiding the transfer of knowledge and skill from the instructional setting to the performance setting. The conditions element is used to specify the most real-world, authentic, or relevant materials and contexts possible given the resources in the instructional setting. Notice in the preceding map-reading examples that students were given a simplified neighborhood map, a commercial city map, or a smartphone with GPS. These are the actual materials learners will be expected to use in the performance context; thus, transfer to the performance setting should be relatively easy for learners.

In deciding the conditions that should be specified, the primary considerations should be the performance and instructional contexts, the nature of the stimulus material, and the characteristics of the target population. Special resources required in either of the two contexts and limitations on task complexity are both conditions that are directly related to the nature of appropriate stimuli and the capabilities of the group.

Conditions for Psychomotor Skills and Attitudes Although the preceding examples focus on intellectual skills and verbal information, conditions appropriate for demonstrating psychomotor skills and attitudinal choices should also be considered carefully. For psychomotor tasks, consider the nature of the context in which the skill will be performed and the availability of any required equipment for performing the task. For example, if learners are to demonstrate that they can drive a vehicle, consider whether they will be required to maneuver a subcompact, an SUV, a pickup truck, a bus, or an eighteen-wheel semi-truck. Also consider whether the driving demonstration will involve inner-city freeways, interstate highways, downtown streets, two-lane country roads, or all of these. Such decisions influence the equipment required, the nature of instruction, the time required for practicing the skills, and the nature of the driving test.

Specifying the conditions under which learners demonstrate that they possess a certain attitude also requires careful consideration. Three important issues are the context in which the choice will be made, the nature of the alternatives from which the learner will choose, and the maturity of the target population. These considerations are important because choices may be situation specific. For example, choosing to demonstrate good sportsmanship during a tennis match may depend on the importance of the match in terms of the consequences for winning or losing. It may also depend on the player's sense of freedom to "act out" feelings of frustration and anger without negative repercussions. It also depends on the age and corresponding emotional control of the players. Demonstrating the true acquisition of a sportsmanlike attitude requires a competitive match where attitudes may be expressed without fear of reprisal. Simply stating the appropriate behavior on a pencil-and-paper test or demonstrating it under the watchful eye of the coach is insufficient.

Specifying conditions for both psychomotor skills and attitudinal choices can be tricky. An appropriate set of conditions may be difficult to implement in the instructional and testing setting. For this reason, simulations are sometimes required. When they are, the designer must remember that the actual demonstration of the attitude has been compromised.

The conditions associated with an objective shape the instruction every bit as much as the behavior in the objective. For example, is it necessary for the learner to memorize the information in the objective? Why must it be memorized? Can the information be looked up in a reference manual, or will there be no time for that? If it is only necessary for learners to be able to find the information, then the instruction consists of opportunities, with feedback, to look for various bits of information related to the objective. If information must be immediately available in a crisis situation, however, then the focus of the practice should be on ways to store and quickly retrieve the information from memory without taking time to look it up in notes or reference materials.

How does the designer decide exactly what the conditions should be? Sometimes it is simply a matter of SME judgment. Often, the designer can use the context analysis as the basis for describing conditions of performance. After all, the context analysis describes the situations under which the desired behavior will occur, and that is what we want to describe in the conditions of an objective.

Derivation of Criteria

The final part of the objective is the criterion for judging acceptable performance of the skill. In specifying logical criteria, you must consider the nature of the task to be performed.

Criteria for Intellectual Skills and Verbal Information Some intellectual skill and verbal information tasks have only one correct response—for example, balancing a ledger sheet, matching the tense or number of subjects and verbs, and stating a company safety policy. In such instances, the criteria are that learners produce the precise response. Some designers add the word *correctly* to this type of objective, whereas others state no criterion and assume that it is implicit in the conditions and behavior. However you choose to treat such objectives, keep in mind that specifying the number of times that learners are to perform the task (e.g., two out of three times, correctly 80 percent of the time) does not indicate the objective criterion. The question of "how many times" or "how many items correct" and similar statements are questions of mastery. The designer must determine how many times a behavior must be demonstrated in order to be sure that learners have mastered it. This decision is usually made when test items are developed. The important point is that the criterion in the objective describes what behavior is acceptable or the limits within which a behavior must fall.

Other intellectual skills and verbal information tasks do not result in a single answer, and learners' responses can be expected to vary, such as dividing a line into equal parts or estimating distance using a scale. In these instances, the criteria should specify the tolerance allowed for an acceptable response. Other tasks that result in a variety of responses include designing a solution to a business problem, writing paragraphs, answering essay questions on any topic, or producing a research report. The criteria for such objectives should specify any information or features that must be present in a response for it to be considered accurate enough. For complex responses, a checklist of response features may be necessary to indicate the criteria for judging the acceptability of a response.

Criteria for complex responses (e.g., an answer, product, or performance) can be complex themselves and specified in a variety of categories. Such categories of criteria might include (1) form of a response (i.e., the physical structure of a response), (2) function of the response (i.e., meeting the specified purpose or intention for the response), and (3) qualities or aesthetics.

Consider the following two examples using these three categories to clarify the idea of complex criteria. Suppose that learners are to produce chairs. The chair can be judged by its features and strength (physical structure), by whether it is comfortable (function or purpose), and by its aesthetic appearance (e.g., color, balance, proportions, coordination).

Now consider the criteria in these categories that might be applied to a written paragraph. Related to form, criteria might include whether it is indented and formatted according to structural rules. For function or purpose, criteria such as conveying information on one topic, persuading a reader, or providing adequate directions might be appropriate. Related to qualities or aesthetics, criteria might include clarity, interest value, logical chronology and transition, and creativity.

Many other different categories of criteria can be applied to learners' answers, products, and performances. Other examples of criteria include such categories as (1) social acceptability, (2) environmental soundness, (3) economic viability, (4) parsimony, and (5) costs.

Designers must analyze the complexity of the task to be performed and, during this analysis, derive appropriate categories of criteria to be considered in judging a learner's response. Mastery should be judged based on whether learners' responses meet the criteria categories and qualities within each category adequately. Many instructional designers manage the complexity of criteria using rubrics or checklists to define criteria for acceptable responses.

Criteria for Psychomotor Skills It may be necessary to specify the criteria for judging the acceptability of a psychomotor skill performance using a checklist to indicate the expected behaviors. Frequency counts or time limits might also be necessary. A description of the body's appearance as the skill is performed may need to be included (e.g., the position of the hands on a piano keyboard). Again, a rubric or checklist might be the best way to manage criteria for performances.

Criteria for Attitudes Specifying criteria for attitudinal goals can be complex. Appropriate criteria depend on such factors as the nature of the behavior observed, the context within which it is observed, and the age of members of the target population. It might include a tally of the number of times a desirable behavior is observed in a given situation. It could also include the number of times an undesirable behavior is observed. You may find that a checklist of anticipated behaviors is the most efficient way to specify criteria for judging the acquisition of an attitude. A frequent problem with criteria for attitude measurement is the evaluator's ability to observe the response within a given time period and circumstance; thus, compromise may be necessary.

Caution One problem that can arise in certain instructional settings is a statement that expert judgment or instructor judgment is the criterion for judging learner performance. It is wise to begin with a determination to avoid listing expert judgment as the criterion for an objective because it is not helpful to you or the learners. It only says that someone else will judge the learner's performance. In situations in which a judge must be used, try to consider the factors you would consider if you were the expert judging the performance. Develop a checklist of the types of behaviors and include these in the statement of the objective to ensure a clear understanding of the criteria.

Process for Writing Objectives

Steps for writing performance objectives include:

1. Edit goal to reflect eventual performance context.
2. Write terminal objective to reflect context of learning environment.
3. Write objectives for each step in goal analysis for which there are no substeps shown.
4. Write an objective for each grouping of substeps under a major step of the goal analysis, or write objectives for each substep.
5. Write objectives for all subordinate skills.
6. Write objectives for entry skills if some students are likely not to possess them.

To make objectives and subsequent instruction consistent with the context analysis, designers should review the goal statement before writing objectives. Does it include a description of the ultimate context in which the goal will be used? If not, the first step should be to edit the goal to reflect that context.

The second step is to write a terminal objective. For every unit of instruction that has a goal, there is a terminal objective. The terminal objective has all three parts of a performance objective, and its conditions reflect the context available in the learning environment. In other words, the goal statement describes the context in which the learner will ultimately use the new skills, whereas the terminal objective describes the conditions for performing the goal at the end of the instruction. Ideally, these two sets of conditions are the same, but, by necessity, they may be quite different.

After the terminal objective has been established, the designer writes objectives for the skills and subskills included in the instructional analysis including intellectual skills, verbal information, and, in some cases, psychomotor skills and attitudes. However, what do you do when you get to the entry skill line? You must make another decision. If the entry skills consist of such basic skills and information that almost all members of the target population know them and would be insulted to be tested on them, then no objectives are required. Conversely, if the entry skills reflect skills and information that may not be known to all learners, then write objectives for these skills.

Writing Objectives into Instructional Materials Consider how a comprehensive list of objectives created during the design process can be modified for inclusion in instructional materials. How do these modified objectives differ from those used by designers? First, few objectives for subordinate skills used during the development of materials are included. Generally, only major objectives are provided in the course syllabus, textbook introduction, main web page, or menu in an e-learning management system. Second, the wording of objectives appearing in such materials is modified. The conditions and criteria are often omitted to focus learners' attention on the specific skills to be learned, resulting in better communication of this information. Finally, students are more likely to attend to three to five major objectives than to a lengthy list of subordinate objectives.

Evaluation and Revision

Evaluating and Revising Objectives

The designer should pause at this point to evaluate the terminal objective and performance objectives that have been drafted. In evaluating performance objectives, you should consider their clarity, feasibility, and criteria.

Clarity, Feasibility, and Criteria

The clarity criterion should apply to the behavior, content, conditions, and criteria included in the objective. One good way to judge clarity is to construct a test item to be used to measure the learners' accomplishment of the task. If you cannot produce a logical item for the objective yourself, then the objective should be reconsidered. Another way to evaluate the clarity of an objective is to ask a colleague to construct a test item congruent with the behavior and conditions specified. If the item produced does not resemble closely the one you have in mind, then the objective is not clear enough to communicate your intentions.

Again, the feasibility criterion should apply to the behavior, content, conditions, and criteria in the objective. The designer might check the feasibility of objectives by asking, "Could I design an item or task that indicates whether a learner can successfully do what is described in the objective?" If it is difficult to imagine how this could be done with the existing learners, facilities, resources, and environment, then the objective should be reconsidered.

You should also evaluate the criteria you have specified in the objective, which may be done by using the criteria to evaluate existing samples of the desired performance or response. These may be samples produced by you, by colleagues, or by anyone who has performed the task. You should specifically attend to whether each criterion named is observable within the specified conditions and time frame. Determining the observability of criteria usually is easier for verbal information and intellectual skill tasks than it is for psychomotor skill and attitudinal objectives, as you might suspect. While writing objectives, the designer must be aware that these statements of criteria will be used to develop assessments for the instruction.

Cautions Do not be reluctant to write objectives using two or even three sentences to describe the desired learning outcome adequately. There is no requirement to limit objectives to one sentence. You should also avoid using the phrase *after completing this instruction* as part of the conditions under which a student will perform a skill as described in an objective. It is assumed that the student will study the materials prior to performing the skill. Objectives do not specify how a skill will be learned.

Do not allow yourself to become deeply involved in the semantics of objective writing. Many debates have been held over the exact word that must be used in order to make an objective "correct." The point is that objectives have been found to be useful as statements of instructional intent. They should convey to the designer or subject matter specialist in the field what it is that the learner will be able to do; however, objectives have no meaning in and of themselves. They are only one piece of the total instructional design process, and they only take on meaning if they contribute to that process. The best advice at this point is to write objectives in a meaningful way, and then move on to the next step in the instructional design process. The following rubric contains a more complete list of criteria for evaluating objectives. It serves as a summary of the qualities of well-written objectives, and it is intended for use by readers who are writing objectives for an ID project.

Rubric for Evaluating Performance Objectives

Criteria for constructing and evaluating elaborated goals, terminal objectives, and performance objectives are summarized in the following rubric to facilitate your work. Space is provided on the left side for marking your judgments, and criteria are listed in the right column. You may want to copy the checklist to provide to various reviewers of your materials.

Designer note: If an element is not relevant for your project, mark NA in the No column.

No	Some	Yes	
			A. Goal Statement Does the goal statement:
___	___	___	1. Describe the ultimate performance context?
___	___	___	2. Describe a context that is authentic and realistic?
			B. Terminal Objective Is there congruence between the terminal objective:
___	___	___	1. Conditions and the context of the learning environment?
___	___	___	2. Behavior and the behavior in the goal statement?
___	___	___	3. Criteria and the criteria in the goal statement?
			C. Performance Objective Conditions Do/will the conditions:
___	___	___	1. Specify the cue or stimulus provided to learners?
___	___	___	2. Specify resource materials/tools needed?
___	___	___	3. Control complexity of task for learners' needs?
___	___	___	4. Aid transfer to performance context (authentic)?
			D. Performance Objective Behavior Is the behavior:
___	___	___	1. Congruent with the behavior in the anchor step of the instructional goal analysis?
___	___	___	2. The actual behavior rather than a description of how learners will respond (e.g., "classify" rather than "circle")?
___	___	___	3. Clear and observable rather than vague?
___	___	___	**E. Performance Objective Content** Is the content congruent with the anchor step in the instructional goal analysis?
			F. Performance Objective Criteria Are/do criteria:
___	___	___	1. Included only when needed to judge a complex task?
___	___	___	2. Include physical or form attributes?
___	___	___	3. Include purpose/function attributes?
___	___	___	4. Include aesthetic attributes?
___	___	___	5. Include other relevant attributes (e.g., social acceptability, health, environment, economy, parsimony)?
			G. Overall Performance Objective Is the performance objective:
___	___	___	1. Clear (you/others can construct an assessment to test learners)?
___	___	___	2. Feasible in the learning and performance contexts (time, resources, etc.)?
___	___	___	3. Meaningful in relation to goal and purpose for instruction (not insignificant)?
			H. Other
___	___	___	1.

Examples

This section contains examples of performance objectives for psychomotor skills and attitudes. To aid your analysis of each example, the conditions are highlighted using the letters *CN*, the behaviors are identified with a *B*, and the criteria are indicated using the letters *CR*. Do not include these letters in your own objectives. Following each set of examples is a discussion that should also aid your analysis. For examples of performance objectives for verbal information and intellectual skills, see the Case Study section of this chapter.

Psychomotor Skills

Figure 4.11 (p. 101) contains an abbreviated goal analysis for changing an automobile tire. The subordinate objectives in Table 6.3 are based on the substeps included in the analysis.

As noted previously, writing performance objectives for psychomotor skills is more complex than writing objectives for verbal information and for many intellectual skills. In this abbreviated list of examples, notice the increased specificity in the conditions. Any special circumstances must be prescribed. Notice in objective 2.4 that the designer does not want the learner to be given blocks or to be reminded to obtain them. Obviously, part of the demonstration is for the learner to recall as well as to perform this step.

Table 6.3 Sample Psychomotor Skills and Matching Performance Objectives

Steps	Matching Performance Objectives
2.1 Determine how to operate jack.	2.1 Given a standard scissors jack and detached jack handle (CN), operate the jack (B). Attach the handle securely, crank the handle so the jack lifts, and lower the jack to its closed position (CR).
2.2 Identify where to attach jack to car.	2.2 Given an unattached scissors jack and a car to be lifted that is perched precariously on the brim of the road (CN), prepare for attaching the jack (B). Relocate the car to a flat, stable location; locate the best place on the frame of the car in proximity to the wheel to be removed; then position the jack squarely beneath the frame at that location (CR).
2.3 Attach jack to car.	2.3 Given a scissors jack placed squarely beneath the frame at the appropriate spot (CN), attach the handle and raise the jack (B). Jack is squarely beneath frame at appropriate spot and raised just to meet car frame. Contact between jack and car is evaluated for balance and adjusted if necessary. Car is not lifted and lug nuts are not loosened (CR).
2.4 Place blocks behind and before wheels that remain on ground.	2.4 Without being given blocks and without being told to locate appropriate blocks (CN), locate blocks and place behind wheels to remain on ground (B). Locate enough brick-size blocks of a sturdy composition and place one before and behind each wheel that is away from jack (CR).
Goal: Change the tire on an automobile.	**Terminal Objective:** Given an automobile with a flat tire, all tools required to change the tire secured in their normal positions in the trunk, and an inflated spare tire secured normally in the wheel well (CN), replace the flat tire with the spare tire (B). Each step in the procedure will be performed in sequence and according to criteria specified for each step (CR).

The verbs are also important and may require some translation to ensure that the behaviors are observable. Notice the shifts in 2.1 from the words *determine how to operate the jack* in the subskill statement to the words *operate the jack* in the objective. To measure whether the learner has *determined how to,* observable behaviors were used in the objective, thus the shift in the wording.

Also notice how the criteria are written. Specifying the criteria for steps in a psychomotor skill typically requires listing the substeps that must be accomplished. The criteria for each of these objectives contain such a list.

Another interesting feature about objectives for psychomotor skills is that although each objective has its own conditions, the conditions, behaviors, and criteria in preceding examples are often conditions for performing any given step. For example, an implied condition for objective 2.2 is the successful completion of objective 2.1. Similarly, an implied condition for objective 2.3 is the successful completion of objective 2.2.

Finally, notice the criteria listed for the terminal objective. Actually listing all the criteria for performing this objective requires listing again all of the specific criteria for each step in the process because completing all the steps constitutes performing the terminal objective. For this reason, the criteria listed for each objective should be placed on a checklist that could be used to guide the evaluation of the learner's performance.

Attitudes

Developing objectives for the acquisition of attitudes can also be complex in terms of conditions, behaviors, and criteria. The examples listed in Table 6.4 are taken from the attitudinal goal on hotel safety included in Figure 4.7 (p. 93), and they serve as good illustrations of problems the designer could encounter.

Table 6.4 Sample Attitudes and Matching Performance Objectives

Attitudes	Matching Performance Objectives
1. Choose to maximize safety from fires while registered in a hotel.	1.1 Unaware that they are being observed during hotel check-in (CN), travelers always (CR) (1) request a room on a lower floor and (2) inquire about safety features in and near their assigned room, such as smoke alarms, sprinkler systems, and stairwells (B).
2. Choose to maximize safety from intrusion while registered in a hotel.	2.1 Unaware they are being observed as they prepare to leave the hotel room for a time (CN), travelers always (CR) (1) leave radio or television playing audibly and lights burning, and (2) check to ensure the door locks securely as it closes behind them (B).
	2.2 Unaware that they are being observed upon reentering their hotel rooms (CN), travelers always (CR) check to see that the room is as they left it and that no one is in the room. They also keep the door bolted and chained (B) at all times (CR).
3. Choose to maximize the safety of valuables while staying in a hotel room.	3.1 Unaware that they are being observed during check-in (CN), travelers always (CR) inquire about lockboxes and insurance for valuables (B). They always (CR) place valuable documents, extra cash, and unworn jewelry in a secured lockbox (B).
	3.2 Unaware that they are being observed when leaving the room for a time (CN), travelers never (CR) leave jewelry or money lying about on hotel furniture (B).

The first thing you should notice about the conditions in these objectives is that they would be very difficult to implement for several reasons. Individual rights and privacy are two problems, and gaining access to rooms to observe whether doors are bolted and jewelry and money are put away is another. In such instances, the designer must compromise, and the best compromise is probably to ensure that individuals know what to do should they choose to maximize their personal safety while in a hotel. An objective test on related verbal information or a problem-based scenario test may be the best the designer can do.

Consider another attitude example that is more manageable. Recall the courteous, friendly bank tellers in Chapter 2. The attitude goal and objectives included in Table 6.5 for teller attitudes appear to be observable and measurable. This particular example enables us to illustrate some important points. First, the conditions are the same for all four of the selected behaviors; thus, they are written once before the behaviors to avoid redundancy. Recall that the measurement of attitudes requires that the tellers know how to act while greeting a customer and why they should act in this manner. They also must believe they are free to act in the manner they choose, which means that they cannot know that they are being observed. Another condition is that they choose to be courteous even when they are very busy. The designer could infer that a teller who chooses to greet customers in a friendly manner under these conditions possesses the desired attitude.

Second, the criterion for acceptable performance, which is *always,* is also the same for all four objectives. This criterion therefore precedes the list of behaviors to avoid redundancy.

Finally, the expected behaviors are listed separately beneath the conditions and criteria. This brief list of behaviors could be expanded to include those behaviors that tellers are never (CR) to exhibit while greeting a customer (e.g., wait for the customer to speak first, fail to look up or acknowledge a customer until ready).

With these objectives, a supervisor can develop a checklist for tallying the frequency with which each behavior occurs. From such tallies, the supervisor can infer whether the teller possesses the prescribed attitude.

Table 6.5 Manageable Attitude and Matching Performance Objectives

Attitude	Matching Performance Objectives
Tellers will choose to treat customers in a friendly, courteous manner.	Unaware that they are being observed during transactions with customers on a busy day (CN), tellers will always (CR): 1. Initiate a transaction with a customer by (a) smiling, (b) initiating a verbal greeting, (c) saying something to make the service appear personalized, (d) verbally excusing themselves if they must complete a prior transaction, and (e) inquiring how they can be of service (B). 2. Conduct a customer's transaction by (a) listening attentively to the customer's explanation, (b) requesting any necessary clarifying information, (c) providing any additional forms required, (d) completing or amending forms as needed, (e) explaining any changes made to the customer, and (f) explaining all materials returned to the customer (B). 3. Conclude each transaction by (a) inquiring about any other services needed, (b) verbally saying, "Thank you," (c) responding to any comments made by the customer, and (d) ending with a verbal wish (e.g., "Have a nice day," "Hurry back," or "See you soon") (B).

Case Study

Group Leadership Training

We pick up the case study again with examples of objectives for verbal information and intellectual skills. Only selected objectives are included here, but a complete ID process includes one or more objectives for each of the subskills identified in the instructional analysis. The conditions are again highlighted using the letters *CN*, the behaviors identified with a *B*, and the criteria indicated using the letters *CR*. As before, ordinarily, these letters are not included in your objectives. A brief discussion follows each set of examples to point out important features of the objectives.

Verbal Information and Intellectual Skills

Table 6.6 includes the instructional goal and the terminal objective for the performance and instructional contexts. The intellectual skills in Tables 6.6 and 6.7 and the verbal information tasks in Table 6.7 are taken from Figure 4.8 (p. 96), which illustrates the instructional analysis for the instructional goal "Lead group discussions aimed at problem solving." Table 6.7 contains the objectives for a sample of subordinate intellectual skills and verbal information tasks depicted in Figure 4.8.

Verbal Information In the example of verbal information objectives in Table 6.7, notice that the conditions specify key terms that must be used in test items presented to learners. For example, in subordinate objectives 6.1.1 and 6.1.2 for skill 6.1, key terms prescribed are "member actions that facilitate cooperative interaction" and "what members should do when their ideas are questioned." These key terms function as cues the learner uses to locate related information stored in memory. Although there are many different ways that corresponding test items could be formatted (i.e., as complete questions or as brief statements), the key terms must be presented to the learner. Notice that the manner in which the key terms are presented to learners is made clear in writing. Notice also that the behaviors used in the subskill and the objective are the same. Even in cases when they are not exactly the same, the behaviors used should enable learners to demonstrate the same covert skill (e.g., *name* versus *list*). Finally, consider the criterion in each objective. Because the number of actions named by learners will undoubtedly vary, the number of actions that should be named by learners is prescribed.

Table 6.6 Sample Instructional Goal with Performance Context and Terminal Objective with Learning Context for the Goal: Lead Group Discussions Aimed at Solving Problems

Instructional Goal	Instructional Goal with Performance Context Added
Lead group discussions aimed at solving problems.	During actual meetings held at designated places on campus and in the community (CN), successfully lead group discussions aimed at solving problems currently existing on campus and in the community (B). Member cooperation will be used to judge achievement of this goal (CR).
	TERMINAL OBJECTIVE WITH LEARNING CONTEXT ADDED
	During simulated problem-solving meetings attended by master's students in the leadership department and held in the department's conference rooms (CN), successfully lead group discussions aimed at solving given problems (B). Member cooperation will be used to judge the achievement of this goal (CR).

Table 6.7 Sample Performance Objectives for Verbal Information and Intellectual Skills Tasks for the Instructional Goal "Lead Group Discussions Aimed at Solving Problems"

Main Step in Instructional Goal	Performance Objective for Main Step
6. Manage cooperative group interaction.	6.1 During simulated problem-solving meetings comprised of master's-level students in leadership and held in the department's conference rooms (CN), manage cooperative group interaction (B). Discussion members should participate freely, volunteer ideas, and cooperate fully with leader and other members (CR).
SUBORDINATE SKILLS	**SAMPLE SUBORDINATE OBJECTIVES FOR MAIN STEP**
6.1 Name member actions that facilitate cooperative interaction.	6.1.1 When requested either orally or in writing (CN) to name group member actions that facilitate cooperative interaction, name those actions (B). At least six facilitating actions should be named (CR).
	6.1.2 When asked either orally or in writing (CN) to indicate what members should do when their ideas are questioned by the group, name positive reactions that help ensure cooperative group interaction (B). Learner should name at least three possible reactions (CR).
6.2 Classify member actions as cooperative behaviors.	6.2.1 Given written descriptions of a group member's actions during a meeting (CN), indicate whether the actions are cooperative behaviors (B). Learner should classify correctly at least 80 percent of the actions demonstrated (CR).
	6.2.2 Given videos of staged problem-solving meetings depicting members' actions (CN), indicate whether the actions are cooperative (B). Learner should classify correctly at least 80 percent of the actions demonstrated (CR).
6.3 Name strategies for encouraging member cooperation.	6.3.1 When asked in writing to name leader actions that encourage and stifle member discussion and cooperation (CN), name these actions (B). Learner should name at least ten encouraging and corresponding stifling actions (CR).
6.4 Classify strategies for encouraging cooperation.	6.4.1 Given written descriptions of group leader's actions during a meeting (CN), indicate whether the actions are likely to encourage or stifle cooperative group interaction (B). Learner should correctly classify at least 80 percent of the actions depicted (CR).
	6.4.2 Given videos of staged meetings depicting staged leader's actions (CN), indicate whether the leader's actions are likely to encourage or stifle member cooperation (B). Learner should classify correctly at least 80 percent of both the encouraging and corresponding stifling actions demonstrated (CR).
6.5 Engender cooperative member behaviors.	6.5.1 In simulated problem-solving meetings with learner acting as group leader (CN), initiate actions to engender cooperative behavior among members (B). Group members cooperate with each other and with leader during discussion (CR).

Intellectual Skills In the intellectual skills examples (e.g., 6.2.1 and 6.2.2 for skill 6.2), notice that the conditions part of the objective is similar to that used in the verbal information objectives. Not only is key terminology included (e.g., "group member's actions during a meeting"), but the manner in which these actions is presented is prescribed as well (e.g., "written descriptions of group actions"; "videos of staged meetings depicting members' actions"). In objective 6.5.1, there are no key terms stated in the conditions; however, the examination will take place in "simulated problem-solving meetings with learner acting as group leader." Notice that the conditions in these three intellectual skills help prescribe the complexity of the task. Detecting positive leader and member actions is probably easier in a written script than in a video of interactive dialogue, which is probably easier than detecting the same actions when you are *ego involved*—leading the meeting yourself and processing the verbal and nonverbal behaviors of colleagues you are actively facilitating. Notice that the behaviors in the subordinate skills and corresponding objectives are congruent. Even when alternative terms are used, the skill demonstrated is the one prescribed in the subordinate skill. Notice the criteria included in these objectives. In subordinate objectives 6.2.1 and 6.2.2, the learner is required to locate 80 percent of the cooperative behaviors demonstrated in the scenarios and videos. However, the criterion for objective 6.5.1 is that members within the leader's interactive groups must cooperate with each other and with the leader. In other words, the behavior of members within the group provides evidence of the leader's success.

Professional and Historical Perspectives

As stated earlier, Mager (1997) first used the term *behavioral objective* in 1975 to emphasize that it is a statement describing what the student will be able to do. During the late 1960s and the 1970s, workshops were set up for public school teachers throughout the country. Thousands of teachers were trained to write behavioral objectives to become accountable for their instruction. Two major difficulties emerged, however, when the process of defining objectives was not included as an integral part of a total instructional design model.

First, without such a model, it was difficult for instructors to determine how to derive objectives. Although instructors could master the mechanics of writing an objective, there was no conceptual base for guiding their derivation. As a result, many teachers reverted to the tables of contents in textbooks to identify topics for which they would write behavioral objectives.

The second and perhaps more critical concern was what to do with the objectives after they were written. Many instructors were simply told to incorporate objectives into their instruction to become better teachers. In reality, most objectives were written and then placed in desk drawers, never to affect the instructional process.

Objections to the use of behavioral objectives have been raised. For example, detractors can point to the seemingly trivial objectives in some instructional materials. However, these objectives typically are not based on a carefully conducted instructional analysis illustrating the relationship of each new skill to ones previously acquired. Similarly, many educators acknowledge that writing objectives in areas such as humanities or interpersonal relations is more difficult than in other disciplines. However, because instructors in these disciplines usually are required to assess learner performance and communicate acceptability (e.g., grades, personnel evaluations), the development of objectives supports these instructors by taking them through the following tasks: (1) specifying the skills, knowledge, and attitudes they will teach; (2) determining the strategy for instruction; and (3) establishing criteria for evaluating student performance when instruction ends.

Although some instructors might see objectives as detrimental to free-flowing classroom discussion, they actually serve as a check on the relevance of discussion. Objectives also can increase the accuracy of communication among instructors who must coordinate their instruction. Statements describing what learners should be able to do when they complete their instruction provide a clear framework for what should be covered, thus helping to prevent instructional gaps or duplication. Objectives can also indicate to parents or supervisors what students or employees are being taught. General course goals, which are often used for this purpose, may sound interesting and challenging but seldom indicate what it is that learners will know or be able to do when instruction is completed.

Researchers have investigated whether using objectives makes any difference in learning outcomes. In almost all the research studies, this question has been asked in the context of an operational instructional setting. In a typical experiment, one group of students receives a sequence of instruction preceded by statements of what they should be able to do when they complete the instruction. A control group receives the same instructional materials but without the statements of the instructional objectives. The results have been ambiguous. Some studies have shown significant differences in learning for those students who receive objectives; other studies have shown no differences. Summary analyses of the research findings indicate a slight but significant advantage for students who are informed of the objectives for their instruction.

Although these investigations are of interest, they do not address the importance of objectives in the process of designing instruction. Objectives guide the designer in tailoring the complexity level of instruction for specific learners, selecting content, developing the instructional strategy, and creating the assessment process. Objectives are critical to the design of instruction, regardless of whether they are presented to learners during instruction.

Process Flowcharts

Writing Performance Objectives

This section contains one main flowchart: writing terminal and performance objectives. Notice that both the terminal and performance objectives contain conditions, performance, and criteria.

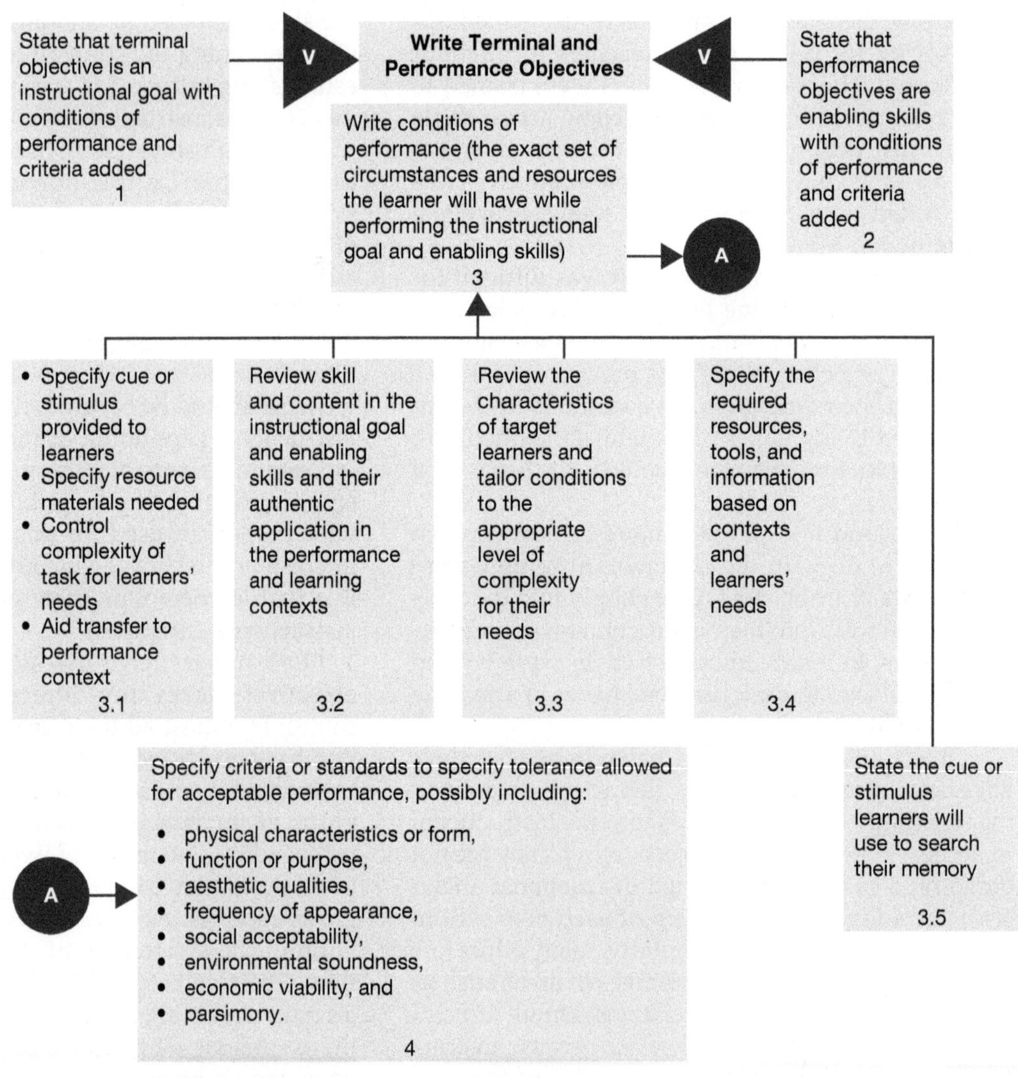

Figure 6.1 Write Terminal and Performance Objectives

Practice

Judge the completeness of given performance objectives. Read each of the following objectives and determine whether it includes conditions, behaviors, and a criterion. If any element is missing, choose the part(s) omitted.

1. Given a list of activities carried on by the early settlers of North America, understand what goods they produced, what product resources they used, and what trading they did.
   a. Important conditions and criterion
   b. Observable behavior and important conditions
   c. Observable behavior and criterion
   d. Nothing
2. Given a list of states and capitals, match at least thirty-five of the fifty states with their capitals without the use of maps, charts, or lists.
   a. Observable response
   b. Important conditions
   c. Criterion performance
   d. Nothing
3. During daily business transactions with customers, know company policies for delivering friendly and courteous service.
   a. Observable behavior
   b. Important conditions
   c. Criterion performance
   d. Both a and b
   e. a and c
4. Students will be able to play the piano.
   a. Important conditions
   b. Important conditions and criterion performance
   c. Observable behavior and criterion performance
   d. Nothing
5. Given daily access to music in the office, choose to listen to classical music at least half the time.
   a. Important conditions
   b. Observable behavior
   c. Criterion performance
   d. Nothing

Convert instructional goals and subordinate skills into terminal and subordinate objectives. It is important to remember that *objectives* are derived from the instructional goal and subordinate skills analyses. Demonstrate conversion of the goal and subordinate skills in the goal analysis by doing the following:

6. Create a terminal objective from the instructional goal:

   In written composition, (1) use a variety of sentence types and accompanying punctuation based on the purpose and mood of the sentence, and (2) use a variety of sentence types and accompanying punctuation based on the complexity or structure of the sentence.
7. Write performance objectives for the following subordinate skills:

   5.6 State the purpose of a declarative sentence: to convey information.

   5.7 Classify a complete sentence as a declarative sentence.

   5.11 Write declarative sentences with correct closing punctuation.

Evaluate performance objectives. Use the rubric in this chapter as an aid to developing and evaluating your own objectives.

8. Indicate your perceptions of the quality of your objectives by inserting the number of the objective in either the Yes or No column of the rubric checklist to reflect your judgment. Examine those objectives receiving No ratings and plan ways the objectives should be revised. Based on your analysis, revise your objectives to correct ambiguities and omissions.

Feedback

1. c
2. d
3. e
4. b
5. d

6–7. Examine the sample terminal objective and performance objectives for the subordinate skills in the writing composition case study in Appendix E.

8. Evaluate your goal elaborations, terminal objectives, and performance objectives using the rubric in this chapter. If you want further feedback on the clarity and completeness of performance objectives you have written, ask a colleague for a critique using the rubric.

References and Recommended Reading

Anderson, L. W., Krathwohl, D. R., Airasian, P. W., Cruikshank, K. A., Mayer, R. E., Pintrich, P. R., Raths, J., & Wittrock, M. C. (2001). *A taxonomy for learning, teaching, and assessing: A revision of Bloom's taxonomy of educational objectives.* Pearson. Revises some terminology from Bloom's original work and presents a two-dimensional matrix framework for relating knowledge outcomes to the hierarchy of cognitive processes.

Brown, A. H., & Green, T. D. (2020). *Instructional design: Connecting fundamental principles with process and practice*. Routledge. This text has good content on writing objectives in a training and development context.

Caviler, J. C., & Klein, J. D. (1998). Effects of cooperative versus individual learning and orienting activities during computer-based instruction. *Educational Technology Research and Development*, *46*(1), 5–17. Demonstrates the effectiveness of providing objectives to learners.

Combs, K. L., Gibson, S. K., Hays, J. M., Saly, J., & Wendt, J. T. (2008). Enhancing curriculum and delivery: Linking assessment to learning objectives.

Assessment and Evaluation in Higher Education, 33(1), 87–102. Argues for accurate statements of objectives that enable a more valid assessment of learning and progress.

Gagné, R. M., Wager, W. W., Golas, K. C., & Keller, J. M. (2004). *Principles of instructional design* (5th ed.). Wadsworth/Thomson Learning. Describes a five-part performance objective and relates objectives to the various domains of learning.

Gronlund, N. E., & Brookhart, S. M. (2008). *Writing instructional objectives* (8th ed.). Pearson. Describes the derivation of objectives for various types and levels of learning and their use in teaching and classroom assessment.

Mager, R. F. (1997). *Preparing instructional objectives* (3rd ed.). Center for Effective Performance. The latest edition of Mager's 1962 book on objectives. Mager's humor is well served by the branching programmed-instruction format.

Marken, J., & Morrison, G. (2013). Objectives over time: A look at four decades of objectives in the educational research literature. *Contemporary Educational Technology, 4*(1), 1–14. Tracks changes in the term *objectives,* finding that more operational definitions are currently used.

Mayer, R. E. (2011). *Applying the science of learning.* Pearson. Describes three levels of instructional objectives, different kinds of knowledge depicted in instructional objectives, and linkage among learning, instruction, and assessment.

Roberts, W. K. (1982). Preparing instructional objectives: Usefulness revisited. *Educational Technology, 22*(7), 15–19. Presents and evaluates varied approaches to writing objectives.

chapter 7

Developing Assessment Instruments

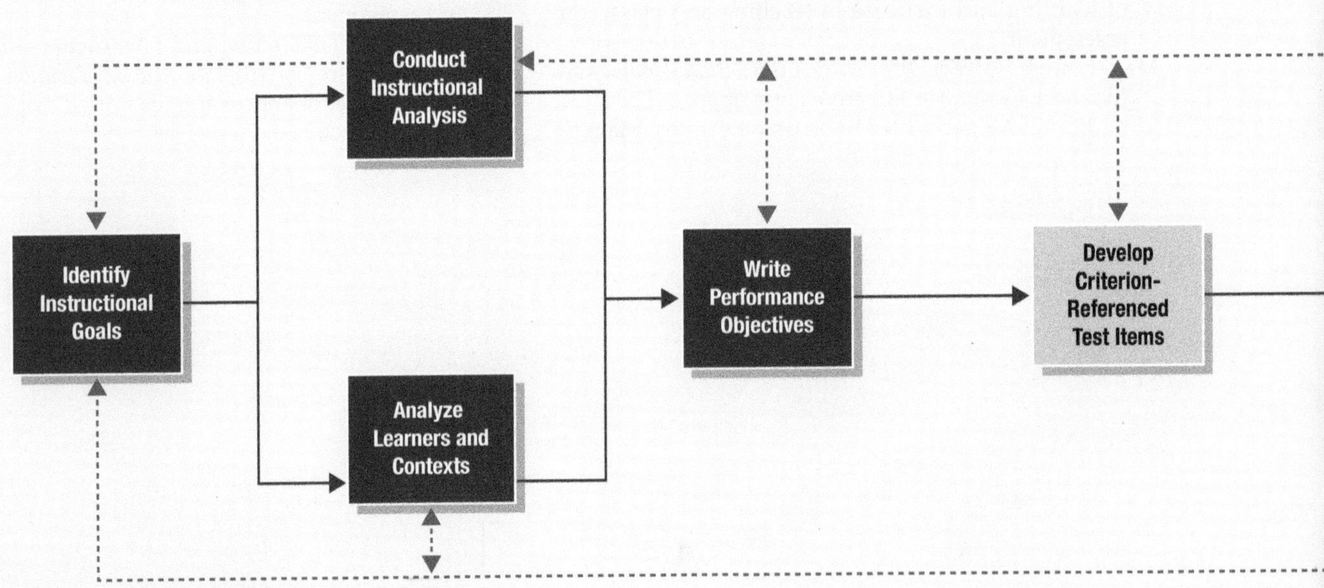

Objectives

- Write criterion-referenced, objective-style test items that meet four categories of quality criteria.
- Create rubrics for product development, live performance, and attitude assessments; develop instructions to guide learners' work.
- Evaluate the congruence among instructional goals, subordinate skills, learner and context analyses, performance objectives, and criterion-referenced test items.

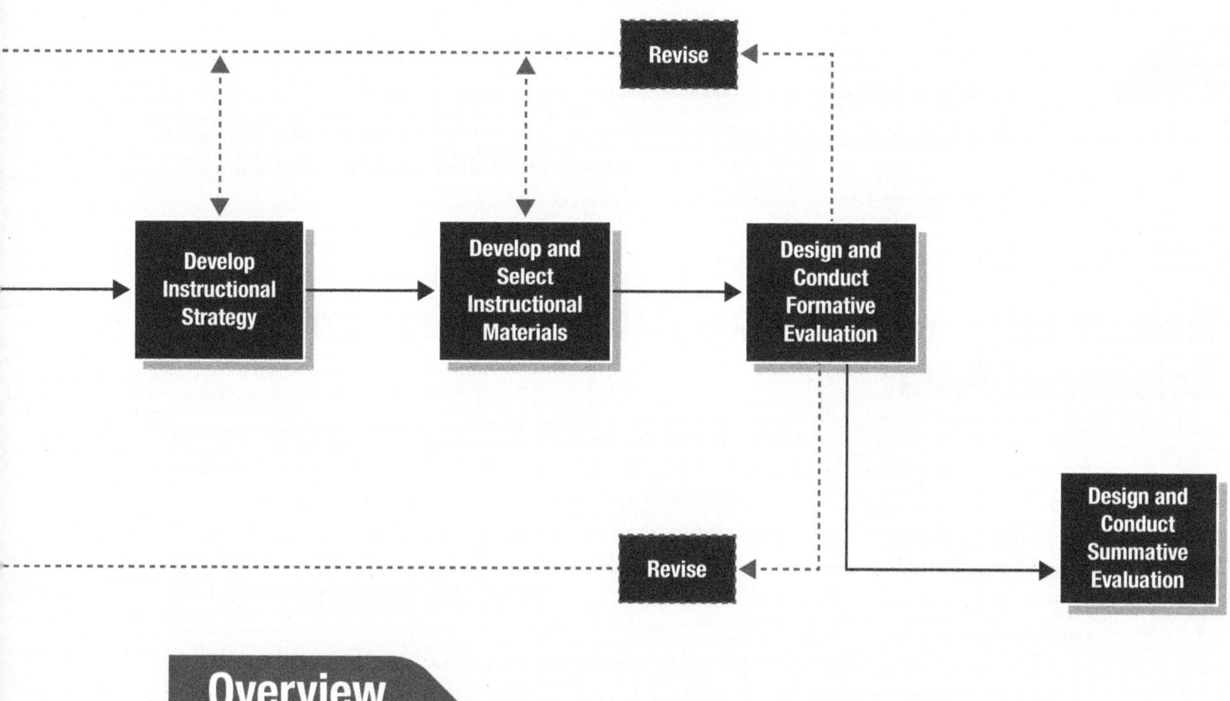

Overview

Criterion-referenced tests are designed to measure performance on an explicit set of performance objectives. In order to develop criterion-referenced tests, you need the list of performance objectives based on the instructional analysis. The conditions, behavior, and criteria contained in each objective help you determine the best format for your assessment instrument.

The term *objective* within the terms *objective test* and *performance objective* are not related. Performance objectives were defined in Chapter 6. Objective tests refer to the format of a test, and they include items that require a short answer of some type. The most common objective test item formats are multiple choice, matching, alternative response, and short answer. An objective test format is best for many verbal information and intellectual skill objectives; however, you still must decide what objective-style item format is most congruent with the prescribed conditions and behaviors. You must also decide how many items are necessary to measure adequately learner performance on each objective by considering how many times the information or skill will be tested. Enough items to support the construction of pretests, practice tests if required, and posttests should be produced. Some intellectual skills cannot be measured using objective test items, such as writing a paragraph, making a persuasive speech, and analyzing and contrasting certain features of two different methods for predicting economic trends. Intellectual skills that result in a product or a performance, psychomotor skills, and behaviors related to attitudes should be measured using tests that consist of instructions for the learner and an observation instrument for the evaluator. In creating these product, performance, or behavior instruments, you must identify, paraphrase, and sequence the observable elements of the product, performance, or behavior.

Before moving forward with your design, it is important to pause at this point to evaluate the congruence between your goals, terminal objectives, subordinate skills, and test items. These elements must be congruent in order for test results to reflect desired information about the quality of instruction and learner achievement related to the instructional goal.

Concepts

We should begin this section by defining and comparing four main types of achievement tests: learner-centered assessment, criterion-referenced tests, objective-referenced tests, and norm-referenced tests.

Learner-Centered, Objective-Referenced, and Criterion-Referenced Tests

These three types of assessments are far more similar than different in terms of format and purpose. Achievement testing remains at the forefront of the school-reform movement in the United States, and learner-centered assessment permeates the school-reform literature. Learner-centered assessment tasks are expected to function as learning events, and in this model, learners are encouraged to engage in self-assessment on their path to assuming responsibility for the quality of their own work.

The definitions of *learner-centered assessment* are congruent with traditional definitions of **criterion-referenced testing**, a central element of systematically designed instruction. Learner-centered assessments are to be *criterion-referenced* (i.e., linked to instructional goals and an explicit set of performance objectives derived from the goals). This type of testing is important for evaluating both learners' progress and instructional quality. The results of criterion-referenced tests indicate to the instructor exactly how well learners were able to achieve each instructional objective, and they indicate to the designer exactly which components of the instruction worked well and which must be revised. Moreover, criterion-referenced tests enable learners to reflect on their own performances by applying established criteria to judge their own work.

In *criterion-referenced assessment,* there is usually an instrument composed of items or performance tasks that directly measure skills described in one or more performance objectives. The term *criterion* is used because assessment items serve as a benchmark to determine the adequacy of a learner's performance in meeting the objectives; that is, success on these assessments determines whether a learner has achieved the objectives in the instructional unit. Increasingly, the term *objective-referenced* is being used rather than *criterion-referenced* in order to be more explicit in indicating the relationship between assessments and performance objectives. Assessment items or tasks are tied directly to the performance described in the objective for the instructional materials. You may therefore consider these three terms—*learner-centered, objective-referenced,* and *criterion-referenced*—essentially synonymous for all practical purposes.

Criterion-Referenced and Norm-Referenced Tests

Norm-referenced tests are quite different in form and purpose than the previous three discussed. It is important to distinguish between criterion-referenced and norm-referenced tests. The two types of tests differ in their central purposes, and the purpose determines the manner in which they are designed, constructed, administered, and interpreted. Norm-referenced tests are used to compare the relative performance of learners in large areas of content, such as a year's content within a specific subject area—for example, mathematics or reading. Using data from norm-referenced tests, we cannot learn exactly what skills John and Mary achieved, but we do know how much more or less they know than each other or than others their age or at their grade level.

In contrast, the main purpose for a criterion-referenced test is to examine a person's or group's achievement in a carefully defined content area; thus, it is focused on specific goals and objectives within a given content area. One type of testing is not superior to the other; each is appropriate for the decisions to be made from the resulting test data. Many of us have seen test companies report both criterion-referenced data and norm-referenced data from the same test. Instructional designers must know that this is more a decision based on how the testing data will be used than anything else, and they should be well versed in the purposes of these tests and the decisions that can be made validly from them.

Instructional designers regularly use data from both types of tests. They use norm-referenced tests to describe learners' general achievement and ability levels using terms such as *above average* (compared to their peers), *average*, or *below average* in a given subject area. Using criterion-referenced tests, we learn exactly which skills within a content area John and Mary have learned. Data from norm-referenced tests are not useful for instructional design and development, but they are useful for selecting students for field-trial groups when developing instructional materials. In contrast, criterion-referenced tests are the backbone of the assessment used for decision making in the development and evaluation of particular instruction. For this reason, we focus on criterion-referenced testing in this text.

Four Types of Criterion-Referenced Tests and Their Uses

The four types of criterion-referenced tests differ by purpose rather than format. There are four types of tests the designer may create: the entry skills test, the pretest, the practice or rehearsal test, and the posttest. These tests may take many formats, from paper-and-pencil objective tests to a product rating scale or an actual physical performance. The most appropriate test format is the one best suited for assessing the performance specified in the objective. Each of these test types has a unique function in designing and delivering instruction. Let's look at each type of test from the viewpoint of the person who is designing instruction. What purposes do they serve within the instructional design process?

Entry Skills Tests The first type of test, an entry skills test, is given to learners before they begin instruction. These criterion-referenced tests assess learners' mastery of **prerequisite skills**, or skills that learners must have already mastered before beginning instruction. Prerequisite skills appear below the dotted line on the instructional analysis chart. If there are entry skills for an instructional unit, test items should be developed and used with learners during the formative evaluation.

It may be found that, as the theory suggests, learners lacking these skills have great difficulty with the instruction. In contrast, it may be found that, for some reason, the entry skills are not critical to success in the instruction. It should be noted that if there are no significant entry skills identified during the instructional analysis, then there is no need to develop corresponding objectives and test items.

Also, if some skills are more questionable than others in terms of being already mastered by the target population, then it is these questionable skills that should be assessed on the entry skills test.

Pretests The purpose of a pretest is not necessarily to show a gain in learning after instruction by comparison with a posttest but rather to profile the learners with regard to the instructional analysis. The pretest is administered to learners before they begin instruction for the sake of efficiency—to determine whether they have previously mastered some or all of the skills to be included in the instruction. If all the skills have been mastered, then the instruction is not needed. However, if the skills have only been partially mastered, then pretest data enable the designer to be more efficient in the creation of instruction. Perhaps only a review or a reminder is needed for some skills, saving time-consuming direct instruction with examples and rehearsal for the remainder.

Designers have some latitude in determining which enabling skills to include on a pretest, and they must use their judgment in selecting the objectives that are most important to test. Deciding which skills to include is probably unique to each instructional goal and particular context. The pretest typically includes one or more items for key skills identified in the instructional analysis, including the instructional goal.

Because both entry skills tests and pretests are administered prior to instruction, they are often combined into one instrument, which does not, however, make them the same test. Different items assess different skills from the instructional goal diagram, and the designer makes different decisions based on learners' scores from the two sets of items. From entry skills test scores, designers decide whether learners are ready to begin the instruction; from pretest scores, they decide whether the instruction is too elementary for the learners and, if not too elementary, how to develop instruction most efficiently for a particular group.

Should you always administer a pretest covering the skills to be taught? Sometimes it is not necessary. If you are teaching a topic that you know is new to your target population and if their performance on a pretest would result in only random guessing, it is probably not advisable to have a pretest. A pretest is valuable only when it is likely that some of the learners have partial knowledge of the content. If time for testing is a problem, it is possible to design an abbreviated pretest that assesses the terminal objective and several key subordinate objectives.

Practice Tests The purpose of practice tests is to provide active learner participation during instruction. Practice tests enable learners to rehearse new knowledge and skills and to judge for themselves their level of understanding and skill. Instructors use students' responses to practice tests to provide corrective feedback and to monitor the pace of instruction. Practice tests contain fewer skills than either the pretest or posttest, and they are typically focused at the lesson rather than the unit level.

Posttests Posttests are administered following instruction, and they are parallel to pretests, except they do not include items on entry skills. Similar to the pretest, the posttest measures objectives included in the instruction. As for all the tests described here, the designer should be able to link the skill (or skills) being tested with its corresponding item on the posttest.

Related to selecting skills from the instructional goal analysis, the posttest should assess all the objectives, especially focusing on the terminal objective. Again, as with the pretest, the posttest may be quite long if it measures all the subordinate skills, and it may be more comprehensive in terms of having more items on more of the skills in the instructional goal analysis. If time is a factor and a briefer test must be developed, then the terminal objective and important subskills should be tested. Items should be included to test those subskills that are most likely to give learners problems on the terminal objective.

Table 7.1 Test Types, Design Decisions, and the Objectives Typically Tested

Test Type	Designer's Decision	Objectives Typically Tested
Entry skills test	• Are target learners ready to enter instruction? • Do learners possess the required prerequisite skills?	• Prerequisite skills or those skills below the dotted line in the instructional analysis
Pretests	• Have learners previously mastered the enabling skills? • Which particular skills have they previously mastered? • How can I most efficiently develop this instruction?	• Terminal objectives • Main steps from the goal analysis
Practice tests	• Are students acquiring the intended knowledge and skills? • What errors and misconceptions are they forming? • Is instruction clustered appropriately? • Is the pace of instruction appropriate for the learners?	• Knowledge and skills for a subset of objectives within the goal • Scope typically at the lesson rather than the unit level
Posttests	• Have learners achieved the terminal objective? • Is the instruction more or less effective for each main step and for each subordinate skill? • Where should instruction be revised? • Have learners mastered the intended information, skills, and attitudes?	• The terminal objective • Main steps and their subordinate skills

Eventually, the posttest may be used to assess learner performance and to assign credit for successful completion of a program or course; however, the initial purpose for the posttest is to help the designer identify the areas of the instruction that are not working. If a student fails to perform the terminal objective, the designer should be able to identify where in the learning process the student began not to understand the instruction. By examining whether each item is answered correctly and linking the correct and incorrect responses to the anchor subordinate skill, the designer should be able to do exactly that.

All four types of tests are intended for use during the instructional design process. After the formative evaluation of the instruction has been completed, however, it may be desirable to drop part or all of the entry skills test and the pretest. It would also be appropriate to modify the posttest to measure only the terminal objective. In essence, much less time would be spent on testing when the design and development of the instruction is complete. A summary of the test types, design decisions, and the objectives typically included on each type of test is included in Table 7.1.

Criterion-Referenced Test Design

How does one go about designing and developing a criterion-referenced test? A primary consideration is matching the learning domain with an item or assessment task type. Objectives in the verbal information domain typically require objective-style test items, including formats such as short-answer, alternative response, matching, and multiple-choice items. It is relatively easy to examine learners' verbal information responses, whether written or oral, and judge whether they have mastered a verbal information objective. Learners either recall the appropriate information or they do not.

Objectives in the intellectual skills domain are more complex, and they generally require either objective-style test items, the creation of a product (e.g., musical score, research paper, widget), or a live performance of some type (e.g., conduct an orchestra, act in a play, conduct a business meeting). At higher levels of intellectual skills, it is more difficult to create an assessment item or task, and it is more difficult to judge the adequacy of a response. What if an objective requires the learner to create a unique solution or product? It is then necessary to write directions for the learner to follow, establish a set of criteria for judging response quality, and convert the criteria into a checklist or rating scale, often called a *rubric,* that can be used to assess whether the characteristics of an adequate response are present in the student's product.

Assessment in the attitudinal domain can also be complex. Affective objectives are generally concerned with the learner's attitudes or preferences. Usually, there is no direct way to measure a person's attitudes (e.g., whether they support diversity within the organization). Items for attitudinal objectives generally require either that the learners state their preferences or that the instructor observes the learners' behavior and infers their attitudes from their actions. For example, if learners voluntarily engage in advocacy for the promotion of minority employees on three different occasions, the instructor may infer that they support diversity. From these stated preferences or observed behaviors, inferences about attitudes can be made.

Test items for objectives in the psychomotor domain are usually sets of directions on how to demonstrate the tasks, and they typically require the learner to perform a sequence of steps that collectively represents the instructional goal. Moreover, criteria for acceptable performances must be identified and converted into a checklist or rating scale that the instructor uses to indicate whether each step is executed properly. The checklist can be developed directly from the skills and execution qualities identified in the instructional analysis. The designer may also wish to test the subordinate skills for the motor skills. Often, these are intellectual skills or verbal information that can be tested using an objective-item format before having the student perform the psychomotor skill. On occasion, the performance of a psychomotor skill, such as making a ceramic pot, results in the creation of a product. It is possible to develop a list of criteria for judging the adequacy of this product.

Mastery Levels

For each performance objective you write, there must be a criterion level specified that indicates how well the learner must perform the skill described in the objective on the assessments you provide. In essence, the criterion indicates the mastery level required of the learner. The concept of **mastery level**, as opposed to *criterion level,* is more often applied to a test for an entire unit of instruction or an entire course. An instructor may state that, in order for learners to "master" this unit, they must achieve a certain level of performance. The question remains "How do you determine what the mastery level should be?"

Researchers who work with mastery learning systems suggest that *mastery* is equivalent to the level of performance usually expected from the best learners. This method of defining mastery is clearly norm-referenced (i.e., a group comparison method), but sometimes it may be the only standard that can reasonably be used.

A second approach to mastery is one that is primarily statistical. If designers want to make sure that learners "really know" a skill before they go on to the next instructional unit, then sufficient opportunities should be provided to perform the skill so that it is nearly impossible for correct performance to be the result of chance alone. When multiple-choice test items are used, it is fairly simple to compute the probability that any given number of correct answers to a set of items could be the result of mere chance. With other types of test items, it is more difficult to compute the probability of chance performance but easier to convince others that performance is not just a matter of chance. Simply exceeding the chance level of performance, however, may not be a very demanding mastery level. Setting it higher than chance often is a rather arbitrary decision.

An ideal mastery level is one defined by an exact and explicit level of performance that defines mastery. It might be argued that in order for soldiers to learn to send encoded messages, they must be able to spell standard military terms. In this circumstance, a mastery level of 100 percent for a unit on spelling military terms is not entirely arbitrary. It is based on the criticality of the skill in question to the learning of subsequent skills. The greater the relationship between the two, the higher the mastery level should be set. As a general principle, mastery level for any performance should be considered with respect to both evaluating the performance at that point in time and enhancing the learning of subsequent related skills in the unit or in the rest of the course.

In some situations, the best definition of *mastery* is the level required to be successful on the job. With many complex skills there is a continuum of performance, with the novice or beginner at one end and the experienced expert at the other. What level is required in the workplace or on the transfer task that the learner is eventually expected to perform? The performance context analysis can yield useful information regarding the expected level of performance and can be used in the design of the criterion-referenced assessment process. If no one is currently using the skills, then managers or subject-matter experts must use their professional judgment to estimate mastery levels. If the levels prove to be unrealistic, they can be adjusted in the future.

Test Item Criteria

Regardless of the type of learning involved in the objective, appropriate test item writing techniques should be applied to the development of criterion-referenced tests. There are four categories of test item qualities to consider during the creation of test items and assessment tasks: goal-centered criteria, learner-centered criteria, context-centered criteria, and assessment-centered criteria. We consider each category next.

Goal-Centered Criteria Test items and tasks should be congruent with the terminal and performance objectives in terms of behavior (action and concepts), conditions, and criteria.

Behavior. They should match the behavior, including the action and concepts, prescribed. To match the response required in a test item to the behavior specified in the objective, the designer should consider the learning task or verb prescribed in the objective. Objectives that ask the student to *state* or *define, perform with guidance,* or *perform independently* require a different format for questions and responses.

It is critical that test items measure the exact behavior described in the objective. For example, if an objective indicates that a student be able to match descriptions of certain concepts with certain labels, then the test items must include descriptions of concepts and a set of labels that the student is asked to match. Let's look at an example.

Objective: Given a scale marked off in tenths and asked to identify designated points on the scale, write the values of the designated points in decimal form in units of tenths.

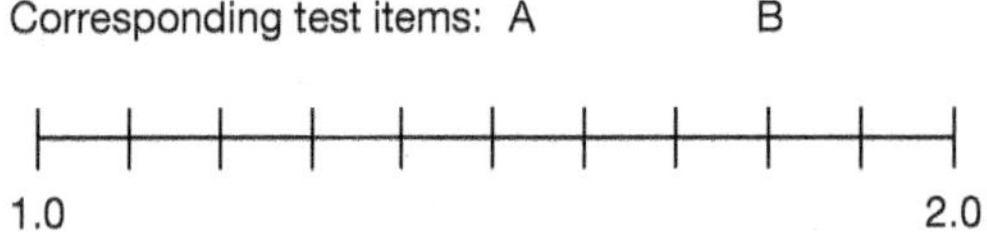

_____ 1. In tenths of units, what point on the scale is indicated at the letter A?
_____ 2. In tenths of units, what point on the scale is indicated at the letter B?

You can see in this example that the objective requires the learner to read exact points on a scale that is divided into units of one-tenth. The test item provides the learner with such a scale and two letters that lie at specified points on the scale, for which the learner must indicate the value of each in tenths.

You will encounter more illustrations similar to this in the Examples, Case Study, and Practice sections. It is important to note carefully the behavior described by the verb of the objective. If the verb is to *match,* to *list,* to *select,* or to *describe,* then you must provide a test item that allows a student to match, list, select, or describe. The objective determines the nature of the item. You do not arbitrarily decide to use a particular item format such as multiple choice. Test and item format depend on the wording of your objectives.

Conditions. Test items and tasks should meet the conditions specified in the objective. If a special item format, equipment, simulations, or resources are prescribed, they should be created for the assessment. An open-book examination differs greatly from an examination in which reference material is forbidden. The expected conditions of performance included in the performance objective serve as a guide to the test item writer.

Criteria. Test items and tasks should provide learners with the opportunity to meet the criteria necessary to demonstrate mastery of an objective. One must determine the number of items required for judging mastery of each objective assessed and whether all the required criteria are included on the checklist or rating scale.

The performance objective also includes the criteria used to judge mastery of a skill. No absolute rule states that performance criteria should or should not be provided to learners. Sometimes it is necessary for them to know performance criteria, and sometimes it is not. Learners usually assume that in order to receive credit for a question, they must answer it correctly.

Note that an assessment for the terminal objective should also be created. Consider how to respond if someone asks how learners demonstrate that they achieved your instructional goal. What can you ask learners to do to demonstrate that they have reached mastery? The answer should describe an assessment that requires the learner to use the major steps in the goal successfully. Typically, there are also separate assessments for each step in the process to determine, as the instruction proceeds, whether learners are mastering each step as it is taught.

Learner-Centered Criteria Test items and assessment tasks must be tailored to the characteristics and needs of the learners, including such considerations as vocabulary and language levels; familiarity of contexts, experiences, and backgrounds; developmental levels for setting appropriate task complexity; motivational and interest levels; special needs; freedom from bias (e.g., cultural, racial, gender); and self-evaluation.

The vocabulary used in the directions for completing a question and in the question itself should be appropriate for the intended learners. Test items should not be written at the vocabulary level of the designer unless that level is the same as that expected for the target learners. Learners should not miss questions because of unfamiliar terms. If the definitions of certain terms are a prerequisite for performing the skill, then such definitions should be included in the instruction. The omission of necessary terms and definitions is a common error.

Another consideration related to familiarity of contexts and experiences is that learners should not miss an item or task because they are asked to perform it in an unfamiliar context or are using an unfamiliar assessment format. Items made unnecessarily difficult by placing the desired performance in an unfamiliar setting not only test the desired behavior but also test additional unrelated behaviors as well. Although this is a common practice, it is an inappropriate item-writing technique. The more unfamiliar the examples, question types, response formats, and test-administration procedures, the more difficult successful completion of the test becomes. One example of this "staged" difficulty is creating problems using contrived and unfamiliar situations. The setting of the problem, whether at the beach, the store, the school, or the office, should be familiar to the target group. Learners can better demonstrate skills using a familiar topic rather than an unfamiliar one. If an item is made unnecessarily difficult, it may hamper accurate assessment of the behavior in question.

An exception to this guideline regarding unfamiliar contexts when assessing higher-order intellectual skills, some psychomotor skills, and some attitudes applies when the successful transfer of newly learned skills into unencountered performance contexts is the goal of the instruction. Even in this circumstance, however, the test item should be situated in a logical performance context for the new skill, and strategies for analyzing and adapting to unencountered contexts should be included in the instruction.

The developmental level, motivation, and interests are all important considerations in designing for particular groups. The ability and maturity of learners dictate how appropriate or complex the same task can be for learners when presented in various formats. Tasks embedded in material that is interesting to the learner will be easier than those presented in ways that are uninteresting to them.

The area of special needs is also a consideration, and there are many areas of special needs. Are the learners, even adults, nonreaders? Do they have test anxiety? Must they have quiet conditions to concentrate? Do they have physical or mental challenges that will impact the practicality of some test and item formats? Each group of learners is different, and designers should learn all they can about their learners' special needs before creating test items and tasks.

Designers must also create tasks and items that are free from bias. They must be sensitive to issues of gender and diversity in creating items and tasks. Items that are biased—either on the surface or statistically against any particular group—are not only inappropriate but unethical as well.

Finally, designers should consider how to aid learners in becoming evaluators of their own work and performances. Self-evaluation and self-refinement are two of the main goals of learner-centered assessment and of all instruction for that matter because they can lead to independent learning. Providing rubrics within the instruction and encouraging learners to use them for self-evaluation as they learn should increase their understanding and skill.

Context-Centered Criteria In creating test items and assessment tasks, designers must consider the eventual performance setting as well as the learning or classroom environment. Test items and tasks must be authentic to the learning and performance context, be feasible in the learning environment, and have adequate resources. Test items should be as realistic or authentic to the actual performance setting as possible. This criterion helps ensure transfer of the knowledge and skills from the learning to the performance environment.

Feasibility and resources in the learning environment are often a consideration as well. Sometimes the learning setting fails to contain the equipment necessary to reproduce exact performance conditions, and designers must be creative in their attempts to provide conditions as close to reality as possible. The more realistic the testing environment, the more valid the learners' responses. For example, if the behavior is to be performed in front of an audience, then an audience should be present for the exam.

Assessment-Centered Criteria Learners can be nervous during assessment, and well-constructed, professional-looking items and assessment tasks can make the assessment more palatable to them. Test-writing qualities focusing on **assessment-centered criteria** include clearly written and parsimonious directions, correct grammar, correct spelling, correct punctuation, accurate resource materials, and direct, clear questions.

There are also many rules for formatting each type of objective test item, product and performance directions, and rubric. These rules are most often related to producing the clearest item and assessment tasks possible. Ideally, learners should err because they do not possess the skill, not because the test item or assessment is convoluted and confusing. Designers who are unfamiliar with formatting rules for items and directions should consult criterion-referenced measurement texts that elaborate formatting rules for assessments.

Mastery Criteria

In constructing the test, a major question that always arises is "What is the proper number of items needed to determine mastery of an objective?" How many items must learners answer correctly to be judged successful on a particular objective? If learners answer one item correctly, can you assume they have achieved the objective? Or if they miss a single item, are you sure they have not mastered the concept? Perhaps if you gave the learners ten items per objective and they answered them all correctly or missed them all, you would have more confidence in your assessment. There are some practical suggestions that may help you determine the number of test items an objective requires. If the item or test requires a response format that enables the student to guess the answer correctly, then perhaps several parallel test items for the same objective should be included. If the likelihood of guessing the correct answer is slim, however, then you may decide that one or two items are sufficient to determine the student's ability to perform the skill.

If you examine the question of the number of items in terms of the learning domain of the objective, it is easier to be more specific. To assess intellectual skills, it is usually necessary to provide three or more opportunities to demonstrate the skill. With verbal information, however, only one item is needed to retrieve the specific information from memory. If the information objective covers a wide range of knowledge (e.g., identify state capitals), then the designer must select a random sample of the instances and assume that student performance represents the proportion of the verbal information objective that has been mastered. In the case of psychomotor skills, there also is typically only one way to test the skill—ask the student to perform the skill for the evaluator. The goal may require the student to perform the skill under several different conditions. These should be represented in repeated performances of the psychomotor skill.

Test Item Format and Performance Objectives

Another important question to consider is "What type of test item or assessment task best assesses learner performance?" The behavior specified in the objective provides clues to the type of item or task that can be used to test the performance.

Table 7.2 Type of Behavior and Related Test Item Types

Type of Behavior Stated in Objective	Types of Test Items: COMPLETION	SHORT ANSWER	MATCHING	MULTIPLE-CHOICE	ESSAY	PRODUCT DEVELOP.	LIVE PERFORM.
State/Name	X	X					
Define	X	X	X	X			
Identify	X	X	X	X			
Discriminate		X	X	X			
Select		X	X	X			
Locate		X	X	X			
Evaluate/Judge		X	X	X			
Solve		X	X	X	X	X	X
Discuss					X		X
Develop					X	X	X
Construct					X	X	X
Generate					X	X	X
Operate/Perform							X
Choose (attitude)							X

In Table 7.2, the column on the far left lists the types of behavior prescribed in the performance objective. Across the top are the types of test items that can be used to evaluate student performance for each type of behavior. The table includes only suggestions. The "sense" of the objective should suggest what type of assessment is most appropriate.

As the chart indicates, certain types of performance can be tested in several different ways, and some test item formats can assess specified performance better than others. For example, if it is important for learners to remember a fact, asking them to state that fact is better than requesting reactions to multiple-choice questions. Using the objective as a guide, select the type of test item that gives learners the best opportunity to demonstrate the performance specified in the objective. There are other factors to consider when selecting the best test item format. Each type of test item has its strengths and its limitations. To select the best item type from among those considered adequate, weigh such factors as the response time required by learners, the scoring time required to analyze and judge answers, the testing environment, and the probability of guessing the correct answer.

Certain item formats are inappropriate even when they speed up the testing process. It is inappropriate to use a true/false question to determine whether a student can state the correct definition of a term. Given such a choice, the student does not state from memory but discriminates between the definition presented in the test item and the one learned during instruction. In addition to being an inappropriate response format for the behavior specified in the objective, the true/false question provides learners with a fifty–fifty chance of guessing the correct response.

Test items can be altered from the "best possible" response format to one that saves testing time or scoring time, but the alternate type of question used should still provide learners with a reasonable opportunity to demonstrate the behavior prescribed in the objective. When the instruction is implemented, it is important that instructors be able to use the evaluation procedures. The designer might use one type of item during development of the instruction and then offer a wider range of item formats when the instruction is ready for widespread use.

The testing environment is also an important factor in item format selection. What equipment and facilities are available for the test situation? Can learners actually perform a skill given the conditions specified in an objective? If equipment or facilities are not available, can realistic simulations, either paper and pencil or other formats, be constructed? If simulations are not possible, will such questions as "List the steps you would take to . . ." be appropriate or adequate for your situation? The further removed the behavior in the assessment is from the behavior specified in the objective, the less accurate is the prediction that learners either can or cannot perform the behavior prescribed. Sometimes the exact performance as described in the objective is impossible to assess, and thus other, less desirable ways must be used. This is also an important consideration when the instructional strategy is developed.

Objective Tests

Objective tests include test items that are easy for learners to complete and designers to score. The answers are short and typically scored as correct or incorrect, and judging correctness of an answer is straightforward. The most common objective formats include completion, short answer, true/false, matching, and multiple choice. Test items that should be scored using a checklist or rubric, including essay items, are not considered to be objective items, and they are described in the next section on alternative assessments.

Writing Objective Test Items Whether centered on goals, learners, contexts, or assessments, designers can use all four main criteria in developing effective objective test items. These criteria were described in detail previously, and they are presented in the rubric at the end of the chapter for your convenience.

Sequencing Items There are no hard-and-fast rules that guide the order of item placement on a test of intellectual skills or verbal information, but there are suggestions that can guide placement. Final decisions are usually based on the specific testing situation and the performance to be tested.

A typical sequencing strategy for designers who must hand-score constructed responses and analyze responses within objectives is to cluster items for one objective together, regardless of item format. The only type of item excepted from this strategy is the lengthy essay question, which typically is located at the end of a test to aid learners in managing their time during the test. A test organized in this fashion is not as attractive as one organized by item format, but it is far more functional for both the learner and the instructor. It enables the learner to concentrate on one area of information and skill at a time, and it enables the instructor to analyze individual and group performance by objective without first reordering the data.

Writing Directions Tests should include clear and concise directions. Beginning a test usually causes anxiety among learners, who are judged according to their performance on the test. There should be no doubt in their minds about what they are to do to perform correctly on the test. There are usually introductory directions to an entire test and subsection directions when the item format changes.

Test directions change according to the testing situation but usually include the following:

- the test title names the content to be covered rather than simply saying "Pretest" or "Test I";
- a brief statement explaining the objectives or performance to be demonstrated;
- information about how the test will be scored, such as the amount of credit given for a partially correct answer, whether they should guess if they are unsure of the answer, and whether words must be spelled correctly to receive full credit;

- whether they should use their names or simply identify themselves as members of a group;
- whether they need anything special to respond to the test, such as number 2 pencils; machine-scorable answer sheets; a special text; or equipment such as computers, calculators, or illustrations; and
- time limits, word limits, or space limits are spelled out.

It is difficult to write clear and concise test directions. What is clear to you may be confusing to others. Write and review directions carefully to ensure that learners have all the information they need to respond correctly to the test.

Objective tests are not the only means of assessment. Next, we consider the procedures for developing alternative assessments, including live performance, product development, and attitudes.

Alternative Assessment Instruments for Performances, Products, and Attitudes

Developing alternative assessment instruments used to measure performance, products, and attitudes does not involve writing test items per se but instead requires writing directions to guide the learners' activities and constructing a rubric to frame the evaluation of the performances, products, or attitudes. Many complex intellectual skills have both process and product goals. For example, consider a course in which this textbook might be used. The instructional goal could be "Use the instructional design process to design, develop, and evaluate one hour of self-instructional materials." Students would be required to document each step in the process and produce a set of instructional materials. The instructor could assess the process by examining the students' descriptions of their use of the process and their intermediate products, such as an instructional analysis and performance objectives. A rating scale could be used to evaluate each step in the process. A separate scale could be used to evaluate the instruction that is produced.

Clearly, there are situations in which the process is the major outcome, with little concern for the product in the belief that with repeated use of the process, the products will continue to improve. In other situations, the product or result is all-important, and the process used by the learner is not critical. As the designer, you must have the skills to develop both traditional tests and novel approaches that use other forms of observation and rating-scale types of assessments. In this section, the methods to use when developing such instruments are described.

Writing Directions Directions to learners for performances and products should describe clearly what is to be done and how, including any special conditions such as resources or time limits. In writing your directions, consider the amount of guidance that should be provided. It may be desirable to remind learners to perform certain steps and to inform them of the criteria to be used in evaluating their work. In such instances (e.g., writing a project proposal, making a sales presentation), examinees can be given a copy of the evaluation checklist or rating scale used to judge their work much earlier as a part of the instruction and as part of the directions. In other circumstances (e.g., answering an essay question, changing a tire), providing such guidance would defeat the purpose of the test. Factors you can use in determining the appropriate amount of guidance are the nature of the skill tested, including its complexity; the sophistication level of the target learners; and the natural situations to which learners are to transfer the skills as determined in your context analysis.

Instructions to examinees related to the measurement of attitudes differ from those given for measuring performances and products. For accurate evaluation of attitudes, it is important for examinees to feel free to choose to behave according to their attitudes. Examinees who are aware that they are being observed by a supervisor or an instructor may not exhibit behaviors that reflect their true attitudes. Covertly observing employees, however, can be problematic in many work settings. Agreements are often made between employees and employers and between employers and unions about who can be evaluated, who can conduct the evaluation, what can be evaluated, whether the employee is informed in advance, and how the data can be used. Even with these understandable limitations, it is sometimes possible through planning and prior agreements to create a situation where reasonable assessment of attitudes can occur.

Developing the Instrument In addition to writing instructions for learners, you must develop a rubric to guide your evaluation of performances, products, or attitudes. There are five steps in developing the instrument:

1. Identify the elements to be evaluated.
2. Paraphrase each element.
3. Sequence the elements on the instrument.
4. Select the type of judgment to be made by the evaluator.
5. Determine how the instrument will be scored.

Identify, Paraphrase, and Sequence Elements. Similar to test items, the elements to be judged are taken directly from the behaviors included in the performance objectives. Recall that categories of elements typically include aspects of the physical form of the object or performance, the utility of the product or performance, and the aesthetic qualities of the product or performance. You should ensure that the elements selected can actually be observed during the performance or in the product.

Each element should be paraphrased for inclusion on the instrument. The time available for observing and rating, especially for an active performance, is limited, and lengthy descriptions such as those included in the objectives hamper the process. Often, only one or two words are necessary to communicate the step or facet of a product or performance to the evaluator. In paraphrasing, it is also important to word each item such that a Yes response from the evaluator reflects a positive outcome and a No response reflects a negative outcome. Consider the following examples for an oral speech:

Incorrect	Yes	No	Correct	Yes	No
1. Maintains eye contact	____	____	1. Maintains eye contact	____	____
2. Pauses with "and, uh"	____	____	2. Avoids "and, uh" pauses	____	____
3. Loses thought, idea	____	____	3. Maintains thought, idea	____	____

In the incorrectly paraphrased list, the paraphrased list of behaviors mixes positive and negative outcomes that would be very difficult to score. In the correctly paraphrased list, items are phrased such that a Yes response is a positive judgment and a No response is a negative one. This consistency enables you to sum the Yes ratings to obtain an overall score that indicates the quality of the performance or product.

After elements are paraphrased, they should be sequenced on the instrument. The order in which they are included should be congruent with the natural order of events, if there is one. For example, an essay or paragraph evaluation checklist should include features related to the introduction first, to the supporting ideas second, and to the conclusions last. The chronological steps required to change a tire should guide the order of steps on the checklist. The most efficient order for bank tellers' behaviors is undoubtedly greeting the customer, conducting the business, and concluding the transaction. In general, the goal analysis sequence is useful for suggesting the sequence of elements.

Developing the Response Format. The fourth step in developing an instrument to measure performances, products, or attitudes is to determine how the evaluator makes and records the judgments. There are at least three evaluator response formats: a checklist (e.g., yes or no), a rating scale that requires levels of quality differentiation (e.g., poor, adequate, and good), a frequency count of the occurrence of each element considered, or some combination of these formats. The best evaluator response mode depends on several factors, including the following:

- the nature and complexity of the elements observed;
- the time available for observing, making the judgment, and recording the judgment;
- the accuracy or consistency with which the evaluator can make the judgments; and
- the quality of feedback to be provided to the examinee.

Checklist. The most basic of the three judgment formats is the checklist. If you choose this method, you can easily complete your instrument by including two columns beside each of the paraphrased and sequenced elements to be observed: a Yes column to indicate that each element was present and a No column to indicate either the absence or inadequacy of an element. Benefits of the checklist include the number of different elements that can be observed in a given amount of time, the speed with which it can be completed by the evaluator, the consistency or reliability with which judgments can be made, and the ease with which an overall performance score can be obtained. One limitation of the checklist is the absence of information provided to examinees about why a No judgment was assigned.

Rating Scale. A checklist can be converted to a rating scale by expanding the number of quality-level judgments for each element where quality differentiation is possible. Instead of using two columns for rating an element, at least three are used and can include either not present (0), present (1), and good (2) or poor (1), adequate (2), and good (3). Including either a (0) or (1) as the lowest rating depends on whether the element judged can be completely missing from a product or a performance. For example, some level of eye contact is present in an oral report, and the lowest rating should be a 1. A paragraph, however, may have no concluding sentence at all; thus, a score of 0 is most appropriate in this instance. The particular ratings selected depend on the nature of the element to be judged.

Similar to checklists, rating scales have both positive and negative features. On the positive side, they enable analytical evaluation of the subcomponents of a performance or product, and they provide better feedback to the examinee about the quality of a performance than can be provided through a checklist. On the negative side, they require more time to use because finer distinctions must be made about the quality of each element evaluated. They also can yield less reliable scores than checklists, especially when more quality levels are included than can be differentiated in the time available or that can be rated consistently. Imagine a rating scale that contains ten different quality levels on each element scale. What precisely are the differences between a rating of 3 and 4 and a rating of 6 and 7? Too much latitude in making the evaluations leads to inconsistencies both within and across evaluators.

Two strategies for developing scales can help ensure more reliable ratings. The first is to provide a clear verbal description of each quality level. Instead of simply using number categories and general terms such as (1) inadequate, (2) adequate, and (3) good, you should use more exact verbal descriptors that represent specific criteria for each quality level. Consider the following example related to topic sentences in a paragraph:

General

	Missing	Poor	Adequate	Good
1. Topic sentence . . .	0	1	2	3

Improved

	Missing	Too broad/ specific	Correct specificity	Correct specificity and interest value
1. Topic sentence . . .	0	1	2	3

Both response scales have four decision levels. The first example contains verbal descriptors for each rating, but the question of what constitutes a poor, an adequate, and a good topic sentence remains unclear. In the improved response format, the criterion for selecting each rating is defined more clearly. The more specific you can be in naming the criterion that corresponds to each quality level, the more reliable you can be in quantifying the quality of the element judged.

The second strategy you can use for developing scales is to limit the number of quality levels included in each scale. There is no rule stating that all elements judged should have the same number of quality levels, say a four- or five-point scale. The number of levels included should be determined by the complexity of the element judged and the time available for judging it. Consider the following two elements from a paragraph example:

	Yes	No					
1. Indented	___	___	1. Indented	0	1	2	3
2. Topic sentence	___	___	2. Topic sentence	0	1	2	3

In the checklist on the left, the elements could each reliably be judged using this list. Considering the rating scales on the right, you can see an immediate problem. Indenting a paragraph and writing a topic sentence differ drastically in skill complexity. Imagine trying to differentiate consistently four different levels of how well a paragraph is indented! Yet, as indicated in the preceding example, specifying four different levels of the quality of a topic sentence is reasonable.

A good rule for determining the size of the scale for each element is to ensure that each number or level included corresponds to a specific criterion for making the judgment. When you exhaust the criteria, you have all the levels that you can judge consistently.

Frequency Count. A frequency count is needed when an element to be observed, whether positive or negative, can be repeated several times by the examinee during the performance or in the product. For example, in a product such as a written report, the same type of outstanding feature or error can occur several times. During a performance such as a tennis match, the service is repeated many times, sometimes effectively and sometimes not. In rating behaviors such as those exhibited by bank tellers, the teller can be observed during transactions with many different customers and on different days.

The instances of positive and negative behaviors exhibited by the teller should be tallied across customers and days.

A frequency count instrument can be created by simply providing adequate space beside each element to tally the number of instances that occur. Similar to the checklist, the most difficult part of constructing a frequency count instrument is identifying and sequencing the elements to be observed.

Scoring Procedure The final activity in creating an instrument to measure products, performances, and attitudes is to determine how the instrument will be scored. Just as with a paper-and-pencil test, you undoubtedly need objective-level scores as well as overall performance scores. The checklist is the easiest of the three instrument formats to score. Yes responses for all elements related to one objective can be summed to obtain an objective-level score, and Yes responses can be summed across the total instrument to obtain an overall rating for the examinee on the goal.

Objective-level scores can be obtained from a rating scale by adding together the numbers assigned for each element rated within an objective. A score indicating the examinee's overall performance on the goals can be obtained by summing the individual ratings across all elements included in the instrument.

Unlike objective tests, checklists, and rating scales, determining an appropriate scoring procedure for a frequency count instrument can be challenging. The best procedure to use must be determined on a situation-specific basis, and it depends on the nature of the skills or attitudes measured and on the setting. For example, when rating the interactive performance of classroom teachers or sales personnel, some instances of the behaviors you want to observe occur during the evaluation, whereas others do not. In such cases, you must consider whether a lack of occurrence is a negative or neutral outcome. In another situation, such as tennis, there are many opportunities to observe an element, such as the service, and to count readily the number of strategically placed first serves, foot faults, or let serves. It is quite easy to tally the total number of serves made by a player and to calculate the proportion of overall serves that were strategically placed first serves, foot faults, let serves, and so forth. Yet, once these calculations are made, you must still decide how to combine this information to create a score on the instructional goal related to serving a tennis ball.

Regardless of how you decide to score a frequency count instrument, it is important that you consider during the developmental process how it will be done and compare the consequences of scoring it one way versus an alternative way. The manner in which you must score an instrument may require modifications to the list of elements you wish to observe; therefore, scoring procedures should be planned prior to beginning to rate learner performances. When no feasible scoring procedure can be found for a frequency count instrument, you might reconsider using a checklist, a rating scale, or a combination format instead.

All the suggestions included in this discussion should be helpful in the development of criterion-referenced tests. If you are an inexperienced test writer, you may wish to consult additional references on test construction. Several references on testing techniques are included at the end of this chapter.

Portfolio Assessments

Portfolios are collections of criterion-referenced assessments that illustrate learners' work. These assessments might include objective-style tests that demonstrate progress from the pretest to the posttest, products that learners developed during instruction, or live performances. Portfolios might also include assessments of learners' attitudes about the domain studied or the instruction.

Portfolio assessment is defined as the process of meta-evaluating the collection of work samples for observable change or development. Objective tests are assessed for learner change or growth from pretests through posttests, and products and performances are tracked and compared for evidence of learner progress. There are at least five criteria for designing quality portfolio assessments:

1. The instructional goals and objectives included in portfolio assessment should be very important and warrant the increased time required for this assessment format.
2. The work samples must be anchored to specific instructional goals and performance objectives.
3. The work samples should be the criterion-referenced assessments that are collected during the process of instruction.
4. The assessments are the regular pretests and posttests, regardless of test format, and typically no special tests are created for portfolio assessment.
5. Each regular assessment is accompanied by its rubric with a student's responses evaluated and scored, indicating the strengths and problems within a performance.

With the set of work samples collected and sequenced, the evaluator is ready to begin the process of assessing growth, which is often accomplished at two levels. The first level, *learner self-assessment,* is one of the tenets of the learner-centered assessment movement. Learners examine their own materials, including test scores, products, performances, and scored rubrics, and they record their judgments about the strengths and problems in the materials. They also describe what they might do to improve the materials. Instructors then examine the materials set, without first examining the evaluations by the learner, and record their judgments. Following the completion of the instructor's evaluation, the instructor and the learner compare their evaluations, discussing any discrepancies between the two evaluations. As a result of this interview, they plan together the next steps the learner should undertake to improve the quality of his or her work.

Portfolio assessment is not appropriate for all instruction because it is very time-consuming and expensive. The instruction must span time, so that the learner has time to develop and refine skills, and must also yield the required products or performances for the assessment.

A course in instructional design is an appropriate situation for portfolio assessment because many products are developed and refined over a span of several months. The products created by the learner include an instructional goal, an instructional analysis, an analysis of learners and contexts, performance objectives, assessment instruments and procedures, an instructional strategy, a set of instructional materials, often a formative evaluation of the materials, and a description of the strengths in the instruction as well as refinement prescriptions for identified problems. During the design and development process, a rubric is used to score each element in the process. At the conclusion of the course, a meta-evaluation of all the materials and initial rubrics is undertaken. This is often the point where learners say, "If only I knew then what I know now."

Evaluation and Revision

This section contains two parts: the rubric for evaluating criterion-referenced assessments and instructions for overall evaluation of the materials developed thus far in the design process.

Rubric for Evaluating Criterion-Referenced Assessments

The following rubric contains a summary of criteria to use in developing and evaluating criterion-referenced assessments. The first section contains criteria appropriate regardless of the assessment format, and the second section describes criteria appropriate for alternative assessments including product development, live performances, and attitudes.

Designer note: If an element is not relevant for your plan, mark NA in the No column.

No	Some	Yes	
			A. All Assessment Formats (Objective and Alternative)
			1. **Goal-Centered Criteria** Are the items, directions, and rubrics congruent with the components of the terminal and performance objectives including:
____	____	____	a. Conditions?
____	____	____	b. Behavior?
____	____	____	c. Content?
____	____	____	d. Criteria?
			2. **Learner-Centered Criteria** Are the items and directions congruent with target learners':
____	____	____	a. Vocabulary, language level?
____	____	____	b. Developmental level (e.g., complexity, abstractness, guidance)?
____	____	____	c. Background, experience, environment?
____	____	____	d. Experience with testing format and equipment?
____	____	____	e. Motivation and interest?
____	____	____	f. Cultural, racial, gender needs (lack bias)?
			3. **Context-Centered Criteria for Assessments** Is/are:
____	____	____	a. Items and directions authentic for the contexts?
____	____	____	b. Items and directions feasible for the contexts?
____	____	____	c. Required equipment/tools available?
____	____	____	d. Adequate time available for administration, scoring, analysis?
____	____	____	e. Adequate personnel available for administration?
			4. **Assessment-Centered Criteria** Is/are:
____	____	____	a. All information required to answer provided?
____	____	____	b. Language clear and parsimonious?
____	____	____	c. Grammar, spelling, and punctuation correct?
____	____	____	d. Item formatting rules followed (consult measurement text)?
____	____	____	e. Format feasible given resources (time, personnel, costs)?
____	____	____	f. Professional looking?
			B. Product, Live Performance, and Attitude Assessments
			1. **Directions** Do directions clearly indicate:
____	____	____	a. What is to be done?
____	____	____	b. How it is to be done?
____	____	____	c. Any needed resources, facilities, equipment?
____	____	____	d. Any constraints on time, format, etc.?
____	____	____	e. Appropriate guidance for task and learner needs?
			2. **Elements or Features to Be Rated** Are elements:
____	____	____	a. Important?
____	____	____	b. Observable?
____	____	____	c. Paraphrased?
____	____	____	d. Sequenced in natural order of occurrence?
____	____	____	e. Stated either neutrally or positively for consistent rating direction?
			3. **Rating or Quality Judgment** Are the rating categories:
____	____	____	a. Consistent in directionality (Yes is positive rating, No is low)?
____	____	____	b. Labeled using both numbers and verbal descriptions?
____	____	____	c. Low in number of rating levels (rarely over three/four)?
____	____	____	d. Fair in that "zero" used only when element is totally missing?
____	____	____	e. Likely to yield reliable ratings (consistent across raters and time)?

Evaluating and Revising the Design

The quality of your items and instruments depends on the quality of your objectives, which in turn depends on the quality of your instructional analysis and goal statement. After reviewing the items you have developed for your objectives, you should stop forward progress in the design process and evaluate your overall design to this point, revising your work if needed for overall quality and congruence.

Quality and Congruence Among Parts

The goal has been identified and analyzed, subordinate skills have been identified, learners and contexts have been analyzed, objectives have been written, and assessments have been developed. It is time to make sure that everything flows together, that the skills, objectives, and assessments are congruent with each other and with the goal of your project.

Taking time to lay out your work to this point may seem redundant because you have already done formative reviews of each step along the way, and as new information, decisions, and assumptions arose in one step, you have already cycled back to reflect your new understanding in previous steps. This is the nature of the ID process. Yes, there is a sequence of steps, but the steps are not discrete; that is, decisions in one step have consequences for both preceding and following steps.

Materials and Procedures for Evaluating the Design You must have all the materials produced thus far to complete the design evaluation, including the instructional analysis diagram, performance objectives, and summaries of learner characteristics, as well as performance and learning contexts, performance objectives, and assessments. Recall that there are four main categories of criteria to be considered for evaluating your overall design to this point—goal, learner, context, and assessment criteria. These criteria are woven through the evaluation of your design. Using the main criteria, there are five steps in evaluating the design:

1. Organize and present the material to illuminate the relationships.
2. Judge the congruence between the information and skills in instructional goal analysis and the materials created.
3. Judge the congruence between the materials and the characteristics of the target learners.
4. Judge the congruence between the performance and learning contexts and the materials.
5. Judge the clarity of all materials.

Organization How can you best organize and present your materials to evaluate them at this point in the instructional design process? Each component builds on the product from the previous one; therefore, the materials should be presented in a way that enables comparison among the various components of your design. The designer should be able to see at a glance whether the components are parallel, which can be achieved by organizing the materials such that related components are together. One way to do this is to construct a design evaluation chart as depicted in Table 7.3. The first column is a list of the subskills from the instructional goal analysis, the second column includes performance objectives for each skill, and the third column shows test items for each objective. The last line contains the instructional goal, the terminal objective, and the test item(s) for the terminal objective. Table 7.4 includes an example of the type of material listed in each section of Table 7.3.

The sequence of subskills presented on your chart is important. If you place them in the order you believe they should be taught, then you can receive additional

Table 7.3 Structure of the Design Evaluation Chart

Subskill	Performance Objective	Sample Assessment
1	Objective 1	Test item
2	Objective 2	Test item
3	Objective 3	Test item
Instructional Goal	Terminal Objective	Test item

Table 7.4 Example of a Design Evaluation Chart

Skill	Performance Objective	Test Item(s)
1. Write the formula for converting yards to meters.	1. From memory, correctly write the formula for converting yards to meters.	1. In the space provided below, write the formula used to convert yards to meters.
2. Convert measures in yards to comparable meters.	2. Given different lengths in yards, convert the yards to meters, correct to one decimal place.	2.5 yds. = _______ meters 7.5 yds. = _______ meters 15 yds. = _______ meters

feedback from a reviewer concerning the logic you have used for sequencing skills and presenting instruction. This additional feedback may save steps in rewriting or reorganizing your materials at a later point. The topic of sequencing skills is addressed in greater detail in Chapter 9.

If others will be collaborating with you, or critiquing your design work, you should have other documents available for review with your design evaluation table, including the instructional analysis diagram, the table of target learner characteristics, and the table describing the performance and learning contexts. All items in the design table should be keyed to the numbering of the subskills in the analysis diagram. This complete set of materials represents your instructional design to this point.

Congruence The second step requires using the goal-centered criteria to judge the congruence among your materials. The congruence among the subordinate skill in the goal framework, its intended performance objective (conditions, behavior, and content), and the intended test items is critically important to the quality of your materials.

A recommended procedure to follow for this part of the analysis is to compare the (1) subordinate skills in instructional goal analysis with the subordinate skills listed in the design evaluation table, (2) subordinate skills in the table with the performance objectives in the table, and (3) performance objectives (conditions, performance, and criteria) with the test items prescribed in the table.

The wording of the subordinate skills in the goal analysis diagram and the design evaluation table should be the same. Once this congruence is established, the goal analysis can be set aside. Your subordinate skills and performance objectives should differ only in that conditions and perhaps criteria have been added. Finally, determine whether the performance objectives and test items match in conditions, performance, and criteria. Are students given the information and materials in the items as prescribed in the objective? Once the design is parallel in content, evaluators can turn to examining the congruence between the performance objectives and the characteristics of the learners.

Learner Characteristics The third step is to compare the materials with the characteristics of the learners. For this analysis, evaluators should judge the congruence between the materials and learners' ability, vocabulary, interests, experiences, and needs. The best materials in the world are ineffective if intended learners cannot use them successfully. Do reviewers believe the performance objectives and assessments are set at the right scope and complexity for the defined target group? Are the objectives broken down finely enough or too much? Are the test items at the appropriate level of complexity for the learners?

Contexts The fourth step is to judge the congruence of the performance and learning contexts with the performance objectives and test items in the design evaluation table. Reviewers should judge the authenticity of the tasks prescribed for the performance context because this authenticity fosters interest value and motivation and helps ensure transfer of skills from the learning to the performance context. They should also examine the feasibility of the tasks for the learning context. Can the designer count on the availability in the learning context of the resources required (e.g., costs, time, personnel, facilities, equipment) to implement the instruction and assessments?

Materials Clarity With congruence among the materials and the goal, contexts, and learners established, the final step is for reviewers to judge the clarity of the materials. Unfortunately, this step is sometimes where the evaluation begins, but without determining the alignment of the design documents, clarity may be a moot point. During this step, evaluators should be asked whether the structure and scope of the goal analysis make sense to them. Are the subordinate and entry skills identified correctly, and are they in the correct order? Are the performance objectives written clearly, and do they know what is meant by each? What is their perception of the quality of the test items, including language clarity; vocabulary level; grammar, spelling, and punctuation; assessment format; and professional appearance?

After you have received feedback concerning the adequacy of your design and made appropriate revisions in your framework, you have the input required to begin work on the next component of the model, namely developing an instructional strategy. Having a good, carefully analyzed, and refined design at this point facilitates your work on the remaining steps in the process.

Examples

When you examine test items and assessments in this section, you can use the four categories of criteria summarized by the rubric at the end of the chapter to help focus your attention on particular aspects of the item.

A Checklist for Evaluating Motor Skills

In measuring the performance of motor skills, you will need instructions for the performance and a rubric you can use to record your evaluations of the performance. The examples provided are based on the automobile tire changing performance objectives included in Table 6.3 (p. 144).

The directions for the examinee are contained in Figure 7.1. The directions differ slightly from the terminal objective in Table 6.3. For the examination, the car will not have the specified flat tire. Instead, the learner is to replace any tire designated by the examiner. Imagine the logistical problems of having to evaluate fifteen or twenty learners on these skills and having to begin each test with a flat

Using the equipment provided in the trunk of the car, remove from the car any one of the tires designated by the instructor. Replace that tire with the spare tire secured in the trunk. The test will be complete when you have (1) returned the car to a safe-driving condition, (2) secured all tools in their proper place in the trunk, (3) secured the removed tire in the spare tire compartment in the trunk, and (4) replaced any lids or coverings on the wheel or in the trunk that were disturbed during the test.

Your performance on each step will be judged using three basic criteria. The first is that you remember to perform each step. The second is that you execute each one using the *appropriate* tools in the *proper* manner. The third is that you perform each step with safety in mind. For safety reasons, the examiner may stop you at any point in the exam and request that you (1) perform a step that you have forgotten, (2) change the manner in which you are using a tool or ask that you change to another tool, or (3) repeat a step that was not performed safely. If this occurs, you will not receive credit for that step. However, you will receive credit for correctly executed steps performed after that point.

Figure 7.1 Directions for a Psychomotor Skill Test (Changing a Tire)

tire on the car. Other information included in the instructions also is based on the practicality of administering the test. Notice that the student is required to return and secure all tools, equipment, and parts to their proper place. While helping to ensure that the examinee knows how to perform these tasks, it also ensures that the equipment and car are ready for the next examinee.

Information is also provided for the examinee about how the performance will be judged. These instructions tell examinees that in order to receive credit, they must (1) recall each step, (2) perform it using the appropriate tool, (3) use each tool properly, and (4) always be safety conscious in performing each step. Given this information, they understand that failure to comply with any one of these four criteria means a loss of credit for that step. They are also told that they can be stopped at any point during the test. Knowing that this can happen, why it can happen, and the consequences of it happening lessens their anxiety if they are stopped during the exam.

A partial checklist used to evaluate performance is included in Figure 7.2. Only main step 2, "Lifts car," is illustrated. Notice that the main headings within step 2 are numbered consistently with the steps in the goal analysis (Figure 4.11, p. 101) and the performance objectives (Table 6.3, p. 144). The criteria listed in each objective in Table 6.3 (p. 144) are paraphrased and assigned letters (e.g., a, b, c) for the checklist. Two columns are provided for the evaluator's response.

The next step in developing the instrument is to determine how learners' scores are summarized. To do this, obtain both main step scores (e.g., Lifts car) as well as a total score for the test. To facilitate this scoring plan, blanks are placed to the left of each main step. The total number of points possible in step 2 is recorded in parentheses beneath the space. The number of points earned by each student can be determined by counting the number of Xs in the Yes column. This value can be recorded in the blank beside main step 2. In the example, you can see that the examinee earned eleven of the possible thirteen points. Summing the points recorded for each main step in the left-hand column yields a total score for the test, which can be recorded at the top of the form beside the name. The total possible points for the test can be recorded in the parentheses beneath the total earned score.

One final observation should be made. The evaluator must determine how to score items 2.2b and 2.3c when no adjustment to the car or jack is needed. One strategy is to place an X or a NA for not applicable in the column for each of these steps even when they are not needed. Simply leaving them blank or checking the No column indicates that the student committed an error, which is not the case.

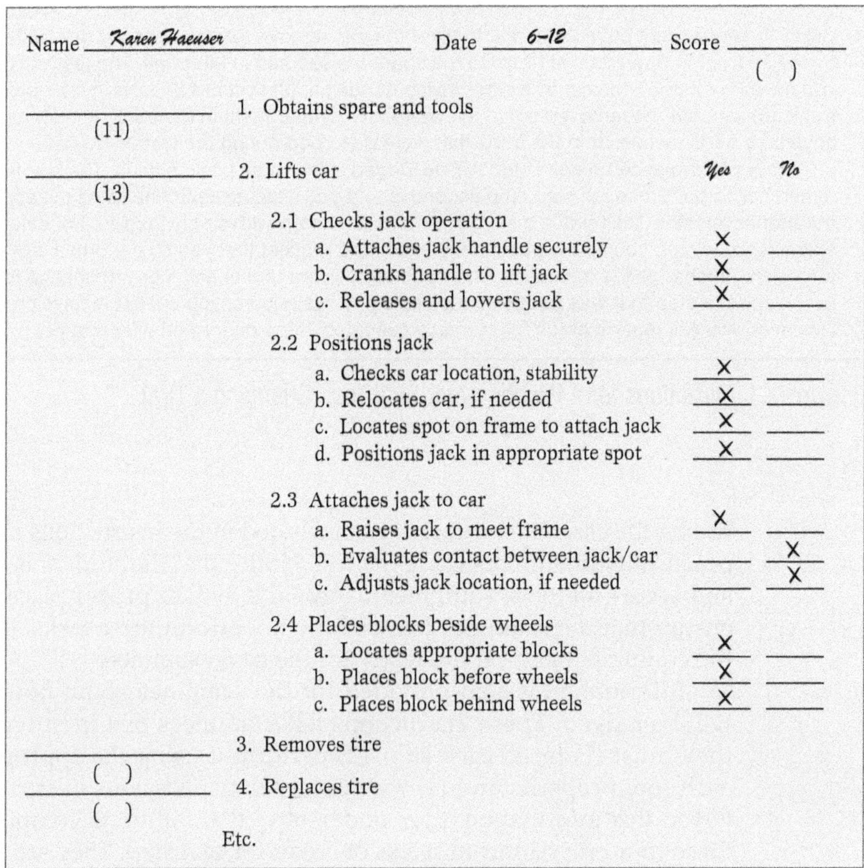

Name *Karen Haeuser* Date *6-12* Score ______ ( )

Score	Item	Yes	No
______ (11)	1. Obtains spare and tools		
______ (13)	2. Lifts car		
	2.1 Checks jack operation		
	a. Attaches jack handle securely	X	
	b. Cranks handle to lift jack	X	
	c. Releases and lowers jack	X	
	2.2 Positions jack		
	a. Checks car location, stability	X	
	b. Relocates car, if needed	X	
	c. Locates spot on frame to attach jack	X	
	d. Positions jack in appropriate spot	X	
	2.3 Attaches jack to car		
	a. Raises jack to meet frame	X	
	b. Evaluates contact between jack/car		X
	c. Adjusts jack location, if needed		X
	2.4 Places blocks beside wheels		
	a. Locates appropriate blocks	X	
	b. Places block before wheels	X	
	c. Places block behind wheels	X	
______ ( )	3. Removes tire		
______ ( )	4. Replaces tire		
	Etc.		

Figure 7.2 Partial Checklist for Evaluating a Psychomotor Skill (Changing a Tire)

Instrument for Evaluating Behaviors Related to Attitudes

For rating behaviors from which attitudes can be inferred, a checklist, rating scale, or frequency count is needed. Our example is based on the courteous bank teller illustrations in Chapter 2 and Table 6.5. Because a teller should be evaluated in the performance site using several example transactions with a customer, a frequency count response format undoubtedly works best. A sample instrument is contained in Figure 7.3.

Notice that at the top of the instrument there is space for identifying the teller and the date or dates of the observations. There is also space for tallying the number of transactions observed. This information is needed later to interpret the data. There is also space to record the total number of positive and negative behaviors exhibited by the teller during the observations.

The particular behaviors sought are paraphrased in the far left column. Similar to the checklist, there are two response columns for the evaluator. The only difference is that space is provided in this example for tallying many behaviors during several different transactions.

In determining how to score the instrument, behaviors perceived as positive (186) and those perceived as negative (19) are tallied. Reviewing the summary of this simulated data, it appears that the teller behaved in a courteous manner toward customers in the vast majority of the instances. This information can be interpreted in two ways, depending on the teller's knowledge of the observations. If the teller was

Name *Robert Jones* Date(s) *4/10, 17, 24*

Total Transactions Observed 卌 卌 卌 Total *+186* Total *−19*

A. Customer Approaches and Teller:	Yes	No
1. Smiles	卌 卌	卌
2. Initiates verbal greeting	卌 卌 卌	
3. Personalizes comments	卌 卌 卌	
4. Excuses self when delayed	////	//
5. Inquires about services	卌 卌 ////	/
6. Attends to all in line	卌 卌	///
7. Other:		
B. During Transaction, Teller:		
1. Listens attentively	卌 卌 卌	
2. Requests clarifying information	卌 ////	
3. Provides forms required	卌 ////	
4. Completes/amends forms	卌 ////	
5. Explains changes made	卌 ////	
6. Explains materials returned	卌 卌 //	///
7. Other:		
C. Concluding Transaction, Teller:		
1. Inquires about other services	卌 卌 卌	
2. Says, "Thank you"	卌 卌 卌	
3. Responds to customer comments	卌 卌	卌
4. Makes concluding wish	卌 卌 卌	
5. Other:		

Figure 7.3 A Frequency Count Instrument for Evaluating Behaviors from Which Attitudes Will Be Inferred (Courteous Service)

unaware of the observations and chose to behave in this manner, then the evaluator could infer that the teller indeed displayed a positive attitude in providing courteous and friendly service. Conversely, if the teller was aware of the examination, then the evaluator could infer that the teller knew how to behave courteously during transactions with customers and chose to do so while under observation.

Case Study

Group Leadership Training

To this point in the case study, we have identified a goal and completed a goal analysis, a subskills analysis, an analysis of learners and contexts, and written performance objectives. Having demonstrated in the Examples section procedures for developing instruments for a psychomotor skill and an attitude, in the case study that follows we demonstrate how test items would be written for several verbal information and intellectual skills objectives. We then pause in the ID process to evaluate the design work to this point.

Recall in Chapter 6 that we created performance objectives for the terminal objective and subordinate skills for main step six in the instructional goal "Lead Group Discussions Aimed at Solving Problems." To jog your memory, one subordinate skill and two sample performance objectives based on it are repeated here from Table 6.7. Notice in the performance objectives that the conditions (CN), behavior, (B), and criteria (CR) are labeled. We will now use this information in the performance objectives to create parallel test items for them.

Subordinate Skills	Sample Subordinate Performance Objectives
6.1 Name member actions that facilitate cooperative interaction.	6.1.1 When requested either orally or in writing (CN) to name group member actions that facilitate cooperative interaction, name those actions (B). At least six facilitating actions should be named (CR).
	6.1.2 When asked either orally or in writing (CN) to indicate what members should do when their ideas are questioned by the group, name positive reactions that help ensure cooperative group interaction (B). Learner should name at least three possible reactions (CR).

Table 7.5 Parallel Test Items for the Verbal Information and Intellectual Skills Performance Objectives in Table 6.7 for the Instructional Goal "Lead Group Discussions Aimed at Solving Problems"

Performance Objectives for Subordinate Skills	Parallel Test Items
6.1.1 When requested in writing to name group member actions that facilitate cooperative interaction (CN), name those actions (B). At least six facilitating actions should be named (CR).	1. List positive actions you and committee members should take to *facilitate* cooperative group interaction during problem-solving meetings. (Create response lines for nine responses.)
6.1.2 When asked in writing to indicate what members should do when their ideas are questioned by the group (CN), name positive reactions that help ensure cooperative group interaction (B). Learner should name at least three possible reactions (CR).	1. Suppose you introduce a new idea during a meeting and the value of your idea is questioned by one or more committee members. What positive reactions might you have to *facilitate* cooperative group interaction? (Create response lines for four responses.)
6.2.1 Given written descriptions of a group member's facilitating actions during a meeting (CN), indicate whether the actions are cooperative behaviors (B). Learner should correctly classify at least 80 percent of the actions described (CR).	1. Read the script of the meeting. Each time the leader or a member of the group exhibits a cooperative behavior, place a check mark beside that line in the script.
6.2.2 Given videos of staged meetings depicting member's actions (CN), indicate whether the actions are cooperative (B). Learner should classify correctly at least 80 percent of the actions demonstrated (CR).	(*Reader note:* This video and the response sheet are both located in the practice test section on the web-based instructional site.) **Directions** **Skill:** Classify Cooperative Leader and Member Actions. Click on the Videos button on the left of your screen and select Video 1 from the video table of contents that appears. Then: (a) Highlight and print the Leader Response Form for Video 1. (b) Study the response form, reading the directions for marking your responses.

Performance Objectives for Subordinate Skills	Parallel Test Items
	(c) Locate the Video 1 title button on your screen and click on the Video 1 title when you are ready to complete the assessment. (d) When you are finished (you may view the video twice in the process of completing your ratings), click on the Feedback-Video 1 title in the video menu. (e) Compare your ratings with those provided in the Feedback-Video 1 and note any discrepancies. (f) Keep your response form and notes about discrepancies, and bring them to the next instructional session at the center.
6.3.1 When asked in writing to name leader actions that encourage and stifle member discussion and cooperation (CN), name these actions (B). Learner should name at least ten encouraging and corresponding stifling actions (CR).	List twelve positive actions and their corresponding stifling actions that you as a group leader can take to affect member interaction during meetings. (Create double response lines for twelve responses with headings of Positive Actions and Stifling Actions.)
6.4.1 Given written descriptions of group leader's actions during a meeting (CN), indicate whether the actions are likely to encourage or stifle cooperative group interaction (B). Learner should correctly classify at least 80 percent of the actions depicted (CR).	1. Read the script of the problem-solving meeting. Each time the leader of the group exhibits a behavior that is likely to encourage member cooperation, place a check mark (3) on the left side of the script in the corresponding script line. In contrast, each time the leader exhibits a behavior likely to stifle member cooperation, place a check mark on the right side of the script beside that line.
6.4.2 Given videos of staged group meetings depicting staged leader's actions (CN), indicate whether the leader's actions are likely to encourage or stifle member cooperation (B). Learner should classify correctly at least 80 percent of the encouraging and stifling actions demonstrated (CR).	(*Reader note:* This video and the response sheet are both located in the practice test section on the web-based class site.) **Directions:** **Skill:** Classify Leader Actions Likely to Encourage and Stifle Member Cooperation. (a) Highlight and print the Leader Response Form 2. (b) Study the sheet, reading the directions for marking your responses. (c) Locate Video 2 in the videos menu on your screen and click on the Video 2 title when you are ready to complete the assessment. (d) When you are finished (you may view the video twice in the process of completing your ratings), click on the Feedback-Video 2 title in the video menu. (e) Compare your ratings of the leader's actions with those provided in the website and note any discrepancies. (f) Keep Response Form 2 and notes about discrepancies, and bring them to the next instructional session at the center.

(*Continued*)

Table 7.5 Continued

Performance Objectives for Subordinate Skills	Parallel Test Items
6.5.1 In simulated problem-solving meetings with learner acting as group leader (CN), initiate actions to engender cooperative behavior among members (B). Group members cooperate with each other and with leader during discussion (CR).	**Directions:** **Skill:** Engender cooperative behavior among members. During the group meeting today, you will serve as leader for thirty minutes. During your meeting, a member (staff) will introduce a problem not previously discussed in the group. You will lead the group discussion as the problem is discussed and demonstrate personal actions before the group that you believe will engender members' cooperative participation. If you have questions about your actions or the actions of others, do not raise them with staff or members of your group until the thirty minutes has passed.
Performance Objective for Main Step	**Prescription for Frequency Count Observation Instrument (used by evaluator during simulations and actual meetings)**
6. During simulated meetings comprised of new leaders and held in the department's conference rooms, manage cooperative group interaction. Discussion members should participate freely, volunteer ideas, cooperate fully with leader and other members. During actual problem-solving meetings held at a designated site on campus or in the community, lead group discussions aimed at solving problems currently existing.	The following categories will be used relative to main step 6: Manage cooperative group interaction in both the learning and performance contexts. A. Engendering actions demonstrated — Frequency 1. ________ ____ 2. ________ ____ (etc.) B. Defusing actions demonstrated — Frequency 1. ________ ____ 2. ________ ____ (etc.) C. Stress-alleviating actions demonstrated — Frequency 1. ________ ____ 2. ________ ____ (etc.) D. Rating of overall quality of cooperative group interaction (circle one) Mild 1 2 3 4 5 Excellent

Test Items for Verbal Information and Intellectual Skills

Sample performance objectives from Table 6.7 (p. 148; Instructional goal, "Lead group discussions aimed at solving problems": step 6, "Manage cooperative group interaction") are repeated in column 1 of Table 7.5. A test item or set of items is illustrated for each of the objectives.

Performance Objectives As you examine the test items, first notice the congruence between the performance objective and the item relative to objective conditions, behavior, and criteria. For example, examine the congruence between performance objective 6.5.1 and its corresponding test directions for learners on the right side of the table. The objective conditions prescribe a simulated meeting with the learner serving as leader. The task directions to the learners describe them as leading the meeting. The behavior in the objective is to initiate actions to engender group members' cooperation. The task directions on the right side prescribe that the leader initiates actions to engender group members' cooperation during the meeting. The criteria in the objective should appear on the designer's rubric for observing leader behaviors during the meeting, not in the task directions to learners.

Congruence with Learner Characteristics Second, examine items for their appropriateness for the master's degree–seeking students in leadership. You need the test items (Table 7.5) and the description of learner characteristics (Table 5.4, pp. 123–124) for this analysis. Judge the complexity of the language used in the items and the complexity of the tasks required. The language and task complexity appear to be at an appropriate level for students preparing to become campus and community leaders.

Performance and Learning Sites Third, examine the test items (Table 7.5) for appropriateness in the learning and performance sites (Table 5.5, p. 124, and Table 5.6, pp. 125–126). The last section of Table 7.5 contains the learning site and performance site assessment for main step 6 to aid your assessment for this criterion. At the posttest point, learners are observed as they lead group discussions, and the evaluator uses an observation form in the learning site to note the behaviors exhibited by leaders and tally the frequency with which each occurs.

Clarity Finally, examine the test items in Table 7.5 for their general clarity. You may wish to use the rubric (pp. 180–182) to assist their evaluation. Note that key terms are highlighted in the items to direct learners' attention. The items appear to be clear in that all information required to answer an item is presented before the learner is expected to respond. Grammar, punctuation, and spelling are correct, and the items have a professional appearance.

Once the items and directions are written, evaluated, and refined, you are ready to create the design evaluation table and review the materials developed to this point. Your role is to organize the materials, locate appropriate reviewers, facilitate the review process, explain materials, answer questions, and take notes. The reviewers' role is to study the documents provided and make the requested judgments.

Design Evaluation

Again, the four main criteria reviewers use to judge the quality of the design to this point involve goal, learner, context, and assessment considerations. In evaluating the congruence among the various design elements, the following steps were taken:

1. Organize and present the materials.
2. Judge the congruence among the materials and the instructional goal.
3. Judge the appropriateness of the materials for the target learners.
4. Judge the congruence of the performance objectives and test items with the performance and learning contexts.
5. Judge the clarity of the materials.

Organization Table 7.6 contains a partial design evaluation chart for the instructional goal on leading group discussions. The first column contains selected subordinate skills for step 6, "Manage cooperative group interaction"; the second column contains the performance objectives for the selected skills; and the third column includes matching test items for each of the objectives. Only a few of the skills, objectives, and test items are needed to illustrate the analysis process. A thorough analysis would include all the skills, objectives, and items developed to this point. In addition to the chart, a copy of the goal analysis (Figure 4.8), learner characteristics (Table 5.4), performance site characteristics (Table 5.5), and learning

Table 7.6 **A Section of a Design Evaluation Chart for the Instructional Goal "Lead Group Discussions Aimed at Solving Problems," Step 6, "Manage Cooperative Group Interaction"**

Performance Skill	Objectives	Test Items
6.3 Name actions for encouraging cooperation.	6.3.1 When asked in writing to name actions for encouraging and stifling discussion member cooperation, name these actions. Learner should name at least ten ways.	1. There are several strategies you can use as a group leader to *encourage and stifle cooperative discussion* during your meetings. What direct actions might you take as the leader to encourage member participation and cooperation? (Create response lines for ten responses.)
6.4 Classify strategies for encouraging and stifling cooperation.	6.4.1 Given written descriptions of group leader's actions during a meeting, indicate whether the actions are likely to encourage or stifle cooperative group interaction. Learner should correctly classify at least 80 percent of the actions depicted.	Place a plus (+) before those group leader actions most likely *to encourage* and a minus (–) before those actions likely *to stifle* cooperative group interaction. _____ 1. Introduces all members who attend the meeting. _____ 2. Emphasizes status differences among group members. _____ 3. Glances around the group welcomingly. _____ 4. Names a particular group member to start discussions. _____ 5. Comments positively after each person has commented (etc.).
6.5 Engender cooperative member behaviors.	6.5.1 In simulated problem-solving meetings with learner acting as group leader, initiate actions to engender cooperative behavior among members. Group members cooperate with each other and with leader during discussion.	As you observe (name) manage the meeting, what actions did he/she take *to engender* or encourage cooperative group behavior? Actions to Engender Cooperation — Frequency 1. ____________ ______ 2. ____________ ______ 3. ____________ ______ (etc.)

site characteristics (Table 5.6) should be available for the reviewers. They could also benefit from the summary of assessment criteria included in the rubric of this chapter. With the materials organized, the second step of judging the congruence between the materials and the goal can be undertaken.

Congruence For this analysis reviewers will need the goal analysis (Figure 4.8) and the subordinate skills in Table 7.6. Notice that the subordinate skills illustrated are worded the same as those in the goal analysis except for the addition of the term *stifling* that has been added to subordinate skill 6.4. Reviewers and designers would need to discuss this addition to determine whether it was appropriate and intended or an inadvertent addition that should be corrected.

Using Table 7.6 only, reviewers should compare the subordinate skills in column one with the performance objectives in column two. The skills do appear to be exactly the same except for skill 6.4, where the action term is *classify,* whereas the objective specifies *indicate.* There is no meaningful difference between these two terms in this instance.

Finally, reviewers should compare the congruence between the performance objectives in column two and the test items in column three. Examine the items for their congruence with the conditions, behavior, and criteria separately rather than holistically. Reviewers followed the same process the designer used in the previous section, and they judged the items and objectives to be congruent across conditions, behavior, and criteria.

Contexts The third step is to judge the congruence of the performance and learning contexts with the goal, objectives, and test items in the design evaluation table. Because reviewers previously judged the goal, subordinate skills, and performance objectives for congruence and decided they were consistent, they can simply concentrate on the performance objectives (Table 7.6) and the description of contexts (Table 5.5 and 5.6). Following their review, they believed that leaders could transfer the skills described in the materials to their campus and community meetings. The meetings will be held on campus or in selected community locations. Little additional resources (e.g., costs, resources, time, personnel, facilities) would be needed, because meetings are likely to occur related to learners' jobs or volunteer activities.

Learners The congruence among the goal, skills, objectives, and test items has already been established; thus, reviewers must review the feasibility of the materials (Figure 4.8 and Table 7.6) for the learner (Table 5.4). Reviewers with greater familiarity with target learners concluded that attaining the instructional goal "Lead group discussions aimed at solving problems" appeared to be feasible for master's-level students in leadership. They also believed that students would most likely succeed in managing cooperative meetings given instruction. They thought the performance objectives and test items were reasonable and should assist the leaders in developing skills that would be usable not only on campus but also in their jobs. In addition, they judged the materials to be free of bias (i.e., gender, cultural, or racial).

Materials Clarity Finally, reviewers considered the clarity of the materials; they needed the goal analysis (Figure 4.8) and the design evaluation chart (Table 7.6) to complete their work. They perceived the structure of the goal analysis to be logical, with the six main steps describing the chronology of events in managing a meeting. The verbal information tables (e.g., Table 4.1) were judged to be necessary to illuminate the designer's intended meaning of the linked subordinate skills. They thought that neither the learners nor the instructors would know what to do if these tables were eliminated from the materials. They also considered the content to be appropriate in scope for student leaders and thought leaders could succeed given instruction in performing the tasks. Reviewers could interpret the performance objectives and test items and thought these materials were clear. In addition, they judged the test items to be consistent with the assessment criteria stated in the rubric.

Professional and Historical Perspectives

For many years, policy makers and citizens demanded accountability in education, and the accountability movement led to assessing learner progress in standards for national, state, and local curriculum. This movement has waned over the past couple of decades, and the testing/accountability movement has come under question. Comments of "too much testing" and "testing programs interfering with meaningful learning" can be heard from politicians, educators, citizens, and parents. None of the controversies or arguments by any of these groups negates the critical requirement for very careful criterion-referenced testing and attitude assessment during the design and development of instruction. Related to classrooms and training offices, however, one might ask, without adequate criterion- and norm-referenced testing, on what are grades, promotion, selection, and placement decisions based?

Process Flowcharts

Developing Assessment Instruments

This section includes flowcharts for developing objective-style, product, performance, attitude, and portfolio assessments.

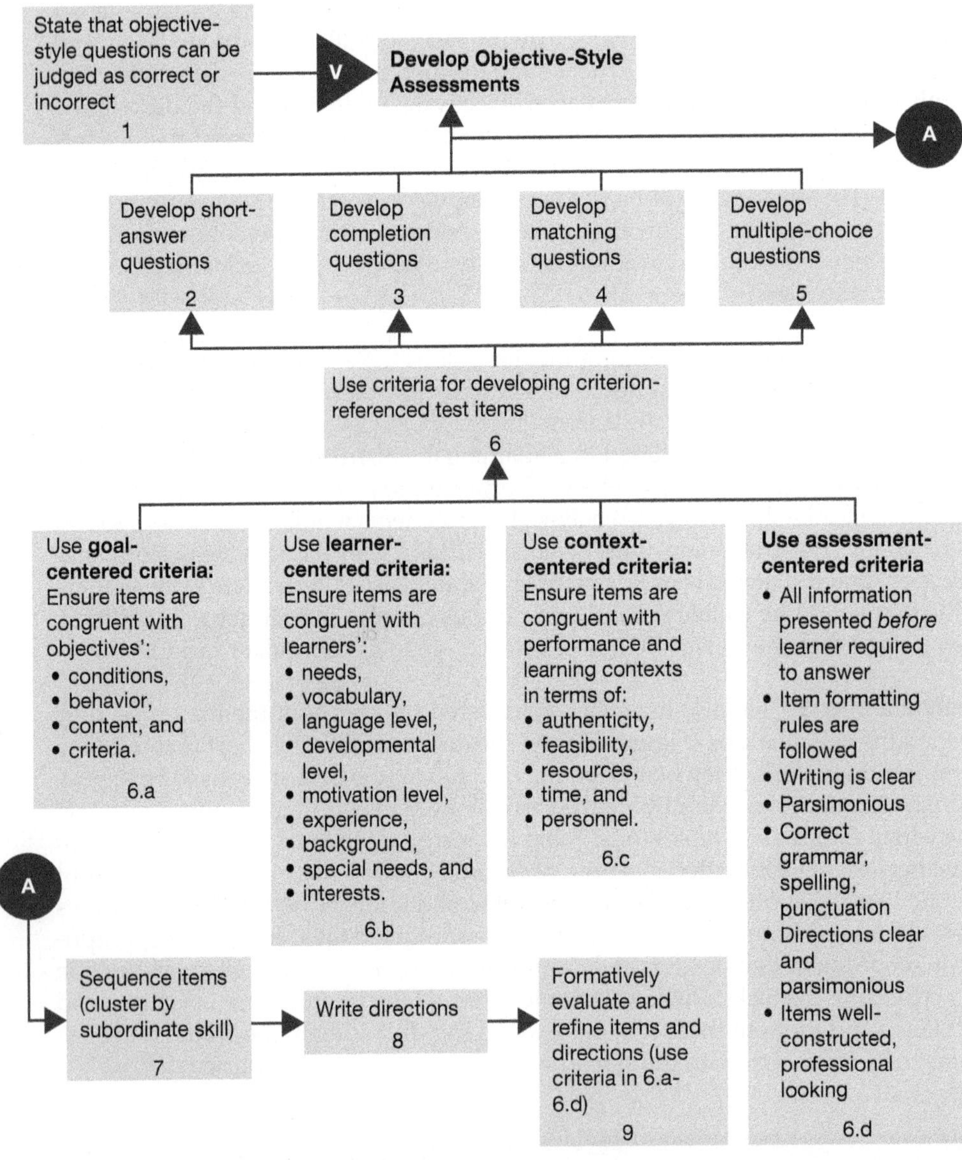

Figure 7.4 Develop Objective-Style Assessments

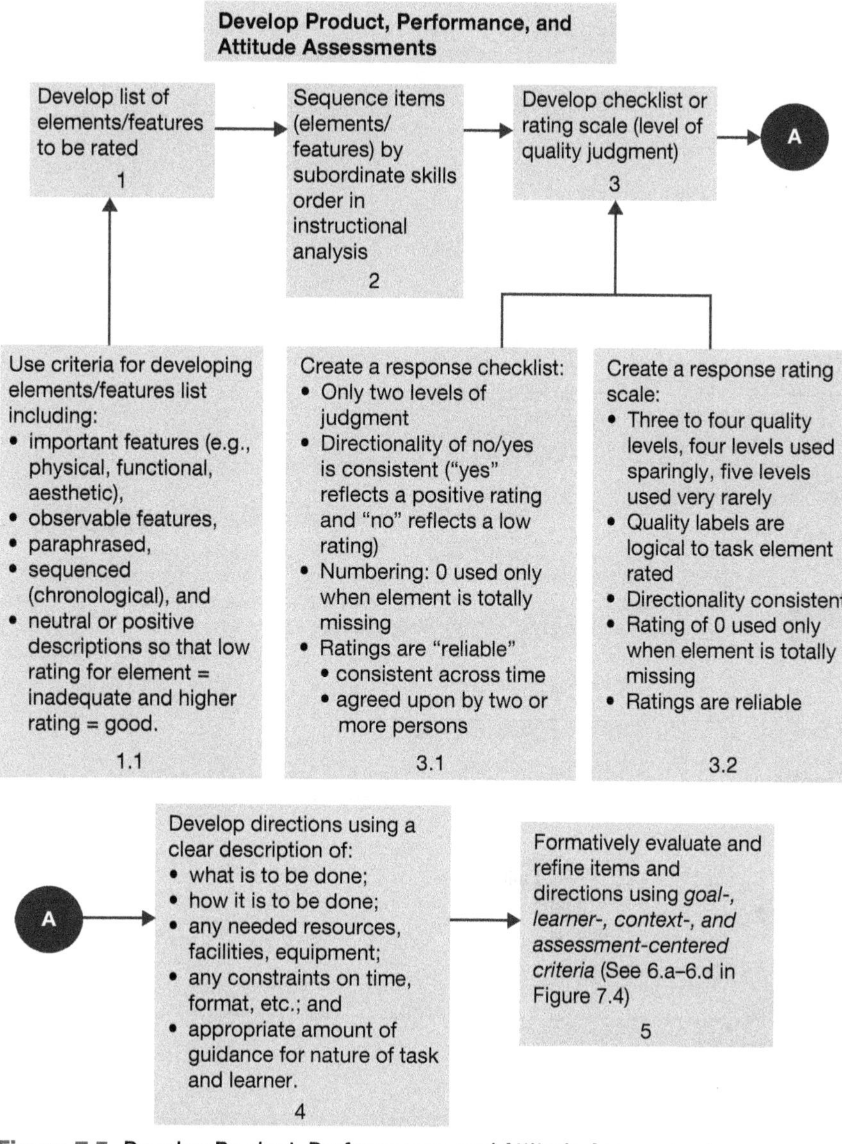

Figure 7.5 Develop Product, Performance, and Attitude Assessments

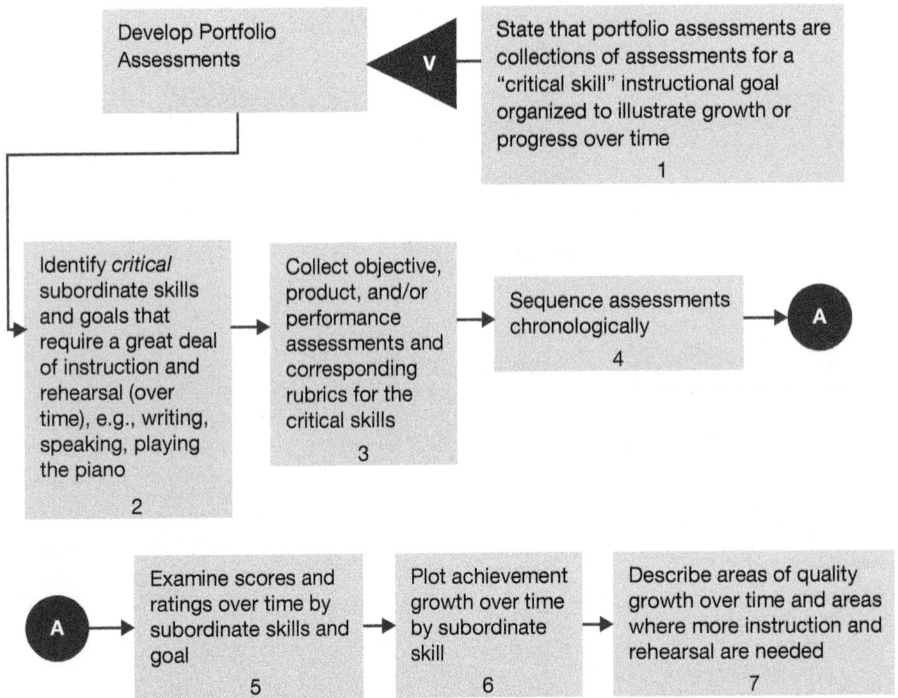

Figure 7.6 Develop Portfolio Assessments

Practice

Judge whether each of the following statements about criterion-referenced tests is correct. If it is, place a C in the space before the item. If it is incorrect, state briefly why it is incorrect. Check your answers in the Feedback section.

_____ 1. A criterion-referenced test is composed of items that measure behavior.

_____ 2. A criterion-referenced test is the same as an objective-referenced test.

_____ 3. Test items in criterion-referenced tests need not measure the exact type of behavior described in a performance objective.

_____ 4. Test items for criterion-referenced tests are developed directly from skills identified in the instructional analysis.

_____ 5. It is always a good idea to construct entry skill test items for the pretest.

_____ 6. Entry skill test items are developed to measure skills learners should possess before beginning instruction.

_____ 7. Pretests are used before instruction to indicate students' prior knowledge about what is to be taught as well as their knowledge of prerequisite entry skills.

_____ 8. Criterion-referenced test items are written directly from performance objectives, which in turn are written directly from the skills in an instructional analysis.

Using the instructional analysis diagram that follows, indicate by box number(s) the skills that should be used to develop test items for the:

_____ 9. Entry skills test

_____ 10. Pretest

_____ 11. Posttest

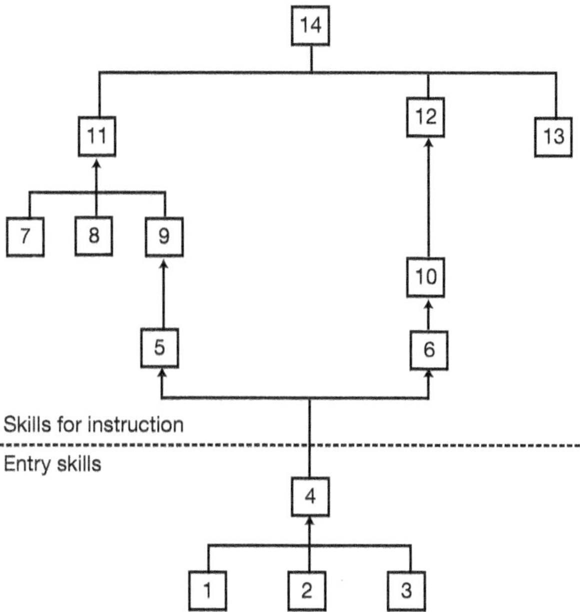

Write parallel assessments for performance objectives. On a separate sheet of paper, write a test item or other assessment that is congruent with the conditions, behavior, and content prescribed in each of the following performance objectives on writing composition. Assume the following:

- Your target group consists of average and above-average middle school students.
- The performance and learning contexts are their school classroom and other areas of the school and community where they might be expected to write. Assume the students have access to their teachers and to Canvas for the instruction and appropriate assessments.

You can use the rubric as an aid to constructing your items and for evaluating those you create.

12. Write a terminal objective for the following: In written composition, use a variety of sentence types and accompanying punctuation based on the purpose, mood, and complexity of the sentence. Sentences will be judged on format for sentence type, punctuation, sentence type by sentence purpose, and sentence variety within paragraphs.
13. Write performance objectives for the following items taken from Appendix D:

    5.6 Given the terms *declarative sentence* and *purpose,* state the purpose of a declarative sentence. The purpose should include to convey/tell information.

    5.7 Given several complete simple sentences that include declarative, interrogative, and exclamatory sentences that are correctly or incorrectly closed using a period, locate all those that are declarative.

    5.11 Write declarative sentences on (1) selected topics and (2) topics of student choice. Sentences must be complete and closed with a period.
14. Develop a test that includes instructions for the learner and evaluation forms for the psychomotor skill of putting a golf ball. The following performance objectives are based on the instructional analysis in Figure 4.6. The test should have two parts, including putting form and putting accuracy. Compare the instructions you write with the ones included in the corresponding item of the Feedback.

    Objectives: On a putting green and using a regulation ball and putter:

    5.1 Demonstrate good form while putting the golf ball. The body must be relaxed and aligned with the target, and the club must be comfortably gripped at the correct height. The stroke must be the appropriate height, speed, and direction for the target and smoothly executed. The face of the putter should be square throughout the stroke.

    6.1 Putt uphill, downhill, and across hill on a sloped putting green; from distances of ten, fifteen, and twenty-five feet; putt accurately enough for the balls to reach a distance of no more than three feet from the cup.
15. Plan a design evaluation, creating a chart with three columns: skills, objectives, and assessments. In addition to the design evaluation chart you construct, what design document helps you determine the congruence of the information in column one of your chart? What information do you need to judge the congruence and quality of the information in column two of your chart? What information do you need to judge the congruence and quality of the information in column three of your chart? How are these various design elements related during the evaluation?

Feedback

1. C
2. C
3. They must measure the behavior in the objective.
4. They are derived from objectives.
5. There may be no entry skills that require testing.
6. C
7. C
8. C

9–11. Generally speaking, performance objectives for which test items should be included are

Entry skills: skills 1 through 4

Pretest: skills 5 through 14

Posttest: skills 5 through 14

12–13. Compare your test items with those in Appendix E. In addition to these examples, you should review the more complete design evaluation chart for writing composition located there.

14. Instructions to learners for the putting exam are provided next.

Putting Assessment Instructions

The putting exam consists of two parts: putting form and putting accuracy. You are required to execute twenty-seven putts for the exam.

Your putting form is judged throughout the test using the top part of the attached rating sheet. The aspects of your form are listed in columns A and B. Your score depends on the number of OKs circled in the column labeled (1). You can receive a total score of ten on putting form if you do not consistently commit any of the mistakes named in the errors column. In the example, the student received a total score of seven. The errors consistently committed were all related to the swing: low backswing and follow-through and slow swing speed.

Your putting accuracy is also judged on the twenty-seven putts. Nine of the putts will be uphill, nine will be downhill, and nine will be across the hill to the cup. From each area, three putts will be from ten feet, three from fifteen feet, and three from twenty-five feet. Your accuracy score depends on the proximity of each putt to the cup. Three rings are painted on the green at one-foot intervals from the cup to make a target area. The following points are awarded for each area:

In cup = 4 points

Within 1 foot = 3 points

Within 2 feet = 2 points

Within 3 feet = 1 point

Outside 3 feet = 0

Balls that land on a ring are assigned the higher point value. For example, if a ball lands on the one-foot ring, you receive three points.

Each of your twenty-seven putts will be tallied on the form at the bottom of the sheet. The example is completed to show you how it will be done. Putting uphill from ten feet, the student putted two balls in the cup and another within the one-foot ring. Eleven points (4 + 4 + 3) were earned for putting uphill from ten feet. Look at the fifteen feet across hill section. One putt was within one foot, one was within three feet, and one was outside three feet for a total of four points (3 + 1 + 0). In summing the student's scores, all putts from each distance and from each area are added. For example, the student has a ten-foot score of 27 and an uphill score of 25. The student's overall score is 56.

The following score levels will be used to evaluate your overall putting performance on the test:

Acceptable = 27 or (27 × 1)

Good = 41 or (27 × 1.5)

Excellent = 54 or (27 × 2)

Perfect! = 108 or (27 × 4)

Before reporting for your test, be sure to warm up by putting for at least fifteen minutes or thirty putts. Remain on the practice greens until you are called for the exam. See Figure 7.7 for tally forms.

15. See Figure 7.8 and the discussion in the text.

Name *Mary Jones* Date *3/26*

A	B	(1)	Type of Errors		
1. Body	Comfort	OK (circled)	TNS		
	Aligned	OK (circled)	RT	LFT	
2. Grip	Pressure	OK (circled)	TNS		
	Height	OK (circled)	HI	LOW	
3. Backswing	Height	OK	HI	LOW (circled)	
	Direction	OK (circled)	RT	LFT	
4. Follow-through	Height	OK	HI	LOW (circled)	
	Direction	OK (circled)	RT	LFT	
5. Speed		OK	FST	SLW (circled)	JKY
6. Club face		OK (circled)	OPN	CLS	
	Total	*7* (10)			

Putting Accuracy Score

Area:	Uphill					Downhill					Across Hill					
Points:	4	3	2	1	0	4	3	2	1	0	4	3	2	1	0	Totals
10'	//	/				/	/	/			/		/	/		*27*
15'		//	/				/	/	/			/		/	/	*18*
25'	/		/		/			/	/	/			/		//	*11*
Totals	*25*					*18*					*13*					*56* Total

Figure 7.7 Checklist and Tally for Evaluating Putting Form and Accuracy

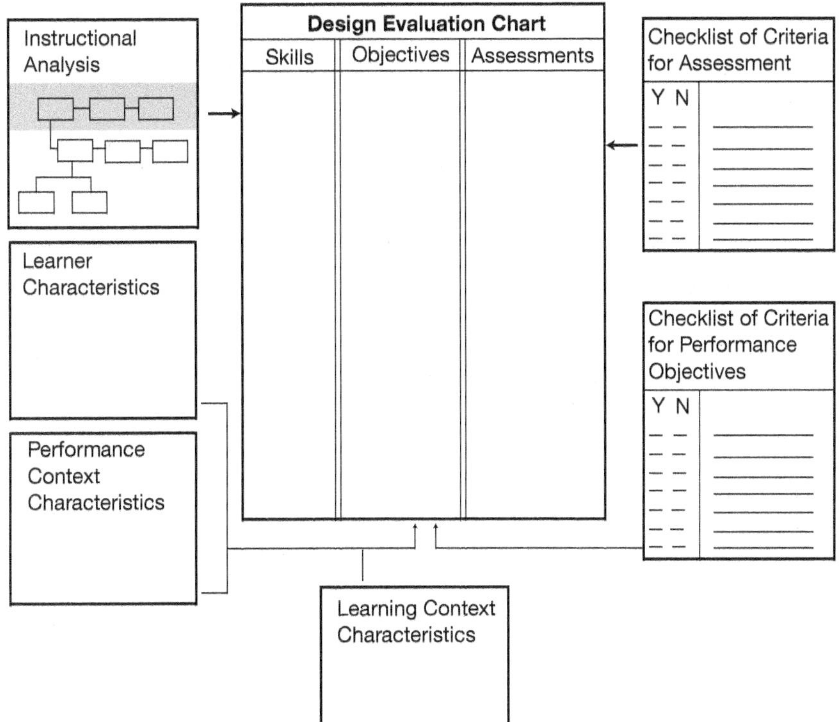

Figure 7.8 Design Elements Gathered and Used in Conducting a Design Evaluation

References and Recommended Readings

Arter, J. A., & McTighe, J. (2001). *Scoring rubrics in the classroom: Using performance criteria for assessing and improving student performance.* Corwin Press. Promotes integrating assessment with instruction to improve student performance.

Arter, J. A., & Chappuis, J. (2006). *Creating and recognizing quality rubrics.* Pearson.

Brookhart, S. M., & Nitko, A. J. (2018). *Educational assessment of students* (8th ed.). Pearson. Includes a good section on assessment of higher-order thinking, problem solving, and critical thinking.

Carey, L. M. (2001). *Measuring and evaluating school learning* (4th ed.). Pearson. Includes deriving and writing test items and rubrics for product, performance, and attitudes, and includes guidelines for portfolio assessment. Terminology is consistent with this text.

Chappuis, J. (2019). *Classroom assessment for student learning: Doing it right—Using it well* (3rd ed.). Pearson. Discusses shift in assessment from ranking students to helping them succeed.

Fishman, J. A., & Galguera, T. (2003). *Introduction to test construction in the social and behavioral sciences: A practical guide.* Rowman & Littlefield. Presents a good perspective on test construction that begins with the end goal as a first consideration in instrument design.

Foshay, W. R., & Hale, J. (2017). Application of principles of performance-based assessment to corporate certifications. *TechTrends, 61,* 71–76. https://doi.org/10.1007/s11528-016-0125-5

Glass, G. V. (2016). One hundred years of research: Prudent aspirations. *Educational Researcher, 45*(2), 69–72. Includes commentary on mastery learning and criterion-referenced testing.

Jonassen, D. H. (1991). Evaluating constructivist learning. *Educational Technology, 31*(9), 28–33.

Kirkpatrick, J. D., & Kirkpatrick, W. K. (2016). *Kirkpatrick's four levels of training evaluation.* ATD Press. Describes the best-known methods of training evaluation.

Kubiszyn, T., & Borich, G. D. (2015). *Educational testing and measurement: Classroom application and practice* (11th ed.). Wiley. Describes criterion-referenced assessment, including information on item-writing criteria, developing alternative assessments, and portfolio assessment.

Mayer, R. E. (2011). *Applying the science of learning.* Pearson. Emphasizes linkage among learning, instruction, and assessment.

McMillan, J. H. (2017). *Classroom assessment: Principles and practice that enhance student learning and motivation* (7th ed.). Pearson. Emphasizes formative evaluation for improving student learning.

Miller, M. D., Linn, R. L., & Gronlund, N. E. (2012). *Measurement and assessment in teaching* (11th ed.). Pearson. Provides comprehensive coverage of classroom assessment from design through interpretation.

Phillips, P. P. (Ed.). (2010). *Measuring and evaluating training.* ASTD Press.

Popham, W. J. (2019). *Classroom assessment: What teachers need to know* (9th ed.). Pearson. Focuses on development and use of classroom testing to increase teaching and learning effectiveness.

Russell, M., & Airasian, P. W. (2011). *Classroom assessment: Concepts and applications* (7th ed.). McGraw-Hill. Provides comprehensive coverage of classroom assessment from design through interpretation.

Shrock, S. A., & Coscarelli, W. C. (2007). *Criterion-referenced test development: Technical and legal guidelines for corporate training* (3rd ed.). Pfeiffer. Focuses on criterion-referenced test development and the importance of linking enabling skills with assessment tasks.

Stanley, P. (2019). *Using rubrics for performance-based assessment: A practical guide to evaluating student work.* Prufrock Press. Straightforward guide to creating, critiquing, and using rubrics for evaluation and grading.

Stevens, D. D., & Levi, A. J. (2013). *Introduction to rubrics* (2nd ed.). Stylus Publishing.

Stiggins, R., & Chappuis, J. (2016). *Introduction to student involved assessment for learning* (7th ed.). Pearson. Promotes quality assessment for the classroom, including designing classroom tests congruent with the purpose for the test.

Zane, T. W. (2009). Performance assessment design principles gleaned from constructivist learning theory (Part 1). *TechTrends, 53*(1), 81–90.

chapter 8

Planning the Instructional Strategy: Theoretical Bases

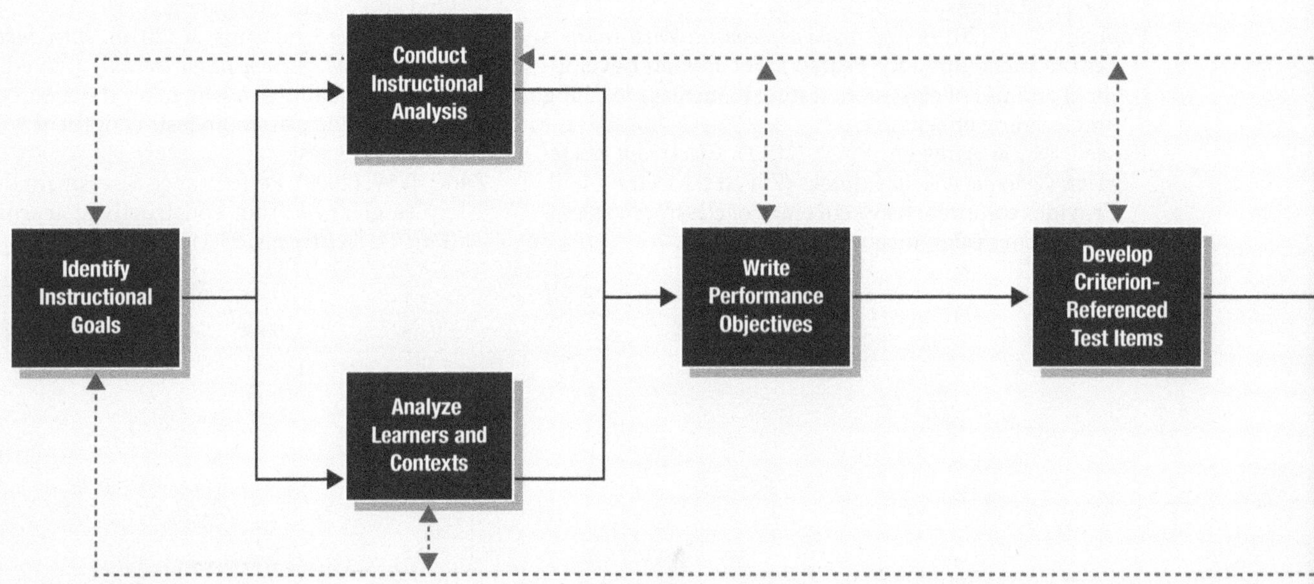

Objectives

- Plan the learning components of an instructional strategy, including preinstructional activities, content presentation and learning guidance, learner participation, assessment, and follow-through activities, for a set of objectives and a particular group of learners.
- Specify learning components congruent with learners' maturity and ability levels.
- Tailor learning components for the type of learning outcome.

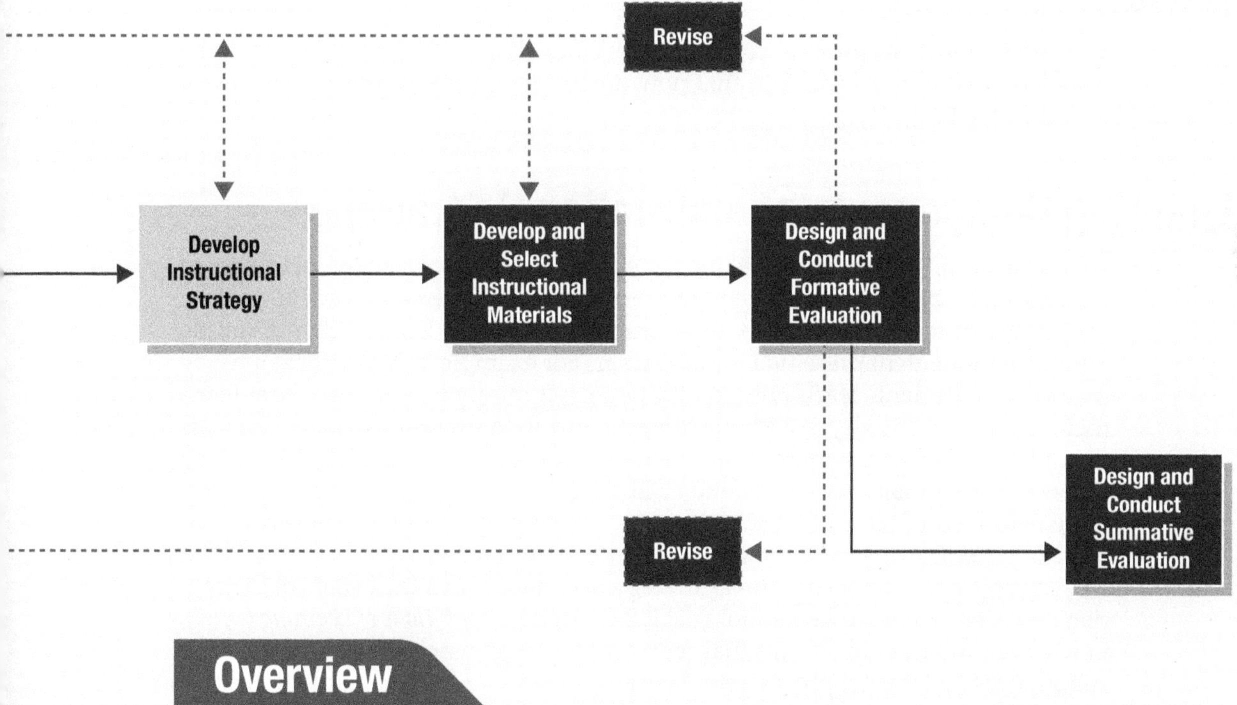

Overview

The instructional strategy is a prescription used for developing or selecting instructional materials. ID products you will need to develop your instructional strategy include all the design materials created thus far, including the instructional goal, the instructional analysis, the learner and context analyses, the performance objectives, and the assessment items. You will need to refer to these materials several times as you design your strategy.

In creating each component of your strategy, you should consider the characteristics of your target students—their needs, interests, and experiences—as well as information about how to gain and maintain their attention throughout the learning components of instruction. Keller's (2010) ARCS model provides a handy structure for considering how to design materials that motivate students to learn.

Instructional designers believe there are five components to a learning strategy. Some educational psychologists, however, view the instructional strategy as having four main learning components that guide learners' intellectual processing through the mental states and activities that foster learning: preinstructional activities, content presentation, student participation with feedback, and follow-through activities. Designers add a fifth learning component—assessment—to facilitate instructional management. Assessment enables us to tailor instruction to the needs of learners, to evaluate the progress of learners, and to evaluate the quality of instructional materials. Although the major function of assessment in the systematic design of instruction is to collect information for determining whether instructional goals have been reached, an equally important function is supporting learning when corrective feedback about performance is provided to learners.

The type of instructional goal is an important consideration when designing your strategy. Whether intellectual skills, verbal information, motor skills, or attitudes, careful consideration of all five of the learning components is important. Each type of goal, however, may require unique activities for each of the learning components.

Concepts

The instructional design steps covered in previous chapters basically deal with the question of what to teach. With that now determined, we turn to the question of how to teach it.

Learning Components of Instructional Strategies

An *instructional strategy* describes the general components of a set of instructional materials and the procedures used with those materials to enable student mastery of learning outcomes. Note that an instructional strategy is more than a simple outline of the content presented to the learner. For example, it is insufficient to say that to have students learn how to add two-digit numbers, you must first teach them single-digit numbers without carrying and then present the main concepts of adding two-digit numbers. This is certainly a part of an instructional strategy and refers to content sequencing and clustering, but this says nothing about what to do before you present that content, what learners will do with that content, or how to test or transfer the content to a performance context.

The concept of an instructional strategy originated with the events of instruction described in cognitive psychologist R. M. Gagné's *Conditions of Learning* (1985), in which he defines nine events that represent external instructional activities that support internal mental processes of learning. Gagné's events of instruction are:

1. Gaining attention
2. Informing learner of the objective
3. Stimulating recall of prerequisite learning
4. Presenting the stimulus material
5. Providing learning guidance
6. Eliciting the performance
7. Providing feedback about performance correctness
8. Assessing the performance
9. Enhancing retention and transfer

Gagné's fifth event, providing learning guidance, has specific meaning within his system of instructional prescriptions for different domains of learning outcomes, but in a general sense, it is useful to think of all of the instructional events as forms of learning guidance. Learning is internal, occurring in the mind of the learner, and the purpose for developing an instructional strategy is planning how to guide learners' internal intellectual processing through the mental states and activities that psychologists have shown foster learning. Gagné's cognitive view of instruction is often characterized as quite purposeful and prescriptive, more content-centered than learner-centered, but we believe this to be a false dichotomy. Yes, there is a definite focus on content because we begin instructional design with needs and goals to preclude aimless wandering through the process; and yes, instruction could be a content-centered lecture/discussion on "textbook" solutions for boosting sales in a certain region. Instruction, however, could also be a learner-centered, problem-based learning team of managers, sales personnel, and selected loyal clients in sessions designed to explore the context, sales processes, causes, possible solutions, and consequences. In our view, the nature of instruction that results from ID is predetermined not by the model but rather by the instructional strategies that are chosen by the designer. The Dick and Carey model is based on this understanding of the cognitive perspective, and we teach it in this text for several reasons:

- It is grounded in learning theory.
- It conforms to currently prevailing views of instruction in public education (standards-based accountability), higher education accreditation (outcomes assessment), and business/industry/military training (performance-based).
- It is a necessary foundational system of instructional design for new students of the field and the most intuitive system to learn.

Later in this chapter, after working through the cognitive approach to ID, we offer our view of blending more learner-centered constructivist learning environments with more guided content-centered strategies.

To facilitate the instructional design process, Gagné's events of instruction are organized here into five major learning components that are part of an overall instructional strategy. The five major learning components of an instructional strategy are:

1. Preinstructional activities
2. Content presentation
3. Learner participation
4. Assessment
5. Follow-through activities

Each of these components is described briefly next, with detailed examples of how strategies could be developed for goals in each domain of learning.

Preinstructional Activities

Prior to beginning formal instruction, consider three factors: motivating the learners, informing them of what they will learn, and stimulating recall of relevant knowledge and skills that they already should know.

Motivating Learners One of the typical criticisms of instruction is its lack of interest and appeal to the learner. One instructional designer who attempts to deal with this problem in a systematic way is John Keller (2010), who developed the ARCS model based on his review of the psychological literature on motivation. The four parts of his model are Attention, Relevance, Confidence, and Satisfaction (summarized in Table 8.1). To produce instruction that motivates the learner, these four attributes of the instruction must be considered throughout the design of the instructional strategy.

The first aspect of motivation is to gain the *attention* of learners and subsequently sustain it throughout the instruction. Gaining attention is also the first of Gagné's nine events of instruction. Learners must attend to a task in order to learn to perform it. Their initial attention can be gained by using emotional or personal information, asking questions, creating mental challenges, and, perhaps the best method of all, using human-interest examples.

According to Keller, the second aspect of motivation is *relevance*. Although you may be able to gain learners' attention for a short period of time, it is difficult to sustain that attention when they do not perceive the subsequent instruction as

Table 8.1 Keller's ARCS Model of Student Motivation

Type of Motivation	Purpose in Instruction	Ways to Bring About
Attention	Gain and sustain learner's attention	Presenting emotional or personal information Questioning Creating mental challenges Using human interest examples
Relevance	Illustrate relevance of instruction for learner	Showing how learning particular skills matches their personal goals (e.g., personal interests, planned progress, employment, success)
Confidence	Demonstrate that learners have the skills and ability to be successful in learning particular skills	Convincing learners who lack confidence that they have the background and ability to succeed Demonstrating to overconfident learners that there remains much to be learned Channeling those who have mastered the skills into more advanced instruction
Satisfaction	Ensure the learner derives satisfaction from the learning experience	Using extrinsic rewards for success such as free time, good grades, promotion, recognition among peers, etc. Focusing on intrinsic rewards such as personally succeeding, building personal capabilities, self-actualization, and experiencing increased self-esteem

relevant to them. When instruction is believed to be irrelevant, learners ask, "Why do we have to study this?" and employees question the relationship between training and their jobs. When you use information from the learner and context analyses (Chapter 5) to help learners understand the relevance of the skills included in instruction, you sustain their motivation; if not, you undoubtedly lose them. In other words, instruction must be related to important goals in the learners' personal lives, student lives, or professional lives.

The third major component of the ARCS model is *confidence*. For learners to be highly motivated, they must be confident that they can master the objectives for the instruction. If they lack confidence, then they are less motivated. Learners who are overconfident are also problematic; they see no need to attend to the instruction because they already know it all. The challenge with under- and overconfident learners is to create the appropriate level of expectation for success. Learners who lack confidence must be convinced that they have the skills and knowledge to be successful, whereas overconfident learners must be convinced that there are important details in the instruction that remain to be learned. However, if learners have, in fact, already mastered the instruction, they should be given more advanced instruction that more nearly meets the four aspects of the ARCS model.

The final component of Keller's model is *satisfaction*. High motivation depends on whether the learner derives satisfaction (also known as *reinforcement*) from the learning experience. Sometimes satisfaction is sustained through the use of extrinsic rewards, such as free time, a high grade, a promotion in the workplace, or some other form of recognition for successful performance. Of greater importance is the intrinsic satisfaction a learner can gain by mastering a new skill and being able to use it successfully. Self-esteem can be greatly enhanced through meaningful learning experiences.

When taken alone, any of the four aspects of Keller's model may not be sufficient to keep a learner on task in a learning situation. However, when you incorporate all four aspects of the ARCS model into your strategy, the likelihood of maintaining the learners' interest is greatly increased.

There is a direct relationship between the five main learning components of the instructional strategy and the four aspects of motivation included in Keller's ARCS model (Figure 8.1). Following exposure to each component of the instruction, learners ask themselves three questions. The first question relates to the relevance of the content presented or activity performed. If the materials are perceived as relevant to personal needs and interests, then attention is gained and maintained. The second relates to how confident they are that they can be successful. If they understand the material and are confident that they will be successful, then motivation is sustained. The third question relates to how satisfied they are that the content presented and activities provided meet their needs. If they are satisfied with each component, then motivation is maintained.

In designing the instructional strategy, we must devise ways to present each component to help ensure that learners continue to answer the three questions affirmatively. To do this, we can use the content from the learner analysis. We must understand their needs, interests, and performance levels well enough to infer how they will perceive the content and activities. In designing each learning component of the instructional strategy for the goal, designers should ask, "How does this relate to the learners' needs and interests and to their feelings of confidence and satisfaction?"

The most important aspect of maintaining learners' perceptions of relevance appears to be the congruence between the learners' expectations and the instruction they encounter. For example, the initial motivating material must be congruent with the learners' perceptions of their needs and interests. What material best meets learners' initial expectations and hooks them into the instruction? If you judge that the congruence of the material in any component would not immediately be obvious to the learner, then devise ways to illustrate the congruence so they perceive it as relevant. Problems result when learners fail to see the relationships among their initial expectations, the content presented, the examples described, the practice activities provided, and the test questions administered.

As you develop the subsequent sections of your strategy, continued in the following pages, you will want to remain aware of motivational concerns.

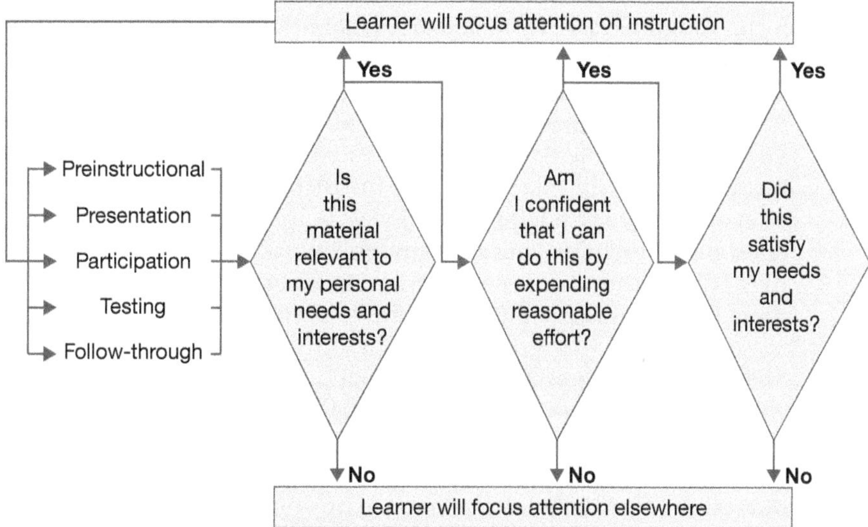

Figure 8.1 The Relationship Between Each Major Component of Instruction and ARCS

Bandura's (1993) work links confidence and motivation, wherein his theory of self-efficacy predicts that students who believe in their ability to achieve a goal are more likely to do so than are students who doubt their ability. For example, present the objectives so that the learners perceive them as achievable instead of overwhelming. A list of thirty or forty technically worded objectives is likely to shatter the learners' confidence, whereas a list of three or four global objectives written in the learners' language tends to build confidence. Learners who are sure that they have previously mastered all prerequisites are more confident than those who doubt their skill and knowledge.

Learners have an immediate reaction to the volume of material presented initially; are learners more likely to feel comfortable and confident or overwhelmed with the amount of material you have chosen? Considering practice exercises, are learners likely to succeed on those you have provided and thus gain confidence in themselves? Has enough instruction preceded the practice for learners to be successful? You should also consider how learners will perceive pretests in deciding whether it is advisable to administer one. Will pretests demonstrate competence in the skills to be learned or create doubt and insecurity instead?

Learner satisfaction is the third general area of consideration. Will learners be rewarded for learning the skills? Will they consider the proposed rewards as adequate for the amount of effort required? Should you provide additional content to point out potential rewards? On your practice exercises, are they likely to succeed and thus gain intrinsic feelings of satisfaction and accomplishment? Are they likely to perceive the feedback you have designed as verification of their success or as criticism? After they complete your posttest, are they likely to be satisfied with their progress? Will they perceive the effort they had to expend to be justified by what they learned? Will they believe that the promises you made in the preinstructional materials were realized? Will they believe that they can do something better? If they believe that the rewards would be forthcoming yet the rewards fail to materialize, then your task in motivating them for a subsequent unit is undoubtedly more difficult. Remember that the most powerful and long-lasting rewards are intrinsic feelings of accomplishment that are relevant to a learner's own internal system of values.

Informing the Learner of the Objectives The second component of the preinstructional activities is to inform the learners of the objectives for the instruction. Have you ever studied a text and wondered which key concepts you should be learning? If you had been informed of the objectives, then you would have known where to focus your attention, what to learn, what to solve, and what to interpret.

By providing learners with the objectives, you help them focus their study strategies on these outcomes. They should feel they are responsible not for knowing everything but rather for being able to do certain specific things. Not only does this information help learners to use more efficient study strategies, but it also helps them determine the relevance of the instruction. A list of objectives at the beginning of instruction may not be the best way to inform and motivate. It might be more appropriate to guide learners through a worked example of the kind of problem they will be learning to solve in the upcoming instruction or model the kind of dramatic presentation they will learn to prepare and deliver.

Stimulating Recall of Prerequisite Skills The third preinstructional component is informing learners of the prerequisite skills required to begin your instruction. This provides a quick reality check to make sure that learners get an initial view of the relationship between the new content and what they already know. This can be done either by briefly testing learners on entry skills and requiring demonstrated mastery before continuing or by briefly describing required entry skills and telling learners that instruction will proceed on the assumption that they can perform these skills. Informing learners of prerequisites prepares them for the instruction that is to follow. If a test is used, it provides designers with information on the variability of students' entry skills, which helps an instructor plan remediation and interpret student achievement in the new instruction.

The second, and more important, purpose for this component is to promote learners' active recall of relevant mental contexts in which the new content can be integrated. In fact, all three preinstructional activities, taken together, can be viewed as the important first step in activating the mental processing that enables learners to tie what they are learning with what they already know. This linking of new with old makes initial learning easier and eventual recall more successful.

Content Presentation and Learning Guidance

The next step is to determine exactly what information, concepts, rules, and principles must be presented to the learner. This is the basic explanation of what the unit is all about. Content presentation usually follows one of two general patterns—deductive or inductive. In the *deductive pattern*, or content-centered approach, a textbook, an instructor, or mediated materials show the learner how to distinguish the pieces of new learning and the structural relationships among the pieces to put them all together into a coherent whole. The *inductive pattern*, or learner-centered approach, is most associated with discovery learning, in which students are guided or guide themselves through experiences from which they glean the pieces of new learning and the structural relationships needed to build the coherent whole. If we consider those in our lives whom we consider to be good teachers, we can usually see how they were able to blend both deductive and inductive patterns in their instruction.

Content presentation is always interwoven with learning guidance, which concerns formatting new content in ways that help us "get it" and remember it when needed in the future. A textbook contains the simplest example of learning guidance in the way text is laid out with section headings, subheadings, paragraph headings, bulleted lists, and so forth. This embedded outline is our cue to the structure of the content and makes it easier to learn and remember. It is important not only to introduce new content but also to explain its structure and interrelationships with other content. Making learning more memorable by depicting structure and relationships can be accomplished in many ways, such as outlining (as in the textbook example); diagramming; modeling (two-dimensional representations and three-dimensional real objects); illustrating with still and motion graphics; highlighting; flowcharting; talking through progressive levels of abstraction; and ranking by size, importance, or complexity.

Another common form of learning guidance is the use of examples. You must determine the types and number of examples to provide with the new content. Many research studies have investigated how we use examples and nonexamples to learn new skills. A *nonexample* is a deliberate attempt by the designer to point out why a particular example is wrong. We know that learning is facilitated by the use of examples and nonexamples, so, generally, they should be included in your instructional strategy. We consider, in more detail, what learning guidance should be included in content presentation and learner participation for objectives in different domains of learning later in this chapter. Throughout this and following chapters, we use the term *content presentation* to mean the totality of what is to be learned along with relevant learning guidance in the form of examples and nonexamples, illustrations, diagrams, demonstrations, model solutions, scenarios, case studies, sample performances, and so on. It is important to remember that the primary error in this step is to present too much content, especially when much of it is unrelated to the objective. Sweller (1994) warns that designers should be aware of the mental processing requirements that too much information and too many intellectual skills can place on a learner's short-term memory (working memory). He uses the term **cognitive load** to refer to one's capacity for holding new information and concepts in mind while processing them and fitting them into the body of knowledge already in permanent memory. Sweller's article suggests ways that designers can manage the cognitive load in instruction.

Learner Participation

Practice with feedback is one of the most powerful components in the learning process. You can enhance the learning process greatly by providing learners with activities that are directly relevant to the objectives, giving learners an opportunity to practice what you want them to be able to do. One approach is to embed practice tests (as described in Chapter 7) into the instruction. The more common approach is to provide informal opportunities within the instruction for students to "try out" what they are learning at the time that they are learning it. Not only should learners be able to practice, but they should also be provided feedback or information about their performance.

Feedback

Feedback is sometimes referred to as *knowledge of results*. For simple learning tasks, students can be told whether their answer is right or wrong or can be shown a copy of the right answer or an example from which they must infer whether their answer is correct. For more complex learning tasks, students can also be told why their practice work is right or wrong, and guidance can be provided to help them understand, learn, and correct their work. Shute's (2008) review of the research on formative feedback is interesting reading and closes with guidelines on what to do, what not to do, how to time feedback, and how feedback relates to learner characteristics.

Feedback is often provided in the form of reinforcement. For adult learners, knowledge of correct completion of a task is often the best reinforcement and can be accompanied by such positive statements as "Great, you're correct." Young children often respond favorably to such forms of reinforcement as an approving look from the teacher in classroom instruction, pop-up animations and audio flourishes in multimedia instruction, recognition in front of peers, special privileges, or the opportunity to do some other activity. Acceptance and approval of peers in small-group interaction can also be very reinforcing and can provide valuable practice and feedback opportunities as learners collaborate to understand concepts and solve problems.

When the learning components are chosen, it is typical to provide content, examples, practice, and feedback for each objective in the instructional analysis. Sometimes, it is more efficient and appropriate to combine several objectives into a cluster in order to provide more integrated content, examples, and practice with feedback. The decision to cluster the objectives is a subjective one, made by the designer based on knowledge of both the content and the learners. When it is an inappropriate decision, it becomes apparent during the formative evaluations.

The learning components chosen for teaching each objective should include components for the terminal objective. It cannot be assumed that just because you have taught each objective in your analysis that learners will be able to integrate all of the skills and information to perform the terminal objective. The final element of your content and learner participation should be a summary of all of the instruction. It is structured like any other objective; namely, there is a summary of the content that has been presented and examples of how to perform the terminal objective. Then the learner is given the opportunity to do a sample activity that includes the terminal objective and to receive feedback on the activity. When that is done, the learner then completes the assessment described in the next section.

Assessment

Four basic criterion-referenced tests are described in Chapter 7: entry skills tests, pretests, practice tests, and posttests. The general function of each was described as well as how to develop them. At this point, you must decide exactly what your strategy as a designer will be for assessing what learners have accomplished. This strategy may differ significantly from that which is eventually chosen by an instructor who uses your completed instruction.

First, you know that you will be using practice tests of some sort, either more or less formal, as part of the learner participation component of your instruction. Then you must make some decisions about what assessment activities to include:

- Should I test entry skills?
- When should the assessment be administered?
- Should I have a pretest over the skills to be taught? When should it be administered? Exactly what skills should be assessed?
- When and how should I administer the posttest?
- Should I question learners' attitudes after the instruction?

A careful distinction must be made here between developing draft materials in preparation for formative evaluation and producing materials in their final form after formative evaluation and revision. The draft form of your instruction developed at this stage may be "test heavy" because you want to be able to locate missing entry skills and track student performance carefully to pinpoint ineffective sequences in the instruction.

In addition to the formal testing already described, the designer may want to consider using embedded attitude questions, which indicate learners' opinions of the instruction at the time that they encountered it. For example, rather than wait until the end of the unit of instruction to ask general questions about the quality of the illustrations, ask questions during the instruction about the illustrations just presented. These attitude or opinion questions can be located directly in self-paced instruction or included in unit guides. Later, after formative evaluation and revision, the embedded attitude questions would probably be removed from the instruction, and the overall testing strategy would become "leaner."

The most helpful types of attitude items are as specific as possible to provide the most information to the designer when the time comes to do the formative evaluation. The questions could refer to such aspects of the instruction as the clarity of a specific example or illustration, the sufficiency of a set of practice problems, or the general interest level of the content.

Sometimes there are parts of the instruction in which the designer uses a special procedure or approach—from either a content or a pedagogical point of view. At these points in the instruction, the designer can insert very specific questions about learners' reactions to what has been done. This approach does not seem to be disruptive to learners during tryouts of draft materials but instead provides on-the-spot specific reactions to the instruction rather than the general reactions that are often received on a questionnaire administered at the end of an instructional unit. The end-of-unit questions can help the designer obtain an overall reaction to the instruction, but the embedded attitude questions provide more precise and targeted information.

Follow-Through Activities

The final learning component in the instructional strategy, *follow-through*, is the strategy for ensuring that learners' memory and transfer needs have been addressed. The key to this step is reviewing the performance context analysis, which should describe the conditions under which the learners must perform the instructional goal.

Memory Skills Consider what learners must recall from memory while performing the instructional goal. Is there anything that must absolutely be retrieved from memory? Must it be done rapidly and without prompts or reference materials? If so, then many of the techniques suggested later in this chapter for teaching verbal information are critical for inclusion in the instructional strategy.

Often the answer to the question of what learners must remember is that memorization is not critical, just as long as they carry out the skill successfully. If this is the case with your goal, then you might want to consider the use of a **job aid**, which is any device used by the performers to reduce their reliance on their memory to perform a task. For example, could the learner follow a checklist while performing the task? If so, this greatly reduces the need to memorize a lot of information and could possibly reduce the length of the instruction.

Transfer of Learning The second question to ask about your instructional goal is "What is the nature of the transfer of learning that must take place?" That is, "How different is the performance context from the learning context?" Let's look at two somewhat extreme examples to make our case.

Suppose the instructional goal is to use a new computer application program, and it is taught in the training center on computers identical to those used in the workplace. During the training, learners work with actual forms used in their department while learning to use the application. It is expected that the learners use the new application after they have completed their training.

From our description, it can be assumed that if the training is well designed, then there should be 100 percent transfer to the workplace. Transfer occurs because the systems and the application are the same and the forms are similar to those used in training. The remaining components in the transfer context are the installation of the application on the learners' computers and the support environment established by their managers for learners' successful use of the new application.

Now consider a situation in which the instructional goal is to become effective participants in employee quality-improvement teams. The employees to be trained are from different divisions within the company; have various types of expertise, levels of education, commitment to the company, and attitudes about their supervisors; and face diverse problems in their respective divisions.

A situation like this requires careful consideration of the transfer of skills learned during training. First, it is assumed that the designer has been able to determine the steps that lead to effective participation on a team. The content and examples should draw on a variety of situations from various parts of the company. The learners should receive ample opportunities to practice working on a team that seeks new solutions to troublesome problems. Unfortunately, the trainer will not be able to create practice situations that exactly match the job conditions because the mix of people on quality-improvement teams varies, as does the nature of the problems. Will the learners be praised for using their new skills? Will anyone even notice them? Will they have the desired effect in terms of increasing the effectiveness of the teams?

Research indicates that, in general, learners transfer only some of what they learn to new contexts (Schunk, 2019). Learning tends to be situation-specific. Therefore, the designer must be aware of the tendency of learning not transferring and must use every means possible to counter this tendency. Broad and Newstrom (2001) reviewed the literature on transfer and organized it in terms of what the trainer, the manager, and the learner can do to increase the probability of transfer.

In addition to making the training and performance as similar as possible, it is also very helpful to require learners to develop a plan that indicates how they will use their new skills in the performance context. The plan should include a list of possible problems the learner may have and suggestions for how these can be overcome. Commitment to and periodic review of the plan help remind the learner of the skills that were learned and how those skills can be used.

Transfer of training from the classroom to the performance site is one of the most critical concerns of educators and trainers. No longer is end-of-instruction posttest performance considered the major criterion by which instructional effectiveness is judged. Instruction is effective if learners can take a step further along the path of self-actualization, use it to further their study of more advanced topics, or perform skills on the job that make a difference in their organization's effectiveness. If these criteria are not met, then there are serious questions about the need for the instruction. Was it the wrong instruction, was it not taught effectively, were learners not motivated, or did it simply not transfer to the performance site? When we examine instruction that does not work, we can find potential problems at a variety of points in the instructional design process—from the needs assessment to the strategy for promoting transfer of learning.

Summary of Learning Components

The learning components of a complete instructional strategy are summarized next in their typical chronological sequence.

A. Preinstructional activities
   1. Gain attention and motivate learners
   2. Describe objectives
   3. Describe and promote recall of prerequisite skills

B. Content presentation
   1. Content
   2. Learning guidance

C. Learner participation
   1. Practice
   2. Feedback

D. Assessment
   1. Entry skills test
   2. Pretest
   3. Posttest

E. Follow-through activities
   1. Memory aids for retention
   2. Transfer considerations

Note that components B, C, and sometimes E.1 are repeated for each instructional objective or cluster of objectives; they are also repeated in summary form for the terminal objective. Components A, D, and E.2 are repeated selectively as needed for objectives or clusters of objectives based on the content, lesson length, flow of the instruction, needs of learners, and so forth.

Learning Components for Learners of Different Maturity and Ability Levels

Let's consider different learners' needs for instructional strategies. First, recall that the learning components of an instructional strategy are intended to guide learners' intellectual processing through the mental states and activities that foster learning. Ideally, all learners could manage their own intellectual processing; that is, they would be independent learners, or we could say that they had "learned how to learn." Indeed, this is an outcome of schooling that is now found in many mission statements for public, private, elementary, secondary, and postsecondary educational institutions.

This ideal exists, to a lesser or greater extent, in all of us. Generally speaking, younger and less-able students cannot manage their learning processes as well as older and more-able students. There is thus a greater need to provide the learning components in an instructional strategy for younger and less-able learners, whereas older and more-able students can provide many of their own learning components. The learning components of an instructional strategy should be planned selectively rather than being provided slavishly for all learners in all instructional settings. Instruction for a first-grade student learning the concept of fractions should include all learning components. In contrast, a one-day in-service seminar for electrical engineers on the latest materials for circuit boards might include only content presentation with examples, practice, and feedback in the form of live question-and-answer discussion sessions. In this situation, a transfer activity might be conducted after the seminar in work-group problem discussions using groupware on the company intranet. The intent in planning instructional strategies should be to match learning components with the amount of guidance needed by the intended learners.

This same consideration is critical when designing instruction for distance students. Moore and Kearsley's (2012) theory of transactional distance is a "pedagogical" theory to be used as guidance for developing a distance course that meets the needs of the intended student population. The implications of the theory are illustrated in Table 8.2; that is, more autonomous distance learners can manage greater transactional distance, thus requiring less course structure and course dialogue (meaning student interaction) for an effective course experience. The opposite is true for less autonomous learners. It can be seen that one would not provide a low-structure, low-dialogue course for students who are not self-directed. However, any combination of structure and dialogue can work quite well for independent learners. Structure makes intellectual content acquisition accessible, manageable, and predictable, whereas dialogue personalizes the student's experience and facilitates learner participation. Although not synonymous with our description of learning components, it is clear that course structure and dialogue are important vehicles for carrying the learning components of an instructional strategy. The value of course structure and learner interaction is supported in studies of distance learning students' perceptions of what works for them in distance courses (Moore & Kearsley, 2012).

Table 8.2 The Structure and Dialogue Dimensions of Moore and Kearsley's Theory of Transactional Distance

Level of Course Structure	Level of Course Dialogue	Transactional Distance	Suitability for Learner Autonomy Level
Low: a flexible course in which student has control of course management	*Low:* little interactive communication with the instructor	*Greater*	Highly autonomous learner
↕	↕	↕	↕
High: a rigid course in which student conforms to a detailed course structure	*High:* lots of interactive communication and guidance from instructor (or through tutor, classmate, course materials, computer, etc.)	*Lesser*	Less autonomous learner who has not "learned how to learn" *or* Any range of learner autonomy up to and including the most independent learner

Learning Components for Various Learning Outcomes

The basic learning components of an instructional strategy are the same regardless of designing instruction for an intellectual skill, verbal information, a motor skill, or an attitude. They can thus be used as an organizing structure for your design. Within each component, however, there are distinctions to consider for each type of learning outcome, as noted in the sections that follow. Developing strategies to help ensure that material is motivational is omitted from this discussion because it was presented earlier in this chapter.

Intellectual Skills

Each of the five learning components should be considered when designing instruction for intellectual skills.

Preinstructional Activities In addition to considering motivation, informing the learner of objectives, and promoting recall of prerequisites, the designer should be aware of both the way learners may have organized their entry knowledge in memory and the limits of their ability to remember new content. The strategy should provide ways for the learner to link new content to existing prerequisite knowledge in memory. When the links may not be obvious to the learner, direct instruction about the links and relationships between existing knowledge and new skills should be provided.

Content Presentation and Learning Guidance In presenting content for intellectual skills, it is important to recall the hierarchical nature of intellectual skills in determining the sequence for presentation. Subordinate skills should always come first. It is also important to point out the distinguishing characteristics of concepts that make up rules, which may include physical characteristics or role and relationship characteristics. It is also important to focus learners' attention on irrelevant characteristics that may be present as well as on common errors that learners make in distinguishing among concepts or in applying rules. These *prompts*, however, must eventually disappear from instruction in ill-defined problem solving because the nature of this type of learning requires that students be able to make their own decisions about the relevance and interrelatedness of various components of the problem being solved.

In selecting examples and nonexamples of a concept, the designer should select both clear and questionable examples and nonexamples to illustrate gross and fine distinctions. It may be necessary to provide direct information about why the examples fit or do not fit the definition. You should also ensure that the examples and illustrations selected are familiar to the learner. Teaching an unknown using an unfamiliar example increases the complexity of the skill for the learner unnecessarily; thus, you should select instances and examples likely to be contained in the learner's experience and memory. To enhance transfer, you could progress from familiar examples to less familiar ones and then to new instances. When students are learning to solve ill-defined problems, the new examples usually take the form of case studies, problem scenarios, and student-selected examples that can be carried over into practice and feedback activities.

The strategy should also provide the learner with ways of organizing new skills so they can be stored along with relevant existing knowledge and thus be recalled more easily. This is particularly critical when students are learning to solve ill-structured problems for which they must "pull together" and synthesize a range of new and old learning to develop solution strategies.

Often at the end of presentation activities, designers say, "I taught all the subordinate skills and each of the steps in the goal. What is left to teach?" Yes, learners have been taught each of the steps, but they have not typically put them all together at one time. Therefore, the content presentation for the terminal objective should at least be a review of all of the steps required to perform the goal, and an example of complete and correct performance of the goal.

Learner Participation There are several important considerations when designing practice exercises for intellectual skills. One is the congruence of the practice to the conditions and behaviors prescribed in the objectives and covered in the instruction, which helps separate relevant practice from busywork. Others are ensuring the link between prerequisite knowledge and new skills and progressing from problems that are less difficult to those that are more complex. Yet another is providing a familiar context within which the skill can be rehearsed. Imagine having to practice analyzing an instructional goal in an unfamiliar skill area or having to write a paragraph on a topic you know nothing about. When you are skilled in performing the instructional goal, you are able to focus on the goal analysis process; when you are familiar with the paragraph topic, you are able to concentrate on the structure of the paragraph and the design of the message. As with designing the presentation of new content and examples, structuring practice exercises using unfamiliar contexts may unnecessarily increase the complexity of the skill for the learner.

There are three caveats regarding the complexity of practice exercises. First, practice toward the end of instruction should replicate conditions found in the performance context for optimum transfer. If this authentic practice seems too unfamiliar to learners, then additional practice (and perhaps content) is required to engage learners in increasingly less familiar contexts until the performance context can be approximated. A second, and related, caveat is that practice for learning to solve ill-defined problems must eventually be in unfamiliar contexts because that is the only way that learners will be able to try out the problem-solving strategies they are learning in a way that enables transfer out of the classroom and into real-world applications. The third is that the learner should be given the opportunity to practice the terminal objective and to receive corrective feedback before the posttest.

The nature of feedback to learners is also important. It should be balanced in focusing on both the successes and failures in students' practice. Focusing only on errors may cause learners to perceive that nothing they did was meritorious, which is seldom the case. When errors are committed, learners should be provided with information about why their responses were inadequate. Learners tend to perceive corrective feedback as information rather than criticism, especially when they can use the feedback to improve their performance. As learners move from lower-level to higher-level intellectual skills, the nature of feedback changes from pointing out features that make practice responses "right" or "wrong" to guidance for students both on their responses and on the process that they used to arrive at their responses.

Assessment The strategy for assessing learners' performance of intellectual skills involves determining when and how to test the skills. To make these decisions, the designer should consider how the test results are used by both the designer and the learner. *Premature testing*, or tests administered prior to learners' readiness for them, can be more damaging than beneficial because they tend to discourage learners and to provide incorrect information about the adequacy of the instruction. In designing tests for complex intellectual skills, it is often desirable to test whether learners have mastered concepts and relationships as well as describe the correct steps for performing a procedure prior to asking them to perform the terminal objective. For example, you may want to test whether students can describe the characteristics of a good paragraph and the criteria for judging paragraph quality prior to asking them to write paragraphs. Practicing incorrect constructions does not improve students' ability to write. Testing their writing skills prior to their mastery of subordinate skills yields paragraphs that require a great amount of feedback from the instructor and frustration for the students.

Just as damaging as premature testing is applying inappropriate standards for judging the quality of intellectual skill products and performances. You should consider carefully the levels of performance that reflect outstanding work, acceptable work, and unacceptable work for a given target group. Setting these standards is somewhat arbitrary, but they must be based on a realistic conception of what is possible for a particular age or ability group in a given situation. Remember that the standard for judging the quality of students' solutions to ill-structured problems cannot be a single correct answer because by their nature, ill-structured problems can have more than one correct solution. Solutions are usually judged using a rubric that accounts for how well the students' solution process identifies and handles the components of the problem as well as how closely the answer embodies the characteristics of an adequate solution to the problem.

Follow-Through It is critical to consider the requirements for retention and transfer of learning for hierarchically related skills, especially when the skills from one instructional unit are subordinate to those in a subsequent one. You must consider whether corrective feedback following the posttest is sufficient or if additional instruction with practice and feedback is required. You should also use data from the posttest to target additional instruction on specific subordinate skills where it is needed.

The review of the strategy for memory and transfer requirements is extremely important with intellectual skills. Where will the skill eventually be used, and has there been sufficient preparation for transfer to occur? Have learners been given authentic tasks to perform and a variety of tasks similar to those encountered in the workplace? If the skill must be used from memory in the performance context, have sufficient cues been provided in the instructional practice? Is it appropriate to create a job aid that enables, for example, animated pop-up explanations for each of the icons in the toolbar of a new computer interface, or could the steps for calibrating a quality-control instrument be listed on a card for use as needed? What about the environment in which the skills will be used? Has this been reproduced, both physically and interpersonally, in the instruction? Finally, is the performance site prepared to support the learner? Are managers and supervisors aware of what is being taught and how the learners expect to use the skills? Are teachers familiar with the performance context, and have they included instruction on how to integrate new skills into the work environment? Prompting the organization to encourage and reward the new skills of learners is a critical aspect of the overall instructional strategy. You can begin this part of the process, if it has not already been done, when you begin to try out the instruction.

A critical transfer requirement for higher-order intellectual skills is learning not only strategies for solving problems but also the ability to reflect on, evaluate, and improve the manner in which one derives and manages those strategies. This ability to monitor and direct one's own cognitive processes is the heart of "learning how to learn" and requires attention throughout all five learning components of an instructional strategy. Briefly, the tactic in all five learning components is to gradually transfer the responsibility for structuring the learning experience from the teacher and materials to the learner. This is the ultimate goal of transfer (e.g., Jonassen, 2011). Our wish for all students-become-citizens is that they have learned to regulate their own learning and profit from their experiences. For further study, readers are referred to Merrill's (2013), Mayer's (2008), and Jonassen's (1997, 2004, 2011) design strategies for teaching problem solving where self-regulated learning is the goal. Kolb's (1984) theory of experiential learning also emphasizes the role of observation and reflection in self-regulation of the learning process. The five learning components and their considerations for intellectual skills are summarized in Table 8.3.

Table 8.3 Learning Components and Considerations to Support Learning for Intellectual Skills

Learning Components	Considerations for Each Component
Preinstructional Activities	Provide for motivation: attention, relevance, confidence, satisfaction Inform learner of objectives Promote recall of prerequisites Link new content to existing knowledge/skills
Content Presentation and Learner Guidance	Sequence based on hierarchy among skills Disclose distinguishing characteristics of concepts (physical, purpose, qualities, etc.) Point out common errors in classifying Illustrate organizing structures (outlines, headings, graphics, job aids, etc.) Point out common errors in classifying Provide examples and nonexamples Create ways of organizing new into existing skills
Learner Participation	Ensure congruence of practice to conditions and behaviors Progress from less to more difficult Use familiar contexts for rehearsal Provide conditions similar to performance context Ensure feedback is balanced with qualities and errors
Assessment	Ensure learners' readiness for testing Accommodate hierarchical nature of skills Apply appropriate criteria for learner age, ability
Follow-Through	Promote transfer (authentic tasks to performance context) Consider memory requirements Consider job aid requirements Ensure job environment receptive Reflect on learning experience and future applications

Verbal Information

Next, we consider each learning component in relation to verbal information goals and subordinate skills.

Preinstructional Activities Designing preinstructional activities is important for verbal information outcomes. Attention and motivation are critical because learning verbal information is just not as exciting as learning new concepts and solving problems. In most instances, verbal information is taught as part of the "body of knowledge" that learners need for mastering other types of skills. To ensure relevance, it should be organized and taught in small doses along with the other skills instead of as a large and isolated group of facts. Make it very clear how the information is used and what value it has. At that point, describing objectives follows naturally, and the question of recalling prerequisite skills can be addressed.

Technically speaking, learning verbal information has no prerequisite skills, but practically speaking, most verbal information is part of a larger body of interrelated knowledge residing in the learner's memory. It also enables performance of intellectual skills that are hierarchically organized. Recall the use of the "V" notation to indicate the position of verbal information in attitudes, intellectual skills, and psychomotor skills. The contexts in which the verbal information will be used should be cued as prerequisites in preinstructional activities.

Presentation Activities In presenting verbal information, the context for storing and recalling it when needed is extremely important. Strategies linking new information to knowledge currently stored in memory, referred to as *elaboration*, improve the effectiveness of the instruction. The more detailed the elaboration or linking procedure, the greater likelihood that learners will store new information in a logical place and recall it later. Elaboration strategies include providing analogies or asking learners to use an imaginary image or example from their own experience for facilitating storage and recall of new information. These contextual links form the cues learners use to recall the information.

Another recommended strategy for presenting verbal information is to group like information in subsets and provide direct instruction relating items in the subset and among different subsets, referred to as *organization*. Procedures recommended for aiding students in organizing new information include providing them with an outline or table that summarizes information by related subsets.

When information is entirely new and unrelated to prior learning, then the strategy should include a memory device, or *mnemonic*, to aid the learner in recalling the information. In developing mnemonics, however, those logically related to the material to be recalled are recommended. Cueing letters that form a familiar word or an easily recalled acronym that is logically related to the information to be remembered can work well. Illogical mnemonics, however, can be as difficult to recall as the information they are designed to help retrieve.

Learner Participation What does it mean to *practice verbal information*? Rote repetition of unrelated facts has limited effectiveness in helping learners recall information over time. Designing practice activities that strengthen elaborations and cues and that better establish an organizational structure are believed to be more useful. Practice generating new examples, forming mental images that cue recall, and refining the organizational structure should also help. Focusing the exercise on meaningful contexts and relevant cues is another consideration for the strategy.

Just as with intellectual skills, feedback about the accuracy of verbal information recalled should be provided. Whenever possible, the feedback should include the correct response as well as information about why a given response is incorrect.

Assessment In testing verbal information, be sure to provide learners with cues that are available in the performance context for recalling the information. Also, sequence verbal information items near related intellectual skills, motor skills, or attitudes to provide a relevant context for recalling the information. As noted previously, such a sequencing strategy for tests suggests that all test items related to definitions and facts not be placed in a separate section at the beginning or end of the test.

Follow-Through Facilitating memorization of verbal information can be problematic, involving additional elaboration and organization strategies; however, it may also require a better motivational strategy. It may be necessary to create something for learners to "do" with the information to hook them into learning it, including such activities as crossword puzzle contests for teams of learners that not only are fun but allow them to aid each other in recalling information as well. Such a team approach may provide them with practice in recalling for themselves as they coach their teammates. Fun for learners, it can enrich elaborations and help ensure that the additional cues provided by teammates are based on prior knowledge and are meaningful to them.

Because this is a verbal information goal, the assumption is that consideration has been given to why the learner must achieve it. With such goals, the learner does not use a job aid or other provided reference material. The motivation of the

Table 8.4 Learning Components and Considerations to Support Learning for Verbal Information

Learning Components	Considerations for Each Component
Preinstructional Activities	Provide for motivation: attention, relevance, confidence, satisfaction Inform learner of objectives
Presentation Activities	Link new information to existing knowledge/skills Place in close proximity to skills information supports Create or illuminate organizational structure (e.g., subset groups, location, order) Point out distinguishing characteristics (physical, uses, qualities, etc.) Introduce logically related mnemonics Provide memory aids (e.g., outlines or tables)
Learner Participation	Practice generating new examples Strengthen elaborations and cues Use meaningful context and relevant cues Provide feedback for accuracy of answers
Assessment	Ensure relevance to performance context Sequence near skills it supports
Follow-Through	Provide additional elaboration and organization strategies Provide recall puzzles or contests

learner and the adequacy of practice are therefore critical. Also, review the context in which the information is used. Is the application context adequately represented in the learning context? The five learning components and their considerations for verbal information are summarized in Table 8.4.

Motor Skills

When thinking about psychomotor skills, our minds seem automatically to jump to sports such as baseball, tennis, or football, but psychomotor skills in trades, manufacturing, and many technical and professional jobs are intricate and demanding and can be dangerous. Consider examples such as learning CPR, learning to operate equipment in a machine shop, or learning to land a single-engine airplane. In these examples, it is easy to imagine the interplay between mind and body.

Initial learning of a motor skill concerns the development of an *executive routine*, which consists of the "directions" that the learner is to follow. The mental statement of each step in the routine is followed by the performance of that step. With repeated practice and appropriate feedback, the steps in the routine begin to smooth out, there is less hesitation between each step, the mental rehearsal of the executive routine decreases, and the skill begins to assume its final form. Expert performance is often represented by the absence of dependency on the executive routine and an automatic execution of the skill. What are the implications of this description of the learning of a typical motor skill for the presentation of content, examples, practice, and feedback? One very apparent implication is the requirement of some form of visual presentation of the skill. Obviously, video can be used to capture movement, but sequences of photos or drawings are often used, at least at the initial stages of learning a motor skill. The categories of content and examples in a strategy usually take the form of a verbal description of the skill followed by an illustration.

Preinstructional Activities It is typically easier to gain learners' attention and motivate them prior to receiving instruction on a motor skill than other types of learning. Motor skills are concrete and can be demonstrated; thus, learners do not need to be "told" what they are going to learn; they can see for themselves. This ability to observe what is to come can be very motivational, and in addition, they can be shown persons they admire performing the skill and receiving praise or coveted rewards. Most of us work very hard for praise, medals, and ribbons. One caution in this situation is how to motivate less able learners who have learned that they do not want to perform psychomotor skills publicly.

Presentation Activities It is important to determine an effective way to group information on a motor skill. It is not unusual to cluster meaningful parts of the skill that can later be integrated into the complete skill. In our earlier example of learning how to putt a golf ball, we showed that this skill can be broken down into lining up the ball with the cup, the backswing, hitting the ball, and follow-through. Whether to present the skill as a whole or in parts may depend on the skill level of the learners, the complexity of the skill, and the time available for learners to master the skill.

Learner Participation Practice and feedback are the hallmarks of psychomotor skills. Research has shown that learners can benefit from mentally visualizing the performance of a skill before they physically engage in it. Actual practice of a skill should be repetitious. Immediate feedback on correct execution of the skill is very important because incorrect rehearsal does not promote skill improvement.

A special problem with a motor skill involving the use of equipment is deciding when the learner should interact with the equipment. At one extreme, the executive routine is learned before the learner practices on the actual equipment. Logistically, this is the easiest approach, but it is not very effective and puts a great burden on the student to remember all the details of the instruction. The other extreme is to have the learner interact with the equipment at each step in the instruction. This is ideal, but this approach can require one piece of equipment per learner.

One solution to this instructional problem, which may later become a performance problem, is to provide the learner with a job aid. For example, perhaps the learner must enter a coded number into a piece of equipment to make it operate in a particular way. If there is no reason to require the learner to memorize all the possible codes, the codes could instead be listed on a plate on the equipment or on a card that the learner could easily review. Job aids can also include lists of steps to be executed or criteria to be used to evaluate a product or performance. If the designer chooses to incorporate a job aid into the training, obviously the learner must be taught how to use it.

Assessment The ultimate question in testing any motor skill is "Can the learner execute the skill that has been taught?" To answer this, they must demonstrate the skill with the intended equipment and environment. Performances may be public, assessment is quick, and learners can be quite ego involved in the situation. If other learners are present during the performance, they must be attentive and supportive of the individual performing or they will have a negative effect on the performance and motivation to participate.

Follow-Through Transfer of learning must also be addressed with motor skills. What are the conditions under which this skill must be performed? If possible, requirements found in the performance context should be present as the skill is practiced during instruction and should also be present for the posttest. Learners should also be encouraged to continue rehearsal following instruction. For example, few if any musicians or athletes become expert following instruction if they do not have the motivation to continue rehearsal on their own.

Mastery of psychomotor skills is reached when learners can demonstrate *automaticity*—that is, they can perform the skill in a smooth and efficient

Table 8.5 Learning Components and Considerations to Support Learning for Motor Skills

Learning Components	Considerations for Each Component
Preinstructional Activities	Provide for motivation: attention, relevance, confidence, satisfaction Illustrate skill to be performed and recall of prerequisites (oral description of plan) Provide information on benefits
Presentation Activities	Plan skill organization for presentation Tell and/or illustrate what to do and how to do it Illustrate physical characteristics and qualities of successful performance Show master performances for age and ability of group
Learner Participation	Plan for repetitious rehearsal Include relevant equipment and environmental considerations Provide immediate feedback illustrating strengths and areas for improvement Provide targeted information for performance improvement
Assessment	Demonstrate skill with intended equipment and in intended environment
Follow-Through	Ensure performance conditions are incorporated in instruction and rehearsal Encourage additional rehearsal following instruction

manner without really thinking about the steps to be followed in the performance. For example, a person driving on a snowy road who automatically corrects a slide by steering in the direction of the slide has mastered that technique of safe driving. In critical psychomotor skills where safety is a concern, automaticity should be reached during training or in follow-through with supervised practice in the performance context. For most motor skills, automaticity is reached after training through practice on the job; thus, steps to ensure transfer to the performance context are required, including cooperation with supervisors and workplace incentives. The five learning components and their considerations for motor skills are summarized in Table 8.5.

Attitudes

Researchers believe our attitudes consist of three components: feelings, behaviors, and cognitive understandings. *Feelings*, in this case, can be described as pleasures or displeasures expressed through our tendency to approach or avoid a situation. This tendency is thought to depend on our success or failure in prior similar situations or our observation of others in these situations. This is the key to a successful instructional strategy for an attitude.

Preinstructional Activities Designing preinstructional activities is also important for attitudes. Similar to psychomotor skills, motivation for acquiring an attitude may best be accomplished through firsthand observation by the learners or through active participation in simulations, through role-playing, or through video or multimedia vignettes. For attitudes, however, the observation should evoke empathic identity with the character observed or portrayed so that learners experientially feel the emotion of the character. In terms of informing the learners of the objectives, it is possible that the objective is communicated through the motivating experience. In other situations, it may be best to state the objectives directly prior to or following the motivating experience. Likewise, linking the upcoming learning to the learner's current feelings, skills, and knowledge may be accomplished through participation in carefully crafted or selected motivational experiences. It may also be helpful to have a recap discussion of the video, where learners reflect on and discuss similar situations and people in their lives.

Presentation Activities The content and example portion of the strategy should be delivered by someone or by an imaginary character who is respected and admired by the learners. This *human model* should display the behaviors involved in the attitude and indicate why this attitude is appropriate. If possible, it should be obvious to the learner that the model is being rewarded or takes personal satisfaction in displaying this attitude.

The substance of the instruction for an attitude consists of teaching the behavior that is to be demonstrated by the learner, such as personal cleanliness, as well as the supporting information about why this is important. The behaviors should be demonstrated under the conditions described in the performance objectives.

Also to be considered in your strategy is whether you are developing an attitude or reshaping one. For existing negative behaviors (and attitudes) such as unrestrained public emotion or anger as a response to frustration, focus instruction on self-awareness and teaching alternative ways of behaving in the circumstance. Creating simulations that evoke emotions that can lead to damaging behaviors may be required. Guiding learners to more positive behaviors as responses to the same emotions can be difficult. Consider strategies such as making a video of them as they respond in context and then working with them as they analyze how they felt and reacted. Have them hear how others in the situation judged their reactions, or have them observe someone they admire react positively in a similar circumstance and, through remaining calm, direct the conclusion of the interaction to the anticipated outcome.

Undoubtedly, the strategy you choose for instruction related to an attitude hinges on multiple factors. In addition to attempting to develop or reshape an attitude, several questions should be considered. Are the learners volunteers for the program because they perceive a need and wish to change? Are they satisfied with themselves but have been directed or "sentenced" to the program by a supervisor, school administrator, or judge? Are the attitude and behaviors ones the learners care little about, or do they represent strong convictions or sensitive feelings? How free can you be in delivering instruction, creating simulations, and providing feedback? Is group instruction sufficient, or is individualized instruction required? The answers to all such questions should be obtained in the learner and context analyses and should also be considered in designing an instructional strategy for attitudes.

Learner Participation How can the learner practice an attitude? First, practice and feedback should be provided for any information, intellectual skills, and motor skills that are part of the attitude. Making inappropriate or ineffective choices that are followed by ineffective or even positive feedback does not help the learner make better choices. Practice, therefore, must incorporate opportunities to choose followed by consistent feedback (rewards/consequences/rationales) to help ensure that a given behavior becomes associated with a given response. Role-playing is frequently used because of the difficulty in recreating the performance context for attitudes within an instructional setting. Opportunities for the learner to give verbal testimonials regarding the desired choices can enhance the effectiveness of role-playing. Feedback should include information about what the learner did right as well as what the learner did wrong. If the learner displays inappropriate responses, information about more appropriate responses should be provided.

Because attitudes can be learned vicariously, mental rehearsals may prove beneficial for practice and might include dramatic scenes that present respected models faced with alternatives. Following the presentation of alternatives, the learners can observe the model reacting in positive ways and observe the model receiving extrinsic rewards or expressing intrinsic satisfaction considered positive and relevant by the learners. In addition, other models could be observed reacting in negative ways and receiving negative consequences. Story simulations are especially useful because characters affected by the negative model's attitudes and behaviors can be observed by learners. When respected characters are injured, insulted, or angered by the "bad" model, the learner can associate or empathize with these reactions, helping the learner rehearse associating the attitude and behavior with the unpleasant consequences. These reactions of the respected characters constitute feedback to the learner. Reactors can be seen discussing the behavior of the negative model, and they can provide informative feedback by describing alternative ways the model should have behaved.

Assessments As discussed previously, an important consideration when designing tests for attitudes is whether learners know they are being observed. Other considerations include tests of verbal information related to knowledge of the expected behaviors and the potential rewards and consequences for behaving in certain ways. The assessment strategy should also encompass any intellectual or motor skills required for exhibiting the required behaviors. For example, it is difficult to demonstrate positive attitudes toward safe driving if one cannot drive a car, cannot state the rules of the road, and cannot solve safety problems encountered while driving. Although this is an extreme example, it illustrates the point.

Questionnaires can be designed with situations and questions for the learners about how they would react to hypothetical circumstances. However, you should be aware that research demonstrates only a moderate relationship between our professed attitudes in a hypothetical situation and our actual behavior when confronted with a similar situation in real life. To the extent possible, the designer should try to create hypothetical situations that simulate those in which the attitude influences learner choices and behaviors.

Follow-Through Perhaps the most important consideration in the instructional strategy for teaching an attitude is the adequacy of the components that promote transfer. Rarely are we interested in a demonstration of an attitude in the presence of an instructor other than to show that the learner has mastered the skills associated with the attitude. We want the attitude to be chosen by the learner as the desired behavior in situations when the instructor is not present. Therefore, it is critical to provide the learner with practice contexts similar to those in which we hope to see the attitude occur. The learner should also be provided with valid feedback to this attitude as part of the practice activity. Support for the attitude must be present in the performance context along with the same kinds of corrective guidance, behavioral modeling, incentives, and rewards as were used for practice and feedback during instruction. Obviously, the organization, all the way down to frontline supervisors, must be on board for desired attitudes to flourish in the performance context. The five learning components and their considerations for attitudes are summarized in Table 8.6.

Table 8.6 Learning Components and Considerations to Support Learning for Attitudes

Learning Components	Considerations to Support Learning for Each Component
Preinstructional Activities	Provide for motivation: attention, relevance, confidence, satisfaction Inform learner of objectives Illustrate benefits and problems (consequences) of a particular attitude Evoke empathetic empathy for character in illustration Provide for reflection or discussion of similar situations or people in their lives
Presentation Activities	Provide respected human model to display the behaviors sought and to describe or show why they are important Illustrate model being rewarded for behaving in a certain way Illustrate model having feelings of satisfaction for having behaved in a certain way Illustrate undesirable consequences to model for behaving in alternative, less desirable way
Learner Participation	Provide opportunities for choosing appropriate behaviors within the context of the information or skills Provide role-playing opportunities for learners to encounter the choices within the appropriate contexts or environments Provide consistent feedback of rewards, consequences, or rationales Encourage learners' verbal testimonials of behaviors linked to rewards or consequences
Assessment	Create scenarios where learners tell their choices and behaviors Test learners' knowledge of desired ways of behaving, rewards and consequences of doing so Create situations for learner to choose to behave in the desired way and then do so Observe learners' choices and behaviors when they are unaware they are being observed
Follow-Through	Provide practice contexts similar to those where the attitude should be displayed

Learning Components for Constructivist Strategies

Overview

Less-prescriptive learner-centered approaches to education and constructivist design theories can have valuable roles in the design and management of instruction. After looking at a radical constructivist view that there is no objective reality and that knowledge is constructed internally and individually by learners and is therefore unpredictable, an instructional designer might ask, "How can instructional designers determine what students need, prescribe instructional activities, and assess learning outcomes?" The answer is that it can be done, but it must be done differently.

As described in Chapter 1, the Dick and Carey model is rooted in cognitive psychology, and we call it a *cognitive model*. Constructivism also has roots in cognitive psychology and has two branches: cognitive constructivism and social constructivism. *Social constructivism* was developed from the work of Russian psychologist Lev Vygotsky in the first part of the twentieth century. His views were similar in many respects to Piaget's developmental theories, but with greater emphasis on social context and social transmission of cultural and intellectual capabilities. Those interested in the origins of his theories may want to read edited translations of some of his original essays (Vygotsky, 1978). In common usage, *social constructivism* is referred to just as **constructivism**, and we follow that convention.

Carey (2005) and Ertmer and Newby (1993) provide balanced analyses of how aspects of a constructivist approach can be compatible with aspects of a cognitive approach for specified types of learners and learning outcomes. Dick (1996) points out the focal points and tasks shared by Willis's constructivist model and the Dick and Carey ID model and views a blending of the two as advantageous; moreover, Dede (2008) suggests that in many situations, a combination top-down (cognitive) and bottom-up (constructive) approach might be the instructional strategy of choice. Anyone familiar with the work of master teachers has observed the beneficial and seamless meshing of these two approaches in the classroom. Readers should be clear about our intent in this discussion of constructivism. It is not to set aside the cognitive model and provide a comprehensive explanation of constructivist instructional design; that has been done well by Jonassen (1999) and others. Our purpose is, rather, to describe aspects of constructivist practice that we believe can be blended effectively into the cognitive ID model. Our approach is to compare the elements of a generic cognitive ID process with planning practices in the design of constructivist learning environments (CLEs). Then we comment on blending CLEs into the Dick and Carey design model and summarize some of the critical aspects of constructivist theory that must be maintained to be faithful to that pedagogy. We finish this section with a brief review of considerations for designing and managing CLEs. For beginning this discussion, a succinct working definition of **constructivist learning environments** is learners in collaborative groups with peers and teachers consulting resources to solve problems. Discovery learning, inquiry-based learning, and problem-based learning are instructional strategies that are roughly synonymous with constructivist learning environments.

Designers considering use of CLEs in their instructional strategy should reread the previous section on Learning Components for Learners of Different Maturity and Ability Levels. Motivation and learning maturity are required of students embarking on instruction with minimal guidance. Unmotivated students who are immature learners tend to become frustrated and flounder because they are unable to manage the cognitive load required for constructivist learning. Articles in the special issue of *Educational Psychologist* (2003) define *cognitive load* and provide useful perspectives on this dilemma in constructivist design, as does Hannafin's (2012) commentary on *optimum guidance*.

Cognitive ID Models and Constructivist Planning Practices

Table 8.7 provides a comparison of the steps in a cognitive ID model with constructivist planning practices. A careful look at the table makes two points very clear. First, constructivism is not an easy way out of the planning process required in cognitive ID. If CLEs are the instructional strategy of choice because designers seek the constructivist learning outcomes predicted by relevant theory, then there are still planning tasks regarding goals, content, learners, contexts, and so forth. Learner-centered instruction does not remove the instructor from planning or participation. The roles still exist; they are just different.

Second, a designer following the Dick and Carey model through Chapter 7 on the design of assessment has completed the planning useful for designing CLEs. There are some theoretical issues in constructivist design that dictate how to use the planning work that has been done for goals, content and objectives, and assessments, and we discuss those shortly. The point here is that the analysis and design work has been accomplished and can be used, so this is an effective place in the Dick and Carey model to introduce a blend with constructivism. Next, we describe how to manage some theoretical issues in blending CLEs into a cognitive model.

Table 8.7 Cognitive ID Models and Constructivist Practices

Cognitive ID Phases	Dick and Carey ID Processes	Constructivist Planning Practices
Analyze	Needs	Places learning within the mission and requirements of the organization.
	Goals	Maintains focus during preparation prior to student engagement and process during student engagement. Includes process outcomes that may not be present in cognitive strategies.
	Content	Assembles and references domain knowledge resources that will be needed by students in the learning environment; seldom done in the detail of a hierarchical subordinates skills analysis.
	Learners	Places learners in zone of proximal social, cultural, and intellectual development (matching learning environment to learners).
	Learning Context Performance Context	Emphasizes situated learning (authentic social, cultural, physical attributes) in constructivist learning environments (CLEs).
Design	Objectives	Usually written but fewer than cognitive frameworks and not stated as formal three-part objectives. Sometimes broken into learning objectives and process objectives because of requirements for learners' collaboration and task management in CLEs.
	Assessments	Mandatory joint responsibility of teacher, learner, and other learners assessing progress, products, and process. More holistic with less focus on testing subskills. No single correct solution, so criteria describe properties of an adequate solution.
	Instructional Strategies • Content clustering and sequencing • Learning components • Student groupings • Delivery system/media	The CLE is the instructional strategy. Learners in collaborative groups with peers and teachers consult resources to solve problems. Group meetings can be face-to-face or computer-mediated in synchronous or asynchronous time or in virtual spaces. Resources must be accessible, pertinent, and sufficient. Problems must be complex, relevant, and situated in the real world. Learners must be actively engaged, reflective, and aware. Teachers must motivate and encourage learners, manage group process/progress, and provide adaptive learning guidance including scaffolding, coaching (tutoring, feedback, and direct instruction), modeling, and mentoring.
Develop	Instructional materials	Focuses less on prescriptive print or mediated instructional materials; focuses more on inquiry, access, and resource-based learning. Carefully describes for students goal, problem scenario, group process, milestones, and resources.
	Assessments	Assessments are usually rubrics and portfolios with guidance on process for collaborative evaluation.
	Course management	Prescriptive instructor's guide is replaced by document describing learning context, intended learners, goal and objectives, content domain and problem scenario, process/activities overview, required tools/resources/scaffolding, and assessment instruments/processes.

Theoretical Considerations

A theoretical difference pervading comparisons of cognitive and constructivist views is rooted in the roles of content and the learner. The cognitive assumption is that the content drives the system, whereas the learner is the driving factor in constructivism. The former focuses more on products and outcomes, whereas the latter focuses more on process. These assumptions cause differences in how cognitivists and constructivists view goals, content and objectives, and assessment, and these differences must be taken into account if one plans to blend CLEs into cognitive ID with theoretical integrity.

Planning and documentation for CLEs always include goals regarding the content domain that will be explored, and just as in cognitive models, these goals should reflect the needs and learning priorities of the organization. The CLE is an instructional strategy; however, that by definition includes goals for learners that spring from the inquiry process instead of from the content domain. These goals are inseparable from constructivist theory and part of the CLE strategy, even if not written out in documentation under the heading of "Goals." Driscoll (2005) describes five aspects of constructivism that should be considered in ID. The five desired outcomes (goals) of learner-centered inquiry when supported by adaptive learning guidance are:

1. Reasoning, critical thinking, and problem solving
2. Retention, understanding, and use
3. Cognitive flexibility
4. Self-regulation
5. Mindful reflection and epistemic flexibility

Points 3, 4, and 5 collectively can be called *metacognition* and are the capabilities that Gagné (1985) terms *cognitive strategies*. The designer who chooses to blend CLEs into the cognitive model should recognize these constructivist goals, make them explicit in project documentation, and account for them in design of the CLE and the assessments. The most compelling reason for choosing CLEs is when the original goal is learning to solve ill-defined problems and develop cognitive strategies; however, the authors have seen many instances in which creative designers have chosen to blend a CLE into the design as a motivational vehicle for other learning outcomes.

Content analysis is completed down through the subordinate skills level in cognitive design to discover the structure of the content, enabling the designer to decide what must be learned in order to master the goal and whether there is a required sequence for learning it. After the analysis, objectives are written that mirror the structure of the content. This objective view of reality becomes a theoretical problem when blending CLEs into a cognitive model. Hannafin et al. (1997, p. 109) make this difference between cognitive and constructivist views clear.

> For constructivists objects and events have no absolute meaning; rather, the individual interprets each and constructs meaning based on individual experience and evolved beliefs. The design task, therefore, is one of providing a rich context within which meaning can be negotiated and ways of understanding can emerge and evolve. Constructivists tend to eschew the breaking down of context into component parts in favor of [learning] environments wherein knowledge, skill, and complexity exist naturally.

If choosing CLEs as the instructional strategy, cognitive designers need not alter the content analysis that has been completed; rather, they must alter the way the content analysis is used. The CLE should not be shaped by imposing a content structure on it; instead, the CLE should be structured so that learners find the content structure within it as part of the process of guided inquiry. The designer can, however, use the content analysis as a resource for selecting a robust problem scenario and providing access to content resources sufficient for solving the problem therein. Another use for the subordinate skills analysis in CLEs is for tutoring and scaffolding in ill-defined problem solving when students need guidance for putting together relationships among concepts, rules, and principles. The content analysis can also be used for designing tutorials as resource material for students in CLEs, following Jonassen's (1997) description of cognitive strategies for teaching well-defined problems. Because objectives mirror the goal analysis and subskills analysis in cognitive design, they are subject to the same theoretical problem denoted in Hannafin's comment. As such, subordinate objectives could be reserved for use in developing tutorials or job aids as resources for learners in the CLE but would not be distributed to learners to guide their progress or process.

As mentioned previously, the cognitive model is content driven, and the result is a parallel relationship among skills, objectives, and assessments. This relationship imposes a structure on the instruction that does not exist in CLEs and influences the nature of assessment. The assessments developed in cognitive design can be used to inform the assessment of constructivist learning but cannot be the assessment of outcomes in CLEs. Ill-structured problems have many correct solutions, so designers choosing to blend CLEs into a cognitive design must create a description of the functional characteristics of correct solutions instead of a description of the correct solution. Designers must also create assessment strategies that address the explicit inquiry goals found in constructivist theory. This requires authentic assessment, characterized by learners performing realistic tasks that typically result in a product of some type (e.g., a problem solution, a journal article, a dramatic video, a computer program) or performances of skills and procedures (e.g., demonstrating steps used to develop a software solution, managing progress of a work team, diagnosing illnesses, producing a newsletter).

A second characteristic of authentic assessment is an interactive joint evaluation of the resulting product or process by the learner and instructor. This evaluation could also include others, such as experts in the field or peer work-team members. Interactive evaluative discussions typically include illuminating first the features of the product or performance that are well done and, from that positive perspective, discussions of other parts of the work that need additional refining.

Finally, these assessments should involve the joint determination of the criteria used to evaluate the quality of students' work. One of the goals of education is for learners to (1) acquire information about the qualities of objects or performances (e.g., form, function, aesthetics, parsimony), (2) use these criteria in judging the work of others, (3) apply the criteria during their own work, and (4) use them in judging the results of their work. The self-assessment aspect moves assessment from being a test of the learner to being a learning outcome. Self-assessment is key to cognitive flexibility, self-regulation, and reflection. We next turn our attention to some details of designing and managing CLEs.

Designing Constructivist Learning Environments

Five theory-based goals of all CLEs were described in the section on theoretical considerations. The five goals can be viewed as a set of minimum specifications or requirements for designing CLEs. They are repeated here with relevant constructivist learning conditions suggested by Driscoll (2005). The discussion follows the pattern of organization used by Chieu (2007).

Reasoning The goal of reasoning—that is, critical thinking—and problem solving is best supported by planning CLEs that are complex, realistic, and relevant. Complexity is required in the problem scenarios used in CLEs if students are to transfer learning experiences to life experiences; however, the range of complexity available within the problem must challenge students of different achievement and ability without inducing undue frustration. The CLE must situate students in a realistic and relevant problem scenario. **Situated learning** requires a context with which students can identify for motivation and transfer. The context should include realistic elements of the physical, social, and cultural world in which the students operate but need not be "the real world." Learning can be situated effectively in such contexts as play-acted fairy tales, mock court trials, computer simulations, serious games, or computer-based micro worlds. A problem scenario should be relevant on two levels. First, problem scenarios must be planned such that students are able to discern pattern and structure in the problem through their inquiry process; otherwise, the problem has little relevance to the desired learning of reasoning and critical-thinking skills. The second level of relevance is in the generalizability of the problem-solving process and strategies that are being learned. Odd, one-of-a-kind problems may be interesting and instructive in some ways but essentially irrelevant for the desired transfer to applying and practicing problem-solving strategies in a variety of unencountered circumstances.

Retention, Understanding, and Use These are best accomplished by providing for interaction among learners, peers, and teachers. The interaction should be integral to the inquiry process such that students are placed in positions where they must probe, consider, defend, refine, and perhaps reconceptualize their construction of new knowledge. This social interaction provides opportunities for the practice and feedback that promote retention and understanding. Social interaction must be managed to maintain a productive balance between what is purely social and what is task oriented, whether organized in face-to-face settings or mediated in chat rooms, blogs, wikis, discussion forums, electronic mailing lists, or social media.

Cognitive Flexibility This is the ability to adapt and change one's mental organization of knowledge and mental management of solution strategies for solving new and unexpected problems. Cognitive flexibility is engendered when students are exposed to multiple representations of the content domain and multiple solution strategies for the same problem and when students are challenged to examine and evaluate their own strategies for solving a problem. CLEs should provide opportunities for confronting dissimilar problems that require reorganization of content domain knowledge and exploration of alternative solutions. Self-assessment and collaborative assessment are critical for developing cognitive flexibility, as they provide opportunities for low-threat encounters with disparate perspectives and opportunities for formative attempts at shaping problem solutions.

Self-Regulation This goal involves identifying learning outcomes of personal interest or value and choosing to pursue them. This goal is best supported by creating environments in which students can practice choosing and pursuing their own learning goals. Less-mature learners typically require guidance as they learn through experience which goals are realistic, achievable, and personally rewarding. CLEs that use project-based learning can offer opportunities for students to choose among multiple problem scenarios within the same general content domain.

Mindful Reflection and Epistemic Flexibility These are reflected by learners who maintain awareness of their own process of constructing knowledge and choosing ways of learning and knowing. Support for this goal is similar to support for cognitive flexibility but goes beyond providing multiple perspectives to encouraging students to weigh, compare, and decide on the merits of differing perspectives. If social negotiation of meaning requires discussion with others to construct meaning, then mindful reflection and epistemic flexibility can be thought of as a mental discussion with oneself about meaning; how one judges something to be true; and whether there are other, perhaps better, ways to know the truth. As with cognitive flexibility, self-assessment and collaborative assessment are critical in acquiring this goal. Next, we turn our attention to some considerations in planning and managing CLEs, providing a template for organizing design and development efforts.

Planning Constructivist Learning Environments

Whether to embark on a cognitive or constructivist instructional strategy—or a blend thereof—requires consideration of several factors, including how well any of the approaches meet the defined needs of the organization. The designer must also decide the best path for learners to achieve the instructional goal approved by the organization. Considerations of learners' characteristics, including their ability, maturity, experience, and knowledge of domain content, are certainly important factors. In choosing a constructivist strategy or blending constructivism with a cognitive strategy, the skills of the teacher, trainer, or instructional manager become an important consideration because managing a CLE and the students engaged in the CLE is quite different from the pedagogical style with which most teachers are accustomed. Moreover, the features of the performance and learning contexts, especially in light of resources, influence the selection of the best strategy for learning.

The planning that goes into CLEs was summarized in the right-hand column of Table 8.7 opposite the "Analyze" and "Design" phases, and the point was made that effective CLEs require thoughtful preparation. Table 8.7 could be used as a template for planning CLEs, but it is focused more on planning needs for a constructivist strategy. For Table 8.7, we assume that the analysis and design steps through Chapter 7 have already been completed and that the designer is choosing to use a CLE instead of the cognitive instructional strategy emphasized in this chapter. Under these assumptions, planning the CLE becomes a combination of modifying existing planning so it addresses constructivist assumptions and addressing additional requirements that are unique to the CLE. Although the table divides planning activities into considerations for the learning environment, learner engagement, learning guidance, and assessment, most of the planning activities can be completed prior to launching the new learning environment and engaging learners.

Authentic assessment and learning guidance are, of course, part of learner engagement, but they are presented in separate rows of Table 8.8 because of their critical contributions to the success of students' progress through CLEs. The popular "5 Es" scheme developed by the Biological Science Curriculum Study (BSCS) team is included in the table for planning for learner engagement, but designers can substitute any scheme that matches their preferences and the pedagogical model being used. In the category of planning for learning guidance in Table 8.8, everything could be considered scaffolding as long as it supports students as needed and is withdrawn as the student develops proficiency. Designers can structure this category in whatever manner suits their concept of learning guidance. See the Examples and Case Study sections at the end of Chapter 9 for examples of how Table 8.8 should be filled out. Note that the "5 Es" are not teacher directed but rather are shared responsibilities of the student, the teacher, the student's peers, the materials and resources, and sometimes the school community, student's family, and the community at large.

Now we shift from our discussion of constructivist ID back to the design of an instructional strategy; however, one final note for those following the Dick and Carey model: If the decision is made to use a constructivist instructional strategy (to use CLEs as the instructional strategy) and to do it with theoretical integrity, then recognize that some assumptions of the Dick and Carey model will be compromised. This will have implications for the assessment of student learning

Table 8.8 Planning for a Constructivist Learning Environment (CLE)

Planning Needs	Planning Activities
Planning the Learning Environment	*Describe here the designs and materials needed to launch the CLE.* • Goal • Learning objectives • Rationale • Constructivist focus • Pedagogical model (problem-based, project-based, case-based, etc.) • Scenario (overview of problem, project, case, etc.) • Learning resource materials • Learner groupings • Delivery system, media, and personnel
Planning for Learner Engagement	*Describe here the procedures and activities anticipated during engagement given the nature of the learners, instructional goal, and pedagogical model.* • Engage (first encounter with problem and material, gain attention, arouse curiosity, establish personal relevance in minds of learners) • Explore (involvement, questioning, hypothesizing, information seeking, interaction, sharing) • Explain (describe phenomena, use terminology, share ideas, propose explanations, test solutions, defend interpretations) • Elaborate (transfer and expand knowledge, apply in new settings, see relationships, recognize patterns, make connections, test in new contexts, relate to life experiences) • Evaluate (collaborate, negotiate outcomes, define criteria, diagnose and prescribe, note incremental improvement, provide product and performance rubrics, reflect, refine)
Planning Learning Guidance	*Describe here materials and activities anticipated for adaptive learning guidance during learner engagement in the CLE.* • Scaffolding • Models • Graphic organizers • Worked examples • Job aids • Concept maps • Questioning • Guided feedback • Coaching • Modeling • Tutoring and peer tutoring • Mediated tutorials • Direct instruction
Planning Authentic Assessment	*Describe here the materials and procedures anticipated for authentic assessment for the goal, the learners, and the CLE.* • Rubrics and other instruments • Categories of criteria • Form • Function • Aesthetic • Legal • Prompts for reflection and self-assessment • Model solutions

outcomes, formative evaluation, revision, accountability, and replicability of instruction. For example, it will be difficult to assess student learning and relate achievement to objectives. That in turn makes formative evaluation and revision difficult, impairs accountability to the sponsoring agency, and makes replication with predictable results doubtful. The instructional strategy specified in the group leadership case study at the end of Chapter 9 is an example of blending a CLE into the Dick and Carey model, but in this instance there would be an impact on some of the cognitive design assumptions. Although the web-based instruction for participants should be provided within typical cognitive-design guidelines, the group-based problem-solving sessions, in which participants set their own agendas and choose their own priorities, result in different learning outcomes for different groups and varying levels of mastery by individual learners within groups. This makes replication with predictable outcomes difficult, and the variability in performance presents problems for formative evaluation, revision, and certification of achievement.

The authors, however, choose to specify the CLE for the case study for two reasons: First, the prerequisite skills were covered in the web-based instruction; and second, the group-based problem-solving sessions should elicit active participation in more authentic performance than could have been offered in direct instruction. As in most decisions for planning instruction, choosing instructional strategies is guided by careful analysis of instructional goals and thorough understanding of the needs of learners and the parent organization.

Evaluation and Revision

Rubric for Evaluating an Instructional Strategy

Before developing materials based on your strategy, you should seek evaluation from content experts as well as from one or more of your target learners. The following is a rubric you can use as a job aid in developing your strategy and reviewers can use to assess it.

Designer note: If an element is not relevant for your plan, mark NA in the No column.

No	Some	Yes	
			A. Preinstructional Activities Is/does the plan:
___	___	___	1. Appropriate for learners' characteristics?
___	___	___	2. Motivational for learners (gain attention, demonstrate relevance)?
___	___	___	3. Inform learners of objectives and purpose for instruction?
___	___	___	4. Cause learners to recall prerequisite knowledge and skills?
___	___	___	5. Inform learners of input needed to complete tasks required?
			B. Presentation Materials Does the plan include:
___	___	___	1. Materials appropriate for the type of learning?
___	___	___	2. Clear examples and nonexamples for learners' experience?
___	___	___	3. Appropriate materials such as explanations, illustrations, diagrams, demonstrations, model solutions, and sample performances?
___	___	___	4. Learner guidance through the presentation materials?
___	___	___	5. Aids for linking new content and skills to prerequisites?
___	___	___	6. Progression from the familiar to the unfamiliar?
___	___	___	7. Organization?

C. Learner Participation Is the plan likely to be:

___ ___ ___ 1. Appropriate for learning type?
___ ___ ___ 2. Congruent with objectives?
___ ___ ___ 3. Congruent with learner characteristics?
___ ___ ___ 4. Congruent with instruction?
___ ___ ___ 5. Likely to be motivational (aid learner in building confidence)?
___ ___ ___ 6. Appropriately placed in instruction (not too soon, often, or infrequent)?

D. Feedback Does the plan appear to be:

___ ___ ___ 1. Appropriate for learning type?
___ ___ ___ 2. Congruent with objectives?
___ ___ ___ 3. Congruent with learner characteristics?
___ ___ ___ 4. Informative, supportive, and corrective?
___ ___ ___ 5. Likely to aid learner in building confidence and personal satisfaction?

E. Assessments Is the plan appropriate for:

___ ___ ___ 1. Readiness/pretests?
___ ___ ___ 2. Posttests?
___ ___ ___ 3. Type of learning (objective, alternative)?
___ ___ ___ 4. Learner characteristics (age, attention span, ability)?
___ ___ ___ 5. Yielding valid and reliable information about learner status and attitudes?

F. Follow-Through Activities Is the plan likely to:

___ ___ ___ 1. Aid retention of the new information and skills?
___ ___ ___ 2. Support transfer of skills from learning to performance environment (e.g., working with supervisors, forming support teams)?

Examples

This section is used to illustrate how theories of learning are linked to specific instructional objectives. Examples are provided for verbal information, intellectual skills, motor skills, and attitudes. The specific instructional goal framework used for these examples is found in Figure 4.6 related to putting a golf ball. This instructional goal framework is chosen because it currently contains intellectual skills and motor skills, and it implies attitudinal and verbal information subordinate skills.

Plan an Instructional Strategy

Need for Instruction

The first step in planning the instructional strategy is to consider the need and purpose for the instruction. Suppose a golf club embarked on a management needs assessment and discovered that in order to sustain a profitable organization, it will need to increase golf memberships in the near future. A club task force was assigned to plan ways the club might increase membership, and several strategies were selected. One strategy the board considered promising was to offer golf instruction to non-member individuals who are preparing to retire or are newly retired in order to interest them in golf and a membership in the club. It added the club's teaching pro to its planning group and settled on a low-cost beginner's clinic to include lessons in putting, chipping, fairway play, and driving. The objective of the clinic will not be proficient golfers embarking on a new career but rather a fun activity for retirees to build interest and camaraderie and hopefully to get new members for the club. There will be four weekly sessions, one for each area, taught by the club's teaching professional. Enrollment is to be limited to sixteen individuals. It is hoped the clinics will be enjoyable and participants will be encouraged to join the club. Depending on the demand for and success of the first clinic, additional clinics may be scheduled.

Characteristics of Target Learners

Next you should consider the characteristics of the target learners, their basic motivations for being in the instruction, and the transactional distance between the instruction and the learners. For this example, assume the learners are mature adults who are heterogeneous in their cognitive abilities but homogeneous in their golfing abilities as beginners. Further, they have volunteered for the lessons, and they have paid a small fee to attend. These facts indicate that the learners are motivated to learn how to play golf. Related to transactional distance, learners are enrolled in small-group instruction with the pro at a local golf club. This means they have direct access to the instructor, and they will be provided with instruction, opportunities to practice, and targeted feedback on their performances. Their level of motivation is quite different from middle and high school students enrolled in a First Tee program and even more different from a typical high school gym class studying a unit on golf.

Plan an Instructional Strategy for Different Types of Learning

Let's link first the attitudinal instructional goal and the theory-based recommendations for shaping attitudes in the instructional strategy. Next, we link the subordinate skills related to verbal information, then intellectual skills, and finally motor skills to the instructional strategy.

Classify Skills by Type of Learning

For our purposes, we expand the framework to include related verbal information for main step I and attitudes. Figure 8.2 includes the amended analysis. The new verbal information tasks are connected to the intellectual skills they support using the traditional "V" in a triangle, and the attitudinal goal is connected to the instructional goal using the "A" in a circle. Several of the original skills are not included to provide space for the additional skills and information. Assume all the original skills are present in the analysis, just not in the portion illustrated in Figure 8.2. We are including only selected subordinate skills in these examples to make specific points.

Notice the attitudinal goal in the top right corner: Chooses physical activity, competition, and golf. This attitudinal goal is the same for the entire instructional unit on golf, not just this section on putting. Enabling skill I.1, Plan the stroke required to putt the ball into the cup, is an intellectual skill. Enabling skill I.4, Execute a practice stroke based on the plan, and I.5, Stroke the ball based on the plan, are motor skills. In addition, four verbal information tasks have been added to support intellectual skills I.1.a(1), I.1.b(1), I.1.d(1), and I.1.e(1). Verbal information supporting following putting rules and putting etiquette are added to support main step I, putting. These example skills and verbal information will be used to show how to link the major subordinate skills to the learning components of instruction and to the recommendations for each type of learning.

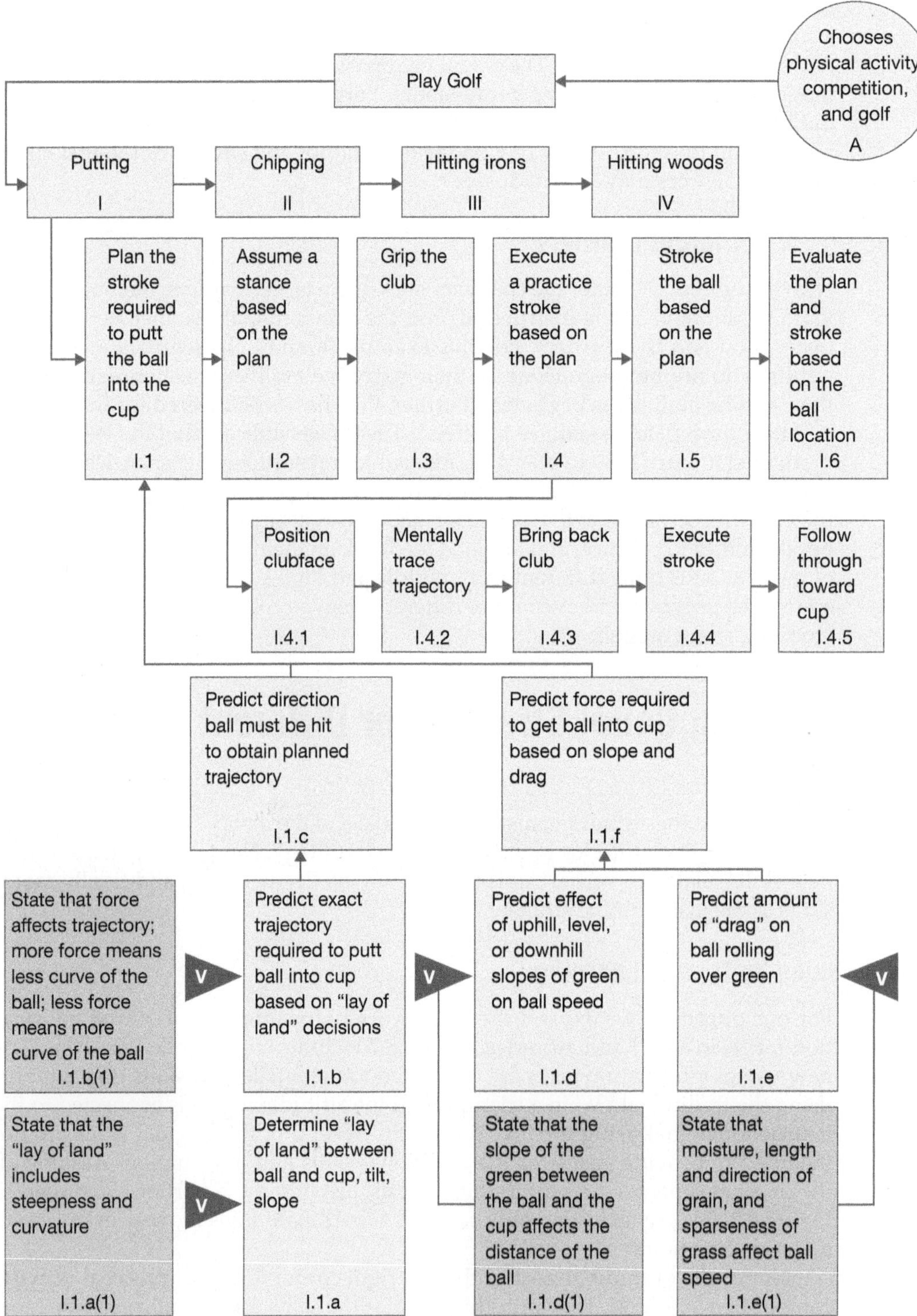

Figure 8.2 Hierarchical Analysis of Putting a Golf Ball from Figure 4.6 with Supporting Verbal Information Added

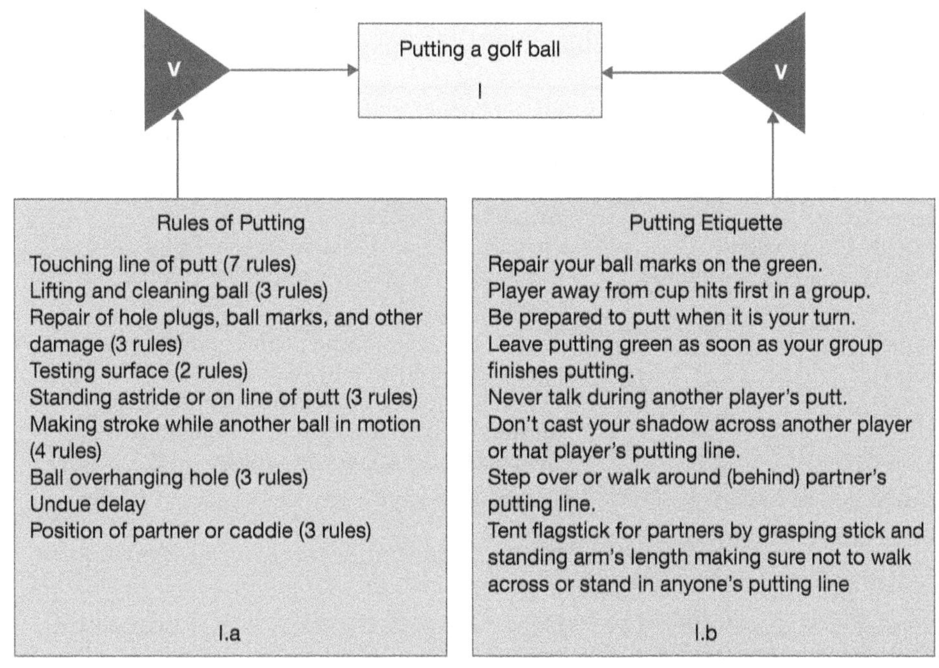

Figure 8.2 Continued

Attitudinal Instructional Goals

Table 8.9 contains the instructional strategy for the attitudinal goal associated with the golf unit. The first column contains the learning components, the second column contains the instructional considerations for the type of learning within each component, and the third column contains the planned instructional strategy. Notice that the information contained in the strategy relates to developing a desire to participate. It relates to recruitment, encouragement, confidence building, camaraderie, and a prescription for various opportunities to participate. It also relates to the overall unit on golf rather than to any selected enabling skills.

Verbal Information Subordinate Skills

Table 8.10 contains an instructional strategy for the few verbal information subordinate skills in Figure 8.2 (i.e., skills I.1.a(1), I.1.b(1), I.1.d(1), and I.1.e(1)). As before, the learning components and considerations for the type of learning are included in the first and second columns, and the instructional strategy is included in the third column. Unlike the attitudinal example, in this case the strategy is directly related to learning the verbal information required to perform the intellectual skills it supports. The strategy is depicted in Table 8.9 for the purpose of illustrating learning components for verbal information; however, in actual putting instruction, the verbal information would be combined with intellectual skills in Table 8.11.

Intellectual Skills

The instructional strategy for intellectual skill I.1 in Figure 8.2 is included in Table 8.11. Learning this skill requires the synthesis of intellectual skills I.1.a through I.1 in Figure 8.2 and the verbal information that supports these skills. Notice in the example that the learners are not putting the ball. The strategy here is to get them actually to learn the factors that influence the accuracy of a putt and make a related plan. The

Table 8.9 Example Instructional Strategy for Golf Objectives Classified as Attitudes

Learning Components	Sample Considerations for Each Component	Instructional Strategy for Attitude: Chooses Physical Activity, Competition, and Golf
Preinstructional Activities	Provide for motivation. Inform learner of objectives. Illustrate benefits and problems (consequences) of a particular attitude.	Advertising video runs in locker rooms during recruitment for class. On video, golf pro tells about benefits of class (e.g., improved game, recognition, companionship, improved flexibility, physical well-being).
	Evoke empathetic empathy for character in illustration.	Testimonials from former clinic members about benefits they personally realized. Run video of local club members attending Masters competition at Augusta showing camaraderie, fun, companionship.
	Provide for reflection or discussion of similar situations or people in their lives.	Testimonials from club members about positive benefits. Pro available to discuss personal benefits of program with interested parties.
Presentation Activities	Provide respected human model to display the behaviors sought and to describe or show why they are important. Illustrate model being rewarded for behaving in a certain way. Illustrate model having feelings of satisfaction for having behaved in a certain way.	Show video of colleagues golfing successfully and praised by companions for improvement. Pro describes score improvement of prior golf class, recognition, and accomplishment.
	Illustrate undesirable consequences to model for behaving in alternative, less desirable way.	Show video of duffers (unknown to club members) unsuccessfully playing golf, showing bad form and resulting poor scoring, and having temper tantrums.
Learner Participation	Provide opportunities for choosing appropriate behaviors within the context of the information or skills. Provide role-playing opportunities for learners to encounter the choices within the appropriate contexts or environments.	Have convenient tee times between lessons for class members to play together practicing the latest lesson (putting, chipping, irons, fairway woods, driving).
	Provide consistent feedback of rewards, consequences, or rationales. Encourage learners' verbal testimonials of behaviors linked to rewards or consequences.	Stage contests and awards (ribbons, certificates) for each main session (putting, chipping, irons, fairway woods, driving). Organize "graduation" golf tournament for class members at completion of instruction.
Assessment	Create scenarios where learners tell their choices and behaviors. Test learners' knowledge of desired ways of behaving, rewards and consequences of doing so. Create situations for learner to choose to behave in the desired way and then do so. Observe learners' choices and behaviors when they are unaware they are being observed.	Observe learners who choose to attend planned instructional sessions as well as attend additional practice after sessions and various contests planned for the group. Observe learners who choose to focus on their skill and form during play.
Follow-Through	Provide practice contexts similar to those where the attitude should be displayed.	Observe those who choose to play additional rounds of golf and choose to enroll in various contests sponsored by the golf course.

Note: This attitudinal instructional strategy covers a monthlong recreational program for learning how to play golf rather than just the putting instructional sessions and the enabling skills included in it.

Table 8.10 Example Instructional Strategy for Golf Objectives Classified as Verbal Information

Learning Components	Considerations for Each Component	Instructional Strategy for Verbal Information Objectives I.1.a(1), I.1.b(1), I.1.d(1), and I.1.e(1) Developed from Figure 8.2
Preinstructional Activities	Provide for motivation: Confidence	Respected golf pro praises group of learners for their putting during warm-up and indicates they will easily master the fundamentals of putting.
	Relevance (why and how to use)	Applying fundamentals of putting will save many strokes during play.
	Inform learner of objectives.	Learn factors that influence the accuracy of a putt related to the slope and surface conditions of the putting green.
	Link new information to existing knowledge/skills (elaboration, analogies, imagining).	Link to pedaling a bike up/down hills: little force to coast down, pedal hard to go up.
Presentation Activities	Place in close proximity to skills information supports.	Keep verbal information together with intellectual skills it supports (e.g., I.1.a(1) with I.1.a)
	Create or illuminate organizational structure (e.g., subset groups, location, order).	Slope issues versus resistance issues (e.g., length and wetness of grass, direction blades of grass grow).
	Point out distinguishing characteristics.	N/A
	Introduce logically related mnemonics.	N/A
	Provide memory aids (e.g., outlines or tables).	Respected pro verbally explains and physically demonstrates how the slope of the green impacts the trajectory and speed of the golf ball. Distribute card with diagrams of known trajectories based on slopes (steep, slight; up, down; right, left), location of ball, and location of cup. Note: At this point the learning of information is blending into the learning of defined concepts, concrete concepts, and rules and is inseparable from these intellectual skills. The verbal information can be "blended" again as part of learner participation in Table 8.11.
Learner Participation	Practice generating new examples. Strengthen elaborations and cues. Use meaningful context and relevant cues. Provide feedback for correctness of answers.	Using cards of various ball locations, slopes, and cups, learner shows (without actually putting) where they should putt the golf ball (trajectory) to get it into the cup.
Assessment	Ensure relevance to performance context. Sequence near skills it supports.	Delayed until intellectual skills I.1 through I.6 assessed.
Follow-Through	Provide additional elaboration and organization strategies. Create recall puzzles or contests.	Talk about other factors they believe might impact the trajectory or distance of their putt.

Table 8.11 Example Instructional Strategy for Golf Objectives Classified as Intellectual Skills

Learning Components	Considerations for Each Component	Instructional Strategy for Objective I.1, Given a putting green with a variety of slopes and resistance conditions, plan the stroke required to putt the ball into the cup.
Preinstructional Activities	Provide for motivation.	Club pro putts several golf balls while class approaches and waits to begin. Invites members of group to "warm up" by putting several balls prior to class beginning.
	Relevance	Golfers often lose tournaments on the putting green.
	Confidence	Plan your stroke carefully to reduce the number of putts you must take.
	Inform learner of objectives.	Plan stroke required to putt the ball into cup (subordinate skill I.1).
	Promote recall of prerequisites.	Remind learners of physical factors that impact putting (the verbal information supporting intellectual skills I.1.a through I.1.e). Ask learners to name: Four characteristics of putting green that create resistance and impact speed of the golf ball (grass, moisture, incline, direction of grass blade growth). Two characteristics of green that impact the trajectory of the golf ball (speed, slope).
	Link new content to existing knowledge/ skills.	Ask learners to explain the impact of these characteristics on the trajectory and speed of the ball. Integrate the five physical characteristics impacting putting into the putting plan.
Content Presentation and Learner Guidance	Sequence based on hierarchy among skills.	I.1.a through I.1 in numerical order (hierarchical).
	Disclose distinguishing characteristics of concepts (purpose, physical, quality).	Grass type, grass length, grass moisture, direction of grass blades.
	Point out common errors in classifying (irrelevant).	Aiming directly for cup without considering slope and trajectory; ignoring speed and distance (over or under shoot).
	Provide examples and nonexamples.	Demonstrate correct and incorrect plans while talking plans through with learners so they learn strategy while watching consequences.
	Create ways of organizing new into existing skills.	Presession video of professionals during a tournament moving around green planning their strokes. (Do not show actual strokes, only planning actions).
Learner Participation	Ensure congruence of practice to conditions and behaviors.	Place various balls around putting green with various slopes and surface conditions, have learners predict the appropriate trajectory for ball to reach the cup.
	Progress from less to more difficult. Use familiar contexts for rehearsal.	Slight slope beneath and above cup; steep slope beneath and above cup; slight slope beside cup; steep slope beside cup.
	Provide conditions similar to performance context.	Roll balls by hand in predicted directions.

Table 8.11 Continued

Learning Components	Considerations for Each Component	Instructional Strategy for Objective I.1, Given a putting green with a variety of slopes and resistance conditions, plan the stroke required to putt the ball into the cup.
	Ensure feedback is balanced with qualities and errors.	For incorrect predictions, show where ball should have been aimed to succeed.
Assessment	Ensure learners' readiness for testing. Accommodate hierarchical nature of skills. Apply appropriate criteria for learner age, ability.	Place ball in various positions on the green varied by slope, direction, and surface conditions. Learners in small groups discuss then tell or walk through the plan they would use to putt the ball into the cup (no putters, only oral or "walked through" plans). Roll balls by hand to test plans. Pro and classmates discuss their perceptions of student's plans and results.
Follow-Through	Promote transfer (authentic tasks to performance context).	Watch postsession video of professionals planning *and* executing putts, describe errors in putting distance and direction made by professionals.
	Consider memory requirements. Consider job aid requirements.	Discuss factors other than physical ones that can affect one's putting.
	Ensure job environment receptive. Reflect on learning experience and future applications.	Each learner assesses the quality of his planned putt.

pro does not want the putt-planning instruction to be a trial-and-error experience with putters. This takes too long for complete discovery, if it ever happens.

Motor Skills

Finally, Table 8.12 contains the events of instruction, considerations for each event and type of learning, and the instructional strategy for motor skills I.4 and I.5 illustrated in Figure 8.2. For motor skills, it is critical that learners are confident they can perform the skill, have seen the skill performed, and have ample opportunities to practice with appropriate feedback. In the situation of putting a golf ball, the resulting proximity of the ball to the cup is the most direct feedback. Based on the actual outcome, the learner can adjust the plan to improve the quality of the putt.

Case Study

Group Leadership Training

Our purpose in this chapter is for you to focus on a theory-based instructional strategy, which includes the five learning components based on Gagné's events of instruction, the considerations designers should have for the type of learning within each component, and the instructional strategy linking the subordinate skills

Table 8.12 Example Instructional Strategy for Golf Objectives Classified as Motor Skills

Learning Components	Considerations for Each Component	Instructional Strategy for Objective I.4: Given a putting green with a variety of slopes and resistance conditions, execute a practice putting stroke based on the plan, and Objective I.5: Given a putting green with a variety of slopes and resistance conditions, stroke the ball based on the plan (Figure 8.2).
Preinstructional Activities	Provide for motivation.	Admired golf pro praises them for the quality of their plans, singles out learners who have made quality plans during the planning stages (vicarious satisfaction).
	Illustrate skill to be performed and recall of prerequisites (oral description of plan).	Using a golf ball on the putting green, pro orally describes putting plan, practices predicted stroke, and executes planned stroke.
	Provide information on benefits.	Regardless of outcome, ball closer to cup than if no plan used.
Presentation Activities	Plan skill organization for presentation.	I.4.1 > I.4.2 > I.4.3 > I.4.4 > I.4.5
	Tell and/or illustrate what to do and how to do it. Illustrate physical qualities of successful performance.	Locating the ball in various positions on the green (slope, distance, surface conditions), orally describe the putting plan, practice the planned stroke, and then execute the stroke.
	Show master performances for age and ability of group.	Discuss outcome (ball in or out of cup) related to the plan and describe and execute new plan if ball not in cup.
Learner Participation	Plan for repetitious rehearsal. Include relevant equipment and environmental considerations. Provide practice close to performance context. Provide immediate feedback illustrating strengths and areas for improvement. Provide targeted information for performance improvement.	Learners move to practice putting green with good balls and their own putters; beginning at simulated hole 1, plan, rehearse, and execute putts through all holes provided. Holes provided should simulate all the green conditions included in instruction. Pro circulates among learners providing information on grip, stance, plan, practice, and execution.
Assessment	Demonstrate skill with intended equipment and in intended environment.	Each learner will perform individually by putting at least three balls under various conditions and will receive personal feedback on their plan, grip, stance, practice stroke, and execution.
Follow-Through	Ensure performance conditions are incorporated in instruction and rehearsal. Encourage additional rehearsal following instruction.	Have a putting contest with learners. Using three or four different holes on the practice green, have all learners put in turn and count the number of strokes. Total score is the number of putts across the number of holes. Encourage learners to remain on the putting green to rehearse their planning and putting. Tell learners hours that putting green is open for their individual practice.

to the learning components and their considerations. To help ensure that we focus on the theoretical basis, we use only one defined concept subordinate skill from the case study. A detailed and more complete instructional strategy is presented in Chapter 9 for the case study on group leadership training using both cognitive and constructivist models.

Verbal Information Subordinate Skills

Table 8.13 contains the instructional strategy for performance objective 6.4.1 from Table 7.5. The objective is as follows:

> Performance Objective 6.4.1 Given written descriptions of a group leader's actions during a meeting, indicate whether the actions are likely to encourage or stifle cooperative group interaction. Learners should classify at least 80 percent of the actions depicted correctly.

As in the examples section, the first and second columns of the table describe the learning components and considerations for types of learning within each component. The third column contains the instructional strategy. In Chapter 9, designers must synthesize these considerations for learning theory in the instructional strategy with other planning needs such as logistics, clustering content, grouping learners, and media selections. Based on these additional considerations, the presentation of materials, groupings, and the order of information will change; however, the theory base should still drive the instructional strategy as it evolves.

Table 8.13 Example Learning Components for Unit on Leading Group Discussions for Subordinate Skill 6.4.1

Learning Components	Considerations for Each Component	Instructional Strategy for Subordinate Skill 6.4.1
Preinstructional Activities	Provide for motivation.	Welcome: Session introduced by speaker who is known to and admired by students.
	Relevance	Speaker indicates that skills in leading group discussion are critical for successful leaders, tells why. Illustrates how managing group discussions helps students achieve personal goals, increase sense of personal worth and value to organization through videotape of leader (attractive to students) managing meeting effortlessly and receiving praise from group leaders and supervisors.
	Confidence	Recognizes and praises group for achievements thus far.
	Inform learner of objectives.	Avoid overwhelming group by managing scope of what presented: Only main step 6, manage cooperative group interaction, presented (subskills addressed later). Active video of meeting paused to illustrate leader managing discussion.
	Promote recall of prerequisites. Link new content to existing knowledge/skills.	Illustrate how skill 6, managing group discussion, fits into overall group leadership skill, especially those skills already mastered by group in main skills 1 through 5.

(continued)

Table 8.13 Continued

Learning Components	Considerations for Each Component	Instructional Strategy for Subordinate Skill 6.4.1
Content Presentation and Learner Guidance	Sequence based on hierarchy among skills.	6.1.1 through 6.5.1, then main step 6 *(Illustrates location of skill 6.4.1 in lesson)*
	Create ways of organizing new into existing skills.	Provide and review list of twelve actions that encourage and stifle member cooperation during a problem-solving meeting (from 3.3.1).
	Disclose distinguishing characteristics of concepts (purpose, physical, quality). Point out common errors in classifying (irrelevant). Provide examples and nonexamples.	Provide meeting scenario in script form with leader demonstrating each encouraging and stifling action. Highlight the twelve actions for learners within the scenario.
Learner Participation	Ensure congruence of practice to conditions and behaviors.	Provide learners with a numbered list of the twelve encouraging and stifling actions a leader can take during a meeting (job aid).
	Progress from less to more difficult. Use familiar contexts for rehearsal.	Create another meeting script with new characters and a leader who demonstrates both encouraging and stifling actions during the meeting.
	Provide conditions similar to performance context.	Ask learners to assess leader comments and actions within the script, classify the action by number, and indicate with a "+" or "−" whether the action would tend to encourage or stifle member cooperation (e.g., "8+" would be a cooperating action for behavior 8).
	Ensure feedback is balanced with qualities and errors.	Provide learners with a completed rating form with all actions numbered and judged as encouraging or stifling. Have learners compare their assessments of the leader in the scenario with the model feedback form and mark where their judgments were or were not consistent.
Assessment	Ensure learners' readiness for testing. Accommodate hierarchical nature of skills. Apply appropriate criteria for learner age and ability.	Actual skill will be assessed on the posttest at the conclusion of the course.
Follow-Through	Promote transfer (authentic tasks to performance context). Consider memory requirements. Consider job aid requirements. Ensure job environment receptive. Reflect on learning experience and future applications.	Discuss with a partner areas of agreement and inconsistency in the assessments. Relate actions of characters in the scenario with those of leaders they have observed in actual meetings at work, on campus, or in the community (no names please). Perhaps prompts such as "Have you heard leaders say, "Let me play the devil's advocate here" or "Well, when I was at . . . "?

Professional and Historical Perspectives

Educational psychologists have conducted much research since the early 1920s to determine how people learn. If you have read this research, you may feel that it often seems esoteric and generally removed from real-life learning situations. Through research, psychologists have been successful, however, in identifying major components in the learning process that, when present, almost always facilitate learning. A few examples include stimulating motivation, sequencing for subordinate and superordinate relations among skills, establishing meaningful relationships between existing knowledge and new knowledge, and providing practice and feedback. Research has also established the effectiveness of many specific instructional practices such as teaching part skills and then whole skills in psychomotor learning, presenting content in both words and pictures, encouraging testimonials in attitude learning, using worked examples in teaching problem solving, spacing several reviews of new learning over time, and so forth. Clark and Mayer (2016) and Park and Hannafin (1993) are just two examples of useful collections of research-based guidelines for designing instruction.

Many of the psychologists whose work influenced the original approaches to instructional design during World War II were behaviorists. As psychologists sought better ways to explain learning and memory, many behavioral psychologists adopted cognitive explanations of learning, with corresponding modifications to their thinking about instruction. This cognitive view of learning that rose from behaviorism was the foundational theory base for instructional systems design and has been dominant in ID practice to the present; however, a parallel line of thinking about teaching and learning grew out of the philosophy of constructivism and the work of Jean Piaget beginning in the 1920s and Jerome Bruner beginning in the 1960s, among others. Piaget's developmental theory, Bruner's discovery learning approach, and other constructivist-influenced instructional theories gained popularity and began to take a prominent position in ID professional organizations and the ID literature. Ertmer and Newby (2013) provide a thorough discussion of behaviorism, cognitivism, and constructivism. As constructivist influence grew, so did the tendency toward polarization, and constructivist criticism of traditional ID became pointed and sharp.

More recently, some pushback from cognitive psychologists has been seen, questioning the efficacy of constructivist designs for learning. Cognitive psychologists contend that students need at least some guidance and in most instances fully guided instruction for efficient and effective learning, and examples of some taking this position include Mayer (2004), Kirschner et al. (2006), and Clark (2012). Constructivists, however, contend that students need minimal guidance during learning, and examples of some taking this position include Hmelo-Silver et al. (2007), Schmidt et al. (2007), and Hannafin (2012). The views of Clark (2012) and Hannafin (2012) are good resources for instructional designers to consult because they are presented in a debate format in Chapter 38 of *Trends and Issues in Instructional Design and Technology* (Reiser & Dempsey, 2012). Tobias and Duffy (2009) use a similar modified debate format in presenting both sides of the issues and sometimes illuminating common ground shared by both camps. Characterizing the argument as maximal versus minimal guidance during teaching/learning oversimplifies a more complex and nuanced controversy of which instructional designers should be aware, arising from philosophical differences regarding the nature of reality and how we know what we know. An interesting aside is that constructivist design, which is well represented in academic instructional design literature, has limited presence in the training, development, and human performance technology literature, and the public debate over constructivism is rarely seen in those ID contexts.

Designers on the extreme ends of the continuum between cognitive and constructive design theories may choose to reject out of hand the design of instruction using the other theory; however, we believe that a blending of these theories can be a productive path for effective instruction and learning. Our experience as professors working with hundreds of university students and their instructional design projects; as instructional designers and developers of our own courses; and as designers, evaluators, and observers of ID projects in school, university, business, military, and government contexts has convinced us that selected constructivist practices can effectively overlay the learning components of a cognitive ID model. Constructivist designers have been particularly effective in describing instructional strategies for learning to solve ill-defined problems, and it is for this domain of learning that a blending of constructivist practices deserves serious consideration. The model used in this text can be viewed as a generic process in which experienced designers can accommodate a variety of philosophical and psychological points of view.

An offshoot of constructivist philosophy called *learning sciences* (LS) began as a formal discipline in the early 1990s, and we mention it here because it has some implications for instructional design. Learning science departments and programs have proliferated, and as of June 2019 there were sixty Ph.D. and master's program members of the Network of Academic Programs in the Learning Sciences (NAPLeS). Sommerhoff et al. (2018) provide an analysis of what is taught in a sample of seventy-five learning science programs. LS is multidisciplinary, drawing from psychological, educational, sociological, and technological fields of study. Among other priorities, LS seeks to understand learning by developing solutions (usually constructivist learning environments) to learning problems and applying them within the teaching/learning context, thereby discovering or confirming principles and theories for future use in solving learning problems. The primary method in LS for pursuing these priorities is design-based research (DBR). In a public education context, a team, perhaps composed of teachers, administrators, students, subject-matter experts, theorists, and designer/researchers, would assemble to consider a learning problem in which they shared interests. The team would analyze the problem, hypothesize causes, consider relevant research and theories, suggest possible solutions, choose a promising solution for tryout, develop research questions, and develop an action plan for implementing and evaluating the proposed solution. So far, this looks similar to ID practice, but there are critical differences. In ID we believe that through careful analysis, we can come reasonably close to accurate descriptions of the nature of a learning problem, related content, learners, contexts, and effective instructional strategies. The assumption in DBR is that many of those details can only be discovered by applying a proposed solution in a field trial, observing and recording, correcting for what was learned, conducting another field trial, correcting, conducting another field trial, correcting, and so on, until the solution is deemed to be satisfactory. This would seem to be the end of the project, but remember that the aim in LS/DBR is twofold: designing and developing of an effective solution to a learning problem *and* discovering or confirming principles or theories. Throughout the iterative formative evaluation and revision cycles, the team would have been collecting qualitative and quantitative information for confirming the validity of the solution as eventually implemented, answering the initial research questions, and making informed observations regarding relevant theory along with suggestions for future implementation.

Instructional systems design and the learning sciences share the outcomes of understanding and improving learning and developing effective solutions to learning problems. Many elements of ISD are shared and practiced in LS, and one will find many LS research references and reports using DBR methodology in the ID literature, but design-based research is not instructional design as we teach it in this text. The goals are different, the methods are different, and the clients are different. The client for a DBR investigation is usually the investigator and a cooperating agency with shared interests, neither of which is pressured for bottom-line results. The client for an ID project is typically the developer's employer or an agency that has contracted for services, neither of which would suffer the sometimes endless calendar of field trial cycles in DBR. Honebein (2017, p. 354) reported that instructional designers are less biased toward personal favorite instructional methods and make better choices of methods when they have richer, more detailed information about the context within which a learning problem exists and concludes at one point that "[t]his result reinforces the well-known principle that instructional designers should invest a reasonable amount of time in front-end analysis to achieve greater precision. With greater precision, designers may reduce the re-work required to revise solutions that fail formative evaluation." DBR has a role in our field for those who subscribe to the philosophical understandings of constructivism, for researchers who choose this methodology as the best approach to answering specific research questions, and for educational or training settings where the choice is made to invest in fine-grained investigations of how learners, teachers, methods, materials, and technology interact in a specific learning context. It is probably not a tool for ID but certainly can be put in one's toolbox for adaptation or use in the broader practice of ISD. Lin and Spector (2017) have edited a very balanced collection of chapters briefly describing LS and ID and then comparing the disciplines, highlighting commonalities, and pointing out opportunities for collaboration.

Process Flowcharts

Planning the Instructional Strategy

The Figures 8.3 through 8.7 illustrate the components of the instructional strategy from preinstructional activities to content presentation and examples, learner participation, assessment, and follow-through.

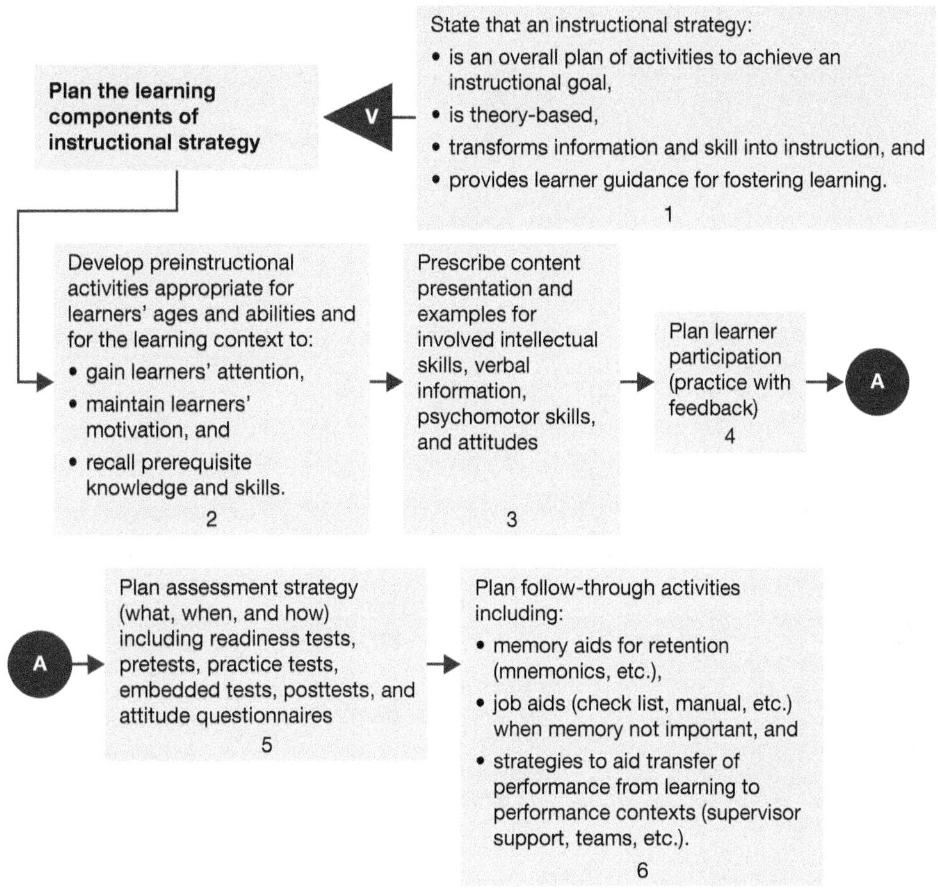

Figure 8.3 Developing Learning Components of the Instructional Strategy

Practice

Examine the instructional analysis in Appendix C for the writing composition goal. Notice that the subordinate skills for each main step have a code that begins with the number of the main step. For example, code 5.4 reflects a subordinate skill for skill 5.5, and 5.32 reflects a subordinate skill for main step 5. Assume the target students are in the sixth grade, and they are average or above average in prior writing achievement. You should follow an educated hunch at this point if you are unfamiliar with sixth-grade students.

1. Preinstructional materials: Motivation. Assume that you are planning the overall motivational presentation for the goal on writing an essay or short story to "hook" the students into the instruction. Which of the following motivational plans would be effective? Choose all the plans that might work.
   a. This step is unnecessary given the limited amount of time available for the unit.
   b. Compare a story or newsletter article written with only declarative sentences and written again with a variety of sentence types based on purpose and mood.
   c. Present a story or article with content of interest to sixth-grade students.
   d. Present the information from the perspective of persons whose opinions the students would value.
   e. Illustrate a student receiving positive attention from teachers and peers for writing a good newsletter article.
2. Design preinstructional materials: Inform learner of objectives. Select the statement that would be most effective for introducing students to the unit: In written composition, use a variety of sentence types and accompanying punctuation based on the purpose, mood, and

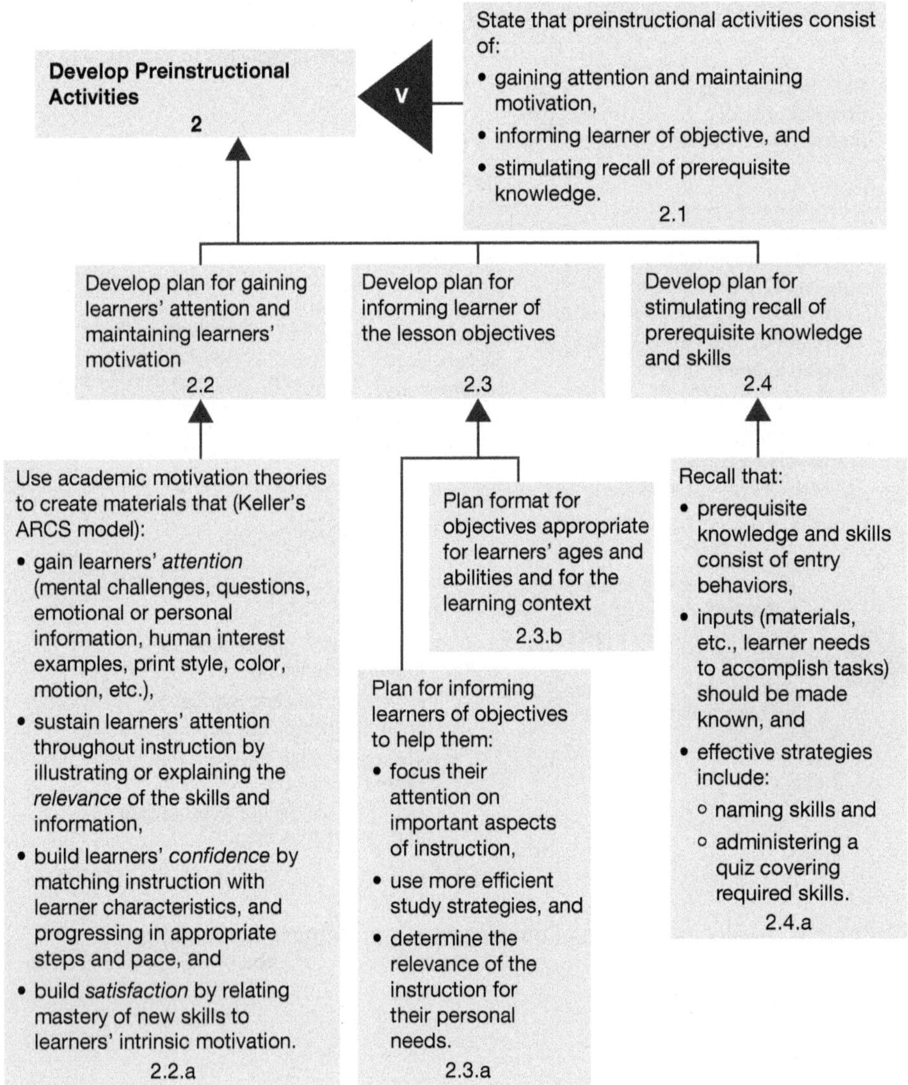

Figure 8.4 Developing Preinstructional Activities

Practice Continued

complexity of the sentence. Choose all that are appropriate.

a. The instruction will be a brief thirty minutes, so there is no need to provide objectives for just this one lesson.
b. Write sentences based on purpose and mood.
c. Write declarative, interrogative, imperative, and exclamatory sentences.
d. Given an assignment to write an interesting newsletter article, write declarative, interrogative, imperative, and exclamatory sentences appropriate for the purpose and mood of the sentence with 90 percent accuracy.

3. Design preinstructional materials: Informing learner of prerequisites. Which of the following plans appears best for the students in the lesson on choosing and writing declarative sentences?
   a. There are no entry skills identified for this unit, so none should be included.
   b. Any entry skills should be identified for the whole unit in the preinstructional materials.
   c. Students should be reminded of skills 5.1 through 5.5.
   d. Prerequisite skills for subordinate skills 5.11, 5.17, 5.24, and 5.31 should be described.
4. Plan content presentation and examples. Consider the following subordinate skill from Appendix C: Classify a complete sentence as a declarative

Develop content presentation and examples for required intellectual skills, verbal information, psychomotor skills, and attitudes

3

Intellectual Skills Provide:
- information, concepts, rules, principles, and relationships among them;
- concept definitions and interrelationships among them;
- clear examples and clear non-examples;
- illustrations, diagrams, demonstrations, model solutions, sample performances;
- learner guidance through the presentation materials;
- a summary of all information and activities;
- aids for linking new content to prerequisites;
- aids for storing new skills with prerequisites;
- familiar examples and illustrations; and
- progression from the familiar to the unfamiliar.

3.1

Attitudes:
Analyze learners and context
Classify learners' purpose as:
- volunteer,
- attending for positive reasons,
- attending for negative reasons,
- needing to change inappropriate feelings and reactions, or
- wanting to develop new feelings and reactions.

Classify attitudes as ones that learners:
- care a lot about (emotional),
- are sensitive about culturally or socially,
- could care less about, or
- are unaware of.

Provide real or imaginary character who is respected by learners to:
- behave in desired manner,
- receive recognition for behaving in desired way, and
- inform learners about why behaving in the desired way is best (rewards and consequences).

Provide:
- focus on self-awareness,
- alternative ways of behaving in context,
- simulations and/or role-playing, and
- opportunities for learners to analyze how they feel and react.

3.2

Verbal Information Provides:
- elaborations to aid linking new information to existing information;
- analogies;
- opportunities for learners to provide example from own experience;
- like information in subsets;
- direct instruction on subsets and relationships among subsets;
- organizing tables, outlines, or schemata; and
- mnemonics as memory aid for remembering lists, etc.

3.3

Motor Skills Provide:
- executive routine for directions the learner is to follow,
- mental rehearsal for execution of each step,
- some form of visual presentation (drawing, video, demonstration), and
- visualization of action.

3.4

Figure 8.5 Developing Content Presentation and Examples

Practice Continued

sentence. How many examples should you include in the instruction?

a. One: This is an intellectual skill rather than verbal information.

b. Two: This is a complex skill and should be demonstrated more than once.

c. Four or more: At least two example sentences and two nonexample sentences should be presented.

d. Twelve: Allow opportunities to illustrate many examples and nonexamples for each type of sentence.

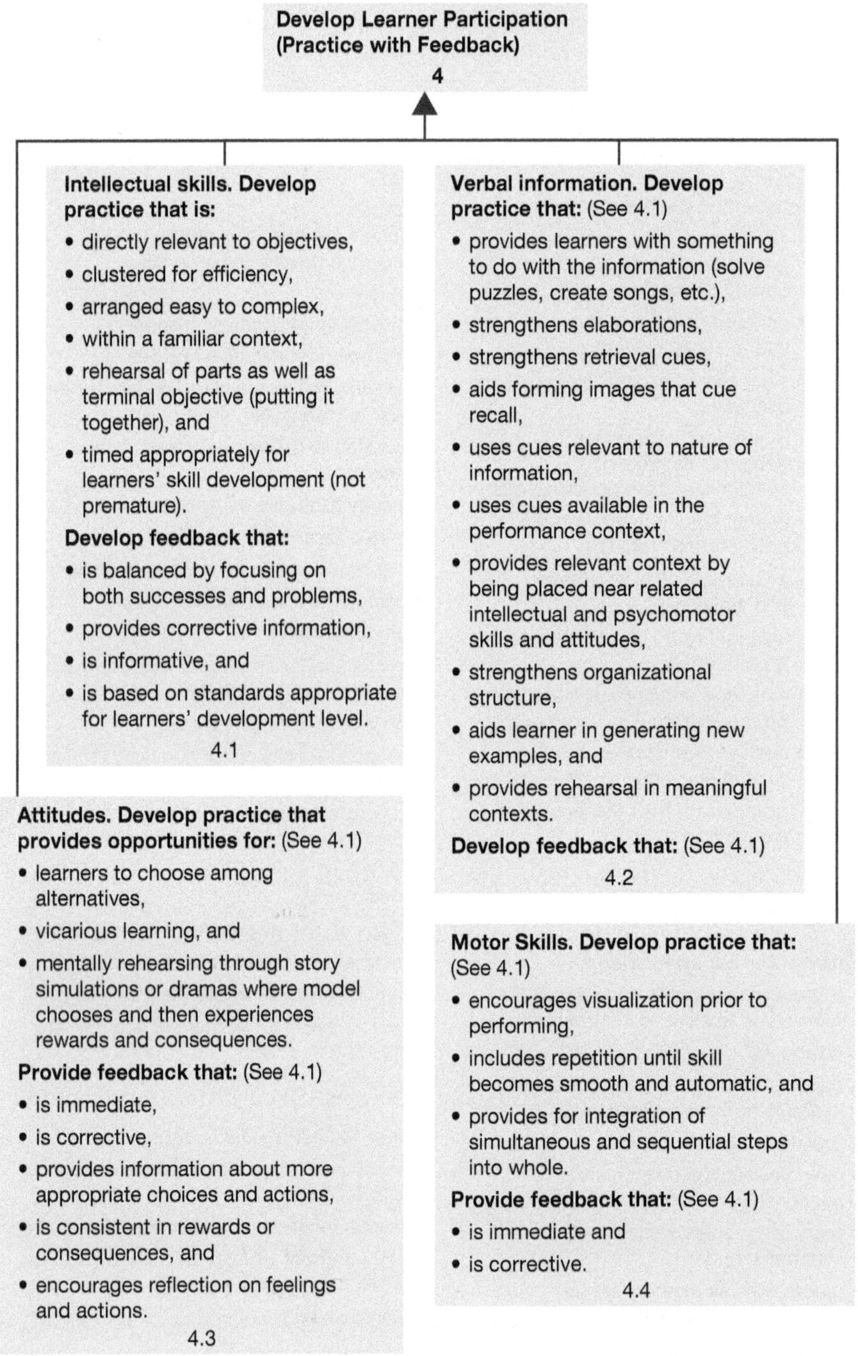

Develop Learner Participation (Practice with Feedback)
4

Intellectual skills. Develop practice that is:
- directly relevant to objectives,
- clustered for efficiency,
- arranged easy to complex,
- within a familiar context,
- rehearsal of parts as well as terminal objective (putting it together), and
- timed appropriately for learners' skill development (not premature).

Develop feedback that:
- is balanced by focusing on both successes and problems,
- provides corrective information,
- is informative, and
- is based on standards appropriate for learners' development level.

4.1

Verbal information. Develop practice that: (See 4.1)
- provides learners with something to do with the information (solve puzzles, create songs, etc.),
- strengthens elaborations,
- strengthens retrieval cues,
- aids forming images that cue recall,
- uses cues relevant to nature of information,
- uses cues available in the performance context,
- provides relevant context by being placed near related intellectual and psychomotor skills and attitudes,
- strengthens organizational structure,
- aids learner in generating new examples, and
- provides rehearsal in meaningful contexts.

Develop feedback that: (See 4.1)

4.2

Attitudes. Develop practice that provides opportunities for: (See 4.1)
- learners to choose among alternatives,
- vicarious learning, and
- mentally rehearsing through story simulations or dramas where model chooses and then experiences rewards and consequences.

Provide feedback that: (See 4.1)
- is immediate,
- is corrective,
- provides information about more appropriate choices and actions,
- is consistent in rewards or consequences, and
- encourages reflection on feelings and actions.

4.3

Motor Skills. Develop practice that: (See 4.1)
- encourages visualization prior to performing,
- includes repetition until skill becomes smooth and automatic, and
- provides for integration of simultaneous and sequential steps into whole.

Provide feedback that: (See 4.1)
- is immediate and
- is corrective.

4.4

Figure 8.6 Developing Learner Participation (Practice with Feedback)

Practice Continued

5. Planning learner participation. Which of the following strategies would be best (considering feasibility or time/resource requirements) for practice and feedback for the skills in the following subordinate skill: Write a declarative sentence using correct closing punctuation? Choose all that apply.
   a. Objective tasks: Multiple-choice format.
   b. Objective tasks: Short-answer format.
   c. Alternative assessment: Live performance with teacher observing.
   d. Alternative assessment: Product development and rubric scoring.

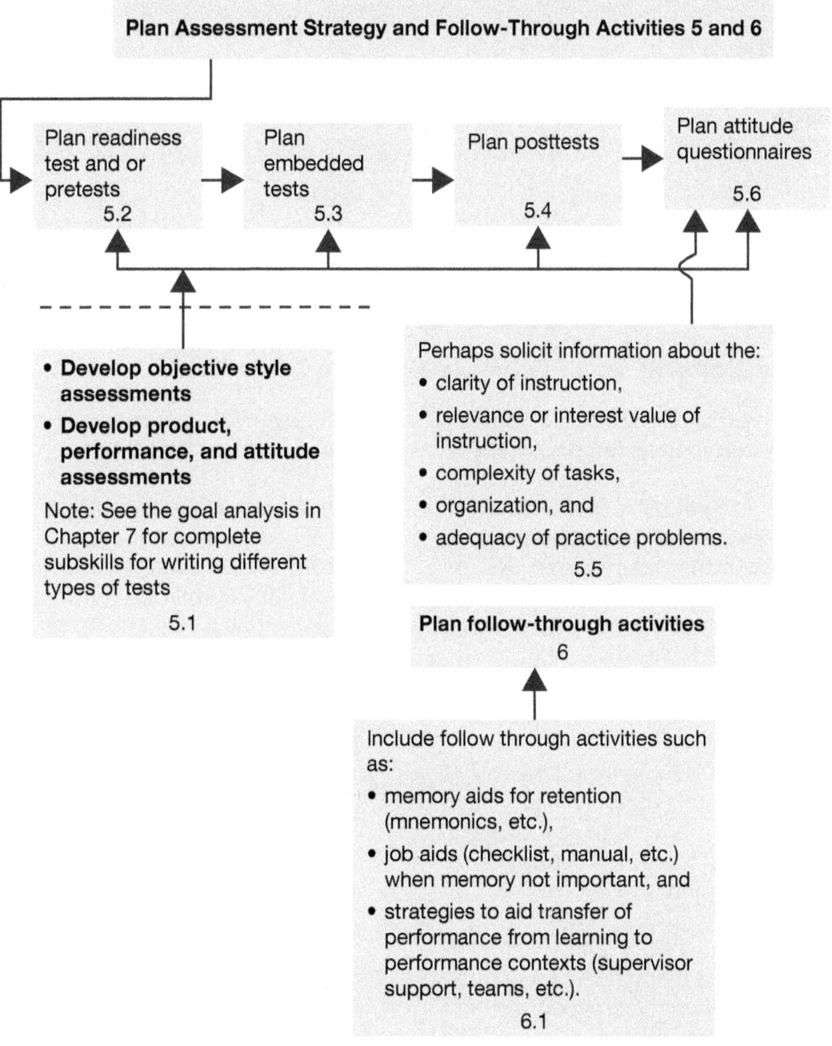

Figure 8.7 Plan Assessment Strategy and Follow-Through Activities (5 and 6)

Practice Continued

e. A combination of objective tasks and alternative assessments.

6. Planning assessment. Which of the following assessment plans appears to be most useful for main step 5 in Appendix C? Choose all that apply.
   a. Administer an objective-style readiness test to ensure that learners can classify complete sentences for all four sentence types.
   b. Administer a readiness/pretest in an objective format covering the entry skills, all subordinate skills, and main step 5.
   c. Administer a posttest in an objective format covering skills 5.11 through main step 5.
   d. Administer an alternative assessment product test over main step 5. The assessment should include directions for the learner and a rubric for scoring students' declarative sentences.

7. Planning for transfer. Which of the following rehearsal and posttest strategies might best support transfer of the writing skills to the home environment? Choose all that apply.
   a. Completing an objective-style posttest and making a good grade.
   b. Completing an alternative assessment in a product development format and making a good grade.
   c. Participating in writing articles for the planned newsletter and posting them on the web for other students.
   d. Participating as an editor or editorial board member for the newsletter.

Feedback

1. b, c, d, e
2. b, c
3. c
4. c
5. b
6. b, c
7. c, d

References and Recommended Readings

Anderson, T., & Shattuck, J. (2012). Design-based research: A decade of progress in education research? *Educational Researcher, 41*(1), 16–25.

Atkinson, R. K., Derry, S. J., Renkl, A., & Wortham, D. (2000). Learning from examples: Instructional principles from the worked examples research. *Review of Educational Research, 70*(2), 181–214. Synthesis of research with principles for providing instructional guidance for teaching intellectual skills.

Bandura, A. (1993). Perceived self-efficacy in cognitive development and functioning. *Educational Psychologist, 28*(2), 117–148.

Besser, E. D., & Newby, T. J. (2019). Exploring the role of feedback and its impact within a digital badge system from a student perspective. *TechTrends, 63*, 485–495. https://doi.org/10.1007/s11528-019-00386-2. A case study describing the role and use of feedback in mastery learning.

Broad, M. L., & Newstrom, J. W. (2001). *Transfer of training*. Da Capo Press. Describes many factors regarding transfer that should be considered before, during, and after instruction by the trainer, the manager, and the learner.

Brown, L. A. (1996). *Designing and developing electronic performance support systems*. Digital Press.

Carey, J. O. (2005). Applying principles of instructional design for quality assurance in e-learning: Issues and dilemmas in higher education. In *Quality assurance of e-learning in higher education*. Report of the National Institute of Multimedia Education International Symposium, November 9–10, 2005 (pp. 69–80). NIME.

Chieu, V. M. (2007). Constructivist learning: An operational approach for designing adaptive learning environments supporting cognitive flexibility. *Educational Technology and Society, 10*(3), 32–46.

Clark, D. (2010). *van Merriënboer's 4C/ID model and instructional design*. http://nwlink.com/~donclark/hrd/learning/id/4c_id.html. Includes a useful graphical representation of inductive and inductive patterns of instruction.

Clark, R. E. (1983). Reconsidering research on learning from media. *Review of Educational Research, 53*(4), 445.

Clark, R. E. (2012). Debate about the benefits of different levels of instructional guidance. In R. A. Reiser & J. V. Dempsey (Eds.), *Trends and issues in instructional design and technology* (3rd ed.). Pearson.

Clark, R. E., & Mayer, R. E. (2016). *e-learning and the science of instruction: Proven guidelines for consumers and designers of multimedia learning* (4th ed.). Wiley.

Dawson, P., Henderson, M., Ryan, T., Mahoney, P., Boud, D., Phillips, M., & Molloy, E. (2018). Technology and feedback design. In M. Spector, B. Lockee, & M. Childress (Eds.), *Learning, design, and technology*. Springer. https://10.1007/978-3-319-17727-4_124-1

Dede, C. (2008). *How Web 2.0 tools are transforming learning and knowledge*. Paper presented at the annual Florida Educational Technology Conference, Orlando, FL.

Dillon, A., & Gabbard, R. (1998). Hypermedia as an educational technology: A review of the quantitative research literature on learner comprehension, control, and style. *Review of Educational Research, 68*(3), 322–349. This summary of research concludes that learning gains from the use of hypermedia are limited.

Dick, W. (1996). The Dick and Carey model: Will it survive the decade? *Educational Technology Research and Development, 44*(3), 55–63.

Driscoll, M. P. (2005). *Psychology of learning for instruction* (3rd ed.). Allyn & Bacon.

Educational Psychologist, 38(1), (2003). Special issue on cognitive load. Addresses the issue of managing cognitive load during instruction.

Educational Technology Magazine, 47(3), (2007). Special issue on highly mobile computing—that is, hold-in-one-hand devices for social interaction and information access including PDAs, cell phones, tablet computers, UMPCs, gaming systems, iPods, motes.

Educational Technology Research and Development, 56(1), (2008). Special issue on scaffolded learning with hypermedia.

Ertmer, P., & Newby, T. (1993). Behaviorism, cognitivism, constructivism: Comparing critical features from an instructional design perspective. *Performance Improvement Quarterly, 6*(40), 50–72. Excellent review of theories that affect instructional design practice. Indicates implications for the instructional designer.

Ertmer, P. A., & Newby, T. J. (2013). Behaviorism, cognitivism, and constructivism: Comparing critical features from an instructional design perspective. *Performance Improvement Quarterly, 26*(2), 43–71.

Gagné, R. M. (1985). *Conditions of learning* (4th ed.). Holt, Rinehart and Winston. Describes in detail the factors that should be present to stimulate learning in each of the learning domains.

Gagné, R. M., & Medsker, K. L. (1996). *The conditions of learning: Training applications*. Harcourt Brace College Publishers. Integrates much of Gagné's early work on conditions of learning with the current world of training in business and industry.

Gagné, R. M., Wager, W. W., Golas, K. C., & Keller, J. M. (2004). *Principles of instructional design* (5th ed.). Wadsworth/Thomson Learning. Chapters 9–12 provide additional guidelines on developing instructional strategies.

Gery, G. (1991). *Electronic performance support systems*. Gery Performance Press. This is the original text by Gloria Gery, who coined the term *electronic performance support systems (EPSS)*.

Hannafin, M. J. (2012). Debate about the benefits of different levels of instructional guidance. In R. A. Reiser & J. V. Dempsey (Eds.), *Trends and issues in instructional design and technology* (3rd ed.). Pearson.

Hannafin, M. J., Hannafin, K. M., Land, S. M., & Oliver, K. (1997). Grounded practice and the design of constructivist learning environments. *Educational Technology Research and Development*, *45*(3), 101–117.

Hannum, W. H. (2007). When computers teach: A review of the instructional effectiveness of computers. *Educational Technology*, *47*(2), 5–13.

Haskell, R. E. (2000). *Transfer of learning: Cognition, instruction, and reasoning*. Academic Press.

Hmelo-Silver, C. E. (2006). Design principles for scaffolding technology-based inquiry. In A. M. O'Donnell, C. E. Hmelo-Silver, & G. Erkens (Eds.), *Collaborative reasoning, learning and technology*. Lawrence Erlbaum Associates.

Hmelo-Silver, C. E., Duncan, R. G., & Chinn, C. A. (2007). Scaffolding and achievement in problem-based and inquiry learning: A response to Kirschner, Sweller, and Clark. *Educational Psychologist*, *42*(2), 99–107.

Honebein, P. C., & Honebein, C. H. (2015). Effectiveness, efficiency, and appeal: Pick any two? The influence of learning domains and learning outcomes on designer judgements of useful instructional methods. *Instructional Technology Research & Development*, *63*, 937–955. Survey research that looked at instructional designers' perceptions of relationships among types of learning, instructional methods, and effectiveness, efficiency, and appeal.

Honebein, P. C. (2017). The influence of value and rich conditions on designers' judgments about useful instructional methods. *Educational Technology Research and Development*, *65*, 341–357. Interesting study that concludes that the more designers know about the context of an ID problem, the more precise their decisions about what instructional methods to choose.

Hooley, D. S., & Thorpe, J. (2017). The effects of formative reading assessments closely linked to classroom texts on high school reading comprehension. *Educational Technology Research and Development*, *65*, 1215–1238. Quasi-experimental study results indicated that formative student assessment with feedback promoted significant increases in student comprehension of text.

Jonassen, D. H. (1991). Objectivism versus constructivism: Do we need a new philosophical paradigm? *Educational Technology Research & Development*, *39*, 5–14. https://doi.org/10.1007/BF02296434

Jonassen, D. H. (1997). Instructional design models for well-structured and ill-structured problem-solving learning outcomes. *Educational Technology Research and Development*, *45*(1), 65–94. Provides examples and procedures for designing and developing both well-structured and ill-structured problem-solving instruction.

Jonassen, D. H. (1999). Designing constructivist learning environments. In C. M. Reigeluth (Ed.), *Instructional design theories and models* (Vol. II). Lawrence Erlbaum Associates.

Jonassen, D. H. (2004). *Learning to solve problems: An instructional design guide*. Pfeiffer.

Jonassen, D. H. (2006). On the role of concepts in learning and instructional design. *Educational Technology Research and Development*, *54*(2), 177–196.

Jonassen, D. H. (2011). *Learning to solve problems: A handbook for designing problem-solving learning environments*. Routledge.

Keirns, J. L. (1999). *Designs for self-instruction: Principles, processes and issues in developing self-directed learning*. Allyn & Bacon. Looks at instructional strategies for individualized learning.

Keller, J., & Burkman, E. (1993). Motivation principles. In M. Fleming & W. H. Levie (Eds.), *Instructional message design*. Educational Technology Publications. Review of both learner and text characteristics that are important to the designer.

Keller, J. M. (2010). *Motivational design for learning and performance: The ARCS model approach*. Springer.

Kirschner, P. A., Sweller, J., & Clark, R. (2006). Why minimal guidance during instruction does not work: An analysis of the failure of constructivist, discovery, problem-based, experiential, and inquiry based teaching. *Educational Psychologist*, *41*(2), 75–86.

Klauer, K. J., & Phye, G. D. (2008). Inductive reasoning: A training approach. *Review of Educational Research*, *78*(1), 85–123. Reports a meta-analysis supporting the positive effects of training on inductive reasoning, problem solving, and transfer.

Kolb, D. (1984). *Experiential learning*. Prentice Hall.

Kruse, K., & Keil, K. (2000). *Technology-based training: The art and science of design, development, and delivery*. Jossey-Bass Pfeiffer.

Lee, W. W., & Owens, D. L. (2004). *Multimedia-based instructional design: Computer-based training; web-based training; distance broadcast training; performance-based solutions* (2nd ed.). Jossey-Bass Pfeiffer. Demonstrates that the same instructional design model can be used for all media.

Liao, Y., Kung, W., & Chen, H. (2019). Testing the effectiveness of creative map mnemonic strategies in a geography class. *Instructional Science, 47*, 589–608. The results of a quasi-experimental study demonstrated significant, positive effects of using a mnemonic on performance, motivation, and creativity.

Lin, L., & Spector, M. J. (Eds.). (2017). *The sciences of learning and instructional design: Constructive articulation between communities*. Routledge.

Mager, R. F. (1997). *How to turn learners on . . . without turning them off: Ways to ignite interest in learning* (3rd ed.). Center for Effective Performance.

Mayer, R. E. (2004). Should there be a three strikes rule against pure discovery learning? The case for guided methods of instruction. *American Psychologist, 59*(1), 14–19.

Mayer, R. E. (2008). *Learning and instruction* (2nd ed.). Pearson.

Mayer, R. E. (Ed.). (2014). *The Cambridge handbook of multimedia learning* (2nd ed.). Cambridge University Press.

Mayer, R. E., & Wittrock, R. C. (2006). Problem solving. In P. A. Alexander & P. H. Winnie (Eds.), *Handbook of educational psychology* (2nd ed.). Erlbaum.

Mayer, R. E., & Alexander, P. A. (Eds.). (2016). *Handbook of research on learning and instruction* (2nd ed.). Routledge.

McKenney, S., & Reeves, T. C. (2013). Systematic review of design-based research progress: Is a little knowledge a dangerous thing? *Educational Researcher, 42*(2), 97–100.

McManus, P., & Rossett, A. (2006). Performance support tools. *Performance Improvement, 45*(2), 8–17.

Merrill, M. D. (2013). *First principles of instruction: Identifying and classifying effective, efficient, and engaging instruction*. Pfeiffer.

Moore, M. G., & Kearsley, G. (2012). *Distance education: A systems view* (3rd ed.). Wadsworth. A good overview of distance education with summaries of research findings.

Mueller, C., Lim, J., & Watson, S. L. (2017). First principles of attitudinal change: A review of principles, methods, and strategies. *TechTrends, 61*, 560–569.

O'Donnell, A. M., Hmelo-Silver, C. E., & Erkens, G. (Eds.). (2006). *Collaborative reasoning, learning and technology*. Lawrence Erlbaum Associates.

Oha, E., & Reeves, T. (2010). The implications of the differences between design research and instructional systems design for educational technology researchers and practitioners. *Educational Media International*, 4(47), 263–275.

Park, I., & Hannafin, M. J. (1993). Empirically-based guidelines for the design of interactive multimedia. *Educational Technology Research & Development, 41*(3), 63–85. Very useful principles with implications for designing interactive multimedia.

Patchan, M. M., & Schunn, C. D. (2015). Understanding the benefits of providing peer feedback: How students respond to peers' texts of varying quality. *Instructional Science, 43*, 591–614. Study concluded that high-ability peer reviewers provide better feedback than low-ability reviewers when critiquing samples of writing.

Reigeluth, C. M., Beatty, B. J., & Myers, R. D. (Eds.). (2017). *Instructional-design theories and models, volume IV: The learner-centered paradigm of education*. Routledge.

Reiser, R. A., & Dempsey, J. V. (Eds.). (2012). *Trends and issues in instructional design and technology* (3rd ed.). Pearson.

Romiszowski, A. J. (1993). Psychomotor principles. In M. Fleming & W. H. Levie (Eds.), *Instructional message design*. Educational Technology Publications. One of the few sources that describes the principles of motor skills instruction for the designer. Excellent summary of the fundamentals.

Rossett, A., & Schafer, L. (2006). *Job aids and performance support: Moving from knowledge in the classroom to knowledge everywhere*. Pfeiffer.

Russell, J., Reiser, R., Hruskocy, C., & Ruckdeschel, C. (1999). Strategies for teaching project-based courses. *Educational Technology, 39*(2), 56–59.

Schmidt, H. G., Loyens, S. M. M., van Gog, T., & Paas, T. (2007). Problem-based learning is compatible with human cognitive architecture: Commentary on Kirschner, Sweller, and Clark. *Educational Psychologist, 42*(2), 91–97.

Schunk, D. (2019). *Learning theories: An educational perspective* (4th ed.). Merrill/Prentice Hall.

Shute, V. J. (2008). Focus on formative feedback. *Review of Educational Research, 78*(1), 153–189.

Schwartz, P., Mennin, S., & Webb, G. (2001). *Problem-based learning: Case studies, experience, and practice*. Kogan Page.

Smith, P. L., & Ragan, T. J. (2020). *Instructional design* (4th ed.). Wiley. In-depth descriptions of a variety of instructional strategies for different types of learning.

Sommerhoff, D., Szameitat, A., Vogel, F., Chernikova, O., Loderer, K., & Fischer, F. (2018). What do we teach when we teach the Learning Sciences? An analysis of 75 degree programs. *Journal of the Learning Sciences, 27*(2), 319–351. doi: 10.1080/10508406.2018.1440353

Sweller, J. (1994). Cognitive load theory, learning difficulty and instructional design. *Learning and Instruction, 4*, 295–312.

Tobias, S., & Duffy, T. M. (Eds.). (2009). *Constructivist instruction: Success or failure?* Routledge.

Vygotsky, L. (1978). *Mind in society: The development of higher psychological processes*. Harvard University Press.

Westera, W. (2019). Why and how serious games can become far more effective: Accommodating productive learning experiences, learner motivation and the monitoring of learning gains. *Journal of Educational Technology & Society, 22*(1), 59–69.

Windschitl, M. (2002). Framing constructivism in practice as negotiation of dilemmas: An analysis of the conceptual, pedagogical, cultural, and political challenges facing teachers. *Review of Educational Research, 72*(2), 131–175. An analysis of the difficulties encountered by teachers implementing constructivist methods in school settings.

Woo, Y., Herrington, J., Agostinho, S., & Reeves, T. (2007). Implementing authentic tasks in web-based learning environments. *Educause Quarterly, 30*(3), 36–43.

chapter 9

Planning Logistics and Management for the Instructional Strategy

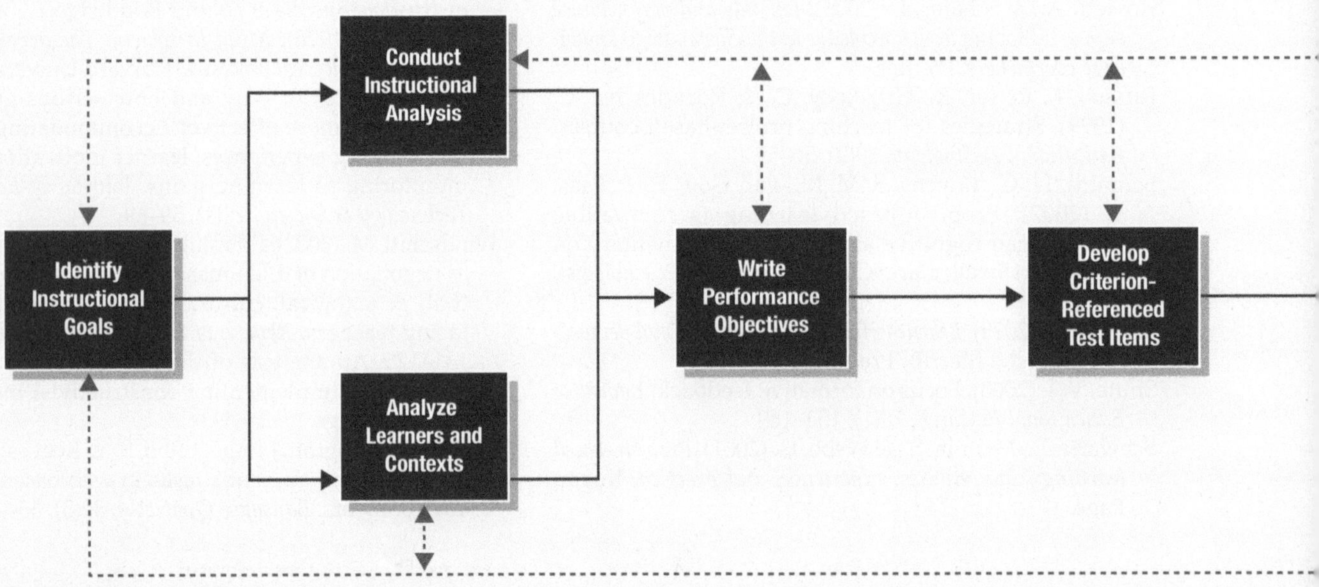

Objectives

- Select a delivery system.
- Sequence and arrange performance objectives in lesson-level clusters.
- Select appropriate learner groupings and media for an instructional strategy.
- Select media and delivery systems.
- Consolidate media selections and confirm or select a delivery system.

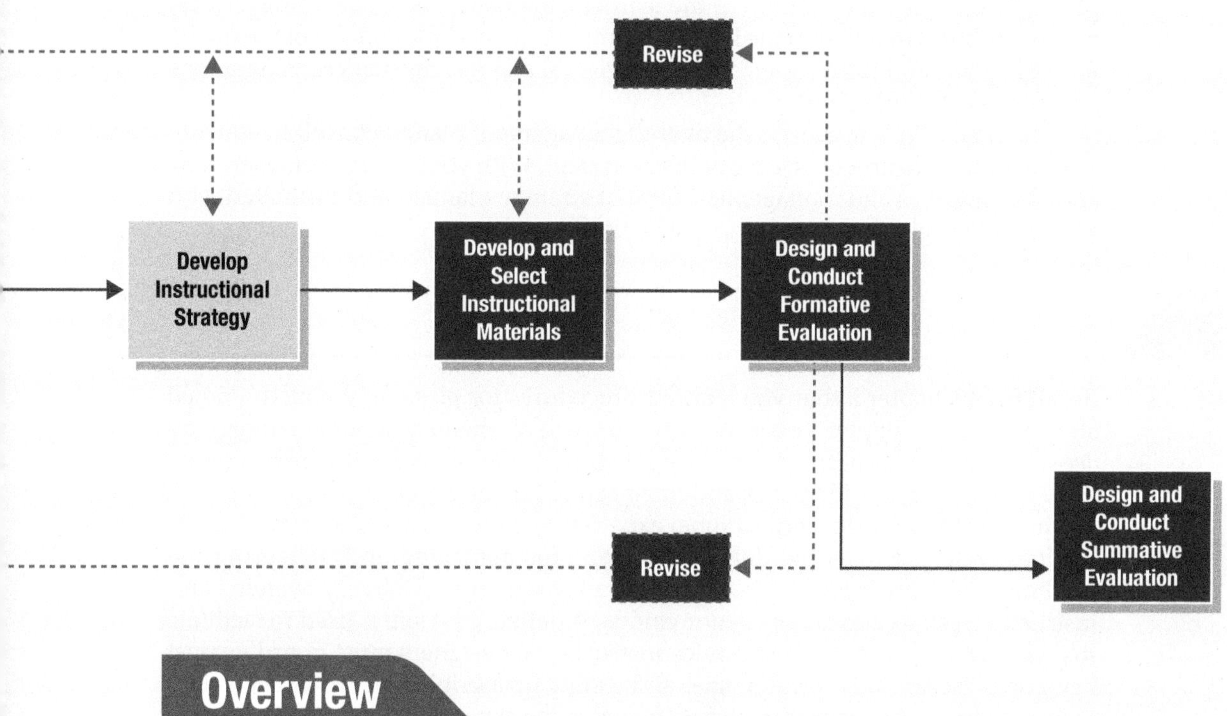

Overview

Recall the instructional strategy is a prescription used for developing or selecting instructional materials, and you bring to this task the work you have already completed, including the instructional goal, the learner and context analyses, the instructional analysis, the performance objectives, and the assessment items. You will need to continue to refer to these design documents as you plan the logistics and management for the instructional strategy.

The first consideration in planning the logistics and management is whether the organization requesting the instruction has already assumed that a specific delivery system will be used. If yes, then you should keep the benefits and constraints in mind as you plan the remaining components. If it is not assumed, then it would be most efficient to plan the delivery system after you have completed most parts of the logistics and management plan.

The second planning activity is related to the sequence of performance objectives and the order of related prescriptions for the learning components. You should sequence the content for teaching, make clusters of logical groupings of skills in the instructional analysis and their performance objectives, and assign objectives to lessons. Accomplishing these tasks efficiently requires consideration of all the previous steps, and it might require adjustment when actually developing instruction and realizing the time required to follow the plan.

With the sequence of skills and clusters of performance objectives in hand, you are ready for the third step, planning the learning components of the instruction. Instruction is presented to learners in the sequence of the named components in the strategy; however, the strategy is not developed in this order. When developing the learning components, first prescribe the preinstructional, assessment, and follow-through learning components and then the content presentation and learner participation components. The preinstructional, assessment, and follow-through components might relate to a single lesson, a group of lessons, or an entire unit of instruction.

The fourth planning activity is to specify learner groupings and select one or more media that can be used to deliver each component. These decisions are based primarily on the characteristics of the learners, the nature of the learning, critical media attributes required in the learning components, and the efficacy of the media for the learners and learning and then on logistical and management considerations such as time, facilities, and funds.

The final step is to review the overall management plan to consolidate media selections and confirm or select a delivery system. With your instructional strategy and your logistics and management for that strategy planned and evaluated, you are ready to begin developing the instruction according to plan.

Concepts

Recall from Chapter 8 that you learned procedures for *planning* the instructional strategy. In this chapter you will continue work on the instructional strategy by *developing* it. This is accomplished by integrating the plans for the instructional strategy with plans for logistics and management of instruction.

In any kind of formal educational experience, there is usually a general methodology, referred to as the **delivery system**, for managing and delivering the teaching and learning activities that we call **instruction**. Delivery systems and instructional strategies are not synonymous. A delivery system is used to facilitate the instructional strategy, and novice instructional designers must guard against being seduced by flashy technologies and ending up ascribing far too much weight to how instruction is packaged and delivered at the expense of the careful planning of the teaching–learning activities that should be included in the instruction. Either the delivery system is an assumption that the designer takes into the development of an instructional strategy, or it is an active decision made as part of developing the management plan. In either case, choosing a delivery system can be a lesson-level, course-level, or curriculum-level management decision.

Selection of a Delivery System

For efficient logistics and management, the instructional designer should first consider whether an imposed or assigned delivery system is specified for the instruction. If there is not, then decisions about the delivery system should be delayed until later in the planning. If there is an imposed system, then its benefits and constraints should be considered in all the remaining steps of the planning process.

The best way to define *delivery system* more precisely is through a list of examples. The following are a few examples of common delivery systems (mixed in with some instructional methods) for conducting instruction:

1. The traditional model is an instructor with a group of learners in classroom, training center, or lab
2. Large-group lecture with small-group question-and-answer follow-up

3. Telecourse by broadcast, webcast, two-way interactive videoconference, or computer-based instruction
4. Computer-based instruction that ranges from (a) independent study to instructor-facilitated and (b) textual drill and practice to fully interactive multimedia (includes simulation, gaming, intelligent tutoring, and virtual reality)
5. Internet or intranet web-based instruction ranges from:
   - independent study to instructor-facilitated;
   - textual drill and practice to fully interactive multimedia;
   - a simple online syllabus to a comprehensive solution organized within a learning portal that includes content, instruction, interaction, and assessment;
   - an individualized course for credit to a group event played out in social media; and
   - a webinar for a small, focused audience to a MOOC for a worldwide audience.
6. Self-paced (sometimes open-entry, open-exit) programs that can include a variety of combinations of instructor or tutor and print or mediated learning
7. Site-based internships, mentoring, and coaching
8. Electronic performance support ranging from simple and searchable job aids to contextually sensitive smart systems
9. Combinations and unique custom systems

Notice that none of these delivery systems indicate what is being learned and by whom. In an ideal instructional design process, first consider the goal, learner characteristics, learning and performance contexts, objectives, and assessment requirements, and then work through the considerations and decisions from Figure 9.1 to arrive at the selection of the best delivery system. Figure 9.1 is an illustration of a recommended sequence for planning the logistics and management for implementation of the instructional strategy. Notice in the figure that planning the instructional strategy appears as the shaded step 2 in the diagram. It is shaded because this task was addressed in Chapter 8: It is repeated in the figure to show its relationship to the logistic and management steps.

The steps in the figure represent an ideal path for choosing a delivery system because the choice is based on careful consideration of needs and requirements before a solution is named. In this view, selecting a delivery system (step 10 in Figure 9.1) is an output of the process of careful deliberation about teaching–learning requirements (steps 2–6). Reversing the sequence and choosing a delivery system first imposes a solution (and its inherent constraints) before the requirements for delivering effective instruction are fully known.

There are three considerations to note about this ideal path to choosing a delivery system. First, it almost never happens this way! One reason is that instructors and instructional designers often have preferred modes of course delivery, so in their minds, the delivery system has been chosen before the instructional design process has even begun. Second, the delivery system can be dictated by the learning context in which the organization delivers its instruction. The designer is typically required to work within this context, changing it only slightly for any given course or workshop. If the designer is working within a public school context, then the assumption may be that the teacher in a traditional classroom setting is the delivery system. The same assumption can be made regarding training in business and industry that still is, for the most part, instructor-led platform instruction in spite of the increase in business training that now assumes web delivery at the outset. Third, increasingly common is the situation in which new delivery systems—such as proprietary software for e-learning portals—have been purchased and installed, and the designer is told that this system will be used for the delivery of instruction, often in an attempt to justify the purchase of the system. Now that

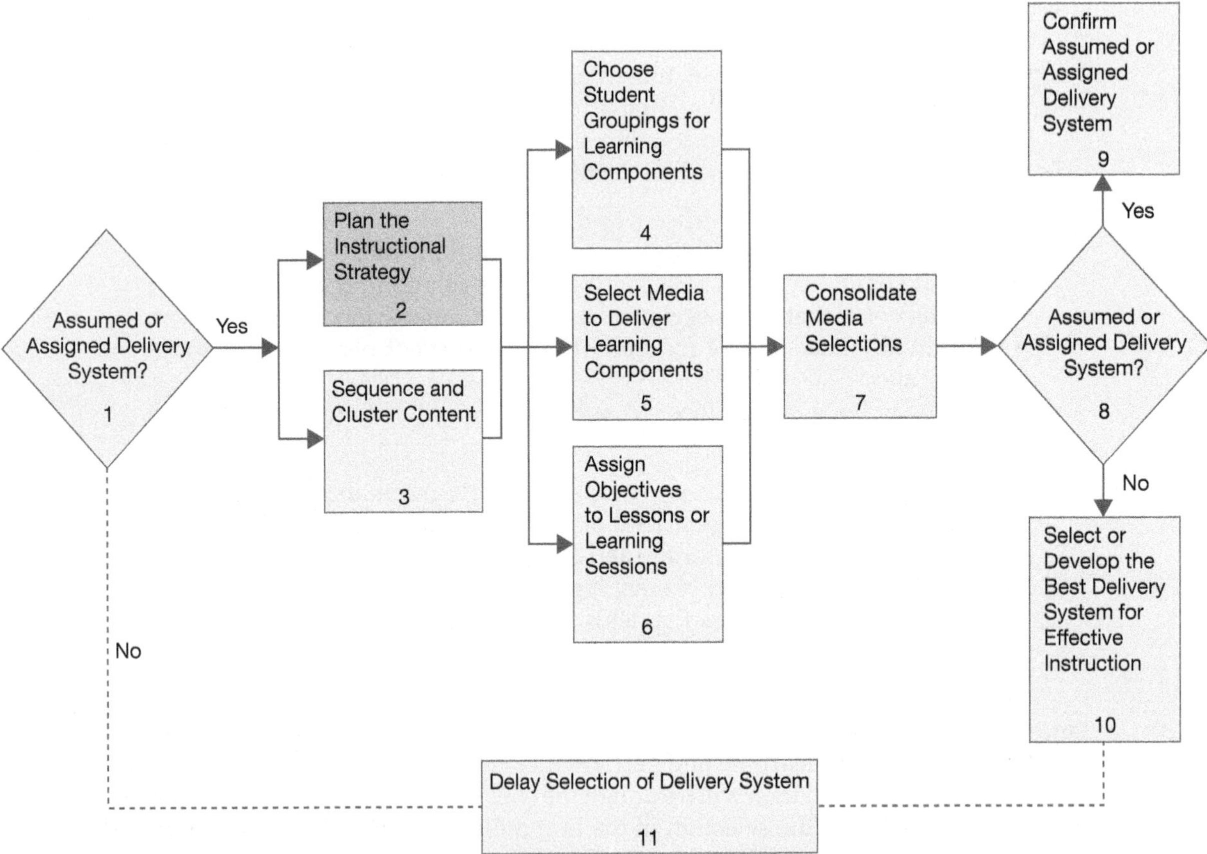

Figure 9.1 Planning Logistics and Management for the Instructional Strategy

Internet (and, in some settings, intranet) access is ubiquitous and web technology has advanced so rapidly, it is often chosen *a priori* as the delivery system when distribution of instruction to the home or desktop is desired across time and distance. When such preestablished situations prevail, as they usually do, the designer must be flexible and get everything out of the system that it is capable of delivering. If there is a mismatch between the skills to be taught and the system specified for delivering the instruction, then the designer must make appropriate adaptations or make the case and propose an alternative system. Figure 9.1 graphically depicts the development of a management plan that distinguishes between assuming a delivery system at the outset of the process and selecting a delivery system as a logical conclusion of the process.

A second consideration to note about the previously described ideal approach to selecting a delivery system is that the numbering in Figure 9.1 gives the appearance of a linear, stepwise sequence, when in fact steps 2, 3, 4, 5, and 6 are frequently considered at the same time. For example, you may decide that a practice and feedback sequence is required for learner mastery (step 3). While specifying that activity, you might also be deciding whether it is most effective to do the practice and feedback in small-group meetings on Skype of three to five learners (step 4) with three different scenarios prerecorded on a video (step 5). The parallel nature of these steps is illustrated in Figure 9.1. Discussion continues later in this chapter about putting together these pieces of a management plan.

A final note is that the systems design model you are using is equally applicable whether the delivery system is chosen earlier or later in the process, and the generic instructional design steps that you are taking in this model are as relevant for an instructor-led videoconferencing delivery system as for a digital, interactive multimedia delivery system. We have included this discussion of selecting delivery systems at this point because it is where it usually happens in practice. The discussion will be reintroduced later in this chapter at the point where specifying media and selecting delivery systems would ideally occur.

Content Sequencing and Clustering

Content Sequence

The second step in developing a logistics and management plan (see Figure 9.1) is identifying a teaching sequence and manageable groupings of content. What sequence should you follow in presenting content to the learner? The most useful tool in determining the answer to this question is your instructional analysis. Begin with the lower-level skills—that is, those just above the line that separates the entry skills from the skills to be taught—and then progress upward through the hierarchy. At no point should you present detailed instruction on a particular hierarchical skill prior to having done so for the related subordinate skills; however, it often is useful to introduce a higher-level skill first as an advanced organizer or as a whole-part-whole instructional sequence.

The instructional sequence for a goal should, of course, logically be sequenced from the left, or the beginning point, and proceed to the right. If there are subordinate capabilities for any of the major steps, then they should be taught prior to going on to the next major component.

Because the goal analysis indicates each step that must be performed and the subordinate skills analysis indicates the skills that must be acquired prior to learning the major steps in the goal, the instructional sequence tends to be a combination of bottom to top and left to right. That is, the subordinate skills for step 1 are taught first and then step 1. Next, the subordinate skills for step 2 are taught and then step 2 itself. This sequence is continued until all the steps are taught. Finally, there is instruction on integrating and practicing all the steps in the instructional goal. See Figure 4.10 (p. 100) for an example of this approach. The boxes are numbered in the sequence in which they should be taught, beginning at the bottom and working up to each major step.

There are three exceptions to this general approach to sequencing. The first occurs when two or more steps in a goal are the same or have the same subordinate skills. In this situation, it is not necessary to teach these skills again. The learner can simply be informed that a skill that has been previously learned will be used again at this point in the procedure.

A second exception to the general sequencing approach is when the instruction includes the use of several pieces of equipment or the parts of a single piece of equipment. The instructional analysis may indicate that the learner will be required, for example, to be able to identify and locate various pieces of equipment at various points in the instruction. To avoid having to go back and forth to make identifications, it is usually both possible and desirable to present all this instruction at the beginning of your unit. Designers are sometimes tempted for logistical reasons to present all the lower-level verbal information objectives, such as definitions, at one time at the beginning of the instruction. Use caution when doing this because you may be removing the context required to make the definitions meaningful. It may also make it more difficult for learners to store the information in memory and to retrieve it using contextual cues. Learners may also think that learning verbal information out of context is irrelevant and boring.

A third exception is when boredom would result from a predictable, tedious, step-by-step sequence. If this is the result, it is better to sacrifice some of the efficiency of the ideal sequence and break it up to sustain interest and motivation.

Clustering Instruction

The next question in your management plan deals with the size of the cluster of material you provide in your instruction. At one extreme of the continuum is the linear programmed-instruction approach, which tends to break all the information down into very small units and requires constant responding by the learner. At the other extreme of the continuum is the conventional textbook, in which a chapter is usually the unit of information. You may decide that you will present your information on an objective-by-objective basis with intervening activities, or you may wish to present the information on several objectives prior to any kind of learner activity.

You should consider the following five factors when determining the amount of information to be presented (or the size of the *cluster*):

1. The age level and learning maturity of your learners
2. The complexity of the material
3. The type of learning taking place
4. Whether the activity can be varied, thereby focusing attention on the task
5. The amount of time required to include all the components in the instructional strategy for each cluster of content presented

For example, how much time will be required for informing learners of the prerequisites, presenting content, and providing practice? For younger children, it is almost always advisable to keep the instruction, and the clusters within it, relatively small. More mature learners are able to handle larger clusters of content. Regardless of the age of the learners, when content is varied with performance and feedback activities, the learners do not seem to tire of the activity as quickly.

The designer is often faced with clustering instruction into two- or three-day workshops or semester-long courses. How much goes into a half-day or a day? The nature of the delivery system makes a big difference. With self-instructional formats, such as stand-alone computer-based instruction and typical e-learning, the designer need not worry about exact time constraints. The nature of these systems allows time to vary among learners; however, instructor-led, group process and video or webcast approaches, for example, require accurate time estimates, and there are no magic formulas for predicting time requirements. Develop a typical segment of instruction and try it out to estimate how long a total course or workshop might take. If timing is an important issue, then do not wait until all of the instruction is developed to estimate how much time is required to deliver it.

Learner Groupings

The primary question to ask when making decisions about learner groupings is whether requirements for social interaction exist in the performance and learning contexts, in the statements of learning objectives, in the specific learning component being planned, or in one's foundational views of the teaching process. The type of learner grouping (e.g., individual, pairs, small group, large group, mixed groupings) depends on specific social interaction requirements and is often mixed within and among the learning strategy in a lesson or unit. Remember that motivation is a key part of the instructional strategy and that social interaction and changes in learner groupings provide variety and interest value even when not specifically required in the performance context or objectives. In other instances, pedagogical methods such as active learning and problem-based learning use a variety of learner groupings for managing different parts of the instructional strategy. The considerations for deciding about learner groupings are the same whether meetings are face-to-face or mediated at a distance through technology.

Step 4 (see Figure 9.1) is to plan for learner groupings. When you are developing the management plan, bear in mind that learner groupings follow the instructional strategy (step 2). This is because the instructional strategy remains the primary planning unit, and it is primary in determining learning effectiveness. The emphasis should always be on planning learner groupings that align with the instructional strategy. If a delivery system requiring distance learning or individualized instruction has been prescribed, then some limits on learner groupings may exist. In most cases, this decision is in the hands of the instructional designer, and web 2.0 and web 3.0 capabilities and social media now make it far easier to "convene" groups of learners who otherwise would be studying independently.

Selection of Media and Delivery Systems

Selections of media and delivery systems are step 5 (see Figure 9.1), and they share many considerations, so the two topics are addressed together. As we begin this discussion of media selection, it is a good time to think back to your own school experiences. Do you remember those few teachers who always seemed to have a video reserved for that last class on Friday afternoon? You remember the routine: class starts—lights off—video starts—video ends—lights on—bell rings—goodbye! Was that good instruction? Usually not, but why not? Think about the learning components of an instructional strategy described in this chapter. Would the Friday afternoon video be a complete strategy or just a part of an overall set of unit activities? The video probably could fit into a unit as part of preinstructional activities and content presentation, but what about the other learning components that are part of a complete strategy? They just did not happen on those Friday afternoons. This example illustrates the point of view in this chapter that media are useful to the extent that they effectively carry some or all of the various learning components of an instructional strategy.

Designing instruction under an imposed delivery system does not particularly limit the media formats available, ranging from text, graphics, audio, hypertext, and motion video through simulations, real objects, and authentic environments. These can be displayed or represented in a low-tech delivery system with an instructor or AV equipment in a classroom or in a high-tech delivery system via computer or the web. Regardless of whether instruction is low-tech, high-tech, or some combination thereof, the instructional strategy is still the key predictor of learner success and must be provided by the instructor, by mediated materials, or by classmates, workmates, colleagues, family, friends, or the learners themselves.

At this ideal point in the instructional design process, once the instructional strategy has been planned and decisions have been made about content sequencing and clustering, appropriate decisions can be made regarding media selection and a delivery system. How are these choices made? Certainly, there are practical considerations one immediately thinks of in terms of availability of resources and personnel, but there are prior decisions that should be made that relate to the selection of appropriate media. Considerations in selecting appropriate media are the following:

1. Instructional strategy
2. Various domains of learning
3. Learner characteristics
4. Task requirements found in objectives
5. Critical needs attributes
6. Practical considerations

Media Selection for the Instructional Strategy

The logic of most current approaches to media selection rests on the cognitive assumption that learning is an internal, mental process that is stimulated by external actions. Psychologists specify those external actions based on the theories about how our minds work. Table 9.1 contains listings of the external actions identified by four cognitive psychologists. The actions are arranged to depict parallel relationships among the four psychologists' suggestions, and in some instances, the arrangements are only rough approximations.

You have seen in Chapter 8 that we organized Gagné's (1985) nine events of instruction into the five learning components of an instructional strategy: preinstructional activities, content presentation, learner participation, assessment, and follow-through activities. Further, note that the five learning components align well with those depicted in Table 9.1, as do those in the table with each other.

So what is the point here for media selection? In their own writings, the instructional theorists in Table 9.1 concur on three general steps regarding media selection:

- First and foremost, develop a theory-based instructional strategy—that is, specifications for what must happen during instruction to ensure efficient and effective learning.
- Second, identify media attributes that are essential for carrying out the instructional strategy.
- Third, select media that possess those attributes.

In light of these recommendations, what criteria should be used for choosing media for delivering instruction? We advocate media selection criteria developed through systematic analysis of needs, content, learners, and contexts and through application of accepted instructional theory as depicted in Table 9.1.

Media Selection for Domains of Learning

Gagné et al. (2004) developed a matrix for choosing effective instructional media and delivery methods that brings together considerations of domains of learning, Gagné's events of instruction, delivery methods and strategies, and types of media. The matrix is accompanied by a table with summary decisions about media characteristics that should be excluded or selected for different domains of learning.

Table 9.1 Psychologists' Theories Underpinning Learning

Gagné (1985) Events of Instruction	Merrill (2002) First Principles	Clark (2010) Guided Experiential Learning	vanMerrienboer (1997) 4C/ID
Attention Objectives Prerequisites Presentation	Activation	Reasons for learning Objectives Overview Conceptual knowledge	Prerequisite information
Guidance	Demonstration	Demonstration	Supportive information
Practice	Application, task centered	Part and whole task practice	Part task practice, whole task practice
Feedback		Corrective feedback	
Assessment		Tests	
Retention/transfer	Integration		

Interested readers should consult the source for details of the media selection logic and the decision table. In our view, the critical decision points in the matrix and table can be distilled down to three questions. Questions in choosing effective instructional media are:

- Is practice with intelligent and adaptive feedback required for learning?
- Is synchronous interaction and feedback required, or can it be asynchronous?
- Is physical practice required for learning?

The answers to these questions are found in the domain of learning represented by the objectives being taught.

Intellectual Skills Consider the analysis of media used to teach intellectual skills. Research suggests that learners should be provided precise corrective feedback to responses made during the learning process. Often, there is more than one "correct answer." To provide responsive feedback to learners' practice, choose interactive media such as a human instructor, a peer tutor, a mentor, a trainer, or a computer-based simulation or smart system. If one-way media such as large-group lecture or informational web pages were chosen, then supplemental learner materials that require responses and provide feedback could be developed, or study groups could be organized. The key is that the medium of choice must be intelligent and adaptive because feedback and guidance to learners will change based on their practice responses.

Verbal Information If the instructional goal is in the domain of verbal information, there is still the requirement of eliciting responses from learners, but there is less need for intelligent and adaptive feedback. Learners can easily compare their own responses to the correct answers, so there is less need for interactive media with verbal information goals.

Psychomotor Skills When learning a motor skill begins by learning an executive routine (describing what the learner should do and how under various circumstances), this first phase can be treated as an intellectual skill. As the learner masters the executive routine, however, practice and feedback are required, either using simulators or in the real physical environment with any real equipment and objects described in the instructional goal. Simulators can be designed to provide feedback, but an instructor often provides a debriefing that includes feedback after a simulation session. When psychomotor learning includes practice with real objects, a peer, a coach, or an instructor is often required for feedback; however, advanced learners can analyze their own performance using practice aids and/or audio-video recordings.

Attitudes Research about how we learn attitudes suggests that one of the most powerful methods is to observe a person we regard highly doing something for which they are rewarded or have received approval. It is then more likely that we will tend to make the same choice when we are in a similar situation. For teaching attitudes, then, the visual media, such as television or digital video, are often suggested. Role-playing, which is also effective for learning attitudes, requires interaction that can be face-to-face, online, or simulated in games or virtual meeting spaces.

The purpose of this review has been to suggest that although media is less important than other factors, some differences in learning outcomes are reflected in the media used to deliver instruction. However, it cannot be assumed that the objectives are all in the same domain. This choice is simpler for a short lesson, in which all of the objectives might be intellectual skills or verbal information. As the size of instruction increases—for example, to a forty-hour course—there is most likely a mixture of domains represented in the objectives, making it necessary to select media for clusters of similar objectives or attempt to mix compatible media for a variety of objectives.

Media Selection for Certain Learner Characteristics

There are two instances in selecting media in which learner characteristics are critical considerations. First, media for learners with sensory, cognitive, or learning disabilities must comply with requirements of the Americans with Disabilities Act for accommodating disabilities, or assistive means must be chosen that supplement the media to accommodate the disabilities. Sometimes it is the design of the medium that enables accommodations for disabilities. For example, blind Internet users have access to design features such as screen-reader software, speech-enabled browsing, or Braille display. The key for enabling such access requires following established design standards for what are termed *accessible web pages*.

The second instance is for a target audience of nonreaders or that includes nonreaders, for whom audio and pictorial media have obvious benefits.

Media Selection for Certain Task Requirements Found in Objectives

In addition to matching media to learning domains and learner characteristics, task requirements found in objectives can limit media choices (step 6 in Figure 9.1). First, the designer should ask whether specific sensory discriminations (e.g., visual, auditory, tactile) are required to master the objective. If the answer is yes, then the medium or combination of media must be capable of managing the sensory requirements in content presentation, learner participation, and assessment. A second question the designer should ask is whether social interaction is required for mastery of the objective. If the answer is yes, this requirement must be accommodated in learner participation and most certainly in assessment. As mentioned previously, social interaction may not require face-to-face encounters and for some purposes could be managed online, through social media, or simulated in virtual reality.

Media Selection for Critical Media Attributes

As a designer begins specific consideration of media for the learning components within an instructional strategy planned in Chapter 8, it is important to ask, "Are there critical media attribute requirements in any of the learning components that would eliminate a particular medium or class of media from consideration?" The critical attributes of media are requirements of:

- practice and intelligent and adaptive feedback,
- synchronous feedback,
- physical practice with real or simulated objects,
- sensory discriminations (visual, aural, olfactory, touch, kinesthetic),
- accommodation of learners' sensory or cognitive challenges,
- accommodation for illiterate or marginally literate learners, and
- social interaction.

If any of these attributes are required in a learning component, then media that cannot provide the attribute are eliminated from consideration for that learning component. If no critical media attributes are required in the learning components, then the designer has an open media selection process governed by practical considerations.

Practical Considerations in Choosing Media and Delivery Systems

An important factor in delivery system selection used to be the projected availability of various media for the environment in which the instruction would be used. If instruction was to be used in the media center of a public school, community college, or university, then a whole array of media devices would have been available to the learner and instructor. In contrast, if instruction was designed for home study or use on the job where equipment is limited, the designer had to develop a means of making that equipment available or limit media selection to reasonable expectations of availability. The ubiquity of computers and online access in recent years really has changed how we think about "reasonable expectations of availability." If an Internet-capable computer is not available at home, then access can be obtained at work, school, or a public library, thus opening media selection to everything that can be delivered by way of the web, even including sophisticated interactive software. Tablets with cellular functionality and smartphones have now extended Internet access without regard to location or time.

Computers, the web, and broadband access have enabled delivery of text, graphics, audio, video, and interactivity by means of a single medium or as discrete items using a single access point. This consolidation of stimulus features into a single delivery system simplifies media selection and distribution of instruction. Concerns regarding the ability of instructors and learners to manage the computer or web interface and associated software are disappearing as children grow up with smart devices, and delivery of audio, video, and interactivity has become increasingly more intuitive, seamless, and platform independent. This trend is seen most clearly in e-learning portals and the porting of web content for e-readers, web books, tablets, and smartphones; the ease of accessing/downloading blogs, RSS feeds, newsfeeds, webcasts, and podcasts; and photo, video, and audio sharing.

A related factor in media selection is the ability of the designer or an available expert to produce materials in a particular medium. For example, you may find that interactive web-based instruction is an ideal medium for a particular instructional objective, but because you do not already have the skills to author web-based instruction or the time to learn them or because there is no staff available to do it, another choice must be made.

The flexibility, durability, and convenience of the materials within a specified medium are other factors. If the materials are designed so that they require equipment found only in a learning center, is there a learning center available? Is it open during hours when learners can participate in independent study? Are the materials in a form that learners can handle alone without destroying either the materials or equipment required for the materials? Should the materials be portable, and if so, how portable can they be with the media you have chosen?

The final factor is the cost-effectiveness, over the long run, of one medium compared to others. Some materials may be initially cheaper to produce in one medium than in another, but these costs may be equalized when one considers costs in other areas, such as lecturers, evaluators, and feedback personnel. It might be cheaper to put a video of a lecture on the web for a large number of learners to view repeatedly as needed, which frees the lecturer or specialist to work with small groups of learners or to help individuals solve problems.

All the factors discussed here represent either theoretical or practical criteria that must be met. These criteria illustrate the importance of media selection in the instructional development process. In theory, it would be ideal to delay the choice of a delivery system until media have been chosen for the components of the instructional strategy; however, in practice, nearly all projects begin with the delivery system already established. Regardless of the circumstance, most delivery systems offer a range of media alternatives. Matched with a thorough front-end analysis and learning context analysis, the designer can maximize the effectiveness of the instruction with a variety of media formats in a course or workshop.

Media Selection for Replacing the Need for Instruction

At this point in the ID process, it is worth reminding designers that education and training are expensive and that alternate paths to mastering skills and improving performance are worth considering. After considering all of the criteria for choosing media, it is natural to focus one's attention narrowly on developing instruction; however, it is possible that job aids, *performance support tools* (PSTs), or *electronic performance support systems* (EPSSs) could replace some or all of the instruction. We mentioned job aids and performance support earlier in this chapter but provide more detail here because they are forms of media. *Job aids* are any tools that support performance of a task or skill, including informative signage in a library to guide learners to information resources, a table of the periodic elements on the front wall for learner reference in a chemistry classroom, a government employee's "cheat sheet" of acronyms for different agencies, a decision map that an auto repair technician uses to troubleshoot your car, or a calculator programmed to run quality-control algorithms for a production manager. PSTs and EPSSs are higher-tech, computer-based forms of job aids. If there is a distinction between the PSTs and EPSSs, it is that PSTs are more stand-alone and not as integrated into the performance context, but the distinctions between the two are disappearing in common usage. Performance support tools basically do three things—streamline and automate procedures, provide information needed for a task, and provide logic required for making decisions—supported through such functional tools as databases, hypermedia, tutorials, expert systems, wizards, task tracking, and process modeling and visualization. Examples of performance support systems include the interview sequence in TurboTax, the templates in Microsoft's PowerPoint software, the tutorials in Adobe Photoshop, the customized software a day trader uses to track the market and time stock trades, and the incident-tracking software integrated with GPS that a police dispatcher uses to route officers to emergency calls.

Using job aids or performance support as a substitute for instruction can be as simple as laminating a "how-to" card for use at a computer workstation or as involved as authoring a complex software system. In most instances, job aids and performance support will not eliminate instruction completely but can shorten learning time and improve precision in job performance. For those interested in investigating job aids and performance support further, we recommend Gery's (1991) original book on EPSSs, Brown's (1996) book on developing EPSSs, Dickelman's (2003) collection of articles, Rossett and Schafer's (2007) book on job aids and performance support, and Gottfredson and Mosher's (2011) book on integrating performance support into the workplace and workflow. Hung and Kalota (2013) wrote an article that is right at the intersection of media selection and EPSS. They report on validation of a performance support system for selecting media.

Consolidate Media Selection and Confirm or Select Delivery System

The last phase of planning is to review the instructional strategy as well as the logistics and management plan to consolidate media selections and ensure compatibility with the delivery system. While planning the management component, consider how to mediate instruction by noting the domain of learning in each objective and examining the conditions, behavior, and content in the objective. Also consider which medium best replicates conditions in the learning and performance contexts. Begin by selecting the ideal media formats for the domains of learning and objective components, but compromise and choose the best medium given constraints such as budget, personnel, equipment, delivery system, and learning site constraints. After choosing the best medium for each objective or cluster of objectives, it makes sense to examine the entire set of selections for patterns or common media prescriptions that can be considered across the objectives.

Evaluation and Revision

Instructional Strategy Evaluation

With the completion of the instructional strategy, you are at another important checkpoint in the instructional design process. Now is a good time to do some more checking with both SMEs and learners. Their reactions will save needless writing and revision later. The time required is small compared to the value of the feedback.

Subject-matter experts and individuals familiar with the needs, interests, and attention spans of learners can be asked to review all three of your strategy tables and to pinpoint potential problems. Spending a short time with selected reviewers now may save hours during later stages of the instructional development process. It may be necessary to provide reviewers with additional information, such as a description of your instructional goal, a list of your objectives, and a description of the characteristics of your intended learners. This information helps reviewers judge the quality of the information included in your strategy.

Now is also the time to try out your instructional strategy and assessments with one or two learners. The procedure is to explain to the learners that you are developing some instruction and would like to see whether you have an adequate outline of what you are going to teach. Go through the strategy just as you have written it, but in this case simply explain it to the learners. You might show them some of the examples and ask them to do the practice activities. Do they understand, and can they participate? Give them some or all of your test items and see how they do. This is a very informal process, but it can yield valuable information that you can use to revise the strategy before you begin to write the instructional materials or instructor guide, create a storyboard, or prepare a web-based instructional lesson.

Rubric for Evaluating an Instructional Strategy

The following is a rubric that you can use as a job aid in developing your strategy and that reviewers can use to assess it. The criteria for judging the learning components is repeated from Chapter 8, and those for judging logistics and management decisions are added so the rubric is complete and useful.

Designer note: If an element is not relevant for your plan, mark NA in the No column.

No	Some	Yes	**A. Content Sequence** Is/does the plan:
___	___	___	1. Appropriate for type of learning?
___	___	___	2. Have logical order (e.g., chronological, simple to complex, concept to rule to principle)?
___	___	___	3. Follow main steps?
___	___	___	4. Cover all skills/information within a main step before moving to next step?

B. Content Clusters (chunks) Is the plan appropriate for:

___ ___ ___ 1. Skill complexity?
___ ___ ___ 2. Learners' age and ability?
___ ___ ___ 3. Type of learning?
___ ___ ___ 4. Content compatibility?
___ ___ ___ 5. Time available (hour, day, week, semester)?
___ ___ ___ 6. Delivery format (self-paced, instructor-led, televised, web-based, combination, etc.)?
___ ___ ___ 7. Time required for all instructional events per cluster?

C. Preinstructional Activities Is/does the plan:

___ ___ ___ 1. Appropriate for learners' characteristics?
___ ___ ___ 2. Motivational for learners (gain attention, demonstrate relevance)?
___ ___ ___ 3. Inform learners of objectives and purpose for instruction?
___ ___ ___ 4. Cause learners to recall prerequisite knowledge and skills?
___ ___ ___ 5. Inform learners of input needed to complete tasks required?

D. Presentation Materials Does the plan include:

___ ___ ___ 1. Materials appropriate for the type of learning?
___ ___ ___ 2. Clear examples and nonexamples for learners' experience?
___ ___ ___ 3. Appropriate materials such as explanations, illustrations, diagrams, demonstrations, model solutions, and sample performances?
___ ___ ___ 4. Learner guidance through the presentation materials?
___ ___ ___ 5. Aids for linking new content and skills to prerequisites?
___ ___ ___ 6. Progression from the familiar to the unfamiliar?
___ ___ ___ 7. Organization?

E. Learner Participation Is the plan likely to be:

___ ___ ___ 1. Appropriate for learning type?
___ ___ ___ 2. Congruent with objectives?
___ ___ ___ 3. Congruent with learner characteristics?
___ ___ ___ 4. Congruent with instruction?
___ ___ ___ 5. Likely to be motivational (aid learner in building confidence)?
___ ___ ___ 6. Appropriately placed in instruction (not too soon, often, infrequent)?

F. Feedback Does the plan appear to be:

___ ___ ___ 1. Appropriate for learning type?
___ ___ ___ 2. Congruent with objectives?
___ ___ ___ 3. Congruent with learner characteristics?
___ ___ ___ 4. Informative, supportive, and corrective?
___ ___ ___ 5. Likely to aid learner in building confidence and personal satisfaction?

G. Assessments Is the plan appropriate for:

___ ___ ___ 1. Readiness/Pretests?
___ ___ ___ 2. Posttests?
___ ___ ___ 3. Type of learning (objective, alternative)?
___ ___ ___ 4. Learner characteristics (age, attention span, ability)?
___ ___ ___ 5. Yielding valid and reliable information about learner status and attitudes?

H. Follow-Through Activities Is the plan likely to:

___ ___ ___ 1. Aid retention of the new information and skills?
___ ___ ___ 2. Support transfer of skills from learning to performance environment (e.g., working with supervisors, forming support teams)?

I. Student Groupings Are groupings appropriate for:

___ ___ ___ 1. Learning requirements (e.g., learning type, interaction, objective clusters)?
___ ___ ___ 2. Learning context (e.g., staff, facilities, equipment, media, delivery system)?

J. Media and Delivery System Are plans appropriate for:

___ ___ ___ 1. Instructional strategy?
___ ___ ___ 2. Assessments?
___ ___ ___ 3. Practical constraints (e.g., context, personnel, learners, resources, materials)?
___ ___ ___ 4. Media and delivery systems available?
___ ___ ___ 5. Materials considerations (durability, transportability, convenience)?

With your strategy complete, you can begin to develop instruction based on the prescriptions in the strategy. For readers who are doing an instructional design project as they work through this text, we suggest that you read Chapter 10 before drafting your instructional materials, paying particular attention to our recommendation that first-time designers plan individualized instruction.

Examples

Now that you have an idea of what is included in an instructional strategy, you can see that it is inappropriate to go directly from a list of performance objectives to writing instructional materials without first planning your instructional strategy as well as the logistics and management necessary to support the strategy. At this time in the design process, the instructional designer must integrate the learning-based instructional strategy with the logistics and management required to develop and implement it.

Recall that the following materials you developed are necessary to finish your instructional strategy and plan the logistics and management required to support it:

- performance objectives,
- prerequisite knowledge (through your analysis of the relationship among subskills in the instructional analysis),
- the sequence for presenting instruction (when you completed your design evaluation table and your analysis diagram),
- the content required (when you analyzed the knowledge and skills during the instructional analysis),
- appropriate test items for each objective, and
- learning component considerations for each learning domain represented in your objectives.

This information, already included in your design evaluation table, serves as input for finishing the development of the instructional strategy.

Integrating Logistics and Management into the Instructional Strategy

Even though we recommend that learning components in an instructional strategy occur in the order presented in Chapter 8, we do not recommend that you try to develop your instructional strategy and management plans in this order. The developmental sequence differs from the suggested order in which learners encounter learning components during a lesson.

Sequence and Cluster Skills and Objectives

You should indicate the sequence of objectives and how to cluster them for instruction. To do this, consider the sequence of subordinate skills and the instructional goal from the instructional goal analysis. With the appropriate sequence selected, identify the size of clusters of skills that are appropriate for the attention span of learners and the time available for each session. Remember to include review or synthesizing activities when needed in your final sequence and cluster.

The decisions you make about sequence and clusters can be summarized using a form such as that shown in Table 9.2. The main skills and subordinate skills included in Table 9.2 are based on the golfing instructional goal in Figure 8.2. Recall that this is a motor skill with subordinate intellectual skills and supporting attitudes and verbal information. Recall that the target learners are beginning adult golfers of retirement age who have enrolled in a golf clinic at a local golf club. The first column in Table 9.2 names the golf clinic session. There will be six total sessions: one for each main skill area, one for the introduction (preinstructional), and one for a capstone golf tournament (follow-through). The second column prescribes the time allotted for each session. Each of the instructional sessions will be two hours in duration to allow time for physical warm-up, motivation, content presentation, learner participation with designated equipment, feedback, and follow-through activities. Session 1, introduction, is assigned one hour, and session 6 is assigned five hours to enable time for the tournament. Each of the instructional sessions includes all the enabling skills for each main step. Necessary verbal information (facts, golf rules, and etiquette) will be included in each main session at the appropriate point for the related enabling skill.

Imagine what would happen to the learners' motivation if all the golf rules and points of etiquette were taught in session 1 prior to any experience on the golf course! As you get further into your instructional strategy, it may be necessary to adjust the clusters you assign for your instructional goal, but for now, you have them planned.

Table 9.2 Sequence and Cluster of Performance Objectives Based on the Instructional Goal Framework for Playing Golf, Putting Section Illustrated in Figure 8.2

Session	Time	Main Skill	Objective Clusters
1	1 hour		Introduction and overview
2	2 hours	I Putting	All objectives associated with main step I: I.1.a through I.6 in hierarchical order
3	2 hours	II Chipping	All objectives associated with main step II in hierarchical order
4	2 hours	III Irons	All objectives associated with main step III in hierarchical order
5	2 hours	IV Woods	All objectives associated with main step IV in hierarchical order
6	5 hours	Goal: Golf	Tournament: 18 holes of golf, learners paired with members

**Note:* The enabling skills for sessions 3 through 5 are not depicted in either Figure 8.2 or Table 9.2.

Preinstructional Activities, Assessment, and Follow-Through

You should indicate your approach to the learning components of preinstructional activities, assessment, and follow-through. Table 9.3 contains the information for session 1: preinstructional, assessment, and follow-through activities for the instruction on golf for beginners. The relevant issues are answered in narrative form with reference to each of the headings in the table. Note that management decisions about learner groupings and media selection are made and recorded while these learning components of the strategy are planned. Note also that preinstructional activities, assessment, and follow-through components can often be applied to all of your objectives; that is, they are usually planned once for your total unit or lesson, if that makes sense for the learners and the content.

Content Presentation and Learner Participation

For each objective or cluster of objectives, indicate the content to be presented and learner participation activities. Table 9.4 includes an instructional strategy for an instructor-led session. The case study that follows illustrates mediated instruction, so it seems appropriate to include an instructor-led example here. When the instruction is instructor-led, you need not create a script for the instructor to follow. Imagine asking a golf professional to memorize a script in order to teach beginning golfers how to golf! Instead, the instructor can use the instructional strategy as a guide for what is to be included in each session and lesson. In Table 9.4, the example uses only the "psycho" part of planning the putt (I.1) from Figure 8.2. The objective number from the list of performance objectives is identified at the top of the form, which includes two main sections: "Content to Be Presented" and "Learner Participation." The presentation section describes briefly the required content and learning guidance. In selecting examples for guidance in your own project, remember to choose congruent examples that are most likely to be familiar and interesting to learners. The participation section describes a practice exercise and the feedback provided.

Notice in Table 9.4 that the designer has included two new headings not included in the instructional strategy in Chapter 8: equipment needed for the lesson and the intended learning context. Notice also that the designer does not wish the instructor or learners to use putters during this portion of the lesson. Instead, the focus is to be only on the psycho portion of the psychomotor skill. Providing putters moves the learners' focus away from the putting green conditions and toward the putting action.

Case Study

Group Leadership Training

There are two versions of an instructional strategy in this case study on group leadership training. The first version illustrates the five phases of a cognitive instructional strategy that follows the Dick and Carey model. The second version uses a constructivist learning environment for the same goal. For additional cognitive and constructivist examples of instructional strategies, refer to the school-based example in the appendices.

Table 9.3 Preinstructional, Assessment, and Follow-Through Learning Components, Including Their Learner Groupings and Media Selections Plans

PREINSTRUCTIONAL ACTIVITIES

MOTIVATION:

Teaching professional:

1. Welcomes group
2. Hypes fun the learners will have
3. Explains benefits of class (e.g., improved putting, recognition, companionship, improved flexibility, physical well-being)
4. Describes score improvement of prior golf class, recognition, and accomplishment
5. Describes learners who joined the club
6. Shows video of:
    - local club members attending Masters' competition at Augusta illustrating camaraderie, fun;
    - colleagues golfing successfully and being praised by companions for improvement;
    - duffers (unknown to club members) unsuccessfully putting, including bad physical form, resulting poor scoring, and temper tantrums (humorous); and
    - other golfers disapproving of bad behavior.

Other club members:

7. Describe score improvement of prior golf class, recognition, and accomplishment
8. Describe benefits to prior learners who joined the club

OBJECTIVES:

1. Lead a healthy, active lifestyle.
2. Learn to play golf, including driving the ball, hitting fairway irons, chipping the ball from sand and fairway, and putting the ball.
3. Join the club to make friends and participate in club-sponsored golf tournaments.

ENTRY SKILLS: Recreational golf, no formal lessons

LEARNER GROUPINGS: One group of sixteen learners located in lounge with video capability

MEDIA SELECTION: Promotional video for golf clinic and club

ASSESSMENT

PRETEST: None

PRACTICE TESTS AND REHEARSAL: Throughout each instructional session at practice putting green and on golf course. Invited to course for individualized practice on putting green and driving range before and between lesson sessions. Learners are to use their own golf equipment.

POSTTEST:

- Contest at conclusion of each instructional session, scoring and prizes (ribbons, certificates).
- Golf tournament (scramble format) in session 6. Each learner is paired with a club member as partner. As tournament progresses, they discuss scoring with club-member partner, keep scores, and submit signed scorecards at the end. Group will lunch together, winners will be announced, and prizes will be awarded. Learners will be reminded that applications for membership are available at pro shop.

LEARNER GROUPINGS: Sixteen learners in class. Grouped together for explanations and demonstrations, pairs for practice, individualized for contests, and foursomes for tournament.

MEDIA SELECTIONS: Video for introductory motivational information. Golf equipment and balls provided by learners. For each contest and tournament, golf scorecards and pencils provided by club.

FOLLOW-THROUGH ACTIVITIES

MEMORY AID: Provide learners with written pamphlet (PGA) containing rules, etiquette, and glossary for golf.

TRANSFER: Learners will be dressed for golf according to club rules, use their personal golf clubs, and use actual scorecards from golf club. Scoring on honor system as with golf game.

Table 9.4 Content Presentation and Learner Participation Learning Components for Instructor-Led Session on Planning a Putt

CONTENT PRESENTATION

OBJECTIVES: I.1.a through I.1 developed from Figure 8.2

CONTENT PRESENTATION:
Content:

- Respected golf pro (instructor) praises group of learners for their putting during warm-up and indicates they will easily master the fundamentals of putting. Applying fundamentals of putting will save many strokes during play. Golf games are lost and won on the putting green.
- Factors that influence the trajectory of a putt (lay of the land: steepness, curvature; force: slope, drag, or surface conditions of the putting green).
- Instructor predicts (talks through) expected trajectory for given hole and then demonstrates exaggeration of each condition by tossing a golf ball toward the cup (e.g., too much and too little force) and then describes the outcome of error.

Examples:
Slope: link to peddling a bike up/down hills: little force to coast down, peddle hard to go up
Curvature: link to walking around a steep hillside, more energy to stay up rather than rolling down
Drag: link to walking through tall or short grass, rolling a ball through smooth putting green and lumpy sand trap

LEARNER GROUPINGS: Group of sixteen learners at side of putting green in location requested by teaching pro to observe particular demonstration; class listens to pro's explanation and observes demonstrations.

EQUIPMENT NEEDED: Pro and learners each need two or three golf balls. Golf balls only, no putters for explanation or demonstration.

INSTRUCTIONAL CONTEXT: Practice putting green at golf club with at least eighteen holes. Putting green must contain holes where skill can be demonstrated.

MEDIA SELECTIONS: None. Instructor-led, live performance on putting green.

LEARNER PARTICIPATION

PRACTICE ITEMS AND ACTIVITIES: Particular holes on green identified that have required conditions. Learners discuss with partners green conditions and predict trajectory and force required to reach hole from a variety of locations around each designated hole. Each learner rolls (by hand) a golf ball at the planned force and predicted trajectory. Partners discuss success of planned ball trajectory on green, ball distance from hole, and location based on resting location of golf ball. Partners then discuss approaches to getting closer to hole. Executes new plan from same original position and compares outcome with first roll.

FEEDBACK: Actual resting location of golf balls tossed by each group member.

LEARNER GROUPINGS: Learners divided into pairs for interaction, discussion, and collegial feedback.

EQUIPMENT: Golf balls only, no putters.

MEDIA SELECTIONS: Instructor-led. Live performance.

Cognitive Instructional Strategy

The five phases of developing the cognitive instructional strategy for a unit of instruction are as follows:

1. Sequence and cluster objectives.
2. Plan preinstructional, assessment, and follow-through activities for the unit, with notes about learner groupings and media selections.
3. Plan the content presentations and learner participation sections for each objective or cluster of objectives, with notes about learner groupings and media selections.
4. Assign objectives to lessons, and estimate the time required for each.
5. Review the strategy to consolidate media selections, and confirm or select a delivery system.

We consider each of these in turn, with examples from the group leadership case study that we have carried throughout the book.

Sequence and Cluster Objectives

The first step in planning the instructional strategy is to sequence and cluster performance objectives. The subskills and instructional goal from Figure 4.8 (p. 96), Lead Group Discussions Aimed at Solving Problems, are included in Table 9.5. Fourteen clusters of objectives are identified, and two hours of instruction are planned for each cluster. Although not broken out for this illustration, the objectives for main steps 1 through 4 are each assigned to their own cluster. The objectives for main step 5, "Manage thought line," are divided into four separate clusters. The objectives for main skill 6, "Manage cooperative group interaction," are broken out into clusters 9 through 12. The content and nature of the objectives in each cluster were analyzed to ensure that they represented a logical set of skills. Cluster 9 contains the objectives related to recognizing and engendering cooperative behavior, and cluster 10 includes objectives for recognizing and defusing blocking behaviors of group members. Cluster 11 deals with recognizing and alleviating group stress. Cluster 12 focuses on objectives for all subordinate skills of main step 6 addressed together. Cluster 13 includes all objectives subordinate to main step 7, "Summarize/conclude discussion." Cluster 14 contains the terminal objective of all seven main steps and their subordinate skills. This cluster reflects the entire leadership process.

The clusters of subskills planned and the amount of time assigned may need to be revised as you continue to develop the strategy. This initial structure, however, helps you focus on lessons rather than on individual objectives.

Table 9.5 Performance Objectives for Main Step 6 from Table 6.7 Sequenced and Clustered

Clusters*	Instructional Goal Steps					
1	Main step 1: Prepare for discussion					
2	Main step 2: Set agenda					
3	Main step 3: Convene group					
4	Main step 4: Introduce task					
5–8	Main step 5: Manage thought line					
	Cluster 5		Cluster 6		Cluster 7	Cluster 8
9–12	Main step 6: Manage cooperative group interaction					
	Cluster 9		Cluster 10		Cluster 11	Cluster 12
	Objectives:		Objectives:		Objectives:	Objectives:
	6.1.1	6.3.1	6.6.1	6.7.1	6.11.1	6.1: Main step 6
	6.1.2	6.4.1	6.6.2	6.7.2	6.12.1	
	6.2.1	6.4.2	6.6.3	6.8.1	6.12.2	
	6.2.2	6.5.1	6.6.4	6.9.1	6.13.1	
			6.6.5	6.9.2	6.14.1	
			6.6.6	6.10.1	6.14.2	
			6.6.7		6.15.1	
13	Main step 7: Summarize/conclude discussion					
14	Terminal objective					

*All clusters are designed to require approximately two hours.

Plan Preinstructional, Assessment, and Follow-Through Activities

These learning components of the instructional strategy relate to the overall lesson or lessons and do not refer to individual instructional objectives within a lesson. First, how will you design preinstructional activities? Remember, this area contains three separate sections: motivation, objectives, and entry skills. Table 9.6 shows the instructional strategy plans for these components. Notice that the information used in the lessons is not included in the figure, the objectives are not written out, and the entry skills are not listed. Instead, there is a brief description of what you must do when developing the instruction, along with notes about learner groupings and media selection.

Focusing now on the assessment and follow-through phases of the instructional strategy for the instructional goal, how would you plan these activities for group leaders? Table 9.7 includes plans for pretests, posttests, and follow-through activities. A pretest focused directly on the objectives included in each session is administered at the beginning of the session except for clusters 8, 12, and 14. No pretest is administered in these sessions because pretest data for these objectives, main steps 5 and 6 and the terminal objective, have been collected in preceding sessions. Likewise, a cluster-focused posttest is administered at the conclusion of each session. A terminal objective posttest is administered during the final session. It should be made clear to learners that the assessments are included to help them focus and practice skills and to help the staff learn about the strengths and weaknesses in the instruction.

The bottom portion of Table 9.7 contains the designers' prescriptions for follow-through activities, including plans for memory aids and transfer support as leaders plan and conduct meetings across campus and in their communities. Student groupings and media selections are also noted in the table.

Table 9.6 Preinstructional Learning Components for Unit on Leading Group Discussion with Student Groupings and Media Selections

PREINSTRUCTIONAL ACTIVITIES
MOTIVATION: Prior to main step 1, "Prepare for discussion," a respected campus leader (e.g., chair, dean, VP, campus student leader) will welcome the new student leaders; provide praise for their choice of leadership on campus, in schools, businesses, and in the community; and discuss the critical role of leaders in improving and maintaining the quality of life on campus and in the community. The respected leader will welcome participants, discuss some critical problems on campus, present statistics on the current problems and trends within the university and across campuses around the state, discuss the financial and emotional costs of such problems, and present actual statistics on the effectiveness of campus leaders in reducing these problems. Actual local instances of student leader effectiveness will be highlighted.
OBJECTIVES: The critical role of the discussion leader in problem-solving groups will be described. An overview of the tasks leaders perform before and during meetings will be presented. A video of an actual group discussion, highlighting the role of the leader at each step, will be shown.
ENTRY SKILLS: Learners will all have completed the instruction on problem-solving group-discussion methods. They will be heterogeneous in their group-discussion skill levels because of their varying ages, education majors, work experience, and group problem-solving experience.
STUDENT GROUPINGS AND MEDIA SELECTIONS: Instructor-led, large-group discussion; streaming video.

Table 9.7 Testing and Follow-Through Learning Components for Unit on Leading Group Discussion

ASSESSMENT

PRETESTS: Because of the heterogeneous nature of the group leaders and the varied group participation experiences they have had, a pretest will be administered at the beginning of each of the sessions. The pretest will be informal and administered as an instructional activity to be collected. For sessions 1 through 3, the pretest will be a print document. For sessions 4 through 14, it will consist of a staged group meeting (video) that leaders watch. During viewing, they will use an observation form to tally the number of times named leader behaviors occur in the meeting. After instructional materials are developed and formative evaluation activities are complete, trainers may choose to dispense with the pretest for evaluation purposes. They may choose, however, to maintain the pretest as a preinstructional learning tool to focus learner attention on the objectives.

STUDENT GROUPING AND MEDIA SELECTION: Individualized, web-based; streaming video; downloadable observation form.

POSTTESTS: A small learning site posttest will be administered at the conclusion of each session. Clusters 8 and 12 will each consist of a performance posttest that requires leaders to manage the discussion thought line and manage the cooperative group interaction.

A final posttest will be administered during the last evening of class, and it will be completed in three sections: a product section, a process section, and an analysis/feedback section.

The product part of the final posttest will require learners to complete the first three main steps (1. Prepare for discussion; 2. Set agenda; and 3. Convene group) in preparation for the first actual group meeting they will lead. Leaders will independently make these preparations between the thirteenth and fourteenth instructional sessions and bring copies of their plans and materials to the last session. They will submit one copy of their plans (product) for review.

For the process portion of the posttest, leaders will break into small groups of four persons. Within their small groups, each member will lead a fifteen-minute group discussion on the "problem" topic he or she has prepared for the meeting. Their leadership performances will be video recorded within each group.

For the last part of the posttest, learners will discuss the leadership performances of members within their groups. During these discussions, members will focus on each leader's strengths relative to introducing the task, managing the thought line, engendering cooperative member behaviors, defusing blocking behaviors, and alleviating group stress. Through these discussions, members will receive feedback on the positive aspects of their performances. Leaders may also review the videos of their own meetings to "watch themselves in action."

The effectiveness of the overall instruction will be assessed through the plans learners submitted, the videos of their leadership, and the interactive discussion in which learners critiqued each other's performances.

STUDENT GROUPING AND MEDIA SELECTIONS: Small and individual grouping; print, video recording with playback.

FOLLOW-THROUGH ACTIVITIES

MEMORY AID: Memory aids planned include checklists of member and leader behaviors that leaders can use to focus their attention as they read meeting transcripts or view videos of simulated meetings. Leaders will take copies of the checklists with them for reference as they plan for meetings in their chosen area.

TRANSFER: The professor schedules follow-up sessions with new leaders. During these meetings, successes, issues, and problems encountered in leading group discussions within the chosen area will be shared. With student permission, leaders will also be given names and e-mail addresses for all class members; it is hoped that these new leaders will form a network of support for each other, sharing ideas and plans.

STUDENT GROUPING AND MEDIA SELECTIONS: Individualized, large- or small-group discussion; print job aid.

Plan Content Presentation and Learner Participation

Content presentation and learner participation sections make up the interactive part of the lesson. They are considered the exchange or interface point. The presentation section has two parts—namely, the content and learning guidance. The learner participation component has two areas: sample practice items and activities and the planned feedback strategy.

Table 9.8 includes performance objectives for main step 6, "Manage cooperative interaction," as an illustration of how this format is used to sketch out the

Table 9.8 **Content Presentation and Student Participation Learning Components for Cluster 9 Performance Objectives (Main Step 6, Manage Cooperative Group Interaction) with Student Groupings and Media Selections**

PERFORMANCE OBJECTIVES SUBORDINATE TO MAIN STEP 6

STUDENT GROUPING AND MEDIA SELECTIONS: All objectives 6.1.1 through 6.4.2, individualized; web-based; streaming video where required; practice and feedback online.

6.1.1 When requested in writing to name group member actions that facilitate cooperative interaction, name those actions. At least six facilitating actions should be named.

CONTENT PRESENTATION

CONTENT: Cooperative interaction within group discussions depends on spontaneous positive actions that group members demonstrate when introducing their own ideas and when reacting to ideas introduced by others. An annotated meeting dialogue will be provided with characters in the meeting demonstrating positive actions that foster cooperative group interaction. The annotation will point out the particular actions used by group members. The dialogue format will be used for its interest value and context validity.

EXAMPLES

Personal actions

1. Prepares for discussion
2. Readily volunteers ideas
3. Invites others to participate
4. Demonstrates goodwill
5. Demonstrates open-mindedness
6. Respects others' loyalties and needs

Reactions to others in discussion

1. Considers all members' ideas before meeting impartially
2. Listens attentively to others' comments
3. Gives others credit for their ideas
4. Demonstrates trust in others' motives
5. Resists pressures to conform

STUDENT PARTICIPATION

PRACTICE ITEMS AND ACTIVITIES

1. List positive personal actions that group members can take to facilitate cooperative interaction during problem-solving discussions.
2. List positive personal reactions to others that group members can take to facilitate cooperative interaction during problem-solving discussions.
3. Think back over interactive discussions you have had in the past. Name the actions and reactions of others that made you feel that those conversing with you were interested in you, in your comments, and in the problem being discussed.

FEEDBACK: Repeat list of positive personal actions and reactions group discussion members can demonstrate.

6.1.2 When asked in writing to indicate what members should do when their ideas are questioned by the group, name positive reactions that help ensure cooperative group interaction. Learner should name at least three possible reactions.

CONTENT PRESENTATION

CONTENT: Problem-solving group discussions naturally require give and take and a good deal of interactive brainstorming that often includes proposals of half-baked ideas. During brainstorming sessions, a member's ideas may be questioned for a myriad of reasons. The manner in which a member responds to these questions can demonstrate her or his goodwill and open-mindedness and can help ensure cooperative group interaction.

EXAMPLES

1. Listens attentively to members' questions (without interrupting)
2. Explains ideas more fully to help others understand the ideas and direction
3. Resists abandoning ideas too quickly just because they are questioned
4. Participates in modifying initial ideas to make them more acceptable to the group
5. Readily admits errors in ideas or judgment

STUDENT PARTICIPATION

PRACTICE ITEMS AND ACTIVITIES

1. List positive reactions a group member can make when her or his proposals or ideas are questioned by other group members.
2. Think back over interactive discussions you have had in the past. Name the positive reactions that you have seen others make when their ideas were questioned or not readily accepted by other members of the group.

FEEDBACK: Restate positive reactions to others' questions.

(continued)

Table 9.8 Continued

6.2.1 Given written descriptions of group members' facilitating actions during a meeting, indicate whether the actions are likely to facilitate cooperative group interaction. Learner should correctly classify at least 80 percent of the actions depicted.

CONTENT PRESENTATION

CONTENT: A written meeting scenario will be presented with actual characters and dialogue. The dialogue will include both positive personal actions and positive personal reactions of meeting participants.

EXAMPLES (See 6.1.1)

STUDENT PARTICIPATION

PRACTICE ITEMS AND ACTIVITIES

Using a checklist of positive personal actions and reactions, identify characters in the written scenario who demonstrate each positive action or reaction.

FEEDBACK: Complete checklist with characters' names inserted for each action and reaction.

6.2.2 Given videos of staged meetings depicting facilitating member actions, indicate whether the members' actions are likely to facilitate cooperative group interaction. Learner should classify correctly at least 80 percent of the actions demonstrated.

CONTENT PRESENTATION

CONTENT: A simulated discussion group will be staged and video recorded with discussion members exhibiting positive personal actions and reactions during the meeting. Learners will watch the group members in action as they propose and discuss ideas.

EXAMPLES (See 6.1.1)

STUDENT PARTICIPATION

PRACTICE ITEMS AND ACTIVITIES

Using a checklist of positive personal actions and reactions, identify characters in the simulated meeting who demonstrate each positive action or reaction.

FEEDBACK: Complete checklist with characters' names inserted for those actions and reactions demonstrated.

6.3.1 When asked in writing to name leader actions that either encourage or stifle discussion and member cooperation, name these actions. Learner should name at least ten encouraging and corresponding stifling actions.

CONTENT PRESENTATION

CONTENT: As the discussion group leader, there are several actions you can take that encourage cooperative group interaction. For each of these cooperating actions, there are corresponding actions that tend to stifle group cooperation.

EXAMPLES

Cooperation-encouraging actions	Cooperation-stifling actions
1. Suggests points of discussion	1. Prescribes topics as questions for the group to consider
2. Uses an authoritative tone	2. Uses an investigative, inquiring tone
3. Uses open terms such as *must* or *should*	3. Uses prescriptive terms such as *perhaps* and *might*
4. Hesitates and pauses between speakers	4. Fills quiet gaps with personal points of view or solutions
5. Willingly turns over the floor to group interrupting member	5. Continues to talk over members who interrupt or interrupts member
6. Encompasses total group with eyes and invites members all to participate freely	6. Focuses gaze on a few
7. Nonverbally (eyes, gestures) encourages speaker to address group	7. Holds speaker's attention
8. Uses comments that keep discussion centered in the group	8. Encourages discussion to flow through leader by evaluating member comments
9. Encourages volunteerism (e.g., "Who has experience with . . . ?")	9. Designates speakers and speaking order (e.g., "Beth, what do you think about . . . ?")
10. Refers to *us, we, our*	10. Refers to *I, me, mine,* or *your*
11. Acknowledges group accomplishments	11. Acknowledges own accomplishments or those of particular members
12. Praises group effort and accomplishment	12. Singles out particular people for praise

Table 9.8 Continued

STUDENT PARTICIPATION

PRACTICE ITEMS AND ACTIVITIES

1. List strategies you can use as group discussion leader to encourage cooperative group interaction.
2. Think back over interactive discussions you have had in the past. Name the actions and reactions of the discussion leader that you believe engendered cooperative interaction among group members.

FEEDBACK: Repeat list of positive leader actions and reactions that engender cooperative interaction among group members.

6.4.1 Given written descriptions of a group leader's action during a meeting, indicate whether the leader exhibits actions that are likely to encourage or stifle cooperative group interaction. Learner should correctly classify at least 80 percent of the actions depicted.

CONTENT PRESENTATION

CONTENT: A written meeting scenario will be presented with actual characters and dialogue. The dialogue will focus particularly on leader actions and reactions designed to encourage positive member interaction and participation.

EXAMPLES (See 6.3.1)

STUDENT PARTICIPATION

PRACTICE ITEMS AND ACTIVITIES

Using a checklist of actions the leader can take to encourage or stifle positive member interaction, identify the particular behaviors exhibited by the leader in the written scenario.

FEEDBACK: Complete checklist with described leader actions checked.

6.4.2 Given videos of staged meetings depicting staged leader's actions, classify the leader's actions that are likely to encourage or stifle member cooperation. Learner should classify correctly at least 80 percent of the encouraging and stifling actions demonstrated.

CONTENT PRESENTATION

CONTENT: A simulated discussion group will be staged and recorded with video. The group leader will exhibit actions designed to encourage or stifle member interaction during the meeting. Learners will watch the leader "in action" managing the group.

EXAMPLES (See 6.3.1)

STUDENT PARTICIPATION

PRACTICE ITEMS AND ACTIVITIES

Using a checklist of actions the leader can take to encourage and stifle positive member interaction, identify the particular behaviors exhibited by the leader in the video.

FEEDBACK: Complete checklist with exhibited leader actions checked.

6.5.1 In simulated problem-solving meetings with learner acting as group leader, initiate actions to engender cooperative behavior among members. Group members cooperate with each other and with leader during discussion.

CONTENT PRESENTATION

CONTENT: Learners will break into small groups of four, and each group will receive a written description and background information for a particular campus or community problem as well as a meeting agenda for discussing the given problem. After reading the material, one member will serve as the discussion leader, and the remaining three members will serve as group members. (Different problem scenarios will be provided for each of the four group members to enable each to rehearse group interaction leadership.)

STUDENT GROUPING AND MEDIA SELECTIONS: Small-group role-play; print scenario.

STUDENT PARTICIPATION

PRACTICE ITEMS AND ACTIVITIES: The leader will introduce the problem to the group, set the climate for cooperative interaction, and lead a simulated group discussion for ten minutes.

FEEDBACK: Following the discussion, group members will discuss positive aspects of the leader's performance. These discussions will be held within the small group only.

STUDENT GROUPING AND MEDIA SELECTIONS: Small-group discussion among group members.

instructional strategy. Each objective is stated, followed by a description of the content and examples to be presented. In cases where videos are used to present content, a description of the action is provided. All instruction and practice is web-based up to objective 6.5.1. Notice that no new content about the objective is included for objective 6.5.1 because the skill-related content was presented online in the preceding objectives. Instead, media, materials, and general instructions for interactive meetings are described. In this instance, the content presentation and student participation components are intertwined. This example illustrates how hierarchical skills build on each other and how the table format can be adapted for each objective.

At this point, we have completed examples of how to design the instructional strategy for the following: (1) sequencing and clustering objectives; (2) planning

Table 9.9 Lesson Allocation Based on Instructional Strategy

Session	Activities
1	Introductory and motivational materials: 1. Respected campus leader gives welcome, praise for student leaders, and overview of course (objectives). 2. Respected campus administrator (chair, dean, VP, etc.) gives welcome, presentation of campus problems (e.g., recruitment, orientation, athletics, safety, etc.), and presentation of impact of campus leaders at the university and across the community related to the problems. 3. Pretest with group discussion feedback pointing to main steps in leadership process.
2	Pretest; introduction; instruction and practice activities on objectives for main step 1,
3	"Prepare for discussion"; and posttest.
4	Pretest; introduction; instruction and practice activities on objectives for main step 2,
5	"Set agenda"; and posttest.
6–9	Pretest; introduction; instruction and practice activities on objectives for main step 3, "Convene group"; and posttest. Pretest; introduction; instruction and practice activities on objectives for main step 4, "Introduce task"; and posttest. Each of these sessions will contain a pretest; introduction; instruction and practice activities on objectives for main step 5, "Manage thought line"; and posttest. Session 6 2 hours; Session 7 2 hours; Session 8 2 hours; Session 9 2 hours
10–13	Sessions 10, 11, and 12 will contain a pretest; introduction; instruction and practice activities on objectives for main step 6, "Manage cooperative group interaction"; and posttest. Session 13 will contain an introduction and interactive groups in which leaders manage group interaction. No pretest or posttest will be administered. A debriefing and discussion session will follow group rehearsals. Session 10 Objectives: 6.1.1, 6.1.2, 6.2.1, 6.2.2, 6.3.1, 6.4.1, 6.4.2, 6.5.1 Session 11 Objectives: 6.6.1, 6.6.2, 6.6.3, 6.6.4, 6.6.5, 6.6.6, 6.6.7, 6.7.1, 6.7.2, 6.8.1, 6.9.1, 6.9.2, 6.10.1 Session 12 Objectives: 6.11.1, 6.12.1, 6.12.2, 6.13.1, 6.14.1, 6.14.2, 6.15.1 Session 13 Objectives: 6.1: Main step 6
14	Pretest; introduction; instruction and practice activities on objectives for main step 7, "Summarize/conclude discussion"; and posttest.
15	Give welcome, instructions for session, and three-part posttest for terminal objective, debriefing.

preinstructional, assessment, and follow-through activities; and (3) identifying content presentation and learner participation activities. Student groupings and media selections have also been noted as the learning components have been planned.

Assign Objectives to Lessons

With this information complete, we should review it and allocate prescribed activities to lessons. Lesson prescriptions are included in Table 9.9 on page 274. Compare the strategy for individual sessions in Table 9.9 with the initial sequence and cluster of objectives in Table 9.5. Notice that we predicted a total of fourteen two-hour clusters in Table 9.5 but added an additional two hours of instruction for fifteen sessions in Table 9.9. This was necessary to allow for preinstructional, motivational, and pretest activities in the first session. Within the remaining sessions, pretest and posttest activities are added. Again, you must consider the timelines tentative until you develop the instruction and test it with actual learners.

Consolidate Media Selection and Confirm or Select Delivery System

Table 9.10 contains a summary of media prescriptions taken from the instructional strategy for the instructional goal, "Lead group discussions aimed at solving problems, Step 6: Manage cooperative group interaction." The first column contains the class sessions, and the second column contains the objectives in each session. The third column identifies the initial media selections based on the domain of learning, the objective, resources available for materials development, and facilities and equipment present in the department. In the fourth column, the media selections are consolidated and final decisions about a delivery system are recorded.

Table 9.10 Consolidation of Media Selections and Choice of Delivery System for Main Step 6, Sessions 10 through 13 (from Table 9.9)

Session	Objectives	Initial Student Groupings and Media Selections	Consolidated Media Selections and Delivery System(s)
10	6.1.1 and 6.1.2	Individualized, web-based distance	Individualized, web-based distance, streaming video
	6.2.1 and 6.2.2	Individualized, web-based distance Individualized, web-based distance, streaming video	
	6.3.1	Individualized, web-based distance	
	6.4.1 and 6.4.2	Individualized, web-based distance Individualized, web-based distance, streaming video	
11	6.6 through 6.9		Individualized, web-based distance, streaming video
12	6.11 through 6.14		Individualized, web-based distance, streaming video
13	6 6.5 6.10 6.15	Large-group presentation for motivation and directions Small group, simulation, and interactions Videos of small-group sessions	Large-group presentation for motivation and directions Small group, simulation, and interactions Videos of small-group sessions and small-group discussion of videos

Considering the entire set of prescriptions in column 3 of Table 9.10, you can see that a pattern exists: live-group simulations, videos, and individualized web-based instruction are each repeated several times. In the performance site, newly trained leaders work interactively within a group, so using live-group simulations during instruction closely resembles the context within which group leaders must work. They must also make inferences from group interactions, so observing televised groups as they interact helps support concept acquisition. Providing printed dialogue scripts of meetings rather than didactic descriptions of meetings is also prescribed for authenticity because interpreting meeting dialogue and members' actions is the focus during learners' actual work.

The first delivery system considered was individualized, web-based distance instruction because of costs and convenience. For authenticity and transfer, however, the live-group simulations must be retained for advanced practice, feedback, and posttesting. These media consolidation and delivery system decisions are reflected in column 4 of Table 9.10.

The decision for independent web-based instruction was made for several reasons. The learners are mature and motivated adults who enrolled in a graduate class in leadership and who are familiar with the value and convenience of distance learning. All learners have computers with Internet access in their homes, in their department's computer laboratory, and within the college and university. From a practical perspective, the distance-learning format teaches the verbal information and discrimination skills economically, standardizes instruction, ensures more uniform results, and reduces learner travel time. Finally, there is sufficient money in the department's budget to pay for web development, formative evaluation, and revision.

After consolidating media selections and confirming or selecting a delivery system, it may be necessary to revisit the previous step, "Allocate activities to lessons," and touch up some of that planning. This is particularly true if selection of a delivery system is delayed until this point in the design process. In most instructional design contexts, the delivery system would be assumed or imposed at the outset of the process, and the designer merely confirms delivery system capability for the media selections. Note in Table 9.10 that skills 6.5, 6.10, and 6.15 have all been moved to session 13 with main step 6 because these skills require learners to come to the department and cannot be delivered via the web. Refer to Figure 9.1 for a visual representation of the overall process of developing an instructional strategy and choosing a delivery system. The instructional strategy for main step 6, "Manage cooperative group interaction," is now complete, and we have the prescriptions necessary to begin developing materials.

Constructivist Instructional Strategy

A constructivist instructional strategy is quite different than the one just described, and it could be created in many different ways due to the flexibility afforded by a constructivist model. Table 9.11 includes a constructivist strategy for main step 6 from the goal analysis in Figure 4.8 (p. 96). The left column focuses the designer on planning needs, whereas the right column identifies planning activities that should be completed. Notice in the sample strategy the increased responsibility placed both on the instructor/coaches and on the learners for creating and managing the learning environment. To assist you in reading Table 9.11, refer to Tables 8.7 and 8.8 on planning a constructivist learning environment (CLE).

Table 9.11 Planning for a Constructivist Learning Environment for Main Step 6, Manage Cooperative Group Interaction

Planning Needs	Planning Activities

Planning the Learning Environment	**Designs and materials needed to launch the CLE**
	• Goal: Lead group discussions aimed at solving problems
	• Learning objectives: Addressed at main step level during sessions; subordinate skills excluded except as job aids or direct requests; fourteen two-hour instructional sessions possible (covered by grant); apportioned to the seven main skills steps; number of sessions per main step negotiated on ongoing basis by the learners and coaches
	• Learning objective for main step 6, "Manage cooperative group interaction": Learners serve as team leaders in a problem-solving meeting and exhibit actions for diffusing committee members' blocking behaviors, engendering members' cooperative behaviors, and alleviating members' stress
	• Rationale: Leaders, through skill in managing problem-solving discussions, encourage campus and community members to become involved and to stay involved in cooperative meetings aimed at improving campus life
	• Constructivist focus: Critical thinking, problem solving, and cognitive flexibility
	• Pedagogical model: Problem-based learning (PBL)
	• Scenario: A group of graduate student leaders addressing problems on campus related to campus life (e.g., recruitment, orientation, registration, graduation, safety, athletics) and identifying ideas for improving management and campus life, key question driving problem scenario for session is "How do I manage my meetings to bring about effective and continued participation by campus and community members?"
	• Learning resource materials
	  • Instructional goal analysis illustrating subordinate skills for main step 6, "Manage cooperative group interaction"
	  • Web-based instruction and quizzes for all subskills for main step 6 to be used as follow-up assignment with groups/individuals if needed
	  • The materials learners produce individually and in groups following their learning interaction in session 2 (meeting agendas) and session 4 (meeting task statements)
	• Job aids
	  • Leader actions that can engender cooperative group behavior (subskill analysis for 6.5)
	  • Recognizing and diffusing members' blocking behaviors (subskill analysis for 6.10)
	  • Actions leader can take to alleviate group stress (subskill analysis for 6.15)
	  • Draft rubric for evaluating leader actions during simulated meeting
	• Learner groupings: Total of twenty learners per class with learners forming own work groups of four individuals (five teams) to ensure that each member has at least fifteen to twenty minutes to serve as leader of a group problem-solving meeting
	• Delivery system, media, and personnel
	• Internet access during sessions and between sessions for learner research
	  • Blogging space for group interaction between sessions
	  • Campus web-based learning portal
	  • Video equipment for recording interactive meetings
	  • Trained facilitator/coach for each meeting group (four TAs)
	  • Technology specialist to manage video recording and playback for teams
	  • Instructional designer to create direct instruction for web-based portal

Planning for Learner Engagement	**Procedures anticipated during engagement** • Engage • View video of campus leaders who express disappointment with their interactions at problem-solving meetings. All cited the cause as ineffective leaders who did not control group stress levels or members' blocking behaviors and who did not make members feel that their ideas were welcome or accepted. Following video, members discuss similar situations in their own experiences and the important role of leaders in gaining and sustaining campus and community member participation in meetings

(continued)

Table 9.11 Continued

Planning Needs	Planning Activities

	• Explore
	  • Group and coach plan session organization to enable both interactive meetings and debriefing, reflection, and review (e.g., group size, meeting length, breaks)
	  • Group and coach discuss the learning outcome related to video interviews as well as the three meeting management job aids they can use (as both leaders and members) during the simulated meetings
	  • Group and coach critique job aids and remove/add leader actions based on their own experiences
	  • Learners take turns serving as group leaders exploring actions they can take to diffuse committee members' blocking behaviors, engender their cooperative behaviors, and alleviate committee members' stress as learners discuss problems on campus and in the community and identify potential solutions and strategies
	  • Explain: Following each person's leadership turn, he or she talks with team members and coach about his or her actions and consequences (actions/feelings) within the group
	• Elaborate: Members share ideas about alternative strategies they or group leader might use for better problem-solving interactions; discuss alternative, effective strategies they have observed leaders use at work and in other meetings within the college and university
	• Evaluate (see "Planning Authentic Assessment" later in this table)

Planning Learning Guidance	**Materials and activities anticipated for adaptive learning guidance**
	• Scaffolding
	  • Demonstrate member blocking behaviors and stress if actions are not forthcoming from group members in meetings
	  • Assist members in focusing on important aspects of leader/member actions
	  • Refer to job aids when needed
	  • Model
	    • Diffusing behaviors when not forthcoming from leader
	    • Stress-alleviating behaviors when not forthcoming from leader

Planning Authentic Assessment	**Materials and procedures anticipated for authentic assessment**
	• Reflection prior to viewing videos; prompts for group members
	• Reflect on consequences of particular actions or reactions within the group
	• Reflect on the effectiveness of leader and committee member actions demonstrated during meeting
	  • Discuss their rational for actions they believe were effective and ineffective in their own leadership
	  • Explain their reasoning about particular actions they judge as effective and ineffective
	  • Evaluate the rubric provided to add/remove actions they believe should be critiqued in their leadership
	• While viewing videos produced of the meetings (which can be paused), prompts for group members when needed
	  • Reflect on consequences of particular actions or reactions observed within the group meeting
	  • Reflect on actions demonstrated that appear to be very effective or those that appear to be ineffective
	  • Consider the types of information needed to refine skills in meeting management
	• Following the reflections, prompts for learner discussion
	  • Whether they want to schedule another meeting simulation where they can serve as leaders and, if so, how they would like it to proceed
	  • The emphasis they would like in a subsequent meeting (e.g., step 5, managing thought line; step 6, managing group interaction; a combination of the two)
	  • Information they believe necessary for the meeting (e.g., actual statistics from the campus and community)
	• Remind learners of group blog, and invite them to reflect on any part of this session's simulated meetings (their role or that of teammates); some members may want to post information or job aids they gather or develop for the group

Professional and Historical Perspectives

Research since the early 1980s confirms that the choice of media for delivering instruction does not make a difference in how much students learn or in their attitudes about what they are learning; rather, it is the design of the instructional experience—the *instructional strategy*—that makes the difference. This is welcome affirmation for instructional designers; however, researchers continue to explore best practices in logistics and management of instruction to optimize the instructional experience for learners as well as for instructional providers and sponsors. The explosion in advances in technology affects how we think about best practices in managing the delivery of instruction, and it ensures continued research in this area for years to come.

This chapter's initial discussion on the selection of a delivery system notes that it most often occurs early in the instructional design process. When working under the constraint of an assigned or assumed delivery system, media selection becomes a choice among those formats available in that system. This limit on available media is not as problematic as one might think. Research on effects of media on students' learning—beginning with military training films in the 1940s and continuing through radio, television, slideshows, computer-based multimedia and simulation, and web-based distance learning—generally concludes that the medium itself does not make a significant difference in how much students learn. Clark's (1983) review of research established the basic argument that the design of instruction rather than the medium used to deliver it determines student learning. In a summary of research eighteen years later, Russell (2001), focusing more on distance learners' achievement, reached conclusions very similar to Clark's. Although Russell's updated website (nosignificantdifference.org) lists several studies reporting improved student performance in mediated distance learning, it is difficult to attribute the positive results to the medium itself because of changes in instructional strategies for the distance learning treatments that were not controlled in the studies. A recent meta-analysis of distance learning studies in higher education conducted by the U.S. Department of Education (2013) reported higher achievement for blended learning versus online learning and face-to-face learning. The report does, however, attribute the elevated achievement to time spent in learning and differences in curriculum and pedagogy rather than to the online media itself. Such empirical findings simply confirm common sense. If the purpose of instruction is to stimulate internal mental processing that causes learning, then any medium capable of stimulating the desired processing is effective. The implication for the instructional designer (with some qualifications discussed in this chapter) is that almost any medium works for most teaching–learning requirements.

Readers familiar with the history of educational technology need fingers on more than two hands to count the "latest and greatest" technology innovations that have been promoted, implemented, and discarded after failing to realize their promised benefits for learners and organizations. Assuredly, the "latest and greatest" criterion is still alive and well in all sectors of public and private education and training, yet it continues to yield solutions unresponsive to the needs of learners or their sponsoring organizations.

Process Flowcharts

Planning Logistics and Management

In planning the logistics and management for the instructional strategy, you should (1) sequence and cluster the content to set lesson size, (2) plan learner groupings, (3) select media, and (4) select or confirm the delivery system (Figures 9.2–9.5).

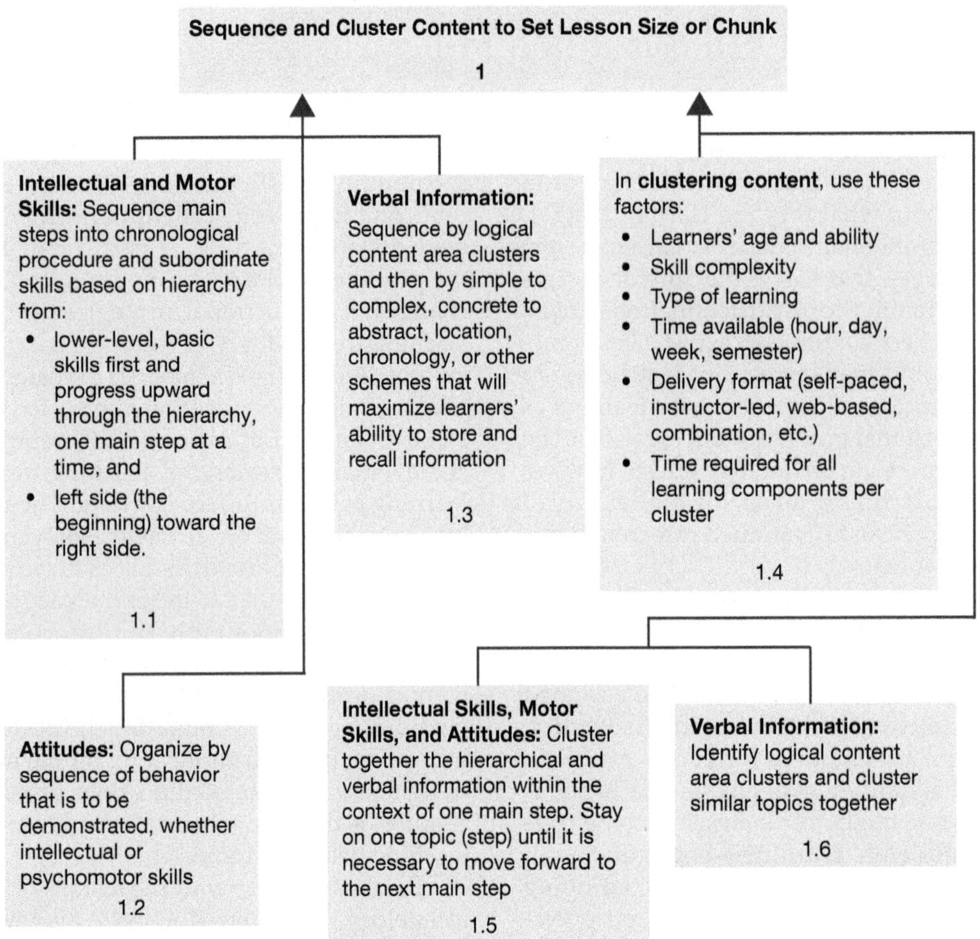

Figure 9.2 Sequence and Cluster Content

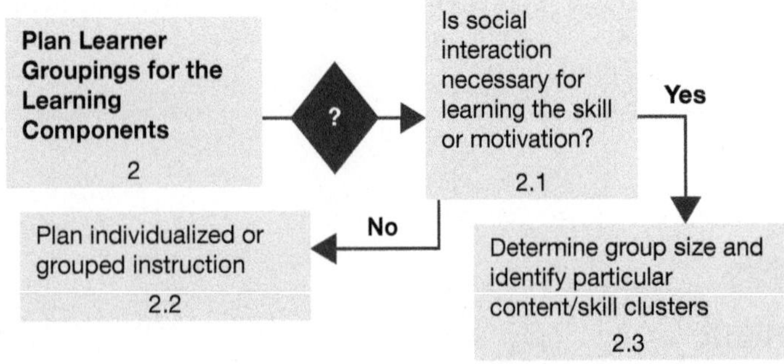

Figure 9.3 Plan Learner Groupings for the Learning Components

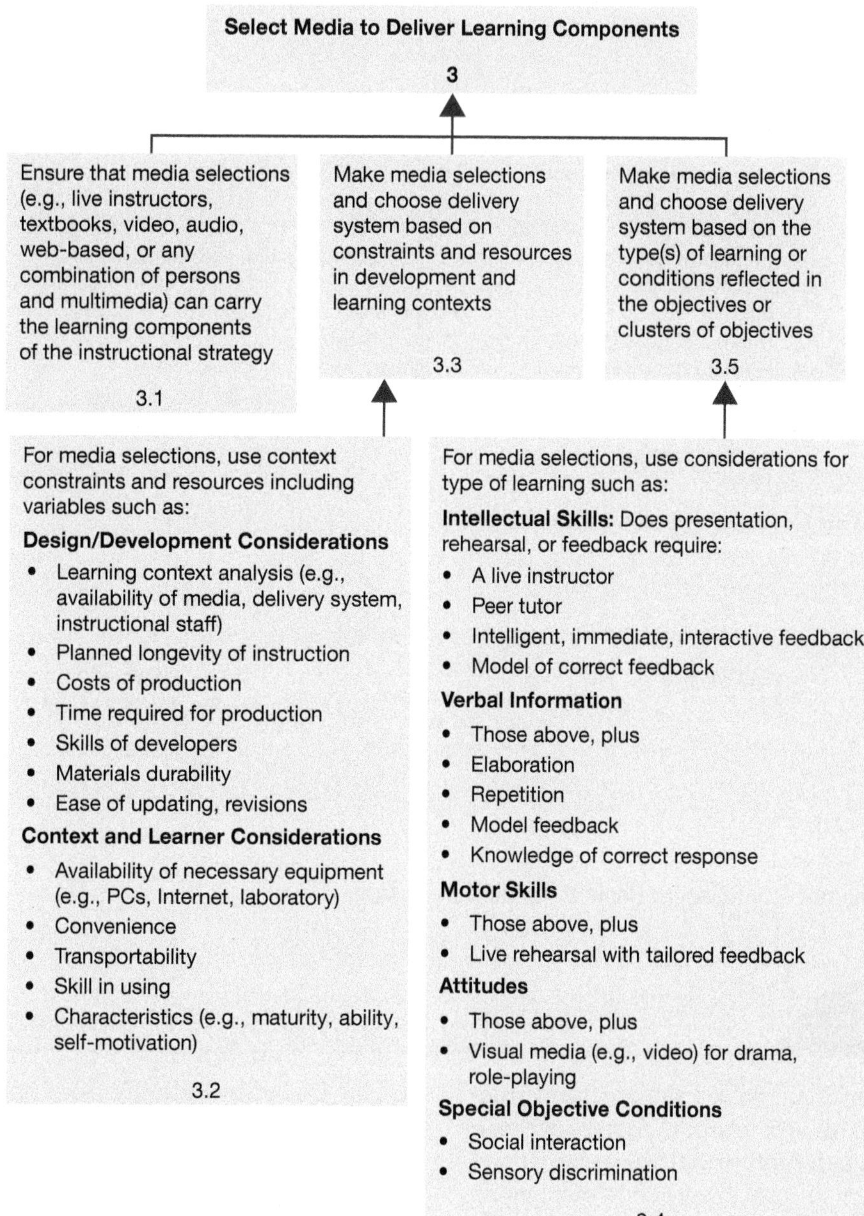

Figure 9.4 Select Media to Deliver Learning Components

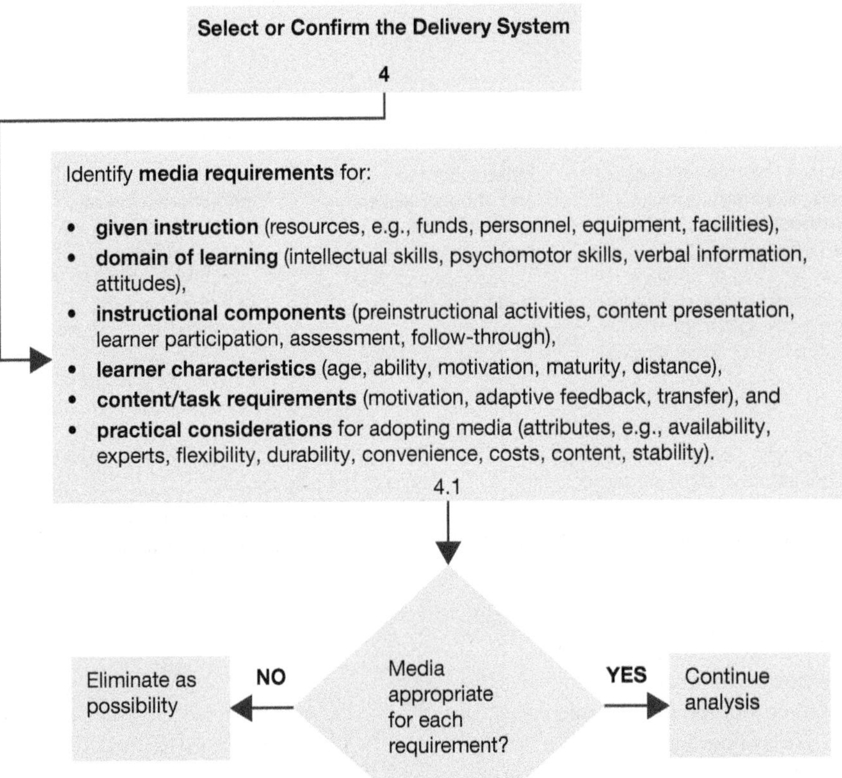

Figure 9.5 Select or Confirm the Delivery System

Practice

1. Sequence subordinate skills. Examine the instructional analysis in Appendix C for the writing composition goal. Notice that the subordinate skills for each main step have a code that begins with the number of the main step (e.g., the code 5.4 reflects a subordinate skill for skill 5.5), and 5.32 reflects a subordinate skill for main step 5. Assume these skill codes signal the order each of the subordinate skills is presented to the learner. Given this information, evaluate the sequence of instruction implied by the skill codes. Is this order correct, or should the skill codes be reordered to reflect a better sequence for learning the skills?
   a. The order of the subordinate skills for instruction is appropriate.
   b. All the verbal information skills should be presented first (e.g., 5.1, 5.2, 5.4, 5.6, 5.8).
   c. Instruction should begin with the discrimination skills (e.g., 5.3, 5.5, 5.7).
   d. The order actually does not matter because these skills can be sequenced in any order as long as they are taught before main step 5.
2. Cluster subordinate skills for instruction. Assume the preinstructional session is complete, you have already planned instruction for main skills 1 through 4, and you are planning a forty-minute instructional session for main step 5. The students are in the sixth grade, and they are average or above average in prior writing achievement. (Follow an educated hunch at this point if you are unfamiliar with sixth-grade students.) Which of the following clusters of objectives would be best for the first forty-minute instructional session related to main step 5?
   a. Main step 5 plus subordinate skills 5.1 through 5.30.
   b. Main step 5 plus subordinate skills 5.11, 5.17, 5.24, and 5.31.

c. Subordinate skills 5.7, 5.9, 5.10, 5.11, and 5.32 (related only to declarative sentences).

d. All subordinate skills from 5.1 through 5.32.

3. Media selection for task requirements. Examine the following enabling skill from Appendix C: Recognize a declarative sentence with correct closing punctuation. Based on the nature of the skill (rather than feasibility and economics), which of the following media do you believe provide a good vehicle for delivering the instruction? Choose all that apply.

   a. Teacher-led instruction.

   b. Inexpensive and practical paper module that can be reused by students next year.

   c. Web-based management program such as Canvas with teacher facilitation and elaboration.

   d. Straight web-based management program such as Canvas.

4. Develop an instructional strategy for the preinstructional activities for the following instructional goal:

   In written composition,

   - use a variety of sentence types and accompanying punctuation based on the purpose and mood of the sentence, and
   - use a variety of sentence types and accompanying punctuation based on the complexity or structure of the sentence.

5. Plan the "learner guidance" component for a constructivist learning environment for the following instructional goal:

   In written composition,

   - use a variety of sentence types and accompanying punctuation based on the purpose and mood of the sentence, and
   - use a variety of sentence types and accompanying punctuation based on the complexity or structure of the sentence.

Consider using a planning template such as the one in Table 8.8 to guide your work. As appropriate for constructivist learning instructional strategies, do not hesitate to add other ideas of interest to you. Compare your ideas with the sample provided in Appendix H and review Sections 1 and 2.

Feedback

1. a
2. c
3. a, b, c, d
4. Plan for a cognitive instructional strategy: Compare your preinstructional activities with those provided in Appendix F. Review the remainder of Appendix F as well as Appendix G to see the entire instructional strategy.
5. Plan for a constructivist learning environment: Compare your plan with the sample provided in Appendix H and review sections 1 and 2 especially.

References and Recommended Readings

Barker, P., & Van Schaik, P. (2016). *Electronic performance support: Using digital technology to enhance human ability*. Routledge.

Bishop, R. (2017). *Multimedia based instructional design*. CreateSpace. Combines an instructional design model with interactive multimedia design.

Brown, L. A. (1996). *Designing and developing electronic performance support systems*. Digital Press.

Clark, R. (1983). Reconsidering research on learning from media. *Review of Educational Research, 53*(4), 445.

Clark, R. E., Yates, K., Early, S., & Moulton, K. (2010). An analysis of the failure of electronic media and discovery-based learning: Evidence for the performance benefits of guided training methods. In J. H. Silber & R. Foshay (Eds.), *Handbook of training and improving workplace performance, vol. 1: Instructional design and training delivery*. Pfeiffer.

Clark, R. E. (2012). *Learning from media: Arguments, analysis, and evidence* (2nd ed.). Information Age Publishing.

Clark, R. C., & Mayer, R. E. (2016). *e-Learning and the science of instruction: Proven guidelines for consumers and designers of multimedia learning* (4th ed.). Wiley.

Dick, W. D. (2016). *A qualitative cross-case analysis of three real-world mobile performance support design models*. http://purl.flvc.org/fsu/fd/FSU_FA2016_Dick_fsu_0071E_13561. Analyzes design process from government, nonprofit, and private-sector organizations for performance support on mobile devices. Reports similarities and differences and makes recommendations for optimizing effectiveness.

Dickelman, G. J. (Ed.). (2003). *EPSS revisited: A lifecycle for developing performance-centered systems*. ISPI. A compilation of articles on EPSS.

Dillon, A., & Gabbard, R. (1998). Hypermedia as an educational technology: A review of the quantitative research literature on learner comprehension, control, and style. *Review of Educational Research, 68*(3), 322–349. This summary of research concludes that learning gains from the use of hypermedia are limited.

Educational Technology Magazine 47(3), (2007). Special issue on highly mobile computing (i.e., hold-in-one-hand devices for social interaction and information access, including PDAs, cell phones, tablet computers, UMPCs, gaming systems, iPods, and motes).

Educational Technology Research and Development, 56(1), (2008). Special issue on scaffolded learning with hypermedia. Focuses on hyperlinking media in constructivist learning environments.

Gagné, R. M. (1985). *Conditions of learning* (4th ed.). Holt, Rinehart and Winston. Gagné describes in detail the factors that should be present to stimulate learning in each of the learning domains.

Gagné, R. M., Wager, W. W., Golas, K. C., & Keller, J. M. (2004). *Principles of instructional design* (5th ed.). Wadsworth/Thomson Learning. Chapters 9–12 in this book provide additional background on developing instructional strategies.

Gery, G. (1991). *Electronic performance support systems*. Gery Performance Press. The original text by Gloria Gery, who coined the term *electronic performance support systems (EPSS)*.

Gottfredson, C., & Mosher, B. (2011). *Innovative performance support: Strategies and practices for learning in the workflow*. McGraw-Hill. Describes performance support on the job as an efficient alternative to formal training.

Hannum, W. H. (2007). When computers teach: A review of the instructional effectiveness of computers. *Educational Technology, 47*(2), 5–13.

Hirumi, A., Bradford, G., & Rutherford, L. (2011). Selecting delivery systems and media to facilitate blended learning: A systematic process based skill level, content stability, cost, and instructional strategy. *MERLOT Journal of Online Learning and Teaching, 7*(4), 489–501. https://jolt.merlot.org/vol7no4/hirumi1211.htm. Describes a very structured approach to media selection in a military context.

Holden, J. T., & Westfall, P. J.-L. (2010). *An instructional media selection guide for distance learning: Implications for blended learning featuring an introduction to virtual worlds* (2nd ed.). United States Distance Learning Association. http://www.usdla.org/assets/pdf_files/AIMSGDL%202nd%20Ed._styled_010311.pdf. Includes a useful table for instructional delivery options for e-learning with descriptions and examples.

Hung, W.-C., & Kalota, F. (2013). Design and validation of MAPS for educators: A performance support system to guide media selection for lesson design. *Performance Improvement Quarterly, 26*(1), 81–99.

Lee, W. W., & Owens, D. L. (2004). *Multimedia-based instructional design: Computer-based training; web-based training; distance broadcast training; performance-based solutions* (2nd ed.). Jossey-Bass Pfeiffer. Demonstrates that the same instructional design model can be used for all media.

Ma, Y., & Harmon, S. W. (2006). Integrating knowledge management systems, electronic performance support systems, and learning technologies: A conceptual model. *Performance Improvement Quarterly, 19*(3), 107–120.

Maughan, G. R. (2005). Electronic performance support systems and technological literacy. *The Journal of Technology Studies, 31*(1), 49–56. A combination of why to use with suggestions of how to use. Also lists a number of computer-based job aids that are not typically thought of as EPSS.

McManus, P., & Rossett, A. (2006). Performance support tools. *Performance Improvement, 45*(2), 8–17. Tools for use as alternatives to formal training.

Merrill, M. D. (2002). First principles of instruction. *Educational Technology Research and Development, 50*(3), 42–59.

Nguyen, F., & Klein, J. D. (2008). The effect of performance support and training as performance interventions. *Performance Improvement Quarterly, 21*(1), 95–114. Reports research findings that support both the efficiency and the effectiveness of EPSS on a tax preparation task.

Richey, R. C., Klein, J. D., & Tracey, M. W. (2011). *The instructional design knowledge base: Theory, research, and practice.* Routledge. Includes topics on media theory, selection, and use in Chapter 6.

Rossett, A., & Schafer, L. (2007). *Job aids and performance support: Moving from knowledge in the classroom to knowledge everywhere.* Pfeiffer.

Russell, T. L. (2001). *The no significant difference phenomenon* (5th ed.). IDECC. The companion website is still available at https://detaresearch.org, but the database search function is very limited and many entries have broken links.

Sugrue, B., & Clark, R. E. (2000). Media selection for training. In S. Tobias & D. Fletcher (Eds.), *Training and retraining: A handbook for business, industry, government, and the military.* Macmillan. Describes selecting media based on comparison of stimulus requirements for instruction with media attributes.

U.S. Department of Education (2013). 2010-11 School Level Leading Indicator Data. ISSN: 1552-583X. press@ed.gov.

Vai, M., & Sosulski, K. (2015). *Essentials of online course design: A standards-based guide* (2nd ed.). Routledge. A step-by-step guide with a rubric for evaluating one's design work.

van Merriënboer, J. J. G. (1997). *Training complex cognitive skills: A four-component instructional design model for technical training.* Englewood Cliffs, NJ: Educational Technology Publications.

chapter 10

Developing Instructional Materials

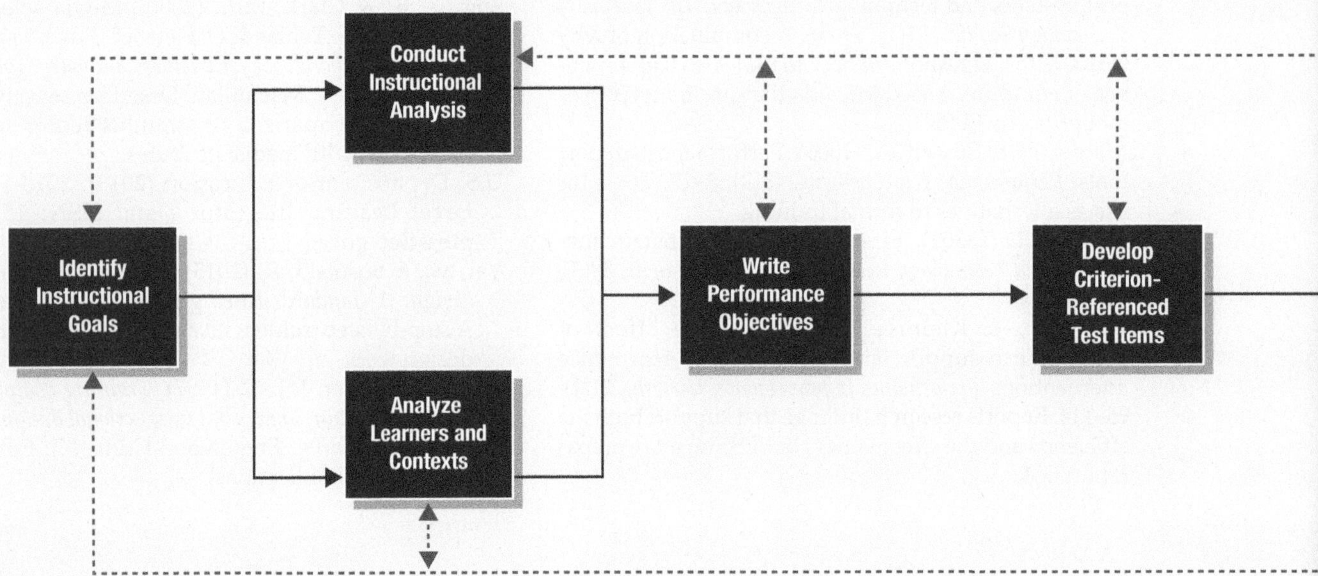

Objectives

- Compare the various roles of instructional designers based on whether they design instruction only; design and develop instruction; or design, develop, and deliver instruction.
- Link the five main categories of quality criteria to components of an instructional package.
- Given an instructional strategy, describe the procedures for developing an initial draft of instructional materials.
- Develop an initial draft of instructional materials based on a given instructional strategy.

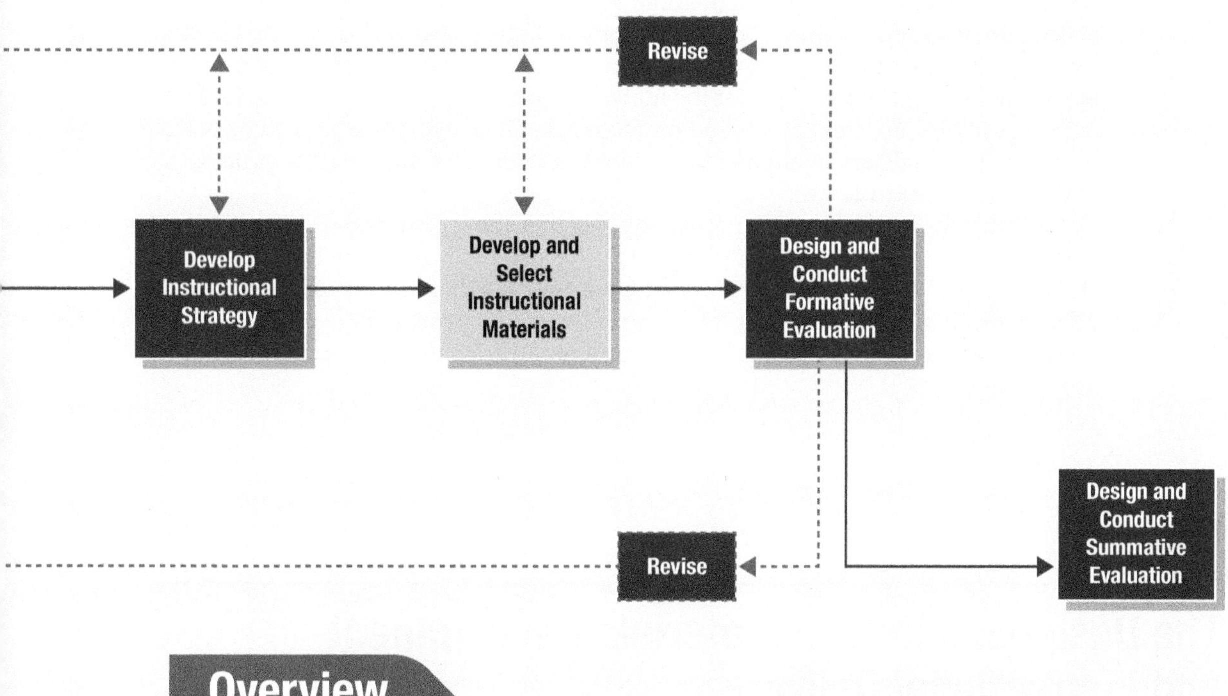

Overview

At the point of beginning to develop instruction, designers need to consider their role in the process, the media and delivery systems specified, and the contents of an instructional package to be created. The role of the instructional designer can vary greatly, from one who completes all required analysis, design, development, implementation, and evaluation tasks to one where only one or a few of these tasks are completed. Designers' skills, the environment within which they work, and the resources available for the instruction are often factors that determine designers' duties. During logistics and management planning, media selections and delivery systems are specified based on types of learning and best practices for learners, contexts, and learning components; however, these ideals are typically modified based on practical constraints. The instructional package to be developed typically includes all materials used by learners during the instruction, assessment materials, and materials for an instructor's guide.

Sometimes existing instructional materials are found that appear to be suitable to aid learners in achieving your instructional goal. Such materials should be evaluated carefully using five categories of criteria: those centered on the instructional goal, learners, contexts, learning, and technical qualities. Regardless of potential cost savings, materials that do not meet any one of these criteria and cannot be modified to do so are of questionable value for your project.

Because creating polished instructional materials can be expensive, designers first create inexpensive rough-draft versions for tryouts with selected learners. This helps ensure that the materials are effective with learners prior to creating more expensive, polished versions. Designers should consider the media for the final version and then use rough-draft formats that best mimic that media.

With the instructional strategy in hand, the designer is ready to bring the instruction to life. Constant reference to your design documents, from the instructional goal through the instructional strategy, while you work keeps your efforts targeted and helps avoid introducing interesting—but extraneous—information. The analysis and design work serves its purpose by ensuring an instructional product that is responsive to the needs that gave rise to the original goal. When you complete this phase of the instructional design, you should have a draft set of instructional materials, draft assessments, and a draft instructor's manual. Do not think that any materials you develop on the first attempt will stand for all time. It is extremely important to consider the materials you develop to be draft copies and to expect review and revision based on feedback. Once developed in rough-draft form, the materials are evaluated and revised as needed following the processes in Chapters 11 and 12.

In this chapter, we consider various roles that the instructional designer can play in materials development and delivery. We also provide concepts, guidelines, and criteria for developing instructional materials. We do not focus on media production techniques because those techniques encompass vast skill sets for which excellent resources are available in books and online text, tutorials, and interactive user groups.

Concepts

The Designer's Role in Materials Development and Instructional Delivery

When the Designer Is Also the Materials Developer and the Instructor

In many instructional settings, the person who designs the instruction also develops materials and teaches students. For example, a human resources generalist in a small company may design, develop, and deliver all new-employee orientation, benefits training, and "soft skills" training; teachers and professors do their own lesson plans and syllabi, materials, and instruction; professionals in all fields routinely design, develop, and present their own workshops and in-service training.

When designers are also developers and instructors, they take on different teaching responsibilities based on the types of materials prescribed in the instructional strategy. When instructors design and develop individualized materials or materials that can be delivered independently of an instructor, their role in instructional delivery is passive, but their role as a facilitator is very active. In this case, their task during instruction is to monitor and guide the progress of students through the materials. Students can progress at their own speed through the instruction, with the instructor providing feedback as needed and additional help for those who seem to get stuck. Except for the pretests and posttests, all learning components are included within the materials. In some materials, even these tests are included and submitted to the instructor when learners complete them, or scoring is automated and entered electronically into the class gradebook. This is a very common model of instruction in e-learning delivered through learning management systems (LMSs), such as Blackboard, Moodle, Canvas, or any of the LMSs now available for K–12, higher education, and professional/technical training.

However, when instructors select and adapt materials to suit their instructional strategy, it is probable that the instructor will have an increased role in delivering instruction. Some available materials may be instructor independent, but when they are not, the instructor must provide learning components specified in the strategy but not found in the materials. This mixed bag of resource-based learning and direct instruction is probably the most common instructor-managed teaching and learning. When an instructor uses a variety of instructional resources, he or she plays a greater role in materials management. By providing a learner guide for available materials, instructors may be able to increase the independence of the materials and free themselves to provide additional guidance and consultation for students who need it.

A third model is the case in which the instructor personally delivers all instruction according to the instructional strategy already developed, common when there is a small budget for materials, very few students, the content to be taught changes rapidly, or the content is so cutting-edge that materials do not exist. The instructor uses the instructional strategy as a guide in producing outlines for lecture notes and directions for group exercises and activities. In professional and technical training, the designer often develops a formal instructor's guide that provides detailed lesson plan–like guidance for lectures, discussions, and participant activities, whereas in educational settings, daily lesson plans or the course syllabus serve this purpose.

This type of instruction has both advantages and disadvantages. A major advantage is that the instructor can constantly update and improve instruction as changes occur in the content. However, a disadvantage is that instructors spend the majority of their time lecturing and delivering information to a group, leaving little time to help individual learners with problems, and when the instructor stops to answer a question for one learner, the progress of the entire group is halted.

The intended delivery mode for instruction is a very important consideration in the development of materials based on the planned instructional strategy. If instruction is intended to be independent of an instructor, then the materials must include all the learning components in the strategy. The instructor is not expected to play a role in delivering instruction.

If the instructor plans to combine available materials, then instructional delivery combines materials and instructor presentation. The instructor may not be required to develop any new materials in this mode but may be required to deliver some of the needed instruction. The amount of original materials developed for this type of instruction depends on available time, budget, and staff support.

If instructors plan to deliver all the instruction with such materials as lecture notes, a multimedia projector, and a whiteboard, then it may be necessary to develop little besides lecture outlines, electronic presentations, practice worksheets or active learning exercises, and formal tests.

As the instructional designer, you made decisions about the intended delivery system and media formats in planning your instructional strategy. Now, when you are also the materials developer and the instructor, it may be necessary to modify and adapt your original decisions to reflect existing materials, the realities of development and production costs, and changes in your thinking about your role as instructor. These decisions affect materials development activities as well as the required budget and staff.

When the designer is also the developer and the instructor, the whole process of materials development is rather informal—that is, much of what would be formal specification and communication between designer and materials developer remains as mental notes or informal planning notes. The thought also tends to reside in the back of the designer's mind that, as the instructor, "I will be able to manage the instruction, adapting and accommodating as needed on the fly." This thought results in less concern for the nitty-gritty details of developing and implementing instruction.

Another commonly practiced arrangement assigns responsibility for design with the instructor, but not sole responsibility for materials production. Unusual in public schools, it occurs more often in higher education, business, government, and military settings, where there is often technical assistance available for production of complex media such as video, web-based, and multimedia. The designer usually works collaboratively with an in-house media production specialist rather than turning over specifications.

When the Designer Is Not the Instructor

In large companies with a significant training and development function, an instructional designer may work with a team responsible for design, development, and implementation of training. There are also similar teams in instructional design (ID) consulting firms, personnel training and development companies, and many universities, where the team usually includes a manager, an instructional designer, a subject-matter expert (SME), a materials developer (or coordinator), and an evaluator.

In a smaller ID setting, one individual may be responsible for more than one function, whereas in a larger setting, multiple individuals may be assigned to each function. The team also interacts regularly with a representative of the internal or external client and sometimes with an instructor or instructional program manager. In ID teams, it is common for the manager to be a senior-level instructional designer and for the instructional designer also to be a materials developer or at least have working-level knowledge of a variety of media formats. The combination of ID and materials development skills is desirable, particularly in computer-based and web-based materials development, because of pressure to bring "just in time" training products to users as quickly as possible. Michael Greer (1994) is a good source for exploring team-based instructional design and ID project management, and Brill et al. (2006) describe project management competencies validated through a Delphi study.

Earlier we mentioned that the process of specifying and developing materials is fairly informal when the designer is also the materials developer and the instructor. When the designer is neither the developer nor the instructor, however, a premium is placed on precision specifications and working in a team environment requiring communication and collaboration skills. There is no such thing as a "standard operating procedure" for the communication that occurs between a designer and a materials developer. It is always a unique collaboration determined by the mix of design and development skills possessed by each participant and the division of responsibilities in the team setting.

For example, a creative instructional designer with good television production skills and the necessary time might turn over a full-production script with storyboarding to the materials developer. At the other extreme, a busy designer without production experience might meet with the developer, go over the learner and context analyses, review the instructional strategy, solicit production ideas from the developer, and then meet later to review a storyboard and script notes prepared by the developer. The best way for a designer to establish methods for communicating media specifications is to meet with and learn from the developer because materials developers already have planning and production tools that they use routinely in their media trade. The instructional designer should adopt the planning tools with which materials developers in a particular shop are comfortable.

Another reason for introducing the idea of an ID team is to point out a common problem in the instructional design process that stems from the relationship, or lack thereof, between the designer and the learners: When the designer is also the instructor of a given set of learners, the designer–instructor has a good understanding of the interests and motivations of the learners, their preferences and expectations, and their general and specific knowledge of the content area. It is often the case, however, in team ID settings that the designer is not the instructor, is unfamiliar with the learners for whom the instruction is intended, and may have little or no direct contact with them. In such cases, the designer can depend on careful learner and context analyses, but in lieu of good information, he or she may depend on personal stereotypes of what the learners are like. Such assumptions may result in more problems than if the designer had no knowledge of the learners at all.

If possible, designers should have conducted the on-site learner and context analyses themselves to observe a sample of the learners for whom the instruction is being designed. This step is equally important whether observing schoolchildren, military recruits, adult volunteer learners, middle-management trainees, or any others for whom instruction is to be designed. If the designer did not do the original learner and context analyses, then an opportunity for at least casual observation should be pursued. Based on these observations, the designer makes decisions as diverse as the size of content clusters, the features of a graphical user interface, or the types of role models that should be used to foster attitudes. Although it is impossible to indicate all the characteristics of a learner population that might be important to the design of new instruction, the instructional designer must become as knowledgeable as possible about the target population.

After considering the roles the instructional designer can play in the development process, focus on the four broad tasks in Table 10.1 that help guide instructional materials development: reconsidering the delivery system and media selection, determining the components of the instructional package, considering existing instructional materials, and developing instructional materials.

Table 10.1 Overview of Instructional Materials Development

Task	Outcome
Reconsider delivery system and media selection	Compromises in delivery system and media selection based on availability of existing materials, cost constraints, and the instructor's role
Determine components of the instructional package	A clear conception of what the materials should include and how they should look
Consider existing instructional materials	Decisions about whether to adopt or adapt any existing materials for use in the instruction
Develop instructional materials	Rough-draft materials and the management information needed for formative evaluation

The Delivery System and Media Selections

At this point in the instructional design process, a delivery system is specified and the instructional strategy has been developed, including clustering and sequencing, learning components, student groupings, and tentative media selections. If the designer is working within an assumed or imposed delivery system, then the range of options is limited and the media selections that have been made are probably fairly stable. If one made open selections of media formats and an ideal delivery system, however, the likelihood is high that specifications will be revised during materials development. The point here is that our choices of theoretically best practice run into a reality check as a natural part of the materials development process; some conflict is expected, and the resulting compromises usually help ensure a workable educational product that fits the learning environment. Three factors often cause compromise in selections of media and delivery system: (1) availability of existing instructional materials, (2) production and implementation constraints, and (3) the amount of facilitation provided by the instructor during instruction.

Availability of Existing Instructional Materials

Sometimes existing materials are an attractive alternative to going through the development and production process. Existing materials could be substituted for planned materials on a scale ranging from a single motivational sequence in one lesson to an entire course or curriculum. Consider the example of our leadership training design. In Chapter 9 we specify a web-based delivery system, but suppose a review of existing materials turned up an appropriate current video series on group leadership skills developed by a junior college consortium. If the duplication and distribution rights are not prohibitive, then with proper permission, appropriate video excerpts could be adapted for web distribution.

Production and Implementation Constraints

Media formats and delivery systems that look expensive are expensive. Cutting production corners to save money usually does not affect student learning, but it does affect attention and perceptions of relevance and authority. Novice designers who have not worked with complex media often severely underestimate the costs of hiring commercial production and equally underestimate the expertise, infrastructure, and time requirements for in-house production. Sometimes after development is completed, the costs of duplication, distribution, and maintenance can be just as prohibitive as unanticipated production costs. It is essential to anticipate such constraints by due diligence during the learning context analysis and to maintain an open and flexible viewpoint when entering the materials production phase. When faced with these dilemmas, the best strategy is to back down to simpler media formats and produce them well rather than sticking with complex media formats and producing them poorly. Using our leadership training example again, if it became apparent that quality, web-based streaming video was simply out of reach, it might be better to drop back to a good PowerPoint presentation developed for web delivery than to do an amateurish video.

Amount of Instructor Facilitation

When describing the designer's role in instructional delivery previously, we noted that different levels of classroom facilitation are provided by the designer when he or she is also the instructor. The discussion of various levels of instructor facilitation also applies in design and development of e-learning. The first steps in adoption of a new technology are usually attempts to replicate the features of the old technology with which we are comfortable; thus, we began delivering learning at a distance using instructional television, the web, and learning management systems. We tried to replicate features of the classroom experience for our students. Instructor facilitation is a particular feature of classroom instruction favored by students and instructors alike, whether meeting face-to-face or at a distance. Instructor facilitation is a point at which distance-learning practices sometimes diverge because of pedagogical philosophies and the ever-present tension between quality and productivity. Table 10.2 compares three levels of instructor facilitation. Note that these three levels are not mutually exclusive and that the features of each are not as discrete as the tabular format might imply.

Table 10.2 Levels of Instructor Facilitation in Three Models of Distance Learning

	e-Classroom Model	e-Lecture Model	e-Complete Model
Purpose	Replicate classroom experience	Replicate lecture hall experience	Replace classroom experience
Context	All learning contexts	Usually higher ed., also meetings and conferences	Usually professional and technical training
Delivery Systems	Web, streaming video, online meeting and conferencing software	Web, broadcast television, streaming video	Web, computer-based training, sometimes field-based on mobile devices
Instructor Facilitation	Instructor centered Learning facilitated by instructor's active participation in group and individual process and peer participation in small-group and peer-to-peer process	Instructor centered or materials centered Learning facilitated by differentiated staff (e.g., proctor, learning center staff, graduate assistant, adjunct, tutor) and peer participation in small-group and peer-to-peer process	Materials and software centered Independent, self-paced learning facilitated by software, sometimes supported by peer participation in small-group and peer-to-peer process
Learners	Suitable for all learner independence levels	Suitable for fairly independent learners	Suitable for highly independent learners
Accountability	Student learning outcomes Student attitude about course Student rating of faculty	Student learning outcomes Student attitude about course Student rating of instructor and differentiated staff	Student learning outcomes Student attitude about course Supervisor rating of student's job performance
Scalability and Per-Student Cost	Limited scalability High per-student cost Add students by adding additional faculty	Scalable Low to moderate per-student cost Add students by adding additional differentiated staff	Scalable Per-student costs dependent on sufficient audience size to amortize cost of development Add students by opening access
Development and Implementation	Low startup costs if technological infrastructure is in place Can be developed and managed independently by a faculty member	Low to high startup costs, depending on medium and sophistication of materials Can require production team and will require network of facilitators	High startup costs for intensive materials development and evaluation Usually requires production team, but primary management task after implementation is maintenance and accountability
Typical Users	All educational and training settings	Usually higher ed. Open University in UK is the model example, also e-universities, e-certificate coursework, large meetings and conferences, and MOOCs	Primarily private sector, military, and government training Limited use in public and higher education

There are several implications in Table 10.2 for the development of materials in distance-learning delivery systems. Recalling our discussion from Chapter 8 of Moore and Kearsley's concept of *transactional distance* (the theory of cognitive space between instructors and learners in an educational setting), high levels of course dialogue in the e-classroom model encourage learners' perceptions of a more personal experience and feelings of group affiliation. Much of this dialogue is instructor participation in synchronous or asynchronous online discussion and practice with feedback, and it is generally reflected in more positive student evaluations of the course and the instructor. This is a feature of classroom instruction that the e-classroom model attempts to replicate in distance learning. When discussion and feedback are provided by the instructor, initial materials development costs are lower; however, per-student costs are high and the course cannot be scaled up in size without overburdening the instructor; hiring additional instructors; or hiring adjuncts, TAs, or other support personnel. The e-lecture–hall model is typified by differentiated staffing to limit instructor costs and still maintain a personalized course that accommodates large student audiences. The per-student costs, however, can still be high because of personnel and administrative expenses.

Practitioners of the e-classroom and e-lecture–hall models worked out innovative strategies for maintaining high levels of interaction in their courses without burdening their instructional personnel by shifting their instructor–student communication to student–student communication. This works well for peer-moderated practice and feedback and for small-group discussion focused on implementation and transfer to the performance context. It also works well when e-space is set up for small-group project and problem-solving interaction. Social media and mobile devices are now being used successfully to lend anywhere, anytime convenience to some of the facilitation and communication in e-learning.

The e-complete model of distance learning opts for higher initial development expenses by assigning learning components to the instructional materials and delivery system rather than to an instructor, and then it relies on distribution to large numbers of students to bring down the per-student cost. In this model, initial choices of ideal delivery system and media formats are often compromised when the instructional designer is faced with distance-learning materials development and delivery cost options that are based on varying levels of instructor facilitation. The decision regarding the role of the instructor in instructional delivery must be considered and affirmed before selecting or developing materials.

The e-classroom and e-lecture–hall models have succeeded beyond expectations, experiencing exponential growth, but reviews in the training and development world have been mixed regarding the success of e-learning. Some training managers and performance consultants cite two problems, among others, in e-learning. One problem occurs when content from instructor-led platform instruction is converted for web delivery without in-depth consideration of the learning components for which the instructor had been responsible in the face-to-face learning environment. Such components as motivating learners, promoting active recall of prerequisites, providing practice with corrective feedback, and promoting transfer could be missing from those e-learning experiences. One response has been to provide an instructor presence in the e-learning environment, and another response is seen in the trend toward **blended learning**, wherein self-paced online and computer-based experiences are joined with face-to-face classroom or workgroup experiences. Blended learning is also a successful alternative for e-classroom and e-lecture–hall learning that would otherwise be completely online, but research indicates that the success is in more positive perceptions of course structure and collaboration rather than improved student achievement (Lim & Yoon, 2008). A second problem occurs when the technologies of e-learning are viewed as solutions. Learning management systems are now very sophisticated with tremendous capabilities for organizing, delivering, managing, and assessing learning, but no advantage will be gained in effectiveness without skillful, creative instructional design. Regardless of the media or the delivery system, the designer's foundation for creating instructional materials must be the learning components specified in the development of the instructional strategy.

Components of an Instructional Package

Having reconsidered the delivery system and media selections, you are ready to start selecting existing instructional materials, developing materials yourself, or writing specifications for someone else to develop the materials. Before you begin, you should be aware of the several components that usually make up an instructional package, noting that the term *package* includes all forms of print and mediated materials.

Instructional Materials

The instructional materials contain the content—whether written, mediated, or facilitated by an instructor—that a student uses to achieve the objectives. This includes materials for the major objectives and the terminal objective and any materials for enhancing memory and transfer to a performance context. ***Instructional materials*** refers to any preexisting materials being incorporated as well as to those materials developed specifically for the objectives. The materials may also include information that the learners use to guide their progress through the instruction. Templates for such student guidance are now available as part of commercial web-based online course management portals such as Blackboard or Canvas, but the instructor must fill in the templates with content specific to a given course. Student workbooks, activity guides, problem scenarios, computer simulations, case studies, resource lists, and other such materials can also be part of the instructional materials.

Assessments

All instructional materials should be accompanied by objective tests or by product or performance assessments and may include both a pretest and a posttest. Embedded tests are built right into the materials, but you may decide that you do not wish to have the pre- and posttests as separate components in the materials, preferring to have them appear as part of the instructor's materials so they are not available to students. The package is incomplete, however, unless you include at least a posttest and the other assessments necessary for using the instructional package.

Course Management Information

Often, there is a general description of the total package, typically called an **instructor's manual**, that provides an overview of the materials and shows how they could be incorporated into an overall learning sequence for students. The manual could also include the tests and other information you judge to be important for implementing the course. In addition to the student guidance templates provided in commercial web-based instructional management systems, there is also facilitation for group and peer interaction and course management support for the instructor, often including automated class listing, student tracking, online testing, project monitoring, grade book, and a variety of communication and messaging mechanisms. Some types of self-paced independent learning do not have course instructors per se, so the instructor's guide is really a course management guide that can be customized for students and site-specific applications. Special attention should be paid to the ease with which course management information can be used by the instructor or course manager, and it should undergo the same type of formative evaluation as tests and instruction.

Considerations for adding suggestions for a constructivist learning environment to the course management information include the needs of the organization, the appropriateness of the environment for the goal and for the learners' ability and motivation, the performance and learning contexts, and the resources available for supporting the environment (e.g., hypertext, knowledge repository, skilled tutor, time, personnel, facilities, equipment, money). Caution must be used in including such information because learning environments are often situation-specific and, by definition, must evolve within the context rather than be prescribed.

Existing Instructional Materials

The next step is to determine whether there are existing materials that fit your objectives. In some content areas there is an abundance of materials available, either superficial or greatly detailed, that are not really directed to the target population in which you are interested. However, occasionally it is possible to identify materials that at least partly serve your needs. Some time spent in library and online research could pay off in time and cost savings if usable resources are found. It is clearly worth the effort to spend several hours examining existing materials to determine whether they meet specified needs when one considers the cost of developing multimedia and courseware for e-learning and mobile learning.

Existing materials for e-learning, called *learning objects*, have become widely available over the past twenty years. As originally envisioned in the e-learning context of the early 1990s, a learning object was what might traditionally be called a reusable *lesson* or *module* that included a minimum of an objective, a cluster of content, practice activities, assessments, and metadata describing the object. The object could also contain additional learning components of an instructional strategy. Such objects reside independently and can be drawn into a "learning space" for instructional purposes. The idea of learning objects was derived from object-oriented computer programming languages like Java, C++, and Visual Basic, wherein a programmer can pick up an object, such as a small scroll bar or drop-down menu, from a digital objects library and plug it into the code for a graphical user interface that is under development. If a learning object complies with one of several industry standards, then it can be "dropped" into a learning management system such as Canvas or Moodle and the LMS will be capable of launching and displaying the object as well as tracking and managing students through the object. The theory of learning objects is that cost savings could be realized by distributing learning objects across agencies that teach the same learning outcomes; for example, many companies teach new employees about 401(k) retirement plans, most universities teach students how to evaluate and cite web pages for use as references in research papers, and all branches of the military teach their military police common tactical procedures. After the concept of reusable learning objects was developed, the term was generalized in common use to refer to any digital content that can be inserted into a user interface to support learning. It could be audio, video, text, multimedia, or any combination of media to carry instructional content and learning guidance. Existing materials for e-learning can be as simple as a three-minute animation on YouTube that helps clarify a concept or as complex as a complete, semester-long course imported from a sister institution and loaded into your learning management system. Regardless of the origin or scope of existing materials, they should be evaluated carefully before use.

To aid planning your evaluations of existing materials, recall from Chapter 7 three of the categories of criteria for creating assessments—goal-centered, learner-centered, and context-centered criteria. We use these and add two more categories—learning-centered and technical criteria.

Goal-Centered Criteria for Evaluating Existing Materials

Goal-centered criteria focus on the content of instruction, and your instructional analysis documents provide a basis for determining the acceptability of the content in various instructional materials. Specific criteria in this area include

(1) congruence between the content in the materials and your terminal and performance objectives, (2) adequacy of content coverage and completeness, (3) authority, (4) accuracy, (5) currency, and (6) objectivity.

Learner-Centered Criteria for Evaluating Existing Materials

Your learner analysis documentation should provide the foundation for consideration of the appropriateness of instructional materials for your target group. Specific **learner-centered criteria** include the appropriateness of the materials for your learners' (1) vocabulary and language levels; (2) developmental, motivation, and interest levels; (3) backgrounds and experiences; and (4) special language or other needs. Other important learner-centered criteria include the materials treatment of diversity and whether gender, cultural, age, racial, or other forms of bias appear to be present. Using these criteria to judge available materials can help you determine the appropriateness of the materials for your specific target group.

Learning-Centered Criteria for Evaluating Existing Materials

Your instructional strategy can be used to determine whether existing materials are adequate as is or whether they must be adapted or enhanced prior to use. Materials can be evaluated to determine whether they include:

- preinstructional materials (e.g., performance objectives, motivational information/activities, prerequisite skills);
- correct content sequencing and presentation that are complete, current, and tailored for learners;
- student participation and congruent practice exercises;
- adequate feedback;
- appropriate assessments;
- adequate follow-through directions that enhance memory and transfer; and
- adequate learner guidance for moving students from one component or activity to the next.

The instructional strategy should be used to evaluate each potential resource. It may be possible to combine several resources to create a complete set of materials. When materials lack one or more of the necessary learning components—such as motivation or prerequisite skills—it may be economically advantageous to make adaptations so that the missing components are made available for use by students. It may also make sense to "complete" existing materials by writing assessments and an instructor's guide.

Context-Centered Criteria for Evaluating Existing Materials

Your instructional and performance context analyses can provide the foundation for judging whether existing materials can be adopted as is or adapted for your settings. **Context-centered criteria** include the authenticity of the materials for your contexts and learners and the feasibility of the materials for your settings and budget.

Technical Criteria for Evaluating Existing Materials

Materials should also be judged for their technical adequacy, according to criteria related to (1) the delivery system and media formats (appropriate for the objectives and the learning context); (2) packaging; (3) graphic design and typography; (4) durability; (5) legibility; (6) audio and video quality; and, when appropriate, (7) interface design, navigation, and functionality.

If suitable materials are found, it may change some of your decisions about delivery system, media, and components of the instructional package. If no appropriate materials are found that can be adopted or adapted for your instructional strategy, you are in the instructional materials development business. You must specify how you or a media production specialist will move from an instructional strategy to an instructional product that you can take into formative evaluation.

Your Instructional Materials

We recommend that you produce self-instructional materials in your first attempt at instructional design—that is, the materials should permit the student to learn the new information and skills without any intervention from an instructor or fellow students. Once having performed this feat, you can move to instructor-led or various combinations of mediated materials with or without an instructor. As a first effort, however, learning components such as *motivation, content, practice,* and *feedback* should be built into the instructional materials.

If you begin your development with the instructor included in the instructional process, it is very easy to use the instructor as a crutch to deliver the instruction. In your first effort as a designer, we recommend that you see how much can be done without having an instructor actively involved in the instructional process. Not only does this test your design skills and give you added insight into the learning components of an instructional strategy, but it also gives you control over a defined and replicable product to take into the formative evaluation process in Chapter 11. We understand, of course, that you may be well along in a design project as you work your way through this text. You may already have planned learning components that cannot be provided by wholly self-instructional means. This is fine; just be aware of the necessity to ensure that the learning components are carried out during instruction as you have designed them.

Rough Drafts

We all know what the term *rough draft* means because we have all written rough drafts of assignments and papers that have subsequently been revised into a final form. *Rough draft* means about the same thing when applied to instructional materials, but it carries the additional meaning that the product is developed in alternate, simpler, less-expensive media formats.

The purpose for doing a rough draft of materials is to create a quick, low-cost version of your design to have something to take into formative evaluation and try out with an SME, several learners, or a group of learners and to guide final production. The thought is that the time to catch any problems with the instructional materials is when they can still be revised without great expenditures of time and money. The design model we follow throughout this text has a feedback line, *Revise instruction*, that marks the point where rough-draft materials encounter that revision process.

A troublesome thought at this point might be "How can I determine whether my instructional planning and materials are effective from a rough-draft version?" Research in learning from different media formats suggests that where actual mastery of knowledge and skills is concerned, there is very little difference between rough draft and finished product. For example, a student most often will learn just as much from watching a video as from looking at hand-drawn storyboard cards and listening to a person read the script. As one might expect, the attention and motivational effects of the experience are different, but rough-draft tryouts are used routinely in formative evaluation of complex and expensive media. Developers even use illustrator art or computer-generated art to determine whether children will like and identify with cartoon characters that will later be created for film or video. Table 10.3 lists examples of rough-draft versions for a few final media formats. As you look them over, recall that the purpose for the draft is a quick and cheap product to take into formative tryouts.

Even those with well-developed skills in multimedia production should keep time commitments in mind and remember that the desired outcome is rough-draft materials for formative evaluation. Anyone with decent word-processing skills can quickly create rough drafts of text and either draw by hand or electronically insert pictures and graphic illustrations; most of us have learned PowerPoint or other simple presentation software for which there are abundant good examples of text design and media formatting that you can emulate for a wide range of content and learner ages. If you start production in PowerPoint, most multimedia authoring programs will import it so you can add features and functionality that you want in your final version and then save your materials in HTML. Even low-end, user-friendly desktop publishing applications such as Broderbund's Print Shop Professional and Microsoft's Publisher include style guides and templates that make good-looking illustrated text easy to produce. Sticking with simple media or illustrated text keeps one's focus on the whole point of this text—that is, the design, development, and validation of effective instruction—rather than production of

Table 10.3 Examples of Suggested Rough-Draft Formats for Formative Evaluation Trials

If Final Medium Will Be	Then Rough-Draft Version Could Be
Illustrated text	Word processed; loose-leaf notebook with hand-drawn or clip-art illustration
Laminated booklet	8½-by-11inch card stock
Activity centers and learning centers	"Flimsy" versions of materials that, in final form, must be "heavy duty" to resist wear and tear
Presentation graphics program, such as PowerPoint	These programs are so user-friendly that it is easiest to create rough-draft materials directly in the presentation program using drawing tools and a good clip-art collection and then type lecture notes or narration into the "notes view."
Video	Hand-drawn storyboards with script notes or full scripts with illustrator art are still used for formative trials, although technological advances have tended to make storyboarding less detailed than it once was. SLR digital video, cell phone video, digital camcorders, and user-friendly desktop video editing programs have made it possible to record inexpensive draft footage and rough-cut it into AVI, WMV, MOV, or QuickTime format for formative tryouts if one has the equipment and skills.
Multimedia computer-based instruction (e.g., Articulate, OpusPro, Flash, Autoplay)	Hand-drawn screen designs (called wireframes in the digital design industry) with flowchart of decision points, media events, and hyperlinks can be used for formative review; mock-ups with realistic screen design but no functionality are often developed for proof-of-concept and esthetic review; prototypes are sometimes developed then refined in user-friendly, lower-tech programs (e.g., rough draft in PowerPoint and then import PowerPoint instruction into Articulate to finish prototype in Flash) for user testing of look, functionality, and learner appeal and effectiveness.
e-Learning (e.g., Articulate, Captivate, Elucidat; as well as LMSs such as Canvas, Absorb, and Moodle, which have extensive course construction tools built in)	Same as above (all programs mentioned can be ported for web delivery)

mediated materials. The purpose for the materials development step in this chapter is to produce only a draft product that communicates well enough to allow a formative tryout with intended learners. Illustrated text or simple media can be used to take a manageable product into formative evaluation, where the focus can be on learning outcomes rather than media production variables.

Materials Development Tools and Resources

Production of mediated materials requires a whole set of skills, both artistic and technical, that can range from simple word processing to creating interactive materials for web-based delivery. To develop familiarity and skills with typical materials planning and production tools, readers are referred to the References and Recommended Readings section at the end of this chapter. Smaldino et al. (2019) provide overviews of current instructional media formats along with guidelines and tips for materials planning, design, and development. Several references at the end of this chapter include instruction on digital audio and video as well as computer-based and web-based multimedia. Technologies change so quickly that listings in this text could soon be outdated; however, there are two good sources for this type of specialized information. Paperback literature available in computer stores, in bookstores, and through web-based vendors make up the "how-to" manuals that quickly follow new releases of computer applications, programming, and authoring tools. The other source is the web itself. To find the most current information on a computer application or authoring tool, just type the brand name into a search engine, and you will likely find websites maintained by the publisher and other users as well as references for user forums, blogs, developer conferences, webinars, YouTube "how-to" videos, and so forth.

Rapid Prototyping

Anyone experienced in multimedia authoring knows the time and energy requirements for developing and testing complex computer-based instruction. The thought of "doing it several times" for the sake of formative evaluation is daunting, but that is exactly what happens in an instructional materials development process called **rapid prototyping**, a term borrowed from manufacturing where computer-aided design (CAD) technology enables direct reproduction of 3-D computer models into physical prototypes that can be 3-D printed in a variety of plastics and metals for evaluating design specifications. In many learning contexts, technologies and training requirements change so quickly that instructional designers have rethought some of the traditional approaches to instructional design. The first strategy used in rapid prototyping is to go light on the early analysis steps of an instructional design model and then develop prototype instructional materials rapidly and use quick iterative cycles of formative evaluation and revision to shape the final form of the materials. Rapid prototyping can be thought of as a series of informed and successive approximations, emphasizing the word *informed* because this developmental approach relies absolutely on information gathered during tryouts to ensure the success of the final product. Jones and Richey (2000) report an interesting case study detailing rapid-prototyping methodology, and Desrosier (2011) provides definitions, rationales, and methodologies for rapid instructional design.

The second strategy is concurrent design and development; that is, much of the front-end analysis work is conducted while the first rough-draft materials are being developed. This might seem like getting the cart before the horse, but recall that rapid prototyping occurs primarily in high-tech and quickly changing learning contexts. The thinking here is that trainers designing cutting-edge technological products will not know answers to critical design questions unless they are also involved in product development with those technologies. Figure 1.2 (p. 6) is a diagram of concurrent design and development. In team instructional design settings, there is a premium on accurate and continuous communication between those working in design and those working in materials development if the benefits of simultaneous activity are to be realized. The concept of using rough-draft materials for tryouts still holds in this type of prototyping, with the focus of early approximations being on the functionality of the user interface, the flow of program events, and learners' navigation through the instruction. In later iterations the focus shifts to learners' performance, and then, as the instruction nears its final form, fancy artwork and graphics and the details of learners' participation are added to the product.

The rapid-prototyping process is quite complex in large instructional development projects involving interactive computer-based and web-based multimedia. In such efforts, many stages of instructional design, materials development, and formative evaluation occur simultaneously. For example, in production of computer-based instruction, one feature could be in the design phase while another is undergoing development and yet another is in prototype testing. It is easy to fall into a pattern of thinking that instructional design is a strictly linear process, but this is misleading because tracking design and development activities reveals a sequence of overlapping and circular patterns that duplicates the iterative product design and development process.

Rapid prototyping is a combination of analysis, design, development, and evaluation and fits loosely in the category of user-centered design methodologies because of its heavy reliance on user involvement in analysis stages and in iterative cycles of formative evaluation. In this regard, rapid prototyping is similar to research-based design and agile design and shares some traits with the successive approximations model, all of which were mentioned in Chapter 8. The task at hand, however, is to get on with preparing rough-draft materials for evaluation with learners.

Job Aid

Developing the First Draft of Your Instruction

The following list should serve as a review of the path you have taken thus far in your own design and remind you of the materials you will need to embark on the development of instruction. You will need (a) instructional goal, (b) instructional analysis, (c) performance objectives, (d) sample test items, (e) characteristics of the target learners, and (f) characteristics of the learning and performance contexts. You will also need an instructional strategy that includes prescriptions for the following: (a) cluster and sequence of objectives, (b) preinstructional activities, (c) assessments to be used, (d) content presentation and learning guidance, (e) learner participation (practice and feedback), (f) strategies for memory and transfer skills, (g) activities assigned to individual lessons, (h) student groupings and media selections, and (i) a delivery system.

The preceding list illustrates how far we have come in the instructional design process. As a job aid, we have outlined the steps needed to develop the first draft of your instruction. You can use it as a checklist to keep you on track as you write your materials to motivate and inform the learners, present content and guidance for each objective, provide practice and feedback, and implement your assessment and memory and transfer strategies.

1. Review the instructional strategy for each objective in each lesson.
2. Review your analysis of the learning context and your assumptions about resources available for developing materials.

3. Reconsider the delivery system and the media chosen to present the materials, to monitor practice and feedback, to evaluate, and to enhance learner memory and transfer.
4. Decide on the components of the package of instructional materials.
5. Survey the literature and ask SMEs to determine what instructional materials are already available.
6. Consider how you might adopt or adapt available materials.
7. Begin organizing and adapting available materials, using the instructional strategy as a guide.
8. Determine whether new materials must be developed.
9. If so, review your analysis of learners. For each lesson, consider the instructor's role in facilitating instruction and determine the degree to which you want the instruction to be self-paced, group-paced, or mixed.
10. Plan and write the instructional materials in rough-draft form based on the instructional strategy. You will be amazed at how stick figures and rough illustrations can bring your ideas to life for a first trial. Printed, visual, or auditory materials in this rough form allow you to check your sequence, flow of ideas, accuracy of illustration of ideas, completeness, pace, and so on. Make a rough set of materials as complete as is reasonably needed for each instructional activity.
11. Review each completed lesson or learning session for clarity and flow of ideas.
12. Using one complete instructional unit, write the accompanying instructions to guide the students through any required activities.
13. Using the materials developed in this first inexpensive rough draft, begin evaluation activities. Chapter 11 introduces and discusses procedures and activities for evaluating and revising instructional materials.
14. You may either develop materials for the instructor's manual as you go along or take notes as you develop and revise the instructional presentations and activities. Using the notes, you can write the instructor's guide later.

Evaluation and Revision

Rubric for Evaluating Instructional Materials

Criteria for evaluating instructional materials are included in the following rubric. This checklist is a useful job aid to evaluate the completed materials you have developed if you are doing a design and development project during this course. You will note that this rubric is a checklist of the criteria discussed earlier in this chapter for evaluating existing materials for use in a new instructional product. The criteria are equally applicable for evaluating newly developed materials. Despite the draft stage of your materials, the last section on technical criteria is useful for selecting existing instructional materials.

Designer note: If an element is not relevant for your project, mark NA in the No column.

No	Some	Yes	**A. Goal-Centered Criteria** Are the instructional materials:
___	___	___	1. Congruent with the terminal and performance objectives?
___	___	___	2. Adequate in content coverage and completeness?
___	___	___	3. Authoritative?
___	___	___	4. Accurate?
___	___	___	5. Current?
___	___	___	6. Objective in presentations (lack of content bias)?

B. Learner-Centered Criteria Are the instructional materials appropriate for learners':

___ ___ ___ 1. Vocabulary?
___ ___ ___ 2. Developmental level (complexity)?
___ ___ ___ 3. Background, experience, environment?
___ ___ ___ 4. Experiences with testing formats and equipment?
___ ___ ___ 5. Motivation and interest?
___ ___ ___ 6. Diversity: cultural, racial, gender needs (lack bias)?

C. Learning-Centered Criteria Do the materials include:

___ ___ ___ 1. Preinstructional materials?
___ ___ ___ 2. Appropriate content sequencing?
___ ___ ___ 3. Presentations that are complete, current, and tailored for learners?
___ ___ ___ 4. Practice exercises that are congruent with the goal?
___ ___ ___ 5. Adequate and supportive feedback?
___ ___ ___ 6. Appropriate assessments?
___ ___ ___ 7. Appropriate sequence and chunk size?

D. Context-Centered Criteria Are/do the instructional materials:

___ ___ ___ 1. Authentic for the learning and performance sites?
___ ___ ___ 2. Feasible for the learning and performance sites?
___ ___ ___ 3. Require additional equipment/tools?
___ ___ ___ 4. Have congruent technical qualities for planned site (facilities/delivery system)?
___ ___ ___ 5. Have adequate resources (time, budget, personnel availability and skills)?

E. Technical Criteria Do the instructional materials have appropriate:

___ ___ ___ 1. Delivery system and media for the nature of objectives?
___ ___ ___ 2. Packaging?
___ ___ ___ 3. Graphic design and topography?
___ ___ ___ 4. Durability?
___ ___ ___ 5. Legibility?
___ ___ ___ 6. Audio and video quality?
___ ___ ___ 7. Interface design?
___ ___ ___ 8. Navigation?
___ ___ ___ 9. Functionality?
___ ___ ___ 10. Other?

Even though your materials are in a rough-draft stage, this is the time in the development process to take action on any concerns that might have been raised as you went through the rubric, and avoid focusing only on technical criteria for your materials. Think carefully through previous decisions you have made regarding goals, learners, learning strategies, and contexts, and then go back and make any adjustments based on any "light bulbs" that blinked on as you were reviewing the rough-draft materials.

Examples

This section includes an example of instructor-led instruction for the instructional goal of playing golf. We illustrate the instruction for session 2 on putting for a reason. The teaching-golf professional leading the interactive sessions is skilled in golf and can easily work from the instructional strategy to prepare for each interactive, live teaching session. Imagine as an expert being expected to memorize a script in order to implement interactive instruction on putting. It is important, however, for the golf pro-instructor to review the instructional strategy in order to be clear about the instructional designer's intentions for the lesson. Thus, the instructional package consists of both a reference copy of the instructional strategy and the knowledge and experience of the teaching professional.

Notice there are some changes from the original instructional strategy depicted in Table 9.4 and this one in Table 10.4. Notice the table is now in outline format to enable easy scanning by instructor. Next, the learning context (environment and facilities), the equipment needed, and the media selection are stated up front for the instructor to facilitate planning. Also note that there are two learner groupings specified: one for the demonstrations and one for the practice activities.

Table 10.4 Instructional Strategy for Instructor-Led Session on Planning a Putt in Golf (Enabling Skill I.1)

Content	Session 2 2 hours Planning the putt portion only (OBJECTIVES: I.1.a through I.1)
Learning Context	Live performance (golf professional and learners) on regulation practice putting green at golf club. Practice putting green must contain holes with typical conditions present (lay of the land: steepness, curvature, and force; surface conditions: slope or drag).
Equipment, Media Selection	Each player has one sleeve of golf balls (three), their own putter, a pamphlet on etiquette and rules of golf, and a YouTube video on putting.
Presession	Following session 1, learners receive YouTube video via their smartphones of various players and their caddies planning putting strokes together, gripping the putter, addressing the ball, and stroking the ball toward the cup. Learners encouraged to physically "warm up" with stretching exercises and then practice individually strokes they saw on the video approximately thirty-plus minutes before the instructional session begins.

Content for I.1 Portion Only	• Respected golf pro-instructor:
	  • praises group of learners for their putting during warm-up,
	  • indicates that they will easily master the fundamentals of putting,
	  • stresses that applying fundamentals of putting will save many strokes during play,
	  • indicates that golf games are lost and won on the putting green,
	  • tells factors that influence the trajectory of a putt (lay of the land: steepness, curvature, and force; surface conditions: slope or drag of the putting green),
	  • predicts (talks through) expected trajectory for given hole,
	  • demonstrates exaggeration of each condition by tossing a golf ball toward the cup (e.g., too much and too little force), and
	  • describes the outcome of error.
	• Examples:
	  • Slope, link to pedaling a bike up/down hills: little force to coast down, pedal hard to go up
	  • Curvature, link to walking around a steep hillside, more energy to stay up rather than rolling down
	  • Drag, link to walking through tall or short grass, rolling a ball through smooth putting green and lumpy sand trap

Learner Groupings for Explanations and Demonstrations	Group of sixteen learners at side of putting green in location requested by instructor to observe particular demonstration; class listens to instructor's explanation and observes demonstrations.

Table 10.4 Continued

Learner Participation and Groupings for Participation	Practice items and activities: Particular holes on green preidentified that have required green conditions. • Learners divided into pairs at different holes. They study and discuss lay of land and slope conditions. • Learners orally predict trajectory and force required to reach hole from a variety of locations around current hole. • After discussing, each learner rolls (by hand) a golf ball at the planned force and predicted trajectory. • Pair then discusses the success of planned trajectory, distance from hole, and location based on resting location of golf ball. • Pair plans approaches to getting closer to hole. • Using a second ball, each member executes new plan from same position and compares new outcome with first outcome.
Feedback	• Actual resting location of golf balls tossed by each group member • Conversation among group members • Comments by professional who circulates among pairs of learners
Follow-Through	Learners return to total group to hear instructor's explanation and watch demonstration of next enabling skill in session 2 (I.2 and I.3, assume stance and grip club). Following instruction and practice for session 2 on all putting skills (I.1 through I.6), learners are encouraged to remain on practice range to continue practicing putting skills.

Case Study

Group Leadership Training

Selected parts of the instructional strategy for the group leadership unit are used to illustrate materials development. From the many performance objectives that could be illustrated, we have chosen two: objective 6.3.1, "Naming strategies that encourage and stifle member cooperation," and objective 6.4.1, "Classifying strategies that encourage and stifle member cooperation." See Table 9.8 (p. 271) for a complete list of the objectives included in session 10.

All materials illustrated are scripts for web-based distance instruction that learners study independently. They come together only for interactive meeting participation and interactive group leadership associated with objective 6.5.1 in Table 9.8, "In simulated problem-solving meetings with learner acting as group leader, initiate actions to engender cooperative behavior among group members."

These examples of rough-draft materials development assume that the instructional designer is sharing development responsibilities with a production specialist. The designer specified web-based instruction in the instructional strategy and has now scripted what will appear on the web pages. For the specific objectives illustrated in the example, the production specialist will use the scripting to create a web page design simulating a comic-book style, with cartoon characters and dialogue balloons. In the example that follows, a comment on mediation is included as each component of the instructional strategy is described. Note that the materials specified for web-based delivery in this example lesson could have been specified with equivalent learning effectiveness for broadcast television with a workbook, illustrated text on DVD, traditional classroom instruction with role-playing, or many other delivery systems. However, any delivery system chosen for the entire unit on group leadership skills must preserve students' opportunities to observe and participate in small-group interaction with adaptive feedback.

Preinstructional Activities

Mediation of Preinstructional Activities

The web-based instructional materials prescriptions for this session are scripts for web presentations as well as any of the inexpensive graphic and color enhancements that are readily available for web-based instruction. These enhancements are intended to stimulate motivation and interest value.

Motivation Materials and Session Objectives

Table 10.5 shows an example of motivational materials and session objectives written by an instructional designer. (See Table 9.6, p. 269, for the instructional strategy for these materials.) The left column identifies particular learning components from the instructional strategy, and the right column contains the instruction, which highlights the links between instruction and instructional strategy, making the relationships easier for you to follow. (The session information and material in the left column do not appear in the actual instruction.)

Figure 10.1 includes an illustration of how photographs and comic book characters can be used to convert these preinstructional activities scripts to web-based instructional materials. This sample of how the materials developer creates the web presentation is provided to spark your imagination and illustrate how scripts can be given personality and interest value. Imagine converting the remaining materials to web-based instruction after you study the scripts, focusing on the nature of the content and its relationship to the components of the instructional strategy.

Table 10.5 **Preinstructional Activities for the Group Leadership Instructional Goal**

Learning Component	Instruction
Introduction/ motivation	Throughout America, we have good intentions of working together to make our campuses safe. We bond together in times of crisis, forming search parties for a missing student or accompanying students to their cars or dorms after an evening class. We always work relentlessly until the crisis is resolved. When there is no immediate crisis, however, we often have difficulty forming cohesive groups that persist in systematic efforts to improve and sustain campus safety. We have seen illustrations of the positive differences that effective leadership can make on our campuses, and we have examined the activities and impact of several campus groups around the state. The key factor in forming and maintaining an effective program is leadership. On your campus, *you* are the key ingredient to an effective program and improved safety for all students, faculty, campus personnel, and guests.
Linking to previous skills	During previous sessions, we practiced group leadership skills related to planning and preparation skills for meetings. You also rehearsed techniques for managing the thought line for the group, and you experienced the difference you can make using thought line management techniques during a problem-solving meeting. To this point in discussion groups, your actions have been rather directive: preparing materials, inviting participants, and keeping the group on the topic with thought line management techniques. Your direction in these areas is critical for helping your colleagues examine different facets of safety issues and plan safety programs.

Table 10.5 Continued

Learning Component	Instruction
Session objectives	There is another important ingredient in effective group leadership: managing cooperative group interaction during meetings. Regardless of the topic of the meeting, the level of members' preparation, or the resulting plan of action, participants are most likely to view your meetings as worth their time and effort when their interaction in the group is comfortable and cooperative. Leader actions for managing cooperative interaction are more democratic than those we have covered to this point; their purpose is to draw out participants. These actions are interwoven in a discussion with actions you use to manage the thought line. In this session, however, we set aside thought line actions and focus specifically on actions for encouraging cooperative group interaction. You can use three main strategies as the leader to manage cooperative group interaction during meetings: 1. Engender cooperative member behaviors 2. Recognize and defuse members' blocking behaviors (if they occur) 3. Recognize and alleviate group stress if it appears You will spend the next four sessions practicing and refining your leadership skills in these three main areas. During this session, our focus will be on skills related to engendering cooperative member behaviors, and we will work on the following three main skills: 1. Recognizing cooperative member behaviors 2. Recognizing leader actions that encourage or stifle member cooperation during meetings 3. Using leader actions ourselves to encourage member cooperation during meetings Many of you have participated in problem-solving discussion groups in the past, and a few of you have served as leaders for discussion groups. As a beginning, watch a leader lead a group-discussion meeting and see how many of these leader behaviors you already recognize.

Figure 10.1 Graphic Example of How Preinstructional Text Material Can Be Converted Using Graphics for Web-Based Delivery

Pretest

The pretest for session 10 covers only objective 6.4.2, "Given videos of staged problem-solving meetings, classify leaders' actions that are likely to encourage or stifle member cooperation." Objectives 6.3.1 and 6.4.1 are both subordinate to 6.4.2 and are embedded in the pretest exercise for 6.4.2. Objective 6.5.1, the highest-level skill in this cluster, is not included in the pretest because it requires the learner to lead an actual interactive group meeting. Requiring a public demonstration of skill prior to instruction on the skills does not seem appropriate for this adult group.

Mediation of Pretest

As prescribed in the objective and instructional strategy, the pretest consists of directions for learners, a learner response form, and a streaming video of a simulated meeting. Learners print a "working copy" of the response form from the website to use as they view the video. For the pretest, they can view the video only twice, marking their responses on the response form as they watch. Following the second viewing, they access the interactive pretest form on the website and respond to questions about the number and type of leader and member actions they observed in the meeting. Table 10.6 contains the directions and the learners' response sheet.

Table 10.6 Sample Pretest for Group Leadership Instructional Goal (Session 10, Objective 6.4.2 in Tables 9.7 and 9.8)

Learning Component	Pretest Directions
Pretest	Detecting leader behaviors that encourage or stifle group cooperation during meetings **Directions:** Print web form 6.1 and then watch web video 6.1: *Leader Behaviors That Encourage and Stifle Cooperative Learning*. In the video, a meeting is underway, and members are discussing problems with campus safety in dorms, in classrooms, and throughout campus. They are examining possible actions they can take to eliminate opportunities for crime and actions that can lessen crime in the future. The form you printed contains twelve specific leader actions that either encourage or stifle group members' cooperation during a meeting. Study the list carefully. Can you pick out these actions used by the group leader in the meeting? As you watch the video presentations: 1. Check all the purposeful actions that Eloise McLaughlin, the group leader, directly makes during the meeting to encourage her colleagues' participation and cooperation. She may exhibit some of the behaviors more than once and others not at all. Each time she exhibits an encouraging behavior, place a check mark (✓) in the "Do" column next to the behavior. 2. Place a check mark in the "Don't" column each time that Eloise takes one of the actions that stifles cooperation. For example, if Eloise uses questions as a way to suggest points of discussion five times, you should place a check mark (✓) in the "Do" column of your checklist each time she demonstrates this skill. However, if she directly tells the group what she wants them to discuss two times, you should place a check mark in the "Don't" column each time she directly tells the group what to discuss. Notice how her actions are recorded on the response form in the following example:

DO TALLY	ELOISE'S COOPERATION-ENCOURAGING ACTIONS	ELOISE'S COOPERATION-STIFLING ACTIONS	DON'T TALLY
✓✓✓✓✓	Suggests points of discussion as questions	Prescribes topics for the group to consider	✓✓

The group meeting segment runs for eight minutes. Watch the video meeting straight through; then watch it a second time. As you watch the meeting progress, use the form to record your judgments about the group management skills Eloise exhibits during the meeting. When you finish marking your checklist, go to web pretest 6.1. Use the form you have been working on to fill in the pretest and click the "Send Pretest" button when you are done.

1. Suggests points of discussion as questions	1. Prescribes topics for the group to consider
2. Uses an investigative, inquiring tone	2. Uses an authoritative tone
3. Uses open terms such as *perhaps* and *might*	3. Uses prescriptive terms such as *must* or *should*

Table 10.6 Continued

4. Hesitates and pauses between speakers	4. Fills quiet gaps with personal points of view or solutions
5. Willingly turns over the floor to group members who interrupt	5. Continues to talk over interrupting members or interrupts member
6. Encompasses total group with eyes, inviting all to participate freely	6. Focuses gaze on a few members
7. Nonverbally (eyes, gestures) encourages speaker to address group	7. Holds speaker's attention
8. Uses comments that keep discussion centered in the group	8. Encourages discussion to flow through leader by evaluating member comments
9. Encourages volunteerism (e.g., "Who has experience with . . .?")	9. Designates speakers and speaking order (e.g., "Beth, what do you think about . . . ?")
10. Refers to *us*, *we*, or *our*	10. Refers to *I*, *me*, *mine*, or *your*
11. Acknowledges group accomplishments	11. Acknowledges own accomplishments or those of particular members
12. Praises group effort and accomplishment	12. Singles out particular people for praise

Content Presentation and Learning Guidance

Mediation of Instruction

We present in this chapter only a segment of the lengthy instruction needed for the objectives in session 10. Assume that instruction for objectives 6.1.1 through 6.2.2 is already complete and that we are developing instruction only for objectives 6.3.1 and 6.4.1. Instruction is web-based and can be accessed by learners in their homes or wherever they have Internet access. The web-based instruction for these two objectives will be created using a comic book instructor and a conversational format, such as illustrated in Figure 10.2 for objective 6.4.1, which roughly illustrates how the committee members will appear in the web-based instruction. Jackson, the leader in this example, is offering introductory comments to the group. Encouraging behaviors are highlighted for learners using callout boxes and arrows.

Figure 10.2 Rough Example of Content Presentation Script in Table 10.5 Converted for Web-Based Instruction

Instruction

Table 10.7 shows the content and learning guidance in session 10 for objectives 6.3.1 and 6.4.1, naming and recognizing leader actions that encourage or stifle cooperative interaction among members. Notice that for objective 6.4.1, an actual script of a meeting is provided. The numbers beside each person's comments during the meeting form a key that links the comments to the leader actions presented in objective 6.3.1. This presentation exercise begins to link verbal information actions to interactive human actions during a meeting.

Table 10.7 Content Presentation and Learning Guidance for Group Leadership Instructional Goal

Session 10, Engendering Cooperative Member Behaviors: Content and Examples for Objective 6.3.1, When Asked in Writing to Name Leader Actions That Encourage or Stifle Member Discussion and Cooperation, Name These Actions

As the discussion leader, there are many actions you can take to encourage cooperation among group members. All these actions are designed to draw out members' ideas and suggestions and to demonstrate the importance of their participation. Your actions during a discussion should place participating members in the foreground while placing yourself in the background. Your personal ideas, solutions, and conclusions are put on hold during the meeting; your job is to get all members actively involved in examining the problem, volunteering ideas and suggestions, weighing the strengths and weaknesses of ideas suggested, and settling on the best solutions that alleviate or minimize given problems in the community. Remember that good solutions identified in meetings are most likely to be carried out if group members participate in forming the solutions and have a personal commitment to them.

Although many actions can encourage or stifle cooperative behavior during a discussion, let's focus our attention on twelve key actions that enhance cooperation, each of which has a complementary stifling counterpart (e.g., do this [*encouraging*] rather than that [*stifling*]). The twelve action pairs (encouraging and stifling) can be divided into four main categories with three pairs each, as illustrated by the following list.

Leader actions that facilitate or stifle cooperative interaction
(Notice that each encouraging and stifling action pair is bridged with the term *rather than.*)

I. Appearing open-minded and facilitating to group members rather than directive when introducing or changing the topic or suggesting paths the group might take. Specific actions to achieve this impression include the following:
   1. Suggesting points of discussion as questions rather than prescribing topics for the group to consider
   2. Using an investigative and enquiring tone rather than an authoritative one
   3. Using open terms such as *perhaps* and *might* rather than prescriptive terms such as *must* or *should*

II. Demonstrating a genuine desire for others to contribute rather than treating them as if they are providing you with an audience. Certain actions effectively leave this impression with your group members:
   4. Hesitating and pausing between speakers rather than filling quiet gaps by offering personal points of view or solutions
   5. Willingly turning over the floor to group members who interrupt you rather than continuing to talk over the interrupting member
   6. Encompassing the total group with your eyes, inviting all to participate freely, rather than focusing your gaze on a few members you know are ready contributors

III. Helping group members focus on themselves, their needs, and their ideas rather than on you as the leader. You can achieve this objective using the following actions:
   7. Nonverbally (eyes, gestures) encouraging speakers to address the group rather than addressing only you
   8. Using comments that keep discussion centered in the group rather than encouraging discussion to flow through you (e.g., "Are there any more thoughts on that idea?" rather than "I like that, Karen, tell me more about it")
   9. Encouraging volunteerism rather than designating speakers and speaking order (e.g., "Who has experience with . . . ?" rather than "Beth, what do you think about . . . ?")

IV. Moving ownership of ideas from individual contributors to the whole group. Ownership transfer can be accomplished in the following ways:
   10. Referring to *us, we,* or *our* rather than *I, me, mine,* or *your*
   11. Acknowledging group accomplishments rather than your own or those of particular members
   12. Praising group efforts and accomplishments rather than singling out particular people for praise

When you exhibit these twelve encouraging behaviors consistently in leading group discussions, group members are more productive and reach better decisions than if you use the alternative stifling behaviors.

Table 10.7 Continued

Session 10, Engendering Member Cooperative Behaviors: Content and Examples for Objective 6.4.1, Given Written Descriptions of a Group Leader's Actions During a Meeting, Indicate Whether the Actions Are Likely to Encourage or Stifle Cooperative Group Interaction

It may be helpful to examine a group leader using each of these twelve cooperation-encouraging actions while leading a group discussion. In the following meeting script, Jackson, the student leader, demonstrates each of the behaviors. The meeting script appears in the right column, and the left column is used to highlight particular actions. The actions are linked to the previous list by number (1–12).

LEADER ACTIONS	MEETING SCRIPT
6. Eyes group inclusively 10. Use of terms *us, our, we* 11. Praises group for accomplishment 12. Does not praise individuals	**Jackson:** *(Smiling, eyes encompassing whole group)* I'm pleased that so many of *us* can be here tonight. During *our* last meeting, *we* discussed the crime problems *we* are having on campus and planned ways to try to reduce the amount of crime *we* see. *Our* three-point program appears to be having an incredible impact; crime statistics are down, and *we* have fewer opportunities for crime on campus. **Sam:** *(Addressing Jackson)* I think the improved lighting along the sidewalks and parking lot by the student union is helping. There have been fewer muggings and no cars stolen since the lighting was installed.
4. Hesitates, waiting for others to join	*(Jackson does not respond verbally; he awaits other members' comments.)* **Beth:** I think the issue of muggings on campus is very important, but I am more concerned with serious crimes like the shootings we see on other campuses. What should we— **Frank:** *(Interrupting Beth)* I see no way this committee can address the possibility of a deranged person entering a dorm or classroom and shooting students. **Beth:** Well, there might be some ways, like locking dorm doors after hours. We should investigate the type of safety measures campuses that have experienced such shootings are putting into place.
6. Eye contact with all 10. Use of terms *we, us* 1. Pose topic as question	**Jackson:** *(Looking around group)* Last meeting *we* agreed to invite Officer Talbot to talk with *us* about ways *we* can help protect ourselves from dorm burglaries. Is this still the area *we* want to address this evening?
9. Not designating speaker	*(Jackson again looks around the group and hesitates without calling on a particular member.)* **Abigail:** *(Addressing Jackson)* I want to talk about ways to protect ourselves from burglars. As I told you, our room was robbed last month while we were visiting Pittsburgh over the weekend. *(Jackson gestures with eyes and hands for Abigail to address her comments to the group.)*
7. Nonverbal gesture for speaker to address group	**Abigail:** *(Continuing to group)* I thought we had done everything we needed to do by telling our neighbors and the dorm supervisor and locking our door and windows, but obviously that wasn't enough.
4. Hesitates	*(Jackson hesitates, awaiting other members' responses to Abigail.)* **Sam:** *(Looking at Jackson)* I'd like some information on the nature of burglaries in our dorms.
8. No comment, evaluation	*(Jackson does not comment; instead, he looks inquiringly at Officer Talbot, the resource officer.)* **Officer Talbot:** During the past year, there were 125 burglaries on our campus, and over 90 percent of them occurred between 10:00 a.m. and 3:00 p.m., when you were at class. Most burglaries have been crimes of opportunity . . . we have made entering our dorm rooms relatively easy. The intruders entered through unlocked doors and windows— **Abigail:** *(Interrupting Talbot)* Our doors and windows were locked, and they still got in. They broke the bathroom window on the back of the building and crawled in over the sink! **Officer Talbot:** It happens, Abigail. I'm sure your intruders felt safer entering your room from the back side. They're typically looking for cash or items they can readily sell for cash, like jewelry, electronic equipment, guns, or other valuables easy to carry away. Typical burglars on this campus are local teenagers and other students. Only 15 percent of our burglaries have been committed by individuals who are considered pros. **Sam:** Thank you.

(continued)

Table 10.7 Continued

LEADER ACTIONS	MEETING SCRIPT
2. Uses enquiring tone 3. Uses terms *perhaps, might*	**Jackson:** *(Using enquiring tone)* It seems that the majority of our crimes are related to opportunities. Perhaps we might consider ways of removing— **Sam:** *(Interrupting Jackson)* Exactly. How can we remove the opportunities? *(Jackson turns interestedly to Sam.)*
5. Willingly turns over floor	**Frank:** I found a dorm security survey that helps students locate areas where they might be a little lax. **Officer Talbot:** I've seen those. What areas does your survey cover? **Frank:** Let's see. It covers examining windows, doors, landscaping, exterior lights, and interior lights. It's in a checklist format and would be easy for us to use and to share with all students who reside on campus.
12. Doesn't praise individual 2. Enquiring tone and response	**Jackson:** *(Does not praise Frank, although he believes that bringing the survey to the meeting was a good idea because it provides a catalyst for further group discussion)* May we make a copy of the survey to share around the group? Is it copyrighted? **Officer Talbot:** These surveys are typically provided by public service groups, and citizens are encouraged to copy and use them. **Frank:** Yes, we can copy and distribute it. It's produced and distributed from the campus police office. In fact, it gives a number here for obtaining more copies. I thought it was a good idea for our meeting this evening, so I brought enough copies for everyone. *(He passes copies of the survey to members around the table.)* **Officer Talbot:** I'll contact the office and get the extra copies. How many copies will we need?
3. Using term *probably* 12. Not praising individual 10. Moving ownership of survey from Frank to group with *our* survey	**Jackson:** We'll *probably* want enough copies for all dorms on campus. *(Turning to the group, without addressing or praising Frank)* Well, what does *our* survey say?

Notice that during Jackson's meeting, he exhibited each of the twelve positive behaviors at least once. Each of these group-encouraging behaviors is so subtle that it often is unnoticed by group members. However, taken together, the behaviors communicate clearly to group members that Jackson believes their input is valuable, he wants them to contribute, and he is not going to broker who gets to speak or when. Jackson's actions demonstrate clearly that he does not perceive his colleagues to be an audience or backdrop for him and one or two of his friends on campus.

Learner Participation

Mediation of Learner Participation and Feedback

The learner participation component is also formatted for web-based instruction, enabling learners to study independently. Learners can print the pages containing the script, locating and marking all instances of behavior directly on the printed pages. After completing the exercise, they can scroll down to the Feedback section, which repeats the meeting script with the behaviors enhancing and stifling marked. Learners can then compare their classification of the behaviors with those made by the designer, marking any discrepancies. These discrepancies can then be discussed in the online discussion board for session 10 or in person when leaders come for the next interactive session.

Learner Participation Script

The learner participation script for the web-based materials is illustrated in Table 10.8. Only a part of the script is illustrated; the actual script would continue until all twelve cooperation-encouraging and corresponding stifling behaviors

Table 10.8 **Learner Participation for the Group Leadership Instructional Goal**

Session 10, Engendering Cooperative Member Behaviors: Learner Participation for Objective 6.4.1

Directions: Can you locate each time one of these twelve key interaction leadership actions occurs in the following meeting? Darcy, the new group leader, is a law student who recently moved to a residence near the university. She has had several leadership roles in college, but this is her first time to work on the problem of campus crime and student safety. Young and inexperienced, she may commit errors or stifling actions as she manages her group's interaction. Having completed communications courses and participated in problem-solving discussions in college, however, she undoubtedly demonstrates several of the encouraging actions as well. Each time Darcy demonstrates an encouraging action, write the number of the action with a plus sign (+) in the left column of the same line. If she uses the action incorrectly (stifling), then write the action number with a minus sign (–). For example, if Darcy suggests a point of discussion as a question, place a +1 in the left column of that line; however, if she tells the group what to discuss, place a –1 in the left column preceding the line. Use a list of numbered leader actions identical to the one used in the pretest to aid your responses.

MARK LEADER ACTIONS IN THIS COLUMN	MEETING SCRIPT
	Darcy: Thank you all for coming this morning. I am so pleased to see this many of you returning and also to see several new faces. Why don't we begin by introducing ourselves? Some of you may want to share your reasons for joining us. Shall we start here on my left?
	(The fourteen graduate students and administrators in attendance begin to introduce themselves.)
	Darcy: At the conclusion of the last meeting, several of you suggested that we discuss ways to be safer as we move about the campus. On this topic, I have invited Sharon Wright to share some of the strategies they use with students who come to the Victims' Advocacy Center on campus.
	Darcy: *(Turning to Sharon)* Thank you for coming this morning, Sharon. Some of you may know Sharon. We are certainly lucky to have her with us. She has a Ph.D. in criminology with a master's in counseling and victim advocacy.
	Sharon: Thank you, Darcy. I'm very pleased to have been invited.
	Darcy: *(Looking around total group, smiling)* I have also made a list of topics suggested in Mann and Blakeman's book *Safe Homes, Safe Neighborhoods* on personal safety in the neighborhood. It appears to me that many of their ideas are appropriate for our housing areas and campus.
	Darcy: *(Continuing)* Our basic plan this morning is to generate information for a personal safety tips brochure that we can stuff in all dorm mailboxes and that Sharon will distribute through the Victims' Advocacy Center. I think we should begin with the issue of safety in the dorm since we're having such problems with robberies.
	Ben: I think that street safety is more problematic here, so—
	Darcy: *(Interrupting Ben)* That's a very good idea, Ben, and we should get to street safety as well.
	(Darcy remains quiet, looking around room for other suggestions from group.)
	Sharon: We should perhaps discuss safety in our parking lots on campus. There are several strategies we can use there to improve our chances of being safe.
	Darcy: That's a good idea, Sharon. Well, that's three good topics: dorm safety, street safety, and parking lot safety. Let's begin with these and see where they take us. Bob, you haven't said anything yet. Where would you like to start?
	Bob: Like Ben, I understand there are a lot of problems on our campus with street crimes such as muggings, purse snatchings, and so forth. Let's consider this area since most of us walk across campus at night following our evening classes. Our campus has some of the most dangerous sidewalks in this city!

The student participation script continues until all twelve cooperation and corresponding stifling behaviors are illustrated. We stop here because the nature of the student participation is established.

are illustrated. We stop before the end of the script because the nature of the student participation is established.

Feedback

Table 10.9 illustrates feedback for a segment of the participation exercise that learners could locate after completing the exercises in Table 10.8. In Table 10.9, the pluses and minuses shown in the left column indicate the designer's classification for whether the action was seen as enhancing (+) or stifling (−). Learners compare

Table 10.9 Feedback for the Group Leadership Instructional Goal

Session 10, Engendering Cooperative Member Behaviors: Feedback for Objective 6.4.1*

Directions: Once you have finished analyzing Darcy's cooperation enhancing and stifling actions, compare your marked script with the following. Each time your behaviors column does not match, circle the behavior on your script that differs from this script. Reread the script at the point of difference to see whether you wish to change your mind about the category. If not, we will discuss differences before moving on.

MARK LEADER ACTIONS IN THIS COLUMN	MEETING SCRIPT
+1 +3, +10 +1	**Darcy:** Thank you all for coming this morning. I am so pleased to see this many of you returning and also to see several new faces. Why don't we begin by introducing ourselves? Some of you may want to share your reasons for joining us. Shall we start here on my left?
	(The fourteen graduate students and administrators in attendance begin to introduce themselves.)
+11, +10 −10	**Darcy:** At the conclusion of the last meeting, several of you suggested that we discuss ways to be safer as we move about the campus. On this topic, I have invited Sharon Wright to share some of the strategies they use with students who come to the Victims' Advocacy Center on campus.
−11, −12	**Darcy:** *(Turning to Sharon)* Thank you for coming this morning, Sharon. Some of you may know Sharon. We are certainly lucky to have her with us. She has a Ph.D. in criminology with a master's in counseling and victim advocacy.
	Sharon: Thank you, Darcy. I'm very pleased to have been invited.
+6 −10	**Darcy:** *(Looking around total group, smiling)* I have also made a list of topics suggested in Mann and Blakeman's book *Safe Homes, Safe Neighborhoods* on personal safety in the neighborhood. It appears to me that many of their ideas are appropriate for our housing areas and campus.
−1, +10 −10, +10 −3, +10	**Darcy:** *(Continuing)* Our basic plan this morning is to generate information for a personal safety tips brochure that we can stuff in all dorm mailboxes and that Sharon will distribute through the Victims' Advocacy Center. I think we should begin with the issue of safety in the dorm since *we're* having such problems with robberies.
	Ben: I think that street safety is more problematic here, so—
−5, −8 +10, −3	**Darcy:** *(Interrupting Ben)* That's a very good idea, Ben, and we should get to street safety as well.
+4	*(Darcy remains quiet, looking around room for other suggestions from group.)*
	Sharon: We should perhaps discuss safety in our parking lots on campus. There are several strategies we can use there to improve our chances of being safe.
−8 −1	**Darcy:** That's a good idea, Sharon. Well, that's three good topics: Dorm safety, street safety, and parking lot safety. Let's begin with these and see where they take us. Bob, you haven't said anything yet. Where would you like to start?
	Bob: Like Ben, I understand there are a lot of problems on our campus with street crimes such as muggings, purse snatchings, and so forth. Let's consider this area since most of us walk across campus at night following our evening classes. Our campus has some of the most dangerous sidewalks in this city!

* To illustrate feedback, only a segment of the exercise is presented.

their classifications with those of the instructor. The right column repeats the script in Table 10.8 so that learners are not required to scroll up and down the screen to match the participation and feedback materials. Learners continue with the feedback material until they have compared all their responses and marked their inconsistent ratings for group discussion.

Following the learner feedback for objective 6.4.1, participants begin instruction for objective 6.4.2, "Classifying leaders' actions during interactive meetings." A streaming video is used in which learners observe segments of three meetings in progress. The information presentation and example segments demonstrate each of the encouraging and discouraging behaviors as well as show how the leader could have molded each of the stifling actions into complementary and encouraging actions.

As a participation activity, learners again classify all the encouraging actions the leader takes during the meeting session. In addition, for each stifling action encountered, they prescribe the action the leader should have taken instead. The feedback for this objective is also delivered using streaming video, with guided trips through the same meeting to revisit particular leader behaviors. During the feedback trip, as each stifling action is revisited, the leader changes actions before the learner's eyes, using complementary and encouraging behavior instead. Following instruction on objective 6.4.2, the learners finish session 10 with objective 6.5.1 and lead a small-group discussion of their own during a face-to-face session.

Professional and Historical Perspectives

New media have always been adopted for educational purposes. We can imagine Egyptian children taking home lessons on papyrus shortly after it was invented in 1000 BC and leafing through books at home after Gutenberg invented the printing press in 1446. Ben Franklin wanted to make books available to everyone and founded the first American public library in 1731. Then came a cascade of media that have uses in formal and informal education, including the phonograph (1877); photographic film (1885); motion pictures (1888); radio (1894); television transmission (1927); audio tape (1940); the large-scale digital computer (1944); color TV (1954); audio cassettes (1963); the Internet, e-mail, microprocessors, VCRs, and Apple I (1970s); PCs, hypertext, CDs, and laptops (1990s); WWW, web browsers, and DVDs (2000s), and so on, into all of the digital formats with which we are familiar today. For each new technology that found uses in education and training, industries developed to supply media materials and software for the *educational technology* market. As more and more sophisticated technologies were developed, so were required materials and software, and both were sold as the newest and best solutions for educational needs. Unfortunately, many of those best solutions spent most of their time on storage shelves in media centers or were considered surplus and sold for scrap. It is natural that newer generations of technology will replace older generations, but many times the technological solutions were developed and sold to solve problems that simply did not exist. Therein lies a rational for systematic design of instruction, where decisions are made about what will be taught, to whom, with what strategies before decisions are made about media and delivery systems. The design of the instruction determines the learning outcome; the medium does not.

This is precisely the point that Clark (1983) made in his controversial article on learning from media that sparked widespread debate among educational technologists and educational psychologists. Kozma (1991) added fuel to the controversy with his rebuttal of Clark's contentions, and the two continued with argument and counterargument in subsequent articles (Clark, 1994; Kozma, 1994). The discussion continues today with frequent citations of both authors in academic and popular literature. Clark's point that the design of instruction is the driver of effective learning is well taken by all, and Kozma's contention that certain affordances available in contemporary media provide unique contributions to learning has gained traction among many instructional designers. A brief article by Moffat (2013) provides a succinct observation on the unavoidable role of media in contemporary teaching and learning.

> Moffat emphasizes how the ubiquity of technology throughout all levels and contexts of education for which we design instruction *requires* ID professionals to meld good learning design with effective, efficient, positive media experiences for learners. Moffat also contends that learners will find media to support their learning whether it is part of their materials or not; so best to design with technology that is integrated for effective teaching and learning at the outset. The practical advice for designers is not Clark or Kozma, but Clark and Kozma; that is, embrace technology but be skeptical of over-hyped media and be open to finding characteristics available in specific media that will enhance the probability of achieving desired learning outcomes.

These authors view instructional media as one part of a system wherein all of the parts work together to achieve the desired outcome of effective learning, so we affirm the positive role of media in systematically designed instruction.

Learning objects were described earlier in this chapter, and technological standards were mentioned. The technological standards allow interoperability; that is, an electronic "handshake" can occur between a learning object and a learning management system that enables the object's features and functions to work as designed. If student interaction, a video, and a test are in the object, then learners will be able to interact, the video will play, learners will take the test, and the object will report the score to the student's profile in the LMS. Four different standards for interoperability are currently popular and built into the top-line LMSs used in business, public schools, and higher education: SCORM, xAPI, AICC, and LTI. Likewise, these standards are available as "save" options for inclusion in most advanced multimedia and e-learning software development programs. Textbook publishers and software developers take advantage of these standards so that a "course core" they have developed can be downloaded and opened with full-featured functionality in a client's LMS. For example, if you are enrolled in a course using this book and the course is housed on an LMS and the instructor has chosen to download the Pearson course core, then you may have access to two practice tests for each chapter, one on information and one on concepts.

That is the background on learning objects, but the real reason for the follow-up on this topic is to introduce a few of the many, many learning object repositories where one can search for all kinds of media that can be used in instruction. These media range from complete courses from Wisconsin that will display in an LMS to brief video clips from YouTube that may explain a concept or demonstrate a process. Browsing several of the following repositories is the best way to get a feel for what might be selected as existing materials for inclusion in an ID project.

MERLOT: https://www.merlot.org/merlot/index.htm

MIT: https://ocw.mit.edu/index.htm

UK Open University: https://www.open.edu/openlearn/

U. Delaware PBL Clearinghouse: https://www.itue.udel.edu/pbl/problems

WISC-Online (Wisconsin Community Colleges): https://www.wisc-online.com/

Kahn Academy: https://www.khanacademy.org/

YouTube: https://www.youtube.com/

eLL eLearningLearning: https://www.elearninglearning.com/

Process Flowcharts

Developing Instructional Materials

The two flowcharts (Figures 10.3 and 10.4) in this section should aid you in evaluating existing instructional materials and creating original rough-draft materials.

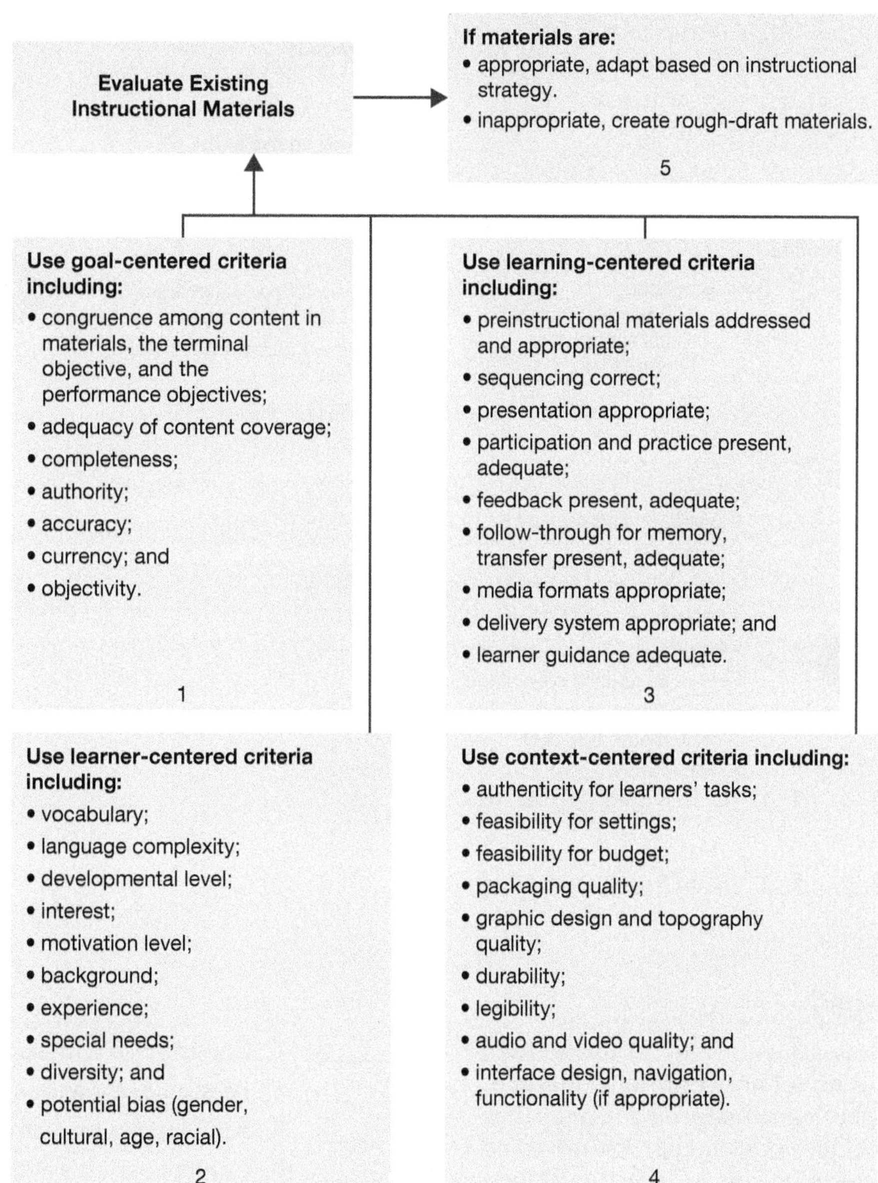

Figure 10.3 Evaluate Existing Instructional Materials

Practice

1. What are the three major components of an instructional package?
2. What types of learning components would you be most likely to include in the instructional materials?
3. What would you be likely to include in the instructor's guide portion of course management information?
4. Number the following materials showing your preferred order of development: ( ) instructional

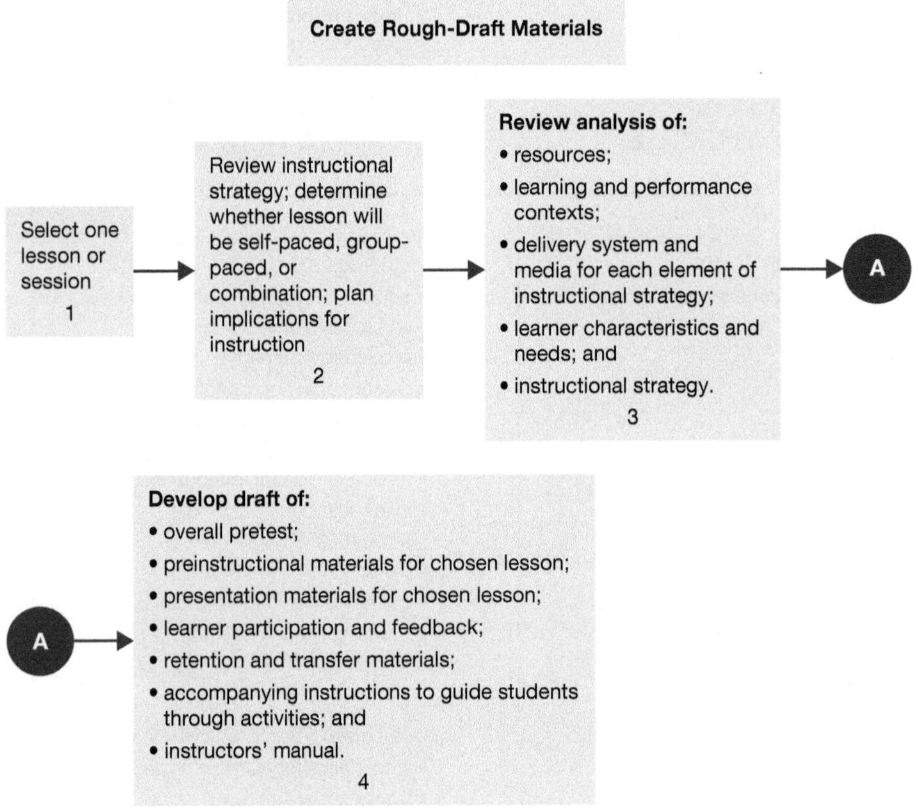

Figure 10.4 Create Rough-Draft Materials

Practice Continued

materials, ( ) assessments, and ( ) instructor's guide. (There is no set answer to this question, but with your developmental project in mind, it is time to give the developmental procedure some thought. This enables you to collect pertinent information at the proper time.)

Designers use five families of criteria to evaluate existing instructional materials. Match each of the following criteria with its family by placing the letter of the family in the space before each criterion.

a. Goal-centered criteria
b. Learner-centered criteria
c. Learning-centered criteria
d. Context-centered criteria
e. Technical criteria

_____ 5. Screen design quality
_____ 6. Complexity of vocabulary
_____ 7. Congruence with subordinate skills
_____ 8. Feasibility for learning environment
_____ 9. Authenticity for learning performance
_____ 10. Content expert's authority
_____ 11. Navigation ease
_____ 12. Adequacy feedback for learners
_____ 13. Audio or video quality
_____ 14. Currency of content

15. If you are creating instructional materials for a class project or some other project, your first step will likely be to create the preinstructional activities of motivation, objectives, and a readiness test for your instruction based on the prescriptions in your instructional strategy. Use your design documents (instructional goal through instructional strategy) to create the first part of your instruction.

Feedback

1. Instructional materials, assessments, and course management information
2. Instructional materials include:
   - preinstructional activities, including objectives and review materials as well as motivational materials and activities;
   - content that must be presented to students to enable them to achieve your objectives, including examples and nonexamples of information, concepts, or skills that must be learned;
   - participation activities that enable students to practice or to try out the concept or skills for themselves, and feedback on students' performance to enable reconsideration of their ideas or adjustment of their techniques;
   - assessments of learners' mastery of new information and skills; and
   - activities that enhance memory and transfer.
3. Instructors' guide should include:
   - information about the target population for the materials;
   - suggestions on how to adapt materials for older, younger, and higher- or lower-achieving students;
   - overview of the content;
   - intended learning outcomes of the instruction;
   - suggestions for using the materials in a certain context or sequence;
   - suggestions for a constructivist learning environment, when appropriate (goals, learners, contexts, resources);
   - suggestions for materials management for individualized learning, small-group learning, learning-center activities, or classroom activities;
   - retention and transfer activities;
   - tests that can be used to evaluate students' performance on terminal objectives;
   - evidence of the effectiveness of the materials when used as suggested with the intended target populations;
   - suggestions for evaluating student work and reporting progress;
   - estimation of time required to use the materials properly; and
   - equipment or additional facilities needed for the materials.
4. No rigid pattern of development exists, although the following order shows an example of procedure suitable for an instructional strategy, a unit of instruction, or whole course (subject to constraints on time, materials, and resources):
   - assessments that were probably completed in a previous design step and may just need final formatting;
   - instructional materials; and
   - course management information, including the instructor's guide and other information for implementing distance learning and self-paced instructional programs.
5. e
6. b
7. a
8. d
9. d
10. a
11. e
12. c
13. e
14. a
15. Once you have the instruction for the preinstructional activities created, use the rubric found just before this practice and feedback section to evaluate your instruction. What appears good? What should be changed? It would also be a good idea to ask a colleague in your group to review your design documents and your preinstructional materials using the rubric. Discuss your evaluations and any changes you believe are needed with your colleague.

References and Recommended Readings

Adnan, N. H., & Ritzhaupt, A. D. (2018). Software engineering design principles applied to instructional design: What can we learn from our sister discipline? *TechTrends, 62*, 77–94. https://doi.org/10.1007/s11528-017-0238-5. Highlights the formative iteration cycles employed in both design practices.

Agola, E. A., & Stefaniak, J. E. (2017). An investigation into the effect of job-aid design on customer troubleshooting performance. *Performance Improvement Quarterly, 30*(2), 93–120. Uses of interactive decision guides were compared with traditional process flowcharts. Users were more positive about their experience with the decision guides but were not more accurate in their troubleshooting decisions.

Aldrich, C. (2007). *Learning by doing: A comprehensive guide to simulations, computer games, and pedagogy in e-learning and other educational experiences.* Jossey-Bass. Integrates content, simulations, games, and pedagogy with training focus.

Allen, M. W., & Sites, R. (2012). *Leaving ADDIE for SAM.* ASTD Press.

Baldwin, S., & Ching, Y. (2019). Guidelines for designing online courses for mobile devices. *TechTrends.* https://doi.org/10.1007/s11528-019-00463-6. Focus is on making online learning accessible for students accessing instruction on smartphones and tablets through a learning management system.

Bates, A. W. (2019). *Teaching in a digital age: Guidelines for designing teaching and learning* (2nd ed.). BC Open Textbooks. https://pressbooks.bccampus.ca/teachinginadigitalagev2/.

Berg, G. A. (2003). *Knowledge medium: Designing effective computer-based learning environments.* IGI Publishing. Includes theory and practices, media theory, and film criticism.

Bishop, M. J., & Sonnenschwin, D. (2012). Designing with sound to enhance learning: Four recommendations from the film industry. *The Journal of Applied Instructional Design, 1*(2), 5–16. This article is addressed to instructional designers and provides guidance on appropriate use of sound in media.

Brill, J. M., Bishop, M. J., & Walker, A. E. (2006). The competencies and characteristics required of an effective project manager: A web-based Delphi study. *Educational Technology Research and Development, 48*(2), 115–140.

Clark, D. R. (2015). *Estimating costs and time in instructional design.* http://nwlink.com/~donclark/hrd/costs.html. The cost estimates on Don Clark's website may be somewhat dated, but he does provide useful information on categories to include in cost and time estimates for design and development of instructional materials.

Clark, R. E. (1983). Reconsidering research on learning from media. *Review of Educational Research, 53*(4), 445–459. Clark's initial argument regarding media effects on learning.

Clark, R. E. (1994). Media will never influence learning. *Educational Technology, Research and Development, 42*(2), 21.

Clark, R. E. (2012). *Learning from media: Arguments, analysis, and evidence* (2nd ed.). Information Age Publishing. A series of point and counterpoint articles regarding the effects of media and media attributes on learning.

Clark, R. E., & Lyons, C. (2010). *Graphics for learning: Proven guidelines for planning, designing, and evaluating visuals in training materials* (2nd ed.). Pfeiffer. Describes guidelines for best use of graphics in instructional materials.

Clark, R. E., & Mayer, R. E. (2011). *E-learning and the science of instruction: Proven guidelines for consumers and designers of multimedia learning* (3rd ed.). Pfeiffer. Provides a comprehensive review of multimedia learning in training and development settings.

Coombs, N. (2010). *Making online teaching accessible: Inclusive course design for students with disabilities.* Jossey-Bass. Presents ways to ensure course content and delivery are accessible to students with disabilities and comply with ADA standards.

Costello, V., Youngblood, E., & Youngblood, S. (2017). *Multimedia foundations: Core concepts for digital design.* Routledge. Describes concepts and skills for multimedia production and digital storytelling.

Dabner, D., Stewart, S., & Vickress, A. (2017). *Graphic design school: The principles and practice of graphic design* (6th ed.). Wiley. Provides applicable principles and examples for all contemporary media.

Desrosier, J. (2011). Rapid prototyping reconsidered. *The Journal of Continuing Higher Education, 59*, 135–145. Thorough discussion of rationale and methods for rapid prototyping instructional design.

Di Paolo, E., Wakefield, J. S., Mills, L. A., & Baker, L. (2017). Lights, camera, action: Facilitating the design and production of effective instructional videos. *TechTrends, 61*, 452–460. https://doi.org/10.1007/s11528-017-0206-0. Contains some information on planning, equipment, and production, but emphasis is on productive uses for video in instruction.

Driscoll, M. (2005). *Advanced web-based training strategies: Unlocking instructionally sound online learning.* Pfeifer.

Educational Technology Magazine, 46(1). (2006). Special issue on learning objects.

Educational Technology Magazine, 47(1). (2007). Special issue on the role of pedagogical agents in providing learning guidance. *Pedagogical agents* are the interface animations that come to life on the screen and provide (1) information, suggestions, and guidance;

(2) *peer buddies* that interact with the user in intelligent tutoring systems; or (3) the interactive avatars in role-playing games.

Fenrich, P. (2005). *Creating instructional multimedia solutions: Practical guidelines for the real world.* Information Science Publishing. Includes information on design teams, authoring tools, and digital media development.

Fleming, M., & Levie, W. H. (Eds.). (1993). *Instructional message design.* Educational Technology Publications. Classic text with excellent chapters on concept learning, problem solving, psychomotor skills, attitude change, and motivation.

Greer, M. (1994). *ID project management: Tools and techniques for instructional designers and developers.* Educational Technology Publications. Describes ID team organization and management with chapters on creating and testing rough-draft materials. This book is no longer in print, but the management model is still applicable. It is available to download from the author's website at http://mikegreersworthsharing.blogspot.com/p/pdf-collection-useful-tools-resources.html

Gustafson, K. L., & Brance, R. M. (1997). Revisioning models of instructional development. *Educational Technology Research and Development, 45*(3), 73–89. Includes commentaries on electronic performance support systems and rapid prototyping.

Halls, J. (2017). *Rapid media development for trainers.* ATD Press. Describes how to create training and instructional media inexpensively in-house.

Hannafin, M. J., & Peck, K. L. (1988). *The design, development, and evaluation of instructional software.* Macmillan. Describes the process of developing computer-based materials from instructional strategy prescriptions. Although an older text, it is still an excellent source.

Hillman, D., Schudy, R., & Temkin, A. (2020). *Best practices for administering online programs.* Routledge. Context for this book is academic higher education. Includes topics on design and development as well as management.

Hoard, B., Stefaniak, J., Baaki, J., & Draper, D. (2019). The influence of multimedia development knowledge and workplace pressures on the design decisions of the instructional designer. *Educational Technology Research and Development, 67*, 1479–1505. https://doi.org/10.1007/s11423-019-09687-y. This study reported that experienced developers tend to select media later in the ID process, and selection can be subject to employer demands, budget, and time constraints.

Horton, W. (2011). *e-Learning by design* (2nd ed.). Pfeiffer. Shows how to develop lessons, tests, games, and simulations and implement individualized instruction.

Jenlink, P. M. (Ed.). (2019). *Multimedia learning theory: Preparing for the new generation of students.* Rowman & Littlefield. Explores foundational concepts from cognitive psychology for use of media and explores generational issues in faculty and students.

Jonassen, D. H., Peck, K. L., & Wilson, B. G. (1999). *Learning with technology: A constructivist perspective.* Merrill/Prentice Hall. Focuses on the use of technology for engaging students in meaningful learning rather than the use of technology to deliver instructional content to learners.

Jones, T. S., & Richey, R. C. (2000). Rapid prototyping methodology in action. *Educational Technology Research and Development, 48*(2), 63–80.

Kozma, R. B. (1991). Learning with media. *Review of Educational Research, 61*(2), 179. Kozma's response to Clark's original article on media effects on learning.

Kozma, R. B. (1994). Will media influence learning? Reframing the debate. *Educational Technology, Research and Development, 42*(2), 7.

Lee, W. W., & Owens, D. L. (2004). *Multimedia-based instructional design: Computer-based training; web-based training; distance broadcast training; performance-based solutions* (2nd ed.). Pfeiffer.

Lim, D. O. O. H., & Yoon, S. W. (2008). Team learning and collaboration between online and blended learner groups. *Performance Improvement Quarterly, 21*(3), 59–72. Describes methods for enhancing learners' online and blended educational experiences.

Macleod, H., Haywood, J., Woodgate, A., & Alkhatnai, M. (2015). Emerging patterns in MOOCs: Learners, course designs, and directions. *TechTrends, 1*(59), 56–63. Not a how-to article; rather, answers questions about who is enrolling in the MOOCs offered at University of Edinburgh and for what purposes.

Mayer, R. E. (2014). *The Cambridge handbook of multimedia learning* (2nd ed.). Cambridge University Press. Describes research and theory in computer-based multimedia learning including learning from words and pictures.

Mayer, R. E. (2009). *Multimedia learning* (2nd ed.). Cambridge University Press. Presents design principles that have direct application in print materials and screen design.

Mayer, R. (Ed.). (2014). *The Cambridge handbook of multimedia learning* (Cambridge Handbooks in Psychology). Cambridge University Press. doi:10.1017/CBO9781139547369. How research-based principles can be applied in multimedia design.

Moffat, D. E. (2013). *Clark and Kozma debate: Is it still relevant?* https://dcmoffat71.wordpress.com/2013/04/17/clark-and-kozma-debate-is-it-still-relevant/

Newby, T. J., Stepich, D. A., Lehman, J. D., Russell, J. D., & Leftwich, A. T. (2011). *Educational technology for teaching and learning* (4th ed.). Pearson. Focuses on integrating instruction and technology for the classroom, including planning and developing instruction; grouping learners; selecting delivery formats, including distance learning; and managing and evaluating instruction.

Park, I., & Hannafin, M. J. (1993). Empirically based guidelines for the design of interactive multimedia.

Educational Technology Research & Development, 41, 63–85. https://doi.org/10.1007/BF02297358. The analytical framework established in this article is as valid today as it was in 1993, as are the twenty principles with implications for designing interactive multimedia.

Pina, A. A. (Ed.). (2017). *Instructional design standards for distance learning*. AECT.

Richey, R. C., Kline, J. D., & Tracey, M. W. (2011). *The instructional design knowledge base: Theory, research, and practice*. Routledge. Describes classic and current theories as frameworks for instructional design practice. Chapter 6 media theory and practice.

Rothwell, W. J., & Kazanas, H. C. (2016). *Mastering the instructional design process: A systematic approach* (5th ed.). Wiley. Includes three chapters on managing ID projects in Part 5.

Santos, S. A. (2006). Relationships between learning styles and online learning: Myth or reality? *Performance Improvement Quarterly, 19*(3), 73–88. Concludes that a student's preferred way of learning does not relate to their success in online learning and does not recommend using learning-style instruments to develop online accommodations or to advise students on taking online courses.

Simpson, O. (2003). *Student retention in online, open, and distance learning*. Kogan Page.

Smaldino, S. E., Lowther, D. L., & Mims, C. (2019). *Instructional technology and media for learning* (12th ed.). Pearson. Includes consideration of all current instructional strategies and media; considered a standard reference in educational technology for K–12 teachers.

Smith, P. J. (2007). Workplace learning and flexible delivery. *Review of Educational Research, 73*(1), 53–88. Organizes research around cognitive conceptualizations of workplace learning and addresses the challenges of delivering flexible learning programs therein.

Spannaus, T. (2012). *Creating video for teachers and trainers: Producing professional video with amateur equipment.* Pfeiffer. Guides trainers through the design and production of video using traditional and digital media.

UBC WIKI. (2014). *Design principles for multimedia.* The University of British Columbia. https://wiki.ubc.ca/Documentation:Design_Principles_for_Multimedia

Vai, M., & Sosulski, K. (2015). *Essentials of online course design: A standards-based guide.* Routledge.

Vaughan, T. (2014). *Multimedia: Making it work* (9th ed.). McGraw-Hill. Describes how to plan, cost, design, and produce multimedia projects for the web, CD-ROM, DVD, and mobile devices.

Wiley, D. A. (2002). (Ed.). *The instructional use of learning objects: Online version.* http://www.reusability.org/read

Zettle, H. (2018). *Video basics* (8th ed.). Cengage. Includes the latest in digital technologies for video design and production.

chapter 11

Designing and Conducting Formative Evaluations

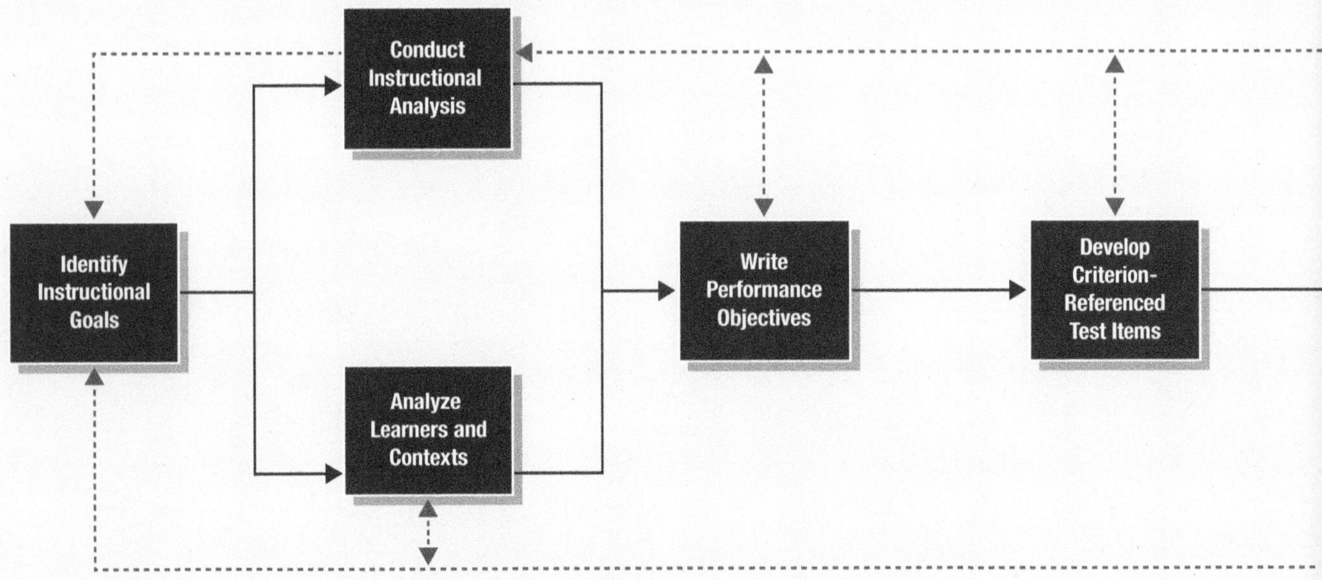

Objectives

- Compare the purposes for and various stages of formative evaluation of instructor-developed materials, instructor-selected materials, and instructor-presented instruction.
- Develop an appropriate formative evaluation plan.
- Construct evaluation instruments for a set of instructional materials or an instructor presentation.
- Collect and organize data according to a formative evaluation plan for a given set of instructional materials or an instructor presentation.

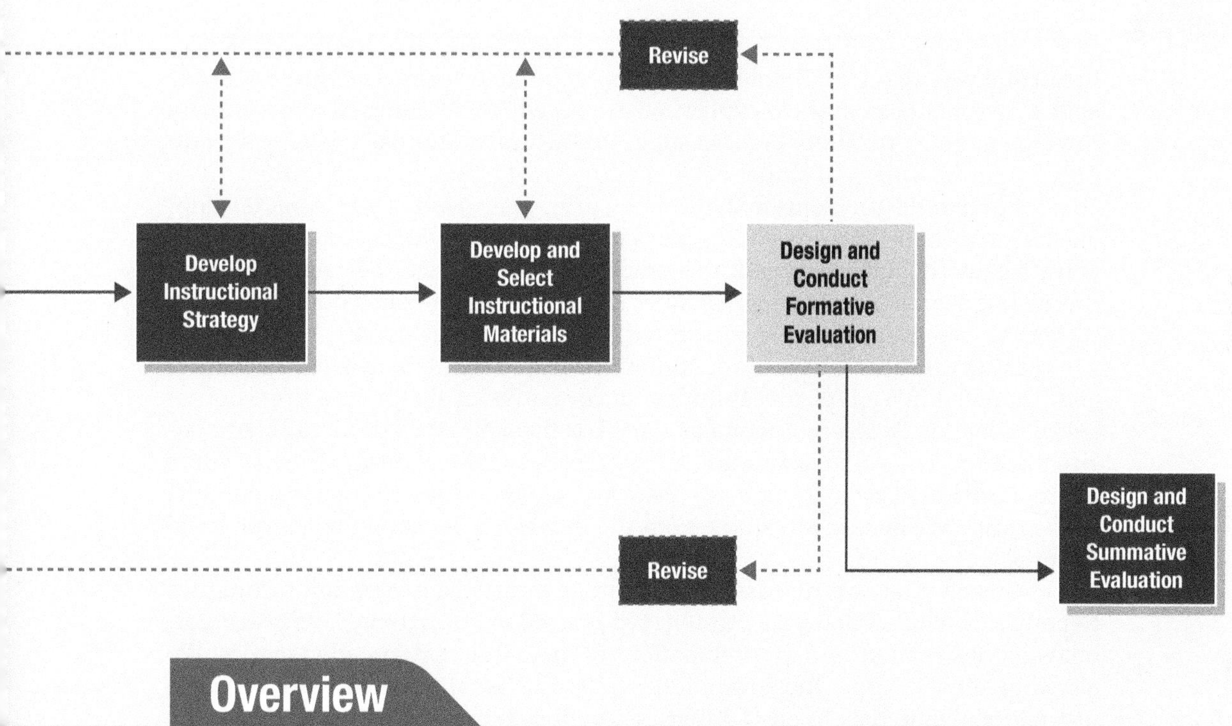

Overview

Formative evaluation of instructional materials is conducted to determine the effectiveness of the materials and to revise them in areas where they are ineffective. Formative evaluations should be conducted on newly developed materials as well as existing materials that are selected based on the instructional strategy. Evaluations are necessary for both mediated and instructor-presented materials. The evaluations should be designed to produce data to pinpoint specific areas where the instruction is faulty and to suggest how it should be revised.

There are three basic phases of formative evaluation. First, in one-to-one or clinical evaluation, the designer works with individual learners to obtain data to revise the materials. The second stage of formative evaluation is a **small-group evaluation**. A group of eight to twenty learners representative of the target population study the materials and are tested to collect the required data. The third stage of formative evaluation is usually a **field trial**. The number of learners is not of consequence; often thirty are sufficient. The emphasis in the field trial is on testing procedures required for installing the instruction in a situation as close to the "real world" as possible. The three phases of formative evaluation are typically preceded by the review of instruction by interested specialists who are not directly involved in the instructional development project but who have relevant expertise.

A variety of qualitative and quantitative instruments and procedures are used to gather data in formative evaluation including but not limited to interviews, observations, checklists, rating scales, surveys, and achievement tests.

Matrix analysis can be used to aid the designer in integrating all the necessary factors in the formative evaluation plan. Main areas to be integrated include all the information gathered in the design documents created from Chapters 2–10.

Concepts

Recall that we suggest in Chapter 5 that during the context analysis you should use your instructional analysis to explain what you will be teaching to some learners from the target population. We also suggested a similar approach when you completed your instructional strategy—that you use it to "teach" some learners in an attempt to find the problems in the strategy prior to its use as a guide for developing the instruction. Both procedures can be referred to as *formative evaluations* in that you are gathering information from learners in order to revise the materials before proceeding with the design process. Now you are doing the same thing, in a more systematic manner, with the instruction that you have developed.

A rather arbitrary division of content has been made between this chapter and Chapter 12. We typically think about formative evaluation and revision of instructional materials as one major step. For the sake of clarity and to emphasize the importance of reexamining the whole instructional design process when instructional materials are to be revised, we separated the design and conduct of the formative evaluation study from the process of revising the instructional materials.

In this chapter, we discuss how to apply formative evaluation techniques to newly developed materials, to selected and adapted materials, to instructor-delivered instruction, and to combinations of these three presentation modes. We also show how to apply these techniques to instructional procedures as well as to instructional materials to ensure that instruction, regardless of the presentation mode, is properly implemented and managed.

The major concept underlying this chapter is **formative evaluation**, which is the process designers use to obtain data for revising their instruction to make it more efficient and effective. Its emphasis is on the collection and analysis of data and the revision of the instruction. When a final version of the instruction is produced, other evaluators may collect data to determine its effectiveness. This latter type of evaluation is often referred to as **summative evaluation**: summative in that the instruction is now in its final form, and it is appropriate to compare it with other similar forms of instruction.

An iterative process of formative evaluation containing at least three cycles of data collection, analysis, and revision is recommended. Each cycle focuses on different aspects of quality. The first cycle, *one-to-one evaluation*, is conducted with three to five members of the target population to pinpoint gross errors in the materials. These errors typically relate to the clarity of vocabulary, concepts, and examples used and to the motivational value of all five learning components of the instructional materials. The rough-draft materials themselves are used during this trial, and learners are instructed to write comments or circle areas of confusion directly on the materials. An interactive interview process is used so the evaluator can learn what was wrong with the materials and why it was wrong. Evaluations can also be conducted with content experts and individuals familiar with the characteristics of target learners; however, these evaluations should be viewed as supplemental rather than a substitute for ones conducted with target learners.

The second cycle, *the small-group evaluation*, follows the correction of major errors identified in the instruction. The group typically consists of from eight to twenty representative members of the target population. The purpose of the small-group evaluation is to locate additional errors in the instructional materials and management procedures. The learning components of the instructional strategy are again the anchor for the evaluation instruments and procedures. During this cycle, the evaluator plays a less interactive role, performance and attitude data are collected, and in-depth debriefings are conducted to obtain both quantitative and qualitative data.

The final cycle, *a field trial*, is conducted following refinement of the materials based on the small-group evaluation. Typically, around thirty representative members of the target learners are included. The materials and procedures used should resemble the anticipated final product. The purpose of this evaluation is to pinpoint errors in the materials when they are used as prescribed in the intended setting. Similar to the first two cycles, evaluation instrumentation and procedures should be anchored in the five learning components of the instructional strategy. Instruments to gather data on learner performance and attitudes are important. The gathering of management data, such as the time required to use the materials and the feasibility of the management plan, is also important. During the field trial, the evaluator does not interfere as data are gathered from the learners or instructor, although observation while materials are used can provide insights for interpreting data.

Formative Evaluation Designs

What frame of reference can you use to design the formative evaluation? Keeping in mind the purpose of formative evaluation is to pinpoint specific errors in the materials in order to correct them, the evaluation design—including instruments, procedures, and personnel—must yield information about the location of and the reasons for any problems. Focusing the design only on the goals and objectives of the instruction is too limited. Data on learners' achievement of goals and objectives is insufficient although important because these data only provide information about where errors occur rather than why they occur. Similarly, a shotgun approach to the collection of data is also inappropriate. Although collecting data on everything you can imagine produces a variety of information, it may yield some data that are irrelevant and incomplete.

Perhaps the best anchor or framework for the design of the formative evaluation is the instructional strategy. Because the strategy was the foundation for creating the materials, it is likely to hold the key to the nature of errors you made in producing them. Using the instructional strategy as the frame of reference for developing evaluation instruments and procedures should help you avoid designing a formative evaluation that is either too narrowly focused or too broad.

One way the instructional strategy can be used to aid the design of the formative evaluation is to create a matrix that lists the learning components of the instructional strategy along one side and the major categories of questions about the instruction along the other. In the intersecting boxes of the component-by-question matrix, you can generate questions that should be answered in the evaluation related to each area and component. Using these questions, you can then plan the appropriate instruments and procedures to use and the appropriate audiences to provide the information.

The different learning components of the strategy should be quite familiar to you by now. What general questions should be asked about each component of the materials? Although there are undoubtedly unique questions for a given set of materials, the five following areas of questions directly related to the decisions you made while developing the materials are appropriate for all materials:

1. Are the materials appropriate for the type of learning outcome? Specific prescriptions for the development of materials were made based on whether the objectives were intellectual or motor skills, attitudes, or verbal information. You should be concerned whether the materials you produced are indeed congruent with suggestions for learning each type of capability. The best evaluator of this aspect of the materials is undoubtedly an expert in the type of learning involved.
2. Do the materials include adequate instruction on the subordinate skills, and are these skills sequenced and clustered logically? The best evaluator for this area of questions is an expert in the content area.
3. Are the materials clear and readily understood by representative members of the target group? Obviously, only members of the target group can answer these questions. Instructors familiar with target learners may provide you with preliminary information, but only learners can ultimately judge the clarity of the materials.
4. What is the motivational value of the materials? Do learners find the materials relevant to their needs and interests? Are they confident as they work through the materials? Are they satisfied with what they have learned? Again, the most appropriate judges of these aspects of the materials are representative members of the target group.
5. Can the materials be managed efficiently in the manner they are mediated? Both target learners and instructors are appropriate to answer these questions.

Table 11.1 contains an example of the suggested framework for designing the formative evaluation. Using such a framework helps ensure that you include relevant questions about different learning components of the materials and that appropriate groups and individuals are included.

Notice the two rows at the bottom of the matrix. The first indicates the individuals or groups most appropriate for evaluating each aspect of the materials; the second provides a reminder that you must consider how to gather each type of information needed from the evaluators. You may want to create a checklist or list of questions to accompany the materials for soliciting information from the specialists you choose. You may also want to interview them to determine why they believe parts of the material are inadequate and to obtain their suggestions about how the materials might be improved.

In designing instrumentation for gathering information from learners, you must consider the phase (i.e., one-to-one, small-group, and field trial), the setting (i.e., learning or performance context), and the nature of the information you are gathering. In the one-to-one evaluations, the materials themselves make up one instrument. Instruct learners to circle words or sentences and to write comments directly in the materials. The questions included in the intersecting blocks of the matrix should help you develop other instruments such as checklists to guide your observations and questions to include in your interviews and questionnaires. It is important to note that although different areas of questions about the materials are described separately here, it does not mean to imply that they must be on separate instruments. The instruments you produce should be efficient in gathering information from participants. At a minimum, the types of data to collect include the following:

1. Reactions of the subject-matter expert, whose responsibility it is to verify that the content of the module is accurate and current

Table 11.1 Example Framework for Designing a Formative Evaluation

	Main Areas of Questions About Materials				
MAIN COMPONENTS OF MATERIALS	TYPE OF LEARNING	CONTENT	CLARITY	MOTIVATION	MANAGEMENT
Preinstructional					
Initial motivation					
Objectives					
Entry skills					
Presentation					
Sequence					
Size of unit					
Content					
Examples					
Participation					
Practice					
Feedback					
Assessment					
Pretests					
Embedded tests					
Posttests					
Follow-through					
Retention					
Transfer					
Performance context					
Who judges?	Learning specialists	Content expert	Target learners	Target learners	Target learners/ Instructors
How are data gathered?	Checklist Interview	Checklist Interview	Observations Interviews Tests Materials	Observations Interviews Surveys	Observations Interviews

2. Reactions of a manager or supervisor who has observed the learner using the skills in the performance context
3. Test data collected on entry skills tests, pretests, and posttests
4. Comments or notations made by learners to you or marked on the instructional materials about difficulties encountered at particular points in the materials
5. Data collected on attitude questionnaires or debriefing comments in which learners reveal their overall reactions to the instruction and their perceptions of where difficulties lie with the materials and the instructional procedures in general
6. The time required for learners to complete various components of the instruction

In the following sections, the roles of subject-matter, learning, and learner specialists in formative evaluation are described. The three learner-oriented phases of formative evaluation are then elaborated.

Role of Subject-Matter, Learning, and Learner Specialists in Formative Evaluation

Although the formative evaluation process focuses on the acquisition of data from learners, it is also important to have the instruction reviewed by specialists. It is assumed that the designer is knowledgeable about the content area or is working with a content specialist and is also knowledgeable about the target population. Still, there are several good reasons to have the instruction reviewed by outside specialists.

When the first draft of the instruction has been written, designers appear to experience a "forest and trees" problem. They have seen so much that they cannot see anything; it is invaluable to the designer to get others to review what has been developed. A *subject-matter expert (SME)*, a type of reviewer outside the project who has special expertise in the content area of the instruction, should comment on the **accuracy** and **currency** of the instruction. Although many suggestions for improvement may be received, the designer should give considerable thought before making any changes that are counter to the instructional strategy already developed. A specialist in the type of learning outcome involved should also be consulted. A *learning specialist*, or a colleague familiar with the suggestions for instruction related to the type of learning, might be able to critique your instructional strategy related to what is known about enhancing that particular type of learning.

It is also helpful to share the first draft of the instruction with a *learner specialist*, or a person who is familiar with the target population—someone who can look at the instruction through the target population's eyes and react. This specialist may be able to provide insights into the appropriateness of the material for the eventual performance context.

The designer is not obligated to use the suggestions of these specialists. There may be some recommendations that the designer may want to consider after data from learners have been collected and summarized. At least the designer is sensitized to potential problems before learners become involved in the formative evaluation process.

One-to-One Evaluation with Learners

In this discussion of the three phases of formative evaluation of instruction, we assume that the designer has developed original instruction. In subsequent sections, we discuss the differences in procedures when existing materials are used or when instructor-led instruction has been created.

The purpose of the first stage of formative evaluation, the **one-to-one evaluation** stage, is to identify and remove the most obvious errors in the instruction and to obtain initial performance indications and reactions to the content by learners. During this stage of direct interaction between the designer and individual learners, the designer works individually with three or more learners who are representative of the target population.

Criteria

During the development of the instructional strategy and the instruction itself, designers and developers make a myriad of translations and decisions that link the content, learners, instructional format, and instructional setting. The one-to-one trials provide designers with their first glimpse of the viability of these links and translations from the learners' perspective. The three main criteria and the decisions designers make during the evaluation are as follows:

1. **Clarity:** Is the message, or what is being presented, clear to individual target learners?

2. **Impact:** What is the impact of the instruction on individual learners' attitudes and achievement of the objectives and goals?
3. **Feasibility:** How feasible is the instruction given the available resources (time/context)?

The one-to-one trials help verify whether the designers' and developers' hunches were correct or reflected misconceptions of the target group.

Selecting Learners

One of the most critical decisions by the designer in the formative evaluation is the selection of learners to participate in the study. This is not an experiment; there is no need for random selection of large numbers of learners. The designer should select a few learners who represent the range of ability in the group because prior learning or ability is usually one of the major determiners of ability to learn new skills and information. The designer therefore selects at least one learner from the target population who is above average in ability (but certainly not the top student), one who is average, and at least one learner who is below average. The designer then works on an individual basis with each learner. After the initial evaluations with the three learners, the designer may wish to select more learners from the target population to work in a one-to-one mode, although three is usually sufficient.

The designer should be aware of learner characteristics other than ability that may be highly related to achievement and therefore should be represented systematically in the formative evaluation. As noted in Chapter 5, attitudes and previous experience can be very important, and such variables should be a consideration during formative evaluation. For the one-to-one phase of the formative evaluation, the designer may wish to select one learner with a very positive attitude toward what is being taught, one who is neutral, and one who is negative. Likewise, if experience on the job is an important factor, select someone who has been on the job ten or more years, one who has been there two to five years, and someone who has been there for less than a year. The point is that ability might not be the only critical factor in selecting learners for a formative evaluation. The designer must make this decision for each particular instructional design situation.

Data Collection

The three main criteria and the decisions to be made during one-to-one trials help evaluators focus on the kinds of information that would be useful. Table 11.2 contains the types of information that can be obtained for comparisons with clarity, impact, and feasibility criteria. The lists in each criterion category are intended to be illustrative rather than exhaustive because the degree of relevance of each kind of information may differ by learner maturity, instructional content, and delivery method.

For clarity of instruction, there are three main categories of illuminating information—message, links, and procedures. The first category, message, relates to how clear the basic message is to the learner, determined by such factors as vocabulary, sentence complexity, and message structures. Regardless of whether the learner reads, hears, or sees the message, he or she must be able to follow it. The second category, links, refers to how the basic message is tailored for the learner, including contexts, examples, analogies, illustrations, and demonstrations. When these links are also unfamiliar to the learner, the basic message is undoubtedly more complex. The third area, procedures, refers to characteristics of the instruction, such as the sequence, the size of segment presented, the transition between segments, the pace, and the variation built into the presentation. The clarity of instruction may change for the learner when any one of these elements is inappropriate for her or him. The instruction can be so slow and iterative that the learner loses interest, or it can proceed so quickly that comprehension becomes difficult.

Table 11.2 Formative Evaluation Criteria for One-to-One Trials and the Types of Information for Each Criterion

Criteria			
	MESSAGE	LINKS	PROCEDURES
Clarity of Instruction	• Vocabulary level • Sentence complexity • Message complexity • Introductions • Elaborations • Conclusions • Transitions	• Contexts • Examples • Analogies • Illustrations • Demonstrations • Reviews • Summaries	• Sequence • Segment size • Transition • Pace • Variation
	ATTITUDES	ACHIEVEMENT	
Impact on Learner	• Utility of the information and skills (relevance) • How easy/difficult the information and skills are to learn (confidence) • Satisfaction with skills learned	• Clarity of directions and items for posttests • Scores on posttests	
	LEARNER	RESOURCES	
Feasibility	• Maturity • Independence • Motivation	• Time • Equipment • Environment	

Descriptive information rather than quantitative data probably yields the best information about clarity for revising the instruction. If the instruction is delivered through print, whether on paper or on a computer screen, the learner can be directed to underline or highlight in some way all unfamiliar words and unclear examples, illustrations, and paragraphs and to mark directions within any figures or tables that are confusing. The learner can be directed to jot down unclear terms and note confusing material when using a video, slides, or multimedia or can be directed to pause the instruction at any point in order to interact with the evaluator about confusing passages or terms. Regardless of the delivery format during a one-to-one trial, the learner can be asked about the procedural characteristics of the instruction, such as segment size and pace. Information about the procedural characteristics can also be collected by observation as the learner listens to the instructor, reads the material, or interacts with a screen. Such observations can help the evaluator determine whether anxiousness, boredom, fatigue, or all three conditions become apparent at different points in the instruction.

The second criterion in Table 11.2, impact on learner, relates to the learner's attitudes about the instruction and her or his achievement on specific objectives. The evaluator must determine whether the learner perceives the instruction as being (1) personally relevant to her or him, (2) accomplishable with reasonable effort, and (3) interesting and satisfying to experience. Related to achievement, posttests help determine whether the individual can recall the information and perform the tasks. The format of these achievement measures differs depending on the instructional delivery medium. Questions or directions for performance can be presented orally by the instructor. Learners can be asked to respond (1) using paper and pencil or keyboard, (2) orally in response to the instructor's questions, or (3) by developing or performing something requested.

The third criterion in Table 11.2, feasibility, relates to management-oriented considerations that can be examined during the one-to-one trial, including the capability of the learner, the instructional medium, and the instructional environment. Examples of questions of interest include the following:

1. How should the maturity, independence, and motivation of the learner influence the general amount of time required to complete the instruction?
2. Can learners such as this one operate or easily learn to operate any specialized equipment required?
3. Is the learner comfortable in this environment?
4. Is the cost of delivering this instruction reasonable given the time requirements?

Procedures

The typical procedure in a one-to-one evaluation is to explain to the learner that a new set of instructional materials has been designed and that you would like his or her reaction to them. You should say that any mistakes learners might make are probably because of deficiencies in the material and not theirs. Encourage the learners to be relaxed and to talk about the materials. You should have the learners not only go through the instructional materials but also have them take the test(s) provided with the materials. Also, note the amount of time it takes a learner to complete the material.

Instructional designers have found this process invaluable in preparing materials. When learners use the materials in this manner, they find typographical errors, omissions of content, missing pages, graphs that are labeled improperly, inappropriate links in their web pages, and other kinds of mechanical difficulties that inevitably occur. Learners often can describe difficulties they have with the learning sequence and the concepts being taught. They can critique the tests in terms of whether they think they measure your objectives. You can use all this information to revise your materials and tests and correct relatively gross problems as well as small errors.

In contrast to the earlier stages of instructional design, which emphasize the analytical skills of the designer, the first critical hallmark of the one-to-one formative evaluation is its almost total dependence on the ability of the designer to establish rapport with the learner and then to interact effectively. The learner has typically never been asked to critique instruction; the assumption has been made that if learning does not occur, it is the student's fault. Learners must be convinced that it is legitimate to be critical of what is presented to them. This is sometimes particularly difficult for the young person who is being asked to criticize an authority figure. The designer should establish an atmosphere of acceptance and support for any negative comments from the learner.

The second critical hallmark of the one-to-one approach is that it is an interactive process. The power of the process is greatly diminished when the designer hands the instruction to the learner and says, "Here, read this and let me know whether you have any problems." Sitting diagonally beside the learner, the designer should read (silently) with the learner and, at predetermined points, discuss with the learner what has been presented in the materials. The dialogue may focus on the answers to practice questions or may be a consideration of special points made in the content presentation. Before each one-to-one session, the designer should formulate a strategy about how the interaction will take place and how the learner will know when it is appropriate to talk with the evaluator.

In most situations a one-to-one session can take place with only one learner at a time. There are exceptions to this rule, especially when learners must work in pairs or teams. The rule of one would then apply to one pair of learners or one team. As the designer proceeds with the evaluation, it is necessary to note the comments and suggestions made by the learner as well as any alternative explanations made by the designer that seem effective. These can be noted on one copy of the instruction, or an audio recording can be used during the session, to which, from our experience, students seem to adapt quite readily.

Assessments and Questionnaires

After the students in the one-to-one trials have completed the instruction, they should review the posttest and attitude questionnaire in the same fashion. After each item or step in the assessment, ask the learners why they made the responses that they did. This helps you spot not only mistakes but also the reasons for the mistakes, which can be quite helpful during the revision process. Also, note that some test items that appear to be perfectly clear to you will be totally misinterpreted by the learner. If these faulty items remain in the assessment for the small-group evaluation, there will be major problems in determining whether only those items or the instruction is defective. Exert as much care in evaluating your assessment instruments as you do the instruction itself.

Test directions and rubrics to evaluate performances and products should also be evaluated formatively before they are used to evaluate examinees' work. Just as with paper-and-pencil tests, you must ensure that the directions are clear to the learner and that learners can follow the instructions to produce the anticipated performance or product.

You must also evaluate the utility of the evaluation instrument, particularly the following elements: (1) the observability of each of the elements to be judged, (2) the clarity of the manner in which they are paraphrased, and (3) the efficiency of the sequencing order. Related to the evaluator's responding format, you should check whether the response categories and criteria are reasonable in terms of the number and type of judgments you must make and the time available for you to observe, judge, and mark the judgment. If you are unable to keep up with the performer, then the accuracy of your judgments will be affected.

The reliability of your judgments should be evaluated by rating the same performance or product two or more times with an intervening time interval. You can also check reliability by having two or more evaluators use the instrument to judge the same performance or product. When the multiple ratings obtained from a single evaluator on a single product differ or the ratings of multiple evaluators differ for a single product, the instrument should be revised in such areas as the number of elements to be judged, the number of levels of judgments to be made, and the clarity of the criteria for each level. The number of elements to be observed and the number of judgment categories should be reduced to a point where consistency is obtained, implying that several iterations of instrument evaluation are necessary to verify the utility of the instrument and the consistency of judgments made using it.

Finally, you should evaluate your scoring strategy. Using the data you gather during the formative evaluation of the instrument, combine or summarize element-level scores as planned. Review these combined scores in terms of objective level and overall performance. Are the scores logical and interpretable? Can they be used to evaluate particular parts of the instruction and performance? If not, then modify the rating or scoring procedure until usable data are obtained.

Learning Time

One design interest during one-to-one evaluation is determining the amount of time required for learners to complete instruction, which is a very rough estimate because of the interaction between the learner and the designer. You can attempt to subtract a certain percentage of the time from the total time, but experience indicates that such estimates can be quite inaccurate.

One final comment about the one-to-one evaluation process: Rarely are learners placed in such a vulnerable position and required to expose their ignorance. Even adults must sometimes admit not knowing the meaning of a common word—they always meant to look it up in the dictionary but forgot. In the one-to-one stage, the designer is in control and thus has the responsibility for providing a comfortable working situation. Because learners may hesitate to reveal deficiencies in their current state of knowledge, every possible effort should be made to be both objective about the instruction and supportive of the learner. Without the learner, there is no formative evaluation.

Data Interpretation

The information on the clarity of instruction, impact on learner, and feasibility of instruction must be summarized and focused. Aspects of the instruction found to be weak can then be reconsidered in order to plan revisions likely to improve the instruction for similar learners. One caution about data interpretation from one-to-one trials is critical: Take care not to overgeneralize the data gathered from only one individual. Although ensuring that the participating one-to-one learner is representative of the intended group helps ensure that reactions are typical of other target group members, there is no guarantee that a second one-to-one learner will respond in a similar manner. Differing abilities, expectations, and attitudes among members of the target group result in different data from each. Information gathered from the one-to-one trial should be viewed as a "first glimpse" that may or may not generalize. Gross errors in the instruction will likely become apparent during the trial and will lead to immediate and accurate revisions. Other areas of the instruction that are questionable may not be revised until after the instruction is retried with other individuals or with a small group.

Outcomes

The outcomes of one-to-one trials are instruction that (1) contains appropriate vocabulary, language complexity, examples, and illustrations for the participating learners; (2) either yields reasonable learner attitudes and achievement or is revised with the objective of improving learner attitudes or performance during subsequent trials; and (3) appears feasible for use with the available learners, resources, and setting. The instruction can be refined further using small-group trials.

In Chapter 12, we discuss how to summarize the information from the one-to-one trials and how to decide what revisions should be made. In this chapter, we continue with our discussion of the next phase of formative evaluation, which takes place after the revisions from the one-to-one evaluation have been completed.

Small-Group Evaluation

There are two primary purposes for the small-group evaluation: First, determine the effectiveness of changes made following the one-to-one evaluation and identify any remaining learning problems that learners may have; and second, determine whether learners can use the instruction without interacting with the instructor. (At this point in our discussion, we continue to assume that the designer is creating some form of self-instructional materials.)

Criteria and Data

Typical measures used to evaluate instructional effectiveness include learner performance scores on pretests and posttests. Pretests typically encompass entry skills as well as instructional objectives, and posttests measure learners' performance on the subordinate and terminal objectives for the instruction. Besides learner performance levels, their attitudes about the instruction are obtained through an attitude questionnaire and sometimes a follow-up interview. Information gathered about the feasibility of the instruction usually includes the following: (1) the time required for learners to complete both the instruction and the required performance measures, (2) the costs and viability of delivering the instruction in the intended format and environment, and (3) the attitudes of those implementing or managing the instruction.

Selecting Learners

For the small-group evaluation, you should select a group of approximately eight to twenty learners. If the number of learners is fewer than eight, the data will probably not be very representative of the target population. However, if you obtain data on many more than twenty learners, you may find that you have more information than you need and that the data from additional learners does not provide a great deal of additional information. The selection of learners to participate in your small-group trial is important. The learners who evaluate the materials should be as representative of your target population as possible. In an ideal research setting, you would select the learners randomly, which would enable you to apply your findings generally to the entire target population. In typical school, business, and adult education settings, however, true randomization is often impossible and perhaps not even desirable. When you cannot select your learners at random or when the group you have available to draw from is relatively small, you should ensure that you include in your sample at least one representative of each type of subgroup that exists in your population, possibly including learners who:

- are low-, average-, and high-achieving;
- have various native languages;
- are familiar with a procedure (e.g., web-based instruction) and learners who are not;
- are younger or inexperienced as well as more mature; or
- are representative of the diversity in the target population (gender, race, culture, special needs, etc.).

When your target group is homogeneous, these subgroups are not a problem. When the target population is made up of persons with varied skills and backgrounds, the designer should consider including representatives of each group in the small-group sample. For example, it is almost impossible to predict how a low-achieving learner will perform on your materials based on the efforts of a high-achieving learner. Selecting a representative sample helps you be more insightful about changes that must be made in your instruction.

Small-group participants are sometimes a biased sample because they consist of people who participate more willingly than the group at large. The designer must be aware of this problem and obtain the most representative group possible, considering all the constraints usually present in obtaining participants for small-group trials. It is also important to note that while this stage is referred to as *small-group evaluation*, the term refers to the number of learners and not the setting in which the learners use the materials. For example, if your materials require the use of highly specialized equipment and you have access to only one piece of equipment, then you should attempt to obtain eight to twenty learners who would use your materials in an individualized setting. It is not necessary to get all the learners together in one room at one time to conduct a small-group evaluation.

Procedures

The basic procedures used in a small-group evaluation differ sharply from those in a one-to-one evaluation. The evaluator (or the instructor) begins by explaining that the materials are in the formative stage of development and that it is necessary to obtain feedback on how they may be improved. Having said this, the instructor then administers the materials in the way they are intended to be used when they are in final form. If a pretest is to be used, then it should be given first. The instructor should intervene as little as possible in the process. Only in those cases when equipment fails or when a learner becomes bogged down in the learning process and cannot continue should the instructor intervene. Each learner's difficulty and the solution should certainly be noted as part of the revision data.

Assessments and Questionnaires

Additional steps in small-group evaluation are the administration of an attitude questionnaire and, if possible, in-depth debriefings with some of the learners in the group. The primary purpose for obtaining learner reactions to the instruction is to identify, from their perceptions, weaknesses and strengths in the implementation of the instructional strategy. The questions should therefore reflect various components of the strategy. The following questions would usually be appropriate:

- Was the instruction interesting?
- Did you understand what you were supposed to learn?
- Were the materials directly related to the objectives?
- Were enough practice exercises included?
- Were the practice exercises relevant?
- Did the tests really measure your knowledge of the objectives?
- Did you receive sufficient feedback on your practice exercises?
- Did you feel confident when answering questions on the tests?

These questions might be included in an attitude questionnaire and then pursued at some depth in a discussion with learners. By using questions directed at learning components of the instructional strategy, such as those just described, it is possible to relate the learners' responses directly to components of the instructional materials or procedures. In the discussion with the learners after the materials have been completed, the instructor can ask questions about such features as the pacing, interest, and difficulty of the materials.

Data Summary and Analysis

Both the quantitative and descriptive information gathered during the trial should be summarized and analyzed. Quantitative data consist of test scores as well as time requirements and cost projections. Descriptive information consists of comments collected from attitude questionnaires, interviews, or evaluator's notes written during the trial.

Outcomes

The goal of the small-group trial and instructional revisions is refined instruction that should be effective with most target learners in the intended setting. Refinements required in instruction may be simple, such as changing examples and vocabulary in test items or increasing the amount of time allocated for study. Modifications might also require major changes in the instructional strategy (e.g., motivational strategies, sequence of objectives, instructional delivery format) or information presented to learners. Once instruction is refined adequately, the field trial can be initiated.

Field Trial

In the final stage of formative evaluation, the instructor attempts to use a learning context that closely resembles the intended context for the ultimate use of the instructional materials. One purpose of this final stage of formative evaluation is to determine whether the changes in the instruction made after the small-group stage were effective; another purpose is to see whether the instruction can be used in the context for which it was intended—that is, is it administratively possible to use the instruction in its intended setting?

To answer these questions, all materials, including the tests and the instructor's manual, should be revised and ready to go. If an instructor is involved in implementing the instruction, the designer should not play this role.

Location of Evaluation

In picking the site for a field evaluation, you are likely to encounter one of two situations: First, if the material is tried out in a class that is currently using large-group, lockstep pacing, then using self-instructional materials may be a very new and different experience for the learners. It is important to lay the groundwork for the new procedure by explaining to the learners how the materials are to be used and how they differ from their usual instruction. Likely, you will obtain an increase in interest, if not in performance, simply because of the break in the typical classroom instructional pattern.

Second, if the materials are tried out in an individualized class, then it may be quite difficult to find a large enough group of learners who are ready for your instructional materials because learners will be "spread out" in the materials they are studying.

Criteria and Data

The field trial is much like the final dress rehearsal in theater because the instruction is polished and delivered in a manner that is as close as possible to the final format. Also similar to dress rehearsals, the main purpose of the field trial is to locate and eliminate any remaining problems in the instruction. There are many similarities between the small-group trial and the field trial. The decisions to be made during both types of trials are whether learner performance is adequate and delivery of instruction is feasible. Another similarity is that information is gathered on learner achievement and attitudes; instructor procedures and attitudes; and resources, such as time, cost, space, and equipment. The main differences between the two trials are in the actual sophistication of the materials, learners, procedures, instructors, and setting.

Selecting Learners

You should identify a group of about thirty individuals to participate in your field trial. Again, the group should be selected to ensure that it is representative of the target population for which the materials are intended. Because a "typical" group is sometimes hard to locate, designers often select several different groups to participate in the field trial, ensuring that data are collected under all intended conditions, such as an open classroom, traditional instruction, Internet-based instruction, or some combination of methods.

The use of multiple tryout sites may be necessary if such sites vary a great deal. The designer may not be able to be present while the instruction is used; therefore, it is important that the designer inform the instructor about the procedures to be followed and the data to be collected.

Procedure for Conducting a Field Trial

The procedure for conducting the field trial is similar to that for the small group, with only a few exceptions. The primary change is in the role of the designer, who should do no more than observe the process. The instruction should be administered or delivered by a typical instructor, for whom the designer may have to design and deliver special training so that he or she knows exactly how to use the instruction.

The only other change might be a reduction in testing. Based on experience in the small group, the pretest and posttest might be modified or reduced to assess only the most important entry behaviors and skills to be taught because by this point in the development process, the main concern in the formative evaluation is feasibility in the learning context.

The questionnaire may be modified to focus on the environmental factors that the designer believes are critical to the success of the instruction. Essentially, the questions should focus on anything that might interfere with the success of the instruction. Observation of the instruction in use and interviews with learners and the instructor are very valuable.

Data Summary and Interpretation

Data summary and analysis procedures are the same for the small-group and field trials. Achievement data should be organized by instructional objective, and attitudinal information from both learners and instructors should also be anchored to specific objectives whenever possible. Summarizing the data in these formats aids in locating areas where the instruction was and was not effective. This information from the field trial is used to plan and make final revisions in the instruction.

Outcomes

The goal of the field trial and final revisions is effective instruction that yields desired levels of learner achievement and attitudes and that functions as intended in the learning setting. Using data about problem areas gathered during the field trial, appropriate revisions are made in the instruction.

Formative Evaluation of Selected Materials

The three phases of formative evaluation previously described are not totally applicable when the instructor has selected existing materials to try with a group of learners. The types of editorial and content changes made as a result of one-to-one and small-group evaluations are typically not used with existing materials. These procedures are avoided not because they would be unproductive in improving the instruction but because the instructor who selects existing materials seldom has the time or resources to conduct these phases. Furthermore, existing materials are typically copyrighted, and changing copyrighted materials is prohibited without adequate permissions. What can and often does occur following formative evaluation of existing materials is the creation of supplemental materials to accompany them, such as syllabi, study guides, practice and feedback activities, student workbooks, additional readings, and so forth.

Formative evaluation of existing materials includes expert judgment studies and field trials. The purpose of the expert judgment phase is to determine whether currently used or other candidate instruction has the potential for meeting an organization's defined instructional needs. The framework for designing a formative evaluation in Table 11.1 is also helpful for designing the expert judgment phase for evaluating existing materials. The left column of the table lists the areas of the materials to be evaluated. Across the top of the table, questions of the appropriateness of the materials for the type of learning can be judged by experts in learning theory. Questions of the currency, completeness, and accuracy of the content can be judged by content experts. If existing materials are judged inadequate by the experts and they are judged not to be easily remedied by supplemental materials, then the remainder of the questions in Table 11.1 about materials clarity, motivation, and management are irrelevant. Likewise, a field trial with inadequate materials seems inappropriate.

Suppose existing materials are judged promising by learning and content experts. In this circumstance, the designer should proceed directly to a field trial with a group of learners, both to determine whether the materials are effective with a particular population and in a specific setting and to identify ways that additions to or deletions from the materials or changes in instructional procedures might be made to improve effectiveness.

Preparations for the field trial of existing materials should be made as they would be for a field trial of original materials. An analysis should be made of existing documentation on the development of the materials, if any exist, including the effectiveness of the materials with defined groups and particularly any description of procedures used during field evaluations. Descriptions of how materials are to be used should be studied, any test instruments that accompany the materials should be examined for their relationship to the performance objectives, and the need for any additional evaluations or attitude questionnaires should be determined.

In the field trial study, the regular instructor should administer the pretest unless he or she knows the learners already have the entry skills and lack knowledge of what is to be taught. A posttest and an attitude questionnaire should certainly be available to evaluate learners' performance and their opinions of the materials.

The instructor who conducts a field trial can observe the progress and attitudes of learners using a set of adopted or adapted materials. It is even possible to examine the performance of different groups of learners using modified or unmodified materials to determine whether the changes increased the effectiveness of the materials. The instructor should certainly take the time following the field evaluation to debrief the learners thoroughly on their reactions to the instruction because additional insights about the materials or procedures can be gained during such debriefing sessions. After completing a field trial of selected materials, the instructor should have collected approximately the same types of data that would have been collected if original materials were being evaluated formatively.

Formative Evaluation of Instructor-Led Instruction

If the instructor plans to deliver the instruction to a group of students using an instructor's guide, then the purposes of formative evaluations are much the same as they are for the formative evaluation of self-paced instructional materials—to determine whether the instruction is effective and decide how to improve it. Once again, the formative evaluation of an instructional plan most nearly approximates that of the field trial phase for instructional materials. Likely, there will be little time for one-to-one or even small-group evaluation.

In preparing for a field trial of instructor-led instruction, the instructor should be concerned with the entry skills and prior knowledge, the posttest performance, and the attitudes of learners. In addition, the instructor is in a unique position to provide interactive practice and feedback, which should be included in the instructional strategy to provide learners with the opportunity to demonstrate specific skills they have acquired. These sessions also serve to identify those skills not yet acquired. This form of in-progress practice and assessment may be administered in one of two formats, either orally to a variety of learners while keeping notes on their performance or by periodically distributing various printed practice and feedback exercises during the lesson. This latter approach provides concrete evidence of learners' progress.

The instructor can also use the field trial as an opportunity to evaluate instructional procedures. Observation of the instructional process should indicate the suitability of grouping patterns, time allocations, and learner interest in various class activities.

Many instructors already use these types of formative evaluation in their instruction. Our point is to stress the thorough and systematic use of these techniques to collect and analyze data in order to revise the lesson plan. To identify weak points in the lesson plan and to provide clues to their correction, in-progress data can be compared to results obtained with the posttest, attitude questionnaire, and students' comments during debriefing sessions.

Very often, the field testing of selected materials and the field testing of instructor-led instruction are interwoven. Frequently, the use of selected materials requires an interactive role for the instructor, and likewise, the use of an instructor's guide may well involve the use of some prepared instructional materials. Under either circumstance, approximately the same types of field evaluation procedures should be used and similar types of revisions carried out.

Data Collection for Existing Materials and Instructor-Led Instruction

Much of the information dealing with the collection of data in a field trial of original instructional materials applies equally well to the data collection procedures used in the evaluation of existing materials and instructional procedures. For example, it is critically important that any equipment to be used during instruction is in good running order and that the environment in which the field trial is conducted be conducive to learning.

When an instructor evaluates self-instructional materials, selected materials, or an instructor's guide, existing rapport with learners can be a great advantage. It is important during the evaluation of materials and guides that students understand the critical nature of their participation in and contributions to the study. The instructor, in working with familiar learners, also has knowledge of the learners' entry skills and, quite possibly, is able to predict accurately the pretest performance of students. The instructor should, however, avoid relying entirely on such predictions. If there is any doubt at all concerning the learners' readiness, they should be pretested to verify their mastery of prerequisite skills.

When the instructor selects materials to implement an instructional strategy, a number of unique concerns arise. Information can be gathered about these concerns by observation and the use of questionnaires. The major question is "Did the instruction have unity?" To answer this question, the instructor should determine the adequacy of the learner guide in directing students to various resources. Redundancy and gaps in the instructional materials should be noted. Was sufficient repetition, practice, feedback, and review built into the strategy? If the instructor is presenting the instruction, then events that reflect the same types of problems should be noted as the presentation progresses. The types of questions raised by learners provide a key to the strategy's inadequacies.

Problem Solving During Instructional Design

In the instructional design process, the designer is often faced with questions that can best be answered with data from learners. It is interesting to find how often it is possible to settle a design argument by saying, "Let's have the learners tell us the answer to that." The whole formative evaluation process is one of gathering data from learners to answer questions you may (or may not) have had about your instruction.

Assume that following a series of one-to-one evaluations, it becomes clear that there is a question about the use of video clips in your instruction. Several students liked and used them, whereas several others said they were of no use. Because it may be expensive to produce video clips for instruction, a significant question must be answered: "Should video clips be used in my instruction?"

In order to answer this question, the designer might develop two versions of the instruction for use in the small-group evaluation. Ten randomly selected learners might receive the instruction with video clips, whereas ten receive it with no video clips. Then the performance and attitudes of both groups could be compared. How did they do on the posttest? How did they do on those items directly related to the video clips? What did they say on the attitude questions about their use of (or the absence of) the video clips? How did the learning times of the two groups compare?

Is this research? Not really. The purpose is to decide about what to do with a unit of instruction, not to determine the benefits of using video clips in instruction. The designer could collect enough data in the formative evaluation about the video clips to make at least a tentative decision about their continued use in the instruction. This same methodology can be used to answer a wide array of questions that inevitably arise during the design process.

Job Aid

Formative Evaluation Activities

The following list summarizes information that you can use for planning a one-to-one, a small-group, and a field trial evaluation. While looking through these suggested procedures, assume that you know your intended target population but are unsure whether they possess the required entry skills. The examples that follow are not offered as the only activities you should pursue in formative evaluation but as a list of suggestions you can use to begin thinking about a design and development project in which you may be involved. You may be able to identify other activities for your project. Four flowcharts are included later in this chapter that graphically depict a typical sequence for the formative evaluation activities in the following job aid.

One-to-One Evaluation

I. Participation by SMEs
   A. You should provide the expert with the following:
      1. Instructional analysis
      2. Performance objectives
      3. Instruction
      4. Tests and other assessment instruments

      These materials should be in rough form because major revisions could well be the outcome of this one-to-one testing. You may want to present your materials in the order described above.

   B. You should be looking for verification of the following:
      1. Objective statements
      2. Instructional analysis

3. Accuracy and currency of the content
4. Appropriateness of the instructional materials in vocabulary, interest value, sequence, chunk size, and learner participation activities
5. Clarity and appropriateness of test items and assessment situations
6. Placement of this piece of instruction relative to prior and subsequent instruction

C. The number of SMEs you should approach for assistance varies with the complexity of the information and skills covered in your materials. For some instruction, one expert is sufficient, whereas for others several may be needed. The nature of the learning task dictates the number and type of expert consultants needed.

II. Participation by learners from the target population
   A. Identify learners who are typical of those you believe will be found in the target population. (Include each major type of learner that can be found in the target population.)
   B. Arrange for the learner(s) to participate.
   C. Discuss the process of a one-to-one evaluation of the materials with each learner separately.
   D. Evaluate the pretest you have constructed to measure entry skills.
      1. Can the learner read the directions?
      2. Does the learner understand the problems?
      3. Does the learner have the required prerequisite skills?
   E. Sit with the learner while he or she studies the materials.
      1. Instruct the learner to write on the materials to indicate where difficulty is encountered or to discuss ideas and problems.
      2. If the learner fails to understand an example, then try another verbal example. Does this clarify the issue? Note in writing the changes and suggestions you make as you go through the materials.
      3. If the learner fails to understand an explanation, then elaborate by adding information or changing the order of presentation. Does this clarify the issue? Note the changes you make in writing.
      4. If the learner appears to be bored or confused while going through the materials, it may be necessary to change the presentation to include larger or smaller bits of information before practice and feedback. Record your ideas concerning the regrouping of materials as you go along.
      5. Keep notes on examples, illustrations, information you add, and changes in sequence during the formative evaluation process; otherwise, you may forget an important decision or idea. Note taking should be quick and in rough form so the learner is not distracted from the materials.

   F. You may choose to test another learner from the target population before you make any changes or revisions in your materials to verify that the changes are necessary. If errors pointed out by your first learner "consultant" are obvious, then it may be necessary to make revisions before conducting a trial with the next learner. This saves testing time and enables the next learner to concentrate on other problems that may exist in the materials.

III. Outcomes of one-to-one formative evaluation
   A. Consider again the types of information you are looking for in the one-to-one testing:
      1. Faulty instructional analysis
      2. Errors in judgment about entry skills of learners in the target population
      3. Unclear or inappropriate objectives and expected outcomes

4. Inadequate information presentation and examples
   a. Examples, graphs, or illustrations that are too abstract
   b. Too much or too little information at one time
   c. Wrong sequence of information presented
   d. Unclear examples
5. Inadequate learner participation
6. Inadequate provision for transfer and retention
7. Unclear test questions, test situations, or test directions
8. Faulty wording or unclear passages

Small-Group Evaluation

I. Participation by learners from the target population
   A. Identify a group of learners that typifies your target population.
   B. Arrange for a group to participate.
      1. Adequate time should be arranged for required testing as well as instructional activities.
      2. Learners should be motivated to participate.
      3. Learners should be selected to represent the types of people expected in the target population. Include several learners from each expected major category in your target population.
   C. During the pretest, instruction, and posttest, make notes about suggestions for instructors who will use the materials. Also, note changes to make in the instruction or procedures as a result of your observation of learners interacting with the materials.
   D. Administer the pretest of required entry skills if one is appropriate.
      1. Check the directions, response patterns, and questions to ensure that the wording is clear.
      2. Instruct learners to circle words they do not understand and place a check beside questions or directions that are unclear.
      3. Do not stop to discuss unclear items with learners during the test unless they become bogged down or stop.
      4. Record the time required for learners to complete the entry test.
   E. Administer the pretest of skills to be taught during instruction. This test and the test of required entry skills could be combined into one pretest, if desirable.
      1. Have learners circle any vocabulary unclear to them.
      2. Have learners place a check beside any directions, questions, or response requirements unclear to them.
      3. Have learners write additional comments in the test if they desire.
      4. Do not discuss problems with learners during the test.
   F. Administer the instructional materials. Have the instructional setting close to reality with all required equipment and materials present. Any instructional assistance required should also be available during the trial.
      1. Instruct learners that you need their help in evaluating the materials.
      2. Have learners sign their work so you can compare their performance on the lesson with their performance based on their entry behaviors.
      3. Instruct learners to circle any unclear words and place a check beside any illustrations, examples, or explanations unclear in the instruction. Learners should keep working through the materials to the end without stopping for discussion.
      4. Record the time required for learners to complete the instructional materials. Time required may be more than anticipated if learners need instruction on unfamiliar equipment or procedures.

G. Administer the posttest.
   1. Have learners sign their posttest to enable comparisons with the pretest and questionnaires.
   2. Have learners circle any unclear vocabulary and place a check beside any unclear directions, questions, or response requirements.
   3. Have learners respond to as many items as they can regardless of whether they are sure of the answer or just guessing. Often, incorrect guesses can provide clues to inadequate instruction. You may want them to indicate which answers reflect guessing.
   4. Record the time required for learners to complete the posttest.

H. Administer an attitude questionnaire to learners.
   1. You may want to ask questions such as the following:
      - Did the instruction hold your attention?
      - Was the instruction too long or too short?
      - Was the instruction too difficult or too easy?
      - Did you have problems with any parts of the instruction?
      - Were the cartoons or illustrations appropriate or distracting?
      - Was the use of color appealing or distracting?
      - What did you like most?
      - What did you like least?
      - How would you change the instruction if you could?
      - Did the tests measure the material that was presented?
      - Would you prefer another instructional medium?

I. Arrange for learners to discuss the pretest, instruction, or posttest with you or their instructor after they have completed all the work.
   1. You may want to structure the discussion with planned questions.
   2. You may want to ask questions such as "Would you change the exercises in section X?" or "Did you like the example in section X?"

Field Trial

I. Select an appropriate sample from the target population.
   A. Arrange for the selected group to try the materials.
      1. Ensure that there is an adequate number of learners in the group. Thirty is often suggested as the number of learners to participate in a field trial.
      2. Ensure that selected learners reflect the range of abilities and skills of learners in the target population.
      3. Ensure that there are adequate personnel, facilities, and equipment available for the trial.
   B. Distribute the instructional materials as well as the instructor's guide, if it is available, to the instructor conducting the field test.
   C. Discuss any instructions or special considerations that may be needed if the instruction is out of context.
   D. Personally play a minimal role in the field trials.
   E. Summarize the data you have collected. Summarized data may include a report of the following:
      1. Scores on the entry skill part of the pretest
      2. Pretest and posttest scores on skills taught
      3. The time required for students to complete each test used
      4. The time required for students to complete the instruction
      5. The attitudes of learners as well as participating instructors

Formative Evaluation of Existing Materials and Instructor-Led Instruction

I. Existing materials

In addition to the formative suggestions for self-instructional materials, you should determine whether the following are true:

A. All parts of the instructional strategy are accounted for in the selected materials or provided by the instructor.
B. The transitions between sources are smooth.
C. The flow of content in the various instructional resources is consistent and logical.
D. The learners' manual or the instructor adequately presents objectives.
E. Directions for locating instruction within each source are adequate.
F. Sections of the instructional strategy that must be supplied by the instructor are complete and adequate.
G. The vocabulary used in all the sources is appropriate.
H. The illustrations and examples used are appropriate for the target group.

II. Instructor-led instruction

A major factor in evaluating instruction that is delivered by instructors is that they are an interactive part of the instruction. In addition to all the considerations mentioned previously, several important evaluation considerations are unique to this type of instruction. Is/does the instructor:

A. Convincing, enthusiastic, helpful, and knowledgeable?
B. Able to avoid digressions to keep instruction and discussions on relevant topics and on schedule?
C. Make presentations in an interesting and clear manner?
D. Use visual aids to help with examples and illustrations?
E. Provide good feedback to learners' questions?
F. Provide adequate practice exercises with appropriate feedback?

You should record events that occur during instruction so that you can study them for what they imply about the effectiveness of the instruction.

Evaluation and Revision

Evaluating and Revising the Formative Evaluation Plan

The formative evaluation component distinguishes the instructional design process from a philosophical or theoretical approach. Rather than speculating about the instructional effectiveness of your materials, you test them with learners; therefore, you should do the best possible job of collecting data that truly reflect the effectiveness of your materials. Just to be clear, the task at this point is to evaluate the formative evaluation plan and make any revisions needed to improve the plan. In the next chapter, with formative evaluation data in hand, you will cycle back through decisions made during analysis, design, and development as necessary for improvement of your product. The hope, of course, is that you will be able to implement your instruction smoothly, that students will enjoy the materials and perform as predicted, and that any needed revisions will be minimal! But first, there are several concerns about the formative evaluation context and the learners who participate in the evaluation that the designer should keep in mind when reviewing the adequacy of planning and procedures for formative data collection.

Context Concerns

For proper evaluation of materials, ensure that any technical equipment is operating effectively. More than one instructor has been discouraged because a new set of instructional materials was tried with particular equipment and the equipment failed to operate correctly. Data from learners were invalid, and the instructor learned little more than that the equipment must operate effectively to try out materials.

It is also important in the early stages of formative evaluation, especially in the one-to-one trials, that you work with learners in a quiet setting in which you can enlist their full attention. At this point, you are concerned about how the materials work under the best possible conditions. As you move to the small-group sessions and field trial, you are increasingly concerned with how the materials work in more typical contexts. If the typical setting is an individualized classroom with a relatively high noise level, then you want to know whether the materials work in that situation; however, you should not begin the formative evaluation under these conditions.

Concerns About Learners

In the selection of learners for participation in any phase of formative evaluation, avoid depending entirely on the instructor to assess entry knowledge of the learners. Whenever possible, administer entry-skills tests to learners to verify that they are members of the target population for whom the materials are intended. Experience has shown that instructors, for whatever reason, sometimes make poor estimates of the readiness of learners who are recommended for participation in formative evaluation studies. Do what you can to verify the entry knowledge of the learners.

When you get the information on entry knowledge and skills of learners, you sometimes encounter the problem of what to do with those learners who have already mastered some or all of the skills to be taught or learners who do not have the required entry skills. Do you drop them from the formative evaluation? It is preferable to include some learners who do not exactly match the skill profile of the real target population. Those who already know some of the content can serve as "subject-matter sophisticates" who can be indicators of how other students who know some or most of the content will respond. You can also determine whether your instruction can bring these learners up to approximately 100 percent performance. If it does not work for these learners, then it is unlikely to be effective with learners who have less entering knowledge.

Learners who do not have the entry skills should also be included in a formative evaluation. The entry skills have been derived theoretically and therefore need validation. If the learners who cannot demonstrate the entry skills do, in fact, struggle through the instruction with little success, whereas those with the entry skills are successful, it suggests that you have identified skills that learners must have to begin the instruction. If, however, learners without the entry skills are successful with the instruction, then you must seriously reconsider the validity of the entry skills you have identified.

We have suggested that in the one-to-one formative evaluation, the designer should use at least three learners—one high, one average, and one low in ability. This is a vague recommendation that can be made more specific by identifying a *high-ability learner* as one who already knows some of the content to be taught. The *average learner* can be identified as one who has the entry skills but no knowledge of the skills to be taught and the *low-ability learner* as one who does not have some of the entry skills. By using these definitions, the designer can be much surer of getting the desired range of abilities. Research indicates that these three types of learners provide different but useful information to the designer, and thus all three should be included in the formative evaluation.

Concerns About Formative Evaluation Outcomes

A final word of caution: Be prepared to obtain information that indicates that your materials are not as effective as you thought they would be after going through such an extensive instructional design process. It is common to become tremendously involved when putting a great deal of time and effort into any kind of project. It is just as common to be sharply disappointed when you find that your efforts have not been entirely satisfactory.

You should note, however, that in the formative evaluation process, positive performance and feedback from students provide you with little guidance for revision but can be very satisfying confirmation of the decisions you have made in the design and development process. Remember, however, that positive feedback only indicates that what you have is effective with the students who used the materials. You can then only make a tentative inference that the materials should be effective with learners who are of similar ability and motivation in your target population.

As you move through the formative evaluation process, it might be helpful to pretend that another instructor has developed the materials and that you are merely carrying out the formative evaluation for that person. We do not suggest that you mislead the learners about it but rather that you adopt this noninvolved psychological mindset in order to listen to what learners, instructors, and SMEs might say. These kinds of feedback must be integrated into an objective assessment of the extent to which your materials are meeting the objectives you have set for them and how they can be improved.

Concerns with Implementing Formative Evaluation

Although the ideal instructional design process is to conduct three phases of formative evaluation prior to distributing instruction for general use, it is sometimes simply not possible to follow this procedure. In many cases, there is not enough time to conduct the formative evaluation or no funds have been budgeted to do so. What responsibility does the designer have in this situation?

The first consideration should be to determine whether any kind of formative evaluation could be conducted before the formal usage of the instruction. Are there ways to combine some of the one-to-one techniques with the field trial? Can we get someone to read through the materials and see whether they make sense? Can we walk through a role-play to make sure it works? Most designers would acknowledge that using newly designed instruction without some type of tryout is extremely risky, but sometimes it is unavoidable.

If instruction is being used with the target population without the benefit of any formative evaluation, it is still possible to use that opportunity to gather information useful for revising the instruction. In these situations, the procedures typically applied are those of the field trial. Just think of it as "going live" with the instruction and a field trial mentality. Questionnaire data and assessment information can be combined with observations of learners and direct discussions of the instruction to determine what kinds of changes should be made.

The general principle for the designer is that formative evaluations are always conducted; it is just a question of when, where, and how. Sometimes there are enough time and resources to conduct the three phases of formative evaluation described here. When it is not possible to do so, the designer's intent should be to improvise ways to gather as much information as possible about the instruction so that it can be revised appropriately.

Rubric for Evaluating Formative Evaluation Procedures

The following summary rubric is appropriate for evaluating the processes used during formative evaluation and will help you focus on the adequacy of your formative evaluation design. The rubric can be used as a preview before conducting the evaluations to alert you to things you may have missed in your planning and then again after the evaluations to assess the job you have done. As you use the rubric, do recall that it is very complete, and you should feel free to use the "NA" option when a criterion doesn't fit your project or circumstances prevent inclusion of the criterion. The rubrics for evaluating the actual materials during a formative evaluation are included in Chapters 8 and 9.

Designer note: If an element is not relevant for your project, mark NA in the No column.

No	Some	Yes	
			A. Overall Formative Evaluation Design Is/does the design:
____	____	____	1. Based on an instructional strategy (i.e., preinstruction, presentation, participation, assessment, and transfer)?
____	____	____	2. Use multiple data-gathering strategies?
____	____	____	3. Include summaries of reviewers' comments to locate strengths and problems?
____	____	____	4. Provide for adjusting/refining materials and procedures prior to subsequent evaluation phases?
			B. Experts Did the evaluation include expert review for:
____	____	____	1. Type of learning by learning specialists?
____	____	____	2. Content accuracy and currency by content specialists?
____	____	____	3. Appropriate complexity by learner specialists?
____	____	____	4. Feasibility and transfer by content specialists?
____	____	____	5. Clarity and effectiveness by target learners?
			C. Target Learners Did learners:
____	____	____	1. Represent target group?
____	____	____	2. Receive an orientation to provide instruction and put them at ease?
____	____	____	3. Receive all necessary materials (preinstruction through transfer)?
____	____	____	4. Complete and comment on pretest (including entry skills)?
____	____	____	5. Mark unclear passages and underline unfamiliar vocabulary?
____	____	____	6. Question unfamiliar examples and suggest alternatives?
____	____	____	7. Question perspectives and focus?
____	____	____	8. Participate in practice and rehearsal activities and comment on the helpfulness of feedback?
____	____	____	9. Complete the posttest and comment on unclear items?
____	____	____	10. Complete the attitude questionnaire and comment on the clarity of questions as well as their opinions?
____	____	____	11. Appear comfortable with media and delivery system?
			D. Evaluators Did evaluators:
____	____	____	1. Interact with learners during one-to-one evaluation to question, clarify, elaborate, etc.?
____	____	____	2. Summarize learners' comments and responses?
____	____	____	3. Identify strengths and pinpoint problems?
____	____	____	4. Revise materials for obvious errors between one-to-one trials and before small-group and field trials?

Examples

The following example continues the golf instruction related to planning the putt. Recall from previous chapters that the main focus of this instruction is promotion of the golf club and recreation. This, rather than actual achievement of golf skills, will temper the format and nature of the evaluation. Recall also that this golf clinic is:

- being provided by a golf club for newly retired or soon-to-retire local people who are prospective members for the club,
- intended for a small group, and
- intended to be instructor-led by the club's golf teaching professional.

These factors will also influence the evaluation. We might ask, why even bother to evaluate? The answers to that question are easy. Should the clinic be successful, the club will want to offer the clinic multiple times to attract new members. The club has invested funds and facilities for the clinic to attract new members and not only recoup its investment but also increase its revenue as a result of new membership. An effective clinic will help ensure that the club realizes its goal.

One-to-One Formative Evaluation

Instructor-led formative evaluations typically require modifications to the basic evaluation design, but the design should be used to guide evaluation planning. In this case, there will be a one-to-one type evaluation except it will be modified to a two-to-two with an evaluator/observer, a teaching professional, and two beginning golfers. The evaluator is teaming with the teaching professional (SME) to make him feel comfortable in the process and to obtain the insights of a professional about the instruction. Two learners rather than one will be included because they will be working as a unit or team similar to a golfer and his or her caddy. During the practice and feedback phase of the strategy, the learners study the putting green together, plan the stroke together, modify the plan based on their joint perspectives, and provide each other with feedback about the adequacy of the plan.

It is critical that the observer/evaluator makes the learners and instructor feel comfortable during the session. When the instructor is also being observed, tension and discomfort are possible should the instructor believe he or she is being judged, especially by someone who is not an expert golfer and in the presence of learners. A good plan might be to encourage the instructor and learners to work as a team as they interact with each other during the lesson and the debriefing that follows the lesson. The format of the evaluation will be an interactive discussion rather than a questionnaire that would undoubtedly be considered too formal in this learning context. The sessions and the evaluation debriefings will be video recorded to free the evaluator to participate as a team member in the live and interactive activity.

Selecting the two learners is important. Many older golfers have played recreational golf and have never had a lesson other than feedback from their companions. Others in this newly retired group have not played much at all. One member of the learner team should have experience without training, and the other should have little or infrequent experience playing the game. In addition, the learners will receive complimentary instruction with no charge since they are helping the club develop the instruction.

As with other formats of instruction, the instructional strategy is used to anchor the questions for instructor-led instruction. Recall from Table 11.1 that the main components of the instructional strategy and main areas of questions are named, and

Table 11.2 contains the three main areas of criteria: clarity, impact, and feasibility. It is best to refer to these tables so you can select those components and criteria most appropriate for your instruction and for the particular stage of formative evaluation. In the following section, we name the learning components from Table 11.1 and then choose the questions to focus the evaluation from the criteria in Table 11.2. For illustration purposes, let's skip the preinstructional component and focus instead on session 2, putting.

Presentation

Recall that this component includes presentation (sequence, size chunk, content, examples, links), participation (practice and feedback), assessment, and follow-through. Appropriate questions for this component might be, did the instructor:

- talk positively about the club, membership, and the clinics (motivation) (goal focus on membership)?
- have a light, recreational, jovial demeanor (goal focus)?
- show enthusiasm for the topic?
- appear interested in the learners?
- stay engaged with the learners throughout the session? and
- present the information and skills in a logical sequence according to the goal analysis?

Appropriate questions for the learners might be, did they:

- see the YouTube video depicting various golfers and their caddies as being relevant and interesting?
- understand why they began by rolling rather than putting balls (clarity)?
- understand the terminology and vocabulary used (e.g., lay of the land, force, trajectory, drag) (clarity)?
- understand the interaction among the physical conditions of the putting green, their mental plans (trajectory and force), and their physical actions in making the putt?
- perceive the instruction as interesting and relevant?
- pay attention to the teaching professional during explanations and demonstrations?
- believe the examples are necessary and clear (clarity)?
- feel the explanations are helpful, too long, or not long enough (clarity and pace)?
- consider the demonstrations to be helpful, too many, not enough (clarity and pace)?
- think the pace of each part (planning, grip, stance, actual putt) is just right, too little, too long (pace)?
- enjoy themselves as they rehearsed (motivation and impact)?

Participation

This component includes practice and feedback. Questions helpful for focusing the evaluation in this area might include, did the learners:

- know what to do for each practice activity (planning, gripping, addressing, stroking) (clarity)?
- think the amount of practice for each activity is just right, too little, too much (pace)?
- provide useful feedback for their partner's putts (impact)?
- enjoy themselves as they rehearsed (motivation and impact)?

Assessment and Follow-Through

There will be no pretest or practice test because this is recreational, and it is assumed the learners will have limited putting skill. The posttest will not be a test but rather a concluding contest to enable learners to integrate the putting skills in a more realistic manner. Appropriate questions for this component might be, did the learners:

- feel the directions for the concluding putting contest are clear and the activity is enjoyable (clarity and motivation)?
- believe they could transfer the skills they learned during instruction to the contest?
- believe they improved their putting skills as a result of the lesson (impact on skill and confidence)?
- score and record their putts accurately for the contest (each stroke is a score point) (transfer)?
- want to play more golf as a result of the lesson (motivation)?

Management and Feasibility

A third criterion area is feasibility, and this is within the management category. We will want to focus on the adequacy of resources. Do the learners and instructor believe:

- the schedule (day, time, week) is convenient?
- there is enough time in the two hours allotted for putting instruction to warm up, learn about putting, and practice their skill?
- they need more time anywhere?
- the practice putting green is physically adequate to practice the trajectory and force skills?
- the club members and the staff are welcoming and helpful?

Formative Evaluation Procedures

These questions will not be placed into a questionnaire and used by group participants. Instead, they will be used by the evaluator to focus the interactive discussions. The session will be video recorded to capture the session events from instructor and learners. Following the instructional session, the observer and golf instructor can review the video together in a debriefing session and discuss what each perceived was happening, what was good, and what might make the session better. Later, the observer can revisit the recorded session to focus on the instructor's adherence to the various components of the instructional strategy, noting any discrepancies and/or improvements to the intended instruction. Also noted can be the instructor's demeanor and attitude and their impact on the learners. The learners' questions and comments to the instructor and each other can be revisited and interpreted considering their comments during the debriefing. Attention should be paid to the clarifications learners request, their actions during the instructor's explanations, their actions during rehearsal, and their level of success in planning the putt and actually putting.

Small Group/Field Trial

There will also be a combined small group/field trial of sixteen learners, which is the number of learners prescribed for the actual golf clinic. This trial will be treated as a regular clinic, and the observer will not interfere with participants or the instructor during any of the sessions. The observer/evaluator will attend all sessions and make notes about the learners' and the golf instructor's activity and conversation. As with the one-to-one format, the observer will video record each of the six sessions, including the actual golf tournament, and then review the recordings and the observation notes with the instructor and perhaps selected learners.

The criteria for reviewing the videos are also the same: adherence to the learning components of the instructional strategy, clarity of the message, impact on the learners, and feasibility. The questions posed during the one-to-one study will again be used to focus the observer and instructor during the debriefing session and video review.

Within the clarity category, they should pay careful attention to the golf instructor's understanding of and adherence to the components of the instructional strategy. If any part was ignored or other strategies were included, the instructor and observer should discuss what and why.

Instructor-led instruction has its benefits and constraints. On the positive side, instructors' experience and knowledge enable them to interact personally with the learners and shift information, activities, timing, and sequence as needed for the learners' attitudes and actions and for environmental and learning context conditions. On the constraint side, instructors may want to proceed through instruction as they have always proceeded: They may leave out some parts of the instructional strategy, not allocate time for adequate practice, or not provide for adequate feedback and transfer. As instructors ourselves, we understand the need for instructors to make strategies and lesson plans their own. Count on even the very best plans being adapted to the judgment and habits of the instructor.

In the feasibility criterion, the observer should have additional questions related to the club's original purpose for offering the golf clinic. Recall that increased membership is the club's main reason for offering the clinic. For example:

1. Is the advertising about the clinic adequate?
2. Do enough people learn about it and sign up?
3. Do they attend all sessions?
4. Do they participate in the end-of-session contests and the capstone golf tournament?
5. Do participants join the club within a reasonable time period?

Case Study

Group Leadership Training

This section includes formative evaluation activities for the group leadership training example as well as a detailed outline of formative evaluation activities to guide your work.

The following illustrations are based on the instructional analysis and strategy of main step 6, "Manage cooperative group interaction," presented in Chapters 8, 9, and 10. Again, the target population is master's-level students in a campus leadership course who have varying levels of knowledge and skills. Conduct of the one-to-one and small-group formative evaluations is described in this section, and examples of the field trial are included in the Practice and Feedback sections. In reading each type of evaluation, you should remember the purposes for the evaluation, the nature of the leadership instruction, and the characteristics of the student leaders.

One-to-One Formative Evaluation Procedures

Materials for the One-to-One Trials

The materials consisted of loose, typed pages containing directions, instruction, and assessments. The videos were presented as paper storyboards at this point. Illustrations consisted of rough hand drawings and clip art. Materials for each objective and any required leader responses were placed on one page, with feedback on the following page. This facilitated evaluating the sequence and clustering of the objectives and ensured that both could be changed readily if needed. The pages were divided into two columns, leaving ample room for tryout students as well as the designer to comment and write suggestions directly in the materials. Six copies of the rough materials were produced: one for each learner, one for the designer, and one for tallying results and making revisions.

Participants and Instructions

Four students in the leadership program were invited to take the course as an independent study and were told of the activities that would be undertaken during the term. The first four students invited to participate agreed, believing it was their first opportunity to study independently with the professor and TAs and with other students in a small-group atmosphere. These four students participated in a semester-long one-to-one evaluation. The sample of four consisted of students with differing undergraduate majors and interests: one was studying to be an athletic director, one wanted to be a high school principal, one wanted to work in student services in higher education, and one was seeking a position in local government. All had experience leading group meetings at work and in the community. Although materials for the entire course were evaluated by this one-to-one group, our discussion here relates only to the portion for main step 6, managing cooperative group interaction.

Participants were thanked for attending, and coffee, soft drinks, and bagels were offered to help ensure a social rather than judgmental environment. The purpose for the session was explained, and participants were told that there were no incorrect answers, only areas in which the developers may not have been as clear or complete as needed. Before beginning, they were told that the developers wished them to check vocabulary, reading level, and pacing as well as the clarity of examples, exercises, and feedback. They were also asked to comment on their experiences in leading group discussions, whether they believe some of the sections could have been skipped, and whether they believe more information and examples should be added.

Preinstructional Materials

As participants worked through each section of the materials, in order to help them begin critiquing, the designers asked them to comment on whether (1) the initial motivation material was clear and interesting, (2) the objectives were clear and relevant to them, and (3) they already possessed any of the skills in the objectives. They were asked to write their comments directly on the pages in the large margin provided. The designer paraphrased their verbal comments in the margin as well.

Content Presentation

Students identified and marked unclear or confusing directions or management information, and they circled unfamiliar vocabulary in the written materials, including the video scripts. The designer asked them to comment orally on the clarity of descriptions and examples used and to suggest orally other examples from their experiences. These experiences were paraphrased in the margin by the designer. They were also prompted to comment on the adequacy of sequence of content and chunk size. It was not possible to judge pace because of the interactive nature of the evaluation.

Learner Participation

Students were asked to complete all practice items and activities and to comment on whether they were interesting and assisted them in learning and remembering the skills. The designer asked the participants to comment on items they missed (without telling the learner that the items were missed) to gather more information on their misconceptions and incomplete learning. Through these conversations, the designer identified areas for which more information and examples were needed. Learners were also asked to evaluate the clarity and helpfulness of the feedback provided and to write in the margin questions that remained after studying the feedback.

Assessments

For both the pretest and the posttest, learners were asked to provide information about the clarity of the test instructions, vocabulary used, and questions or tasks required. They marked unclear or confusing words, questions, or directions. As participants responded, the designer asked probing questions when an item was missed on the posttest to identify the source of errors or misconceptions. Learners' comments were paraphrased by the designer in the margins beside the missed questions.

Following the one-to-one evaluation, learners were asked to reflect on the instruction and comment on its clarity and utility overall. This interview provided insights into the relevance of the instruction for their tasks as leaders and for its utility in helping them perform their jobs better. They were also asked to comment on any materials they believe should be improved or eliminated.

After each one-to-one evaluation, the comments of the learner were reviewed and synthesized, and the materials were revised to eliminate obvious mistakes. The revised set of materials was then produced for the next evaluation session. With the one-to-one evaluations completed and the materials revised as needed, the instruction should undergo a small-group evaluation to identify any problems with the materials or their administration in the intended format.

Small-Group Formative Evaluation Procedures

Materials for the Small-Group Trial

The small-group trial was conducted the following semester. By this time, the instructional materials were completely developed to the intended level of sophistication, including the web-based instruction, simulations, instructor-led sessions, videos, and assessments, so that either management or learning problems could be identified during the evaluation. The instructor's guide was also complete and tested to help ensure that various faculty members could use the materials effectively. To facilitate learners' evaluation of the instructor-led, web-based, and video instruction, an evaluation form naming each objective and its related activities was given to learners to complete immediately after they completed each part of the instruction. The form also included a rating scale for judging the interest, clarity, and utility of each activity as well as a column for their suggested improvements. It used the general format shown in Table 11.3.

Table 11.3 Form Learners Can Use During the Formative Evaluation of Nonprint Materials

Group Leadership Training Materials Evaluation Form for Nonprint Media

Rating responses
1 = Not at all
2 = Somewhat
3 = Mostly
4 = Very

Use this column to write your ideas and suggestions for how to improve this piece of the instruction.

INSTRUCTIONAL PIECE	PLEASE CIRCLE THE QUALITY LEVEL	WHAT WOULD MAKE IT BETTER?
6.1.1 Pretest	Interesting: 1 2 3 4	
Video on website	Clear: 1 2 3 4	
Video #6	Useful: 1 2 3 4	
6.2.2 Website	Interesting: 1 2 3 4	
Video of meeting	Clear: 1 2 3 4	
Discussion group	Useful: 1 2 3 4	

(And so forth for the remaining nonprint objectives and activities.)

Participants and Instructions

All twenty members of the leadership class were selected for the small-group formative evaluation. Again, they were all master's-level students with differing undergraduate majors and varying areas of interest. Some of the participants had prior experience with group leadership, either at work or in the community. Two of the participants had formal coursework in communication and group discussion management.

Only one small-group evaluation could be conducted because there was only one class this term; it may be necessary to schedule another class next semester after the results are evaluated and the materials and instructor's guide revised. Some of the revisions may result in learning or management improvements; others may not.

Preinstructional Materials

Learners followed directions and participated as instructed. For the web-based pretest, a free-response form was inserted following the pretest, and learners were invited to enter comments on any unclear information in the directions. Learners were directed to answer all the questions on the pretest to the best of their ability. Following the pretest, learners received another essay-style response form, and they were invited to identify and comment on any questions that were unclear or confusing. Questions were organized within objectives, and objectives were organized within instructional goals. Data were summarized by identifying the percentage of students in the group answering each question correctly and the percentage of items answered correctly by each learner. In addition, the designer tallied items and directions marked as unclear and vocabulary words marked as unfamiliar. Learners were not stopped to ask questions about the interest value or clarity of the motivational materials or objectives.

Content Presentation and Practice

Learners were not stopped or interviewed during instruction. Prior to beginning, however, they were invited to mark directly on print materials any explanations, examples, illustrations, vocabulary, practice, and feedback that they considered unclear. For video- and web-based materials, the evaluation form was again provided for learners to mark as they worked through the instruction. Learners were instructed to complete all participation items and activities within the materials.

Assessments

The posttests were marked in the same manner as the pretests. Similarly, questions were organized within objectives, and objectives were organized within instructional goals. Data were summarized by identifying the percentage of learners in the group answering each question correctly as well as the percentage of items and objectives answered correctly by each participant. Again, a tally of questions marked as unclear and vocabulary words marked as unfamiliar was made. Finally, the time required for learners to complete the pretest, instruction, and posttest was recorded, including the shortest time, longest time, and average time taken by the group. With these data gathered and organized by objective and goal, the process of identifying problems and solutions began.

Instruments for Assessing Learners' Attitudes About Instruction

Instruments for assessing learners' achievement of group leadership skills were illustrated and discussed in Chapter 10. No attitude questionnaires, however, were presented, and good formative evaluation includes assessing both achievement and attitudes.

Table 11.4 contains an attitude questionnaire for the instructional goal, "Lead group discussions aimed at solving problems." The questionnaire is designed to be administered following session 10: "Engender cooperative member behaviors" (objectives 6.1.1 through 6.5.1 in Table 6.7, p. 148). It contains six sections. Four of the sections relate to facets of Keller's ARCS model: attention, relevance, confidence, and satisfaction. Another section enables learners to rate the clarity of instruction.

Table 11.4 Attitude Questionnaire for Main Step 6: Manage Cooperative Group Interaction, Session 10, Objectives 6.1.1 through 6.5.1

Session 10: Engendering Cooperative Member Behaviors **Date** ________

Instructions: Use the following questionnaire to judge the effectiveness of today's session on engendering cooperative member behaviors. Please rate the quality of the instruction in each of the five main categories included on the form. For each of the instructional areas listed on the left, circle the response on the right that best reflects your perception of the quality level. At the bottom of the form, please comment on aspects of tonight's session that you consider to be strengths or problems. Thank you.

I. **Attention:** To what degree did the following instructional activities hold your interest or attention?

INSTRUCTIONAL AREAS	ATTENTION LEVEL (CIRCLE ONE LEVEL FOR EACH AREA)
A. Reading, analyzing annotated dialogues of meetings illustrating:	
1. Member actions that aid cooperative interaction	Little 1 2 3 4 5 Very attentive
2. Strategies leaders use to encourage group cooperation	Little 1 2 3 4 5 Very attentive
B. Watching, analyzing videos of meetings depicting:	
3. Positive member actions that aid cooperative interaction	Little 1 2 3 4 5 Very attentive
4. Leaders engendering cooperative member behaviors	Little 1 2 3 4 5 Very attentive

(Continued)

Table 11.4 Continued

Session 10: Engendering Cooperative Member Behaviors	**Date** ________
C. Performing myself as group leader to:	
5. Engender cooperative member behaviors in my group	Little 1 2 3 4 5 Very attentive
II. **Relevance:** To what degree do you believe the following skills are relevant for helping you provide effective leadership in problem-solving meetings?	
	RELEVANCE LEVEL
6. Recognizing cooperative member behaviors during meetings	Little 1 2 3 4 5 Very relevant
7. Engendering cooperative member behaviors during meetings	Little 1 2 3 4 5 Very relevant
III. **Confidence:** What level of confidence do you have that you can use these group interaction management skills effectively in problem-solving discussions?	
	CONFIDENCE LEVEL
8. Recognizing cooperative member behaviors during meetings	Little 1 2 3 4 5 Very confident
9. Engendering cooperative member behaviors during meetings	Little 1 2 3 4 5 Very confident
IV. **Clarity:** What level of clarity do you believe the following instructional materials and activities have?	
	CLARITY LEVEL
10. Session introduction	Little 1 2 3 4 5 Very clear
11. Objectives for session	Little 1 2 3 4 5 Very clear
12. Annotated written dialogues of meetings	Little 1 2 3 4 5 Very clear
13. Videos of meetings	Little 1 2 3 4 5 Very clear
14. Performing ourselves as group leaders	Little 1 2 3 4 5 Very clear
15. Instructions for our group leadership activity	Little 1 2 3 4 5 Very clear
16. Checklists we used to find positive leader actions	Little 1 2 3 4 5 Very clear
17. Feedback on exercises for positive member and leader actions	Little 1 2 3 4 5 Very clear
V. **Satisfaction:** Overall, how satisfied were you with:	
	SATISFACTION LEVEL
18. The facilities	Little 1 2 3 4 5 Very satisfied
19. The instructor(s)	Little 1 2 3 4 5 Very satisfied
20. The pace	Little 1 2 3 4 5 Very satisfied
21. The instruction	Little 1 2 3 4 5 Very satisfied
22. Yourself, relative to the new skills you have developed/refined	Little 1 2 3 4 5 Very satisfied

Table 11.4 Continued

Session 10: Engendering Cooperative Member Behaviors **Date** ___________

VI. **Comments:** Please comment on aspects of this session that were strengths or problems for you personally.

	Strengths	Problems
Introduction:		
Objectives:		
Annotated dialogues:		
Videos:		
Interactive leadership session:		
Assessments:		
Other:		
Other:		

The last section asks learners to provide their comments on the strengths and weaknesses of instruction from their perspective. To aid their work, different aspects of instruction are named in the far-left column. The last two rows, marked "Other," are included to invite learners to comment on aspects of the instruction that were not specifically named on the form.

In addition to evaluating the instruction, instruments used to gather information are also assessed for their clarity and utility during the formative evaluation. For example, if several learners ask questions about instructions or particular items on the attitude questionnaire or tend to leave items or sections blank, then the related areas should be examined for clarity and modified. In addition, if any section of the instrument does not yield data useful for pinpointing strengths and weaknesses and for revising instruction, then it should also be revised or eliminated.

For additional learning support, the school curriculum case study in the appendices should be reviewed.

Professional and Historical Perspectives

If you had been developing instructional materials in the early 1960s, it is likely that your initial draft, or perhaps a revised draft, of those materials would have been put into final production and distributed to the target population. The almost-certain problems that would occur as a result of untested, first-draft instructional materials probably would have been blamed on poor teaching and unmotivated students when, in fact, the materials may not have been sufficient to support the instructional effort at the time of publication.

The problem of untested materials was magnified in the 1960s and 1970s with the advent of large, federally funded curriculum development projects and the influence of the abundance of publishers in a highly competitive education market that developed textbooks, audiovisual products, and grade-level learning materials kits that were distributed nationwide. Komoski (1974) describes and documents the explosion of instructional materials in that time period when the concept of materials evaluation tended to be defined as a comparison of the effectiveness of an innovation with other existing products. When such studies were carried out, researchers often found relatively little difference in student achievement between existing products and the new curriculum materials. Several studies reported by Baker and Alkin (1973) that were conducted between 1963 and 1967 had concluded that revising materials after trials with only one reviewer resulted in improved performance. In reviewing this situation, Scriven et al. (1967) and Cronbach (1975) concluded that our concept of evaluation should be expanded to include what has come to be called **formative evaluation**—the collection of data and information during the development of instruction that can be used to improve the effectiveness of the instruction.

During that time period, the concept of formative evaluation of instructional materials made its way from instructional systems design into the public eye under the terminology *learner verification and revision* (LVR). California in 1972 and Florida in 1974 were pioneers in legislation requiring publishers to demonstrate that the effectiveness of textbooks had been "verified" by learners and revised accordingly (Carey & Carey, 1980). After extensive reviews, Komoski and Lennon (1979) and Komoski and Woodword (1985) pointed out that the LVR reports provided by publishers were largely summaries of teachers' and administrators' anecdotal comments about how much they liked the textbooks in question. When publishers did document studies of effectiveness, they were usually reporting large-scale comparisons of students' achievement gains from beginning to end of a school year. Typical gains were normative measures of about one year of growth, which would have been expected due to maturation and other schooling factors regardless of whose textbooks and materials were used. Komoski (1985) makes clear distinctions between contemporaneous understandings of LVR as used in the commercial materials market and formative evaluation as used in the field of instructional design.

The LVR movement died a slow, predictable death in the face of pushback from textbook selection committees, state legislators, and intense lobbying from the publishing industry. Most evaluation of textbooks and other instructional materials now uses comparisons between the contents of given materials and the relevant state and/or national student learning benchmarks. The benchmarks are learning goals, but the textbook is content, so no conclusions can be drawn regarding how effective the materials may be. Student learning would be a product of the kinds of factors we have described in evaluating instructor-led instruction. One initiative that goes beyond simple content comparisons is Project 2061, begun in 1985 and sponsored by the American Association for the Advancement of Science. The first report from Project 2061 was *Science for All Americans*, a characterization of basic learning goals; that is, the knowledge, skills, and attitudes that all students, K–12, should acquire in their schooling in science, mathematics, and technology. The project then focused on developing clear benchmarks for student outcomes, for instructional support for teachers, and for learning support for students. Project 2061 has gone on to produce benchmarks-based evaluations of popular textbooks in each of four content areas: algebra, high school biology, middle grades mathematics, and middle grades science. In this report on the middle grades mathematics evaluations (Kulm et al., 1999), only four of the twelve textbooks that were evaluated were judged acceptable. The report is good reading for the descriptions of SME and connoisseur evaluation methodology and results, and the project home page is a good starting point for exploring the project's broad reach into science curriculum and methods (American Association for the Advancement of Science, 2000). Although formative evaluation plays no role in Project 2061's evaluation methodologies, its process does include consideration of research-based benchmarks that are correlated with effective teaching methodologies and improved student learning outcomes. Formative evaluation was originally defined and used as a process to improve learning outcomes after the first draft of instruction was developed. All experienced designers, however, will confirm that formative evaluation is not a single event; rather, it is a process that is employed for continuous improvement throughout the ID process. Agile design and research-based design, two contemporary relatives of classic ISD, even rely on formative evaluation as their primary quality control methodology. All designers have found that it was better to question decisions and assumptions early and often, thereby avoiding many problems that would otherwise not be discovered until after the draft of the instruction is complete.

Process Flowcharts

Formative Evaluation

You should design your formative evaluations to develop a frame of reference to ensure your approach is not too narrow or broad. Figures 11.1 through 11.4 depict formative evaluation activities with experts and with learners in one-to-one, small-group, and field trial settings.

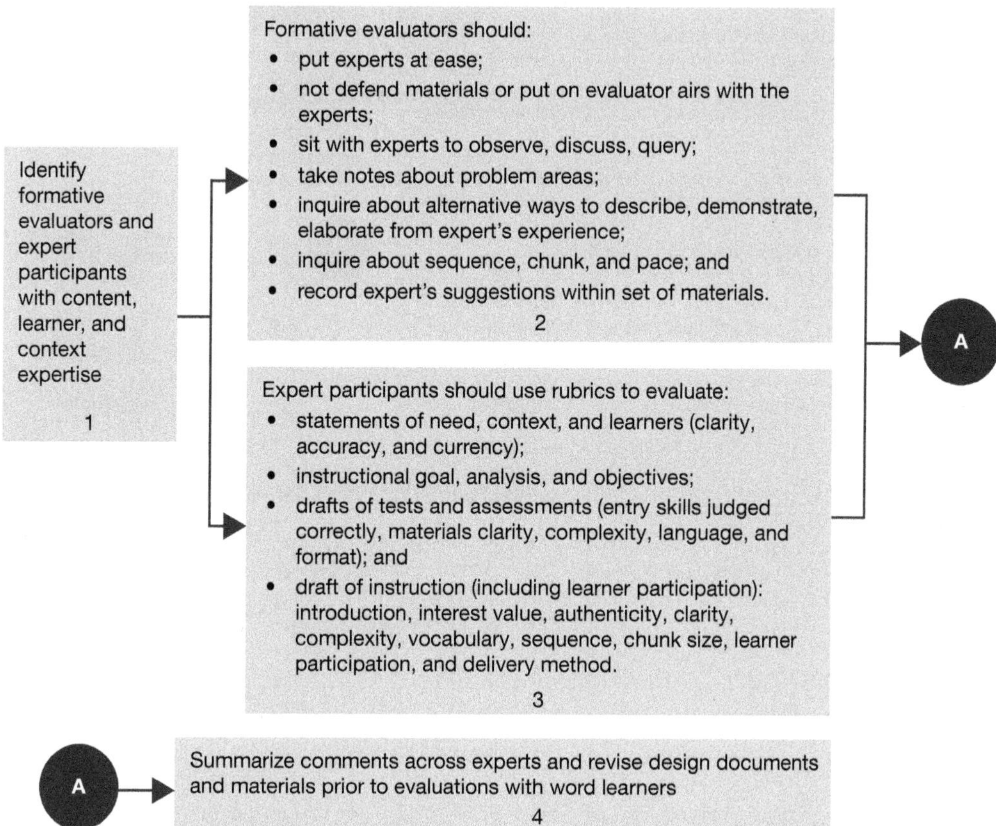

Figure 11.1 Conduct One-to-One Formative Evaluations with Experts

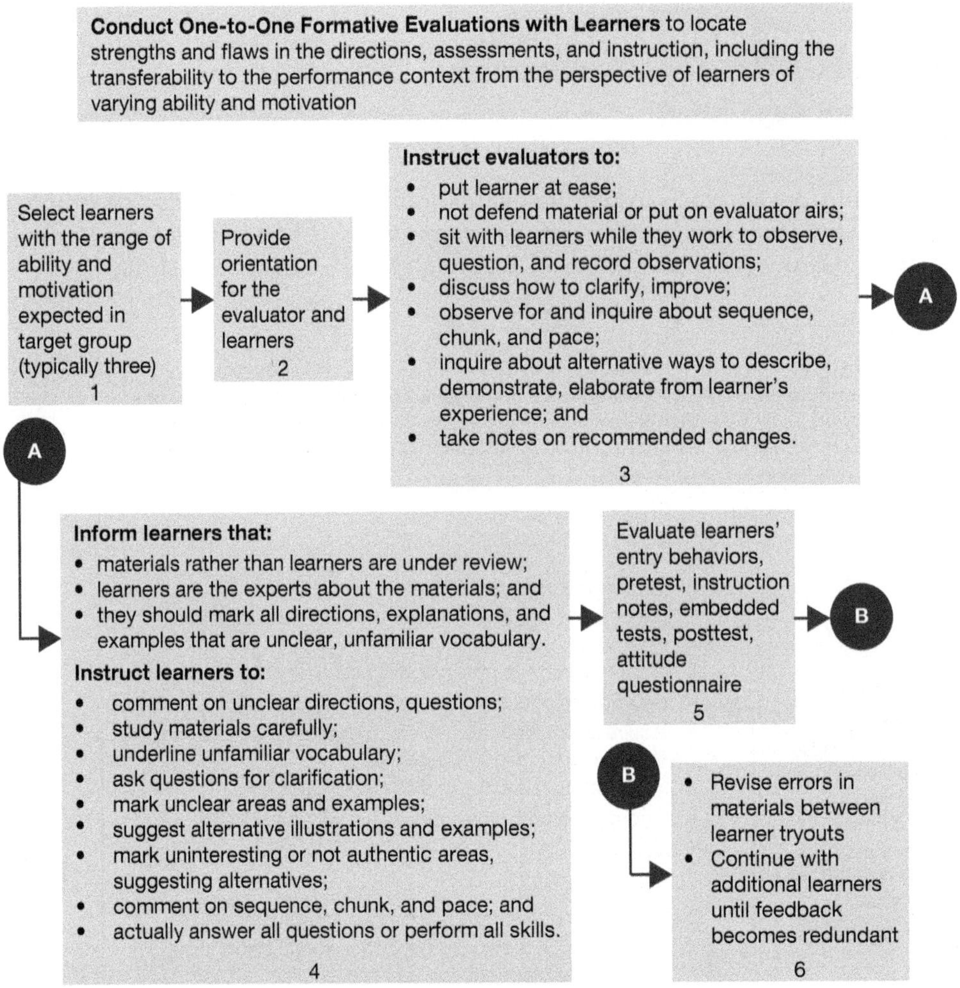

Conduct One-to-One Formative Evaluations with Learners to locate strengths and flaws in the directions, assessments, and instruction, including the transferability to the performance context from the perspective of learners of varying ability and motivation

Select learners with the range of ability and motivation expected in target group (typically three)
1

→ Provide orientation for the evaluator and learners
2

→ **Instruct evaluators to:**

- put learner at ease;
- not defend material or put on evaluator airs;
- sit with learners while they work to observe, question, and record observations;
- discuss how to clarify, improve;
- observe for and inquire about sequence, chunk, and pace;
- inquire about alternative ways to describe, demonstrate, elaborate from learner's experience; and
- take notes on recommended changes.

3

→ A

A → **Inform learners that:**

- materials rather than learners are under review;
- learners are the experts about the materials; and
- they should mark all directions, explanations, and examples that are unclear, unfamiliar vocabulary.

Instruct learners to:

- comment on unclear directions, questions;
- study materials carefully;
- underline unfamiliar vocabulary;
- ask questions for clarification;
- mark unclear areas and examples;
- suggest alternative illustrations and examples;
- mark uninteresting or not authentic areas, suggesting alternatives;
- comment on sequence, chunk, and pace; and
- actually answer all questions or perform all skills.

4

→ Evaluate learners' entry behaviors, pretest, instruction notes, embedded tests, posttest, attitude questionnaire
5

→ B

B →

- Revise errors in materials between learner tryouts
- Continue with additional learners until feedback becomes redundant

6

Figure 11.2 Conduct One-to-One Formative Evaluation with Learners

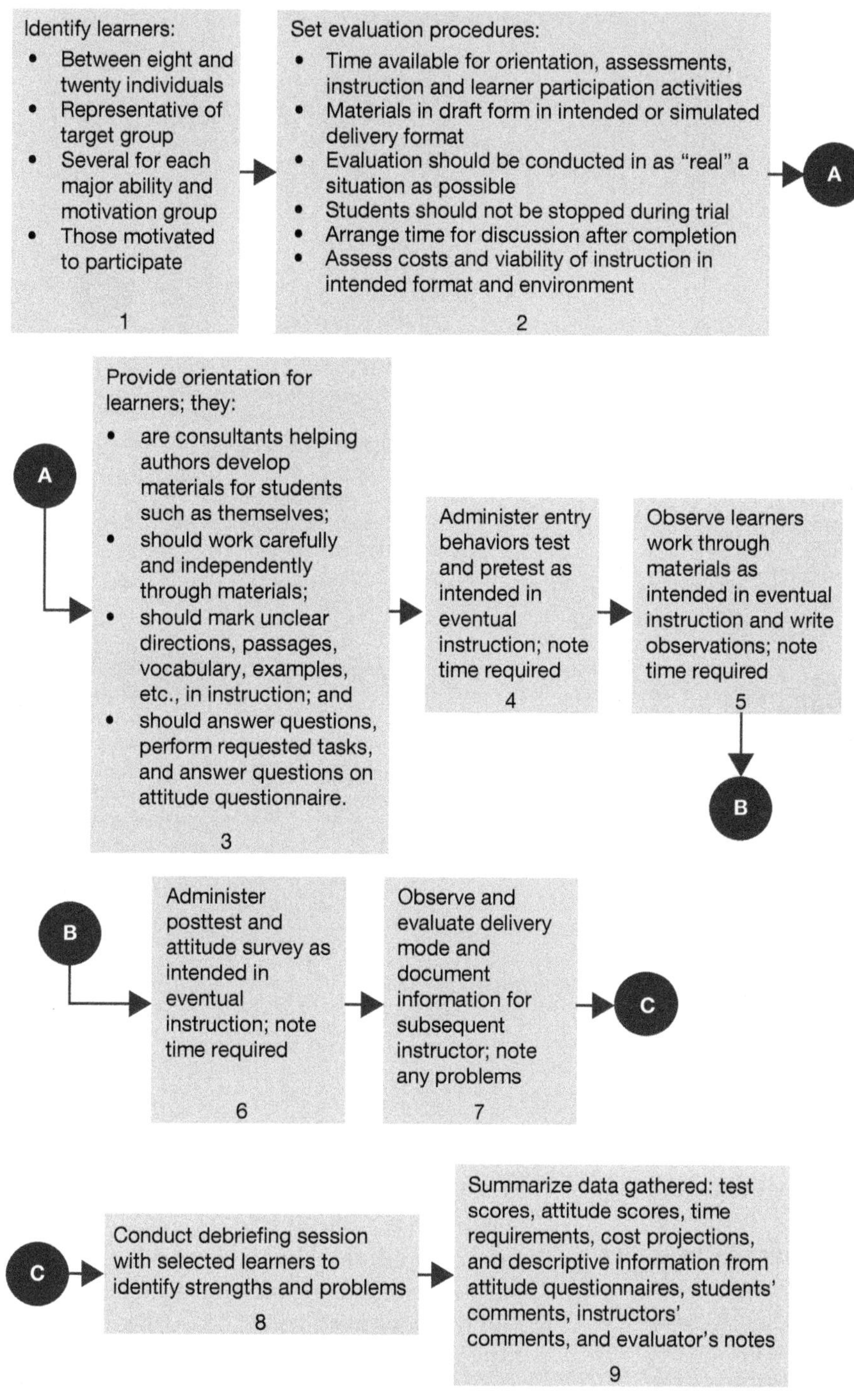

Figure 11.3 Conduct Small-Group Formative Evaluation

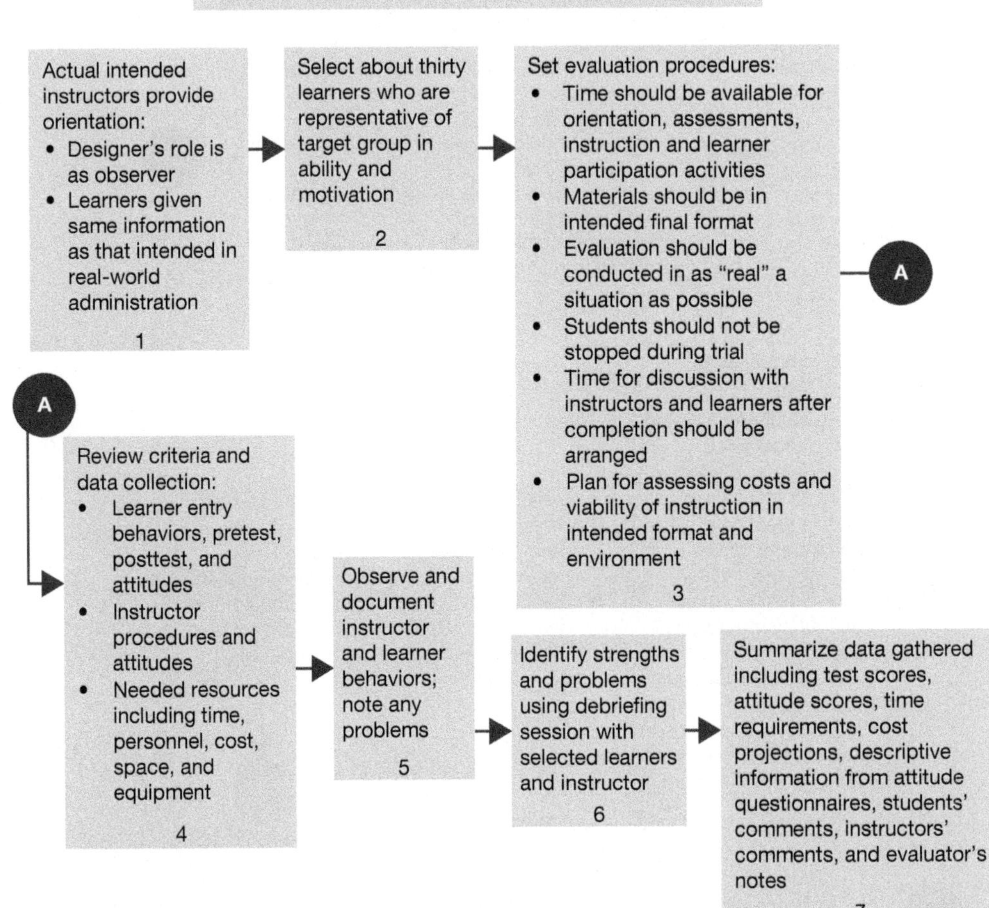

Figure 11.4 Conduct Field Trial Formative Evaluation

Practice

The following exercises are based on the instructional analysis and strategy of main step 5, "Select sentence type to convey mood or emphasis," "Prescribe best sentence type(s) to introduce and develop each main point," presented in Appendices C, F, and G. Assume the primary medium for the instruction is individualized, web-based instruction using an instructional delivery system such as Canvas. Assume also the target population is sixth-grade students who are average and above average in writing skills. Additionally, the instruction is using the writing of newsletter articles for the school as the motivational tool. For a field trial formative evaluation, consider the questions and identify decisions you would make based on the purposes of the evaluation, the nature of the instruction, and the target population.

1. Why should the designer be interested in a field trial of the materials on writing composition?
2. What information should the designer collect during the field trial for this instruction that would not have been collected during the small-group evaluation session?
3. Describe an appropriate sample group and instructional setting that could be used to evaluate the instructional materials.
4. What materials should the designer include in the field trial?
5. How should the designer's procedures differ if he or she conducts a field trial of adapted or adopted materials rather than a set of original materials?

6. Describe the major procedural differences between the field trial of selected materials and the field trial of instructor-led instruction.
7. Develop an attitude questionnaire to use with learners when conducting the small-group evaluations and field trials. Make your questionnaire appropriate for sixth-grade students who are participating in the formative evaluation of the writing composition materials.

Feedback

1. Materials are field-tested to determine their effectiveness with the target population when used under specified conditions. Field trials answer the question "Do these materials work for given learners when used in the planned learning context, and are there any improvements that can be made?" It helps to determine the instructional effectiveness of the materials in the absence of coaching by an instructor. It also aids in determining whether the materials are ready for use. The materials, tests, and instructions for both learners and instructors should be examined during the field trial. Have the materials had enough revision, or is more revision required? Revision at this point can be either in the materials themselves or in suggestions for using the materials.
2. The designer should collect:
   - achievement data using entry behaviors tests (entry skills 5.1 through 5.5), pretest, embedded test, and posttest data (subordinate skills 5.7 through 5.29 and main step 5);
   - students' motivational attitudes (interesting, relevant, confident, satisfied);
   - their perceptions of the materials related to each of the five learning components;
   - the clarity of the materials (spelling, punctuation, sequence, pace); and
   - the ease of accessing the instruction, rehearsal, feedback, and assessments using the learning management system.

   These are the same types of information that would be obtained during the small-group evaluation. Other information might include learners' attitudes about the following:
   - Was instruction interesting?
   - Was instruction too easy, too difficult, or just right?
   - Was instruction too fast, too slow, or just right?
   - Were the materials easy to use, or were they complicated?

   The designer should also include instructors' attitudinal information: whether the materials are easy to use, complicated, or just right and why the instructors hold these opinions.
3. An appropriate population for a field trial for the writing composition instruction would be one or more sixth-grade classes in the district that are heterogeneous in writing achievement (e.g., contains both average and above-average students). The class or classes should have teachers who are interested in the project and who are experienced in using Internet-based instruction with the class. They should also be experienced in working with students who are receiving their instruction using personal computers because this introduces new challenges for group management (e.g., students working on lessons rather than communicating with friends or surfing the Internet).
4. All materials developed should be included and evaluated in the field trial. This should include all print materials, web-based materials, equipment, assessments, and the instructor's guide.
5. The major difference between field evaluation of selected materials and original materials is that the instructor is present during the evaluation of selected existing materials. This provides the instructor with the opportunity to observe the use of the materials and to determine the adequacy of the various components of the instructional strategy.
6. With instructor-led instruction, the instructor interacts with the learners while delivering the instruction, controls the practice and feedback components of the instruction, and is more passive when evaluating selected materials.
7. The attitude questionnaire (see Appendix L, section 7) can be given to learners to complete during the small-group and field trials. During the one-to-one trials, however, you should use the questionnaire as an interview form. You can write responses learners make on the form. The one-to-one trials help you evaluate the attitudinal questionnaire formatively to determine whether the questions you have asked are clear. If you get several "I don't know" responses, then rephrase the questions until the learner understands the question and expresses an opinion. Note on the

questionnaire the changes you must make to clarify what you are asking. The attitudinal questionnaire can be used as an interview guide during the debriefing session as well; it helps you focus the evaluation on important components in the materials.

References and Recommended Readings

American Association for the Advancement of Science. (2000). *Project 2061 home page*. https://www.aaas.org/programs/project-2061

Baker, E. L., & Alkin, M. C. (1973). ERIC/AVCR annual review paper: Formative evaluation of instructional development. *AV Communication Review, 21*, 389–419.

Bernhardt, V. (2007). *Translating data into information to improve teaching and learning*. Routledge. Describes procedures for summarizing data for decision making at the school level.

Black, P., & William, D. (2009). Developing a theory of formative assessment. *Educational Assessment, Evaluation, and Accountability, 21*, 5–31. Describes formative evaluation at the curriculum and classroom levels.

Bodzin, A. M., Price, B., & Heyden, R. (2001). A formative evaluation approach to guide the development of a webtext biology curriculum. Paper presented at the National Association of Biology Teachers Annual Meeting, November 7–12, 2004, Montreal, Quebec, Canada. http://www.lehigh.edu/~inexlife/papers/nabt2001.pdf. Reports methods for a formative evaluation of a large-scale field trial of online biology curriculum.

Brandon, P. R., Young, D. B., Shavelson, R. J., Jones, R., Ayla, C. C., Ruiz-Primo, M. A., Yen, Y., Tomita, M. K., & Furtak, E. M. (2008). Lessons learned for the process of curriculum developers' and assessment developers' collaboration on the development of embedded formative assessments. *Applied Measurement in Education, 21*(4), 390–402. Focuses on formative evaluation at the curriculum and classroom levels.

Cambre, M. (1981). Historical overview of formative evaluation of instructional media products. *Educational Communications and Technology Journal, 29*(1), 1–25. Presents historical perspective on formative evaluation. An older but useful article for those interested in historical perspectives in ID.

Carey, J. O., & Carey, L. M. (1980). Using formative evaluation for the selection of instructional materials. *Journal of Instructional Development, 3*, 12–18. https://doi.org/10.1007/BF02909013

Carey, L. M. (2001). *Measuring and evaluating school learning*. Allyn & Bacon. Chapter 10, "Evaluating Group Performance"; Chapter 11, "Analyzing Items, Tasks, and Tests"; and Chapter 12, "Evaluating Individual Performance and Instruction" are all very helpful for the designer interested in more detail in synthesizing and interpreting data to evaluate learning and instruction.

Cronbach, L. J. (1975). Course improvement through evaluation. Reprinted in D. A. Payne & R. F. McMorris (Eds.), *Education and psychological measurement*. General Learning Press, 243–256. Describes need for formative evaluation of instructional materials.

Dick, W., & Carey, L. M. (1991). Formative evaluation. In L. J. Briggs, K. L. Gustafson, & M. H. Tillman (Eds.), *Instructional design: Principles and applications*. Educational Technology Publications. Describes formative evaluation from the instructional designer's perspective.

Druin, A. (Ed.). (1999). *The design of children's technology*. Morgan Kaufmann Publishers. Includes methodology for formative evaluation and revision of computer-based instruction and support.

Dziuban, C. D., Picciano, A. G., Graham, C. R., & Moskal, P. D. (2015). *Conducting research in online and blended learning environments: New pedagogical frontiers*. Routledge. Focus is on research paradigms and methods but contains discussions of variables that are of interest for formative and summative evaluation.

Flagg, B. N. (1990). *Formative evaluation for educational technologies*. Lawrence Erlbaum. Describes formative evaluation procedures for training programs using electronic technology.

Glaser, N. J., Schmidt, M., Wade, S. L., Smith, A., Turnier, L., & Modi, A. C. (2017). The formative design of epilepsy journey: A web-based executive functioning intervention for adolescents with epilepsy. *Journal of Formative Design in Learning*, 1(2), 126–135. A case study reporting iterative cycles of small-group formative evaluation and revision.

Heritage, M. (2010). *Formative assessment: Making it happen in the classroom*. Corwin Press. Stresses the use of learner performance data in improving instruction and learning.

Hunsaker, E., & West, R. E. (2020). Designing computational thinking and coding badges for early childhood educators. *TechTrends, 64*, 7–16. https://doi.org/10.1007/s11528-019-00420-3. A case study that takes the reader through the design, development, formative evaluation, and revision of media and materials.

Johnson, R. B., & Dick, W. (2012). Evaluation in instructional design: A comparison of evaluation models. In R. A. Reiser & J. V. Dempsey (Eds.), *Trends and issues in instructional design and technology* (3rd ed.). Allyn & Bacon. Describes formative evaluation from the instructional designers' perspective.

Kaufman, R., Guerra-Lopez, I., & Platt, W. A. (Eds.). (2005). *Practical evaluation for educators: Finding what works and what doesn't*. Corwin. Chapter 8 is on evaluating for continuous improvement.

Kenny, R. (2017). Introducing Journal of Formative Design in Learning. *Journal of Formative Design in Learning, 1*, 1–2. https://doi.org/10.1007/s41686-017-0006-0. The editor of this new AECT publication introduces the purposes and topical areas of interest for the journal in its first issue. The conceptual base is design-based research (DBR), but the principles of formative evaluation and revision in DBR processes apply to ID as well.

Kulm, G., Roseman, J., & Treistman, M. (1999). *A benchmarks-based approach to textbook evaluation*. Science Books & Films, *35*, 4. http://www.project2061.org/publications/textbook/articles/approach.htm

Komoski, P. K. (1974). An imbalance of product quantity and instructional quality: The imperative of empiricism. *AV Communication Review*, *22*(4), 357–386. Early arguments for learner verification in the face of an explosive proliferation of instructional materials in the education marketplace. The logic of the LVR argument remains viable today.

Komoski, P. K., & Lennon, R. T. (1979). Learner verification of instructional materials. *Educational Evaluation and Policy Analysis*, *1*(3), 101–103. Makes a clear distinction between learner verification and revision and materials validation studies. Lennon writes a counterpoint view from the perspective of the publishing industry.

Komoski, P. K., & Woodward, A. (1985). The continuing need for learner verification and revision of textual materials. In D. H. Jonassen (Ed.), *The technology of text: Volume two* (pp. 396–417). Educational Technology Publications.

Martin, F., & Dunsworth, Q. (2008). A methodical formative evaluation of computer literacy course: What and how to teach. *Journal of Information Technology Education*, *6*, 123–134. http://www.jite.org/documents/Vol6/JITEv6p123-134Martin217.pdf. Describes a case study of formative evaluation in a university setting.

Moseley, J. L., & Dessinger, J. C. (Eds.). (2010). *Handbook of improving performance in the workplace*. International Society of Performance and Instruction and Pfeiffer. Provides summary of ideas in performance, theory, and practice and includes section on formative evaluation.

Nathenson, M. B., & Henderson, E. S. (1980). *Using student feedback to improve learning materials*. Routledge. Describes the use of the formative evaluation process with Open University courses in England.

Performance and Instruction Journal, *22*(5). (1983). Special issue on formative evaluation. This issue carries several articles of interest to the designer. See especially: Wager, One-to-One and Small Group Formative Evaluation; Komoski, Formative Evaluation; Lowe, Clinical Approach to Formative Evaluation; and Golas, Formative Evaluation Effectiveness and Cost.

Phillips, J., Klein, J. D., Dunne, E., & Siriwardena, M. (2019). Using formative data to make evidence-based decisions during re-design. *Journal of Formative Design in Learning*, *3*, 133–145. https://doi.org/10.1007/s41686-019-00036-z

Reeves, T. C., & Hedberg, J. G. (2003). *Interactive learning systems evaluation*. Educational Technology Publications. Presents six levels of evaluation and includes formative techniques for e-learning processes and materials.

Royse, D. D. (2001). *Program evaluation: An introduction*. Brooks/Cole–Wadsworth Thompson Learning. Contains a chapter on formative and process evaluation readers will find informative.

Russell, J. D., & Blake, B. L. (1988). Formative and summative evaluation of instructional products and learners. *Educational Technology*, *28*(9), 22–28. Distinguishes between the formative evaluation of instruction and the formative evaluation of learners.

Scott, R. O., & Yelon, S. R. (1969). The student as a co-author—The first step in formative evaluation. *Educational Technology*, October, 76–78. Describes procedures to be used in one-to-one formative evaluation with students.

Scriven, M., Tyler, R., & Gagné, R. (1967). *Perspectives of curriculum evaluation*. AERA Monograph Series on Curriculum Evaluation. Rand McNally. Makes the first functional distinction between formative and summative evaluation.

Smith, P. L., & Ragan, T. J. (2020). *Instructional design* (4th ed.). Wiley. Contains chapters on formative and summative evaluation, with data displays and interpretations for revision.

Spector, J. M. (2015). Evaluation of educational practice, programs, projects, products, and policies. In J. M. Spector, B. Lockee, & M. Childress (Eds.), *Learning, design, and technology*. Springer, Cham. https://doi.org/10.1007/978-3-319-17727-4_1-1. Summative evaluations are discussed, but the emphasis is on formative evaluations. Author stresses the importance of research on evaluation methodology for progress in the field.

Spector, J. M., & Yuen, A. H. K. (2016). *Educational technology program and project evaluation*. Routledge. Chapter 17 focuses on continuous formative evaluation.

Tessmer, M. (2005). *Planning and conducting formative evaluations*. Routledge reprint of the original 1993 book. A complete description of the major phases of formative evaluation.

Weston, C. B., LeMaistre, C., McAlpine, L., & Bordonaro, T. (1997). The influence of participants in formative evaluation on the improvement of learning from written instructional materials. *Instructional Science*, *25*(5), 369–386. This empirical study using print materials concluded that formative revisions that incorporate learner feedback have the most impact on improving student learning.

Weston, C. B., McAlpine, L., & Bordonaro, T. (1995). A model for understanding formative evaluation in instructional design. *Educational Technology Research and Development*, *43*(3), 29–49. The article presents a model that depicts the feedback relationships among various ID processes.

Williams, D. D., South, J. B., Yanchar, S. C., Wilson, B. G., & Allen, S. (2011). How do instructional designers evaluate? A qualitative study of evaluation in practice. *Educational Technology Research and Development*, *29*(6), 885–907. Many of the references at the end of Chapter 7 are useful sources for data synthesis, analysis, and interpretation during the formative evaluation process.

chapter 12

Revising Instructional Materials

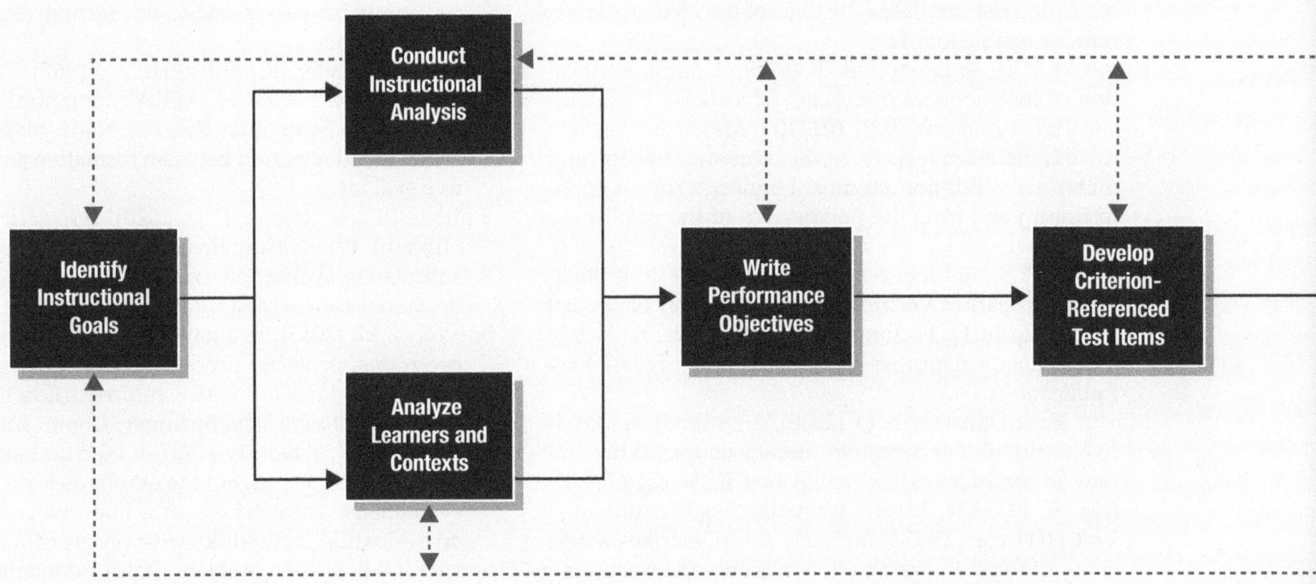

Objectives

- Describe various methods for summarizing data obtained from formative evaluation studies.
- Summarize data obtained from formative evaluation studies.
- Use summarized formative evaluation data to identify weaknesses in instructional materials and instructor-led instruction.
- Use formative evaluation data to identify problems in instructional materials and suggest revisions.

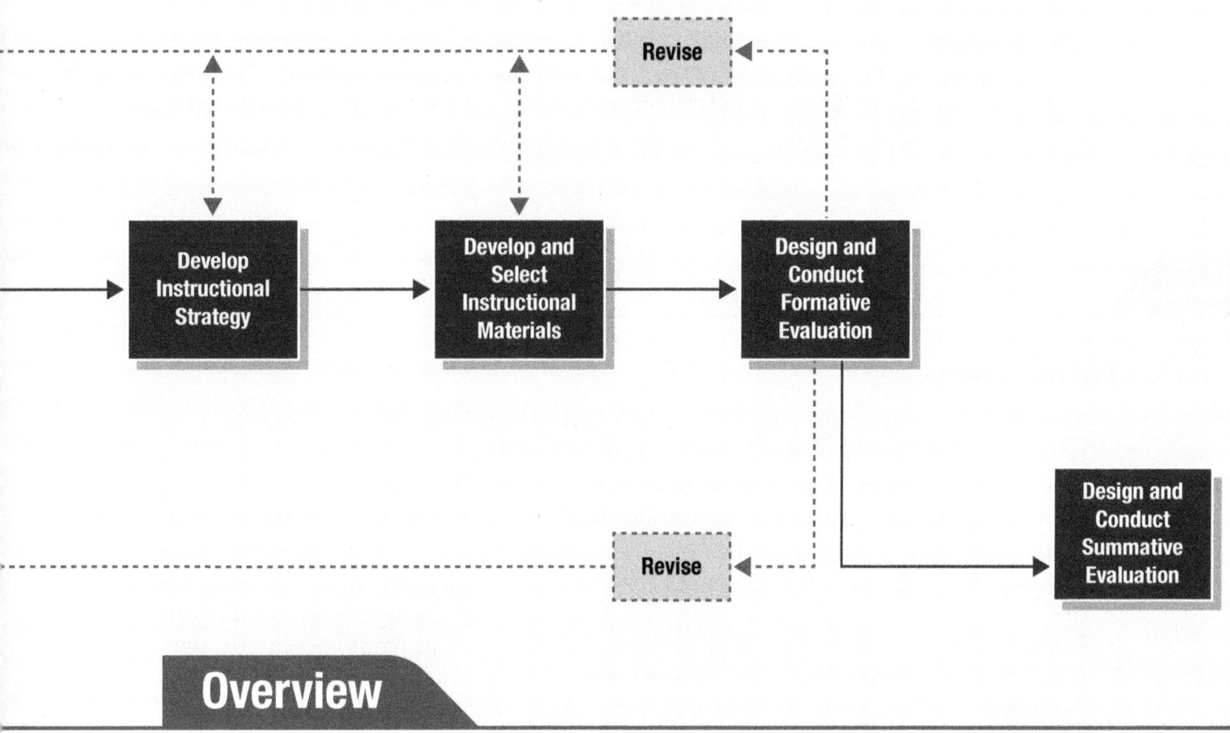

Overview

The data you collect during the formative evaluation should be synthesized and analyzed to locate potential problems in the instructional materials. Your data summaries should include analysis of information about the instructional materials obtained from content experts, learners' remarks in the materials, their performance on the pretest and posttest, their responses on the attitude questionnaire, their comments during debriefing sessions, and information gained from the performance context. Once you summarize the data, you are ready to analyze and evaluate various components of the instruction.

Begin by summarizing comments by content and learning experts, learner experts, and performance context experts and revise instruction accordingly. Second, study learners' achievement prior to and following instruction. Examine the summarized data relative to entry skills and draw implications about the entry behaviors of students in your target group. Review summarized pretest and posttest data for both total performance and objective-by-objective performance. Relate learners' objective-by-objective performance to the subordinate skills in your instructional analysis chart. Draw inferences about your group's performance on each test item and each objective. Compare data obtained from the entry skill items with pretest and posttest data as well.

Locate areas where learners' performance did not meet your expectations. Examine the objectives, test items, and instructional strategy for those objectives.

Analyze the objectives, test items, vocabulary, sequence, and instructional strategy carefully prior to making direct changes in the instructional materials. Examine also data related to learners' attitudes and their comments within the materials, during observations, and on checklists and surveys.

Begin your materials and procedures revision. Check procedures and implementation directions as well as equipment required for instruction for possible guides to revision. Develop an *instructional revision analysis form* that integrates learning components from the instructional strategy with identified problems, changes, evidence that changes are needed, and sources of evidence cited for each component in the materials.

Revise instruction based on your prescriptions in the instructional revision analysis form. Delay any revisions that may depend on information from the field testing of other lessons. These data synthesis and analysis activities are undertaken following each of the one-to-one, small group, and field trial formative evaluations. If you make major revisions in your materials following the field trial, then another trial is advisable to check the effectiveness of your revisions.

Concepts

Analyzing Data

There are many ways in which the data collected in a formative evaluation may be summarized to point to areas of learner difficulties and possible revisions. The methods we describe here are merely suggestions. As you begin to work with your own data, you may find other techniques that help you derive more insight from them. Note that you need not be concerned about the use of complex statistics in this step of the instructional design process because simple descriptive summaries of the data are sufficient. Elaborate statistical tests are almost never used in the formative evaluation and revision process. We first look at what you can do with the data and information from expert reviewers and then data from one-to-one formative evaluation and then consider the small-group and field trial phases.

Data Analysis from Expert Reviewers

One often begins this data analysis by organizing information about the materials from content, learning, learner, and performance context experts. Data from these specialists can be summarized together to determine whether there are common problems. Examining the reviewers' comments about the instructional materials across the instructional strategy, the designer can identify particular problems, propose changes to alleviate the problems, and seek evidence to support the conclusions. The materials designer might use a summary form such as the one in Table 12.1 to record judgments across experts. Such a summary makes clear common problems and aids revisions prior to learner trials.

Data Analysis for One-to-One Trials

Following the one-to-one formative evaluation, the designer has very little data because information typically is available for only three to five learners. Because these learners were selected based on their diversity, the information they provide will, in all likelihood, be very distinct rather than blending into some type of group average. In other words, the designer must look at the similarities and differences among the responses of the learners and determine the best changes to make in the instruction.

Table 12.1 **Summarize and Analyze Data from Experts and Prescribe Revisions**

A. Template for Summarizing Information:

	MATERIALS CONGRUENT WITH INSTRUCTIONAL ANALYSIS?	MATERIALS APPROPRIATE FOR LEARNER CHARACTERISTICS?	MATERIALS APPROPRIATE FOR LEARNING CONTEXT?	MATERIALS APPROPRIATE FOR PERFORMANCE CONTEXT?
I. Content Expert(s)	*Summarize +/– comments here*			
II. Learning Expert(s)	*Summarize +/– comments here*	*Summarize +/– comments here*	*Summarize +/– comments here*	
III. Learner Expert(s)		*Summarize +/– comments here*	*Summarize +/– comments here*	*Summarize +/– comments here*
IV. Performance Context Expert				*Summarize +/– comments here*

B. Template for Prescribing Revisions:

INSTRUCTIONAL STRATEGY COMPONENT	Problem Identified	PROPOSED CHANGES TO INSTRUCTION	EVIDENCE AND SOURCE
Entry skills test			
Motivational introductory material			
Pretest			
Information presentation			
Learner participation			
Posttest			
Attitude questionnaire			

The designer has five kinds of basic information available: (1) learner characteristics and entry skills, (2) direct responses to the instruction including practice activities, (3) learning time, (4) posttest performance, and (5) responses to an attitude questionnaire (if used).

The first step is to describe the learners who participated in the one-to-one evaluation and to indicate their performance on any entry-skill measures. Next, the designer should bring together all the comments and suggestions about the instruction that resulted from going through it with each learner, which can be done by integrating everything on a master copy of the instruction using a color code to link each learner to his or her particular problems. It is also possible to include comments from a subject-matter expert (SME) and any alternative instructional approaches that were used with learners during the one-to-one sessions.

Next, posttest data are summarized by obtaining individual item performance and then combining item scores for each objective and for a total score. It is often of interest to develop a table that indicates each student's pretest score, posttest score, and total learning time. In addition, student performance on the posttest should be summarized, along with any comments, for each objective. The same type of summary can be used for examining the data on the attitude questionnaire, if one is used at this point in the instruction. The designer might summarize this information-by-student in a form similar to the one in Table 12.2 to assist with materials revisions.

With all this information in hand, the designer is ready to revise the instruction. Of course, certain obvious revisions may have been made before completing the one-to-one sessions; now the more difficult revisions must be made. Certainly, the place to begin is within those sections that resulted in the poorest performance by learners and those that resulted in the most comments.

Table 12.2 **Summarize Information Gathered from One-to-One Formative Evaluations with Learners and Prescribe Revisions**

A. Create Data Summary Table

LEARNER CHARACTERISTICS	ENTRY SKILLS TEST	PRETEST	PRACTICE TESTS	POSTTESTS	ATTITUDE QUESTIONNAIRE
Low Ability/ Experience	*List # for items and objectives not mastered*	*List # for items and objectives not mastered*	*List # for items and objectives not mastered*	*List # for items and objectives not mastered*	*List +/– comments about instruction*
Average Ability/ Experience	*List # for items and objectives not mastered*	*List # for items and objectives not mastered*	*List # for items and objectives not mastered*	*List # for items and objectives not mastered*	*List +/– comments about instruction*
High Ability/ Experience	*List # for items and objectives not mastered*	*List # for items and objectives not mastered*	*List # for items and objectives not mastered*	*List # for items and objectives not mastered*	*List +/– comments about instruction*
Totals	*List all items and objectives problematic for group*	*List all items and objectives problematic for group*	*List all items and objectives problematic for group*	*List all items and objectives problematic for group*	*List all items and objectives problematic for group*

B. Summarize Information Within Instructional Materials

- Create a master "analysis" copy of all assessments, including the attitude questionnaire as well as the instructional materials.
- Summarize all learners' comments directly within materials at appropriate places. This includes unclear vocabulary, information, and examples; time for completion; and so forth.

First, try to determine, based on learner performance, whether your rubric or test items are faulty. If flawed, then changes should be made to make them clearer or consistent with the objectives and the intent of the instruction. If the items are satisfactory and the learners performed poorly, then the instruction must be changed. You have three sources of suggestions for change: learner suggestions, learner performance, and your own reactions to the instruction. Learners often can suggest sensible changes. In addition, the designer should examine carefully the mistakes made by learners to identify the kinds of misinterpretations they are making and, therefore, the kinds of changes that might be made. Do not ignore your own insights about what changes will make the instruction more effective. You used systematic design procedures, so you made careful descriptions of what is to be learned and provided examples; you offered students the opportunity to practice each skill, and they received feedback. The basic components are there! The usual revisions at this stage are ones of clarification of ideas and the addition or deletion of content, examples, and practice activities. Hopefully, the three sources of data suggest the most appropriate steps to take.

There are times when it is not obvious what to do to improve your instruction. It is sometimes wise simply to leave that part of the instruction as is and see how it works in the small-group formative evaluation. Alternatively, the designer can develop several approaches to solving the problem and try these out during the small-group evaluation.

Data Analysis for Small-Group and Field Trials

The small-group formative evaluation provides the designer with a somewhat different data summary situation. The data from eight to twenty learners are of greater collective interest than individual interest—that is, these data can show what problems and reactions this representative group of learners had. The available data typically include item performance on the pretest and posttest, responses to an attitude questionnaire, learning and testing time, and comments made directly in the materials.

The fundamental unit of analysis for all the assessments is the individual assessment item. Performance on each item must be scored as correct or incorrect. If an item has multiple parts, then each part should be scored and reported separately so the information is not lost. This individual item information is required for three reasons:

1. Item information can be useful in deciding if there are particular problems with the item or if it is measuring the performance described in its corresponding objective effectively (described later).
2. Individual item information can be used to identify the nature of the difficulties learners are having with the instruction. Not only is it important to know that, for example, half the learners missed a particular item, but it is also as important to know that most of those who missed it picked the same distractor in a multiple-choice item or made the same type of reasoning error on a problem-solving item.
3. Individual item data can be combined to indicate learner performance on an objective and, eventually, on the entire test. Sometimes, the criterion level for an objective is expressed in terms of getting a certain percentage of items correct on a set of items. The individual item data can be combined to show not only the percentage of items correct for an objective but also the number and percentage of learners who achieved mastery.

After the item data have been collected and organized into a basic item-by-objective table, it is then possible to construct more comprehensive data tables.

Group's Item-by-Objective Performance The first data summary table that should be constructed is an item-by-objective table, as illustrated in Table 12.3. Assume that we have a ten-item test that measures four objectives. Twenty learners were in the small-group formative evaluation.

Although any number of computer-based programs for data analysis can be used to create students' performance summaries, we recommend spreadsheet programs because they are readily available and easy to use. Simply set up the analysis table in the program to reflect the structure of your test. Notice in Table 12.3 that the objectives are listed across the top of the table and items are inserted in the second row within the objectives they measure. Learners are listed down the left side of the table, and their data are recorded in the rows beneath the items and objectives. A number 1 in the column beneath an item indicates a correct response; a blank indicates an incorrect response for each learner. Using the number 1 to indicate correct answers makes it very easy to sum correct answers and calculate all the other summary data you need.

With the raw data displayed in this manner, we can use the table to create two summaries for analysis: item quality and learner performance. You should analyze item quality first because faulty items should not be considered when analyzing learner performance. The bottom rows contain the data summaries needed for the item analysis. The first row contains the number of the twenty students who answered each item correctly. The next row contains the percentage of learners who answered each item correctly. These figures are obtained by dividing the total number of students in the evaluation into the number of students who answered correctly—that is, for item 1, 18/20 = 0.90, or 90 percent. The last row contains the percentage of the group that mastered each objective. This value is calculated by dividing the number of students who mastered each objective by the total number of students in the analysis. In this example, learners must answer all the questions correctly for an objective in order to master the objective. The purpose for the

Table 12.3 Item-by-Objective Analysis Table

Objectives		1		2		3			4			Items		Objectives	
ITEMS		1	2	3	4	5	6	7	8	9	10	NO.	%	NO.	%
Students	1	1	1	1	1	1	1	1	1	1	1	8	100	4	100
	2	1	1	1	1	1	1	1	1	1	1	8	100	4	100
	3		1	1	1	1	1	1	1	1	1	7	88	3	75
	4	1			1	1	1		1		1	4	50	0	0
	//														
	20	1	1			1	1	1	1			4	50	2	50
No. of students correct		18	19	15	17	17	6	18	18	10	9				
Percentage of students correct		90	95	75	85	85	30	90	90	50	45				
Percentage mastering objectives		90		75		85			45						

(Item total summaries are calculated after two potentially faulty items, 6 and 8, are removed from the analysis.)

Note: Although there were twenty students in the analysis group, data for only five students are illustrated.

item-by-objective analysis is threefold: (1) to determine the difficulty of each item for the group, (2) to determine the difficulty of each objective for the group, and (3) to determine the consistency with which the set of items within an objective measures learners' performance on the objective.

An **item difficulty index** is the percentage of learners who answer an item correctly. Item difficulty values of more than 80 percent reflect relatively easy items for the group, whereas lower values reflect more difficult ones. Similarly, consistently high or low values for items within an objective reflect the difficulty of the objective for the group. For example, the difficulty values for items 1 and 2 in Table 12.3 (90 and 95) indicate that nearly all the learners mastered the items associated with objective 1. If these data were from a posttest, we could infer that the instruction related to objective 1 is effective. Conversely, if they are low, they point to instruction that should be considered for revision.

The consistency of item difficulty indices within an objective typically reflects the quality of the items. If items are measuring the same skill and if there is no inadvertent complexity or clues in the items, then learners' performance on the set of items should be relatively consistent. With small groups, differences of 10 or 20 percent are not considered large, but differences of 40 percent or more should cause concern. Notice in Table 12.3 that item data are consistent within objectives 1 and 2. In contrast, the data are inconsistent within objectives 3 and 4. For objective 3, two items are quite consistent (85 and 90), whereas one item, number 6, yielded a much lower difficulty index (30). Such a pattern reflects either inadvertent complexity in the item or a different skill being measured. The pattern in objective 4 illustrates two consistent items (50 and 45) and one outlier (90). This type of pattern reflects either a clue in item 8 or a different skill being measured. When inconsistent difficulty indices are observed within an objective, it indicates that the items within the set should be reviewed and revised prior to reusing them to measure learner performance. If the item is judged sound, then it reflects an aspect of instruction that should be reconsidered.

Learners' Item-by-Objective Performance The second type of analysis is individual learner performance. Before conducting this analysis, you should eliminate any items judged faulty during the item analysis. The last four columns in Table 12.3

contain the individual performance data. The first two of these columns contain the number and percentage of items answered correctly by each learner. The last two columns contain the number and percentage of objectives mastered by each learner. Answering correctly all items within an objective was set as the criterion for mastery.

The hypothetical data for learners in Table 12.3 illustrate that individuals in the group performed quite differently on the test. Two individuals mastered all four objectives, and the scores for the other three learners range from no objectives mastered to 75 percent. If these data represented performance on entry behaviors or skills to be included in the instruction, then they would suggest who was ready for instruction and whether instruction was actually needed by some members of the sample. In contrast, if they reflected posttest performance, then the designer could make inferences about the necessity of revising the instruction. Data about learners' performance on items and objectives provide different information, and for the formative evaluator, data on objectives mastered are more informative than raw scores.

Learners' Performance Across Tests The item-by-objective table provides the data for creating tables to summarize learners' performances across tests. Table 12.4 illustrates how learner-by-objective mastery can be illustrated across tests administered. The table illustrates pretest and posttest data; however, some designers may also have data from embedded tests, and, when available, these data can be included in such a table as well. The data are presented for only five of the twenty students in the analysis, and a summary for the twenty students is presented at the bottom of the table. The first row identifies the objectives, the second row identifies the tests, and subsequent rows are used to record students' mastery of objectives on each test. The two summary rows at the bottom of the table contain the percentage of the twenty learners who mastered each objective on each test and the increase or decrease in percentages from pretest to posttest for each objective. Ideally, the percentages of learners who mastered each objective should increase from pretests to posttests. Such a pattern is illustrated for four objectives in Table 12.4.

You may also want to summarize learners' performances across tests using the percentage of objectives mastered on each test, as illustrated in Table 12.5. The top row identifies the test and the number of objectives measured by each one. Subsequent rows contain the percentage of objectives mastered by each student on each test. The bottom row contains the average percentage of objectives mastered by

Table 12.4 Student Performance on the Pretest and Posttest by Objective

Objectives		1		2		3		4	
TEST		PR	PS	PR	PS	PR	PS	PR	PS
Students	1		1		1	1	1	1	1
	2		1		1		1		1
	3	1	1		1	1	1		
	4		1		1		1		1
	//								
	20		1		1	1	1		1
Percentage		20	100	10	100	50	100	40	60
mastering diff.		80		90		50		20	

PR = pretest; PS = posttest; 1 = mastered.

Note: Table includes data for only five of twenty students in the evaluation, but summary percentages reflect data for entire group.

Table 12.5 Entry Skill, Pretest, and Posttest Data Summarized by the Percentage of Total Possible Objectives

Student Number	3 Entry Skill Objectives	9 Pretest Instructional Objectives	9 Posttest Objectives
1	100	11	89
2	100	22	89
3	100	22	89
4	100	11	100
//			
20	67	0	67
Mean	92	14	88

Note: The mean scores are based on the performance of all twenty students even though the data for only five are illustrated.

the group on each test. From these data, the designer could infer that (1) the group selected was appropriate for the evaluation, (2) the instruction covered skills not previously mastered by the group, and (3) the instruction was effective in improving learners' skills.

Graphing Learners' Performances Another way to display data is through various graphing techniques. A graph may show the pretest and posttest performance for each objective in the formative evaluation study. You may also want to graph the amount of time required to complete the instructional materials as well as the amount of time required for the pretest and posttest. Figure 12.1 offers an example of a pretest/posttest performance graph.

Another graphic technique for summarizing formative evaluation data involves the instructional analysis chart. This procedure requires the determination of the average pretest and posttest performance of learners participating in the formative evaluation on each of the skills indicated on the instructional analysis chart. The designer uses a copy of the instructional analysis chart without the statement

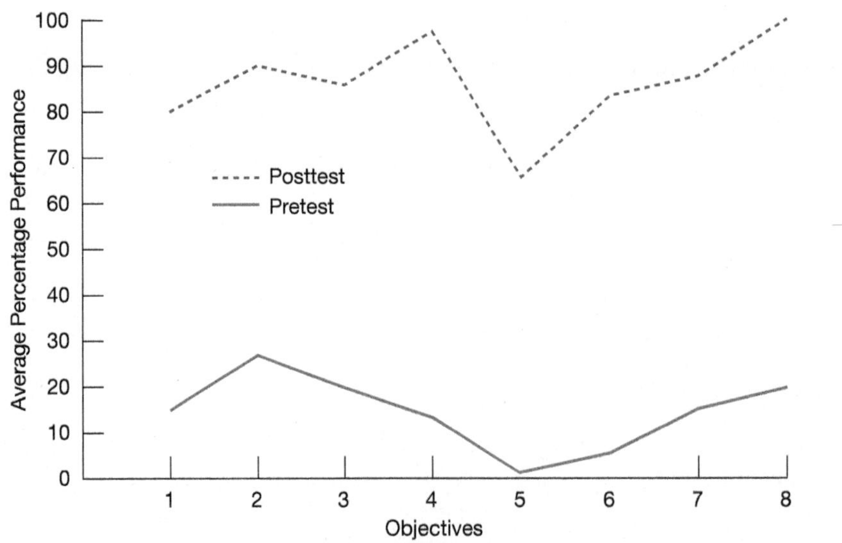

Figure 12.1 Pretest/Posttest Graph Showing Learner Performance

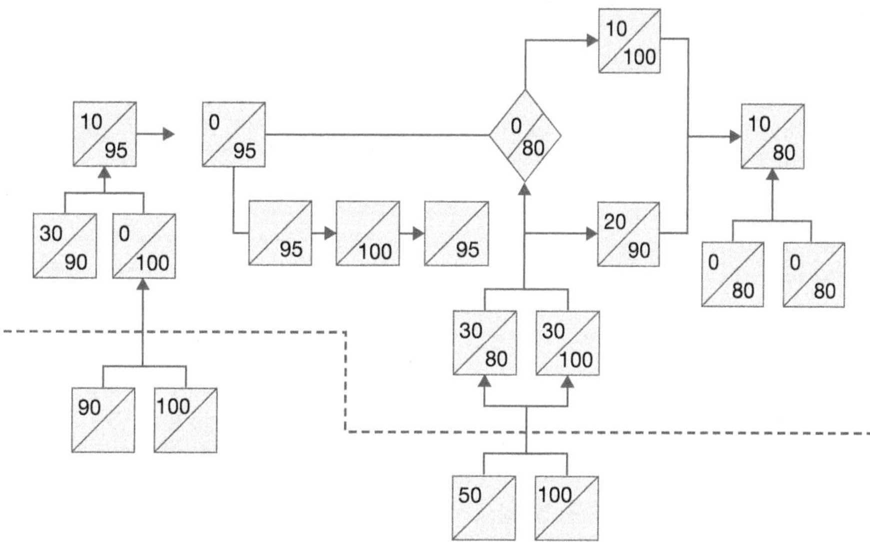

Figure 12.2 Summary of Pretest and Posttest Scores for a Hypothetical Instructional Analysis Chart

of skills. Figure 12.2 shows an example of this technique. The pretest and posttest scores for each objective are entered in the appropriate boxes; the top number in each box is the group's average pretest score, and the bottom number is their average posttest score. This provides an interesting display of the interrelationships of the scores on the various skills in the instructional materials. It becomes apparent if learners' performances decline as they approach the top of the hierarchy. You may also find a skill mastered by only a few learners that seems to have little effect on the subsequent mastery of superordinate skills.

Other Types of Data There are other kinds of data to summarize and analyze in addition to learners' performance on objectives. It has been found that a good way to summarize data from an attitude questionnaire is to indicate on a blank copy of the questionnaire the percentage of learners who chose each alternative to the various questions. If you also request open-ended, general responses from the learners, then you can summarize them for each question.

Other important types of data are the comments obtained from learners, from other instructors involved in the formative evaluation, and from SMEs who react to the materials. Because it is almost impossible to summarize these comments in tabular or graphic form, it is better to try to relate each of these comments to the instructional materials themselves or to the objective in the materials to which they refer. These comments can be written directly on a copy of the materials. The final type of data summary to prepare is results of measures that were taken on any alternative approaches you may have used during either the small-group evaluations or field trials. These data may be performance on specific test items, responses on an attitude questionnaire, or even an indication of total learning time.

Sequence for Examining Data

As you prepare summaries of your data, you quickly begin to get an overall picture of the general effectiveness of your instructional materials and the extent of revisions that may be required. Remember to be open to revisions of your design and materials in all steps of the model. After generally examining the data, we suggest that you use the data in the following sequence.

Instructional Analysis and Entry Skills

First, after removing data for any defective items, you should examine the remaining data with regard to the entry skills of learners. Did the learners in the formative evaluation have the entry skills you anticipated? If so, did they succeed with the instructional materials? If they did succeed but did not have the required skills, then you must question whether you have identified critical entry skills.

Objectives, Pretests, and Posttests

The second step is to review the pretest and posttest data as displayed on the instructional analysis chart (see sample in Figure 12.2). If you sequenced the materials appropriately and if you identified skills that are hierarchically dependent on each other, then learners' pretest performances should decrease as you move upward through the hierarchy—that is, there should be poorer learner performance on the terminal objective than on the earlier skills. When the instruction is working well, there will, of course, be no decline in learner performance as learners complete the skills at the top of the analysis. These data help you identify exactly where problems exist and perhaps even suggest a change in the instructional sequence for certain skills.

Third, you might examine the pretest scores to determine the extent to which individual learners, and the group as a whole, had already acquired the skills that you were teaching. If they already possess most of the skills, then you receive relatively little information about the effectiveness of the instruction or how it might be improved. If they lack these skills, you have more confidence in the analyses that follow.

By comparing pretest with posttest scores objective by objective, which is the usual procedure when you examine the instructional analysis chart, you can assess learner performance on each particular objective and begin to focus on specific objectives and the related instruction that appear to need revision. It may be necessary to revise the conditions or the criteria specified in the objectives. Recall that conditions are used to control the complexity of performance tasks, and your criteria may be too lenient or harsh for the target group.

As you identify objectives on which the learners performed poorly, examine the exact wording of the objective and the associated test items and the exact student answers to the items. Before revising the instructional materials, refer to your item analysis table (see sample in Table 12.3) to see whether poor test items, rather than the materials, indicated poor learner performance. All that may be needed are revised test items rather than a major revision of the instructional materials.

Learning Components of Instructional Strategy and Materials

The next step is to examine the instructional strategy associated with the various objectives with which learners had difficulty. Was the planned strategy actually used in the instructional materials? Are there alternative strategies that might be used? The final step is to examine the materials themselves to evaluate the comments about problem areas made by learners, instructors, and SMEs.

Learning Time

An important concern in any formative evaluation is the amount of time required by students to complete the instructional materials. It may be necessary for you to revise the materials to make them fit within a particular time period. This is an extremely difficult task, and it must be done with great care. With individualized materials, it is not unusual for the slowest learner to take two or three times longer than the fastest learner. Knowing what to remove from the materials or to change without interfering with learning is very difficult to determine. Often the decision can be made only after a trial/revise/trial/revise process with target learners.

Media, Materials, and Instructional Procedures

Data that relate to the implementation of the instructional materials must also be examined. We suggested earlier that you might gather misleading data because of the faulty operations of media equipment or software problems. There may also have been disruptions in the classroom, an extended lunch break, or any one of a variety of other kinds of activities that are common to various instructional settings. Because these disruptions cannot be controlled, they simply must be noted and explained.

However, there are procedural concerns that can be controlled. Were learners hindered by the logistics required to use the materials? Were there questions about how to proceed from one step to the next? Were there long delays in getting test scores? These are the kinds of implementation procedural problems often identified in questionnaires and debriefing discussions. Solutions to such problems must be found and incorporated into either the instruction or the instructors' manual to make the instructional activity run more smoothly.

Revision of Selected Materials and Instructor-Led Instruction

The data summary and revision procedures described previously are equally appropriate whether the instructor develops original instructional materials, uses a variety of selected materials, or works from an instructor's guide. The types of data collected, the ways in which they are summarized, and the ways in which they are used to direct the revision process are all similar. When working with selected materials, however, there is little opportunity to revise the materials directly, especially if they are commercially produced and copyrighted. With copyrighted materials, the instructor can consider the following adaptations for future trials: (1) omit portions of the instruction, (2) include other available materials, or (3) simply develop supplementary instruction. Procedures for the use of materials should also be reconsidered in light of formative evaluation data.

Instructors working from an instructor's guide have the same flexibility as the developer for changing instruction. A pretest and a posttest, together with an attitude questionnaire, should provide data for a thorough analysis of the instruction. Summary tables that indicate performance on each objective should be prepared. Examine learner performance on test items and objectives and then relate learner performance by objective to the instructional analysis diagram.

The instructor's notes from the guide should reflect questions raised by learners and responses to those questions. Learners' questions should be examined to determine whether basic misunderstandings have developed. Were the responses to the questions sufficient to provide adequate performance by learners on the related test items?

An instructor who used an instructor's guide is also likely to obtain a greater "spread" in the scores on tests and reactions on attitude questionnaires. Research data indicate that, by the very nature of group-paced, interactive instruction, some students are unlikely to understand the concepts as rapidly as others during a given class period. Because there are typically no embedded remedial strategies in group instruction, such learners learn progressively less during a series of lessons and receive progressively poorer scores; their attitudes will likely reflect this situation. In this interactive, group-paced mode, learners' initial performance is likely to resemble a bell curve distribution (i.e., a few high scores, a few low scores, and mostly average scores); however, as instruction progresses in hierarchical content, the performance curve will tend to become bimodal. Learners who are less able or who simply do not progress through new content as quickly for any number of reasons will tend to aggregate toward the bottom of the curve as they miss skills prerequisite for subsequent learning. Hierarchical content includes subjects such as mathematics, foreign language, most science, computer coding, statistics, and so forth.

Identifying learners who are performing poorly and inserting appropriate activities are important components of the revision process for the instructor using an interactive instructional approach. Unlike using written instructional materials, the instructor can revise the presentation during its implementation and note the reasons for the change.

One final observation: We have stressed that you are working with a systems approach to build an instructional system, and when you change one component of the system, you are changing the whole system. You must be aware, therefore, that when you make changes through the revision process, you cannot assume that the remaining unchanged instruction will necessarily maintain its initial effectiveness. You may hope your changes are for the better, but you cannot assume that they always are.

Evaluation and Revision

Evaluating and Revising Data Summary and Interpretation

We suggest that as you begin the revision process, your mindset is to think extensively about all that has led to this point in the ID process rather than intensively about just the instructional materials you have in front of you. Question whether decisions made along the analysis, design, and development path have led to problems revealed by the data from formative evaluation. Did SME reviews raise questions about whether attaining the goal will solve the original performance problem when learners apply new skills in the performance context? Did learners have problems in the instruction because of the materials or because your analysis of learners was off the mark? Did learners find the objectives trivial and not worth their time? We are sure you get the idea at this point in the ID process that looking backward and forward is required for optimizing your instructional product. Section E in the rubric that follows is a reminder to consider what has gone before as you look forward to making revisions.

After you have summarized your data as suggested in this chapter, consider Table 12.6 for organizing the information gathered from all sources. The table uses the components of the instructional strategy as the framework in the left column, and additional columns are provided for summarizing (1) any problems identified with a component, (2) the changes being proposed based on the problems, and (3) the evidence gathered illustrating the problem. The evidence might name sources such as the materials, assessments, data summaries, observations, or interviews. Such a summary helps focus the designer on work to be done, and when a design team is involved, it enables conversations and negotiations about next steps in the project.

We recognize that the needs of instructional designers differ according to the type of materials with which they are working; however, the strategy suggested

Table 12.6 Template for an Instructional Revision Analysis Form for Summarizing Information from a Formative Evaluation

Instructional Strategy			
COMPONENT	PROBLEM IDENTIFIED	PROPOSED CHANGES TO INSTRUCTION	EVIDENCE AND SOURCE
Entry skills test			
Motivational material			
Pretest			
Information presentation			
Learner participation			
Posttest			
Attitude questionnaire			
Transfer to performance context			

here should apply to almost any instructional design effort. For example, if you taught a psychomotor skill, then your posttest performance should be recorded on a rubric of some sort and summarized on your instructional analysis chart. There might also be a paper-and-pencil test of subordinate skills and knowledge. These scores should be examined in connection with their associated motor skills. The use of attitude responses and learning time should be the same for any type of instruction.

Given all the data from a small group evaluation or field trial, the designer must make decisions about how to make the revisions. It is almost always apparent where the problems are, but it is not always apparent what changes should be made. If a comparison of several approaches has been embedded in the formative evaluation, then the results should indicate the type of changes to be made. Otherwise, the strategies suggested for revising instruction following the one-to-one evaluations also apply at this point—namely, use the data, your experience, and sound learning principles as the bases for your revisions.

One caution: Avoid responding too quickly to any single piece of data, whether it is the learners' performance on an objective, a comment from an individual learner, or an observation by an SME. They are all valuable pieces of information, but you should attempt to corroborate these data with other data. Look for performance as well as observational data that help you focus on deficiencies in the instructional materials.

An additional suggestion: When summarizing data from the field evaluation, be careful to summarize it in an accurate and clear fashion. You will find that these data not only are of interest to you as the instructional designer but also serve as an effective vehicle to show others how learners performed with your instruction. The table and graphs can provide both a general and a detailed description of the overall performance of the learners and can be a valuable piece of reporting to sponsoring agencies, instructors, and training managers.

Rubric for Evaluating Data Summary and Interpretation

The following rubric contains criteria for evaluating data summary and interpretation. Use it to plan data analysis for your own project, evaluate your analysis materials, or share with others for evaluating your materials.

Designer note: If an element is not relevant for your project, mark NA in the No column.

No	Some	Yes	
			A. Experts Do the information summaries include data from:
____	____	____	1. Content experts?
____	____	____	2. Managers and supervisors (performance context)?
____	____	____	3. Trainers/teachers (learning context)?
			B. Learners Do the information summaries include data from:
____	____	____	1. Readiness for instruction (entry skills)?
____	____	____	2. Pretest–posttest growth by skill?
____	____	____	3. Attitudes?
____	____	____	4. Comments within materials (clarity, sequence, chunk, etc.)?
____	____	____	5. Total learning times for each session?
			C. Procedures Do the information summaries include data about:
____	____	____	1. Media and equipment?
____	____	____	2. Personnel?
____	____	____	3. Facilities?
____	____	____	4. Budget?
____	____	____	5. Schedules?
____	____	____	6. Management of learners through materials?
			D. Analysis Were issues and problems summarized by and linked to:
____	____	____	1. Participants (e.g., experts, learners)?
____	____	____	2. Preinstructional activities?
____	____	____	3. Readiness/pretest?
____	____	____	4. Information presentation?
____	____	____	5. Learner participation?
____	____	____	6. Assessments?
____	____	____	7. Follow-through for transfer?
			E. Revision Strategy Do suggested revisions reflect systematic thinking in that they are logical and linked to problems identified in the:
____	____	____	1. Design decisions (e.g., analysis of needs, solutions, goals, learners, contexts, instructional strategy)?
____	____	____	2. Instructional materials?
____	____	____	3. Instructional procedures?
____	____	____	4. Media and delivery system?
____	____	____	5. Resources (funding, personnel, time, facilities, equipment, etc.)?

The final revision of your materials should be effective in bringing about the intended learning with members of your target audience. Then you are ready to reproduce, publish, or set up your instruction for e-distribution.

Examples

The examples in this section are based on the golf instructor-led session on putting a golf ball. Recall from Chapter 11 that there were a modified one-to-one formative evaluation and a combined small-group/field trial formative evaluation. The questions asked are similar across these two types of evaluation; therefore, we will illustrate only the field trial because it has more questions and learners.

Small-Group Evaluation

Participants in this evaluation included the evaluator, the instructor, and sixteen learners. Instructional session 2, putting, was interactive on the practice putting green, and it was video recorded. Following instruction, a debriefing session was held where the evaluator and instructor viewed and discussed the video together. The evaluator asked prompting questions when the conversation lagged. Later the evaluator viewed the videos for information missed during the instructional session and completed the questionnaire in summary form. Neither the instructor nor the learners completed the questionnaire. It is based solely on the judgment of the evaluator and must be interpreted as such.

Table 12.7 contains a copy of the questionnaire with the evaluator's summary ratings inserted. Notice that the evaluator assigned the highest rank to the teaching professional in all motivational categories but gave him the lowest rating related to following the enabling skills in the goal framework. This low rating was due to the instructor skipping the planning part of the putt and going directly to skills related to gripping the putter.

Table 12.7 Evaluator's Summary of Instructor Actions

Motivation of Learners Did the instructor:	No①	Rarely②	Usually③	Always④
1. Talk positively about the club, membership, and the clinics?	①	②	③	●
2. Have a light, recreational, jovial demeanor?	①	②	③	●
3. Show enthusiasm for the topic?	①	②	③	●
4. Appear interested in the learners?	①	②	③	●
5. Stay engaged with the learners throughout the session?	①	②	③	●
6. Present the information and skills in a logical sequence according to the goal analysis (content presentation)?	●	②	③	④

Table 12.8 contains the evaluator's ratings of the learners' attitudes and actions. The anchors for these ratings are the elements of the instructional strategy from motivation through transfer. To be considered problematic, the evaluator's rating needs to be lower than three. All ratings were in the acceptable range except B.1 and B.2 within

Table 12.8 Evaluator's Perceptions of Learner Attitudes and Actions

A. Motivation Did the learners:	No①	Rarely②	Usually③	Always④
1. See the YouTube video depicting various golfers and their caddies as being relevant and interesting (motivation)?	No①	Yes●		
2. Perceive the instruction as interesting and relevant?	No①	Rarely②	Usually●	Always④
3. Pay attention to the teaching professional during explanations and demonstrations?	No①	Rarely②	Usually●	Always④
4. Appear confident they could perform the putting skills?	No①	Rarely②	Usually●	Always④
5. Appear to be satisfied with their progress?	No①	Rarely②	Usually●	Always④

Table 12.8 Continued

B. Content Presentation Did the learners:	
1. Understand why they began by rolling rather than putting balls (clarity)?	No● Mostly② Yes③ (*This didn't happen.*)
2. Understand the interaction among the physical conditions of the putting green, their mental plans (trajectory and force), and their physical actions in making the putt (clarity)?	No● Mostly② Yes③ (*This didn't happen.*)
3. Believe the examples are necessary and clear?	No① Yes●
4. Feel the explanations are helpful?	Too short① Long② Helpful●
5. Consider the demonstrations to be helpful?	Too few① Many② Helpful●
6. Think the pace of each part (planning, grip, stance, actual putt) is just right?	Too little① Long② Just right●
C. Participation (Practice and Feedback) Did the learners:	
7. Know what to do for each practice activity (planning, gripping, addressing, stroking)?	① ② ● ④
8. Think the amount of practice for each activity is just right?	Too little① much② Just right●
9. Provide useful feedback for their partner's putts?	① ② ● ④
10. Enjoy themselves as they rehearsed?	① ② ● ④
D. Assessment and Follow-Through Did the learners:	
1. Feel the directions for the concluding putting contest are clear?	No① Somewhat② Yes●
2. Feel the concluding putting contest is enjoyable?	No① Somewhat② Yes●
3. Believe they could transfer the skills they learned during instruction to the contest?	No① Somewhat② Yes●
4. Believe they improved their putting skills as a result of the lesson?	No① Somewhat② Yes●
5. Score and record their putts accurately for the contest (each stroke is a score point)?	No① Somewhat② Yes●
6. Want to play more golf as a result of the lesson?	① ② ③ ●

content presentation related to planning the putt. These did not happen, which tends to remove the *psycho* from *psychomotor*.

Table 12.9 contains the evaluator's ratings of management and feasibility. The evaluator judged all but one criterion within this category to be met. The inadequacy of the physical structure of the putting green for slope and force is again cited. Notice that half the criteria in this category are related to the golf club's goal of increasing membership and thereby increasing revenue.

The summary data from the rating scales are presented in the instructional revision plans in Table 12.10. The only areas where changes are proposed relate to information presentation and learner participation. The likelihood of the designer getting these changes made is questionable because the golf professional does not believe putts should be planned without putters in hand and an improved practice green for putting is not available at the course. In this circumstance, the designer

Table 12.9 Evaluator's Summary of Management and Feasibility

Management and Feasibility — Do the learners and instructor:	
1. Believe the schedule (day, time, week) is convenient?	No① Yes●
2. Believe there is enough time in the two hours allotted for putting instruction to learn about putting and to practice their skill?	No① Yes●
3. Think the practice putting green is physically adequate to practice the trajectory and force skills?	No① Yes●
4. Believe the club members and the staff are welcoming and helpful?	① ② ③ ●
5. Is the advertising about the clinic adequate?	No① Yes●
6. Do enough people learn about it and actually sign up?	No① Yes● *(10 on waiting list)*
7. Do they all attend the putting session?	No① Yes● *(15 of 16 participated)*
8. Do they participate in the end-of-session putting contest?	No① Yes● *(15 of 16 participated)*
9. Do participants actually join the club within a reasonable time period?	No① Yes● *(3 of 16 joined by session 2)*

Table 12.10 Plans for Revising Instruction for Session 2, Putting

Instructional Strategy Source	Problem	Proposed Change in Instruction	Evidence and Source
Motivational, Introductory Material	None	None	Observation, learner and instructor comments
Pretest and Posttest	None given		
Information Presentation	Instructor avoided skill on planning putt without putter	Request instructor to include in lesson; investigate whether this step is necessary	Observation during presentation; instructor commented not necessary
Learner Participation	Practice green physically not adequate to practice trajectory and force skills	Investigate whether other greens on course have more contour	Comments of instructor, learners, and observation
Transfer	None	None	Learners could apply skills and tally score during the putting contest
Management and Feasibility	Putting green physically inadequate	None: no other facility availability. Point out to learners particular holes on course where slope and surface enable better application of these skills.	Comments by learners, instructor, and observation

Club goals met? No problems with putting clinic and no changes requested. Evidence: Waiting list of ten for next clinic; fifteen of sixteen participants attended putting session; three participants joined by the time of the putting session; positive comments by teaching professional and club membership chair; evaluator observations must ponder whether, given the success of the club's goal of increased membership and recreation, these are important issues to pursue. Two questions that immediately come to mind for the instructional designer are: First, did I overdesign the instruction, and second, should I have included the golf professional early and often in planning the instructional strategy?

Case Study

Group Leadership Training

Data from the instructional goal on leading group discussions are used to illustrate techniques for summarizing and analyzing data collected during formative evaluation activities. Examples provided in this case study are designed to illustrate procedures you might use for either a small-group evaluation or a field trial of materials and procedures. Of course, the types of tables, graphs, and summary procedures you actually use should be tailored to your instructional materials, tests, instructional context, and learners. These examples simply show some ways the information gathered could be summarized for the group leadership unit.

Small-Group or Field Trial Evaluation

Recall that, based on interviews with leaders in the performance context (school principals, campus administrators, training directors in businesses, and municipal government personnel), some decisions were made about how these adult learners would be tested. Because of learner sensitivity, they should not be pretested on verbal information or leadership performance objectives; pretests should simply assess their ability to recognize leadership skills demonstrated by others during staged meetings. The decision was also made not to have individual learners identify themselves on their pretest or practice exercise papers. Learners were identifiable on the posttests because these consisted of actual performance in group leadership simulations. Not having identified the learners, individual member performance cannot be traced across tests; however, total group performance can be monitored, which provides evidence of instructional effectiveness.

Formative evaluation data for twenty learners were collected during a field trial of the instruction. Assessment data were collected for the twelve leader actions that encourage and stifle group cooperation contained within objectives 6.4.2 and 6.5.1. Recall that the same twelve actions are embedded within these two objectives. During the pretest, learners viewed a simulated meeting on video and marked their observation form each time the leader exhibited one of the twelve enhancing or stifling actions (objective 6.4.2). Assessment data for objective 6.4.2 were also collected during learner participation activities within the instruction. Posttest data were collected only for the learners' group leadership actions exhibited during simulated meetings (objective 6.5.1). Attitudinal data were collected using a questionnaire and debriefing at the end of session 10.

Analysis of Item-by-Objective Data Across Tests

The first step in summarizing performance data from any test is to determine how to score learners' responses. When an objective-style test is administered, obtaining a score is relatively easy for each learner by counting the number of test items answered correctly. Scoring live performance assessments, however, requires some planning.

See, for example, the following excerpt from the pretest in Table 10.6, p. 308.

DIRECTIONS: The group meeting segment runs for eight minutes. Watch the video meeting straight through; then watch it a second time. As you watch the meeting progress, use the form to record your judgments about the group management skills Eloise exhibits during the meeting.

Do Tally ✓✓	Eloise's Cooperation-Encouraging Actions	Eloise's Cooperation-Stifling Actions	Don't Tally ✓✓
✓✓✓	1. Suggests points of discussion as questions	1. Prescribes topics for the group to consider	✓✓
✓✓✓	2. Uses an investigative, inquiring tone	2. Uses an authoritative tone	✓✓
✓✓✓	3. Uses open terms such as *perhaps* and *might*	3. Uses prescriptive terms such as *must* or *should*	✓✓✓
✓✓✓	4. Hesitates and pauses between speakers	4. Fills quiet gaps with personal points of view or solutions	✓✓
✓✓✓	5. Willingly turns over the floor to group members who interrupt	5. Continues to talk over interrupting members or interrupts member	✓✓✓

In scoring the pretest, the designer made the following decisions. Each of the enhancing and stifling actions was exhibited by the leader three times during the simulated meeting. Learners were given credit if their tally was within one point of the exhibited actions; thus, a tally of two, three, or four occurrences earned credit, and a 1 was placed in the student-by-behavior cell in the summary chart.

Table 12.11 contains a summary of learners' responses on the pretest for objective 6.4.2. There are twelve behaviors within the objective, and they are summarized similarly to test items within an objective on an objective-style test. Each of the twelve encouraging and stifling actions is listed across the top of the table, and the twenty learners are listed in the far-left column. Further, enhancing and stifling behaviors for each of the twelve actions were combined to create a total test score from zero to twelve. To receive credit for any one of the twelve actions, learners had to classify correctly both the enhancing and stifling behaviors within a skill. For example, if they classified correctly the enhancing behaviors for action 3 but not the stifling behaviors for action 3, they did not receive credit for action 3. Notice the shaded pairs of cells for each learner in the table; these reflect the skills for which learners received credit.

The row totals (each learner's score in the far-right column) were obtained by summing the shaded action pairs within each learner's row. The first row of column totals at the bottom of the table reflects the percentage of learners classifying each enhancing and each stifling action correctly. The last row on the bottom of the chart contains the percentage of the group that classified each of the twelve pairs of actions correctly.

With the pretest data summarized in this manner, the analysis and interpretation began. First, individual learner performance (far-right column) was examined. Was the group heterogeneous in their group leadership skills as anticipated? The designer concluded that their performance on the pretest was heterogeneous or very different. The highest possible score on the test was twelve points, and their scores ranged from zero to eleven. Three of the learners earned scores of nine (75 percent) or higher, four earned scores between six and eight, four earned scores of four and five, and nine—almost half the group—earned scores of three (25 percent) or less.

Table 12.11 Pretest Data Summarized by Learners Across Behaviors (Horizontal) and Behaviors Across Learners (Vertical)

Encouraging (+) and Stifling (−) Behaviors Exhibited by Leaders

LRNS	1		2		3		4		5		6		7		8		9		10		11		12		TOTAL
	+	−	+	−	+	−	+	−	+	−	+	−	+	−	+	−	+	−	+	−	+	−	+	−	
1	1	1	1	1	1	1	1	1	1	1	1	1	1	1	1	1	1	1	1	1	1	1	1		11
2	1	1	1	1	1		1	1	1	1	1		1	1	1				1	1	1	1	1		7
3	1	1	1	1	1	1	1		1	1	1	1	1	1		1	1	1	1	1	1		1		8
4	1	1	1	1	1	1	1	1				1	1	1	1		1		1		1	1		1	6
5	1	1	1		1					1	1	1	1	1	1				1	1	1	1	1		5
6	1	1	1	1	1	1	1		1	1			1				1	1					1		5
7	1	1			1						1	1	1	1	1	1			1	1	1	1	1		6
8	1		1	1	1	1	1	1		1	1				1						1	1			4
9	1				1								1	1						1	1	1			2
10		1	1	1	1	1	1	1	1		1	1	1		1	1	1	1	1	1	1	1	1	1	9
11										1				1					1		1				0
12	1	1	1	1	1								1							1					2
13			1	1	1	1		1	1	1	1	1	1	1	1	1	1	1	1		1	1	1	1	9
14	1	1	1									1	1						1		1	1			2
15													1	1	1	1	1		1		1				2
16	1		1	1	1	1					1	1		1							1		1		3
17	1		1	1	1	1	1						1						1	1		1	1		3
18					1					1		1	1			1					1				0
19	1			1	1	1				1							1		1						1
20			1		1	1					1	1	1	1	1		1		1	1	1	1	1		5
*	70	50	70	60	85	55	40	30	30	50	50	55	80	60	50	35	45	25	70	50	80	60	55	15	
**	45		55		55		25		25		40		50		25		25		40		55		10		

*Percentage of learners receiving credit for classifying correctly each enhancing (+) and stifling (−) behavior.

**Percentage of learners receiving credit for classifying correctly both the enhancing and the stifling actions within a skill.

The next step was to examine the total group's performance on each of the behaviors (bottom row). A reasonable question to answer from pretest data is "Do the learners need this instruction, or do they already possess the skills?" Between 10 and 55 percent of the group classified each pair of skills correctly. From these data, the designer can conclude that, with the possible exception of learner 1, instruction in enhancing cooperative group interaction was warranted. In addition, their performance in classifying the enhancing and stifling actions (next to last row) was contrasted. The learners were better at recognizing the enhancing behaviors demonstrated than the stifling ones. In fact, they were better at classifying stifling behaviors for only one skill, number 5: Willingly turns over the floor to group members who interrupt rather than talking over interrupting members.

In this instruction, objective 6.4.2 was not included on the posttest because the posttest consisted of demonstrating the twelve encouraging actions and avoiding the stifling ones while leading a discussion group. The designer contrasted the learners' pretest performance for objective 6.4.2 with their performance on the participation exercise embedded within instruction. Although this is not typical, there were no other data following instruction that could be used to compare with their pretest performance. This contrast allowed loosely examining the effects of instruction for objectives 6.1.1 through 6.4.2. Learner participation data should always be considered tentative; however, it might provide some evidence of growth or change from the pretest. The observation sheet learners used in the learner participation exercise was scored in the same manner as the pretest, which made comparisons possible.

Analysis of Data Across Tests

Figure 12.3 contains a graph of learners' achievement for objectives 6.4.2 and 6.5.1. The left side of the graph contains percentage levels used to identify the percentage of the twenty students who mastered each of the twelve behaviors. The twelve actions are listed along the bottom of the graph. With the data arranged as in Figure 12.3, the designer was able to make observations about instruction related to the encouraging actions and the learners' achievement.

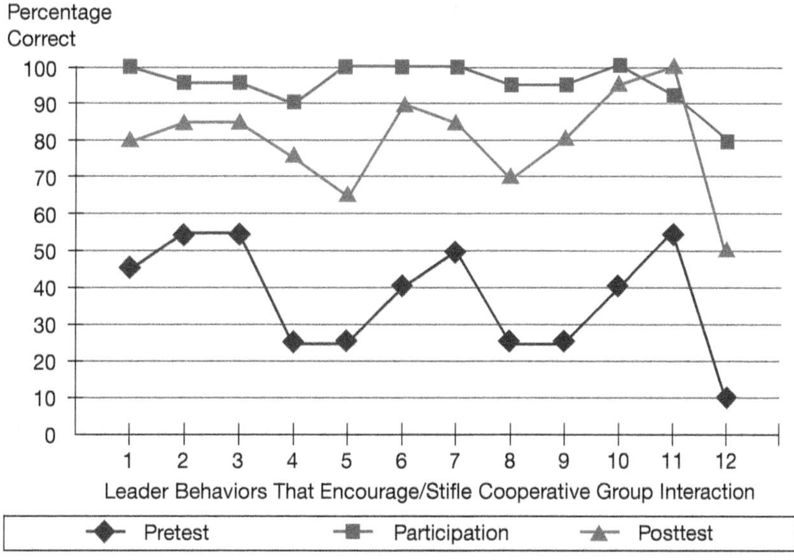

Figure 12.3 Percentage of Group Recognizing Twelve Leader Actions That Encourage and Discourage Cooperative Group Interaction on the Pretest and Posttest (Objective 6.4.2) and Demonstrating Encouraging Behaviors as They Lead Group Discussions (Objective 6.5.1 Posttest Only)

The lower line in the figure represents learners' pretest performance on objective 6.4.2, and these data were transferred directly from the bottom row of Table 12.11. The top row of data illustrates their classification skills on the learner participation activity that was included within the instruction. This activity followed instruction on objectives 6.1.1 through 6.4.2. Notice that at this point in the instruction, 80 percent or more of the group classified all twelve of the leader behaviors correctly. This high level of performance across the twelve skills and the learners' growth between the pretest and the practice activity indicate that instruction was effective in helping learners recognize these encouraging and stifling actions when they are exhibited by others.

The center row of data illustrates learners' demonstration of the twelve behaviors during the posttest administered at the end of session 10. Setting the criterion for effective instruction at 80 percent of the group demonstrating each skill successfully, the designer concluded that instruction was adequate for eight of the twelve behaviors. It was ineffective, however, for helping learners demonstrate the following encouraging actions consistently:

4. Hesitates and pauses between speakers rather than filling quiet gaps with personal points of view (75 percent)
5. Willingly turns over floor when interrupted rather than continuing to talk or interrupting group members (65 percent)
8. Uses comments to keep the discussion centered on the group rather than encouraging the discussion to flow through the leader (e.g., evaluating speaker's comments) (70 percent)
12. Praises group effort and accomplishment rather than singling out particular people for praise (50 percent)

Notice in these data that learners were better at recognizing the twelve encouraging or stifling behaviors in other leaders than they were at consistently exhibiting the actions themselves during a meeting. This differentiation is consistent with the hierarchical order of these two skills in the instructional goal analysis.

Analysis of Attitudinal Data

At the end of session 10, learners were asked to complete the attitudinal questionnaire contained in Table 11.4 (p. 357). The questionnaire was scored by summing the ratings of all learners (twenty) for each question and then dividing the sum by twenty to obtain the group's mean rating for each question. These values were then rounded to the nearest whole number. The range of responses (highest and lowest rating given for each question) was also identified.

These data are recorded on a blank copy of the questionnaire included in Figure 12.4. The mean rating for each item is circled on the questionnaire, and the range is indicated using a vertical mark above the lowest and highest rating for each item. The mean rating is calculated by summing all learners' responses to an item and then dividing this sum by the number of learners who answered the item. At this point, items indicating potential problems can be flagged. In this instance, a potentially problematic question was defined as one having a mean or average score of three or lower, and an asterisk was placed to the left of items with means in this area.

Related to learners' perceptions of their attention levels during instruction, they were attentive during all activities, and they believed all objectives covered were relevant to their goals as group leaders (mean four or higher). Moving to the confidence questions, the range of responses, or distance between the lowest and highest rating, increased, and the mean score for their confidence in actually using these actions dropped to three. Within the clarity category, all instruction was rated satisfactorily for the videos of simulated meetings. For overall satisfaction, problems were identified for pace of instruction and self-satisfaction.

At this point, the four questions with means at or below the criterion for unsatisfactory ratings were examined. Instructional parts with potential problems are the following:

9. Confidence in engendering cooperative group behavior
13. Videos of meetings
20. Pace of instruction
22. Self-satisfaction with new skill levels

It is possible that these four questions were related. For example, questions 9 and 22, confidence and self-satisfaction, could have been linked; they could also have been related to the reported pacing and video problems.

I. Attention: To what degree did the following instructional activities hold your interest or attention?	
Instructional Areas	**Attention Levels (Circle one level for each area)**
A. Reading and analyzing annotated dialogues of meetings illustrating the following:	
1. Member actions that aid cooperative interaction	Little 1 2 3 (4) 5 Very Attentive
2. Strategies leaders use to encourage group cooperation	Little 1 2 3 (4) 5 Very Attentive
B. Watching and analyzing videotapes of meetings depicting the following:	
3. Positive member actions that aid cooperative interaction	Little 1 2 3 4 (5) Very Attentive
4. Leaders engendering cooperative member behaviors	Little 1 2 3 4 (5) Very Attentive
C. Acting as group leader to:	
5. Engender cooperative member behaviors in my group	Little 1 2 3 4 (5) Very Attentive
II. Relevance: To what degree do you believe the following skills are *relevant* for helping you provide effective leadership in problem-solving meetings?	**Relevance Levels**
6. Recognizing cooperative member behaviors during meetings	Little 1 2 3 4 (5) Very Relevant
7. Engendering cooperative member behaviors during meetings	Little 1 2 3 4 (5) Very Relevant
III. Confidence: What level of *confidence* do you have that you can effectively use these group interaction management skills in problem-solving discussions?	**Confidence Levels**
8. Recognizing cooperative member behaviors during meetings	Little 1 2 3 (4) 5 Very Confident
*9. Engendering cooperative member behaviors during meetings	Little 1 2 (3) 4 5 Very Confident
IV. Clarity: What level of *clarity* do you believe the following instructional materials and activities have?	**Clarity Level**
10. Session introduction	Little 1 2 3 (4) 5 Very Clear
11. Objectives for session	Little 1 2 3 4 (5) Very Clear
12. Annotated written dialogues of meetings	Little 1 2 3 (4) 5 Very Clear
*13. Videos of meetings	Little 1 (2) 3 4 5 Very Clear
14. Performing ourselves as group leaders	Little 1 2 3 4 (5) Very Clear
15. Instructions for our group leadership activity	Little 1 2 3 (4) 5 Very Clear

Figure 12.4 Summary of Field Test Group's Responses on the Attitude Questionnaire for Main Step 6: Manage Cooperative Group Interaction, Session 10, Objectives 6.1.1 Through 6.5.1

16. Checklists we used to find positive leader actions	Little 1 2 3 (4) 5 Very Clear
17. Feedback on exercises for positive member and leader actions	Little 1 2 3 (4) 5 Very Clear
V. Satisfaction: Overall, how satisfied were you with the following:	**Satisfaction Level**
18. The facilities	Little 1 2 3 4 (5) Very Satisfied
19. The instructor(s)	Little 1 2 3 (4) 5 Very Satisfied
* 20. The pace	Little 1 2 (3) 4 5 Very Satisfied
21. The instruction	Little 1 2 3 (4) 5 Very Satisfied
* 22. Yourself, relative to the new skills you have developed/refined	Little 1 2 (3) 4 5 Very Satisfied

VI. Please comment on aspects of this session that were strengths and problems for you personally.

	Strengths	Problems
Introduction:	*Good, interesting*	*Need food*
Objectives:	*Good; Clear; Liked outline format; Easy to follow*	
Annotated dialogues:	*Easy to follow; Easy to find actions; Relevant topics*	
Video:	*Relevant topics; Interesting new groups*	*Moved too fast; Would like to stop video while marking observation form; Help!*
Interactive leadership session:	*Liked problem areas; Relevant topics for our own meetings*	*Too hurried—not enough time to get into leadership role; Some people not serious*
Assessments:	*Like checklists; Like testing format—Seemed like part of instruction*	*Videos were too fast, missed stuff; Frustrating*
Other:	*Will be able to use skills on job for quality team*	*Some stifling actions conflict with good manners (e.g., should comment on speaker's ideas to demonstrate attentiveness and understanding)*

Figure 12.4 Continued

Learners' open comments provided more information on these topics. Each learner's comments were content analyzed, similar comments were clustered across learners, and a summary of the issues they discussed were included on the questionnaire form. Related to the video problem, they thought the televised meetings went too fast for careful observation, and they were unable to watch the meeting progress and mark their observation forms at the same time. They also reported not having enough time to practice their leadership skills in the interactive meetings. Finally, several noted that they had trouble with some of the cooperation-stifling actions and believed the actions were in direct conflict with conventions of polite conversation. In follow-up interviews, the designer discovered that learners believed it was polite to comment when someone suggests a new idea because the comment illustrates to the speaker that others were listening and understood the comment. The difference between conventions of polite conversation and leader behaviors that stifle cooperative interaction could have accounted for learners' poor posttest performance in actions 4, 5, 8, and 12. It is typically not considered polite to leave a large, obvious gap in a conversation (4), allow others to interrupt (5), not comment on others' ideas (8), and not praise individuals for particularly good ideas and contributions (12). The designer concluded that the difference between cooperation-engendering behaviors in a group and conventions of polite conversation should be addressed directly in the instruction. The designer also decided to revisit authoritative reference resources in the group communications field and consult with additional SMEs regarding social convention versus effective group management actions.

Plans for Revising Instruction

At this point in formative evaluation of the leadership training instruction, it is premature to make final decisions about changes in the materials for one segment of a total unit of instruction. Before actually making some changes, other lessons should be field tested and analyzed. The changes should be made based on the overall effectiveness of the unit; however, data gathered in session 10 were used to create an instructional revision analysis table such as the one in Table 12.12. The table has four parts. The component being evaluated is listed in the left column, problems identified and potential changes are described in the next two columns, and the last column contains the evidence used to justify the change and its source. The resources used to complete the table are (1) test data and observations of students using the materials, (2) notes and remarks students made in the materials, and (3) information taken from the attitude questionnaire. The materials revision prescriptions are drawn directly from the verbal descriptions of each item analysis table made previously.

As the designers moved through the formative evaluation process, they noted that changes made in the materials could have consequences other than the ones anticipated. If extensive changes were made, such as inserting instruction for skills considered previously to be prerequisites for the students and excusing those with formal coursework and leadership experience from selected lessons, then another field trial should be conducted with these changes in place to see whether the desired impact was realized.

Table 12.12 Instructional Revision Analysis Form

Instructional Strategy Source	Problem	Proposed Change in Instruction	Evidence and Source
Motivational, introductory material	None	None	Learners reported good attention levels, clarity of purpose, and relevance of instruction (attitude questionnaire and debriefing session).
Pretest	Video meeting was too quick; learners had difficulty watching meeting and marking their observation form at the same time.	Add instructions to pause video while marking the observation form.	Comments came from attitude questionnaires, instructor comments, and debriefing session.
Information presentation	Performance levels on skills 4, 5, 8, and 12 were inadequate. Conflict was reported between stifling behaviors and conventions of polite conversation.	Add more information and examples of these behaviors in the presentations. Directly address the differences between leadership actions that engender cooperative group behavior and conventions of polite conversation. State differences and explain the purpose for the differences.	Information came from the following sources: • Posttest scores for these skills • Attitude questionnaire • Debriefing session • Observation during interactive meetings
Learner participation	(6.4.2) Video meeting was too quick; learners had difficulty watching meeting and marking their observation form at the same time.	Add instructions to pause video while marking the observation form.	Attitude questionnaire
Posttest	There was inadequate time available for each learner to perform.	Move learners into groups as they finish individualized activities. Watch, however; this may tend to place all the strong performers together and the novices together.	Attitude questionnaire
Attitude questionnaire	None	None	Questionnaire did detect areas of weakness and obtain explanations for them. Information obtained was corroborated with posttest data, debriefing, and instructor's comments.

Professional and Historical Perspectives

Examine almost any instructional design model and you find major emphasis on the concept of *formative evaluation*—that is, on collecting data to identify problems and to revise instructional materials. During the revision process, designers must keep a systems perspective on their work and remain open to possibilities that revisions may be warranted in any stage of the design process. Notice the dotted feedback line in the model shown in the opening graphic of this chapter. From formative evaluation, the feedback line traces back, indicating possible revisions in all stages of the design.

Models often indicate that after data have been collected and summarized, you should revise the materials "appropriately." In our approach to revising materials, we summarize the data that have been collected and then make changes that seem to be indicated by the data and our understanding of the goal, the learners, the instructional and performance contexts, and the instructional strategy we have chosen. The professional and historical perspectives section in the previous chapter on formative evaluation is equally applicable for this chapter on revision of materials.

Process Flowcharts

Revising Instructional Materials

There are several figures (Figures 12.5–12.8) included within this section to aid you in planning your documentation for your formative evaluation. They include (a) the sequence for examining your formative evaluation data, (b) summarizing data from experts and prescribing revisions, (c) analyzing data from one-to-one formative evaluations and prescribing revisions, and (d) analyzing data from small-group and field trial formative evaluations.

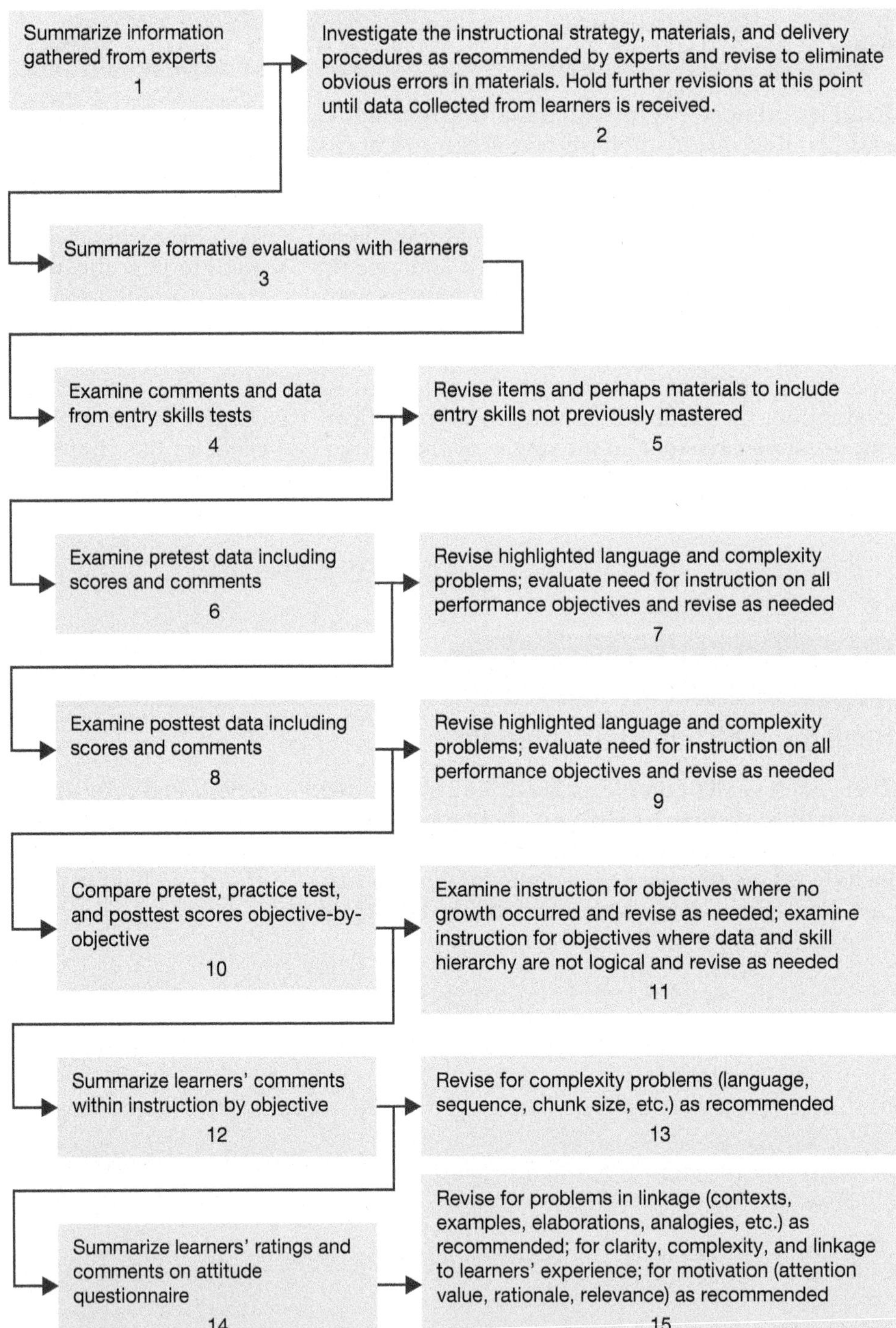

Figure 12.5 Plan Sequence for Examining Formative Evaluation Data

A. Template for Summarizing Information:

	MATERIALS CONGRUENT WITH INSTRUCTIONAL ANALYSIS?	MATERIALS APPROPRIATE FOR LEARNER CHARACTERISTICS?	MATERIALS APPROPRIATE FOR LEARNING CONTEXT?	MATERIALS APPROPRIATE FOR PERFORMANCE CONTEXT?

B. Template for Prescribing Revisions:

INSTRUCTIONAL STRATEGY COMPONENT	PROBLEM IDENTIFIED	PROPOSED CHANGES TO INSTRUCTION	EVIDENCE AND SOURCE
Entry skills test			
Motivational introductory material			
Pretest			
Information presentation			
Learner participation			
Posttest			
Attitude questionnaire			

Figure 12.6 Summarize and Analyze Data from Experts and Prescribe Revisions

A. Create Data Summary Table

LEARNER CHARACTERISTICS	ENTRY SKILLS TEST	PRETEST	PRACTICE TESTS	POSTTESTS	ATTITUDE QUESTIONNAIRE
Low Ability/ Experience	*List # for items and objectives not mastered*	*List # for items and objectives not mastered*	*List # for items and objectives not mastered*	*List # for items and objectives not mastered*	*List +/– comments about instruction*
Average Ability/ Experience	*List # for items and objectives not mastered*	*List # for items and objectives not mastered*	*List # for items and objectives not mastered*	*List # for items and objectives not mastered*	*List +/– comments about instruction*
High Ability/ Experience	*List # for items and objectives not mastered*	*List # for items and objectives not mastered*	*List # for items and objectives not mastered*	*List # for items and objectives not mastered*	*List +/– comments about instruction*
Totals	*List all items and objectives problematic for group*	*List all items and objectives problematic for group*	*List all items and objectives problematic for group*	*List all items and objectives problematic for group*	*List all items and objectives problematic for group*

B. Summarize Information Within Instructional Materials:

- Create a master "analysis" copy of all assessments, including the attitude questionnaire as well as the instructional materials.
- Summarize all learners' comments directly within materials at appropriate places. This includes unclear vocabulary, information, and examples; time for completion, and so forth.

Figure 12.7 Summarize and Analyze Data from One-to-One Formative Evaluations with Learners and Prescribe Revisions

C. Create Instructional Revision Analysis Form

INSTRUCTIONAL STRATEGY COMPONENT	PROBLEM IDENTIFIED	PROPOSED CHANGES TO INSTRUCTION	EVIDENCE AND SOURCE
Entry skills test			
Motivational introductory material			
Pretest			
Information presentation			

Instructional Revision Analysis Form Continued

INSTRUCTIONAL STRATEGY COMPONENT	PROBLEM IDENTIFIED	PROPOSED CHANGES TO INSTRUCTION	EVIDENCE AND SOURCE
Learner participation			
Posttest			
Attitude questionnaire			

Figure 12.7 Continued

A. **Create Sample Graphs of Learners' Pretest, Practice Test, and Posttest Scores for Analysis** (Data Reflect the Percentage of Students Who Master Each Objective)

1. **Create Bar Graph (Examples of hypothetical data are filled in)**

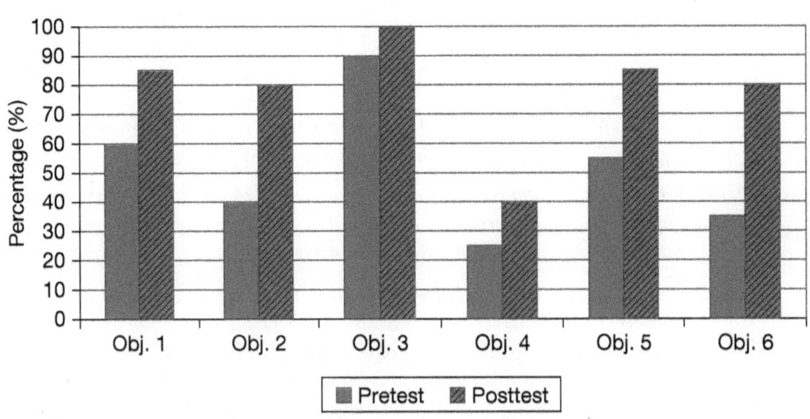

Example Data Analysis:

- Look for evidence of effective learning from pretest to posttest: Objectives 1, 2, 3, 5, 6
- Look for evidence of problems: Objective 4

Figure 12.8 Summarize and Analyze Data from Small-Group and Field Trial Formative Evaluations

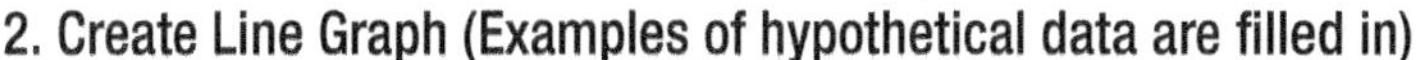

2. Create Line Graph (Examples of hypothetical data are filled in)

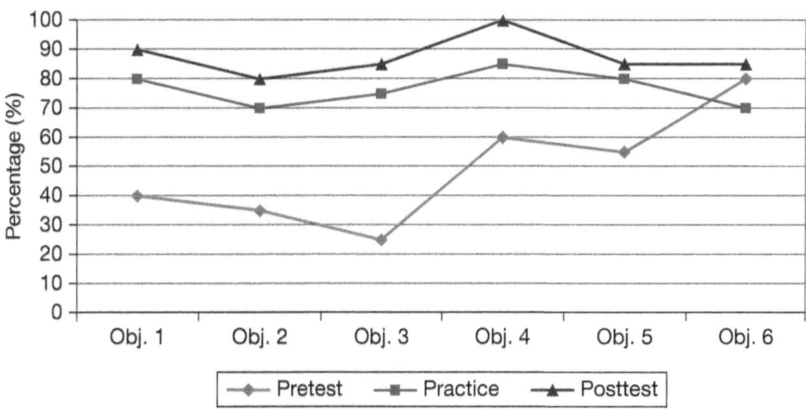

3. Create Flow Chart (Examples of hypothetical data are filled in)

Skeleton of instructional analysis with pretest/posttest percentage of students mastering each skill (problem skills are shaded)

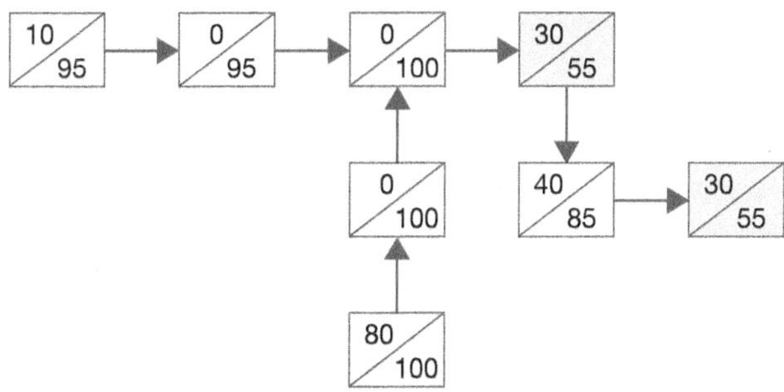

B. Summarize Information Within Instructional Materials: Create a master "analysis" copy of all assessments, including the attitude questionnaire as well as the instructional materials. Summarize all learners' comments directly within materials at appropriate places. This includes unclear vocabulary, information, and examples; time for completion; and so forth.

Figure 12.8 Continued

C. Summarize Information from Attitude Questionnaire.

1. Bar Chart with Examples of Hypothetical Group Mean Ratings, Items within Rating Categories

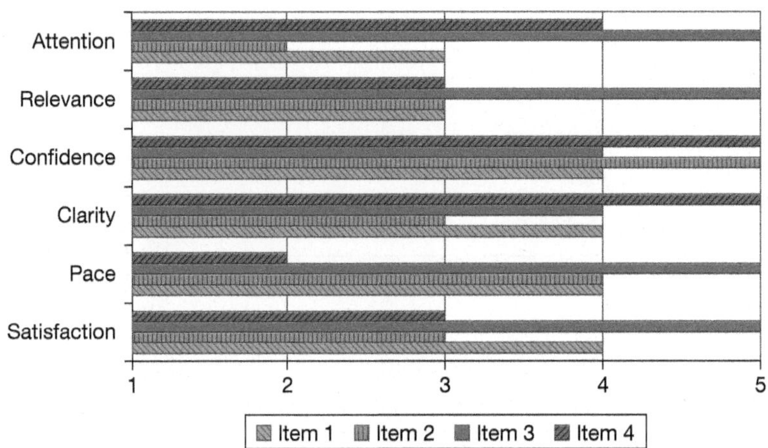

2. Summary Table of Learner Comments

INSTRUCTION	STRENGTHS	PROBLEMS	SUGGESTIONS FOR IMPROVEMENT
Introduction	*Summarize comments here*	*Summarize comments here*	*Summarize comments here*
Pretest	*Summarize comments here*	*Summarize comments here*	*Summarize comments here*
Information presentation	*Summarize comments here*	*Summarize comments here*	*Summarize comments here*
Examples	*Summarize comments here*	*Summarize comments here*	*Summarize comments here*
Pace	*Summarize comments here*	*Summarize comments here*	*Summarize comments here*
Practice activities	*Summarize comments here*	*Summarize comments here*	*Summarize comments here*
Posttest	*Summarize comments here*	*Summarize comments here*	*Summarize comments here*

D. Create Instructional Revision Analysis Form

INSTRUCTIONAL STRATEGY COMPONENT	PROBLEM IDENTIFIED	PROPOSED CHANGES TO INSTRUCTION	EVIDENCE AND SOURCE
Entry skills test			
Motivational introductory material			
Pretest			
Information presentation			
Learner participation			
Posttest			
Attitude questionnaire			

Figure 12.8 Continued

Practice

1. What data should you use to determine whether learners in your target group actually possessed the entry skills identified in your instructional analysis and whether those you identified were relevant to your instruction?
2. When should you develop instruction for prerequisite skills?
3. What type of data table should you create to provide the information necessary to determine the exact nature of problems that learners have with the instruction?
4. Why should you construct a narrative explanation from data tables of problems that are identified with each test?
5. Why should you summarize performance by objective across pretest and posttest?
6. What materials should you evaluate using an attitude questionnaire?
7. What information should you include in an instructional revision analysis table?
8. Table 12.13 contains an incomplete item-by-objective table for five learners. Use the raw data to calculate the following:
    - Raw score for each learner
    - Percentage of items correct for each learner
    - Number of objectives passed by each learner. Assume answering all three items within an objective correctly is required to pass.
    - Number of learners answering each item correctly
    - Percentage of learners answering each item correctly
    - Percentage of learners passing each objective

    You may want to transfer the data to a spreadsheet to complete your calculations.

    Four students who participated in the field trial of the writing composition materials demonstrated on the entry skills test that they had not mastered the entry skills. They were included in the field trial to determine whether the subordinate skills identified as entry skills were classified correctly for the instructional goal. Figure 12.9 contains the percentage of these four students who mastered the declarative sentences subordinate skills on the pretest, embedded test, and declarative sentences portion of the posttest. Answer the following questions based on their performance data in the chart.
9. Did students appear to need instruction on all of the skills?
10. Based on pretest and posttest data, for which skills did students appear to benefit from the instruction?
11. Apart from those skills students had mastered prior to instruction, for which skills was instruction not effective?
12. Based on their achievement in the unit, what would you recommend as next steps for these students?

Table 12.13 **Item-by-Objective Analysis Table**

Objective	1			2			3			4						
ITEM	1	2	3	4	5	6	7	8	9	10	11	12	RAW SCORE	PERCENTAGE CORRECT	OBJECTIVES PASSED	PERCENTAGE OF OBJECTIVES PASSED
Student 1	1	1	1		1	1				1	1					
2	1	1	1	1	1	1	1	1	1	1	1					
3				1	1	1				1	1					
4	1			1	1	1	1	1	1	1	1					
5	1	1	1	1	1	1	1	1	1	1	1					
Total correct																
Percentage correct																
Percentage passing objective																

1 = Correct answer.
Incorrect answer is left blank.
To pass an objective, all items within the objective must be correct because each item was constructed to test a different facet of the objective.

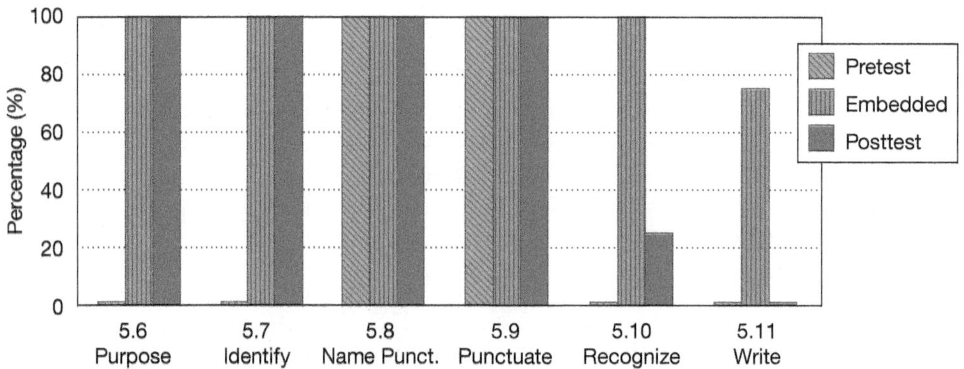

Figure 12.9 Mastery of Each Objective on the Pretest, Embedded Items, and Posttest for Four Students Who Did Not Possess the Required Entry Skills

Feedback

1. Use item and objective analysis data from the items on the pretest and posttest. Data from the entry skills pretest tell you whether students possessed the entry skills. Data from tests used with the instructional materials tell you whether you actually identified relevant entry skills. If students perform poorly on the entry skills items yet are successful on subsequent tests, then you must reexamine the entry skills you identified.
2. Do not develop instruction for prerequisite skills prior to at least the one-to-one evaluation of your materials. As shown in the Case Study section, data from the field test tell you whether and for what specific objectives such materials are needed.
3. Construct an item/objective analysis table. It should be constructed in a manner to enable you to analyze both correct and incorrect answers. Correct answer analysis tells you whether your instruction was effective; incorrect answer analysis tells you what went wrong and helps you focus on revisions that might help.
4. Construct a narrative analysis from the data for each test while the information is fresh in your mind because this information becomes one basis for the instructional revisions analysis table. If you do not do it and have many raw data tables from several tests before you, it is very difficult to focus and pinpoint problems that occurred.
5. The summary tables highlight trends in performance. If learners failed to master an objective on the pretest, was it mastered on the posttest?
6. All components of the materials should be evaluated on the attitude questionnaire. It is recommended that an attitude questionnaire be administered at the same time that materials are used by learners. We recommend embedding attitude questions within the lessons so students comment while the material is fresh in their minds. If this approach is used, then care must be taken not to disrupt the flow of learning.
7. An instructional revision analysis table should contain five types of information: (1) the name of the learning component from the instructional strategy; (2) problems identified with the component; (3) changes to be made in the instruction; (4) evidence from either test or questionnaire data, remarks in materials, and observations of how procedures worked; and (5) the source of evidence cited as the reason(s) for changes.
8. See Table 12.14.
9. Based on the pretest/posttest data in the chart, students do not appear to need instruction for subordinate skills 5.8 and 5.9.
10. Based on pretest and posttest data, students appeared to benefit from instruction for subordinate skills 5.6 and 5.7.
11. Instruction was not effective for subordinate skills 5.10 and 5.11.
12. These four students should be branched to individualized instruction covering recognizing the elements of complete sentences as well as additional instruction on recognizing and writing declarative sentences.

Table 12.14 Item-by-Objective Analysis Table

Objective	1			2			3			4						PERCENTAGE OF OBJECTIVES PASSED
ITEM	1	2	3	4	5	6	7	8	9	10	11	12	RAW SCORE	PERCENTAGE CORRECT	OBJECTIVES PASSED	
Student 1	1	1	1		1	1				1	1		7	58	1	25
2	1	1	1	1	1	1	1	1	1	1	1		11	92	3	75
3				1	1	1				1	1		5	42	1	25
4	1			1	1	1	1	1	1	1	1		9	75	1	50
5	1	1	1	1	1	1	1	1	1	1	1		11	92	3	75
Total correct	4	3	3	4	5	5	3	3	3	5	5	0				
Percentage correct	80	60	60	80	100	100	60	60	60	100	100	0				
Percentage passing objective			60			80			60			0				

1 = Correct answer.
Incorrect answer is left blank.
To pass an objective, all items within the objective must be correct because each item was constructed to test a different facet of the objective.

References and Recommended Readings

All references at the end of Chapter 11, "Designing and Conducting Formative Evaluations," are appropriate for this chapter on instructional materials revision.

Ainsworth, L. B., & Viegut, D. J. (Eds.). (2006). *Common formative assessments: How to connect standards-based instruction and assessment*. Corwin Press. Focuses on how to create assessments for formative evaluation to identify students' learning needs.

Ayala, C. C., Shavelson, R. J., Ruiz-Primo, M. A., Yin, Y., Furtak, E. M., Young, D. B., & Tomita, M. (2008). From formal embedded assessments to reflective lessons: The development of formative assessment studies. *Applied Measurement in Education, 21*(4), 315–334. Focuses on the impact of formative assessment on the curriculum, learners, and student motivation.

Bodzin, A., Price, B., Cates, W., Williamson, B., & Campbell, N. (2002). *Formative evaluation of the design and development of a web-based biology curriculum: Y1 findings*. Paper presented at the National Association for Research in Science Teaching Annual Meeting in New Orleans, LA., April 7–10, 2002. http://www.phschool.com/usingexploringlife/downloads/narst2002.pdf. The report describes the iterative formative evaluation process used and includes a table on pages 30–31 that displays problems found, feedback sources, and resulting product changes.

Cifuentes, L., Mercer, R., Alverez, O., & Bettati, R. (2010). An architecture for case-based learning. *TechTrends*, 54, 44–50. https://doi.org/10.1007/s11528-010-0453-9. Describes a testing, evaluation, and revision cycle.

Gagné, R. M., Wager, W. W., Golas, K. C., & Keller, J. M. (2004). *Principles of instructional design* (5th ed.). Wadsworth/Thomson Learning. Includes a chapter on assessing student performance for not only the development of objective-referenced assessments but also the concept of "mastery" and norm-referenced measures.

Hattie, J., & Temperley, H. (2007). The power of feedback. *Review of Educational Research, 77*(1), 81–112.

Le Maistre, K., & Weston, C. (1996). The priorities established among data sources when instructional designers revise written materials. *Educational Technology Research and Development, 44*(1), 61–70. The results of this study indicated that designers tend to rely more heavily on their own knowledge in making revisions than they do on feedback data.

Luo, H., Koszalka, T. A., Arnone, M. P., & Choi, I. (2018). Applying case-based method in designing self-directed online instruction: A formative research study. *Education Technology Research & Development, 66,* 515–544. https://doi.org/10.1007/s11423-018-9572-3. The case study includes descriptions of two iterations of pilot testing with revisions based on results.

Mordacq, J. C., Drane, D. L., Swarat, S. L., & Lo, S. M. (2017). Development of course-based undergraduate research experiences using a design-based approach. *Journal of College Science Teaching, 46*(4), 64–75.

Park, S. (2019). A developmental study on a SPAT design model for mobile learning. *Education Technology Research & Development, 67,* 123–159. https://doi.org/10.1007/s11423-018-9630-x. This study reports a development process that includes iterative cycles of review and revision.

Phillips, J., Klein, J. D., Dunne, E., & Siriwardena, M. (2019). Using formative data to make evidence-based decisions during re-design. *Journal of Formative Design in Learning, 3,* 133–145. https://doi.org/10.1007/s41686-019-00036-z

Rusman, E., Ternier, S., & Specht, M. (2018). Early second language learning and adult involvement in a real-world context: Design and evaluation of the "ELENA Goes Shopping" mobile game. *Journal of Educational Technology & Society, 21*(3), 90–103. Follows development through good descriptions of cycles of evaluation and revision.

Sahrir, M. (2012). Formative evaluation of an Arabic online vocabulary learning game prototype: Lessons from a Malaysian institute of higher learning experience. In N. Alias & S. Haashim (Eds.), *Instructional technology research, design, and development: Lessons from the field* (pp. 357–368). IGI Global. Detailed analysis of the formative evaluation and revision phase of the ID model.

Tessmer, M. (1994). Formative evaluation alternatives. *Performance Improvement Quarterly, 7*(1), 3–18.

Tessmer, M. (2005). *Planning and conducting formative evaluations*. Routledge reprint. A complete description of the major phases of formative evaluation.

Vanderhoven, E., Schellens, T., Vanderlinde, R., et al. (2016). Developing educational materials about risks on social network sites: A design-based research approach. *Educational Technology Research & Development, 64*, 459–480. https://doi.org/10.1007/s11423-015-9415-4. Describes four trial and revision cycles in interactive, classroom-, and home-based instruction. Includes very detailed descriptions of the rationale for theory-based revisions following each cycle.

Weston, C., Le Maistre, C., McAlpine, L., & Bordonaro, T. (1997). The influence of the participants in formative evaluation on the improvement of learning from instructional materials. *Instructional Science, 25*, 369–386. This empirical study using print materials concluded that formative revisions that incorporate learner feedback have the most impact on improving student learning.

chapter 13

Designing and Conducting Summative Evaluations

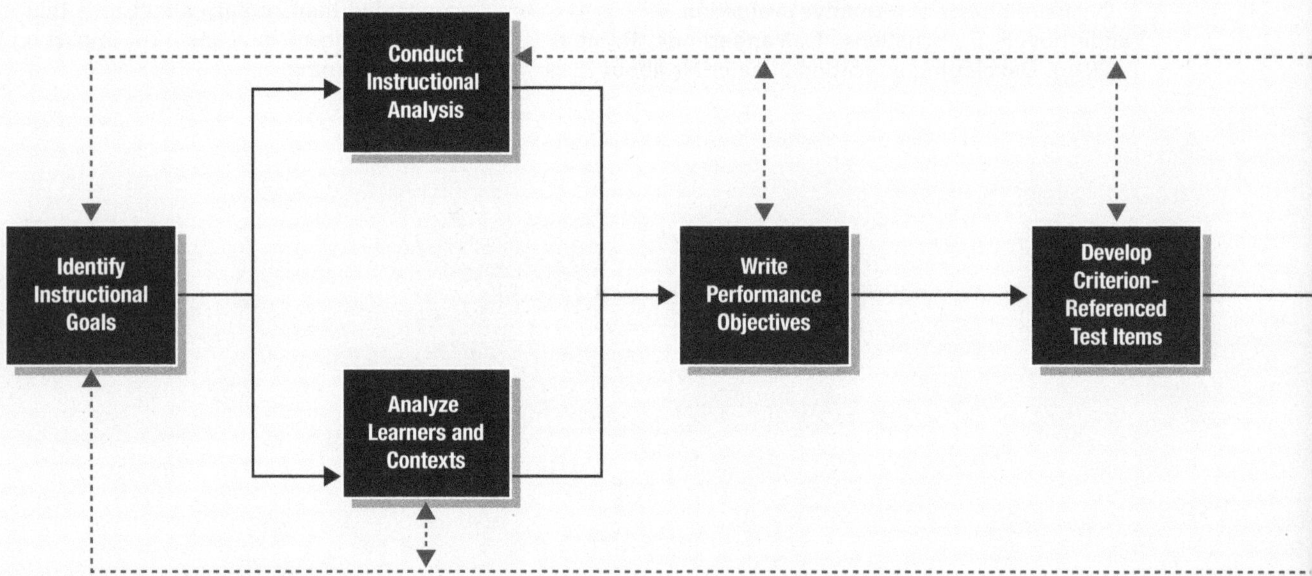

Objectives

- Contrast formative and summative evaluation by purpose and design.
- Describe the purpose of summative evaluation.
- Describe the two phases of summative evaluation and the decisions resulting from each.
- Design an expert judgment phase of summative evaluation.
- Design an impact phase of summative evaluation.

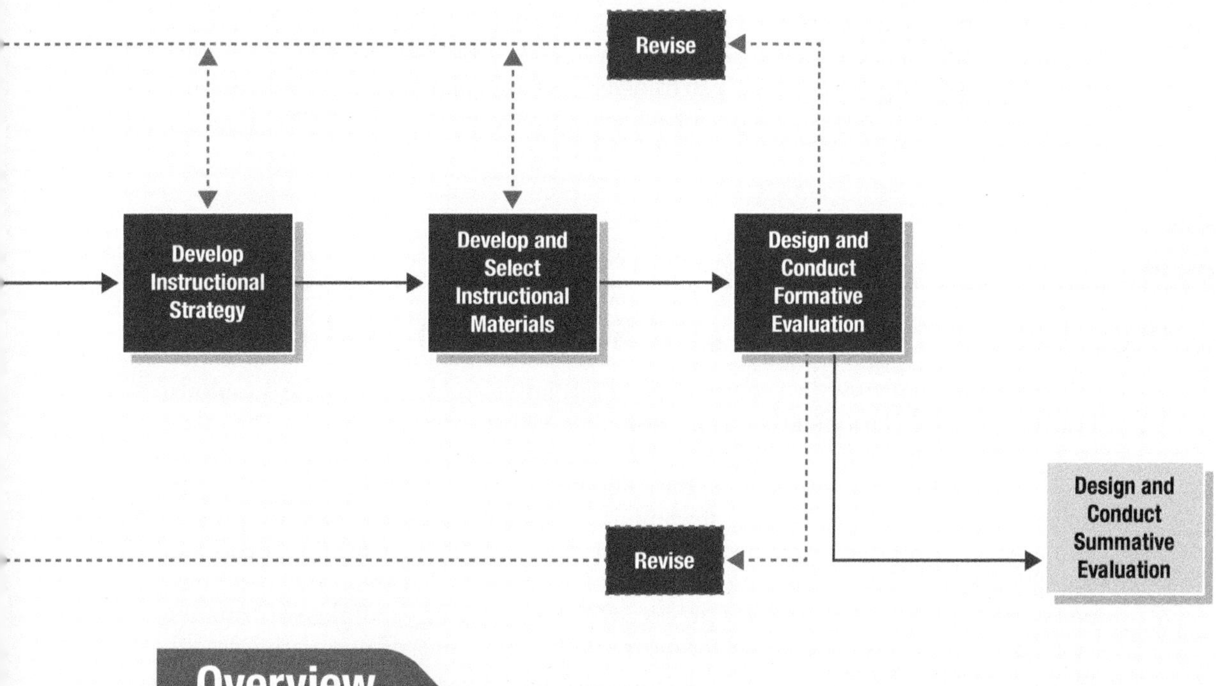

Overview

Formative and summative evaluations differ by purpose and design. Formative evaluations are conducted for the purpose of identifying the strengths and weaknesses in newly developed instruction, whereas summative evaluations are intended to make decisions about whether to maintain, adopt, or adapt existing instruction. The primary evaluator in a formative evaluation is the designer or developer of the instruction, whereas the primary evaluator in a summative evaluation is frequently unfamiliar with the materials, the organization requesting the evaluation, or the setting in which the materials are evaluated. Such evaluators are referred to as *external evaluators*; these evaluators are often chosen for summative evaluations because they have no personal investment in the instruction and are likely to be more objective about the strengths and weaknesses of the instruction.

If designers of a particular piece of instruction can step back from their work and take an objective point of view, they can be excellent summative evaluators because of their understanding of the instructional design process, the characteristics of well-designed instruction, and the criteria for evaluating instruction. These skills provide them with the expertise for designing and conducting the expert judgment as well as the impact analysis phases of summative evaluation. In professional and technical training settings, a performance improvement specialist or team is frequently responsible for the whole process from identifying goals to evaluating the eventual impact of training in the workplace.

The design of the expert judgment phase of summative evaluation is anchored in the model for systematically designing instruction. Similar to initially designing instruction, the materials evaluator begins by judging the congruence between the instructional needs of an organization and the goals for instructional materials. Next, the completeness and accuracy of the content presented in the materials are evaluated. The standard for this evaluation is an instructional goal analysis with required subordinate skills. Content experts are involved in either producing or verifying the quality of the skills diagram. The instructional materials are then evaluated for the quality of their instructional strategies and their potential for supporting transfer of knowledge and skills from the learning to the performance context.

The impact analysis phase of summative evaluation is focused on the jobsite, and it examines whether (1) an organization's needs were met following use of the instruction, (2) employees are able to transfer new information and skills to the job, and (3) an improvement in job performance or productivity is realized.

Concepts

Comparison of Formative and Summative Evaluations

We begin this chapter with a comparison of formative and summative evaluations, but first we will clarify some terminology. One distinction that should be made is that the terms *formative* and *summative* are frequently paired with *assessment* instead of *evaluation*. In this syntax, the reference is to student achievement, so formative assessment is measuring student achievement for the purpose of guiding and improving student learning, and summative assessment is for the purpose of establishing a student's standing relative to a learning goal or standard. Test items embedded within instruction and practice with feedback are examples of formative assessment, and final exams and term projects are examples of summative assessment. In our ID context, assessments are focused on students and evaluations are focused on instructional materials and processes, but we are sure that you recognize how useful assessments are in doing our evaluations.

You have just studied formative evaluation and are very familiar with its characteristics, and what you know about formative evaluation will aid you in putting summative evaluation into perspective. Although there are many similarities, formative and summative evaluations differ in several aspects. These differences are summarized in Table 13.1. The first difference is related to the purpose for conducting each type of evaluation. Formative evaluations are undertaken to locate weaknesses and problems in the instruction in order to revise it. Summative evaluations are undertaken after instruction is completed to determine the impact of the instruction for the learners, their jobs, and the organization. It is not undertaken to revise instruction but to document the findings for decision makers who must decide whether to obtain or maintain the materials.

The second difference involves the stages of the evaluations. The formative evaluation includes three stages—the one-to-one, small-group, and field trial—all conducted directly with target learners. During each stage, a great deal of time is spent observing and interviewing learners in order to understand the nature of problems they encounter with the instruction. The summative evaluation, conversely, contains only two stages: expert judgment and impact analysis. The **expert judgment stage** resembles evaluative decisions made by the designer and the context and content experts during the design and development of materials.

Table 13.1 A Comparison of Formative and Summative Evaluation

	Formative Evaluation	Summative Evaluation
Purpose	Locate weaknesses in instruction in order to revise it	Document the degree to which skills learned during instruction transferred to the jobsite
Phases or Stages	One-to-one Small group Impact evaluation	Expert judgment Impact analysis
Instructional Development History	Systematically designed in-house and tailored to the needs of the organization	Produced in-house or elsewhere, not necessarily a systems approach
Materials	One set of materials	One set of materials
Position of Evaluator	Member of design and development team	Typically an external evaluator
Outcomes	A prescription for revising instruction	A report documenting the soundness of the instruction and the impact the instruction had on the worker, the job, and the organization

Target learners are not involved in this stage of summative evaluation. The **impact evaluation stage** is conducted with target learners after they have returned to their jobs and focuses on the jobsite and examines three things: (1) if an organization's needs were met following use of the instruction, (2) whether employees are able to transfer new information and skills to the job, and (3) if an improvement in job performance or productivity is realized. Outcome data are typically obtained through unobtrusive observations, questionnaires, document analysis, and job performance ratings in the performance context.

The materials subjected to formative and summative evaluations typically have different developmental histories. Instruction subjected to formative evaluations usually has been designed and developed systematically and thus holds promise for being effective with target learners. Conversely, materials included in a summative evaluation may or may not have been developed following systematic design procedures. The expert judgment phase of summative evaluation provides evidence of the materials' developmental history, and should materials be judged as lacking by experts, then the impact evaluation may or may not be performed. Another contrast is the relationship of the evaluator to the materials. Typically, formative evaluators have a personal investment in the materials and thus seek valid judgments about the materials to produce the best materials possible. Evaluators with personal investments in the outcome of the evaluation are called *internal evaluators*. It is wise for summative evaluators not to have a personal investment in the materials being evaluated because such detachment helps them maintain objectivity in designing the evaluation and in describing both the strengths and weaknesses in the materials. Detached evaluators are commonly referred to as *external evaluators*.

The final difference between formative and summative evaluations is the outcome. The results of a formative evaluation include prescriptions for revising the instruction and the actual materials revisions among the three stages of the evaluation. The outcome of the summative evaluation could lead to materials revision, but it is not a prescription for revisions. Instead, it is a report for decision makers that documents how well skills learned during instruction were transferred to the jobsite and the impact of using the new skills on the workers' productivity and the organization.

Burke and Hutchins (2008) and Hutchinson (2009) describe three areas of consideration for summative evaluations including characteristics of the instruction, characteristics of the trainee/employee, and characteristics of the workplace. These three areas and considerations within them are presented in Table 13.2. Look carefully at the information in the table. Assume for a moment that you are a designer who has been called to do an expert judgment review in a summative evaluation. As a designer/evaluator, you are pleased to recognize that you already possess the conceptual knowledge for the evaluation because you will be using skills and strategies for your summative evaluation work that you use in designing instruction. You recognize the instructional characteristics within the first column as the five main learning components you use in design that are based on Gagné's nine events of instruction to support learning. This evaluation is conducted during the expert judgment phase of summative evaluation.

In the second column, person characteristics, you recognize factors to consider in analyzing your learners, including the ARCS model of motivation. You also recognize most of the considerations included in the third column as factors to consider in analyzing the performance context. Considerations of the learner/employee and the workplace environment are typically investigated during the impact phase of summative evaluation.

The designer/evaluator also incorporates front-end analysis considerations, especially as they relate to an organization's goals and the alignment of those goals with those in particular instruction. This information is used both in the expert judgment and in the impact phases of summative evaluation. Summative

Table 13.2 Factors to Consider in Summative Evaluations of Transfer of Skills to the Workplace

Instructional Characteristics	Person Characteristics	Work Environment Characteristics
Preinstruction	Cognitive ability	Supervisors
Motivation	Special needs	Positive feedback for worker
Clear understanding of knowledge and skills required for job	Self-efficacy	Involvement in training
Appropriate difficulty level for ability	Motivation	Discuss skills among employees
Links to prior knowledge and job needs	Perceptions of relevance for immediate needs, confidence, and personal satisfaction for learning and performing	Consequences for correct use
Content	Expectations	Remediation for incorrect use
Relevant to job/career needs	Affinity for or commitment to company	Improvement following related training
Learner guidance		Positive transfer climate
Elaboration		Organizational commitment
Learner participation		Hold supervisors and employees accountable for performance improvement related to training
Ample opportunities to practice		Discuss new skills with peers
Practice congruent with job performance		Opportunities to use skills
Relevant and targeted feedback		Support during implementation of skills
Assessment		Cues that prompt use of new skills
Adequate transfer strategies		Social support as incentives and feedback
Mental rehearsal, conversing about, goal setting, job aids		

evaluators incorporate all these steps from the instructional design process into their quest to determine the quality of existing instructional materials and how well information and skills are transferred to the workplace. They also must consider other factors unique to the organization or to the instruction.

Expert Judgment Phase of Summative Evaluation

The expert judgment phase of summative evaluation includes five types of analyses:

- Congruence analysis
- Content analysis
- Design analysis
- Transfer possibility analysis
- Existing materials analysis

Congruence Analysis

The purpose of congruence analysis is to examine the congruence between the organization's stated needs and the instructional materials as well as their resources and those required to implement the instruction.

Organization's Needs We are still assuming that you are in the role of an evaluator. To perform the congruence analysis, you should first obtain copies of the organization's strategic plans, its current goals and objectives, and its stated needs for the training. You can then infer how closely the training goals are aligned with the organization's goals and needs. The closer the training is aligned to the organization's strategic plans and goals, the better the support that managers and employees will receive when instituting new training for improving skills in the workplace.

Next, obtain any job analysis documents available as well as any descriptions the organization has about related problems it wishes to address through instruction. Compare this information with the description of the goals and objectives of the instruction. The closer the tasks in the job analysis description and the current organization's needs match the goals and objectives of the instruction, the more likely learners will achieve the skills and transfer them to the worksite. This information for the instruction can usually be obtained from the group that designed the materials.

The evaluator also needs an accurate description of the characteristics of the organization's employees/students. Their learning characteristics (e.g., attitudes, motivations, abilities, special needs, experiences, goals) should be compared with those of the learners for whom the instruction was intended. The organization's employees selected for training and the target learners for the instruction should be relatively similar in experience, abilities, and motivations.

Resources Analyze the congruence between the resources the organization has available for the instruction and the costs of obtaining and implementing the instruction. Materials that are too costly, however effective, often run out of budget for maintenance by an organization. The facilities and equipment available in the organization and those required to implement the instruction should also be contrasted.

Once adequate descriptions are obtained, compare (1) the organization's needs versus needs addressed in the materials, (2) the organization's target groups versus target groups for the materials, and (3) the organization's resources versus requirements for implementing the instruction. The information from your congruence analysis should be shared with appropriate decision makers. Although you may be asked to make recommendations, the persons who make the final decisions about what to include in a summative evaluation, or whether to even continue the evaluation, vary greatly from one organization to another. Three questions related to the design of quality materials should be addressed for any summative evaluation. These questions include:

1. Are the materials and any accompanying assessments accurate and complete?
2. Is the instructional strategy adequate for the anticipated types of learning outcomes?
3. How likely is it that knowledge and skills from training will transfer to the workplace?

Content Analysis

Because you may not be a content expert in the materials you evaluate, it may be necessary to engage a content expert as a consultant. What you must consider is how best to use this expert. One strategy is to provide the experts with copies of all materials and ask them to judge the accuracy, currency, and completeness of the materials for the organization's stated goals; another strategy is to obtain the design documents from the group that produced the instruction and ask the expert to use them as a standard against which to evaluate the accuracy and completeness of the instructional materials. How can the instructional goal framework be used to evaluate the materials? The skills included in the framework can be converted to a checklist or rating scale the evaluator uses to judge the quality of the materials and any accompanying tests.

Design Analysis

The evaluator should judge the adequacy of the components of the instructional strategy included in the materials. As an external evaluator, you may not know whether the materials are adequate for the given learners' needs, but you should take steps to find out about the learners' characteristics in order to make these determinations. The designer's instructional strategy, including the preinstructional information, content presentation, learner participation, assessment, and follow-through, should be used as a template for reviewing the materials.

Although the basic components of an instructional strategy do not change, it may be necessary to adopt criteria related to each component based on the type of learning outcome(s) addressed in the materials and the learners' motivation and capabilities. For example, advanced training for experienced, motivated employees may well be light on learning components, while the opposite would be true for initial training for new employees. It may also be necessary to assess the materials from logistics and management points of view. These aspects of the strategy, rather than the learning foundation, may be the cause of some problems uncovered in the instruction.

If some or all of the instructional materials are judged to be unsound in these important aspects, then continuing the summative evaluation could be fruitless. Supervisors should be informed of your judgments about the content and instructional strategy, and again they should be asked whether they wish to continue the evaluation.

Transfer Possibility Analysis

The fourth area of questions about the instructional materials relates to their potential for transferability of knowledge and skills from the learning context to the jobsite. Consider such factors as learner guidance and support as the learner bridges the gap between instruction and the job. Learner guidance and support include such questions as the following:

- Are they permitted to take any instructional materials with them to the jobsite?
- Are there learner guides, checklists, or outlines to consult?

- Is there an app for their smartphones or easy ways to contact support?
- Is there an electronic performance support system on their tablet or at the jobsite?
- Are any just-in-time materials available to support the transfer process?
- Are any required software and instructional programming platform-neutral for implementation in the maximum number of work environments?
- Were critical aspects of the job adequately simulated in the learning context?
- Are supervisor capabilities, equipment, or environments compatible with the organization's goals and learners' newly acquired skills?
- Are there factors that might enhance or restrict the utility of the materials for the organization?
- Did employees actually learn the knowledge and skills during training?

If the information and skills are not learned, then it is not likely that transfer will occur.

Some of us have known groups and individuals who consider the "in-service training" experience to be points on a certificate, a day away from the job, lunch out with colleagues, and home early. The potential for transfer within such cultures is slim. How can the designer/evaluator assess potential for transfer when this may be the circumstance? Evaluators can request posttest data from the organization providing the instruction to determine whether the skills were actually learned. Information about individuals is not necessary, but group achievement data could be helpful. Examining a copy of the posttest also helps determine whether the skills were tested or if, instead, a "smile" survey was administered. Yet other evidence may be obtained by interviewing the individuals who provided the training and, of course, the learners themselves; they are well aware of the learning that did or did not occur.

Existing Materials Analysis

A new model for summative evaluation is not required for this type of evaluation because the expert judgment phase of summative evaluation works quite well through all its stages. For these evaluations, one does not assume that all stages will be undertaken; instead, following each analysis, a decision is made about whether to continue. The analysis of existing materials follows the same sequence as used to analyze materials that have just been designed and developed. The analysis begins with congruence analysis, followed by content analysis, design analysis, and transfer feasibility analysis.

Figure 13.1 summarizes the sequence of tasks involved in the expert judgment phase of evaluating the potential of materials for an organization's needs. Congruence analysis should obviously be undertaken first. Regardless of the quality of materials reviewed, its lack of congruence with an organization's needs means it is inappropriate and should not be considered further. If the materials are congruent, then move to content analysis. Again, should the content not be judged to be complete, current, and accurate, the materials should be dismissed from further consideration. This step-down expert judgment process helps ensure that the evaluation is as economical as possible.

At this point, you have concluded the expert judgment phase of the summative evaluation. The evaluation design and procedures used to conduct this part of the evaluation should be documented in your evaluation report, together with your recommendations and rationale. If the materials are judged to be unsound in these important aspects, then continuing the summative evaluation would be fruitless. Supervisors should be informed of your judgments following this phase of the summative evaluation, and again, they should be asked whether they wish to continue the evaluation to the workplace.

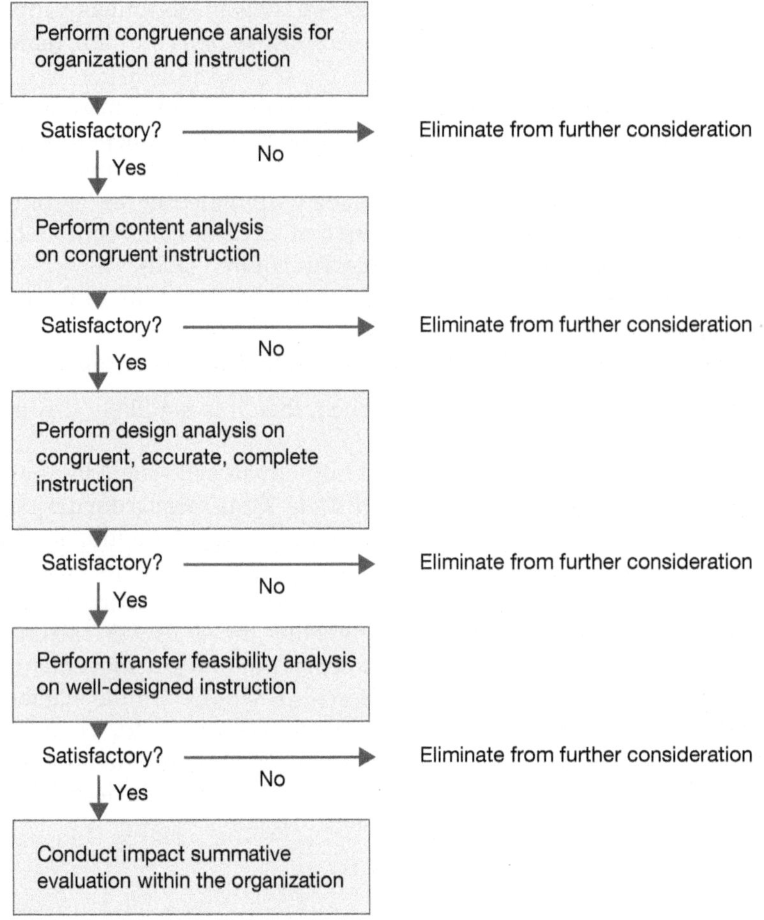

Figure 13.1 Sequence of Stages of Analysis During the Expert Judgment Phase of Summative Evaluation

Impact Phase of Summative Evaluation

The second phase of summative evaluation is **impact analysis**, which is conducted within the organization. The impact analysis is sometimes called **outcomes analysis.** Impact analysis typically includes the following activities:

- focusing the impact study,
- establishing criteria and data needs,
- selecting respondents,
- planning study procedures,
- summarizing and analyzing data,
- reporting results, and
- negotiating resources.

Focusing the Impact Study

The first planning activity is to center your study in the workplace. The evaluator must shift from the perspective of the instruction to a perspective on the organization. Review the organization's goals, their defined needs, and their relationships to the specific goals for the instruction and to their employees who participated in the instruction. With these as a resource, describe clearly the questions to be answered during the site study. Basically, your questions should yield information for the impact analysis (outcomes for learner, job, and organization).

It is always a good idea to plan how you will introduce the study and interact with employees. Even your initial contact can sink a study if company personnel are not approached appropriately. All participating personnel must understand that you are evaluating specific training and instructional materials and not them or their company. Individuals and organizations are often justifiably wary of strangers asking questions. The focus of and purpose for your evaluation should be made clear to all.

In your initial contact, introduce yourself, the purpose of your study, and the ways in which the personnel can help. It is never a good idea to simply show up or to send unexpected questionnaires. You need your participants to feel as positively as possible toward you, your organization, and your study. Building trust and being sensitive to participants' needs help ensure your access to the setting and to the data. In fact, it may be a good idea to refer to participants as *evaluators* throughout the study.

Establishing Criteria and Data

Again, the criteria and data in the performance site vary greatly from one context to another, and appropriate methods for the evaluation must be tailored to the site. The criteria or questions here are whether:

- persons in the worksite believe the learner has transferred the skills learned during instruction to the worksite,
- learning the skills met the organization's defined needs or progress has been made toward meeting them, and
- physical or attitudinal evidence of use or impact exists within the worksite.

The data to answer these questions can include:

- ratings of learner performance and attitudes on the job;
- supervisor, peer, and customer attitudes;
- employees' performance ratings by supervisors;
- supervisors' performance ratings by managers; and
- physical improvements in products, performances, or services.

Data-gathering methods depend on the resources available for the study. With adequate resources, site visits with personnel interviews and observations would be the ideal. With limited resources, surveys and questionnaires might suffice.

Selecting the Respondents

The nature of information you need and the particular questions will assist you in planning the types and number of persons who are included in your study. This typically includes target learners, peers, supervisors, managers, and sometimes customers. It may be necessary to interview the persons in the organization who requested the evaluation. Through discussions with them, you can ensure that you have identified their needs, resources, and constraints accurately. They also may help identify questions that you may not have considered, and they should be able to assist you with access to the organization's personnel and to records you may need. With these persons identified, you can make arrangements to visit the site at a future date and interact with appropriate people.

Learners/employees have insight into whether they use the new skills (and if not, why?) and how they use the skills. Peers and subordinates of the learners selected may also offer insights into the effectiveness of the instruction. Did they notice the learners using the skills? Were the learners effective? How could they have performed better? Did the learners receive attention or any other kinds of rewards for trying the new skills? Did they talk with the learners about the new skills? They might also shed light on constraints present in the environment that work against applying the new skills.

The managers or supervisors of the learners chosen should be included because their perceptions of the utility of the instruction and the application of the skills in the workplace might be identical to the learners or quite different. They can also provide insight into their role, if any, in planning or delivering the training and personal support they give employees trying the new skills in the workplace. They also have information about changes in the organization resulting from the training and the fit between the skills learned and the defined needs of the organization. Supervisors might also have access to company records and worker performance ratings related to applying the new skills in the workplace.

Planning Study Procedures

In selecting the most appropriate procedures for collecting evidence of training impact, you should consider when, where, and how to collect the information.

When to Collect Data The timing for collecting the information is best decided based on the nature of the instruction, the nature of the work in the jobsite, and the needs of the organization. Consider whether you need preceding posttest data from the training organization. It is possible that the inability of target groups to transfer skills to the jobsite is their lack of competence in performing the skills at the conclusion of instruction. If this is important to know, then obtain this data for the evaluation. The needs of the organization also dictate whether you perform an impact study after thirty days, six months, or a year or whether you will follow up multiple times and examine the data for change across time. Evaluators may wish to observe at varying times following instruction because some skills take longer to install for routine use than others.

Where to Collect Data Again, this depends on the organization's needs. In some instances, the study may be undertaken by one organization's training group and one of their departments within one site. However, it can be undertaken for training provided by a company's training group across multiple jobsites. Some organizations have similar missions and employees in various locations, and they may wish to investigate the nature of transfer of skills from a single training program into their various sites. In this case, the focus of the enquiry remains the same within each site, but the outcomes can be quite different with differing managers, supervisors, employees, peers, and social environments. A benefit of such studies is that you may discover that some groups are better at installing new skills in the jobsite than others, and strategies for success can be shared across groups. You can also locate implementation and transfer problems that are common across groups. Such a discovery should undoubtedly result in the instruction being refined to address better ways to promote transfer of the skills. It can also potentially answer nagging questions about whether observed problems were with the instruction and the embedded transfer strategies or with situations within a given jobsite. If several groups are successful in installing the skills and procedures and a couple are not, then it appears the instruction might be good. However, if only a few sites are successful whereas most are not, the evaluator should examine and document the strategies and support provided in the few successful sites.

How to Collect Impact Data Decisions about how to collect impact data include issues of sampling, data collection, and data analysis, all of which must be considered in light of the organization's expectations and needs. Related to sampling, you must decide whether you can study the entire target group who completed the instruction along with those who supported them during their transfer experience.

If this group is too large, then you must consider how to identify a representative subgroup of the target group. You might wish to select a subgroup representing varying levels of ability, posttest performance following instruction, experience on the job, career goals, years with the company, attitudes such as self-efficacy and motivation for learning (levels of attention, perceptions of relevance, perceptions of competence, and personal satisfaction), and perhaps supervisors' ratings of job performance. Once you have selected your learner/employee sample, their supervisors and peers are also included, as you are seeking information about the social and work environment that may influence your selected workers' implementation of new skills in the workplace.

Data Collection Procedures These depend on the type of data you have decided to collect. For example, will you need surveys and questionnaires, observation forms, interview protocols, rating scales, or company records? Examine each question to be answered, and ask yourself what information you need to answer it. The anchors for the questions within should be the overall questions of the summative evaluation, the skills learned in the instruction, the job skills, aspects of the work environment, and theoretical underpinnings such as learning and change theory.

Summarizing and Analyzing Data Data analysis procedures should be straightforward and descriptive. Data should be summarized within study questions for easy interpretation, and the summaries can include item frequency counts or content analysis of respondents' comments. There is no need here for fancy statistics—unless you have fancy questions and a sophisticated design, such as measuring change in performance or attitudes over time. Keep in mind that razzle-dazzle results will most likely confuse those who requested the study, so keep the results accurate, direct, and easy to read and interpret.

Reporting Results The nature of your summative evaluation report depends on your design. If you included both the expert judgment and impact analysis phases, then both should be documented in the report. For each one you should describe the general purpose, the specific questions, the design and procedures, the results, and your recommendations and rationale. The rationale for your recommendations should be anchored in the data you present in the results section.

You should always consider the reader as you design and produce your report. After analyzing several program evaluation reports, Fitzpatrick et al. (2004) concluded that, although the reports were informative, they were also arsenic in print! Consider following their formatting suggestion for remedying this problem: Begin the report with an executive summary or abstract that highlights your final recommendations and rationale. Readers can then read the remainder of the technical documentation selectively to verify the quality of your procedures or the validity of your conclusions. (You can evaluate technical reports formatively just as you would evaluate instruction formatively.)

Negotiating Resources Now is the time to plan initially for the resources you need to conduct the study. You should have determined the information you will need, the number of people to contact, the number of sites to be visited, the data-gathering instruments and methodology needed, and the expert personnel required to conduct the study; thus, it is time to estimate carefully the resources you will need. It is not uncommon for organizations to want a first-class study from a very small budget. If the ideal study is not feasible given the resources, then it is time to adjust the plan and to be clear about what can be done and how results will be analyzed and delivered.

Evaluation and Revision

Evaluating and Revising Summative Evaluations

Table 13.3 contains a summary of the expert judgment and impact phases of summative evaluation for comparison. Recall that if instructional materials are judged inadequate during the expert judgment phase, there would be little if any reason to continue with an impact study. It stands to reason then, if no expert judgment analysis has been done, then an impact analysis study could be wasted time or misleading.

Table 13.3 The Expert Judgment and Impact Phases of Summative Evaluation

Summative Evaluation	
EXPERT JUDGMENT PHASE	IMPACT PHASE
Overall Decisions	
Did the materials follow best practice and meet this organization's needs?	Were the materials effective with transfer of skills to the prescribed setting (work, next course)?
Specific Decisions	
Congruence Analysis: Are the needs and goals of the organization congruent with those in the instruction? **Content Analysis:** Are the materials complete, accurate, and current? **Design Analysis:** Are the principles of learning, instruction, and motivation clearly evident in the materials?	**Outcomes Analysis:** **Impact on Learners:** Are the achievement and motivation levels of learners satisfactory following instruction? Were the employees selected for training a match for the training (e.g., entry skills, complexity, motivation, personal goals)? **Impact on Job:** Are learners able to transfer the information, skills, and attitudes from the instructional setting to the job setting or to subsequent units of related instruction? **Impact on Organization:** Are learners' changed behaviors (performance, attitudes) making positive differences in the achievement of the organization's mission and goals (e.g., reduced dropouts, resignations; improved attendance, achievement; increased productivity, grades)? **Management Analysis:** 1. Does the organization maintain a positive transfer climate? 2. Are supervisors' attitudes and behavior supportive of transfer? 3. Are implementation procedures supported by management? 4. Were costs related to time, personnel, equipment, and resources appropriate given the outcomes?

Rubric for Evaluating Summative Evaluations

The following is a rubric that designers can use to review summative evaluation procedures. The evaluation should include the expert judgment (if one was conducted), the impact phases of the evaluation, and an examination of the final evaluation report submitted to the organization.

Designer note: If an element is not relevant for your project, mark NA in the No column.

No	Some	Yes	
			A. Expert Judgment Phase Are the following analyses included:
_____	_____	_____	1. Congruency (instructional goals, organizational needs, and resources)?
_____	_____	_____	2. Content analysis (complete, accurate, and current)?
_____	_____	_____	3. Design analysis (instructional strategy and motivation)?
_____	_____	_____	4. Impact feasibility analysis (learners exit instruction competent, job aids provided, skills a priority for organization, consequences for not using skills, etc.)?
_____	_____	_____	5. Clear data summaries and analyses in report to organization?
			B. Impact Analysis Phase (Outcomes Analysis) Are the following areas examined for their impact on the organization:
_____	_____	_____	1. Learners' achievement and attitudes?
_____	_____	_____	2. Transfer of skills to performance context?
_____	_____	_____	3. Frequency of skill application (actual/ideal)?
_____	_____	_____	4. Context for skill application?
_____	_____	_____	5. Positive changes in learners' skills, work, or attitudes related to instruction?
_____	_____	_____	6. Factors inhibiting use of the skills on the job?
_____	_____	_____	7. Management attitudes concerning transfer of skills and impact on work environment and productivity?
_____	_____	_____	8. Evidence that original problems within organization were resolved?
_____	_____	_____	9. Organization better meeting mission and goals?
			C. Reports to Organization Do reports contain clear:
_____	_____	_____	1. Executive summary?
_____	_____	_____	2. Descriptions of evaluation procedures used?
_____	_____	_____	3. Data summaries and descriptions?
_____	_____	_____	4. Conclusions?
			D. Other
_____	_____	_____	1.
_____	_____	_____	2.

Examples

This section contains examples of evaluation instruments for the expert judgment and impact phases of the summative evaluation. Basically, the instruments required for the expert judgment phase consist of information summary charts and product evaluation checklists or rating scales to be completed by the evaluator.

Rating Form for Congruence Analysis

Table 13.4 contains an example information summary form for completing the congruence analysis. The first column is used to describe the instructional needs of the organization, the entry skills and characteristics of the target group in the organization, and the organization's resources for obtaining and implementing the instruction. The second column contains related information from the instruction. The third column contains a scale with ratings from one to four, enabling the reviewer to judge the level of congruence between the organization's documents and the materials. The final column can be used to jot notes the reviewer may want to review in preparing the summary report. Summarizing the information in this manner enables both you and the decision makers to make judgments about the appropriateness of the materials for the organization's needs.

Table 13.4 Congruence Analysis Information Summary Form

Instruction reviewed ____________________

Reviewer ____________________

Circle level of congruence observed

1 = Not congruent, 2 = Some congruence, 3 = Mostly congruent, 4 = Right on

Statements of Organizations' Characteristics	Instructional Materials	Level of Congruence	Reviewer's Comments
Organization's instructional needs (goals and main objectives)	Stated goals and objectives in materials	1 2 3 4	
Entry skills of organization's target group	Stated entry skills for learners	1 2 3 4	
Characteristics of organization's target group Characteristics of performance contexts	Stated characteristics of learners and contexts accommodated in instruction	1 2 3 4	
Organization's resources available for implementing instruction	Costs and other resources within budgeted amounts	1 2 3 4	

Rating Form for Content Analysis: Evaluating the Completeness and Accuracy of Materials

A hypothetical goal framework and materials rating form are illustrated in Figure 13.2. The goal analysis appears in the top portion of the table, and the rating form appears in the lower portion. You could develop any number of response formats to record your judgments. In the example, five response columns are used to rate the accuracy, completeness, link to the job analysis, inclusion on the posttest, and summary comments. A simple three-point scale is used to compare subordinate skills and the materials: Not Included, Included, and Congruent.

After evaluating the materials for accuracy, you can tally the number of positive marks in the bottom row of the table. Recall from our previous discussion of content analysis in the expert judgment phase that these criteria should be rated one at a time. If the materials are judged to be inaccurate, then there is no need to continue. Materials judged to be accurate can be evaluated further. In the hypothetical example, the instruction appears to be promising because it includes all five main steps and their subordinate skills identified by content experts. The bottom row of Figure 13.2 shows that 100 percent of the skills are portrayed accurately in the instruction. In contrast, the evaluator judged that only 79 percent of the instruction was complete and only 79 percent was completely linked to the job analysis. The posttest column is interesting in that only 64 percent of the skills were included on the posttest. This can potentially signal a problem for the transfer analysis. Employees' skills in almost 40 percent of the goal framework were not assessed at the conclusion of instruction. This can be fine if only main step skills are included on the posttest; however, if the skills not tested include main steps as well as subordinate skills, this situation should be flagged. In the example in Figure 13.2, main step 2 and its subordinate skills were not included on the posttest. The reviewer noted this in the comments column.

Following your data analysis, you may wish to use the data to answer questions about the instruction from a systematic instructional design perspective. Sample questions include the following:

1. How clear are the goal(s) and the main objectives of this instruction?
2. How accurate and current is the information included in the instruction?

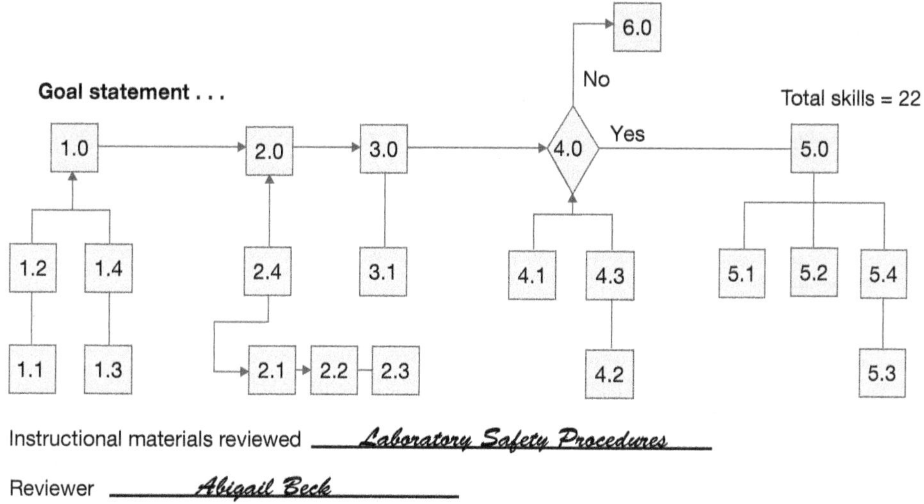

Instructional materials reviewed *Laboratory Safety Procedures*

Reviewer *Abigail Beck*

Rate each subordinate skill within the instruction as: Circle
1 = Not included, 2 = Included, 3 = Congruent

Subordinate Skills Statements	Content Accurate	Content Complete	Linked to Job Analysis	Included on Posttest	Reviewer's Comments
1.0	1 2 (3)	1 2 (3)	1 2 (3)	1 2 (3)	
1.1	1 2 (3)	1 2 (3)	1 2 (3)	1 2 (3)	
1.2	1 2 (3)	1 2 (3)	1 2 (3)	1 2 (3)	
1.3	1 2 (3)	1 (2) 3	1 2 (3)	1 2 (3)	
1.4	1 2 (3)	1 2 (3)	1 2 (3)	1 2 (3)	
2.0	1 2 (3)	1 2 (3)	1 (2) 3	(1) 2 3	*No evidence*
2.1	1 2 (3)	1 2 (3)	1 (2) 3	(1) 2 3	*learners*
2.2	1 2 (3)	1 2 (3)	1 (2) 3	(1) 2 3	*acquired*
Etc.	1 2 3	1 2 3	1 2 3	1 2 3	*these skills*
TOTAL	100%	79%	79%	64%	

Figure 13.2 A Framework for Evaluating the Accuracy and Completeness of Instructional Materials and the Content Validity of Accompanying Tests

3. How logical is the sequence of information in the instruction?
4. How appropriate is the instruction for the entry skills and characteristics of target learners (e.g., skills; contexts; understandings; gender, racial, cultural bias)?
5. Are measures of performance (paper-and-pencil tests and rubrics) congruent with the goals and objectives in the instruction and the target learners' characteristics?

Rating Form for Design Analysis

Instructional designers conducting a summative evaluation of their own materials are keenly aware of the foundational principles of learning and instruction for their materials. Independent evaluators not involved in the production of the materials should determine whether these principles were used in the creation of the instruction.

Evaluating the Learning and Instructional Strategies in Materials

Motivation You should particularly focus on the potential of the instruction for motivating learners and learners' perceptions of how interested they were in learning the information and skills presented. The ARCS model (Keller, 2010) provides a helpful summary of the motivational principles that can be used by designers in producing instructional materials and by evaluators in determining the quality of existing instruction. Recall from Chapter 8 that ARCS represents the principles for (1) gaining and then maintaining learner *attention* through instruction that is (2) perceived by the learners to be *relevant* for their personal needs and goals (3) at the appropriate level of difficulty so that learners are *confident* they can succeed if they try and (4) perceived by learners as *satisfying* in terms of rewards for their investments. The concepts in this principle of motivation can be converted to complementary summative evaluation questions such as those presented in Table 13.5.

Table 13.5 Summative Evaluation Questions from Principles of Motivation (Attention, Relevance, Confidence, Satisfaction)

Materials ______________________________

Reviewer ______________________________

1 = Not present, 2 = Some coverage, 3 = Adequately addresses (Circle one) Rate each criterion in the materials as:

ARCS Motivation Model	Question Areas for Summative Evaluation	Ratings	Reviewer's Comments
Attention	1. Are strategies used to gain and maintain the learners' attention (e.g., emotional or personal appeals, questions, thinking challenges, human interest examples)?	1 2 3	
Relevance	2. Is the instruction relevant for given target groups?	1 2 3	
	3. Are learners informed and convinced of the relevance (e.g., information about new requirements for graduation, certification, employment, advancement, self-actualization)?	1 2 3	
Confidence	4. Are learners likely to be confident at the outset and throughout instruction so that they can succeed? • Informed of purposes • Likely to possess prerequisites • Instruction progresses from familiar to unfamiliar • Concrete to abstract • Vocabulary, contexts, and scope appropriate • Challenges present but realistic	1 2 3	
Satisfaction	5. Are learners likely to be satisfied from the learning experience? • Relevant external rewards such as free time, employment, promotion, recognition • Actual intrinsic rewards (e.g., feelings of success, accomplishment, satisfaction of curiosity, intellectual entertainment)	1 2 3	

Types of Learning The principles of instruction for different types of learning can be used as anchors for focusing the expert judgment phase of a summative evaluation. Table 13.6 contains a checklist based on principles of instruction for intellectual skills, verbal information, attitudes, and motor skills. The questions contained in the checklist are not intended to exhaust the list of learning principle–based questions that could be posed; instead, they are intended to illustrate the role of these principles in the design of a summative evaluation. Readers who want more information on these principles or their derivation and use in instruction should review the section in Chapter 8 on learning components for various learning outcomes.

Table 13.6 **Rating Form for Examining Characteristics of Instruction Based on Principles of Instruction for Intellectual Skills, Verbal Information, Attitudes, and Motor Skills**

Materials Reviewed ____________________

Reviewer ____________________

1 = Not included, 2 = Somewhat, 3 = Clearly addressed Circle rating:

Intellectual Skills	Rating	Comments
1. Are learners reminded of prerequisite knowledge they have stored in memory?	1 2 3	
2. Are links provided in the instruction between prerequisite skills stored in memory and new skills?	1 2 3	
3. Are ways of organizing new skills presented so they can be recalled more readily?	1 2 3	
4. Are the physical, role, and relationship characteristics of concepts clearly described and illustrated?	1 2 3	
5. Are application procedures clearly described and illustrated for rules and principles?	1 2 3	
6. Are quality criteria (characteristics) directly addressed and illustrated for judging adequate versus inadequate results such as answers, products, or performances?	1 2 3	
7. Are obvious but irrelevant physical, relational, and quality characteristics and common errors made by beginners directly addressed and illustrated?	1 2 3	
8. Do the examples and nonexamples represent clear specimens of the concept or procedure described?	1 2 3	
9. Are examples and contexts used to introduce and illustrate a concept or procedure familiar to the learners?	1 2 3	
10. Do examples, contexts, and applications progress from simple to complex, familiar to unfamiliar, and/or concrete to abstract?	1 2 3	
11. Do practice and rehearsal activities reflect application of the intellectual skills or merely recall of information about the performance of the skill?	1 2 3	
12. Does feedback to learners provide corrective information and examples, or does it merely present a correct answer?	1 2 3	
13. When appropriate, are follow-through activities such as advancement, remediation, and enrichment present and logical (e.g., address prerequisites, focus on improved motivation, provide additional examples and contexts)?	1 2 3	

(continued)

Table 13.6 Continued

Intellectual Skills	Rating	Comments
II. VERBAL INFORMATION		
1. Is new information presented in a relevant context?	1 2 3	
2. Are strategies provided for linking new information to related information currently stored in memory (e.g., presentation of familiar analogies, requests for learners to imagine something or to provide examples from their own experiences)?	1 2 3	
3. Is information organized into subsets, and are the relationships of elements within and among subsets explained?	1 2 3	
4. Are lists, outlines, tables, or other structures provided for organizing and summarizing information?	1 2 3	
5. Are logical mnemonics provided when new information cannot be linked to anything stored in memory?	1 2 3	
6. Does rehearsal (practice) include activities that strengthen elaborations and cues (e.g., generating new examples, forming images that will cue recall, refining organizational structure)?	1 2 3	
7. Does feedback contain information about the correctness of a response as well as information about why a given response is considered incorrect?	1 2 3	
8. Does remediation include additional motivational strategies as well as more rehearsal for recall cues?	1 2 3	
III. ATTITUDES		
1. Are the desired feelings clearly described or inferred?	1 2 3	
2. Are the desired behaviors clearly described or inferred?	1 2 3	
3. Is the link (causality) between the desired feelings and behaviors and the link between them and the subsequent positive consequences clearly established?	1 2 3	
4. Is the link between the undesirable feelings and behaviors and the link between them and the subsequent negative consequences clearly established?	1 2 3	
5. Are the positive and negative consequences that are presented true and believable from the learners' perspective?	1 2 3	
6. Are the positive and negative consequences that are presented ones that are likely to be considered important by target learners?	1 2 3	
7. If vicarious learning is involved, are the target learners likely to generate emotions such as admiration, scorn, empathy, or pity for characters and situations presented to tap these emotions?	1 2 3	
8. If vicarious learning is involved, are the contexts and situations presented familiar and relevant to target learners?	1 2 3	
9. In the feedback, are the positive and negative consequences promised for specific actions experienced either directly or vicariously by learners?	1 2 3	

IV. MOTOR SKILLS	
1. Does the instruction address similar skills the learner can already perform?	1 2 3
2. Does the instruction include a visual presentation of the motor skill that illustrates its sequence and timing?	1 2 3
3. Are complex skills broken down into logical parts for learners' analysis, experimentation, and rehearsal?	1 2 3
4. Is there provision for integrating the logical parts into performance of the complete skill?	1 2 3
5. Are common errors and strategies for avoiding them directly addressed?	1 2 3
6. Is repetitive practice provided to enable learners to smooth out the routine and automate the skill?	1 2 3
7. Is immediate feedback provided to help learners avoid rehearsing inaccurate executions?	1 2 3

Instructional Strategies Effective instruction, regardless of whether it is for learning verbal information, intellectual skills, attitudes, or motor skills, has certain characteristics based on the research of educational psychologists and instructional theorists. Quality instruction should gain attention and spark motivation in the learner. It should also help the learner focus on the relevant aspects of what is to be learned, store the information logically in memory, and recall the information and skills efficiently at a later time. The summative evaluator should be aware of the current principles for designing effective instruction and use these design principles in criteria and standards for the evaluation of the materials. Instructional principles that should be used in designing summative evaluations should at least include motivation, types of learning (i.e., intellectual skills, verbal information, attitudes, and motor skills), and the instructional strategy.

Table 13.7 contains a sample rating form for evaluating the instructional strategies contained in the materials. The left-hand column contains the parts of the instructional strategy, excluding pretests and posttests. One column is used for rating the adequacy of each element in a strategy within the instruction. Space is provided for two more response columns to jot the strengths or the problems for each part of the strategy. These ratings and brief notes help you create the final documentation.

Table 13.7 Rating Form for Judging the Instructional Strategy in Instructional Materials

Instructional Materials ______________________________

Reviewer ______________________________

1 = Missing from materials, 2 = Present in materials, 3 = Good, 4 = Excellent Circle your judgment:

Learning Components	Rating	Qualities	Problems
I. Preinstructional			
A. Initial motivation	1 2 3 4		
B. Objectives	1 2 3 4		
C. Entry skills			
1. Described	1 2 3 4		
2. Sample items	1 2 3 4		
II. Information Presentation			
A. Organizational structures			
1. Headings	1 2 3 4		
2. Tables and illustrations	1 2 3 4		

(continued)

Table 13.7 Continued

Learning Components	Rating	Qualities	Problems
B. Elaborations			
1. Analogies/synonyms	1 2 3 4		
2. Prompts to imagine/consider	1 2 3 4		
3. Examples and nonexamples	1 2 3 4		
4. Relevant characteristics of examples	1 2 3 4		
5. Summaries/reviews	1 2 3 4		
III. Learner Participation			
A. Relevant practice	1 2 3 4		
B. Feedback			
1. Answers	1 2 3 4		
2. Example solutions	1 2 3 4		
3. Common errors and mistakes	1 2 3 4		
IV. Follow-Through Activities			
A. Memory aids	1 2 3 4		
B. Transfer strategy	1 2 3 4		

Judging the instructional materials in this way (Tables 13.4–13.7), you can begin to form a clear picture of the promise the instruction has for meeting the needs of the organization. Information you gather from this review is invaluable for assisting you in planning your focus for your impact evaluation.

Rating Forms for Impact Analysis

External evaluators can often gather information from individuals in the workplace using either surveys or site visits depending on the nature of the instruction, the characteristics of the workplace, and the evaluation budget. Figure 13.3 contains a template the evaluator can use to gather survey data on perceptions of target learners at a designated follow-up date. It includes:

- an introduction section,
- a list of the learning outcomes for the instruction,
- questions about the participants' level of use of the skills taught in the instruction,
- questions about the relevance of the particular skills for their work,
- questions about additional support needed for any of the skills,
- free-response questions for reasons they are not using particular skills, and
- free-response forms for positive changes they have observed in themselves or the organization as a result of the instruction.

Other questions can be added to tailor the form to particular instruction of organizations.

Table 13.8 can be used as a template to design inquiry forms and procedures for a site visit. The first column identifies questions you might want to ask employees at the jobsite. The second column in the table names groups of personnel you might want to include in your evaluation. The questions can be reformatted depending on the particular respondent's job. Other questions tailored to specific instruction and jobs can be added. The third column lists methods of collecting data that you

Reflections on Residuals from (*name instruction/workshop here*)

During (*date*) you were selected to participate in (*name of workshop, training, course*) that had the defined expected outcomes of: (*insert your goals and objectives here*)

1. *Name first goal/objective*
2. *Name second goal/objective*
3. *Name third goal/objective*
4. *Etc.*

(*name, time*) has passed since the conclusion of the (*instruction*), which has provided time for you to transfer the new knowledge and skill to your job and to reflect on how you and your work have been influenced by the (*workshop*) experience. We would like for you to share your reflections on how you and your work have been influenced by the experience. Your comments are anonymous, and all information gathered will be used to assess the effectiveness of the (*workshop*). Thank you in advance for your time.

A. To what degree are you using these skills in your work?

Outcomes	Not using	Planning to use	Starting to use	Using routinely	Was using before
1. *Insert outcome 1 here*	○	○	○	○	○
2. *Insert outcome 2 here*	○	○	○	○	○
3. *Etc.*	○	○	○	○	○

B. If you responded "not using" to any of the intended outcomes, please indicate your reason. For any outcome, choose as many reasons as apply. *Designer note: Add your own reasons below that are relevant to the organization and skill.*

Outcomes	Not relevant for my work	Need more training	Need more supervisor support	Need more resources	Need more assistance
1. *Insert outcome 1 here*	○	○	○	○	○
2. *Insert outcome 2 here*	○	○	○	○	○
3. *Etc.*	○	○	○	○	○

Please comment here on other reasons why you are not currently using the skills learned in the instruction.

C. As a direct result of the workshop, have you noticed positive changes related to these outcomes in your knowledge, skills, and attitudes/perspectives?

1 = No, 2 = Some, 3 = A lot

Outcomes	Knowledge	Skills	Attitudes
1. *Insert outcome 1 here*	① ② ③	① ② ③	① ② ③
2. *Insert outcome 2 here*	① ② ③	① ② ③	① ② ③
3. *Etc.*	① ② ③	① ② ③	① ② ③

D. For each outcome, please comment on the course strengths and your suggestions for improvements.

Outcomes	Strengths	Suggestions for Improvement
1. *Insert outcome 1 here*		
2. *Insert outcome 2 here*		
3. *Etc.*		

Figure 13.3 Template for Assessing Learners' Perceptions of the Impact of Instruction in the Performance Context

Table 13.8 Questions, Data Sources, and Methods for Impact Summative Evaluation in the Jobsite

Sample Questions	Data Sources	Methods
1. Did the information and skills learned transfer to the job (all, some, none)? 2. How are the skills used (frequency, context)? 3. What physical, social, managerial factors support the use of the skills? 4. What physical, social, managerial factors inhibited the use of the skills? 5. Are you able to experiment with the new skills to adapt them to the job? 6. Does using the skills help resolve the original need? How? What is the evidence? 7. Are the information and skills learned • better than the ones used before? • directly related to the job tasks? • appropriate for your expectations? • relatively easy to learn and use? • discussed with your peers? • discussed with your supervisors? • discussed with peers outside the organization? 8. Were you involved in planning the instruction? How? 9. Do you respect the group providing the training/instruction? 10. Would you attend training/instruction sponsored by providers again? 11. Have you recommended the training/instruction to others? 12. What physical/social evidence do you have of improved job performance (e.g., time, profit, resources, pleased workers, customer satisfaction, supervisor satisfaction)? 13. Does acquiring and using these skills enhance your career path? How?	Learners Supervisors Customers Company records Colleagues/peers of learners Subordinates of learners Trainers	Interviews Questionnaires Observations Records analysis Product/performance evaluations Ratings of job performance or behavior

might want to consider. Resources available for the study will undoubtedly influence how data are gathered. A very limited budget means that you will use more surveys and distance interviews. If there are ample resources and time, you will surely want to include site visits, personal interviews, focus groups, and direct observations of the learners performing on the job.

Case Study

Group Leadership Training

The following illustration is based on the instructional analysis and strategy of main step 6, "Manage cooperative group interaction," presented in Chapters 8 and 9. Recall that the target population is master's-level students in a campus leadership course who have varying levels of knowledge and skills, various prior major areas of study, and varied interests and professional goals.

Recall that our target learners completed a one-semester-hour course as participants in one-to-one, small-group, or field trial evaluations over a two-semester time period during the development and refinement of a new group leadership course. The impact evaluation was undertaken with all thirty of these learners to determine whether they were able to apply their group leadership skills during the year following the course. As can happen, very limited funds were provided for the study, and it was assigned as a part of a graduate assistant's duties.

Rating Form for Target Learners' Attitudes

One year following course completion, a survey was sent to alumni requesting information about how well they were able to transfer the group leadership skills they learned during instruction to their work within the college, university, and community. Figure 13.4 contains the survey participants will receive through an e-mail invitation to participate and a link to an online survey program such as SurveyMonkey, Zoho Survey, SoGoSurvey, or Qualtrics (recommended for advanced users). On the actual form sent, all skills should be included; however, we include only two in Figure 13.4 to illustrate the procedure.

Reflections on Residuals from the Group Leadership Training

Last year, you participated in the group leadership course for school, business, and community leaders. The course had the defined expected outcomes that you would use effective group leadership skills in conducting meetings for solving problems, including the following:

1. Preparing for meetings and discussions
2. Setting meeting agendas
3. Convening the group
4. Introducing the task
5. Managing the thought line
6. Managing cooperative group interaction
7. Summarizing and concluding the discussion

One year has passed since you successfully completed the course. Hopefully, this has provided the time necessary for you to transfer your leadership skills to your work with groups in the university and community. We would like you to share your reflections on how you and your work have been influenced by the leadership course. The survey will take only a few minutes, and your comments are anonymous. All information gathered will be used to assess the effectiveness of the course for our students. Thank you in advance for your time.

A. To what degree are you using these skills in your work as a group leader?

Outcomes	Not using	Planning to use	Starting to use	Using routinely	Was using before
1. Managing the thought line	○	○	○	○	○
2. Managing cooperative group interaction	○	○	○	○	○
3. *Etc.*	○	○	○	○	○

Figure 13.4 Survey for Assessing Learners' Perceptions of the Impact of Instruction in the Performance Context

B. If you responded "Not Using" to any of the skills, please indicate your reason. For any outcome, choose as many reasons as apply.

Outcomes	Not relevant for my work	Need more training	Need more supervisor support	Need more resources	Need more assistance
1. Managing the thought line	○	○	○	○	○
2. Managing cooperative group interaction	○	○	○	○	○
3. *Etc.*	○	○	○	○	○

Please comment here on other reasons you are not currently using the skills learned in the instruction.

C. As a direct result of the course, have you noticed *positive* changes related to these outcomes in your knowledge, skills, and attitudes/perspectives?

1 = No, 2 = Some, 3 = A lot

Outcomes	Knowledge	Skills	Attitudes
1. Managing the thought line	① ② ③	① ② ③	① ② ③
2. Managing cooperative group interaction	① ② ③	① ② ③	① ② ③
3. *Etc.*	① ② ③	① ② ③	① ② ③

Please comment on how your work in the university and community has been influenced.

D. For each outcome, please comment on the course strengths and your suggestions for improvements.

Outcomes	Strengths	Suggestions for Improvement
1. Preparing for meetings and discussions		
2. Setting meeting agendas		
3. *Etc.*		

Figure 13.4 Continued

Professional and Historical Perspectives

The need for summative evaluation became apparent in the early 1970s when advocates for each new public-school curriculum and each new media delivery system claimed that it was better than its competitors'. Studies were conducted as soon as possible to determine the "winner." Often, the innovation did not do as well as traditional instruction. This came as no surprise to experienced evaluators who knew that the innovation was really in draft form or in its first edition, whereas the traditional instruction may have been used, reviewed, and revised for many years.

Persuasive arguments were made to postpone such comparisons until an innovation had been evaluated formatively and revised to the point that all the major problems were removed and it was suitable for routine use. Only then would it be appropriate to evaluate exactly what the innovation could do in terms of learner performance, attitudes, instructor reactions, costs, and durability. In "Professional and Historical Perspectives" in Chapter 12, we described the short-lived learner verification and revision movement and saw that it had little impact on enhancing the effectiveness of publishers' and technology producers' products. Thus, summative evaluation as originally conceived as a data-based comparison of two or more competing products never really occurred in the educational materials marketplace. This classical application of summative evaluation, however, was and still is universally applied when soliciting proposals or going to bid for high-dollar products and services in all public and private settings.

The summative evaluations that were done in the late 1970s and early 1980s were called learner validation studies where students' achievement gains were tracked over a school year. When it came to an impartial study to validate the effectiveness of an innovative delivery system or an innovative curriculum (or both), most decision makers did not want the study to be conducted by a developer or advocate for the product; thus, external or third-party evaluators were often hired to conduct this type of summative evaluation. External evaluators are still used in many instances where an impartial judgment of something's worth is required.

The tenor of summative evaluations has changed over the years. The question is no longer "Which is better?" Instead, it is "Did the intervention, including the instruction, solve the problem that led to the need for the instruction in the first place?" In other words, instruction is being considered as a solution to a problem, and the ultimate summative evaluation question is "Did it solve the problem?" or "Did it meet the stated goals for which it was developed?" The evaluations that are now used to answer those questions have many names and nuances, but all are summative in nature. Some of these are fidelity of implementation studies, quality assessments, outcomes assessment, product evaluation, design verification, quality control studies, impact evaluation, confirmation studies, and transfer of training studies.

The proliferation of e-learning over the past twenty-five years has many organizations scrambling for quality software and learning materials for this delivery format. Public schools, universities, and continuing professional education as well as training groups in business, government, and the military have all realized the economics and convenience of distance education, and they are seeking quality instructional materials. One need look no further than the coronavirus pandemic of 2020 to see how a public health emergency created a huge demand for remote access to educational materials and programs. Most policy makers now believe that the emergency brought e-learning responses that will persist into the future well after vaccines and cures have ameliorated the effects of the virus and social interaction has returned to (somewhat) normal. As e-learning comes to the forefront of public thinking about education, the public and private education sectors will look more and more to experts who can lead the way in designing, developing, and evaluating instructional materials, processes, and systems. In retrospect, Kyle Peck's musings in his 2015 article in *TechTrends* seemed prescient:

> I've been advocating for and working toward changes in teaching and learning for four decades, and I know how stable education is, but I am convinced that a "perfect storm" of forces both within and outside education are about to accelerate the evolution of learning and learning design, increasing the demand for well-prepared learning designers, learning-related tool builders, and learning-related researchers.

He sees a bright future for instructional designers and educational technologists.

Process Flowcharts

Summative Evaluation

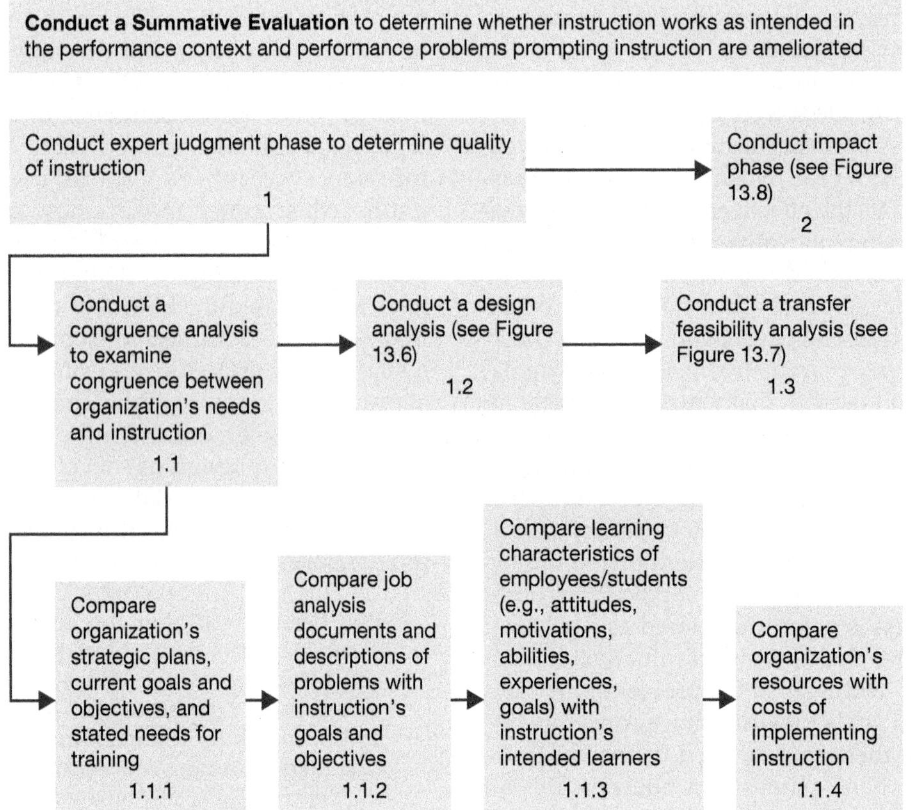

Figure 13.5 Conduct a Summative Evaluation

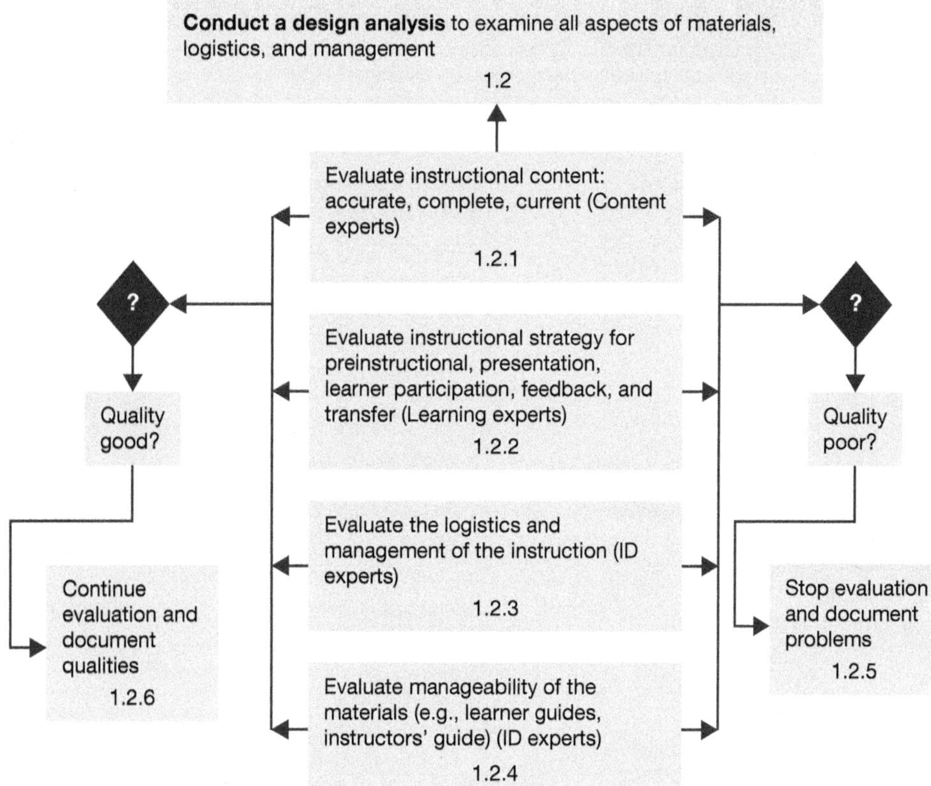

Figure 13.6 Conduct a Design Analysis Summative Evaluation

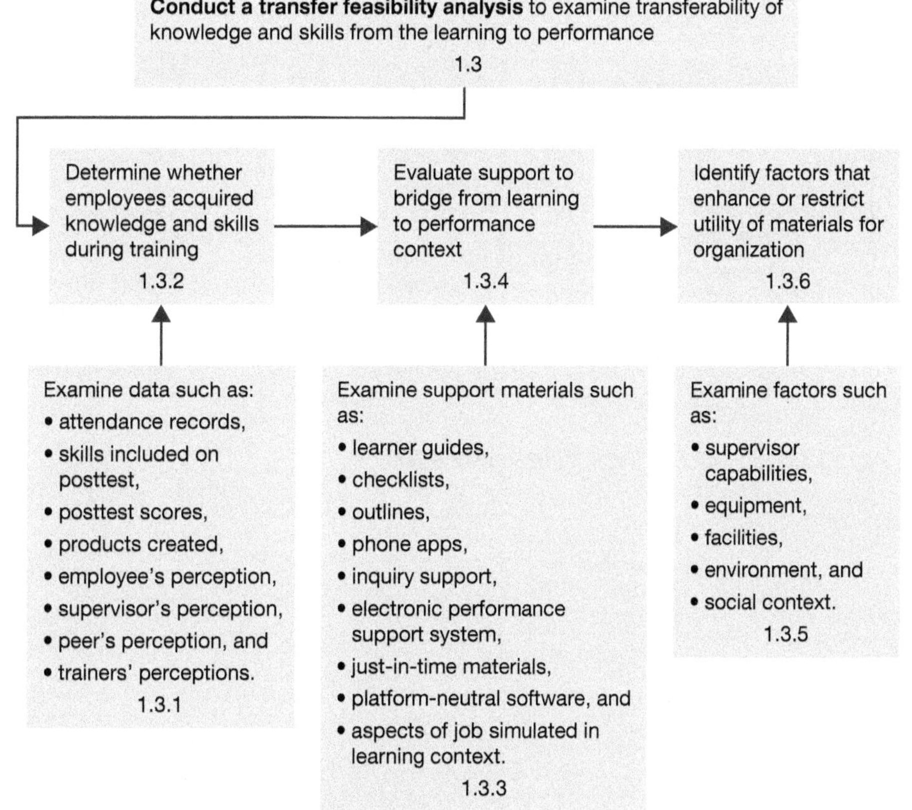

Figure 13.7 Conduct a Transfer Feasibility Analysis

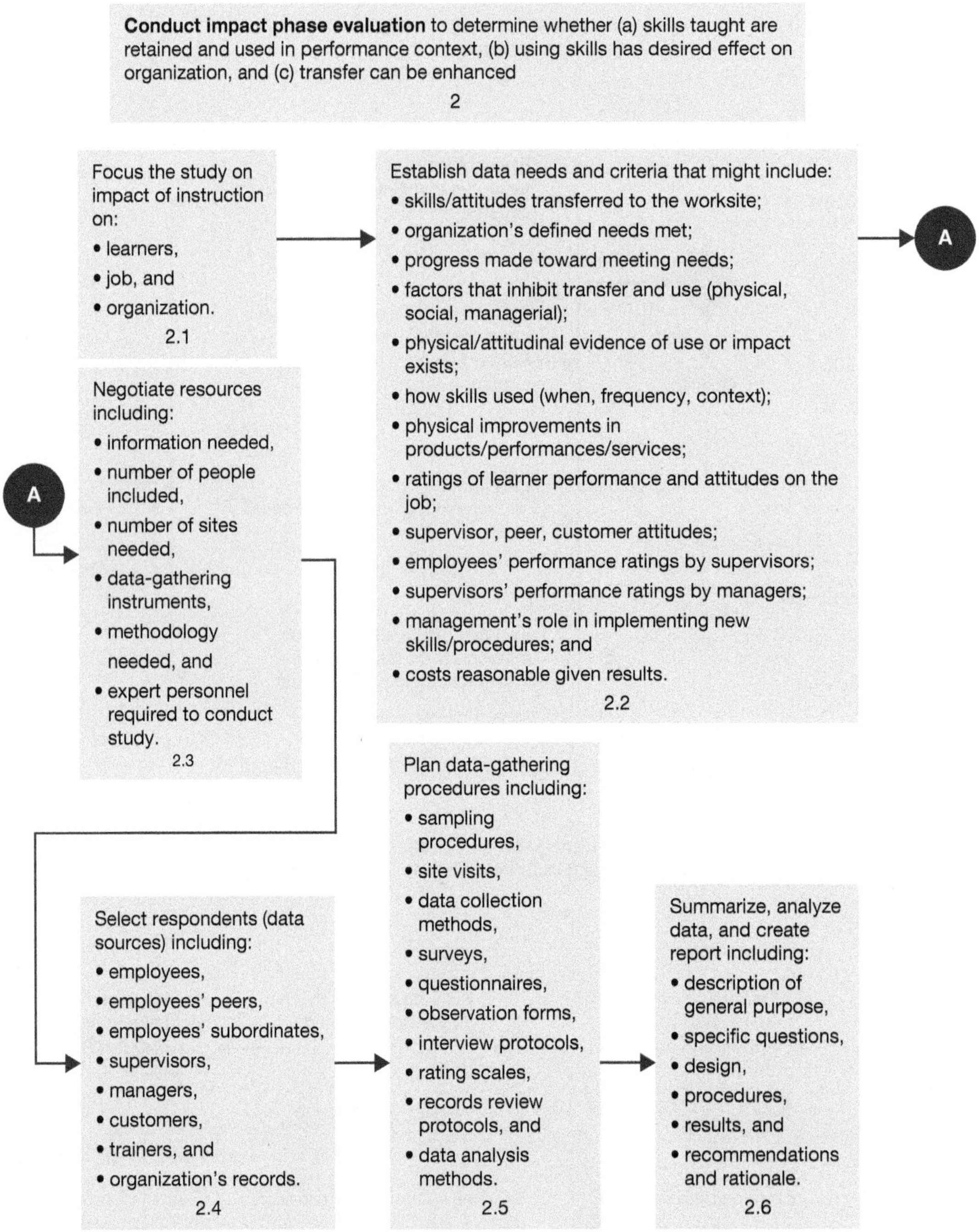

Conduct impact phase evaluation to determine whether (a) skills taught are retained and used in performance context, (b) using skills has desired effect on organization, and (c) transfer can be enhanced
2

Focus the study on impact of instruction on:
- learners,
- job, and
- organization.

2.1

Establish data needs and criteria that might include:
- skills/attitudes transferred to the worksite;
- organization's defined needs met;
- progress made toward meeting needs;
- factors that inhibit transfer and use (physical, social, managerial);
- physical/attitudinal evidence of use or impact exists;
- how skills used (when, frequency, context);
- physical improvements in products/performances/services;
- ratings of learner performance and attitudes on the job;
- supervisor, peer, customer attitudes;
- employees' performance ratings by supervisors;
- supervisors' performance ratings by managers;
- management's role in implementing new skills/procedures; and
- costs reasonable given results.

2.2

A

A

Negotiate resources including:
- information needed,
- number of people included,
- number of sites needed,
- data-gathering instruments,
- methodology needed, and
- expert personnel required to conduct study.

2.3

Select respondents (data sources) including:
- employees,
- employees' peers,
- employees' subordinates,
- supervisors,
- managers,
- customers,
- trainers, and
- organization's records.

2.4

Plan data-gathering procedures including:
- sampling procedures,
- site visits,
- data collection methods,
- surveys,
- questionnaires,
- observation forms,
- interview protocols,
- rating scales,
- records review protocols, and
- data analysis methods.

2.5

Summarize, analyze data, and create report including:
- description of general purpose,
- specific questions,
- design,
- procedures,
- results, and
- recommendations and rationale.

2.6

Figure 13.8 Conduct an Impact Phase Evaluation

Practice

1. What is the main purpose of a summative evaluation?
2. What are the two main phases of a summative evaluation?
3. Why is the first phase of a summative evaluation often necessary?
4. Name four different types of analyses conducted during the first phase of a summative evaluation and the types of instruments used to collect the information.
5. What is the main decision made following the second phase of a summative evaluation?
6. Who participates in the second phase of summative evaluation, and what procedures are used to collect information?
7. Contrast the purposes for formative and summative evaluations.
8. Contrast the position of the evaluator in formative and summative evaluations.
9. Contrast the final products of formative and summative evaluations.

Feedback

1. Purpose: to document the impact of instruction
2. Phases: expert judgment and impact analysis
3. Expert judgment: to determine the potential of instructional materials for meeting the needs of the organization
4. Types of analyses conducted during expert judgment phase:
   - Congruence analysis—information summary form
   - Content analysis—product checklist or rating scale
   - Design analysis—product checklist or rating scale
   - Transfer analysis—product checklist or rating scale
5. Impact evaluation: to document the degree to which information and skills were transferred to the jobsite (performance context)
6. Participants: External evaluator and organizations employees, including those who have completed training, their peers, supervisors, and managers; those who identified problems and arranged for the instruction; and possibly customers. Data collection methods include surveys, attitude questionnaires, interviews, observations, job performance ratings, and company records.
7. Purpose
   - Formative evaluation: To collect data in order to revise instruction
   - Summative evaluation: To collect data in order to determine whether information and skills learned during instruction are transferred to the workplace and meet the organization's needs
8. Evaluator Position
   - Formative evaluation: Evaluators are typically designers with a personal investment in the improvement of the instruction
   - Summative evaluation: Evaluators ideally are external personnel who can objectively evaluate the quality of instruction produced by others and its impact on the organization
9. Final Products
   - Formative evaluation: Prescriptions for the revision of materials and revised materials
   - Summative evaluation: An evaluation report for decision makers that documents the purpose, procedures, results, and recommendations from the study

References and Recommended Readings

Alexander, M. E., & Christoffersen, J. (2006). The total evaluation process: Shifting the mental model. *Performance Improvement, 45*(7), 23–28. The authors argue for establishing return on investment considerations during initial performance analysis work and then addressing considerations throughout design, development, and implementation.

Broad, M. L. (2005). *Beyond transfer of training: Engaging systems to improve performance*. Pfeiffer. Links results of training to original performance improvement needs.

Brown, S. M., & Seidner, C. J. (Eds.). (2012). *Evaluating corporate training: Models and issues*. Springer (reprint). Describes evaluation models and standards from business and education. Includes chapters on return of investment, impact evaluation, and formative evaluation.

Budd, M. L., & Hannum, W. H. (2016). A new vision for HRD to improve organizational results. *Educational Technology, 56*(4), 21–25.

Burke, L. A., & Hutchins, H. M. (2007). Training transfer: An integrative literature review. *Human Resource Development Review, 6*, 263–269. Summarizes studies investigating factors related to successful transfer of training illustrating the many and varied influences on the transfer process.

Burke, L. A., & Hutchins, H. M. (2008). A study of the best practices in training transfer and proposed model of transfer. *Human Resource Development Quarterly, 19*(2), 107–128. Proposes a model for building transfer strategies into the instruction.

Carey, L. M., & Dick, W. (1991). Summative evaluation. In L. J. Briggs, K. L. Gustafson, & M. H. Tillman (Eds.), *Instructional design: Principles and applications*. Educational Technology Publications. Summaries of summative evaluation procedures.

Chyung, S. Y. Y. (2015). Foundational concepts for conducting program evaluations. *Performance Improvement Quarterly, 27*(4), 77–97. Theory and practice of program and product evaluation in business settings.

Cronbach, L., & Associates. (1980). *Toward reform of program evaluation*. Jossey-Bass. Proposes that the evaluator serves in a supportive role in the instructional design process.

Dessinger, J. C., & Moseley, J. L. (2011). *Confirmative evaluation: Practical strategies for valuing continuous improvement*. Wiley. Describes techniques for evaluation of the impact of training several months after the implementation of instruction.

Dick, W., & King, D. (1994). Formative evaluation in the performance context. *Performance and Instruction, 33*(9), 3–10. Discusses follow-up evaluation in the workplace.

Draper, S. W. (1997). The prospects for summative evaluation of CAL in HE. *Association of Learning Technology Journal, 5*(1), 33–39. Describes the utility of summative evaluation and some strategies for evaluating instructional software for computer-assisted learning. His article can be accessed at http://www.psy.gla.ac.uk/~steve/summ.html#CAL

Ensmann, S., Ward, A., Fonseca, A., & Petersen, E. (2020). A case study for the 10-step approach to program evaluation. *TechTrends, 64*, 329–342. https://doi.org/10.1007/s11528-019-00473-4. Presents a case study of a summative evaluation with conclusions that were later reconsidered.

Farrington, J. (2011). Training transfer: Not the 10% solution. *Performance Improvement Quarterly, 24*(1), 117–121. Reminds readers that the 10 percent solution was introduced to gain readers' attention and was not based on reality.

Ford, J. K., Bhatia, S., & Yelon, S. L. (2019). Beyond direct application as an indicator of transfer: A demonstration of five types of use. *Performance Improvement Quarterly, 32*(2). Argues for the expansion of training transfer measures to include a broader view of application of new skills and knowledge over time.

Gagné, R. M., Wager, W. W., Golas, K. C., & Keller, J. M. (2004). *Principles of instructional design* (5th ed.). Wadsworth/Thomson Learning. Includes a brief description of the summative evaluation process from the instructional designer's point of view.

Giberson, T. R., Tracey, M. W., & Harris, M. T. (2006). Confirmative evaluation of training outcomes: Using self-report measures to track change at the individual and organizational level. *Performance Improvement Quarterly, 19*(4), 43–61. Proposes an evaluation model that includes formative and summative aspects.

Guerra-Lopez, I., & Leigh, H. N. (2009). Are performance improvement professionals measurably improving performance? What PIJ and PIQ have to say about the current use of evaluation and measurement in the field of performance improvement. *Performance Improvement Quarterly, 22*(2), 97–110. Presents a content analysis of a decade of *Performance Improvement* and *Performance Improvement Quarterly* articles.

Performance Improvement Quarterly, 22(1), 69–93. Published online in Wiley InterScience (http://www.interscience.wiley.com). Reports a qualitative study of trainers' perspectives on best practices in promoting transfer to the workplace.

Kalman, H. K. (2016). Integrating evaluation and needs assessment: A case study of an ergonomics program. *Performance Improvement Quarterly, 29*(1), 51–69. This case study describes how a confirmatory (summative) evaluation of a ten-year-old course was integrated with a needs assessment for revision of the course.

Keller, J. M. (2010). *Motivational design for learning and performance: The ARCS model approach*. Springer. The full ARCS model with a process for integrating motivational design with instructional design, including worksheets and tools for obtaining audience information and analyzing the audience.

Kirkpatrick, D. L. (2006). *Evaluating training programs: The four levels* (3rd ed.). Berrett-Koehler. In Kirkpatrick's model, evaluation is the tenth of ten steps that resemble the Dick and Carey ID process. Their four levels of evaluation are reaction, learning, behavior, and results. Describes the levels, includes considerations for e-learning and transfer of learning, discusses a fictional model case, and provides case studies of a wide range of successful applications.

Kirkpatrick, J. D., & Kirkpatrick, W. K. (2016). *Kirkpatrick's four levels of training evaluation*. ATD Press. Chapter 8 is on Kirkpatrick's level 4 evaluation of results.

Marshall, J., & Rossett, A. (2014). Perceptions of barriers to the evaluation of workplace learning programs. *Performance Improvement Quarterly, 27*(3), 7–26.

O'Neill, J. L. (2016). Weeding with ADDIE. *Reference & User Services Quarterly, 56*(2), 108–115. A case study of development of a training program for university librarians on weeding their collection. Includes descriptions of formative evaluation and revision during development and summative evaluation in a follow-up after a year of implementation.

Meeker, D., Cerully, J. L., Johnson, M. D., Iyer, N., Kurz, J. R., & Scharf, D. M. (2015). Summative evaluation. In *SimCoach evaluation: A virtual human intervention to encourage service-member help seeking for posttraumatic stress disorder and depression* (Chapter 3, pp. 19–32). Rand Corporation. Report of a thorough summative evaluation of an intervention designed to encourage service men and women to seek help for PTSD and depression.

Peck, K. (2015). The future of learning design: "The future's so bright I gotta wear shades." *TechTrends, 59*(1), 24–29.

Phillips, J. J. (2016). *Handbook of training evaluation and measurement methods* (4th ed.). Routledge. Includes procedures for data management and has several chapters on analysis of return on training investment.

Rogers, E. M. (2003). *Diffusion of innovations* (5th ed.). The Free Press.

Sloan, V., Haacker, R., Barnes, T., & Brinkworth, C. (2017). Long-term impacts of a career development workshop for undergraduates. *Bulletin of the American Meteorological Society, 98*(9), 1961–1968. This project used a two-phase summative evaluation plan, but the first phase became formative in the use of results while the one-year follow-up was summative.

Saettler, P. (1990). *The evolution of American educational technology*. Libraries Unlimited. Saettler does an excellent job in his book of defining formative and summative evaluation in the context of the work the Children's Television Workshop did on designing and developing *Sesame Street* and *The Electric Company*.

Spector, J. M. (2015). Evaluations of educational practice, programs, projects, products, and policies. In M. Spector, B. Lockee, & M. Childress (Eds.), *Learning, design, and technology*. Springer. Good discussions of summative evaluation and evaluating fidelity of implementation.

Stolovitch, H. D. (Ed.). (1997). Special issue on transfer of training-transfer of learning. *Performance Improvement Quarterly, 10*(2). Includes a summary of thirty years of diffusion of innovations studies.

Stufflebeam, D. L. (2007). *CIPP evaluation model checklist: A tool for applying the CIPP model to assess long-term enterprises* (2nd ed.). https://kwschochconsulting.com/wp-content/uploads/2017/04/cippchecklist_mar07.pdf. This is a checklist for documenting and reporting on project evaluation rather than a "how to" of CIPP evaluation. The final letter in Stufflebeam's CIPP acronym stands for product evaluation, and in this checklist it is broken into impact, effectiveness, sustainability, and transportability evaluations, all of which are summative considerations.

Stufflebeam, D. L., & Coryn, C. L. S. (2014). *Evaluation theory, models, and applications* (2nd ed.). Jossey-Bass. A complete textbook for the social sciences on evaluation theories, models, and methods. Several of the models include both formative and summative evaluation.

Stufflebeam, D. L., & Zhang, G. (2017). *The CIPP evaluation model: How to evaluate for improvement and accountability*. Guilford Press. Excellent resource for summative evaluation. Pairs well with the CIPP checklist referenced in Stufflebeam (2007).

Thiagarajan, S. (1991). Formative evaluation in performance technology. *Performance Improvement Quarterly, 4*(2), 22–34. Discusses follow-up evaluation six months after implementation. Excellent references.

Vishwanath, A., & Barnett, G. A. (Eds.). (2011). *The diffusion of innovations*. Peter Lang Publishing. Includes essays on current aspects of diffusion research.

Yang, M., Lowell, V. L., Talafha, A. M., & Harbor, J. (2020). Transfer of training, trainee attitudes, and best practices in training design: A multiple-case study. *TechTrends, 64*, 280–301.

Yelon, S. L., Kevin Ford, J., & Bhatia, S. (2014). How trainees transfer what they have learned: Toward a taxonomy of use. *Performance Improvement Quarterly, 27*(3), 27–52.

Glossary

Alternative assessment Describes evaluation instruments and procedures other than objective-style tests; includes the evaluation of live performances, products, and attitudes; format includes directions for the learner and a scoring rubric.

Agile design A generic design process that uses iterative cycles for product development. Originally used in the software development process, it has applications in ID project management and ID product design and development.

ARCS model Keller's theory of motivation: attention, relevance, confidence, and satisfaction.

Assessment-centered criteria Test or item criteria used to judge item writing qualities such as grammar, spelling, punctuation, clarity, parsimony, and the use of recommended item formatting rules.

Assessment instruments Materials developed and used to assess learners' status and progress in both achievement and attitudes. For achievement, objective tests, product development activities, and live performances are included. For attitudes, both observation and self-report techniques are included.

Attitude An internal state that influences an individual's choices or decisions to act under certain circumstances. Attitudes represent a tendency to respond in a particular way.

Authentic assessment Assessment in meaningful real-life contexts (or simulations thereof) in which newly acquired skills will ultimately be applied.

Behavior An action that is an overt, observable, measurable performance.

Behavioral objective *See* Objective.

Blended learning At its most basic, it is a combination of any two or more learning environments. In common practice, it is typically a combination of web-based and classroom instruction in the same course or training program.

Candidate media Those media that can present the desired information without regard to which may be the most effective. The distinction is from noncandidate media. A book, for example, cannot present sound and thus would be an inappropriate choice for delivering instruction for certain objectives.

Chunk of instruction All the instruction required to teach one objective or a combination of two or more objectives.

Cluster analysis A technique used with goals in the verbal information domain to identify the specific information needed to achieve the goal and the ways that information can best be organized or grouped.

Cognitive flexibility The ability to adapt and change one's mental organization of knowledge and mental management of solution strategies for solving new, unexpected problems.

Cognitive load The amount of information that a person can manage in working (short-term) memory while participating in a learning activity. The theory predicts detrimental effects on learning and retention from instructional content that is either too much or too complex.

Cognitive maps The graphical representation of how conceptual knowledge is structured (e.g., flowcharts, hierarchies, circles, spider webs).

Cognitive strategy Metaprocesses used by an individual to manage how he or she thinks about things in order to ensure personal learning.

Cognitive task analysis Method of identifying the information and skills required to perform complex tasks. Uses rigorous observation and interview protocols to access the required information from an expert.

Cognitivism A learning theory in which learning is viewed as active mental processing to store new knowledge in memory and retrieve knowledge from memory.

Cognitivism emphasizes the structure of knowledge and external conditions that support internal mental processes.

Complex goal A goal that involves more than one domain of learning.

Concept A set of objects, events, symbols, situations, and so on, that can be grouped together on the basis of one or more shared characteristics and given a common identifying label or symbol. *Concept learning* refers to the capacity to identify members of the concept category.

Conditions A main component of a performance objective that specifies the circumstances and materials required in the assessment of the learners' mastery of the objective.

Congruence analysis Analyzing the congruence among (1) an organization's stated needs and goals and those addressed in candidate instruction; (2) an organization's target learners' entry skills and characteristics and those for which candidate materials are intended; and (3) an organization's resources and those required for obtaining and implementing candidate instruction. It is conducted during the expert judgment phase of summative evaluation.

Constructivism A postmodernist philosophy that rejects the existence of objective reality, contending instead that reality is constructed in the mind of each individual. Also a corollary pedagogical or learning theory in which learning is viewed as an internal process of constructing meaning by combining existing knowledge with new knowledge gained through experiences in the social, cultural, and physical world. Constructivism emphasizes the processes and social interactions in which a student engages for learning.

Constructivist learning environment (CLE) Learners in collaborative groups with peers and teachers consulting resources to solve problems. Collaboration can be face-to-face or managed at a distance by media. Collaboration can be real or simulated in virtual learning spaces.

Content stability The degree to which information to be learned is likely to remain current.

Context-centered criteria Test or item criteria used to judge the congruence between the situations used in the assessments and the learning and performance contexts. Authenticity of examples and simulations is the main focus.

Criterion A standard against which a performance or product is measured.

Criterion-referenced test items Items designed to measure performance on an explicit set of objectives; also known as objective-referenced test items.

Delivery system The means by which instruction will be provided to learners. Includes instructor-led instruction, distance education, computer-based instruction, and self-instructional materials.

Design-based research (DBR) An interdisciplinary research methodology for both improving educational practices and developing insight into learning theories through iterative development and analysis cycles. Also called educational design research and associated with the learning sciences and constructivist philosophy.

Design evaluation chart A method for organizing design information to facilitate its evaluation. The chart relates skills, objectives, and associated test items, allowing easy comparison among the components of the instructional design.

Discrepancy analysis Investigations of the gap between an organization's current status and their desired status on defined goals.

Discrimination Distinguishing one stimulus from another and responding differently to the various stimuli.

Domain of learning A major type of learning outcome that can be distinguished from other domains by the type of learned performance required, the type of mental processing required, and the relevant conditions of learning.

Electronic performance support system (EPSS) An application embedded in a software system that can be accessed as needed to support job performance. The application could supply algorithms, expert systems, tutorials, hyperlinked information, and so forth.

Embedded attitude question Question asked of learners about the instruction at the time they first encounter it.

Entry skills Specific competencies or skills a learner must have mastered before entering a given instructional activity. Also known as *prerequisite skills.*

Entry-skill test item Criterion-referenced test items designed to measure skills identified as necessary prerequisites to beginning a specific course of instruction. Items are typically included in a pretest.

Evaluation An investigation conducted to obtain specific answers to specific questions at specific times and in specific places; involves judgments of quality levels.

Expert judgment evaluation Judgments of the quality of instructional materials made by content experts, learner specialists, or design specialists. The first phase of summative evaluation.

Feedback Information provided to learners about the correctness of their responses to practice questions in the instruction.

Field trial The third stage in formative evaluation, referring to the evaluation of the program or product in the setting in which it is intended to be used. Also, the second phase of summative evaluation.

Formative evaluation Evaluation designed to collect data and information that is used to improve a program or product; conducted while the program is still being developed.

Front-end analysis A process used for evaluating instructional needs and identifying alternative approaches to meeting those needs. It includes a variety of activities including, but not limited to, performance analysis, needs assessment, job analysis, training delivery options, and feasibility analysis.

General learner characteristics The general, relatively stable (not influenced by instruction) traits describing the learners in a given target population.

Goal A broad, general statement of an instructional intent, expressed in terms of what learners will be able to do.

Goal analysis The technique used to analyze a goal to identify the sequence of operations and decisions required to achieve it.

Goal-centered criteria Test or item criteria used to judge the congruence between the instructional goal, performance objectives, and test items of any format that is used to monitor learning.

Group-based instruction The use of learning activities and materials designed to be used in a collective fashion with a group of learners; interactive group-paced instruction.

Hierarchical analysis A technique used with goals in the intellectual skills domain to identify the critical subordinate skills needed to achieve the goal and their interrelationships. For each subordinate skill in the analysis, this involves asking, "What must the student know how to do in order to learn the specific subskills being considered?"

Human performance technology Setting instructional goals in response to problems or opportunities within an organization.

Impact analysis The influence of given training or instruction on the organization requesting the instruction. It questions whether information, skills, and attitudes covered in the learning environment transferred to the jobsite and whether, as a result, identified problems were solved and defined needs met.

Impact evaluation stage Focuses on the jobsite and examines whether (1) an organization's needs were met following use of the instruction, (2) employees are able to transfer new information and skills to the job, and (3) an improvement in job performance or productivity is realized.

Individualized instruction The use by students of systematically designed learning activities and materials specifically chosen to suit their individual interests, abilities, and experience. Such instruction is usually self-paced.

Instruction A set of events or activities presented in a structured or planned manner, through one or more media, with the goal of having learners achieve prespecified behaviors.

Instructional analysis The procedures applied to an instructional goal to identify the relevant skills and their subordinate skills and information required for a student to achieve the goal.

Instructional materials Print or other mediated instruction used by a student to achieve an instructional goal.

Instructional strategy An overall plan of activities to achieve an instructional goal. The strategy includes the sequence of intermediate objectives and the learning activities leading to the instructional goal as well as specification of student groupings, media, and the delivery system. The instructional activities typically include preinstructional activities, content presentation, learner participation, assessment, and follow-through activities.

Instructor's manual The collection of written materials given to instructors to facilitate their use of the instructional materials. The manual should include an overview of the materials, tests with answers, and any supplementary information thought to be useful to the instructors.

Intellectual skill A skill that requires some unique cognitive activity; involves manipulating cognitive symbols as opposed to simply retrieving previously learned information.

Item analysis table A means of presenting evaluation data that show the percentage of learners who answered each item correctly on a test.

Item difficulty value The percentage of learners who answer a test item or perform a task correctly.

Job aid A device, often in paper or computer form, used to relieve the learner's reliance on memory during the performance of a complex task.

Job analysis The process of gathering, analyzing, and synthesizing descriptions of what people do, or should do, on their jobs.

Learner analysis The determination of pertinent characteristics of members of the target population. Often includes prior knowledge and attitudes toward the content to be taught as well as attitudes toward the organization and work environment.

Learner-centered criteria Criteria used to judge the congruence among the appropriateness of achievement level, language, contexts, and experiences of target learners and that presented in instructional materials.

Learner-centered design An approach to creating instruction focused less on learning outcomes and more on the learners themselves. Characterized by highly flexible learning environments that change as learners' needs evolve. Also known as user-centered design and associated with constructivist designs for learning.

Learner performance data Information about the degree to which learners achieved the objectives following a unit of instruction.

Learner specialist A person knowledgeable about a particular population of learners.

Learner verification and revision (LVR) A formative evaluation and revision process for quality improvement once used by publishers of educational texts and materials.

Learning context The actual physical location (or locations) in which the instruction under development will be used.

Learning management system (LMS) A digital platform, usually web based, for housing and managing teaching/learning materials, activities, and processes.

Learning objects Any digital resource that can be imported, exported, accessed, and reused; usually in a learning management system.

Learning sciences An interdisciplinary, research-based discipline that seeks to understand learning and the construction of learning environments. Associated with constructivist philosophy and design-based research methodology.

Learning tools interoperability (LTI) A technical standard adopted by learning management systems and learning materials developers that ensures compatibility between the system and the materials (learning objects).

Mastery level A prespecified level of task performance, with no gradations below it, that defines satisfactory achievement of an objective.

Media The physical means of conveying instructional content (e.g., drawings, slides, audio, computer, person, models).

Mindful reflection In constructivist learning, it is the internal mental process in which learners consider their own past and present process of learning for the purpose of confirming or adjusting the process for future learning encounters.

Mobile learning The use of mobile devices to provide content, strategies, and management support for learning.

Model A simplified representation of a system, often in picture or flowchart form, showing selected features of the system.

Module An instructional package with a single integrated theme that provides the information needed to develop mastery of specified knowledge and skills and serves as one component of a total course or curriculum.

Need A discrepancy between what should be and the actual current status of a situation.

Needs assessment The formal process of identifying discrepancies between current outcomes and desired outcomes for an organization.

Noninstructional solution Means of reducing performance discrepancies other than the imparting of knowledge; includes motivational, environmental, and equipment factors.

Objective A statement of what the learners will be expected to do when they have completed a specified course of instruction, stated in terms of observable performances; also known as *performance objective, behavioral objective,* and *instructional objective.*

One-to-one evaluation The first stage in formative evaluation, referring to direct interaction between the designer and individual tryout student.

Outcomes analysis *See* Impact analysis.

Performance analysis An analytical process used to locate, analyze, and correct job or product performance problems.

Performance-based instruction The use of job performance measures or estimates as inputs for designing training and assessing learning.

Performance context The setting in which it is hoped that learners will use the skills they are learning successfully; includes both the physical and social aspects of the setting.

Performance objective *See* Objective.

Performance support tool (PST) A small-scale, usually stand-alone electronic performance support system designed to support a limited range of job tasks.

Performance technology Application of relevant theories of human learning and behavior to improve human performance in the workplace; synonymous with *human performance technology.* A performance technologist practices performance technology.

Personas Fictional persons who represent predominant characteristics of target learners. Profiles are typically developed using samples of large groups of intended learners and summarizing biographical information such as education levels, career interests, and motivational factors.

Portfolio assessment The process of meta-evaluating a collection of work samples or assessments to determine observable changes over time in skill level and/or attitudes. All test formats can be used, including objective tests, products, and live performances.

Posttest A criterion-referenced test designed to measure performance on objectives taught during a unit of instruction; given after the instruction. Typically does not include items on entry behaviors.

Practice test A criterion-referenced assessment, typically at the skill or lesson level, used to provide the learner with active participation and rehearsal opportunities and the designer with opportunities to monitor learner progress.

Preinstructional activities Techniques used to provide the following three events prior to delivering instructional content: (1) get the learners' attention, (2) advise them of the prerequisite skills for the unit, and (3) tell them what they will be able to do after the instruction.

Prerequisite skills Also known as *entry skills.*

Pretest A criterion-referenced test designed to measure performance on objectives to be taught during a unit of instruction and/or performance on entry skills; given before instruction begins.

Problem, ill-structured Situation in which neither the exact rules to be applied nor the exact nature of the solution is identified in the problem statement. Multiple solutions may be acceptable.

Problem, well-structured Situation in which the nature of the solution is well understood, and there is a generally preferred set of rules to follow to determine the solution.

Procedural approach (for goal analysis) The process of listing chronologically, in a step-by-step manner, all the substeps required to perform an instructional goal.

Psychomotor skill Execution of a sequence of major or subtle physical actions to achieve a specified result. All skills use some type of physical action; the physical action in a psychomotor skill is the focus of the new learning and is not merely the vehicle for expressing an intellectual skill.

Rapid prototyping In software development, it is also called *rapid application design (RAD)* and is the process of using prototype approximations of a software design in order to test whether the application meets the design specifications. In instructional design, it is use of iterative cycles of formative evaluation and revision as a substitute for time-consuming front-end analysis.

Reliability The consistency or dependability of a measure.

Research An investigation conducted to identify knowledge that is generalized.

Return on investment (ROI) In training and development, it is a comparison between the costs incurred for training and the benefits realized from training.

Revision The process of producing an amended, improved, or up-to-date version of a set of instructional materials.

Rough-draft materials The development of instructional materials in quick and inexpensive media formats for formative tryout.

Scaffolding Teacher, peer, or mediated guidance for students' learning provided when support is needed for progress and withdrawn as students develop proficiency.

Sharable Content Object Reference Model (SCORM) A series of e-learning standards for ensuring interchangeability of course objects within SCORM-compliant course management systems.

Situated learning The concept that learning occurs best through engagement in a process or activity that should be placed in (situated in) a context that is relevant to the learner and the knowledge to be gained.

Skill An ability to perform an action or group of actions; involves overt performance.

Small-group evaluation The second stage of formative evaluation, referring to the use of a small number of tryout students who study an instructional program without intervention from the designer and are tested to assess the effectiveness of the instruction.

Step One skill identified in the analysis of an instructional goal. Describes a complete task, behavior, or decision that must be completed when someone performs the instructional goal. Most goals include five or more steps. *See also* Substep.

Strategic planning A planning process used to determine and describe future organizational directions, how to achieve the prescribed directions, and how to measure whether the directions are achieved; encompasses a variety of models and processes.

Subject-matter expert (SME) A person knowledgeable about a particular content area. Also known as a *content specialist; see also* Subject-matter specialist.

Subject-matter specialist A person knowledgeable about a particular content area. Also known as a *content specialist* or a *subject-matter expert (SME).*

Subordinate objective An objective that must be attained in order to accomplish a terminal objective. Also known as an *enabling objective* or an *intermediate objective.*

Subordinate skill A skill that must be achieved in order to learn a higher-level skill. Also known as a *subskill* or an *enabling skill.*

Substep One component of a major step in a goal. There must be two or more substeps to justify a substep analysis. Performing each of the substeps in sequence is equivalent to performing the step from which they were derived.

Summative evaluation Evaluation designed and used after an instructional program has been implemented. The purpose is to make decisions concerning whether the instruction actually works as intended in the performance context and whether progress is being made in ameliorating the performance problems that prompted the instructional design and development effort. It includes two phases: expert judgment and impact. The expert judgment phase includes congruence, content, design, and transfer feasibility analyses; the impact phase includes analyses of instructional effectiveness on learners, job, and organization.

Superordinate skill Higher-level competency composed of and achieved by learning subordinate skills.

System A set of interrelated parts working together toward a defined goal.

Systems approach Procedure used by instructional designers to create instruction. Each step requires input from prior steps and provides input for the next step. Evaluation provides feedback used to revise instruction until it meets the original need or specification.

Systems approach and models for instruction A logical and iterative process of identifying all the variables that can affect the quality of instruction, including delivery, and then integrating information about each variable in the design, development, evaluation, and revision of the instruction.

Table of test specifications Prescriptions for a test that include information such as level of learning, the task, performance objective, test item format, and the number of items to present for each task.

Target population The total collection of possible users of a given instructional program.

Terminal objective An objective the learners will be expected to accomplish when they have completed a course of instruction, made up of subordinate objectives; often, a more specific statement of the instructional goal.

Training A prespecified and planned experience that enables a person to do something that he or she could not do before.

Transfer of learning The process whereby the learner applies skills learned in one context to another, similar context. Also referred to as *transfer of training.*

Tryout students A representative sample of the target population; may be used to test an instructional program prior to final implementation.

Validity The degree to which a measuring instrument actually measures what it is intended to measure.

Verbal information Requirement to provide a specific response to relatively specific stimuli; involves recall of information.

xAPI An interoperability standard for learning objects that is slowly replacing the Sharable Content Object Reference Model (SCORM).

4C/ID A four-component ID model originated by Joreon J. G. van Merriënboer for developing instruction for complex learning. Elaborated in a ten-step design process.

Appendices

Many readers of this textbook are educators. The examples in this section relate to school curriculum to aid in applying the Dick and Carey model to school learning. Many of you are using this textbook as a resource for developing your own instruction. We thought it would be helpful for you to see abbreviated example products from each step in the design model collected together in one place. It should benefit those of you who are required to document your design process and develop materials as a course project. The following list will help you locate materials in the appendices.

Note: The case study progresses from this point with only direct instruction to illustrate creation of materials rather than prescriptions for teacher-led or interactive teacher–student learning. These latter two formats of instruction cannot be illustrated in this medium. We recommend that designers begin with direct instruction that requires them to be responsible for all aspects of the instruction created.

Appendix J Session 2: Pretest: Writing Newsletter Article and Using Rubric to Evaluate Article

Appendix K Session 3: Pretest and Instruction in Subordinate Skills 5.6 Through 5.11

Appendix L Group's and Individual's Achievement of Objectives and Attitudes About Instruction

1. Student-by-Item-by-Objective Data Array for Entry Skills
2. Student-by-Item-by-Objective Data Array for Declarative Sentence Portion of Posttest
3. Student Performance by Objectives on the Pretest, Embedded Items, and Posttest
4. Percentage of All Fifteen Students Who Mastered Each Objective on the Pretest, Embedded Items, and Posttest
5. Percentage of Four Students (Students 1–4) *Not* Possessing the Required Entry Skills Who Mastered Each Objective on the Pretest, Embedded Items, and Posttest
6. Percentage of Ten Students (Students 6–15) Possessing the Required Entry Skills Who Mastered Each Objective on the Pretest, Embedded Items, and Posttest
7. Attitude Survey and Summary of Students' Ratings and Comments About the Materials and Lesson

Appendix M Materials Revision Matrix Analysis

Appendix A

Design Decisions from Front-End Analysis and Instructional Goal for Writing Composition

Front-End Analysis	Design Decisions
I. Needs assessment	During a middle school faculty meeting called to discuss problems of students' written composition, teachers decided to conduct a needs assessment study. Each teacher assigned a short essay for his or her students to be written on a common topic. A newly formed evaluation team of teachers from across the school district reviewed the themes to identify possible common problems. They reported that students typically use one type of sentence—namely, declarative, simple sentences—to communicate their thoughts rather than varying their sentence structure by purpose or complexity. Additionally, punctuation other than periods and commas was absent from students' work, and commas were rare.
II. Instructional goal and relationship to needs	Teachers decided to design special instruction that focused students on: • writing a variety of sentence types based on sentence purpose, • writing using a variety of sentence structures that vary in complexity, and • using a variety of punctuation to match sentence type and complexity. Through instruction focused directly on the problems identified in the needs assessment, they hoped to change the current pattern of simplistic similarity found in students' compositions.
III. Clarifying the instructional goal	They decided to create two units of instruction with the following goals. In written composition, students will: 1. Use a variety of sentence types and accompanying punctuation based on the *purpose* and *mood* of the sentence. 2. Use a variety of sentence types and accompanying punctuation based on the *complexity or structure* of the sentence.
IV. General description of the intended learners	The composition units with their special emphasis on sentence variety were judged most appropriate for sixth-grade classes that contain students presently achieving at average and above-average levels of language expression. These groups will be very heterogeneous in their current writing skill; therefore, instruction on writing sentence types as well as on using sentence types in compositions should be included in the materials.
V. General description of the performance context	The performance context is the school regardless of the subject area, any community group or organization where students may need to produce written work, and jobs they may have that require it.
VI. General description of the learning context, if different	The learning context is the school classroom and web-based instruction that can be accessed by students in the classroom, in the school media center/library, and at home.
VII. Description of any tools the learners will need to accomplish the goals	Students will need a personal computer with word processing to practice their writing skills, and they will need an instructional system (such as Canvas) that delivers and manages instruction and assessments. Personal computers were loaned to all sixth-grade students in the district at the beginning of the year. Most schools in the district have wireless Internet connections within the upper-grades classrooms, the learning center/libraries, and the teachers' work rooms. The district also has acquired Canvas to enhance instruction within the schools and support student access of instruction from home.

Appendix B

Goal Analysis of the Instructional Goal on Writing Composition

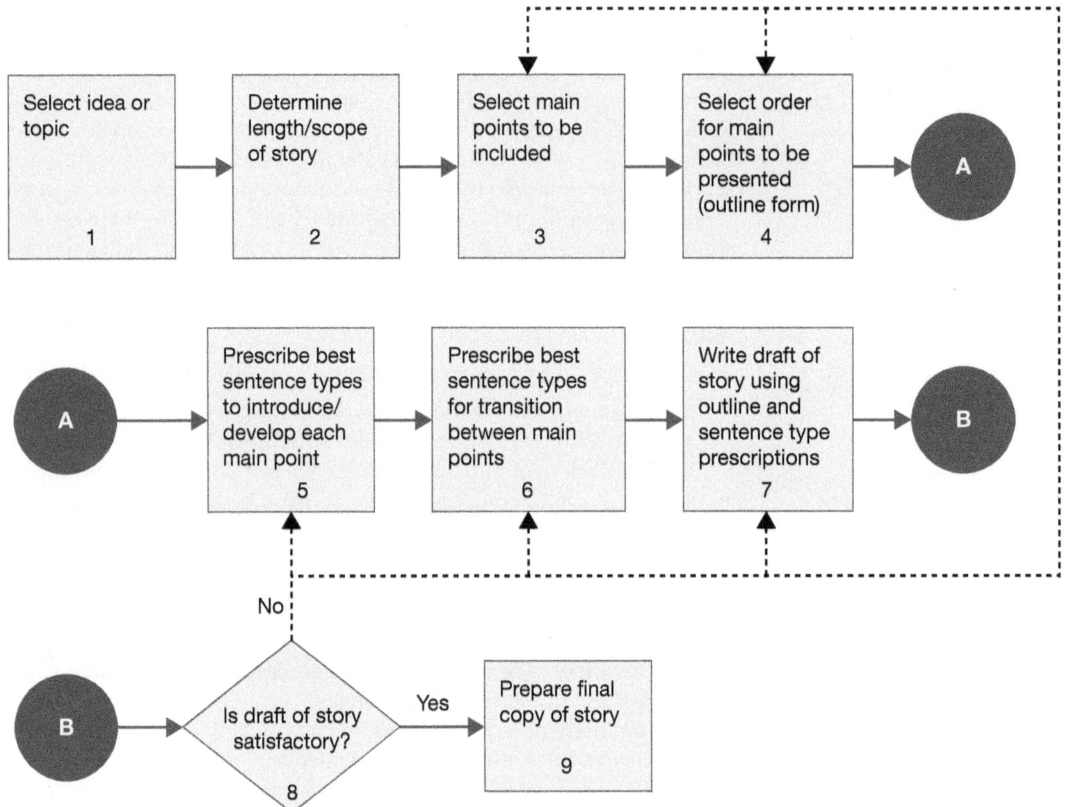

Appendix C

Hierarchical Analysis of Declarative Sentence Portion of Writing Composition Goal with Entry Skill Lines

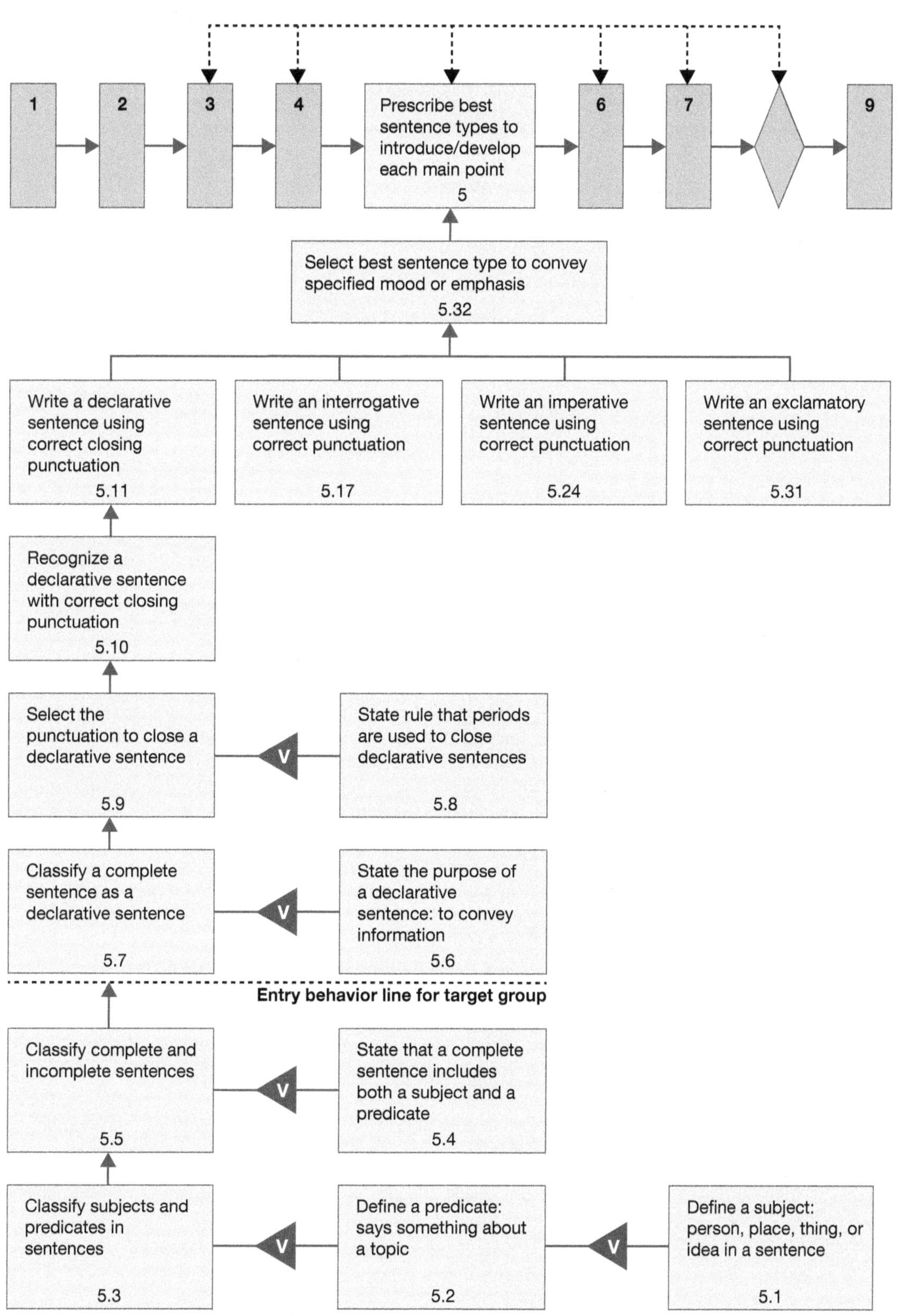

Appendix D

Analysis of Learner Characteristics, Performance Context, and Learning Context

1. Learner Characteristics for Sixth-Grade Students in Writing Instruction

Information Categories	Data Sources	Learner Characteristics
I. Abilities		
A. Entry skills	Needs assessment data from students' writing tests Interviews with teachers	Students tend • to write using simple, declarative sentences and • to use only periods and commas to punctuate their work.
B. Prior knowledge of topic area	Needs assessment data from students' writing tests Interviews with teachers	Students have completed five grades in school where sentence types, structure, and punctuation have been covered in regular instruction.
C. Educational and ability levels	Permanent records Interviews with teachers	Students in the group are average and above average in their abilities (e.g., stanines 4–9, percentile scores 27–99). Teachers indicate that all students in the group are very capable of learning and rehearsing the writing skills.
D. General learning preferences	Interviews with teachers and students	Students enjoy working with the computer and enjoy learner participation activities. They like working in class rather than being asked to complete large writing assignments as homework.
II. Attitudes		
A. Attitudes toward content	Interviews with teachers and tryout students	Teachers report that students vary widely in their receptivity to writing instruction and their willingness to practice their writing in journals and other writing assignments. Students interviewed verified this diverse opinion. For some it was their favorite subject, while for others it was their least favorite and a chore.
B. Attitudes toward potential delivery system	Interviews with teachers and tryout students	Teachers believe that the web-based instruction as well as the laptops students have for their writing assignments will be good motivators for students. They also think that an additional motivator or "hook" will be needed to motivate all of the students. Students want to be selected for the new writing program to gain access to computers in the classroom.
C. Motivation for instruction (ARCS)	Interviews with teachers and students	Students expect to pay attention to the computer. Most would like to write better (some said faster). They think they can learn to use sentence variety. Some think that learning to write better would make others respect them more. Teachers again indicate a diverse group with some students well motivated and others not motivated at all.
D. Attitudes toward training organization	Interviews with teachers and students	Varied perceptions of the effectiveness of the teachers and school. Most students are very positive, while some appear negative and disgruntled with both school and teachers.
III. General group characteristics	Overall impressions	Group very heterogeneous in achievement and motivation. All in group can learn and improve their writing skills. Students need a writing vehicle (e.g., story) that is motivational and that enables students to learn skills and practice in short rather than long writing assignments.

2. Performance and Learning Contexts for Writing Composition

Reader note: In this school, the learning and performance contexts are the same, so no separate analysis of the performance context is required.

Information Categories	Data Sources	Performance Site Characteristics
1. Managerial/ supervisory support	Interviews with: Principals Teachers Parents	• All are pleased with the use of computer-based, individualized instruction and the word processors as part of an overall program to improve students' writing skills. • The principal has suggested creating a sixth-grade newsletter as a motivational tool and an outlet for students' writings as long as all sixth graders are allowed to participate. She also suggested that the "newsletter" be distributed via the school district's Canvas Learning Management System in which the teaching and learning will be organized and delivered, thereby eliminating the costs of printing and distribution and initiating a "green" activity for the school. Parents are pleased with the new emphasis on writing, and they are willing to support their children's and the school's efforts. • The PTA has agreed to fund a sixth-grade newspaper if articles are written by sixth graders but for all grades in the school (supporting reading and writing). The leadership can be described as very positive and supportive of the planned writing initiative.
2. Physical aspects of the site	Interviews with: Students Teachers Media/Library Center Directors Parents District Director, Learning Support Center	All sixth-grade students were loaned personal computers at the beginning of the year. About 90% of the computers are working at any one time. Schools within the district, including the classrooms and learning centers, are wireless. The district learning support center provides the Canvas teaching/learning system to teachers and students throughout the district and provides regularly scheduled training for teachers in *using* the system and *managing* students receiving instruction through the system. Teachers are expected to teach their students how to use their computers, how to access the instructional system, and how to use the system. They are also expected to support students and provide elaboration when necessary.
3. Social and learning aspects of site	Interviews with: Students Teachers Media/Library Center Directors	Students can work individually in Canvas to access the direct instruction using their laptops. They can access the instruction from their classrooms, from the media/library centers, and from home if they have a computer and Internet access. The direct instruction provides: • preinstructional information including motivational material, performance objectives, and information about prerequisites; • presentation with examples and nonexamples; • rehearsal with feedback; and • assessment to check whether students have acquired the skills at least at a basic level.
4. A description of any tools the learners will have to accomplish the goals		Laptops (personal or school loaned)

Appendix E

Design Evaluation Chart Containing Subordinate Skills, Performance Objectives, and Parallel Test Items

Instructional Goal In written composition, students will (1) use a variety of sentence types and accompanying punctuation based on the *purpose* and *mood* of the sentence and (2) use a variety of sentence types and accompanying punctuation based on the *complexity or structure* of the sentence.

Terminal Objective In written composition, use a variety of sentence types and accompanying punctuation based on the *purpose, mood, and complexity* of the sentence. Sentences will be judged on format for sentence type, punctuation, sentence type by sentence purpose, and sentence variety within paragraphs.

Parallel Test Item Write a one-page description or story that includes different kinds of sentences to hold your readers' interest. In your story, remember to use:

1. At least **two** of each of the following types of sentences: declarative, interrogative, imperative, and exclamatory.
2. Only complete sentences.
3. Correct punctuation based on the type of sentence and mood.
4. The best type of sentences to convey the idea you wish.

Subordinate Skills	Performance Objectives	Parallel Test Items
5.1 Define subject.	5.1 Given the term *subject*, define the term by purpose.	1. Define the subject part of a sentence. 2. What does the *subject* part of a sentence do? The subject ❍ shows the sentence is beginning. ❍ is capitalized. ❍ shows action. ❍ names the topic.
5.2 Define predicate.	5.2 Given the term *predicate*, define the term. The definition must include that the predicate says something about the subject or topic.	1. Define the predicate part of a sentence. 2. What does the *predicate* part of a sentence do? The predicate tells something about the ______. ❍ subject ❍ verb ❍ adjectives ❍ prepositions
5.3 Classify subjects and the predicates in the complete sentences.	5.3 Given several complete, simple declarative sentences, locate all the subjects and predicates.	Is the subject or the predicate underlined in these sentences? If neither is underlined, choose "Neither." 1. <u>The carnival</u> was a roaring success. ❍ Subject ❍ Predicate ❍ Neither 2. <u>The</u> soccer team was victorious this season. ❍ Subject ❍ Predicate ❍ Neither 3. Susan got an <u>after-school job</u> weeding flower beds. ❍ Subject ❍ Predicate ❍ Neither

Subordinate Skills	Performance Objectives	Parallel Test Items
5.4 State that a complete statement includes both a subject and a predicate.	5.4 Given the term *complete sentence*, define the concept. The definition must name both the subject and the predicate.	1. A complete sentence contains both a(n) ____ and a(n) ____. 2. What is a complete sentence? A complete sentence contains ______. ❍ a subject ❍ a predicate ❍ neither a subject nor a predicate ❍ both a subject and a predicate
5.5 Classify complete and incomplete sentences.	5.5.1 Given several complete and incomplete declarative sentences, locate all those that are complete.	Are these sentences complete or incomplete? 1. John closely followed the directions. ❍ Complete ❍ Incomplete 2. The team that was most excited. ❍ Complete ❍ Incomplete 3. The dog sled bumped over the frozen land. ❍ Complete ❍ Incomplete 4. Found the lost friends happy to see her. ❍ Complete ❍ Incomplete
	5.5.2 Given several complete and incomplete declarative sentences, locate all those missing subjects and all those missing predicates.	Are these sentences missing a subject *or* a predicate? If they have both a subject and predicate, mark "Have both." 1. John closely followed the directions. ❍ Subject ❍ Predicate ❍ Have both 2. The team that was most excited. ❍ Subject ❍ Predicate ❍ Have both 3. The dog sled bumped over the frozen land. ❍ Subject ❍ Predicate ❍ Have both 4. Found the lost friends happy to see her. ❍ Subject ❍ Predicate ❍ Have both
5.6 State the purpose of a declarative sentence.	5.6 Given the terms *declarative sentence* and *purpose*, state the purpose of a declarative sentence. The purpose should include to convey/tell information.	1. The purpose of a declarative sentence is to _____. 2. What *purpose* does a declarative sentence serve? A declarative sentence _____ something. ❍ tells ❍ asks ❍ commands ❍ exclaims
5.7 Classify a complete sentence as a declarative sentence.	5.7 Given several complete simple sentences that include declarative, interrogative, and exclamatory sentences that are correctly or incorrectly closed using a period, locate all those that are declarative.	Ignore the missing punctuation marks and tell which of these sentences are declarative. 1. Are you hungry ❍ Declarative ❍ Not declarative 2. Put down your pencils please ❍ Declarative ❍ Not declarative 3. The woods looked quiet and peaceful ❍ Declarative ❍ Not declarative 4. Wow, look at that huge fire ❍ Declarative ❍ Not declarative

Subordinate Skills	Performance Objectives	Parallel Test Items
5.8 State that periods are used to close declarative sentences.	5.8 Given the terms *declarative sentence* and *closing punctuation*, name the period as the closing punctuation.	1. The closing punctuation used with a declarative sentence is called a _____. 2. Declarative sentences are closed using what punctuation mark? ❍ Quotation ❍ Exclamation point ❍ Question mark ❍ Period
5.9 Select the punctuation used to close a declarative sentence.	5.9 Given illustrations of a period, comma, exclamation point, and question mark and the terms *declarative sentence* and *closing punctuation*, select the period.	1. Circle the closing punctuation used to end a declarative sentence. , ! . ? " 2. Which one of the following punctuation marks is used to end a declarative sentence? ❍ , ❍ ! ❍ . ❍ ? ❍ "
5.10 Recognize a declarative sentence with correct closing punctuation.	5.10 Given several simple declarative sentences with correct and incorrect punctuation, select all the declarative sentences with correct closing punctuation.	Which of these sentences have the *correct* ending punctuation mark? 1. John likes to read space stories? ❍ Correct ❍ Incorrect 2. I ride two miles to school on the bus. ❍ Correct ❍ Incorrect 3. Sometimes I go skateboarding! ❍ Correct ❍ Incorrect
5.11 Write declarative sentences with correct closing punctuation.	5.11 Write declarative sentences on: (1) selected topics and (2) topics of student choice. Sentences must be complete and closed with a period.	1. Directions: Write five declarative sentences that describe today's school assembly. 2. Directions: Choose an event that happened in our class during the last two weeks. Write five declarative sentences about the event that could be used in a "news" story.

Appendix F

Instructional Strategy for Cognitive Instruction: The Objective Sequence and Clusters, Preinstructional Activities, and Assessment Activities

Component	Design
Objective Sequence and Clusters	Six lessons (each column below) with objectives clustered by lesson and sequenced within and across lessons. Allow one hour for each lesson.

1	2	3	4	5	6
5.6	5.12	5.18	5.25	5.11	5.32
5.7	5.13	5.19	5.26	5.17	
5.8	5.14	5.20	5.27	5.24	
5.9	5.15	5.21	5.28	5.31	
5.10	5.16	5.22	5.29		
5.11	5.17	5.23	5.30		

Preinstructional Activities

Motivation

1. Learning Environment: The class will begin a school newsletter to be distributed throughout the school and perhaps the district using the district's Canvas organization site. Sixth-grade students will plan for and manage the newsletter, and they will write the articles for it.
2. Writing Different Types of Sentences: A newsletter article will be used as an introduction. It will be on a topic of high interest to sixth graders, and it will contain all four sentence types to illustrate the point of variety and increased interest of the article through varying sentence type.

Objectives Each of the four types of sentences in the sample story will be highlighted and described in the introduction. The purpose of the unit, learning to write stories that contain a variety of sentence types, will be included.

Entry Skills

1. Newsletter: Students will be reminded of the classes' problem-solving steps applied on previous assignments and use them for planning and developing the newsletter (clarify problem, look for solutions, try out and refine solutions, and monitor effectiveness).
2. Writing: Because there are several entry skills noted in the instructional analysis, a test including entry skills will be developed and administered to determine whether students have the required prerequisite skills.

Assessment

Entry Skills The test will be short and consist of items covering skills 5.1, 5.2, 5.3, 5.4, and 5.5. If some learners do not have the prerequisites, then they will be directed to instruction for them as the first lesson (individualized through Canvas). The assessment will be developed and administered through Canvas.

Pretest The pretest will have two parts. Students will be asked to write a short newsletter article using the four types of sentences, and their articles will be assessed using a scoring rubric. Each lesson (e.g., declarative sentences) will also have an objective test within Canvas that is administered just prior to the lesson, and it will include only the subskills for that lesson. This assessment can eventually function as a branching mechanism for students who have previously mastered the skills. This test will be referred to using terms such as *recap* or *review* in directions to students.

Embedded Tests An embedded test will be administered immediately following each lesson, and it will cover the subordinate skills from the lesson. These tests will be used to diagnose problems students may be having with these subordinate skills, and they will eventually become practice or rehearsal with feedback. In discussions with students, these assessments will also be referred to using terms such as *recap* or *review* in directions to students.

Component	Design
	Posttests Students will be administered two forms of posttests. One will be administered after instruction is completed for the unit, it will be objective in format, and it will enable checking whether students have the basic skills mastered. The second will be an alternative assessment format in the form of a newsletter article (monitor effectiveness step from problem-solving strategy). The instructor, young author, and young colleagues will review the article(s) and provide (1) praise for validation and (2) suggestions for improvement for each student. This particular review will focus on the use of the four sentence types. The article assessment will occur many times over the year and focus on a variety of writing skills (e.g., paragraphs, complex sentences, transition, sequence, elaboration, narratives, various sentence structures). The articles along with the reviews will become part of the students' writing portfolios. These portfolios will enable the teacher, student, and parents to monitor writing progress over the year.
Follow-Through Activities	**Memory Aid:** Students will develop a checklist of criteria for judging sentence types and articles that they can use to evaluate their stories and articles. The teachers will provide the first simple rubric based on the lesson, and students will modify it for their work. Students will be reminded to use the checklist in reviewing and editing their stories and in assisting their colleagues.
	Transfer Strategy: There are two transfer strategies used: (1) applying their problem solving strategy from a previous unit in this new newsletter environment and (2) reinforcing writing for reasons other than "The teacher assigned it."

Appendix G

Instructional Strategy for the Content Presentation, Student Participation, and the Lesson Time Allocation Based on the Strategy

Learning Components	Design
Objective 5.6 State Purpose of Declarative Sentence	Content Presentation **Content:** Declarative sentences are used to convey information, to tell the reader something. **Examples:** Use declarative, simple sentences on the topics of interest students named in their newsletter interest inventory. Make all the example sentences on the same topic with a beginning, middle, and end sequence. For example: (1) Tom really enjoys space stories. (2) He has a subscription to a science-fiction magazine. (3) He can't wait for each edition to come in the mail each month. (4) He reads it cover to cover before he does anything else. Student Participation **Practice items:** Direct students to tell what a declarative sentence does and what each of the sentences presented tells them. For example, What does a declarative sentence do? What does Tom like to read? Where does he get his information? **Feedback:** Tell again that a declarative sentence is used to convey information, and point out *what* each of the sentences tells the reader.
Objective 5.7 Classify a Complete Sentence as Declarative	Content Presentation **Content:** Declarative sentences are used to convey information, to tell the reader something. **Examples:** Use declarative, simple sentences on the topics of interest students named in their newsletter interest inventory. Make all the example sentences on the same topic with a beginning, middle, and end sequence. (See previous example in 5.6.) **Nonexamples:** Use interrogative, imperative, and exclamatory sentences as nonexamples, and point out why each is not an example without teaching about them. Stay focused on declarative sentences. For example, (1) What does Tom like to read? (2) Where does he get his stories? (3) What does he get in the mail? (4) Tom stop reading right now. Student Participation **Practice items:** Give students a list of sentences *on the same topic* and have them classify the declarative ones. Use interrogative, imperative, and declarative sentences in the set. *Remove the punctuation* from the sentences so they must classify using only the message as a clue. **Feedback:** Restate rule for declarative sentences and show *why* sentences presented are or are not declarative sentences.
Objective 5.8 State Periods Used to Close Declarative Sentences	Content Presentation **Content:** Periods are used to close declarative sentences. **Examples:** Use three to five declarative, simple sentences with their periods highlighted (e.g., bold print, color) on the topics of interest students named in their newsletter interest inventory. Make all the example sentences on the same topic with a beginning, middle, and end sequence. (See previous example in 5.6.) Student Participation **Practice items:** Have students name *period* or select the name from among a list of punctuation mark names. For example, (1) What punctuation mark is used to close declarative sentences? (2) Does a period, comma, or exclamation point close a declarative sentence? **Feedback:** Restate that the period is used to close declarative sentences.

Learning Components	Design
Objective 5.9 Select Punctuation to Close Sentence	**Content Presentation** **Content:** Periods are used to close declarative sentences. **Examples:** Same format as subordinate skill 5.8, but different examples. **Nonexamples:** Repeat the example sentences but replace the punctuation marks with punctuation from other sentence types, and point out the mismatch between sentence content and incorrect punctuation mark. **Student Participation** **Practice items:** Present three to five simple declarative sentences on the topics of interest with their periods omitted. Make all the example sentences on the same topic with a beginning, middle, and end sequence. (See previous example in 5.6.) Have students select the punctuation mark (i.e., period [.], question mark [?], exclamation mark [!]) to close the sentences. **Feedback:** State that periods should be used to close all the declarative sentences. Show correct punctuation for illustration sentences.
Objective 5.10 Recognize Declarative Sentences with Correct Punctuation	**Content Presentation** **Content:** Only periods are used to close declarative sentences. **Examples:** Use three to five declarative, simple sentences with their periods highlighted (e.g., bold print, color) on the topics of interest students named in their newsletter interest inventory. Make all the example sentences on the same topic with a beginning, middle, and end sequence. (See previous example in 5.6.) **Nonexamples:** Present another set of simple declarative sentences on the same topic with correct and incorrect ending punctuation. Explain why each of the sentences is or is not correct. **Student Participation** **Practice items:** Provide an additional set of simple declarative sentences on one topic of interest with correct and incorrect ending punctuation. Have students select the correctly punctuated declarative sentences. **Feedback:** Indicate *why* declarative sentences with incorrect punctuation are incorrect.
Objective 5.11 Write a Declarative Sentence with Correct Punctuation	**Content Presentation** The content for this skill was covered in its subordinate skills. At this point, students should be encouraged to write on a topic they know about. Figuring out what to write is a very different skill than recognizing correctly written declarative sentences. The content will be the directions of what to do. **Student Participation** **Practice 1:** Have students convert other types of sentences to declarative sentences. In their conversions, students should stay with the same topic but expand the meaning and add content as needed to change the format. Examples include the following: Directions to students: Change the following sentences to declarative ones. Keep with the same topic, but expand or change the information in the sentence as you need to in order to convert the sentence to a declarative one. a. How did (somebody they know from film or literature) look? b. Where did (somebody they know from town, class, story, or literature) go? c. Watch out for lightning! d. Finish your chores before you go outside. **Feedback:** Show examples of how sample sentences can be rewritten as declarative sentences. Remember to tell them that there are many ways to convert the sentences correctly. **Practice 2:** Have students write a series of three to five declarative sentences on one topic of their choice. Topics they have chosen for their newsletter columns make a good list of topics from which to choose. Another writing idea may be to describe events or places around the classroom or school.

Learning Components	Design	
	Feedback: Provide students with a brief list of criteria they can use to evaluate their sentences as they write them; for example: Do your sentences ___ have a subject? ___ have a predicate? ___ tell something to the reader? ___ have a period at the end? ___ all describe the same topic?	
Lesson Allocation Based on Instructional Strategy	**Activity**	**Minutes Planned**
Session 1	1. Introductory, motivational materials 2. Entry skills assessment	55
Session 2	Newsletter article writing pretest	
Session 3	Pretest and instruction on objectives 5.6–5.11, declarative sentences	55
Session 4	Pretest and instruction on objectives 5.12–5.17, interrogative sentences	55
Session 5	Pretest and instruction on objectives 5.18–5.24, imperative sentences	55
Session 6	Pretest and instruction on objectives 5.25–5.31, exclamatory sentences	55
Session 7	Review of objectives 5.11, 5.17, 5.24, and 5.31, all four sentence types	55
Session 8	Instruction on objective 5.32, selecting best sentence type for a particular purpose or mood	55
Session 9	Objective posttest on objectives 5.6–5.32	60
Student Groupings	Students will work individually using their laptops, and they may work with teacher or small group for question/answer, extra practice, and customized feedback.	
Consolidation of media selection and choice of delivery system for main steps	The primary medium will be individualized, web-based instruction, but the teacher will be prepared with extra examples, nonexamples, and practice to support small-group work when needed.	

Appendix H

Plans for a Constructivist Learning Environment

1. Plans for Constructivist Learning Environment (CLE)

<table>
<tr><th>Planning Needs</th><th>Planning Activities</th></tr>
<tr><td>Planning the Learning Environment</td><td>Designs and materials needed to launch the CLE
<ul>
<li>Goal: Improved writing composition using a variety of sentence types</li>
<li>Learning objectives: Main step 5: Prescribe best sentence types to introduce/develop each main point (in article)</li>
</ul>
Rationale: During a middle school faculty meeting called to discuss problems of students' written composition, teachers decided to conduct a needs assessment study. Each teacher assigned a short essay for his or her students to be written on a common topic. A newly formed evaluation team of teachers from across the school district reviewed the themes to identify possible common problems. They reported that students typically use one type of sentence—namely, declarative, simple sentences—to communicate their thoughts rather than varying their sentence structure by purpose or complexity. In addition, punctuation other than periods and commas was absent from students' work, and commas were rare. Teachers decided to design special instruction that focused students on (1) writing a variety of sentence types based on sentence purpose, (2) writing using a variety of sentence structures that vary in complexity, and (3) using a variety of punctuation to match sentence type and complexity. Through instruction focused directly on the problems identified in the needs assessment, they hoped to change the current pattern of simplistic similarity found in students' compositions.
<ul>
<li>Constructivist focus: Reasoning, critical thinking, problem solving, retention, understanding, and use</li>
<li>Pedagogical model: Project-based learning</li>
<li>Scenario: The newsletter (suggested earlier by the needs assessment team and principal) will be used to create the desired learning environment. Students will work in cooperative teams to plan and produce their newsletters for student colleagues throughout the school and perhaps the district. The newsletter will provide opportunities for:
<ul>
<li>Natural motivation or a reason for practicing their writing skills</li>
<li>Student-centered learning as students plan and manage their newsletter as well as plan what to write and how to write their articles (e.g., sports, nature, school events, community events, student heroes, health)</li>
<li>Practicing, applying, and assessing sentence and paragraph construction skills in an authentic performance context</li>
<li>Applying the classes' problem-solving strategies from earlier instructional units (i.e., prerequisite skills: clarify problem, seek solutions, try out ideas, refine, and monitor effectiveness)</li>
<li>Working cooperatively with their student colleagues and teacher advisors</li>
<li>Applying criteria from multiple perspectives to judge their writing (i.e., format, content, interest, aesthetics, values or appropriateness, and legal considerations)</li>
</ul></li>
<li>Learning resource materials:
<ul>
<li>Structure for student activity for managing the newsletter (see section 2 following matrix).</li>
<li>List of newsletter columns (topics) selected by students</li>
<li>Individualized, web-based instruction on writing various types of sentences (simple, complex, and compound), paragraphs, and articles</li>
<li>Policies for use of the site to disseminate information established by district's legal personnel, administrators, and parents' advisory team, including:
<ul>
<li>Legal considerations the district has in providing the site</li>
<li>Individuals/groups given access to the site (e.g., students in class, across school, across district; teachers, parents, administrators)</li>
<li>Types of access groups/individuals have (i.e., authorship; site leader for loading, editing, and deleting submitted materials, reader only)</li>
<li>Content permitted in district-disseminated materials (e.g., age appropriate, lacks bias, meets community and school values)</li>
</ul></li>
<li>Job aids for:
<ul>
<li>Sample middle-school-level newsletters and newsletter articles on topics selected by students</li>
<li>Other products as identified during the production of the newsletter</li>
</ul></li>
</ul></li>
</ul></td></tr>
</table>

Planning Needs	Planning Activities

	• Learner groupings: There will be two different categories of work teams: the newsletter management teams (e.g., content, graphic design, editorial, production) and the column content (creative) teams (e.g., sports, science, school events). All students may choose to serve on one or more of the management teams based on their interest, and they may switch management teams for new experiences or colleagues. All members of the class will serve as a writer on one or more of the column content (creative) teams. Students will monitor the monthly newsletter's progress to see whether they have the teams necessary for the tasks that evolve.
	• Delivery system, media, and personnel:
	  • Canvas organization site for disseminating the newsletter created by district's learning support center
	  • E-learning portal to deliver individualized web-based instruction on various types of sentences and composition
	  • Students' laptops for content research for articles
	  • Library/media specialists for assisting with topic research
	  • Sixth-grade language arts teachers
	  • District instructional designers and instructional technologists
	  • The teachers and students will identify other school personnel who want to become involved (e.g., art teachers for graphic design, physical education teachers for the sports column, social studies teachers for the history group, science teachers for the space group, and music/drama/language arts teachers for the arts column, library/media specialists for content research and technology).

Planning for Learner Engagement	**Procedures and activities anticipated during engagement** • Engage: Engagement will be initiated by discussion within the classes about a middle-school group who last year created and published their own newsletter. Positive benefits of the existing newsletter will be discussed, and the teacher will raise questions about whether the class would like to start their own newsletter this year. When, through their discussion with the teachers, the group decides to seek more information about publishing a newsletter, each class will choose one sixth-grade representative from each school to take a field trip to the county office to seek more information. At the school district office, the representatives will meet with the director of learning and technology and request permission for sixth graders to produce and publish their own newsletter. The representatives will report the content of the meeting to their classmates, and the classes will then wait one week to learn the verdict (prearranged) of the director's agreement to support the newsletter. Official letters will be sent from the director to the student representatives, who will read the letters to their classmates. • Explore: Students seek information about the types of management teams that will be necessary to produce and publish the newsletter and the reading interests of sixth-grade students (columns and articles). They also seek information about the appearance of other student newsletters (graphics, distribution format) and the types of articles produced in them (e.g., topics, length, tone). They will also explore the types of articles they would like to write (e.g., sports, science, arts, school events, town history). • Explain: Students within work teams plan and explain the tasks to be accomplished and their ideas for articles to one another, to their parents, and to the teachers and advisors. They explore with the teacher whether they must write articles individually or can write in pairs or triads. • Elaborate: Their problem-solving, teamwork, and writing skills will be used in other classes in the school, at home, and for a few, on their jobs. • Evaluate: See authentic assessment in subsequent section of table.

Planning Learning Guidance	**Materials and activities anticipated for adaptive learning guidance**
	• Scaffolding
	• Models:
	  • Newsletters
	  • Articles
	• Coaching, questioning by teachers and content advisors
	• Peer tutoring from team members and editorial committee
	• Individualized instruction in Canvas on sentence, paragraph, and article types

Planning Needs	Planning Activities
Planning Authentic Assessment	**Materials and procedures anticipated for authentic assessment** • Individual articles during development: Students will reflect on the rubrics suggested by the teacher and add criteria they believe should be included. They will use writing format, content interest value, legal and policy criteria to form and critique their articles individually. They will also work with their teacher advisors (e.g., art, physical education, media specialist) to reflect on and improve their articles. • Single newsletter issue prepublication: Learners who serve on the editorial teams will work with writers to critique single issues of the newsletter prior to production and suggest ideas for revision and refinement. • Post publication: Students will get "natural" feedback on their articles from siblings, parents, other students in the school, and other teachers. • Portfolio: Individual student's articles will be gathered over the year into a writing portfolio. Student and teacher will review the portfolio each grading period to examine writing progress overall and progress related to the particular lessons covered during the term (e.g., declarative sentences, transition).

2. Procedural Analysis for Management of Newsletter (Constructivist Learning Environment)

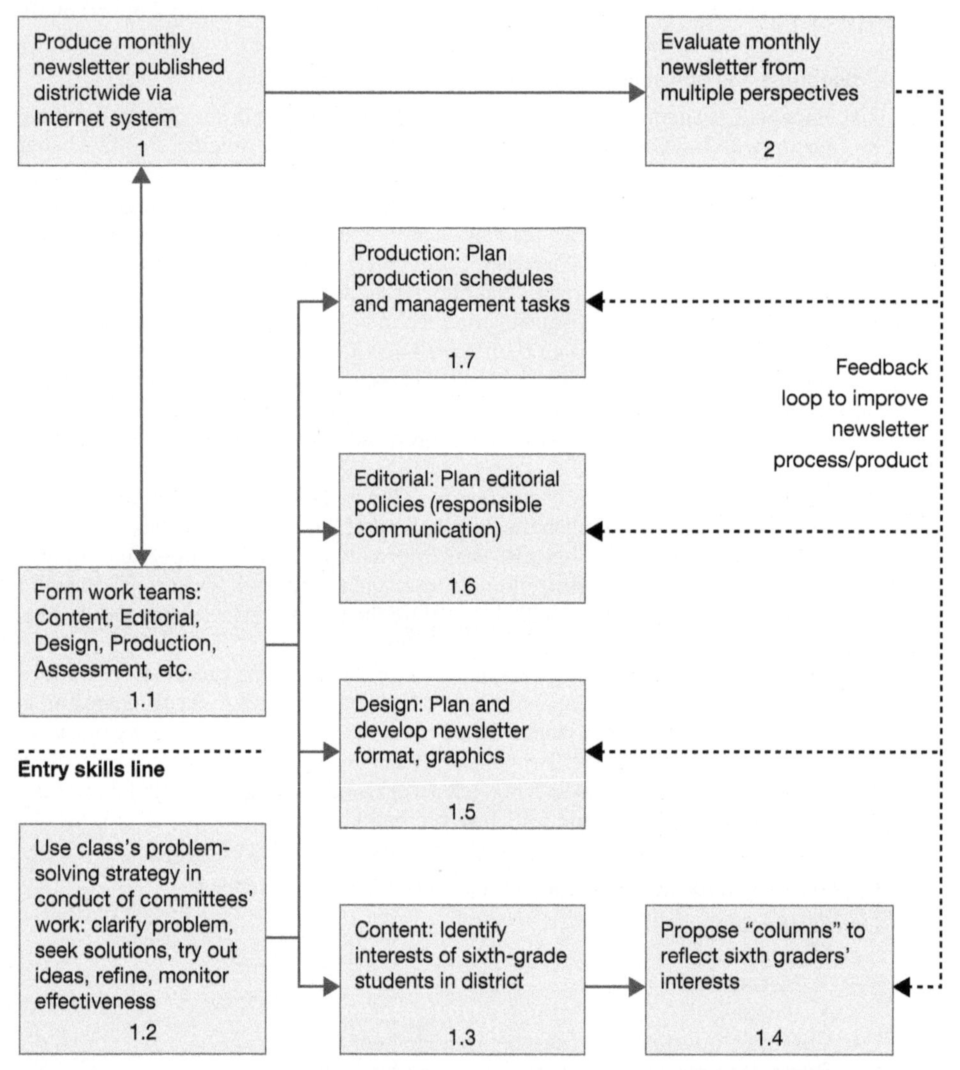

Appendix I

Session 1: Motivational Materials, Unit Objectives, and Assessment for Entry Skills

Designer note: These materials are intended to be delivered via Canvas where space and color are not issues.

Component	Subskill	Text
Motivation		

Now that the work teams are busy planning for our newsletter, we can begin thinking about writing interesting articles for it. To make our articles interesting, we are going to use many different styles of writing and types of sentences. Are you wondering how you can make your articles most interesting for other sixth graders?

One way we can make our articles more interesting is to use *different types* of sentences when we write them. Using different types of sentences does not change the message, it only changes the way we tell it.

Different kinds of sentences help our readers know what we want to say and how we feel about what we have said. It involves them in what they are reading because it helps the article come alive.

To show you how using several different kinds of sentences makes a newsletter article more interesting, I have written the same article for the next Science Column two ways.

My story on the left side has only declarative sentences in it, while my story on the right side uses four different kinds of sentences.

Read both stories and compare them.

There Is No Dark Side of the Moon

by
Lauren Hauser

They say there is no dark side of the moon. Next they will be telling us there is no boogey man or no tooth fairy. The source of ideas about the dark side of the moon needs some explanation. There must be something behind the idea. Rock bands sing about it, and it appears in space stories all the time.

The explanation is simple. Our Earth rotates on an axis. As it turns, it exposes all of its sides every day to anyone watching Earth from the moon. Unlike Earth, our moon does not rotate, so people looking at our moon from Earth always see the same side. When we go to the moon, we will see both daylight and darkness there, because both our Earth and our moon orbit the sun.

What songs and stories refer to as the moon's dark side is actually its far side. The side of the moon facing away from us is called the far side. The side facing us from space is called the near side. Go outside some night this week and look at the *near side* of the full moon.

There Is No Dark Side of the Moon!

by
Lauren Hauser

What? There is no dark side of the moon? Next they will be telling us there is no boogey man or no tooth fairy! If there is no dark side of the moon, where did the idea come from? There must be something behind the idea! Rock bands sing about it, and it appears in space stories all the time.

The explanation is simple. Our Earth rotates on an axis. As it turns, it exposes all of its sides every day to anyone watching Earth from the moon! Unlike Earth, our moon does not rotate, so people looking at the moon from Earth always see the same side. When we go to the moon, will we see both daylight and darkness there? Yes, because both our Earth and our moon orbit the sun.

What songs and stories refer to as the moon's dark side is actually its far side. The side of the moon facing away from us is called the far side. What do you think the side we always see is named? The side facing us from space is called the near side. Go outside some night this week and look at the *near side* of the full moon.

Don't you think the second article tells exactly the same information, only it's more interesting to read? It makes me wonder whether I will ever see Earth from the moon. It also makes me wonder what is on the far side that I can't see. I hope Lauren writes about that in her next column.

When we write our own newsletter articles, we should remember that using several different kinds of sentences will make them more interesting for students all across town.

Component	Subskill	Text
Unit Objectives		

It will be fun to learn to write newsletter articles that have different kinds of sentences in them. Right now let's focus on the following kinds of sentences and choose the type that best fits what we want to say.

Of course, writing articles that have all four kinds of sentences will require some practice. I want to show each of the sentence types to you and help you practice writing each one.

After writing all four sentence types, we are going to use them to create interesting newsletter articles for our first edition.

Let's start with declarative sentences.

Four Types of Sentences

- Declarative sentences *tell* the reader something.
- Interrogative sentences *ask* questions.
- Imperative sentences *command*, *direct*, or *request* something.
- Exclamatory sentences *show emotion* or excitement.

Component	Subskill	Text
Entry skills	5.1–5.5	

First, refresh your ideas about *complete* sentences because we will need to use them regardless of the type of sentence we write.

Please click on the **"Review"** button below to check your memory about complete sentences. To check your answers when you finish, click **"Submit"** and then click **"OK."**

Review

Designer note: The skill codes in the left column would not be present on the entry skills test for students; they are included here to enable you to link the entry skills with the items. In addition, the selected response items were chosen from the design table to be compatible with the Canvas "quick" test administration and feedback format.

Skills	Item
Entry Skills Test	

5.1. 1. What does the *subject* part of a sentence do? The subject _____.
- ❍ shows the sentence is beginning
- ❍ is capitalized
- ❍ shows action
- ❍ names the topic

5.2. 2. What does the *predicate* part of a sentence do? The predicate tells something about the ___________.
- ❍ subject
- ❍ verb
- ❍ adjectives
- ❍ prepositions

5.3. **Is the subject or the predicate underlined in these sentences? If neither is underlined, choose "Neither."**

3. American students ride Amtrak trains. ❍ Subject ❍ Predicate ❍ Neither
4. European students ride Eurail trains. ❍ Subject ❍ Predicate ❍ Neither
5. Students in Japan ride white bullet trains. ❍ Subject ❍ Predicate ❍ Neither

5.4. 6. What is a complete sentence? A complete sentence contains ___________________.
- ❍ a subject
- ❍ a predicate
- ❍ neither a subject nor a predicate
- ❍ both a subject and a predicate

5.5. **Are these sentences complete or incomplete?**

7. The Iditarod Trail Sled Dog Race. ❍ Complete ❍ Incomplete
8. Dry, bumpy, cold, dark, and wind-blown. ❍ Complete ❍ Incomplete
9. The winner took about nine long, dark days to finish. ❍ Complete ❍ Incomplete

Are these sentences missing a subject or a predicate? If they have both a subject and a predicate present, choose "Have both."

10. The Iditarod Trail Sled Dog Race. ❍ Subject ❍ Predicate ❍ Have both
11. Dry, bumpy, cold, dark, and wind-blown. ❍ Subject ❍ Predicate ❍ Have both

Session 2: Pretest: Writing Newsletter Article and Using Rubric to Evaluate Article

Designer note: For space reasons in this book, we cannot continue the motivational aspect of direct instruction from peer tutors using photographs and text "callouts." To see the instruction as intended on Canvas, please review the materials in the Course Management site. We will continue here with straight text and use the symbol 📷 to indicate where a peer–tutor photograph is to be inserted and used with conversation callouts.

1. Pretest Directions to Students

Component	Subskill	Text
Alternative Assessment Pretest and Rubric	Instructional Goal	

📷 It is time to write your first article for the newsletter because the content team has tallied the results of their survey on our interests and picked topics for columns. Choose any one of these column topics for your first article. If you have a better idea for a column, please name it and write your article for that column.

Newsletter Columns

a. East Side West Side (All About the Town)
b. Entertainment
c. Environment
d. Our Town in History
e. Space
f. Sports
g. Technology in the News
h. Upcoming School Events

📷 Use your laptops and Word to write your two- to three-paragraph article for the newsletter. Your article should include different kinds of sentences to hold your readers' interest. In your story, remember to use the following:

Article Characteristics

1. At least **two** of each of the following types of sentences: declarative, interrogative, imperative, and exclamatory.
2. Only complete sentences.
3. Correct punctuation based on the type of sentence and mood.
4. The best type of sentences to convey the idea you wish.
5. Correct spelling. Remember to spell-check your work. Put any words you misspell (not typos) on your spelling list.

📷 When you finish your draft article, look it over. Can you find ways to make it more interesting for our readers? Make the changes that you need.

POST your article to Mr. Brown in Canvas by the end of the period this morning.

📷 You might want to use this rubric to help review your article.

2. Sample Rubric for Scoring Students' Pretest Articles

Criteria	Sentence Types DECLARATIVE	INTERROGATIVE	IMPERATIVE	EXCLAMATORY
1. Total number of sentences				
2. No. of sentences complete				
a. No. of subjects missing				
b. No. of predicates missing				
3. No. of correct ending punctuation				
4. No. of sentences appropriate for idea				
5. No. of sentences appropriate for mood				

Designer note: Criteria not covered in this unit are omitted from the rubric purposefully.

Session 3: Pretest and Instruction in Subordinate Skills 5.6 Through 5.11

Designer note: Recall that symbol 📷 is used to indicate where a peer–teacher photograph will be inserted and used with conversation "callouts" to enter the text.

Component	Subskills	Text
Objective Pretest and Instruction	5.6–5.11	

📷 Let's turn our attention to *declarative* sentences. First, refresh your ideas about them because they form the skeleton of all writing.

Please click on the "**Review**" button below to check your memory about declarative sentences. To check your answers when you finish, click "**Submit**" and then click "**OK.**"

Subordinate Skills Pretest

5.6. 1. What *purpose* does a declarative sentence serve? A declarative sentence ______ something.
- ❍ tells
- ❍ asks
- ❍ commands
- ❍ exclaims

5.7. **Ignore the missing punctuation marks and tell which of these sentences are declarative.**

2. Camping with the girl scouts was fun last Saturday
   - ❍ Declarative
   - ❍ Not Declarative
3. Should we have pitched our tents in a circle
   - ❍ Declarative
   - ❍ Not Declarative
4. Always clean up the dishes before campfire begins ❍ Declarative ❍ Not Declarative
5. We heard scary stories about bears around the campfire ❍ Declarative ❍ Not Declarative
6. Oh no, there's a bear outside the tent ❍ Declarative ❍ Not Declarative

5.8. 7. Declarative sentences are closed using a ______________.
- ❍ quotation
- ❍ exclamation point
- ❍ question mark
- ❍ period

5.9. 8. Which of these punctuation marks is used to end a declarative sentence?
❍ , ❍ ! ❍ . ❍? ❍ "

9. Which of these punctuation marks is used to close a declarative sentence?
❍ . ❍ ! ❍ ; ❍ ? ❍ :

5.10. **Which ones of these declarative sentences end with the correct punctuation mark?**

10. An Iditarod sled dog racer is called a *musher*? ❍ Correct ❍ Incorrect
11. Last year's last-place musher had a team of 16 dogs. ❍ Correct ❍ Incorrect
12. The losing musher took 16 days to finish the race. ❍ Correct ❍ Incorrect
13. The race is so hard that even the last person gets a trophy? ❍ Correct ❍ Incorrect
14. The trophy for the last musher is called the Red Lantern Award! ❍ Correct ❍ Incorrect

5.11. **Directions:** Choose any event that happened in our class during the last two weeks. In the space below, write four *declarative sentences* about the event that might be used in a "news" story.

SUBMIT

Student Management	Please go to Instruction and click on the title: Session 1 Declarative Sentences. *Designer note:* Teacher should determine whether to split students for subsequent instruction based on mastery scores for the pretest.

Component	Subskill	Text
Content Presentation	5.6	Declarative Sentences

A declarative sentence is used *to tell the reader something or describe something*. When you want to state a fact or describe something in a direct manner, you write a declarative sentence.

Here are some declarative sentences used to state facts.

Examples

1. Chiniqua is growing a spice garden beside her back porch.
2. She has five different spices in her garden including mint and basil.
3. She has to finish her homework before she can go to the garden.
4. The whole family loves meals made with her spices.

A declarative sentence tells us something. Notice that sentence 1 tells us *what* Chiniqua has. She has a garden. Sentence 2 tells us *what* she has in her garden. Sentence 3 tells us *when* she works in the garden, and sentence 4 tells us how her family feels about her garden. All these sentences *tell us something*.

Declarative sentences can also be used *to describe something*. The following sentences are descriptions.

Examples

1. It rained really hard the day of the school picnic.
2. The sky was so dark the streetlights in the park came on.
3. We were all soaking wet and so were the hot dogs.

Sentence 1 *describes* the day as rainy, sentence 2 *describes* the picnic day as very dark, and sentence 3 *describes* the students and food.

Component	Subskill	Text
Content Presentation	5.7	

Look at the next two sentences. One is a declarative sentence, and one is not. Can you tell the difference? Which one is the declarative sentence?

Nonexample

1. Georgia really enjoyed the soggy picnic.
2. What did Georgia enjoy?

Sentence 1 is the declarative sentence since it tells us *what* Georgia enjoyed. Sentence 2 is NOT declarative. After reading this sentence, we do not know what Georgia liked. Because sentence 2 does not give the reader information, it is NOT a declarative sentence.

continued

Component	Subskill	Text
Practice and Feedback	5.6–5.7	

Let's practice. Read the following pairs of sentences. Which of the sentences are declarative and why?

A.1 What are Segway PTs?
A.2 Segway PTs are battery-powered personal transporters.

B.1 Segway PTs can stand still, turn in place, and travel at the speed of walkers.
B.2 What can you do with a Segway PT?

In the first pair of sentences, sentence A.1 does not tell us what a Segway PT is, so it cannot be declarative. Sentence A.2 describes a Segway PT, so it is declarative. It tells us something about a Segway.

In the second pair of sentences, the declarative sentence (B.1) tells us what a Segway PT can do, but sentence B.2 does not provide any clues about what we can do with one. Sentence B.2 is NOT a declarative sentence.

Component	Subskill	Text
Content Presentation	5.8–5.9	Punctuation for Declarative Sentences

Punctuation marks are used to close complete sentences. The *period* (.) is the punctuation mark that is *always* used to close a declarative sentence.

When you see a period at the end of a sentence, it is a clue that the sentence may be a declarative one.

Other types of sentences may use a period, but a sentence that

- *provides information* and
- is *closed with a period*

is always a declarative sentence.

Here are some declarative sentences that are correctly punctuated with periods at the end.

Examples

1. Our solar system has the sun and eight planets that are bound to it by gravity.
2. The eight planets share well over 166 moons among them.
3. There are also three dwarf planets: Ceres, Pluto, and Eris.
4. The solar system has billions of small bodies that include asteroids, meteoroids, comets, and interplanetary dust.

We know these four sentences are declarative because they *describe* our solar system and what it contains, and they are *closed using periods.*

If a sentence appears to be declarative because it tells something or describes something yet the punctuation mark at the end of the sentence is NOT a period, then the sentence is NOT a declarative one.

Some sentences tell the reader something, and this is a clue that they *might* be declarative. *However*, when a period is NOT used to close the sentence, it is NOT declarative. Look at these sentences taken from a science-fiction story.

Nonexamples

1. The meteoroid may hit Earth!
2. Earth will be destroyed for humans if it hits!

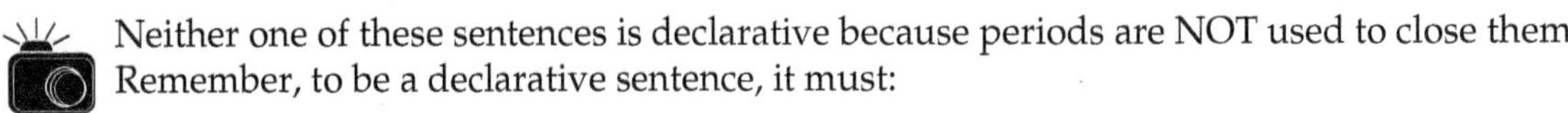

Neither one of these sentences is declarative because periods are NOT used to close them. Remember, to be a declarative sentence, it must:

- tell the reader something and
- close with a period.

Component	Subskill	Text
Practice and Feedback	5.8–5.9	

Let's practice! Look at these sentences. Which ones are declarative?

1. Welcome to Explore America Camp!
2. Welcome to Explore America Camp.
3. Where are you going to camp this summer?

The first sentence is NOT declarative. Although it welcomes us to a new camp, it does NOT end with a period. The second sentence is declarative. It welcomes us to the new camp, and it ends with a period. The third sentence is not declarative because it does NOT convey information, and it does NOT end with a period.

Component	Subskill	Text
Embedded Test Items	5.6–5.11	

Let's review declarative sentences. Please click on the review button below to get the review questions. After you answer all of the questions, remember to "submit" your answers and carefully review the feedback for each question. Pay attention to any mistakes you see and try to figure out why. You may review the information you have just read about declarative sentences after your review if you wish.

Subordinate Skills

5.6. 1. Why do we use declarative sentences in our writing? We use them to _______.

❍ ask something
❍ command something
❍ exclaim something
❍ tell something

5.7. **Ignore the missing punctuation marks and tell which of these sentences are declarative.**

2. In the fifteenth century, Native Americans lived right here in our town
❍ Declarative ❍ Not Declarative
3. What kind of Indians were they ❍ Declarative ❍ Not Declarative
4. Did they live near the school grounds ❍ Declarative ❍ Not Declarative
5. Wow, I really wish I had known some of them ❍ Declarative ❍ Not Declarative
6. Read the book about Native Americans first ❍ Declarative ❍ Not Declarative

5.8. 7. Declarative sentences are closed using a _______.

❍ question mark
❍ period
❍ exclamation point
❍ quotation

continued

5.9. 8. Which one of the following punctuation marks is used to end a declarative sentence?

❍ ; ❍ ! ❍ . ❍ ? ❍ :

5.10. Which of these declarative sentences end with the correct punctuation mark?

9. Each planet's distance from the sun determines how long its year lasts?
❍ Correct ❍ Incorrect
10. An Earth year lasts about 365 Earth days! ❍ Correct ❍ Incorrect
11. Mercury's year lasts only about 88 Earth days. ❍ Correct ❍ Incorrect
12. Neptune's year lasts almost 165 Earth years? ❍ Correct ❍ Incorrect

5.11. 13. **Directions:** Choose any one of the topic columns for our newsletter, and write four related *declarative sentences* in the space below that could be used in the column. Remember, the columns are:

a. East Side West Side (All About the Town),
b. Entertainment,
c. Environment,
d. Our Town in History,
e. Space,
f. Sports,
g. Technology in the News, and
h. School Events.

SUBMIT

Designer note: Assume that the portion of the objective posttest covering declarative sentences would be constructed using the prescriptions in the instructional strategy and formatted in the same manner as the pretest and embedded test. All test items on the posttest would contain different example sentences.

Appendix L

Group's and Individual's Achievement of Objectives and Attitudes About Instruction

1. Student-by-Item-by-Objective Data Array for Entry Skills

Obj	5.1	5.2		5.3		5.4		5.5						
Itm	1	2	3	4	5	6	7	8	9	10	X	%	Obj	%
STD														
1							1		1		2	20	0	0
2			1	1	1		1		1		5	50	1	20
3			1	1	1		1		1		5	50	1	20
4	1		1	1	1		1		1		6	60	2	40
5	1	1	1	1	1		1	1	1	1	9	90	4	80
6	1	1	1	1	1	1	1	1	1	1	10	100	5	100
7	1	1	1	1	1	1	1	1	1	1	10	100	5	100
8	1	1	1	1	1	1	1	1	1	1	10	100	5	100
9	1	1	1	1	1	1	1	1	1	1	10	100	5	100
10	1	1	1	1	1	1	1	1	1	1	10	100	5	100
11	1	1	1	1	1	1	1	1	1	1	10	100	5	100
12	1	1	1	1	1	1	1	1	1	1	10	100	5	100
13	1	1	1	1	1	1	1	1	1	1	10	100	5	100
14	1	1	1	1	1	1	1	1	1	1	10	100	5	100
15	1	1	1	1	1	1	1	1	1	1	10	100	5	100
# Std. correct	12	11	14	14	14	10	15	11	15	11				
% Std. correct	80	73	93	93	93	66	100	73	100	73				
% Obj	80	73		93		66		73						

Note: 1 = correct response; blank = incorrect response; Obj = Objective, Itm = Item; Std = Student

2. Student-by-Item-by-Objective Data Array for Declarative Sentence Portion of Posttest

Obj Items	5.6		5.7			5.8	5.9		5.10				5.11					
	1	2	3	4	5	6	7	8	9	10	11	12	13	14	15	X	%	Obj
STUDENTS																		
1	1	1	1	1	1	1	1	1		1	1		1		1	12	80	5
2	1	1	1	1	1	1	1	1	1	1	1	1	1	1	1	15	100	6
3	1	1	1	1	1	1	1	1	1	1	1	1	1	1	1	15	100	6
4	1	1	1	1	1	1	1	1	1	1	1	1	1	1	1	15	100	6
5	1	1	1	1	1	1	1	1	1	1	1	1	1	1	1	15	100	6
6	1	1	1	1	1	1	1	1	1	1	1	1	1	1	1	15	100	6
7	1	1	1	1	1	1	1	1	1	1	1	1	1	1	1	15	100	6
8	1	1	1	1	1	1	1	1	1	1	1	1	1	1	1	15	100	6
9	1	1	1	1	1	1	1	1	1	1	1	1	1	1	1	15	100	6
10	1	1	1	1	1	1	1	1	1	1	1	1	1	1	1	15	100	6

continued

Obj Items	5.6		5.7			5.8	5.9		5.10				5.11					
	1	2	3	4	5	6	7	8	9	10	11	12	13	14	15	X	%	Obj
STUDENTS																		
11	1	1	1	1	1	1	1	1	1	1	1	1	1	1	1	15	100	6
12	1	1	1	1	1	1	1	1	1	1	1	1	1	1	1	15	100	6
13	1	1	1	1	1	1	1	1	1	1	1	1	1	1	1	15	100	6
14	1	1	1	1	1	1	1	1	1	1	1	1	1	1	1	15	100	6
15	1	1	1	1	1	1	1	1	1	1	1	1	1	1	1	15	100	6
# Students Correct	15	15	15	15	15	15	15	15	14	15	15	14	15	14	15			
% Students Correct	100	100	100	100	100	100	100	100	93	100	100	93	100	93	100			
% Obj	100		100			100	100		100				93					

Note: 1 = correct response; blank = incorrect response; Obj = Objective, Itm = Item; Std = Student

3. Student Performance by Objectives on the Pretest, Embedded Items, and Posttest

Obj	5.6 Purpose			5.7 Identify			5.8 Select Punctuation			5.9 Punctuate			5.10 Recognize			5.11 Write		
TEST	PR	EM	PO	PR	EM	PO	PR	EM	PO	PR	EM	PO	PR	EM	PO	PR	EM	PO
1		1	1		1	1	1	1	1	1	1	1		1				
2		1	1		1	1	1	1	1	1	1	1		1			1	
3		1	1		1	1	1	1	1	1	1	1		1			1	
4		1	1		1	1	1	1	1	1	1	1		1	1		1	
5		1	1		1	1	1	1	1	1	1	1		1	1		1	
6		1	1		1	1	1	1	1	1	1	1		1	1		1	1
7		1	1		1	1	1	1	1	1	1	1		1	1		1	1
8		1	1		1	1	1	1	1	1	1	1		1	1		1	1
9		1	1		1	1	1	1	1	1	1	1		1	1		1	1
10	1	1	1		1	1	1	1	1	1	1	1		1	1		1	1
11	1	1	1	1	1	1	1	1	1	1	1	1	1	1	1	1	1	1
12	1	1	1		1	1	1	1	1	1	1	1	1	1	1	1	1	1
13	1	1	1	1	1	1	1	1	1	1	1	1	1	1	1	1	1	1
14	1	1	1	1	1	1	1	1	1	1	1	1	1	1	1	1	1	1
15	1	1	1	1	1	1	1	1	1	1	1	1	1	1	1	1	1	1
# Passing	**6**	**15**	**15**	**4**	**15**	**15**	**15**	**15**	**15**	**15**	**15**	**15**	**5**	**15**	**12**	**5**	**14**	**10**
% Passing	**40**	**100**	**100**	**27**	**100**	**100**	**100**	**100**	**100**	**100**	**100**	**100**	**33**	**100**	**80**	**33**	**93**	**66**
Diff		**+60**	**0**		**+73**	**0**		**0**	**0**		**0**	**0**		**+67**	**−20**		**+60**	**−27**

Note: 1 = objective mastered, blank = objective not mastered; Pr = Pretest, Em = Embedded test or rehearsal, Po = Posttest; Diff = Difference between students passing pretest and posttest on declarative sentences portion of goal; Students 1–5 had not mastered entry skills before beginning instruction.

4. Percentage of All Fifteen Students Who Mastered Each Objective on the Pretest, Embedded Items, and Posttest

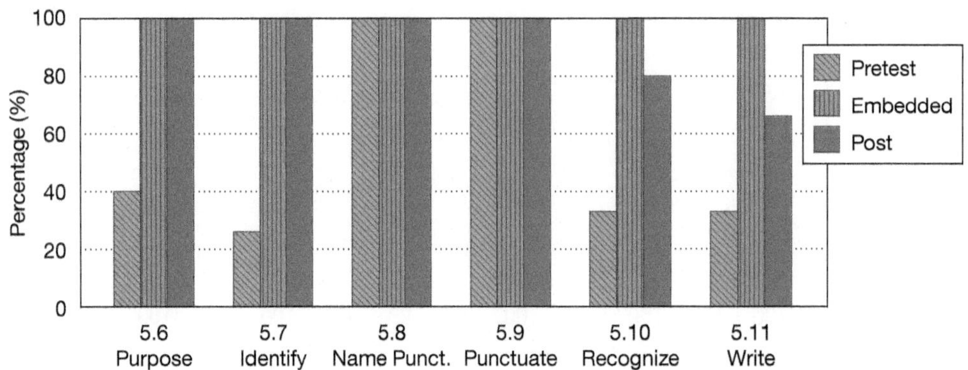

5. Percentage of Four Students (Students 1–4) *Not* Possessing the Required Entry Skills Who Mastered Each Objective on the Pretest, Embedded Items, and Posttest

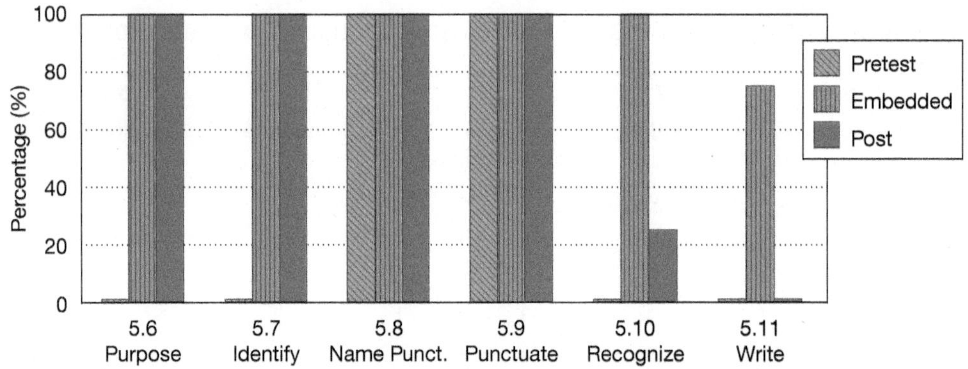

6. Percentage of Ten Students (Students 6–15) Possessing the Required Entry Skills Who Mastered Each Objective on the Pretest, Embedded Items, and Posttest

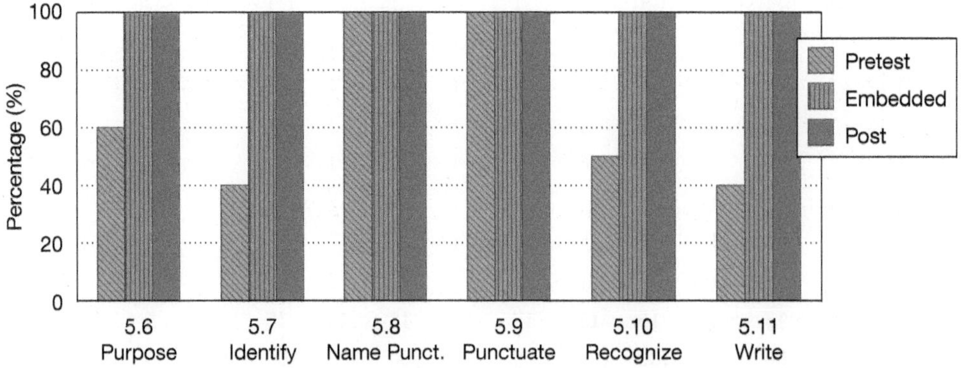

7. Attitude Survey and Summary of Students' Ratings and Comments About the Materials and Lesson

Help Us Make the Lesson Better

Please answer the following questions to help us understand what you think about the lesson on writing different kinds of sentences. Your comments will help us make better lessons for you. Thanks.

Name Summary Date 1/6 Class Small Group

A. Motivation

1. Would you like to make a newsletter for sixth-grade students to read? ☐ Yes ☐ No
   Yes = 11111 11111 111 13; No = 11 2
2. Did you like the sixth graders in the lesson? ☐ Yes ☐ No
   Yes = 11111 11111 11111 15; No = 0
3. Do you enjoy working at your speed in Canvas? ☐ Yes ☐ No
   Yes = 11111 11111 11111 15; No = 0
4. Did you enjoy the article about the dark side of the moon? ☐ Yes ☐ No
   Yes = 11111 11111 11111 15; No = 0
5. Did you think the story with all types of sentences was more interesting? ☐ Yes ☐ No
   Yes = 11111 11111 11111 15; No = 0
6. Would you like to write more interesting stories? ☐ Yes ☐ No
   Yes = 11111 11111 111 13; No = 11 2
7. What types of stories do you most like to read?
   horses, pets, space, sports, nature, cars, mysteries

B. Objectives

1. Did you understand that you were going to learn to write interesting newsletter articles?
   ☐ Yes ☐ No
   Yes = 11111 11111 11111 15; No = 0
2. Did you understand that you were going to learn to use the four different types of sentences in your stories? ☐ Yes ☐ No
   Yes = 11111 11111 11111 15; No = 0
3. Did you want to write different types of sentences? ☐ Yes ☐ No
   Yes = 11111 11111 11111 15; No = 0

C. Entry Behaviors

1. Were the questions about subjects, predicates, and complete sentences clear to you?
   ☐ Yes ☐ No
   Yes = 11111 11111 11111 15; No = 0
2. Did you already know about subjects, predicates, and complete sentences before you started?
   ☐ Yes ☐ No
   Yes = 11111 11111 1111 14; No = 1

3. Do you wish information about subjects, predicates, and complete sentences had been included in the lesson? ☐ Yes ☐ No
   Yes = 0; No = 11111 11111 11111 15

D. Tests

1. Were the questions on the pretest clear? ☐ Yes ☐ No
   Yes = 11111 111 8; No = 11111 117 Didn't know the answers, Vocabulary clear
2. Did you know most of the answers on the pretest? ☐ Yes ☐ No
   Yes = 11111 1111 9; No = 11111 1 6
3. Were the questions in the lesson clear? ☐ Yes ☐ No
   Yes = 11111 11111 11111 15; No = 0
4. Were the questions on the posttest clear? ☐ Yes ☐ No
   Yes = 11111 11111 11111 15; No = 0

E. Instruction

1. Was the lesson on declarative sentences interesting? ☐ Yes ☐ No
   Yes = 11111 11111 11111 15; No = 0
2. Was the lesson clear to you? ☐ Yes ☐ No
   Yes = 11111 11111 11111 15; No = 0

   If not, what wasn't clear?

   Where were the newsletter articles?
3. Were the example questions helpful? ☐ Yes ☐ No
   Yes = 11111 11111 10; No = 11111 5
4. Were there too many examples? ☐ Yes ☐ No
   Yes = 11111 5; No = 11111 11111 10
5. Were there too few examples? ☐ Yes ☐ No
   Yes = 11111 11111 10; No = 11111 5
6. Did the practice questions in the lesson help you? ☐ Yes ☐ No
   Yes = 11111 11111 10; No = 11111 5

   If not, why not?
7. Did the feedback for the questions in the lesson help you? ☐ Yes ☐ No
   Yes = 11111 11111 10; No = 11111 5

   If not, why not?

F. Overall

1. Generally, did you like the lesson? ☐ Yes ☐ No
   Yes = 11111 11111 11111 15; No = 0
2. Did you learn to do things you couldn't do before? ☐ Yes ☐ No
   Yes = 11111 11111 10; No = 11111 5
3. What do you think would improve the lesson most?

   More example articles to see. The lesson wasn't about writing articles. We learned this before.

Appendix M

Materials Revision Matrix Analysis

Instructional Strategy	Problem Identified	Proposed Changes to Instruction	Evidence and Source
Preinstruction Motivation	**OK**	**None**	**Questionnaire Interview**
Entry Skills	Four students did not have required entry skills (1, 2, 3, & 4); Student 5 missed skill 5.4, was able to classify sentences (skill 5.5), but had problems writing (5.11). Students without entry skills performed well on embedded tests but did not retain skills for posttest. Students who did not have entry skills did not want to make a newsletter.	Ensure all students entering the instruction possess entry skills. Develop lesson on entry skills for students who need it.	Entry skills test Embedded test Posttest Observation
Presentation	Group appears not to need instruction in skills 5.8 and 5.9. Five students (11–15) in group did not need instruction, and another five (6–10) only needed to review. Several students said they already knew how to write declarative sentences. High-ability students dissatisfied with lesson.	Move 5.8 and 5.9 to entry skills for unit and remove from instruction and assessments. Branch students based on pretest data; instruction is individualized.	Pretest Embedded test Posttest Questionnaire
Student Participation (Practice with Feedback)		Students wanted more information about newsletter. Refocus objective items and/or examples/nonexamples toward newsletter content. Remove imperative items as distractors in assessments because they are too difficult to distinguish at this point. Reintroduce them following instruction on content differences between declarative and imperative sentences.	Embedded Test Posttest Questionnaire Interview
Assessment	None	None	Pretest separated skilled and unskilled in objective and alternative assessment. Vocabulary OK. Time OK. Scoring within Canvas OK. Students liked the name *review* rather than *quiz*, and they liked the immediate feedback they could check themselves.

Instructional Strategy	Problem Identified	Proposed Changes to Instruction	Evidence and Source
Transfer	Students without entry skills did not think the newsletter would be a good idea; those with entry skills liked it very much.		Questionnaire Interview
General	Most students could master the items on the objective posttest, but many still struggle with coming up with their own ideas and writing their own content. Practice using the newsletter and working in writing teams should help. Work with library/media specialist to work with article research in the library/media center. Monitor writing to ensure that all students are participating rather than allowing others to accomplish their writing for them.		

Index

A

B

C

T

U

V

W

Y